THE PILGRIMAGE
OF GRACE

❖▪▪▪❖

This book studies the largest insurrection to occur in
England between the Peasants' Revolt of 1381 and the
English Civil War of the 1640s. It concentrates upon the
nine rebel armies that were mobilised in the North during
the month of October 1536, examining their recruitment,
organisation, grievances and aims, as well as the impact
they made upon the government of Henry VIII. Operating principally from original sources, it revises the standard work of the Dodds and appraises the research
produced in the subject over the last thirty years.

Bush proposes that, as a rising of the commons, the
aim of the rebellion was to safeguard the commonwealth
as well as to protect Christ's faith, arguing that it cannot
be fully explained as a reaction against the Henrician
Reformation. On the other hand, in adopting the idiom
of a rising of the commons, it did not become simply a
popular uprising, but was rather a conjunction of protest,
with gentlemen, clergy and commons establishing working alliances with each other against the government.
Besides a study of revolt, this book provides a vital
insight into the cultural, religious, political and social
beliefs of sixteenth-century England.

*Michael Bush is former Reader in History
at the University of Manchester*

Michael Bush

THE PILGRIMAGE OF GRACE

A STUDY OF THE REBEL ARMIES OF OCTOBER 1536

MANCHESTER UNIVERSITY PRESS
Manchester and New York

distributed exclusively in the USA
and Canada by St. Martin's Press

Published by Manchester University Press
Oxford Road, Manchester M13 9NR, UK
and Room 400, 175 Fifth Avenue, New York, NY 10010,
USA

Distributed exclusively in the USA and Canada
by St Martin's Press, Inc., 175 Fifth Avenue, New York,
NY 10010, USA

British Library Cataloguing-in-Publication Data
A catalogue record is available from the British Library

Library of Congress Cataloguing-in-Publication Data
Bush, M. L.
The pilgrimage of grace: a study of the rebel armies of
October 1536/Michael Bush.
p. cm.
ISBN 0–7190–4696–3
1. Great Britain——History——Henry VIII, 1509–
1547. 2. Insurgency——England, Northern——History——16th century. 3. Great Britain——History,
Military——16th century. 4. Pilgrimage of Grace
1536–1537. I. Title.
DA339 B87 1996
95–1037
942.05'2—dc20
CIP

ISBN 0 7190 4696 3 *hardback*

First published 1996

99 98 97 96   10 9 8 7 6 5 4 3 2 1

Typeset in Horley Old Style by J&L Composition Ltd,
Filey, North Yorkshire
Printed in Great Britain
by Biddles Ltd, Guildford and King's Lynn

120396 - 8796X8

Contents

████████████████████████████████████

X   The convocation of the hosts

XI   Conclusion   407

Maps

Foreword

This study of the pilgrimage of grace concentrates upon the uprisings that broke out over much of northern England in October 1536. True, it pays some attention to the Lincolnshire uprising but does not explore it with the same intensity, largely because it was a separate revolt: a preamble to, rather than an integral part of, the pilgrimage of grace. Principally, the east midland revolt is examined for its effect upon the pilgrimage of grace for which it served as an initial inspiration and example. Likewise, the study has little to say about the northern revolts of early 1537, on the grounds that they were the aftermath of the pilgrimage of grace, important for allowing the government to proceed against the pilgrim high command but, quintessentially, a consequence of the earlier insurrection. Rather than a part of the pilgrimage of grace, they were a reaction against it, in the sense that their participants were rebelling against the settlement the pilgrim leadership had reached with the government the previous December.

The pilgrimage of grace proper, then, is defined as the insurrections that occurred north of the Trent between 8th October, when the first revolt started in Beverley, and 27th October, when the government and the rebels agreed upon a truce. Since the October truce became a pardon in the first week of December, the study also shows, by looking in detail at the intervening events and negotiations, how this conversion was achieved. The selectiveness of the study is justified by the importance of what it has chosen to dwell upon. At the crux of the whole insurrectionary movement of late 1536 and early 1537, and responsible for its impact, was the formation of the pilgrim army. The uprising was a military achievement for the pilgrims, even though they won no battles. To approach it from a military angle therefore makes good sense. Yet its military organisation was only one of its distinguishing marks. Any attempt to give the pilgrimage of grace its true meaning must examine the motivation of the rebels in all its complexity. To reduce the motive to a religious protest is to misrepresent it. The same could be said of singling out the secular complaint. This study therefore seeks to stress the variety of grievance rather than to identify any prime cause. Another central feature of the pilgrimage was its broad social appeal: the way that aristocratic, clerical and commoner rebels interrelated. This study therefore seeks to appreciate the contributions respectively made by the social groups involved. To characterise the movement as either aristocratic or popular, this study contests, is to get it wrong.

The pilgrimage of grace was a spectacular event of the English Reformation. Moreover, in view of its size and impact – with allegedly over 60,000 rebels up in arms in late October, it was the largest rebellion to occur in England between the peasants' revolt of 1381 and the civil war of the 1640s – it was an outstanding event of the late middle ages and the early modern period. For this very reason, it deserves to be studied at length. In addition, its evidence reveals how religion, the state and society were perceived. The insights it provides on the cultural, political and social attitudes of the time justify a full and careful examination.

For granting me access to the evidence, I am grateful to the P.R.O., the British Library, the county record offices north of the Trent and the Trustees of Chatsworth House (especially Tom Askey). The book also owes much to generations of undergraduates who, thanks to the Manchester B.A. thesis, were able to do research for their first degree. It is especially indebted to the members of my special subject class of 1993–4 who, without knowing it, were subjected to the following book and whose response to it, in class discussions and in their written work, caused changes to be made. So, thanks to James Cooper, Brett Welch, Mark Walker, Arlene Graham, Christine Ford, Marissa Handley and Julian Luke. It has also benefited from the shrewd comments of David Bownes, who is the specialist on the post-pardon revolts of 1537, and Christine Hallett whose speciality was the Lincolnshire rebellion of October 1536.

The idea was born back in 1989 when, in the Round Room of the Chancery Lane Public Record Office, first Leigh Beier and then Cliff Davies provokingly said: "Why don't you write a book on it?" My greatest debt is to Sarah Bush, the historian of the silk industry, who accompanied me in visiting all the sites associated with the pilgrimage of grace, helping me to locate them as well as to appreciate their significance.

To avoid pedantry and antiquarianism, the spelling of all quotations from the documents has been modernised.

M. L. Bush
Didsbury, Manchester
September 1994

Abbreviations

Bateson Mary Bateson (ed.), "The pilgrimage of grace and Aske's examination", *E.H.R.*, 5 (1890), pp. 330–48 and 550–78.

Bindoff S. T. Bindoff (ed.), *The House of Commons, 1509–1558* (London, 1982), three vols.

B. L. British Library.

C.W.A.A.S. *Cumberland and Westmorland Antiquarian and Archaeological Society, Transactions.*

C. R. O. Cumbria Record Office (Kendal and Carlisle).

Dodds M. H. and R. Dodds, *The Pilgrimage of Grace, 1536–7, and the Exeter Conspiracy, 1538* (Cambridge, 1915), two vols.

Ducatus Lancs *Ducatus Lancastriae (London, 1823), three vols.*

E.H.R. *The English Historical Review.*

H.R.O. Humberside Record Office (Beverley).

Index of Wills Y.A.S.R.S., 11 (1891).

Hughes and Larkin P. L. Hughes and J. F. Larkin (eds.), *Tudor Royal Proclamations* (London, 1964), I.

I.P.M. Henry VII *Calendar of the Inquisitions Post Mortem, Henry VII* (London, 1898–1956), three vols.

L.P. *J. S. Brewer, James Gairdner and R. H. Brodie (eds.) Letters and Papers, Foreign and Domestic, of the Reign of Henry VIII, 1509–47* (London, 1862–1910), twenty–one vols., plus *Addenda* (London, 1929–32).

P.R.O. Public Record Office.

Stapulton J. C. Cox (ed.), "William Stapleton and the pilgrimage of grace", *Transactions of the East Riding Antiquarian Society*, 10 (1903).

Star Ch. Yorkshire, II H. B. McCall (ed.) *Yorkshire Star Chamber Proceedings*, Y.A.S.R.S., 45 (1911).

Star Ch. Yorkshire, III William Brown (ed.) *Yorkshire Star Chamber Proceedings*, Y.A.S.R.S., 51 (1914).

Star Ch. Yorkshire, IV John Lister (ed.) *Yorkshire Star Chamber Proceedings*, Y.A.S.R.S., 70 (1927).

St.P. *State Papers, King Henry VIII* (London, 1830–52), eleven vols.

Statutes of the Realm A. Luders, T. E. Tomlins, J. Raithby et al. (eds.) (London, 1810–28), eleven vols.

Toller T. N. Toller (ed.), *Correspondence of Edward, Third Earl of Derby*, Chetham Society, new ser. 19 (1890).

Tonge *Heraldic Visitation of the North Counties in 1530 by Thomas Tonge, Norroy King of Arms*, Surtees Society, 41 (1863).

V.E. John Caley and Joseph Hunter (eds.), *Valor Ecclesiasticus* (London, 1810–34), six vols.

V.C.H. Cumberland *The Victoria History of the County of Cumberland* (London, 1901–5), two vols., James Wilson (ed.).

V.C.H. East Riding *A History of the County of York, East Riding* (London, 1969–89), six vols., ed. K. J. Allison.

V.C.H. Lancashire *The Victoria History of the County of Lancaster* (London, 1906–14), eight vols., William Farrer and J. Brownbill (eds.).

V.C.H. North Riding *The Victoria History of the County of York, North Riding* (London, 1914–23), two vols., W. Page (ed.).

V.C.H. Yorkshire *The Victoria History of the County of Yorks* (London, 1907–13), three vols., W. Page (ed.).

Y.A.S.R.S. Yorkshire Archaeological Society, Record Series.

Yorkshire Chancery Proc. *Monastic Chancery Proceedings*, Y.A.S.R.S. 88 (1934), J. S. Purvis (ed.).

Glossary

Affinity: a lord's connexion, consisting of those dependent upon him as allies, tenants, servants, retainers and relatives.

Agistment: a charge exacted by the landlord for the right to graze cattle and sheep, usually on enclosed land.

Alarum: a form of bell-ringing, the peal rung backwards to summon men to arms.

Almain rivets: light, body armour, comprising plates sliding on rivets to allow some flexibility.

Amercement: a punishment by fine.

Appointment: the making of a treaty, agreement or settlement.

Appropriation: the assignment to a religious institution of the revenues and offices originally intended for the maintenance of a parish church.

Approvement: measures of estate management to increase the profitability of rented farmland, usually by means of enclosure, for the benefit of the landlord.

Augmentations: the royal court established in 1536 to oversee the suppression of religious houses and to administer the revenues accruing to the Crown from these suppressions and also from other estates newly acquired by the Crown.

Baronage: 1) that part of the peerage with the title of baron; 2) the holders of fiefs with feudal obligations to the Crown.

Bidding, of beads, of holy days: the injoining of prayers by the priest; his announcement of imminent religious festivals.

Bills: 1) a halberd or combination of spike and axe on a long wooden shaft; 2) letters.

Body politic: a conventional, contemporary image of the state as an organic interrelationship, in which the various parts of society were assigned complementary functions as if they were the parts of a body. In the political thought of the time the image was closely associated with the notion of the society of orders.

Burgess: a resident of a town who possessed special commercial and governmental municipal rights and, recognised as a freeman, was distinguished within the town from the unfranchised.

Common bell: town bell.

Common council: the council directly representing the burgesses as opposed to the council of the mayor and aldermen.

Common hall: town hall.

Commonalty, commons, commonty: the order of society comprised of all subjects lacking the status of gentleman or cleric.

Commoning rights: rights within the manorial system, possessed by both lord and tenant, 1) to the waste (for grazing livestock and collecting wood, nuts, mushrooms, bracken etc.); 2) to the cultivated parts immediately after haymaking or the corn harvest (for grazing).

Commonweal, commonwealth: 1) the wealth of the commons; 2) the material good of the realm and all its inhabitants.

Cornage: a freehold tenure, distinct from socage or fief, in which the tenant owed military service specifically for the defence of the northern border and was subject to the payment of noutgeld.

Customary tenant: a tenant holding land once regarded as held in villeinage and therefore unfreely. In the law such a tenure was regarded as held at the will of the lord; but, by virtue either of the custom of the country or of the custom of the manor, it was assumed in practice that the tenure was held by hereditary right and for an unrevisable rent. The principal forms of customary tenure were copyhold and tenant right tenancy.

Custumal: a declaration of manorial rights and obligations agreed by the lord of the manor and the tenantry.

Debateable lands: a region on the border to which both the English and the Scottish Crowns laid claim to ownership.

Demesne: that part of the manor regarded as being directly under the control of the lord. In this respect it was distinguished from the part of the manor comprised of customary and free tenures. If rented out, the demesne was leased on short-term, rank-rent leases. In sharp contrast the tenures were held hereditarily and their rents were fixed by custom. From the viewpoint of the law and the landlord, another part of the manor regarded as demesne was the waste, although the lord's control of it was restricted by the tenants' commoning rights.

Estates society: see society of orders.

Estovers: a commoning right within the manorial system, allowing the collection of whatever grew naturally upon the waste.

Farm, farmhold, farmer: 1) lease, leasehold, lessee; 2) cultivate, unit of cultivation, cultivator.

Feodary: official involved in the collection of feudal dues and the enforcement of feudal obligations.

Feudal dues: the payments made either in place of the military service owed by the fief holder (i.e. scutage) or to ensure the overlord's recognition of the transmission of a fief from father to son (i.e. relief).

Fiefs: freehold tenures feudally obliged to provide an overlord with military service and other payments and services in recognition of vassalage.

Fifteenth and tenth: a direct tax levied by the government, characterised by a fixed yield and indirect assessment (i.e. by the community's own officials rather than commissioners appointed by the Crown). In this respect, the government's role was simply to seek parliament's authorisation for the tax and to see to its collection. In contrast, the other direct tax at the government's disposal, the subsidy, was open yield and directly assessed, with government officials assessing the wealth of subjects each time the tax was granted, exacting it at a variable rate, set by parliament, of so much in the pound and organising its collection. Both taxes were alike in being irregular: that is, to be raised only in a situation of emergency, notably war. Neither was intended to finance everyday government.

First fruits and tenths: a perpetual tax upon the clergy introduced by statute in 1534, allowing the Crown to levy each year a tenth of clerical incomes and to exact a first fruits tax equivalent to one year's revenues upon each new clerical incumbent.

Fiscal feudalism: a royal policy of exploiting feudal rights, notably associated with wardship and marriage, for financial gain.

Franchises: areas of independent jurisdiction where the king's writ could not normally run and where a range of regalian rights were enjoyed by the owner. Their jurisdictional independence was abolished in 1536.

Freehold: 1) tenure in socage; 2) tenure by enfeoffment; 3) free, as opposed to customary, tenancy.

Garth: a courtyard.

God's penny: a payment made by some customary tenants in lieu of the gressum. In some cases it was paid in place of the gressum due upon a change of lord. In other cases it excused the tenant of the gressum due upon a change of tenant. In parts it totally replaced the gressum. In other parts it merely relieved the tenant of the gressum due upon change of lord.

Harnessed: a bowman or billman equipped with jack, sallet and a pair of splints was regarded as fully harnessed.

Herbage: right of pasturage.

Holy days: days recognised as religious festivals, in connexion with the commemoration of sacred persons, notably saints, and sacred events. Most were abrogated by the government in 1536.

Honour: a tenurial barony, without franchisal rights but with the feudal authority to command the service of its fiefholders.

Host: army.

Hundred: see wapentake.

Intakes: enclosures extending the area of cultivation at the expense of the waste.

Intermission: the power of mediation between man and God which popular catholicism attributed to saints if sufficiently venerated.

Jack: a protective, sleeveless jacket or jerkin made of either layers of leather or resined linen.

Liberties: see franchises.

Manred: the men a lord could call upon in a private capacity for waging war (i.e. to form a private army).

March treason: from the English point of view, criminal offences incurred by aiding and abetting the Scots in their designs against England.

Men of worship: a synonym for gentlemen.

Mesne lords, mesne manors: lords who held estates (i.e. mesne manors) of another lord in such a way as to be his feudal vassal, the result of subinfeudation, which had awarded tenants-in-chief of the Crown fief holders of their own.

Mosstroopers: border warriors inhabiting the peaty wastes of the northern frontier.

Musters: periodic assemblies convoked for each wapentake, ward or hundred by commissions of array. Their purpose was to mobilise the militia: based upon the obligation, of all able men between sixteen and sixty, to serve for the defence of the realm with equipment appropriate to their wealth, in keeping with the statute of Winchester (1285). The pilgrims employed the same system for gathering together their hosts.

Noutgeld: the annual payment required of freeholders in cornage. It was normally paid to the Crown, but, as in the barony of Westmorland, it could be alienated to a subject.

Oaths: in connection with the pilgrimage of grace they came in two basic forms: 1) the commons' oath imposed by the rebels and requiring allegiance to God, the king and the commons or commonweal; 2) the king's oath, produced as a counter to the commons' oath and requiring obedience to the Crown.

Orders: see society of orders.

Peasants: members of families who cultivated smallholdings with family labour essentially for a subsistence purpose.

Predial tithes: the tenth exacted of the cultivated produce of the land, as opposed to the personal tithes exacted of labour and occupation, and normally consisting, for example, of corn, hay and fruit.

Purgatory: according to catholic practice, the repository for the souls of the dead whilst they awaited the grace of God to admit them to Heaven. During this wait the intercession of saints, achieved by lights, oblations and prayers, as well as the ministrations of the clergy, were regarded as especially efficacious in deciding the fate of these souls. Protestantism regarded purgatory as an invention of the catholic church, created to exploit the wealth of the laity. Lacking scriptural authority and unnecessary since salvation, it was thought, was achievable by faith alone, protestants advocated its repudiation.

Quondam: a former head of a religious house.

Regulars: monks, nuns or canons.

Reivers: border warriors dependent for their living on rustling sheep and cattle.

Risings of the commons: a genre of revolt lasting from 1381 to 1549 in which large-scale uprisings, enlisting support from the whole range of society, complained that the health of the body politic was being impaired particularly because of the commons' maltreatment.

Sallet: a helmet protecting the back of the neck, made either of steel or hardened leather.

Sanctuary men: criminals who have legitimately escaped the law through taking refuge in a place with recognised rights of sanctuary such as a church or a liberty.

Scrimmage: a skirmish.

Secular clergy: clerics who are not regulars: that is, who are not bound by the vows of a religious order.

Sergeant corn: a payment in kind, usually oats, made to the sheriff by the tenantry of certain communities for feeding the horses of his staff (i.e. the sergeants) when on his tourn.

Sheriff's tourn: the circuit made by the sheriff twice yearly to preside over each hundred, wapentake or ward court within his county.

Socage: land held as freehold in the manner of a fief, but without the obligations of knight's service.

Society of orders: a social system subscribing to the belief that society was best organised as a formal hierarchy of complementary orders or estates. The recognised orders were the gentlemen, the clergy and the commons. Each order was distinguished by its obligatory functions. Thus, the gentlemen were expected to aid the king in running the state and also to protect the commonalty from abuse; the clergy were expected to maintain the spiritual welfare of the realm, whilst the commons were expected to produce wealth. Since each order had a specific and equally necessary role to play - political in the case of the gentlemen, religious in the case of the clergy, economic in the case of the commons - it was felt that a society organised in this manner would be harmonious, with discordancy arising only if members of one order sought to exercise the functions of another, or if the functions of each order were neglected by its members.

Splints, pair of: pieces of plate armour worn on the arms.

Subsidy: see fifteenth and tenth.

Suzerainty: the supreme overlordship within a system of feudalism conferred by final ownership of the land. It was usually vested in the monarch.

Tenant right: a peasant tenure found in the northern border counties, in the palatinate of Durham, in north Lancashire and in the northerly parts of the North and West Ridings of Yorkshire. Its terms placed the tenant under obligation to provide free military service in the defence of the northern border when summoned by the wardens of the marches. Although regarded in the law as a customary tenure held at the will of the lord, in practice, thanks to the custom of the country or of the manor, it was considered to be an hereditary tenancy and, thanks to the military obligation, it was thought, both by peasant and Crown, to deserve lenient landlordship.

Tillage laws: legislation passed under the early Tudors to curtail the development of sheep-farming and to preserve the land under plough. Through enclosure and engrossment (i.e. the amalgamation of farms), the extension of pastoral farming was thought to be depopulating the countryside, especially by reducing the number of peasant farmsteads. Promoting this legislation was the fear that the military capacity of the realm, which was thought to depend upon the sturdy yeoman, was being impaired and that inflation was being generated by the decreasing production of corn.

Tolbooth: an office for the collection of customs dues.

Use: a device for escaping feudal payments and the feudal obligation of wardship and marriage. Since they mostly fell due upon the death of a fiefholder, placing the fief under the legal ownership of a self-perpetuating trust or use was a simple and effective means of avoiding their liability: that is, until the enactment of the statute of uses in 1536 which, by declaring the beneficiency of the use to be the legal owner of the fief to which it applied, deprived the use of its intended purpose.

Van, vanguard: The front portion of an army as arrayed for battle: the forward as opposed to the middleward or rearward.

Vassal: a fief holder, owing homage, services and dues to a feudal overlord who might be the suzerain or a tenant-in-chief.

Visitation: 1) an examination of the clergy by officials appointed either by episcopal or royal authority; 2) an examination of the gentlemen, conducted by royal heralds, county by county, to assess their entitlement to a coat of arms.

Wapentake: a variant term for hundred or ward. It represented the largest public subdivision in the shire, an administrative unit for the collection of the subsidy, the organisation of the militia and the sheriff's tourn.

Ward: see wapentake.

Wardship and marriage: the right of the feudal overlord to take possession of fiefs where the holder has been succeeded by a minor and to retain it until the minor came of age, as well as to decide whom the minor should marry. The right was normally vested in the Crown, although often sold to subjects.

Water towns: a group of small townships situated along the River Hull which, in conjunction with the town of Beverley, comprised the Liberty of Beverley and were subjected to the manorial lordship of the archbishop of York.

Waste: that part of the manor which was uncultivated and to which the all-year-round commoning rights of lord and tenantry attached.

I

⬛⬛⬛⬛⬛⬛⬛⬛⬛⬛⬛⬛⬛⬛⬛⬛⬛⬛⬛⬛⬛⬛⬛⬛⬛➤

INTRODUCTION

Some historiographical observations

Since the publication of Madeleine and Ruth Dodds' magnificent book *The Pilgrimage of Grace and the Exeter Conspiracy* (1915), much of the work done on the revolts of October 1536 has been impaired by special pleading and oversimplification. In addition, the documentary evidence has been inadequately explored, mainly because of the willingness of historians to accept at their face value the documentary summaries provided by the *Letters and Papers Foreign and Domestic of the Reign of Henry VIII*. As a result, the actual language of revolt has largely escaped analysis.[1]

The special pleading has mostly derived from a persistent struggle between a catholic and a protestant interest, each engaged in a face-saving attempt to absolve its own religion. Thus, the catholic interest presented the uprising as a necessary and spirited defence of the old religion by the people of the east midlands and the north against a reformation of callous radicalism. It has used the pilgrimage of grace to show that at the time the old religion was very much alive and that the reformation was imposed upon the country by a small band of heretics who only succeeded by virtue of their control of the government. As part of the same *apologia*, they proposed that the uprising was defeated by trickery. In contrast, the protestant interest needed to show that the reformation was essentially benign: in fact, far too moderate and

---

1 M. H. and R. Dodds, *The Pilgrimage of Grace, 1536–7, and the Exeter Conspiracy, 1538* (Cambridge, 1915), two volumes; J. Gairdner (ed.), *Letters and Papers, Foreign and Domestic, of the Reign of Henry VIII* (London, 1864–1932), volumes XI and XII.

reasonable to provoke a great rebellion. It thus proposed that there were other causes of revolt, of a secular rather than religious vein, and concerned with material rather than with spiritual matters.

The protagonist of the catholic interest was the monk Dom David Knowles, supported by J. J. Scarisbrick.[2] The protagonist of the protestant interest was A.G. Dickens, supported by Joyce Youings. Youings opined: "The dissolution of the majority of smaller monasteries, it is now generally agreed, was only a minor cause of the rebellion of 1536", making reference to Dickens' work *The English Reformation*.[3] Of the Lincolnshire uprising, Dickens wrote: " It was a chaotic, ignominious and rather sordid affair which can scarcely be dignified as the protest of a catholic society against the Reformation" . Of the pilgrimage of grace, he wrote: "The roots of the movement were decidedly economic, its demands predominantly secular, its interest in Rome almost negligible. . . . In short, the English remained incapable of staging genuine Wars of Religion".[4] Needless to say, not all engaged in this controversy have been defending their own religion. Some supporters of the catholic interest have been protestant or agnostic - notably C. S. L. Davies and Christopher Haigh - who, in properly reacting against the prejudices of Dickens, were innocently drawn into the catholic camp.[5]

However, the special pleading associated with the revolts of October 1536 cannot be explained wholly in terms of sectarian strife. In recent years it has also resulted from various attempts to whitewash key figures in the uprising, notably the Earl of Cumberland and Lord Cromwell. Thus, G. R. Elton has presented the uprising as small in scale, essentially the work of a defeated court faction which went to the country and manipulated the commons to come out against the government. For this reason it cannot be said to have expressed widespread hostility in the north to the rule of Thomas Cromwell who

---

2 See D. Knowles, *The Religious Orders in England* (Cambridge, 1959), III, ch. 25; and J. J. Scarisbrick, *Henry VIII* (London, 1968), pp. 338–45.

3 J. Youings, *The Dissolution of the Monasteries* (London, 1971), p. 53.

4 A. G. Dickens, *The English Reformation* (London, 1964), pp. 125 and 128. For his appreciation of the secular grievances and their importance, see his "Secular and religious motivation in the pilgrimage of grace", *Studies in Church History*, 4 (1967), pp. 39–64.

5 For C. S. L. Davies, see his "The pilgrimage of grace reconsidered", *Past and Present*, 41 (1968), pp. 54–75 and his "Popular religion and the pilgrimage of grace", in A. Fletcher and J. Stephenson (eds.), *Order and Disorder in Early Modern England* (Cambridge, 1985), pp. 58–91. For C.A. Haigh, see his *Reformation and Resistance in Tudor Lancashire* (Cambridge, 1975), ch. 9 and his *English Reformations* (Oxford, 1993), p. 148.

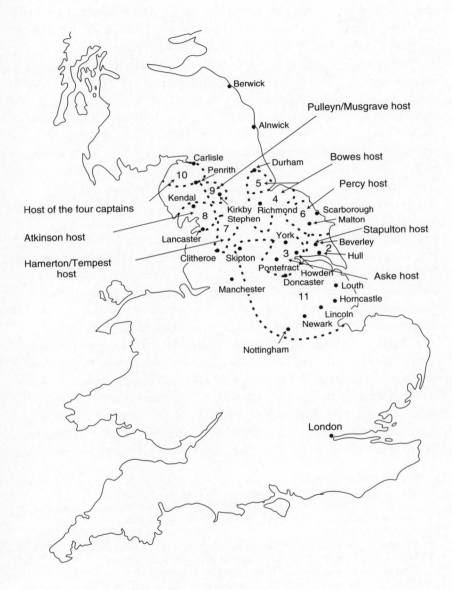

Map 1 The hosts in the pilgrimage of grace
(The numbers are those of the regional maps.)

therefore cannot be regarded as a prime cause of the uprising.[6] R. W. Hoyle sought to exculpate the Earl of Cumberland. Reacting against the charges brought against the earl by M. E. James, Hoyle argued that the rebel opposition to him, as it was made evident in the siege of Skipton Castle, simply came of his loyalty to the government.[7]

Yet special pleading accounts only for part of the oversimplification evident in interpretations of the pilgrimage of grace. Some of it stems from a preference for monocausal explanations, coming of the need to put the answer in a nutshell. In spite of the multiplicity of grievances contained in the rebels' own declarations of complaint, the uprising is normally presented as having either religious or temporal motives.[8] Moreover, in spite of the plurality of social movements in the pilgrimage of grace, with protests from the commons, the clergy and the gentlemen, and in spite of the broad spectrum of society in its leadership, with captains drawn from all three orders, the uprising is usually regarded as either aristocratic or popular in character.[9] A further source of oversimplification has been the tendency to dismiss it as a tragic failure, the pathetic victim of government manipulation. For some reason or other, it has not proved possible to appreciate it as partly successful and partly a failure, or as successful at one, if unsuccessful at another, stage of its development.

Much of the research on the subject has repeatedly returned to certain basic themes, notably causation and leadership. In spite of its obvious importance, the organisation of revolt hardly gets a mention: oath-taking, the holding of assemblies, the formation of armies, the enlistment of neighbouring regions, the drafting of manifestos, the summoning of councils to frame policy, the drawing up of petitions. These were all vital parts of the pilgrimage of grace, yet none has

6 See G. R. Elton, "Politics and the pilgrimage of grace", in *After the Reformation* (Manchester, 1980), B. Malament (ed.), pp. 25–56.

7 See R. W. Hoyle, "The first earl of Cumberland: a reputation reassessed", *Northern History*, 22 (1986), pp. 63–94.

8 See nn. 2, 4 and 5.

9 For the presentation of the pilgrimage of grace as an aristocratic revolt, see R. B. Smith, *Land and Politics in the England of Henry VIII* (Oxford, 1970), ch. 5 and Elton, op. cit., passim. For its presentation as a popular revolt, see R. W. Hoyle, "Henry Percy, sixth earl of Northumberland and the fall of the house of Percy, 1527–1537" in G. W. Bernard (ed.), *The Tudor Nobility* (Manchester, 1992), p. 197. The same idea is suggested in his "Thomas Master's narrative of the pilgrimage of grace", *Northern History*, 21 (1985), pp. 61–3. The Lincolnshire uprising has received a similar treatment, with Hoyle and S. J. Gunn presenting it as a popular revolt (see ibid., pp. 55–61 and below, n. 73);and with M. E. James emphasising the leadership role of the local aristocracy (see also n. 73).

received careful analysis; and none has been described since the Dodds did it in 1915.

Furthermore, much of the research published on the pilgrimage of grace has tended to take the overview. This has caused the neglect of another vital characteristic: its episodic nature. The pilgrimage of grace proceeded through several stages. These were interrelated, but each possessed a discrete existence of its own. Rather than be viewed as one coherent, fluid movement, the uprising needs to be perceived as a succession of episodes: i.e. the October mobilisation; the November Truce; the December Pardon; the final showdown. Each episode, arguably, demands its own careful and separate study.

As well as a succession of episodes, the pilgrimage of grace comprised a series of regional revolts. These also require to be studied separately, as well as in relation to the whole, in order to be properly understood. Examining the uprising as local history, rather than simply as a national event, has made progress in the last thirty years, with studies on Lancashire, Cumbria, Durham and the West Riding. Unfortunately, much of this work is seriously flawed and needs to be redone. Thus R. B. Smith made the basic mistake of assuming that the revolts in the West Riding could only be one of two types of insurrection: either popular or aristocratic. In doing so, he overlooked a third type, proposed earlier by Rachel Reid who conceived the pilgrimage of grace as an uprising that came form below and was promoted by the unwillingness of discontented gentlemen to co-operate with the government in its suppression.[10] Smith also made the untenable assumption that, because the gentlemen did nothing to stop it, they were guilty of starting it. Haigh produced two studies of Lancashire in the pilgrimage of grace.[11] Both are marred by his failure to analyse the full significance of the rebels' complaint against the dissolution of the lesser monasteries, the result of his labelling it as just a religious grievance. In addition, he failed to appreciate the fact that much of the actual revolt in Lancashire was imported by invading armies: in north Lancashire by the Atkinson host from Westmorland; in east Lancashire by the Tempest/Hamerton host from Yorkshire. As for S. M. Harrison's study of the Cumbrian revolts, it failed to identify the basic nature of the agrarian grievances present, largely by ignoring its close association

10 Smith, op. cit., ch. 5; R. R. Reid, *The King's Council in the North* (London, 1921), pp. 136–9.
11 See his *Reformation and Resistance in Tudor Lancashire*, ch. 9 and his *The Last Days of the Lancashire Monasteries and the Pilgrimage of Grace*, Chetham Society, 3rd series, 17 (1969), passim.

with the custom of tenant right.[12] Moreover, he failed to distinguish
between the uprisings in Cumberland and the barony of Westmorland. And so he found in the Cumbrian region two revolts whereas
in reality there were three. Finally, his book is weak in descriptive
narrative, concentrating instead upon explanation and analysis, and
therefore offers an inadequate account of the course of each revolt.
The local study of the pilgrimage of grace, then, has still a long way
to go before it can be said to have covered the subject adequately.

Although published long ago, the Dodds' study remains the
standard account of the pilgrimage of grace. For the detailed story of
the uprising as a whole, it is the only authority. That it should
dominate the subject for so long is quite remarkable and probably
without equal for an historical work. Its outlook is pleasantly open-
minded, if rose-tinted and romantic. The Dodds had no axe to grind
and they brought out the plurality and variety evident in the uprising's
grievances and social roots. In fact, they provided an impressive
appreciation of the uprising's complexity. However, the book tells a
fine story but one littered with minor errors. Its dates, for example, are
frequently wrong, even if only by a day or two. As a piece of analysis, it
offers little more than the occasional, and often nonsensical, general-
isation. In surveying the October uprisings, the Dodds placed too
much emphasis upon the ones that occurred on Humberside. Their
mistake was to regard the Lincolnshire uprising as an integral part of
the pilgrimage of grace, so much so that they devoted two substantial
chapters to it.[13] Another mistake was to include in the same book the
unrelated Exeter conspiracy of 1538. This left them with insufficient
space to treat fully the whole range of revolts of which the pilgrimage
of grace was composed. Consequently, the uprisings in the North
Riding, in the palatinate of Durham, in the northern wolds of the
East Riding, in the uplands of the West Riding, in Lancashire and
Cumbria are all crammed together in one breathless chapter.[14]

What is badly needed is a new narrative: one which incorporates
the complexity of the regional revolts with an account of the successive
stages of the uprising's development. What is also needed is sustained
comparative analysis of its pre-conditions, aims, leadership, organisa-

12 S. M. Harrison, *The Pilgrimage of Grace in the Lake Counties, 1536–7* (London,
   1981), pp. 47–56. He simply stresses that entry fines were being raised and the
   tenantry were therefore "hard pressed", whereas the issue in contention related to
   the system of border service tenant right and concerned an alleged breach of the
   custom.
13 Dodds, I, chs. 5 and 6.
14 Ibid., ch. 9.

tion and impact, as well as examination of the light the uprising throws upon the social, religious and political attitudes of the time. This study offers a small contribution to this large task. Its subject is the formation of the rebel armies (i.e. hosts) which, in just over a fortnight, obliged the government to concede the truce of 27th October. Its basic aim is to examine, in all its regional diversity, the creation of the uprising.

The nature of revolt

With autumn slipping into winter, October 1536 was a most unlikely time to mount a rebellion; yet in the first week of the month two large rebel hosts were mobilised in Lincolnshire and, in the second and third weeks another eight sprang up in the north, one of which, the Bowes host, divided into two separate forces, producing nine armies in all. Each of these armies was several thousand strong; each professed to be a rising of the commons; each was similarly moved by a concern for both the faith of Christ and the commonwealth; each hated the government for being extortionate and heretical. All recruited from the whole range of society, their supporters including gentlemen and clerics as well as townsmen and peasants. Some of the participants claimed they were compelled to join, but clearly evident was not only the fury of all three orders but also their ability to find a common accord, especially in their shared hostility to the government and Thomas Cromwell. None of these hosts was the work of one particular social group. Moreover, in each case gentlemen and clerics sought to manipulate the people. But from the latter came a strong drive of protest and rage which rendered the uprisings, in initiative and impetus, popular movements.

The hosts of October 1536 were undoubtedly part of a long tradition. As the product of so-called risings of the commons which aimed to put the government to right, they belonged to a genre of protest that had its beginnings in 1381; that declared itself again in Jack Cade's uprising of 1450 and in the Lincolnshire revolt of 1470; and that came to spectacular fruition between 1489 and 1549. In that period six such uprisings occurred: in Yorkshire in 1489; in Cornwall in 1497; in Lincolnshire and the north in 1536; in Norfolk and Cornwall in 1549. Each rebellion took the form of an army acting in the name and interest of the commons. The purpose in each case was to denote that within the body politic things were out of joint and to propose that, since remedy seemed beyond the capacity of the designated ruling element and therefore unachievable in the normal way, a topsy-turvy means of action was required.

Within this tradition of revolt, the northern uprising of October 1536 was certainly distinctive. As well as a rising of the commons, it was uniquely conceived as a pilgrimage. Also distinguishing it was the importance the rebels attached to oath-swearing. An exceptionally large number of gentlemen and clerics were involved. Finally, in its opening stages it enjoyed remarkable success. With five of its hosts converging upon Pontefract in late October, and two more confronting the loyalist Earl of Derby in Lancashire and a further one pinning down the loyalist Earl of Cumberland in Skipton Castle, and with the government having at its disposal no more than a pathetic, disease-ridden army, part of which was occupied in holding down Lincolnshire, the king was forced on 27th October to agree to a humiliating truce whose terms obliged him to consider seriously the rebels' grievances as they were set out in five general articles delivered to him by the rebel leaders, Sir Ralph Ellerker and Robert Bowes.

The northern uprising was first presented as a pilgrimage on 13th October when the Aske and Stapulton hosts met on Weighton Hill, just outside Market Weighton in the East Riding. Accompanying Stapulton were two messengers from the Lincolnshire uprising. In conversation with them Aske remarked that "they were pilgrims" and had a "pilgrimage gat to go".[15] Soon afterwards the term appeared in various manifestos, all produced by Robert Aske between 16th and 18th October when he was resident in York. A letter addressed to the gentlemen, usually termed his second proclamation, referred to "this assembly or pilgrimage" and was signed by Aske "in the name of all pilgrimage and commonalty".[16] Three other written statements made by Aske at this time associated the alleged pilgrimage specifically with a bid for grace. Thus, an order for religious houses was issued "by all the whole consent of all the headmen of this our pilgrimage for grace". It represents the first known usage of this term.[17] In the same period Aske also composed a letter of protection for the abbey of York St. Mary, which stated that the monks had

---

15 *L.P.* XI. 828/xii, p. 327. The term was not used in the proclamation of 11th October (*L.P.* XI. 622); and was presumably concocted either at the Skipwith Moor assembly of 12th October; or *en route* to meet up with the Beverley and Holderness rebels at Weighton Hill.

16 Several variants of this letter have survived. See *St.P.* I, pp. 466–7 (*L.P.* XI. 705{2}); P.R.O. SP1/108 (*L.P.* XI. 705{3}) and P.R.O. E36/118, f. 21 (*L.P.* XI. 705{4/ii}).

17 Toller, p. 51 (*L.P.* XI. 784/ii). For the order in which these statements were issued, see below, pp. 90–2.

promised to aid the rebels "in this our pilgrimage of grace" and an elaborate oath for swearing in the gentlemen called "the oath of the honourable men".[18] The latter contained the first mention of the variant term "our pilgrimage of grace for the commonwealth".

The meaning of this particular term was made evident in Aske's second proclamation which declared that the purpose of the pilgrimage was to petition the king "for the reformation of that which is amiss" and to seek "the punishment of the heretics and subverters of the laws" in order to preserve "Christ's church" and also "this realm of England", along with its king, nobility and commonalty.[19] Further light is thrown upon its meaning by Aske's encounter with Lancaster Herald at Pontefract Castle on 21st October, the day after the castle's submission. When the herald asked him for the content of the rebels' articles, Aske blustered, not having as yet drawn them up, saying "he and his company would go to London, of pilgrimage to the king's highness, and there to have all vile blood of his council put from him, and all noble blood set up again; and also the faith of Christ and his laws to be kept and full restitution of Christ's church of all wrongs done unto it, and also the commonty to be used as they should be".[20] Yet another insight into its meaning was provided by Aske during his final examination when he remarked that the purpose of assembling was "for grace by petition to [the king] for remedy for their faith".[21] The uprising was conceived, then, as a pilgrimage to invoke grace which would proceed by petitioning the king to terminate the government's pact with heresy and to revive respect for the society of orders and its abiding principles. Whose grace was being sought? Although the second proclamation is somewhat ambiguous, implying that God's favour was being invoked to oblige the king to grace his northern subjects with redress of grievance, the general tenor of the evidence suggests that it was the king's.

Not all the hosts presented themselves as being on a pilgrimage of grace, but the usage of the term spread beyond the movements led by Aske. Thus, when the Hamerton/Tempest host sought to raise east Lancashire in order to prevent the Earl of Derby from suppressing the restored Sawley Abbey, it issued a proclamation signed, in reflection of the order for religious houses, "by all the whole consent of the headmen in this our pilgrimage for grace to the commonwealth".[22] The

18 SP1/110, f. 210b (*L.P.* XI. 784/iii); Toller, p. 50 (*L.P.* XI. 892 {3}).
19 See above, n. 16.
20 *St.P.* I, pp. 486–7 (*L.P.* XI. 826).
21 Bateson, p. 571.
22 Toller, pp. 51–2 (*L.P.* XI. 892{2}).

Atkinson host also used the term, informing the Earl of Derby when he ordered it to go home that "they had a pilgrimage to do for the commonwealth".[23] And in November John Atkinson, its head captain, informed John Towneley of Burnley that he had received a letter from Aske "in this our pilgrimage of grace for the commonwealth".[24] The hosts which made no reference to the pilgrimage of grace subscribed to Captain Poverty. They presented themselves as under instruction from this allegorical figure. By doing so, they implied a pilgrimage. Presenting the image of a movement led by a figure who was thought to be both Christ and the commons, the hosts of Cumberland, Westmorland, Richmondshire and Durham were calling upon the Piers Plowman story which, as told by William Langland, featured in book six a pilgrimage of the whole range of society that looked to a ploughman for leadership and direction.[25] Not surprisingly in view of the context, the term "pilgrimage" had for the rebels a strong and significant religious connotation. Thus, its very usage marked a protest against the government's recent campaign to root out saint-worship, in which it had condemned the traditional practices associated with seeking the grace of God through the intercession of saints. Prominent among these practices, as defined in the royal injunctions enforcing the Ten Articles, had been pilgrimages.[26] But neither the purpose nor the provenance of the term "pilgrimage of grace" was simply religious. Part of the idea was probably adopted from the Lincolnshire uprising which did not regard itself as engaged in a pilgrimage but may well have described the supplication that it sent to the king as a "humble petition for grace".[27] The concerns of this petition were preponder-

---

23 Toller, p. 44 (*L.P.* XI. 947{2}).
24 SP1/108 (*L.P.* XI. 804).
25 M. L. Bush, "Captain Poverty and the pilgrimage of grace", *Historical Research*, 65 (1992), pp. 17–36.
26 No mention is made of pilgrimages in the Ten Articles, but the injunctions produced shortly afterwards by Cromwell warned priests against "alluring" the people "by any enticement to the pilgrimage of any saint"; and whilst not forbidding them, they called upon priests to discourage people from going on them. At issue was the belief that the remission of sin could only be granted by God and through Christ. The corollary was that saints had no power to remit sin and therefore nothing was to be gained by beseeching them to do so by venerating their images or relics. See G. Burnet, *The History of the Reformation of the Church of England* (Oxford, 1829), I(ii), pp. 250–56 (for injunctions) and pp. 459–73 (for articles).
27 This phrase was used in the king's letter to the Duke of Suffolk, dated 15th October [SP1/110 (*L.P.* XI. 971)]. It seems to relate to the petition addressed by the rebels to the king and dispatched on 9th October. See below, p. 15.

antly secular.[28] Moreover, the fact that it was addressed to the king suggests that "grace" in this context simply meant "royal favour". Aske was well aware of this petition, its content and its purpose. In the first week of his revolt, he used it to declare their grievances.[29] The likelihood, then, is that, whilst the concept of rebellion as a pilgrimage was the clever creation of Robert Aske, the attached "for grace" or "of grace" was adopted from the Lincolnshire uprising and had a secular connotation.

Furthermore, of the variants used, the term most frequently employed was not "pilgrimage of grace" but "pilgrimage of grace for the commonwealth".[30] It seems that the usage of the term developed as follows: first "pilgrimage for grace" was used which, in order to avoid the repetition of the preposition "for", had to be altered to "pilgrimage of grace" when the phrase "for the commonwealth" was tacked on.[31] "For the commonwealth" meant either "for the commons" or "for the material good of the realm".[32] Both meanings denoted material, as opposed to spiritual, benefits. No matter how used, it marked another pointed reaction against the government. Just as the rebels' designation of the revolt as a pilgrimage was a provocative rejoinder to a government which had recently dismissed the practice as a superstitious indulgence, so its presentation of the revolt as a defence of the commonwealth was an attempt to brand a government, which repeatedly justified its reforms by declaring that they were good for the commonwealth, as either hypocritical or capable only of achieving the opposite of what it intended. The northern uprisings thus declared through their very title an avowed

28 The text of the petition has survived only in an incomplete form. See P.R.O. SP1/ 108(*L.P.* XI. 705). One article is missing: i.e. the objection to the tax of clerical first fruits. See M. L. Bush, "Up for the commonweal; the significance of tax grievances in the English rebellions of 1536", *E.H.R.*, 106 (1991), pp. 303–4. Of the six articles of complaint, one deals with spiritual matters alone and three deal solely with material matters. The other two deal with both material and spiritual matters. See below, pp. 17–18.

29 Bush, op. cit., pp. 306–7.

30 For the various usages, see Toller, pp. 50–51 (*L.P.* XI. 705{4}); *L.P.* XI. 892{2}; SP1/108 (*L.P.* XI. 804); *L.P.* XI. 785; Toller, p. 44 (*L.P.* XI. 947{2}); *L.P.* XI. 1218.

31 As in the order for religious houses [Toller, p. 51 (*L.P.* XI. 784/ii)] and in the letter of protection for York St. Mary Abbey [SP1/110, f. 210b (*L.P.* XI. 784)]. A variant which preserved the original "pilgrimage for grace" was "our pilgrimage for grace to the commonwealth" [see *L.P.* XI. 892{2}]. The original manuscript, once located in the P.R.O., is now lost.

32 Bush, "Captain Poverty", p. 30.

opposition not simply to the Henrician reformation but also to some of the government's secular policies.

Needless to say, the uprising was a pilgrimage only in name and conceit. Essentially, it consisted of a number of horsed and harnessed armies which marched to places of no religious significance, which sought to gain support by the threat of military force and which planned to do battle if its petition beseeching the king to show grace and favour failed.[33]

Both the Lincolnshire uprising and the pilgrimage of grace were distinguished from the other risings of the commons in the emphasis each placed on taking oaths of allegiance to the rebellion. Thus, as a preliminary to forming the host, confederations were formed bound by oath. The oath came in two basic forms: either "to be true to God, the king and the commonwealth" or "to be true to God, the king and the commons". Both forms were first created by the Lincolnshire rebels and then adopted by the northerners who added a third variation, Aske's oath of the honourable men, which was specially designed to declare the grievances of the uprising prior to the drawing up of a petition.[34] The business of taking oaths, however, was simply in imitation of the Succession Act of 1534 which made all adult Englishmen liable to an oath binding them to accept the king's divorce and remarriage and to reject the pope's jurisdiction in the matter. Following this legislation, royal commissions had enforced it, obliging selected subjects to take the oath and proceeding against those who refused.[35] So again, as with their use of the term "commonwealth", the rebels imitated the government, creating and applying the commons' oath in the manner of the king's oath.

The Lincolnshire uprising and the pilgrimage of grace were also distinguished from the other risings of the commons by their success in enlisting large numbers of gentlemen. However, all the risings of the commons drew support from the other two orders. With clerics and gentlemen involved they were never popular movements *tout court*. The ones most inclined to appear popular had overriding agrarian grievances: i.e. certain strands of the peasants revolt of 1381, Ket's rebellion of 1549 and the Cumbrian revolts of 1536. In these instances the participating gentlemen did not become leaders but were rather borne along by the commons. Yet when political grievances were

---

33 For the military plan, see *L.P.* XI. 705{2} and Bateson, pp. 569 and 571.
34 As Aske made clear to Lancaster Herald when he met him on 21st October. See *St.P.* I, pp. 486–7 (*L.P.* XI. 826). For the oath, see Toller, pp. 50–51.
35 G. W. O. Woodward, *The Dissolution of the Monasteries* (London, 1966), pp. 50–1. The statutes are 25 Henry VIII, c. 22, revised by 26 Henry VIII, c. 13.

dominant, a rising of the commons could be led by gentlemen. This was very much the case in 1536, in Lincolnshire, Yorkshire and the palatinate of Durham. With the social hierarchy enlisted, the government lost its local means of suppressing disorder and the commons were given the assurance that their disobedience was warranted. Such revolts, initially small in scale, had the chance to escalate into extensive rebellions as the government was driven to look elsewhere for a means of suppression.

In Lincolnshire the uprising suddenly folded as the gentry lost their nerve and unconditionally surrendered.[36] In the north, however, the uprising persisted as the gentry remained true to the rebel cause although determined to defeat the government by extracting from it concessions rather than by brute force. Thus, the hosts failed to march on London, but, having organised themselves for military action in October, the rebels remained ready for further action if the government failed to offer satisfaction. As a result, concessions were gained: the October Truce, then the December Pardon. Also secured was the promise of a parliament, to be held in York, to consider the grievances specifically set out in the rebels' twenty-four articles. The only fly in the ointment was that the uprising expressed not simply an aristocratic and clerical protest but also a revolt of the people. This was made evident in popular suspicions of the government's trustworthiness which developed as soon as the October Truce was signed.[37] These led to further revolts which the rebel leadership could not stop, revolts which rocked without capsizing the Truce in November and eventually destroyed the December agreement in the course of January and February 1537.[38] With promises broken, and with the organisation of the uprising as a society of orders having been fractured by the persistence of revolt and the contempt of the commons for what the gentlemen rebels had achieved, the government was able to exchange policy for the sword. Unfurling the banner, it could now resort to a military solution.[39]

A final distinguishing feature of the pilgrimage of grace was its dependence upon the Lincolnshire uprising. In the early stages the pilgrimage was but an adjunct of the movement south of the Humber. It raised troops simply to march them to the aid of the Lincolnshire men; during the first week of revolt, it relied upon the petition

36 See below, p. 16.
37 Dodds, I, chs. 12 and 13.
38 Ibid., II, chs. 16–18.
39 Ibid., ch. 18.

produced by the Lincolnshire rebels to state its own grievances; and its procedure and organisation were utterly derivative, relying not simply upon the tradition of risings of the commons but also upon the example set by the Lincolnshire uprising.

The Lincolnshire prelude

Characterising the Lincolnshire uprising was the speed at which it became a substantial rebellion and the suddenness of its termination.[40] Breaking out in the episcopal town of Louth on 2nd October, initially in defence of the treasures belonging to its church, it recruited support from the surrounding countryside, burned heretical books and captured the commissioners engaged in dissolving Legbourne Priory. Then, on 3rd October, the Louth rebels captured the subsidy commissioners, obliging them to compose a letter of complaint to the king which was immediately dispatched to him. The following day, having mustered at Julian Bower to form a host captained by the captured gentlemen, it resolved to march on Lincoln which it had reached by 6th October. *En route* the Louth host held a series of musters, at Towes and Hambleton Hill on 5th October and at Dunholm on 6th October. At these musters it recruited support from the vicinity and linked up with other hosts, one recruited from the town of Caistor and its surroundings, another recruited from West Ancholme: that is, the region between the rivers Ancholme and Trent which prior, to its absorption into the Louth host, was temporarily under the captaincy of Robert Aske.[41] Then in Lincoln the Louth host met up with the host recruited from the Horncastle region. This had likewise organised itself as a society of orders under the captaincy of gentlemen, one of whom was sheriff of the county, Sir Edward Dymmoke. Together, the two hosts formed an army reckoned at 20,000 men, all raised from the region of Lindsey.[42]

---

40 Dodds, I, chs. 5 and 6; A. Ward, *The Lincolnshire Rising, 1536* (Nottingham, 1986), passim.

41 For the West Ancholme revolt, see below, p. 78. For the link–ups, see *L.P.* XI. 828/i, 853–4 and 971.

42 This figure was provided by Guy Kyme when he related what had happened in Lincolnshire to the Yorkshire rebels on 11th October. See Stapulton, p. 89. The same figure was quoted by Marmaduke Constable and Robert Tyrwhit on 5th October as the size of the force provided by the market towns of Lindsey: i.e. Louth, Horncastle, Caistor and Market Rasen (*L.P.* XI. 553). Other figures quoted at the time were 10,000–12,000 spears with 30,000 others, given in a report to Cromwell (*L.P.* XI. 567) and over 40,000 in a report to Audley on 7th October (*L.P.* XI. 585). It was clearly a very large army. The figures vary because some include all supporters whilst others include only those selected to man the host.

By this time the Horncastle revolt had already produced and distributed a statement of grievance in the form of a set of articles. This was revised by the gentlemen on 7th October, approved by the commons on 8th October and dispatched on 9th October, southwards to the Court and northwards into the East and West Ridings. It was sent into Yorkshire in response to letters from the towns of Halifax and Beverley offering support and requesting further information. The articles were presented as a petition. In the manner of a bill of complaint exhibited to a court of equity, they were addressed "to the king, our sovereign lord".[43]

So far, the host had recruited its support from the clay lands and chalk wolds north of Lincoln. It now sought to involve southern Lincolnshire, especially Holland. In doing so, however, it suddenly lost momentum and confidence, probably because of the differences developing between the gentlemen and the commons on how to proceed. On 6th October a link-up with fenland Lincolnshire was planned, with Sheriff Dymmoke summoning the people of Holland to an assembly at Ancaster Heath on 8th October.[44] But no such assembly took place, presumably because the gentlemen in Lincoln, reacting against the impatience of the commons to set forward, successfully urged that, before proceeding further, they should await the king's reply to their letter of 3rd October.[45] The king's reply to this letter arrived on 10th October.[46] Its reception widened the gulf between the two orders, especially after the commons had demanded to hear its contents and learned, thanks to the parson of Snelland, that in reading it out to them Thomas Moigne had omitted a certain passage.[47] This omission was undoubtedly the statement which contemptuously dismissed the rebels' request for a general pardon and instead ordered them to hand over one hundred ringleaders with halters about their necks. Moigne probably left it out to prevent the commons from insisting upon an immediate march on London. The exposure of his treachery brought the rebel gentlemen and commons almost to blows and made the commons even more determined not to wait but to act.[48] Although the king's reply had offered them little comfort, however, the gentlemen insisted upon awaiting the king's

---

43 Bush, "Up for the commonweal" , p. 303. For the articles, see SP1/108 (*L.P.* XI. 705).
44 *L.P.* XI. 571.
45 *L.P.* XI. 971.
46 *L.P.* XI. 569.
47 *L.P.* XI. 665 and 971.
48 Ibid. and Hoyle, "Thomas Master's narrative", pp. 65–6.

answer to their petition of 9th October.[49] Then, on 12th October, the
uprising suddenly collapsed. This was in response to a proclamation
from the Earl of Shrewsbury which ordered the rebels to disperse,
threatening to wage battle against those who did not.[50] At this point
the rebels decided to disband their host and the gentlemen rebels
resolved to visit the Duke of Suffolk, the man in charge of the
government's military operation against the uprising, to seek his
intercession with the king for the general pardon which both the letter
of 3rd October and the petition of 9th October had requested and the
king's reply had refused.[51]

Staggered by the sudden collapse of the uprising, the government
was slow to react. Not until 15th October was the Duke of Suffolk
ordered to occupy Lincoln; and not until 17th October did he actually
do so.[52] As for the uprisings in Yorkshire, the abrupt end of the
Lincolnshire uprising left them policyless. This was because of their
reliance upon the Lincolnshire petition to articulate their own complaint and because of their plan of joining up with the midland revolt
in order to confront the government together. At first they refused to
believe what they heard.[53] Subsequently, they came to believe that the
Lincolnshire host had dispersed because it had gained what it wanted:
the general pardon and some redress.[54] It therefore became an urgent
matter to press for the same treatment; but the decision made by the
leadership was to do so not by an act of submission but by maintaining
a military presence. As the news seeped through that the Lincolnshire
rebels had surrendered unconditionally, Aske summoned a convocation of the hosts and, backed by a considerable force, obtained from
the government what the midlanders had been denied.[55]

Throughout October the pilgrimage of grace remained dominated
by the example of the Lincolnshire uprising and the lesson to be
learned from its sudden demise. It imitated its procedures; it adopted
its grievances; it applied its remedies. The Lincolnshire rebels declared
their grievances and remedies in two letters to the government: that is,
the letter of 3rd October from the subsidy commissioners and the
petition of 9th October. What is noticeable about their grievances is

49 Ibid.
50 G. W. Bernard, *The Power of the Early Tudor Nobility: a Study of the Fourth and
    Fifth Earls of Shrewsbury* (Brighton, 1985), p. 34.
51 *L.P.* XI. 971.
52 *L.P.* XI. 715; *L.P.* XI. 747 and 939.
53 Stapulton, p. 96.
54 See below, p. 98.
55 See below, ch. X.

the prominence given to complaints against the government's exploitation of the realm. Thus, the letter of 3rd October presented the cause
of the uprising as first, the rumours that "all the jewels and goods of
the churches of the country should be taken from them and brought to
your grace's council" and secondly, the rumour that the king's loving
subjects "should be put of new to enhancements and other importunate charges" which "extreme poverty" prevented them from paying.
In addition, the letter implied an objection to a peace-time subsidy in
its declaration that the rebels were prepared to sacrifice "their bodies,
lands and goods . . . for the defence of your person or your realm", a
complaint confirmed by an anonymous report from Gosperton to
Chancellor Audley which revealed that the rebels wished the king
would not demand further supplies from his subjects except in time
of war and specifically for the defence of the realm.[56]

The letter of 3rd October was essentially a complaint against
government exploitation. It contained no reference to the faith and
claimed that the rebels' purpose was the maintenance of the king and
commonwealth. The material concerns of the letter are confirmed as
genuine statements of complaint by the early actions of the rebels, the
Louth revolt beginning as a defensive action to safeguard the treasures
of Louth church from imminent confiscation[57]; the Caistor revolt
beginning as a tax protest against the subsidy commissioners, the
rebels asserting that "they would pay no more silver"[58]; the Horncastle rebels initially moved by the Louth men's protest against the
rumoured plans to confiscate church goods and then driven to murder
Dr. Raynes, chancellor to the Bishop of Lincoln, who was thought to
be about to implement them.[59]

The material emphasis of the grievances is also made evident in the
petition of 9th October and its articles. They amounted to six complaints, four of them claiming that various forms of taxation were
threatening the well-being of the commonwealth.[60] Thus, the fiscal
feudalism unleashed by the recent Statute of Uses, the new clerical
taxes of first fruits and tenths, and the fifteenth and tenth due in 1537
without the traditional rebate for poverty, were all three presented as
harmful and insupportable, while a further article blamed their introduction upon persons of low birth who, it was suggested, had misused
their closeness to the king to procure what was "most especially for

56 Dodds, I, pp. 98–9 (*L.P.* XI. 534); *L.P.* XI. 585.
57 *L.P.* XI. 828/i; *L.P.* XII{1}. 380.
58 SP1/106 (*L.P.* XI. 533).
59 *L.P.* XI. 828/i/2; *L.P.* XII{1}. 70/xii.
60 Bush, "Up for the commonweal", pp. 303–4.

their own advantage". The corollary of this point was to deplore the
exclusion of true noblemen from the government.[61] No wonder that
when the Lincolnshire articles were encountered in Yorkshire, it was
reported there that they "were up in Lincolnshire for the commonweal".[62]

But the Lincolnshire uprising was not simply provoked by the
government's plunder of the realm. Another of its concerns was the
defence of the faith. This failed to feature in the letter of 3rd October
but appeared in three of the articles contained in the petition of 9th
October. Thus, the suppression of abbeys was opposed "whereby the
service of God is minished"; objection was also made to the "late
promotion" of a number of bishops "that hath subverted the faith of
Christ"; and the article blaming ministers of low birth for the government's obnoxious policies could be taken to deplore their promotion of
heresy as well as their extortionate ways.[63] Furthermore, associated
with the uprising was the burning of heretical books.[64] This was
accompanied by complaints about the abrogation of holy days[65]; the
destruction of parish churches[66]; the termination of the pope's overlordship of the Anglican church[67]; the reduction of the sacraments
from seven to three[68]; and the new teaching "touching our lady and
purgatory".[69]

On the other hand, the complaint against the suppression of
religious houses was so phrased in the petition of 9th October as to
give it a temporal as well as a spiritual meaning. The point it made was
that, on account of the Dissolution, "the poorality of your realm be

61 This point was not made explicitly in the petition, but it was in the rebels' minds
    at the time. See *L.P.* XI. 828/v.
62 E36/119, f. 35 (*L.P.* XII{1}. 201/vii).
63 SP1/108 (*L.P.* XI. 705).
64 *L.P.* XI. 828/iii and 853.
65 *L.P.* XI. 553 and 970.
66 See *L.P.* XII{1}. 70/xii and 380.
67 Simon Maltby reported bidding the beads in the traditional manner on 8th
    October which involved praying for the pope and the cardinals [E36/118, f. 4
    (*L.P.* XI. 975)]. Thomas Kendall, vicar of Louth, claimed that people begrudged
    the king's headship of the church (*L.P.* XI. 970). There were other rebels,
    however, who declared that they were not against the king's headship of the
    church. See Porman's declaration (*L.P.* XI. 853) and Nicholas Leach's declara-
    tion (*L.P.* XII{1}. 70/xi).
68 This point was made by the chronicler Edward Hall but by no one else. See E.
    Hall, *The Reign of Henry VIII*, ed. C. Whibley (London, 1904), p. 269.
69 *L.P.* XII{1}. 70/i/5.

unrelieved, the which we think is great hurt for the commonwealth".[70]
Likewise, the complaint against heretical bishops in the same petition
was given a temporal twist since the article that made it referred to
"the vexation that hath been taken of your subjects" by the Bishop of
Lincoln as "the beginning of all the trouble", a reference, among other
things, to the confiscation of church treasures which it was feared he
was about to implement.[71] On the other hand, some of the complaints
made by the Lincolnshire rebels against the government's plunder of
the realm may have had spiritual as well as material significance. For
example, the rumoured tax on births, deaths and marriages could be
seen as doing spiritual harm because it was understood that an
inability to pay would bar people from receiving the associated sacrament; and the confiscation of church treasures could be seen not only
as an appropriation of wealth but also as the removal of aids to efficacy
in the business of interceding with God for the living and the dead. In
this respect, whilst the grievances of the Lincolnshire rebels can be said
to have fallen into two categories, the one centring on the defence of
the faith from heresy, the other on defending of the commonwealth
from government greed, some of the grievances, having both temporal
and spiritual implications, fit into both.

The Lincolnshire grievances, in taking this basic faith and commonwealth form, were very similar to those of the pilgrimage of grace.
They differed in two respects. First, they showed no concern for
infringements of the constitution. Unlike the northern revolts, there
was no talk of the laws of the realm being subverted; and when concern
was shown for the privileges of the church it was related specifically to

---

70 SP1/108 (*L.P.* XI. 705). The petition objected to the suppression that had so far
   occurred. In support of this view, one of the first acts of the Louth rebels was to
   go to Legbourne Priory. There they stopped the dissolution, taking captive the
   commissioners involved. But the surviving evidence offers a variety of views on
   the Dissolution, some of them tolerant of it. One rebel point of view was that
   no more suppressions should take place (see *L.P.* XI. 853), presumably a
   response to the rumour that all abbeys were about to be dissolved (see *L.P.*
   XII{1}. 70/x), but implying that the dissolution of the lesser monasteries was
   acceptable on condition that it did not go any further. Another rebel point of
   view thought that suppressions "for the king's pleasure" should be allowed
   (*L.P.* XI. 585), implying that those carried out for the benefit of his ministers
   should be disallowed. There is no good evidence to prove that the Lincolnshire
   rebels restored any religious houses. Christopher Ascough reported to Cromwell
   on 6th October that "they have made a nun in your abbey of Legbourne and an
   abbot in Louth Park" (*L.P.* XI. 567), but this overlooks the fact that Legbourne
   had yet to be dissolved and it is also contradicted by Guy Kyme who told the
   Yorkshire rebels on 11th October that there had been no restorations in
   Lincolnshire (*L.P.* XI. 828).
71 *L.P.* XI. 828/i/2; *L.P.* XII{1}. 70/xii; E36/118, f. 4 (*L.P.* XI. 975).

the fiscal issue of the new taxes imposed upon the clergy in the form of first fruits and tenths.[72] Secondly, the Lincolnshire rebels appeared to lack agrarian complaints: the agrarian problems identified by the northern rebels went totally unmentioned in Lincolnshire.

Not only in the basic nature of its grievances but also in the method of revolt, the pilgrimage of grace followed the example of the Lincolnshire uprising. Both rebellions were self-consciously and reputedly risings of the commons. But this did not render them popular revolts since central to their organisation were gentlemen and central to their inspiration were clerics. Moved themselves by grudges against the government, the gentlemen promoted the Lincolnshire uprising.[73] But this does not mean that it was their creation. Initially, their contribution to the development of revolt lay only in their failure to take counteraction. Then actual participation came of their enforced enlistment. As for the clergy, they certainly played a part in provoking the uprising. Alienated by the government's religious reforms and tax demands, they appeared to create the rumours which sparked it off. Fearing that large numbers would be deprived of their livings so that first fruits could be exacted of their successors, and pressured by impending visitations, organised by the Bishop of Lincoln and carried out by his chancellor, Dr. Raynes, the secular clergy spread the rumour that the visitors would not simply examine the clergy to see that they were fit to have the cure of souls but would also confiscate all church treasures and destroy some parish churches.[74] In response, the commons rose to defend their parish churches against this onslaught. In addition, the clergy helped to incite revolt by returning home with the news, after being present in large numbers in Louth and Caistor at the start of the uprising because of the episcopal visitation to which they had been summoned; by ringing the bells of their churches on 2nd and 3rd October and by encouraging the commons to take action.[75] Having

---

72 E36/121, f. 116 (*L.P.* XI. 585).

73 M. E. James in his "Obedience and dissent in Henrician England; the Lincolnshire rebellion, 1536", *Past and Present*, 48 (1970) makes a case for an aggrieved gentility. This is criticised but not totally demolished by S. J. Gunn in his "Peers, commons and gentry in the Lincolnshire revolt of 1536", *Past and Present*, 123 (1989), which proposed a revolt driven by popular initiative and involving a gentry which had been compelled to participate.

74 See *L.P.* XI. 975 and *L.P.* XII{1}. 380 and 481. Also see Dodds, I, pp. 91–2.

75 Dodds, I, p. 94. On 2nd October sixty parish priests were assembled in Louth for the visitation. With the visitation stopped, they returned home and rang their church bells. For the part played by the clergy in initially arousing the commons, see M. Bowker, "Lincolnshire 1536: heresy, schism or religious discontent", *Studies in Church History*, 9 (1972), pp. 200–201. For the eight score priests assembled in Caistor, see *L.P.* XI. 853.

urged the men of Louth to defend their church crosses, Thomas Kendall, vicar of Louth, was reported to have slapped the backs of the rebels bidding them: "Go in their journey".[76] Nicholas Leach, vicar of Belchford, appeared to play a similar role in the Horncastle revolt.[77] Besides the secular clergy, the regulars were also very much involved: not just ex-monks like William Morland but also the monks and canons of the remaining houses, moved by the fear that they were next in line for suppression. Barlings, Bardney, Kirkstead, Grimsby all provided money and men.[78] One calculation put the number of priests and monks openly engaged with the rebels at seven to eight hundred.[79]

The Lincolnshire uprising began as a movement of burgesses and peasants summoned by the ringing of bells to assemble in certain townships, notably Scunthorpe, Caistor, Louth and Horncastle where they formed confederations bound by the oath to be true to God, the king and the commons, or some close variant of that formula.[80] The initial leadership was provided by commoners or very minor gentlemen: i.e. Nicholas Melton, a shoemaker of Louth; William Leach, yeoman of Horncastle; and George Huddiswell, yeoman but sometimes described as gentleman, of Horkstow near South Ferriby, who was elected captain of the Caistor uprising on 3rd October and who, "with a black coat and a grey beard", took Robert Aske captive on 4th October and made him swear the commons' oath.[81] The commons then sought to involve the gentlemen and clergy of the region by imposing upon them the same oath. Having subjected them to the commons' oath, they then tried to re-enact the society of orders by forming an army led by gentlemen. In the case of the Louth host, this was organised exactly in accordance with the normal administration of the region, with the rebels divided up into the wapentakes from which they came and with each wapentake captained by its leading gentleman.[82] Also in keeping with the society of orders, the gentlemen were obliged to formulate statements of grievance. However, having recruited the county establishment and having required of it a role in keeping with the society of orders, the Lincolnshire uprising did not cease to be a rising of the commons. The declarations of complaint

---

76 *L.P.* XI. 854.
77 *L.P.* XI. 828/i/2.
78 Dodds, I, pp. 104–5. For the view that the government was planning to suppress all religious houses, see *L.P.* XII(1). 70/x; *L.P.* XI. 853; *L.P.* XII{1}. 702.
79 *L.P.* XI. 854.
80 For the oath and its variants, see *L.P.* XI. 568, 571, 585, 853, 854, 968.
81 For Melton, see *L.P.* XI. 568 and 828/iii. For Leach, see *L.P.* XI. 828/i/2. For Huddiswell, see *L.P.* XI. 568 and 853; Bateson, p. 332.
82 *L.P.* XI. 853–4 and 971.

produced by the gentlemen had to be subjected to the assent of the rank and file. This was given, after they had been read out, by a holding up of staves and a shout of "yea, yea, yea" or "we like them very well".[83] Moreover, the gentlemen were expected to serve the cause of the commons both in keeping with their oath and in compliance with the popular perception of how things should be done.

That the commons did not become the subservient followers of the enlisted gentry was made evident in the frictions which developed between the two orders and which intensified once the rebels had assembled in Lincoln.[84] These frictions did not arise from disbelief in, or scepticism about, the notion of orders but stemmed rather from a clash of concepts of how the society of orders should operate. On the one hand, the gentry were keen to curtail their disobedience to the king and therefore insisted upon an approach which emphasised humble supplication and focused the complaint upon evil ministers. Essentially, they followed a procedure which accorded with that of the equity courts in which, in theory at least, private complaints were brought to the king's notice and his justice was awaited. On the other, the commons were keen to insist that the gentlemen remained true to them and that, of their two basic obligations, their duty of obediently serving the king should give way to their duty of protecting the commons from the government. For this reason the commons were more dedicated to military action. As a result, besides presenting the government with a petition, the rebels established hosts. The uprising quickly ceased to be a mere gathering of the people and became a military organisation whose principal task was to defeat all opposition, to race upon London and to seek remedy by removing the base-born ministers, specifically Richard Riche and Thomas Cromwell, and the heretical bishops, to enforce the repeal of their policies and to obtain a free and general pardon which, without exception or payment,would exempt from punishment everyone associated with the uprising. In the final analysis, it seems, the rebels believed that a solution to the kingdom's problems would come from a meeting of the king and his commons. Brought together, the virtue of the prince and the practical wisdom of the commons would interact to cure the ills of the body politic, principally by placing government policy in the hands of the king rather than in the control of evil ministers. Future ills would be avoided by ensuring that the body politic was run according to the society of orders, with matters of religion determined by the clergy and

83 *L.P.* XII{1}. 70/viii and xi.
84 *L.P.* XI. 971.

matters of state directed by the king through the peerage and the gentry. In these circumstances, the commons would have no cause to rise and the king, aided by a council of true gentlemen and clerics as well as by a free parliament and convocation, would be able to uphold the faith of Christ and safeguard the commonwealth.

Besides these obvious similarities, there were also striking differences between the Lincolnshire uprising and the pilgrimage of grace. Lacking in the latter was the violence of the former. The pilgrims spoiled property but committed no murders.[85] Lacking in the Lincolnshire uprising was the participation of peers.[86] Lords Burgh, Clinton and Hussey all made their escape whereas actively serving the pilgrimage of grace were Lords Latimer, Neville, Scrope, Lumley and Darcy; and sworn to the cause were the Earls of Westmorland and Northumberland. Lacking in the Lincolnshire uprising was the conceit of a pilgrimage. Moreover, whilst its supporters stopped one suppression, that of Legbourne Priory, it did not restore any of the religious houses already dissolved. Nonetheless, a great deal of affinity existed between the two rebellions. In fact, the Lincolnshire uprising signposted the way for the pilgrimage of grace. This was vividly illustrated by the procedure of following the crosses which the Louth rebels first advocated and which the rebels of Yorkshire and Cumberland came to practise.[87] The pilgrimage of grace also adopted the grievances of the Lincolnshire uprising, thereby becoming a bifocal movement for the defence of both faith and commonwealth. It adopted its methods, forming confederations bound by the commons' oath which quickly organised themselves as horsed and harnessed hosts captained, if possible, by gentlemen. It adopted the same aims, all of which rested upon seeking the king's favour and forgiveness: to restore the dissolved monasteries, to replace base by noble councillors, to oppose fiscal innovations, to slam the door on heresy and to receive the king's unconditional pardon. Essentially, the Lincolnshire uprising belonged to the same type of revolt as the pilgrimage of grace. Both were revolts of all three orders, with each order seeking to use the other two for its own particular end. Both adopted the language of the rising of the commons, thus placing themselves squarely within a tradition of revolt which began in 1381 and ended in 1549. Both were alike in being principally against the government. Finally, the Lincolnshire uprising

85 For the three murders committed by the Lincolnshire rebels, see Dodds, I, pp. 98 and 101–2.
86 Ibid., pp. 109–10, 112–13 and 132.
87 SP1/109 (*L.P.* XI. 823/iii); *L.P.* XI. 854.

provided the original inspiration for the pilgrimage of grace which it preceded only by one week and imparted to it the lesson that, to ensure the success of any supplication made to the king, it was a vital necessity to have a host at hand or at least on call.

II

▰▰▰▰▰▰▰▰▰▰▰▰▰▰▰▰▰▰▰▰▰▰▰▰▰▰

THE STAPULTON HOST

The uprising around Beverley

This uprising began on Sunday 8th October, six days after the start of the Lincolnshire rebellion and exactly a week after the citizens of Louth had locked up their church to prevent the confiscation of its treasures. Incited and inspired by the Lincolnshire example, it was the first revolt in the north to form a host, which was initially placed under the captaincy of William Stapulton, a common lawyer, and eventually led by the knights, Sir Thomas Percy, Sir Ralph Ellerker the younger and Sir William Constable. Essentially the uprising was, as it claimed to be, a movement of the commons.[1] It became a considerable insurrection partly because the gentry of the East Riding either fled or remained passive; and partly because the surrounding areas, Holderness to the east and Yorkswold to the west and north, found with it a common cause. In this way it became an uprising of the wapentakes of Harthill and Holderness. Having formed a confederation bound by oath to be true to God, the king and the commons, it created an army with the intention of "going forward", hoping to aid the cause of the Lincolnshire rebels. But from 15th to the 19th October it was fully occupied in besieging Hull, and by the time the siege was over the Lincolnshire rebels had been fully subjugated. Instead, it linked up

---

1 Evident in the various forms in which the oath was presented: i.e. "to the commons" (Stapulton, p. 84); "sworn to take the commons' part for the commonwealth" [Hallom: E36/119, f. 27b (*L.P.* XII{1}. 201/iv)]; to be sworn "to be true to God and to the king and to the commons and to maintain holy church and to take such part as the commons do take" [Wilson: SP1/109, f. 39b (*L.P.* XI. 841)]; sworn to be "true and faithful to you and other commons of the realm" [town of Beverley to commons of Lincolnshire: SP1/107 (*L.P.* XI. 645)].

with the other Yorkshire uprisings, sending its army to join theirs in the pilgrim host which confronted the government at Doncaster on 26th and 27th October.[2]

Revolt in the Liberty

The uprising broke out in the town of Beverley, after a day or two of agitated talk which had been provoked by the sighting of beacons alight in Lincolnshire on 4th October and also incited by a letter from the Archbishop of York who, as lord of the Liberty of Beverley, had warned Robert Creke, his receiver there, to watch out for "light heads" and who, in reporting upon the Lincolnshire rebellion, informed the townsmen that the Earl of Shrewsbury was planning military counteraction.[3] Another cause of agitation in the town was the arrival of *agents provocateurs* from Lincolnshire, notably the two canons, Sir John Bowton and Sir William Mowde, who are first encountered on 7th October at Hessle, the landing on the Yorkshire side of the Humber for the Barton ferry. They had with them a bill authorising their journey into Yorkshire which was addressed "to all our true friends" from the gentlemen Sir William Sandon, William Willoughby and Arthur Dymmoke "with all other of our company".[4] This was the first message received in Yorkshire that denoted the Lincolnshire uprising to be gentry-led. Arriving at the Tabard Inn in Beverley, the two canons declared that the Lincolnshire host was "a good company", nudgingly regretted that "they were no more in number" and presented the cause of revolt as "the wealth of holy church".[5] In reporting upon them, William Breyar, a roving ex-sanctuary man, recorded the talk of the town on the same day, relating that men in the market place had excitedly discussed the prospect of a march on London which would allow them to sort out "deceivers" and rob Cheapside. It was not simply the townsmen who were worked up; in the market place a man told Breyar that "all the countryside hereabouts is in a rout"; and at the Tabard Breyar overheard a gentleman from Holderness say that, if the Lincolnshiremen needed support, "they should be sure of all that country".[6]

The following day, the uprising began, in the Louth manner, with a ringing of the common bell.[7] This followed the arrival of William

2 See below. ch. X.
3 For beacons, see *L.P.* XI. 563. For archbishop's letter, see *L.P.* XII{1}. 1022. For proof that his letter had reached Beverley by 7th October, see *L.P.* XI. 841.
4 P.R.O. SP1/113, f. 248 (*L.P.* XI. App. 10). Also see *L.P.* XI. 647.
5 SP1/109, f. 39 (*L.P.* XI. 841).
6 SP1/109, fos. 38b–39 (*L.P.* XI. 841).
7 For outbreak, see the accounts by Breyar (*L.P.* XI. 841), Kitchen (*L.P.* XII{1}. 201/vii) and Stapulton (printed in full in *Transactions of the East Riding Antiquarian Society*, 10 (1903), pp. 83ff).

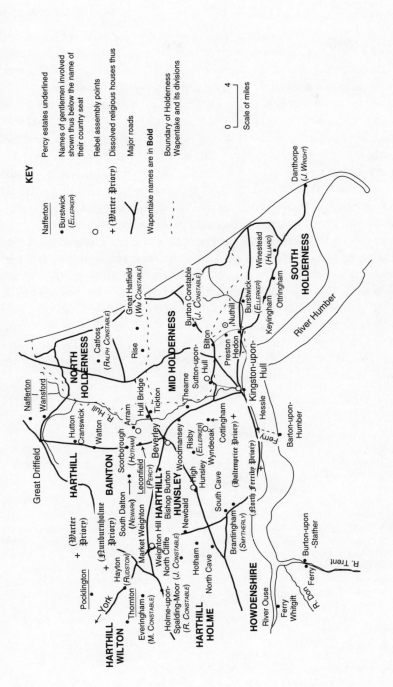

KEY

Nafferton — Percy estates underlined

• Burstwick (ELLERKER) — Names of gentlemen involved shown thus below the name of their country seat

○ — Rebel assembly points

+ (Warter Priory) — Dissolved religious houses thus

— Major roads

Wapentake names are in **Bold**

- - - — Boundary of Holderness
Wapentake and its divisions

0 —— 4
Scale of miles

Map 2 The uprising around Beverley

Woodmancy from Lincolnshire with further news of that rebellion and
a copy of its articles, presumably the set composed by the Horncastle
host.[8] In addition, there now came to light a letter sent earlier to
Robert Raffles, one of the town's twelve governors, allegedly from
Robert Aske, who on 5th October had been a temporary leader of
the West Ancholme strand of the Lincolnshire revolt.[9] The letter
provided instructions on how to mount a rebellion.[10] Raffles had
concealed its existence as long as he could.[11] Although Aske later
dismissed it as a forgery, its content, as evident in the accounts
made of it by Breyar and Stapulton, seems to echo his earliest
pronouncements – the oath of the honourable men and his first two
proclamations.[12] Aske at the time had two opportunities to deliver the
letter personally: on 7th October when he travelled from Howden to
Lincoln, probably via the Hessle – Barton ferry, or when he returned
to Yorkshire on 8th October by the same ferry to dine with William
Babthorpe at Osgodby.[13] The letter apparently ordered a ringing of the
town bell; the swearing of an oath of allegiance to the commons; and
the holding of a muster. And this is what was done.[14] The operation
was masterminded by two Beverley burgesses, Richard Wilson and
Richard Hendyke, advised by Woodmancy, Roger Kitchen, another
burgess of the town, and the priest, Sir John Tuvye.[15]

After dinner and in the early afternoon, Wooodmancy rang the

---

8 M. L. Bush, "Up for the commonweal: the significance of tax grievances in the
English rebellions of 1536", E.H.R., 106 (1991), p. 305.
9 See below, p. 78.
10 The text of the letter has not survived. Its content can be extracted from Breyar's
account of the events in Beverley of 8th October [SP1/109, f. 39b (L.P. XI. 841)].
11 According to Kitchen's account (L.P. XII{1}. 201/vii).
12 For Aske's allegation of forgery, see Bateson, p. 333. Breyar provides most
information about the letter and its effect [SP1/109, f. 39b (L.P. XI. 841)]. His
account was made soon after the event, on 22nd October 1536, and, since he left
the north about 10th October he could not have been confusing it with Aske's
later declarations. For the later declarations, see SP/108 (L.P. XI. 622); SP1/108
(L.P. XI. 705 {4}); St. P., I, pp. 466–7 (L.P. XI. 705{2}). Stapulton suggested, in
his account of its effect upon Kitchen, that Aske's letter to Beverley had ordered
the ringing of the town bell (Stapulton, p. 83).
13 See below, p. 81.
14 For the effectiveness of the letter in provoking revolt, see the accounts by
Stapulton (Stapulton, p. 83), Breyar [SP1/109, f. 39b (L.P. XI. 841)], the
archbishop of York [SP1/119, f. 2 (L.P. XII{1}. 1022)] and Marmaduke Neville
[P.R.O. E36/118, f. 118 (L.P. XII{1}. 29 {2})]. Breyar claimed that Hendyke and
Wilson were the agents of Robert Aske (SP1/109, f.40). For this there is no
corroboration. Hallom claimed to have heard on 7th October that "Aske had been
with the first tidings where began the first commotion" [E36/119, f. 27b (L.P.
XII{1}. 201/iv)].
15 Stapulton, pp. 83–4; L.P. XII{1}. 201/vii; L.P. XI. 841.

common bell with the consent of the others. In response the townsmen flocked into the market place already armed, suggesting that they had been awaiting the call and that the revolt was started not simply by an act of manipulation but by an upsurgence of popular rage. Directed to the garth (court yard) of the town hall, they were ordered by Wilson to take the oath. In the name of Robert Aske, and presumably quoting from his letter, he required every man to be true to God, the king and the commons in order to maintain the holy church, to "take such part as the commons do take", and to resist any opposition to this cause.[16] Then, having read out the Lincolnshire articles, he swore the townsmen *en masse*, "to go forward for the reformation" of them, holding a copy of the articles in one hand and a missal in the other.[17] Finally, after they had composed a letter of support for the Lincolnshire uprising which Woodmancy then took to the rebels in Lincoln, a muster was proclaimed, again in the name of Aske, to be held at four o'clock on one of the town's common pastures, Westwood Green.[18]

The muster was disrupted by a row between a faction supporting the lordship rights of the Archbishop of York and a faction supporting the rights of the municipality.[19] It was also spoiled by Sir Ralph Ellerker the younger's failure to attend.[20] In the Lincolnshire manner, the uprising, although initiated by the commons, sought to enlist gentlemen as captains of the host. Let down by Ellerker, it latched onto the Stapulton family whose seat and estate were situated west of York in the Ainsty but who happened at the time to be on holiday in Beverley, staying at the Greyfriars which overlooked Westwood Green.

The first encounter with the Stapulton family took place through the hedge which separated the green from the friary. Lady Stapulton, the wife of the ailing Sir Christopher Stapulton and close friend of an enthusiastic friar, Sir Thomas Johnson, made contact with the rebels, as they retired from their first muster, by calling out "God's blessing have you" and "speed you well in your good purpose".[21] Admitting that her family was resident within, she exhorted: "Go pull them out by the heads". The following day, when the rebels returned to muster on the green, they found themselves urged on by Lady Stapulton and

---

16 P.R.O. SP1/109, f. 39b (*L.P.* XI. 841).

17 For the ceremony, see Stapulton, p. 84. For the oath, see E36/119, f. 35 (*L.P.* XII{1}. 201/vii).

18 For the letter, see Stapulton, p. 84 and *L.P.* XI.971. For the muster, see SP1/109, f. 39b (*L.P.* XI. 841) and Stapulton, p. 84.

19 Stapulton, p. 85.

20 For the expectation that he would be there on 8th October, see SP1/109, f. 39b (*L.P.* XI. 841). For his refusal to become involved, see Stapulton, p. 85.

21 Stapulton, p. 84.

Friar Johnson, both of whom expressed delight with the uprising, the
friar not only offering, in an appropriately clerical manner, biblical
justification for the rebels' activities, but also promising his military
service if it came to a fight. It was he who proposed that William
Stapulton, Sir Christopher's brother, would make a good captain. The
outcome was that, after reassembling on the morning of 9th October,
this time with horse and harness, and after being let down again by Sir
Ralph Ellerker the younger who refused to take the oath, a group of
commoners led by Richard Wilson, visited the friary, swore the
Stapulton family and took to the assembly on the green the adolescent
Brian Stapulton, Christopher's son and heir and stand–in for his father
who was too ill to attend, and his uncle William, who bore a remarkable resemblance to Robert Aske: a practising London lawyer, even a
member of the same inn of court, a younger son of a middling
Yorkshire gentry family, and a familiar through service with the sixth
Earl of Northumberland.[22] Also like Aske, Stapulton was prevented by
the outbreak of the Lincolnshire uprising from returning to London
for the new law term.[23]

That the purpose of the rebels' visit to the friary was to recruit
captains became evident in the shout "Captains, captains!" that went
up from the assembled host as the two Stapultons were seen approaching. That the host was fully in support of Stapulton's captaincy was
evident in the chant "Master William Stapulton shall be our captain",
which issued from it as he sought to make up his mind.[24] Thus, by
the end of the second day a host had been organised, recruited from
the two components of the Liberty, the borough itself and the so–
called water towns. Yet it amounted to no more than four to five
hundred men; that is, roughly the equivalent of the force that the
town of Beverley could muster for the militia.[25] Moreover, its
appointed captains consisted of a boy and his uncle, neither of
them native to the Beverley region and both totally unfamiliar with
military matters.

According to Stapulton, he agreed to lead the rebels in order to

22 Stapulton, pp. 85–7; Bindoff, III, pp. 375–6. For Stapulton's fellowship of Gray's
   Inn, see *L.P.* XI. 818.
23 Stapulton, p. 83; Bateson, p. 331.
24 Stapulton, p. 86.
25 Ibid. The water towns consisted of Tickton Stork, Hull Bridge and Eske to the
   north–east of Beverley and Thearne, Woodmancy and Weal to the south–east of
   it. See *V.C.H. East Riding*, VI, pp. 161, 278ff and 210. At the muster of 1539, 451
   men from the town were declared able for military service, eighty of them with
   horse and harness. The water towns provided another sixty-nine, including
   thirteen horse. See E36/39.

restrain them.[26] Apparently, he had tried to stop the ringing of the
town bell the previous day; and now that they had assembled and
formed a host, he argued that they should do nothing until further
instructions came from Lincolnshire.[27] But this argument had little
effect. It was disobeyed immediately as Roger Kitchen, running with
his horse on Westwood Green, exhorted: "As many as be true to the
commons follow me"; and that, without more ado, they should raise
Cottingham, Hessle and the other towns about.[28] That night Hunsley
beacon was without authorisation fired. As a result, the region was
aroused and further assemblies were held on Westwood Green, on
10th and 11th October, as newcomers from Newbald, Cottingham
and North Cave came in, were sworn and excitedly demanded
"when we would forward".[29] In response Stapulton urged them to
await a response to the letter which they had dispatched to the
Lincolnshire host on 8th October.[30]

To make his policy of restraint more acceptable he proposed the
appointment of two commoners as petty captains (i.e. Richard Wharton, a substantial yeoman from Hull Bridge and Nicholas Horncliffe,
bailiff of Beverley, the one representing the water towns, the other, the
borough of Beverley).[31] He also allowed a second letter to be sent into
Lincolnshire. This letter of 10th made no mention of the previous
letter of 8th. Probably it was a duplicate, with the addition of presenting itself as coming from not just the commonalty of the town but also
"the country thereabouts".[32] There were several possible reasons for
sending it: apprehension, largely arising from the absence of a reply,
that the previous letter had gone astray; the need to announce that the
Beverley revolt now involved a region rather than one urban community; the need to assure the latest recruits, and to reassure the Beverley
commons, that the adopted policy of consulting the Lincolnshire
rebels before proceeding further was a genuine one and not simply a
ploy to stay the uprising. From the commons' point of view its aim was
to extract the awaited reply so that the uprising could move on to the
next stage; from Stapulton's point of view it was a device to maintain
control of the commons and to safeguard his policy of restraint.

Apart from the letter of 8th October, it is the only declaration of

26 Stapulton, pp. 86–7.
27 Ibid., pp. 83–4 and 87–8.
28 Ibid., p. 87.
29 Ibid.
30 Ibid., pp. 87–8.
31 Ibid., p. 87.
32 SP1/107 (*L.P.* XI. 645).

grievance known to have been made by this uprising. It stated that the rebels had taken an oath to be true "to God and our prince and his lawful acts and demands", as well as "to you and other commons of the realm". Its declared aim was to aid the commons in Lincolnshire and elsewhere in resisting "all them that be councillors, inventors and procurers" who were planning "utterly to undo . . . the commonalty of the realm". It closed with the request that the Lincolnshire men should send them advice on what to do, signing off with the oath "God save the king, the church and the commonalty". Appended was the common seal depicting St. John of Beverley in the attire of the Archbishop of York, a dormant beaver under his feet. Clearly evident in the letter was subscription to the belief that throughout the realm there existed a social group, the commons, with an identical interest and a shared cause, the latter created by government oppression resulting from "unlawful acts and demands". Not only the language of the letter but its sentiments betokened a firm belief in the society of orders. It expressed not class hostility but alarm that the society of orders, essentially an organisation of society for the maintenance of good governance, was failing to fulfil its very purpose. A further and related point in the letter was that the society of orders was also threatened by attempts "to undo . . . the church". Again, the acknowledged enemy was the government, trampling upon the corporate rights and expectations that the society of orders held dear.

The response from Lincolnshire arrived the following day, on 11th October. In anticipation, the people had assembled, again on West-wood Green.[33] Drawn from the surrounding townships and hamlets, they were reckoned to number 4,000.[34] To calm matters down, Sir Ralph Ellerker the elder arrived and was allowed to attend unsworn. He and a priest, Sir John Miller, were deeply anxious about the approaching letter and the explosive effect it might have. Miller even proposed a reception party to intercept the letter at Hessle and to amend it, if necessary, before it was declared to the commons. But then Woodmancy rode onto the green, followed shortly afterwards by three messengers from Lincolnshire, Guy Kyme, Anthony Curtis and Thomas Dunne. Ellerker proposed that the letter should be vetted before it was made public. The Lincolnshire men, however, required it to be "read and declared openly".[35] With them they had not only the

---

33 Stapulton, p. 88.
34 *L.P.* XI. 828/xii.
35 Stapulton, pp. 88–9.

letter but also a set of articles, presumably the petition finalised in
Lincoln and sent to the king on 9th October. Both were read out to the
host; and, in addition, Kyme gave a stirring account of the Lincolnshire uprising and its achievements so far.[36]

Kyme and Dunne stayed with the Beverley host for three days,
whilst Anthony Curtis travelled into Holderness.[37] Ignorant of the
collapse of the midland uprising, they inspired the Beverley rebels
with news of the two Lincolnshire hosts, the one led by the subsidy
commissioners, the other by Sheriff Dymmoke, both of them well
supplied with horse and harness, able to give battle to any "king
christened" and totalling 20,000 men.[38] They also instructed the
Yorkshiremen on how to proceed, urging them to oblige gentlemen
to join by threats to spoil their property. Moreover, in fulfilment of
their own main purpose, they sought to persuade the Beverley host to
march south, offering "comfortable words" from the Abbot of Barlings – probably an assurance that those falling in battle would achieve
salvation.[39] Moved in this manner, and needing to enlist more support,
the Beverley rebels fired both Hunsley and Tranby beacons on 11th
October; and, on the following day, the highly revered St. Wilfred's
Day, they held another muster, this time at Hunsley, which is about
five miles south—west of Beverley, where, it was estimated, 3,000 troops
met. At this muster stirring news was brought: that "all Holderness
was up to the seaside", the result of Curtis' visit, and that Robert
Aske, having raised Marshland and Howdenshire, was marching his
army to join up with the Stapulton host.[40] Added to Aske's original
instruction, the one that aroused the townsmen of Beverley on 8th
October, was now another, calling upon them to join him at Market
Weighton. With his proposal that the two forces should muster
together on 13th October at Weighton Hill, the Stapulton host readily
complied.[41] The outcome of the meeting was to send a joint delegation
of gentlemen to Hull in order to persuade it to join the uprising.[42] It

36 Ibid., p. 89. Kyme in his account presents Dunne as the reader of the letter and
   articles (L.P. XI. 828/xii).
37 Stapulton, p. 90.
38 Ibid., p. 89.
39 Ibid., pp. 89–92; E36/119, f. 27b (L.P. XII{1}. 201/iv).
40 Stapulton, pp. 89–91. For the 3,000 figure given by Kyme, see L.P. XI. 828/xii.
   Since Holderness had yet to join and the military capacity of the whole of Harthill
   wapentake was no more than this figure, it is undoubtedly an exaggeration. See
   Appendix I.
41 Stapulton, pp. 91–2. See Map 2.
42 Ibid., p. 92.

was the failure of this delegation that caused the two hosts to go their separate ways, one to York and the other to Hull.

Revolt in the lordship of Watton

On 12th October an extensive region to the north of Beverley joined the Stapulton host after the parts along the river Hull between Beverley and Great Driffield had been recruited by John Hallom, yeoman of Calkeld. He first made a stand on 8th October when, at the Sunday service in the parish church of Watton, the priest, in the new manner, omitted to announce the forthcoming St. Wilfred's Day, traditionally celebrated on 12th October. Challenged by Hallom who accused him of breaching custom, the priest claimed to be acting on the king's authority and with the consent of convocation. This answer was found unsatisfactory; and after mass the congregation resolved to have the holy days bidden and kept "as before".[43] But they did not immediately take up arms and they also failed to respond to the firing of Hunsley beacon on 9th October. Hallom, however, visited Beverley on 11th October. At the house of John Crowe, in which the rising of the 8th October had been planned, he met Guy Kyme and Thomas Dunne. From them he learned of the grievances that had raised Lincolnshire, later recalling them, in a selective manner which indicated his own concerns, as an objection to the dissolution of the monasteries and to the expected onslaught on parish churches, especially the plans to confiscate their relics and ornaments, to leave only one church standing in every four miles and to allow the surviving churches only one chalice, cross and cope apiece. He also recalled that Kyme and Dunne presented their revolt as a tax protest, against the fifteenth and tenth, the first fruits and tenths "and divers other payments".[44] In Crowe's house Hallom was sworn. According to his own account, he was obliged "to take the commons' part for the commonwealth but not against the king".[45] Hallom claimed that all strove to secure copies of the Lincolnshire articles. He failed to obtain one but returned home with the copy of a letter composed by a friar of Knaresborough who resided in Beverley and was spreading horrifying rumours, by means of bills passed by hand and nailed to church doors, about the dissolution of parish churches and the imposition of new taxes on sacraments, food, ploughs and cattle.[46] This particular letter

43 E36/119, f. 27 (*L.P.* XII{1}. 201/iv).
44 E36/119, fos. 27–27b.
45 Ibid., f. 27b.
46 Ibid. For the activities of the friar, see below, pp. 60–1.

ordered an assembly on St. Wilfred's Day at Hunsley beacon, in support of the Lincolnshire cause. Equipped with it, and also with the news that both Lincolnshire and Beverley had risen against "the plucking down of the abbeys and other things touching the common-weal", Hallom had no difficulty in raising the neighbouring townships of Watton and Hutton Cranswick as well as the countryside between Watton and Great Driffield.[47] The enthusiasm of the people was so great that, as Hallom put it, "from that time forward no man could keep his servant at plough but everyman that was able to bear a staff went forward towards Hunsley".[48] On the other hand, the actual size of his company was probably no more than 230 men.[49]

Hallom's company celebrated St. Wilfred's Day by joining up with the Beverley rebels at Hunsley beacon and by holding a second assembly at Arram where they linked up with other woldsmen, probably the rebels of north Holderness and a contingent drawn from the region north of Great Driffield, notably from Nafferton and Kilham and the estates of Bridlington Priory.[50] The size of this force was not all that large, perhaps no more than the four to five hundred woldsmen who arrived at the siege of Hull on 19th October.[51] This was undoubtedly because many from that region served in yet another host, the one led by Sir Thomas Percy.[52]

The Watton revolt took the form of a popular uprising led by a peasant. But this state of affairs was unintentional and shortlived. Hallom became sole captain because the three others elected as captains of the commons (Henry Newark, Robert Hotham and William Cowsor), all of them gentlemen, "slinked away", leaving him "alone to guide them". Moreover, the company raised from the Watton area soon fell under the charge of the gentlemen, Nicholas and Robert Rudston.[53]

47 E36/119, f. 21 (*L.P.* XII{1}. 201).
48 E36/119, f. 27b (*L.P.* XI{1}. 201/iv).
49 Calculated from Hallom's statement that when £46 were divided up among his company, it yielded four shillings a head [E36/119, f. 28 (*L.P.* XII{1}. 201/iv)].
50 For the Hunsley muster, see *L.P.* XII{1}. 201/iv and Stapulton, p. 90. For the Arram muster, see E36/119, f. 28 (*L.P.* XII{1}. 201/iv). Hallom merely says "and there mustered more of the country" (ibid.). That there was a movement of revolt beyond Great Driffield, see *L.P.* XII{1}. 201/iv and *L.P.* XII{1}. 1020 {2}.
51 Stapulton, p. 98.
52 See below, ch. V.
53 For the gentlemen slinking away, see *L.P.* XII{1}. 201/iv. On 15th October the Yorkswold men were led to York by Robert Rudston (Stapulton, pp. 94–5, but he mistakenly calls him Richard) and on 19th October they were led to Hull by Nicholas Rudston (ibid., p. 98).

Revolt in Holderness

Absent from the Hunsley Beacon gathering on 12th October were the Holderness men. However, Holderness had already risen, a day after Anthony Curtis brought it news of the Lincolnshire revolt.[54] In January 1537 Sir Ralph Sadler, after visiting the region to make enquiries about its involvement in the pilgrimage of grace, attributed the Holderness revolt to Robert Aske who allegedly entered the wapentake and deliberately raised it by means of bills that claimed churches were to be limited to one in every five miles and that the king was bent on exacting fees for marriages, christenings and burials.[55] Sadler was probably confusing Robert Aske with Anthony Curtis and the friar of Knaresborough.[56] Otherwise, his account has the ring of truth, suggesting that the friar and his letters were inciting an audience in the wapentake of Holderness as well as in the wapentake of Harthill.

A brief first–hand account of the start of the Holderness revolt was provided by the husbandman William Nicholson who claimed that, when the news of the Lincolnshire uprising reached him, it was couched in terms of "the spoiling of Holy Church and divers other things".[57] On the same day, 11th October, the people were summoned to Nuthill by the common bell of the town of Preston (just north of Hedon) and were sworn by the vicar of Preston, again upon a book. The following day, at a second assembly on Sutton Ings, each of the three component bailiwicks of Holderness chose a captain: Richard Tenand for the Middle Bailiwick, William Barker for the North Bailiwick, and William Ombler for the South Bailiwick.[58] Their company was again small, numbering something like three hundred men;[59] but fierce and aggressive, it took a number of gentlemen, including Sir Christopher Hilliard, and caused others to flee to Hull.[60] At night on 12th October it appeared outside Hull demanding to have Sir John Constable, Sir William Constable and Sir Ralph Ellerker the elder, who had taken refuge there.[61] On the evening of 13th October it reached Beverley.[62] On 14th October it met up with

---

55 *L.P.* XII{1}. 200.
56 Lumley when examined gave the same impression, declaring that "Aske was gone to Holderness to stir them there" [SP1/115, f. 212 (*L.P.* XII{1}. 369)].
57 E36/119, f. 32b (*L.P.* XII{1}. 201/v).
58 Ibid.
59 Stapulton, p. 94.
60 Stapulton, p. 91. The gentlemen were Sir Christopher Hilliard, William Grymeston, Ralph Constable and John Wright.
61 *L.P.* XI. 818.
62 *L.P.* XII{1}. 201/v.

the Stapulton host in a muster at Westwood Green.[63] Thereafter the two revolts became jointly involved, first in besieging Hull and then in marching to meet Robert Aske at Pontefract.[64] In contrast, the company from Yorkswold joined Aske in the taking of York and only rejoined the Stapulton host on 19th October for the final taking of Hull.[65]

The siege of Hull

The original impressiveness of the Lincolnshire uprising lay in the speed at which it was able to enact the society of orders. This was done by capturing and converting into captains the heads of county families. In contrast, the uprising in the Beverley region had much greater difficulty in enlisting gentlemen. For the first few days the latter furthered the rebel cause only by running away. Some went to Hull; others took refuge in Scarborough, Pontefract and Cawood Castles.[66] Determined to recruit them, the rebels of the Beverley region followed in pursuit. Thus, on 13th October George Bawne of Kilham offered to attack Scarborough Castle; but the more accessible Hull became the target of the Stapulton host.[67]

On the night of 12th October, Hull received a visit from the captains of the Holderness revolt and later from four deputies representing the Stapulton host.[68] Four messengers from Hull then returned to Beverley with the four rebel deputies but only to declare why the town of Hull would not participate in the uprising.[69] On the 13th October, and after consultation with Robert Aske at Weighton Hill, four more deputies were sent. Whereas three of the deputies on the 12th October had been commoners, the deputies of 13th October were all gentlemen, two of them (i.e. Nicholas Rudston and George Metham) drawn from Aske's host and the other two (William Stapulton and Robert Hotham) from the Beverley uprising.[70] It was clear that, although the townsmen of Hull were ambivalent and wavering, steeling the town's resistance was the presence within its walls of Sir

---

63 Stapulton, p. 94.
64 For the siege of Hull, see Stapulton, pp. 93 and 95 and *L.P.* XII{1}. 201/v. For Pontefract, see Stapulton, p. 100.
65 *L.P.* XII{1}. 201/iv; Stapulton, pp. 94–5; *L.P.* XII{1}. 306; Stapulton, p. 98.
66 See below, nn. 260–63.
67 Stapulton, p. 92.
68 Ibid., p. 91.
69 Ibid.
70 Ibid., pp. 92–3. The deputies of 12th October had been the commoners Richard Wharton, Richard Wilson and one Smith and the gentleman, William Grymeston (Stapulton, p. 91).

Ralph Ellerker the elder and Sir John Constable.[71] In the circumstances it made sense to send gentlemen; and this was now possible
partly because of the conjunction made with the Howdenshire uprising, which had been more successful in drawing in the gentry, and
partly because of the capture of Robert Hotham, a servant to the Earl
of Westmorland and a resident of Yorkswold.[72] Yet his stay with the
uprising was a very short one since he fled the same day. Without him
the three deputies proceeded to Hull, meeting the mayor that evening
and the following morning the refugee gentlemen. Sir John Constable
was the sticking point. His refusal to submit caused the mayor, aldermen and the other gentlemen to hold out and to deny the rebels men,
money and provisions.[73] Sir Ralph Ellerker was less strongly placed to
resist since it was now clear that two of his sons, Sir Ralph and
Thomas, had been taken.[74] At this point he offered to take the
rebels' articles of grievance to the king on condition that they allowed
him to remain unsworn, an offer the rebels rejected.[75]

By the 15th October the Stapulton host had yet to enlist the town
of Hull but had gained the support of the surrounding area, notably
Hullshire (i.e. the parishes of Hessle, North Ferriby and Kirk Ella),
Cottingham and south Holderness.[76] Moreover, it had at last recruited
substantial gentry support, now having, in all probability, two knights
under oath – Sir Ralph Ellerker the younger and Sir Christopher
Hilliard – as well as a number of esquires and plain gentlemen,
notably Robert Hotham, Robert Rudston, Henry Newark, William
Grymeston, Ralph Constable, John Wright, Richard Smytherly, Philip
Wardby and James Constable.[77] Yet most of these gentlemen had been
made to participate and some (e.g. Hotham and Newark) had already
fled. After being captured they were sworn to support the uprising
under pain of having their property attacked.[78] Furthermore, although
they were appreciated for their support, the commons held them in
suspicion especially because of their delaying tactics: for the gentlemen
had insisted that nothing be done until the Lincolnshire rebels

71 Ibid., p. 93.
72 *L.P.* XII{1}. 29 {2} and 201/iv.
73 Stapulton, p. 92.
74 Ibid., p. 93.
75 Ibid.
76 Ibid., pp. 89 and 94–5.
77 See below, pp. 63–4.
78 The possible exceptions were Robert Rudston who appeared with Aske at Market
    Weighton on 12th October with his nephew, Nicholas (Stapulton, p. 92) and
    James Constable of North Cliffe and Philip Wardby, whom Stapulton reported
    simply as coming in on 12th October (ibid.).

responded to the Beverley letters of support, and now they appeared to be delaying the conquest of Hull. The latter policy provoked hostility from the commons on 14th October when, in seeking how to deal with the town, the Stapultons met Sir Christopher Hilliard and other unnamed gentlemen at Bishop Burton and having decided to besiege it, arranged another meeting for 15th October at Wyndeoak in the lordship of Cottingham. Only then did the Stapultons contact their host which anxiously awaited them at Market Weighton. Expecting the two to return earlier that day, the Beverley commons had become deeply unsettled by their absence, suspecting presumably that, like Hotham and others, they had fled. Crying "down with them", they deplored the fact that "the gentlemen counselled too much and would betray them".[79]

Another outburst of suspicion occurred on 15th October at the Wyndeoak meeting when, instead of proceeding to Hull, the two Stapultons expressed the wish to go to York, allegedly to visit the family home at Wighill and pick up their harness. The Beverley commons would not hear of it; and the two Stapultons were therefore obliged to join the siege of Hull. Yet, whilst fearing betrayal, the Beverley commons were deeply appreciative of the Stapultons' leadership and very much under their influence. Thus, in travelling to the Wyndeoak assembly on 15th October, William Stapulton upbraided the commons for being so suspicious of him and offered, since he was "a stranger among them", to "withdraw from the captaincy". The reaction of the commons was to shout: "We will have none other captains; and whosoever after speak against our captain, the rest to strike him down". Stapulton therefore agreed to continue in the post, but, according to him, only on condition that the men refrained from pillage and paid a fair price for what they requisitioned.[80]

On 15th October the Stapulton host divided into two. The one part, a company of four to five hundred woldsmen led by Robert Rudston and probably Sir Ralph Ellerker the younger, went to join Aske at York.[81] The other part, led by the Stapultons, Sir Christopher Hilliard and Thomas Ellerker, Sir Ralph the younger's brother and also by the commoners, Barker, Tenand and Ombler, took up positions around Hull. This force consisted of recruits from Holderness, Hull-

79 Ibid., pp. 93–4.
80 Ibid., p. 94.
81 Ibid., pp. 94–5. For proof that Ellerker went with them, see *L.P.* XII{1}. 306.
   The size of the company is assumed from the number of woldsmen who rejoined
   the Stapulton host on 19th October(Stapulton, p. 98 and *L.P.* XII{1}. 201/iv).

shire, Beverley and Cottingham.[82] The siege lasted five days.[83] The fall
of the town on 19th October was a more impressive achievement than
Aske's taking of York and Pontefract Castle, both of which submitted
without the need for military action. In the early stages of the siege, the
Stapulton host received the devastating news that the Lincolnshire
rising, the *modus vivendi* for its own uprising, had collapsed; but in
compensation it learnt that York was taken, that both Richmondshire
and the region around Malton were up and that, making up for the
stand–offishness of the Yorkshire aristocracy, Sir Thomas Percy,
brother of the ineffectual Earl of Northumberland and, at the time,
resident with his mother at Seamer near Scarborough, had come out in
support of the commons.[84]

A number of pressures, the fear of being put to the torch and a
shortage of provisions, eventually reduced Hull to subjection.[85] But
what placed it in the rebels' hands was the decision made by Sir Ralph
Ellerker the elder and Sir William Constable, first thing on 18th
October, to negotiate, possibly as a result of receiving a persuasive
letter asking them to do so from Thomas Percy.[86] In accepting Sir
Ralph's terms, which traded their compliance in return for an immu-
nity from taking the oath and from serving as captains, the rebels were
able to detach him from Sir John Constable who was then browbeaten
into submission, although earlier he had stated a preference to die
rather than yield. His submission followed the arrival of the woldsmen
who, having been sent to York, had now been dispatched by Aske to
Hull, in response to Stapulton's call for assistance.[87] According to
Richard Cromwell, who from south Humberside was reporting upon
events for the benefit of his father, this brought the total of the
besieging force to 6,000, undoubtedly an exaggerated figure but one
which made the point that Hull had come under attack from a
considerable force.[88]

Having taken Hull and ended the resistance of the Ellerkers, the
Constables and their clients, the question for the Stapulton host was
what to do next, especially as the Lincolnshire rising was no longer
showing the way and the Aske uprising, also deflated of purpose by the

82 Stapulton, pp. 94–5.
83 Ibid., pp. 95–8.
84 Ibid., p. 96.
85 The point of view of the besieged was made in a letter from the corporation of
   Hull to the king [SP1/112 (*L.P.* XI. 1285)].
86 Stapulton, pp. 97–8. For Percy's letter, see Stapulton, p. 96.
87 Ibid., pp. 94 and 97–8.
88 For this estimate of the besieging force, see *L.P.* XI. 789.

collapse of the midland revolt, had yet to reformulate its own strategy. In these circumstances, on 20th October, the Stapulton host met again at Hunsley beacon, this time with the gentlemen taken from Hull.[89] The intention was to draw up a petition, now that it was no longer possible to use the Lincolnshire articles. For the purpose, a council was appointed, its membership chosen by the commons and consisting of William Grymeston of Cottingham, John Wright of Holderness, the ex-Percy servant William Worme and William Stapulton, all of them minor gentlemen and two of them lawyers. Its aim was to produce "articles of our griefs" and to send them to the Duke of Suffolk with the request that he act as their petitioner to the king.[90]

But as they were working out the articles, a messenger arrived from Aske whose host was now at Pontefract Castle. Just as the Beverley men were first agitated by the news that Shrewsbury was preparing to crush the Lincolnshire uprising, they were now moved by the news that he was about to give battle to Aske. Abandoning the articles, they sent two hundred men of Holderness to keep Hull, obliged Sir Ralph Ellerker the elder to keep Hunsley beacon and prepared to leave for Pontefract at seven o'clock the following morning.[91] Travelling via York, and forming two contingents, the one led by Sir Ralph Ellerker and the Rudstons, the other by Brian and William Stapulton, they had reached Pontefract by nine o'clock on the morning of 22nd October where the high command ordered them to serve with Sir Thomas Percy in the vanguard of the pilgrims' army. With him they lodged at Wentbridge on 22nd October, Hampole Nunnery on 23rd October and Pickburn on 24th October.[92] In this manner the uprising took on the appearance of a Percy revolt placed at the service of pilgrimage of grace; but in reality the uprisings about Beverley had been something else: a movement of the commons inspired by the Lincolnshire uprising and whose signal achievement was the taking of Hull and the gentlemen who had taken refuge within its walls.

89 E36/119, f. 28 (*L.P.* XII{1}. 201/iv).
90 Stapulton, pp. 98–9. The two lawyers were Wright and Stapulton.
91 Ibid., p. 99; *L.P.* XII{1}. 201/iv.
92 Stapulton, pp. 99–101. The two basic accounts of the pilgrim host, Stapulton's Confession and Aske's Narrative, appear contradictory on this point, with Stapulton declaring that his host served in the van under Sir Thomas Percy (Stapulton, p. 100) and with Aske claiming that it served in the middleward under Sir Robert Constable (Bateson, pp. 336–7). In all probability the host served in both wards between 22nd and 27th October through being shifted from one to the other. See below, pp. 376–8.

Grievances and aims

At the start of his confession William Stapulton helpfully listed the
causes of revolt, but how many of them appertained to his own
uprising?[93] Some reference is made to other areas of revolt: for
example, the evidence he provides to illustrate the fear that churches
would go the way of the lesser monasteries is taken from the West
Riding, that is, from the wapentake of Ainsty where the Stapultons'
estate and seat were situated.[94] It is also clear that the list fails to
include all the grievances held by the Stapulton host. A major
complaint of the Beverley rebels was the way the government had
interfered – through subpoenas, decrees and injunctions issued by
the Court of Star Chamber – in the town's struggle with its manorial
lord, the Archbishop of York, over the election of its twelve governors.[95] To this matter Stapulton makes reference only later, in his
narrative of events.[96] Nor does he mention anywhere in his account
the fiscal grievances present in the revolt; nor the objection made to the
king's headship of the church; nor the feared consequences of the act of
succession.[97]

As a statement of the complaints moving the rebels of the
Beverley region, then, Stapulton's confession is incomplete, approx-
imate and misleading. Yet, in spite of these shortcomings, it has a
use. In listing the grievances against the government, Stapulton first
specified "the common bruit" in Yorkshire that certain parish
churches would be dissolved and their goods expropriated by the
king. Secondly, he stated the fear that, from the churches that
survived, their treasures would be taken and that, for the future
ministration of their services, they would be provided with articles
of little value, such as copper chalices. Stapulton singled out for
special notice these two related grievances. He then linked them
with the suppression of religious houses, the abrogation of holy
days and "the new opinions of certain persons concerning the faith"
as being, along with certain agrarian complaints, the ones that "did
move, grudge and stir the people much to such rebellion".[98] Apart

93 Stapulton, p. 82.
94 Ibid. The parishes he singled out for mention were Wighill, Walton and Thorp
   Arch (to be incorporated in the parishes of either Tadcaster or Bolton Percy) and
   Askham Richard and Askham Bryan (to be incorporated in the parish of Long
   Marston).
95 See below, pp. 50–3.
96 Stapulton, p. 85.
97 See below, pp. 47–8(taxes), p. 46(headship), p. 50 (succession).
98 Stapulton, p. 82.

from the agrarian grievances, all this can be corroborated as applying to the uprising about Beverley.

In view of the impact that the Lincolnshire uprising had upon the Beverley region, it appears that the grievances of the two revolts had much in common. They largely fall into three categories: the spoliation of the church; the subversion of Christ's faith; and the exploitation of the commonalty. All three were seen, and interlinked, as essentially the work of the government, especially of the king's councillors and particularly Thomas Cromwell.[99]

Like the Lincolnshire rebels, the rebels about Beverley were agitated by the dissolution of the monasteries. Hallom was reported, by William Horsekey, a yeoman of Watton, as having raised the people between Watton and Great Driffield "for such pretences . . . concerning the plucking down of abbeys", declaring that "all Lincolnshire and Beverley were up for throwing down of the abbeys".[100] The aim of the Beverley rebels, as reported by the servant of Robert Hotham, receiver to the Earl of Westmorland, was to "put in religious persons in their houses again".[101] The degree of concern for the dissolution in the region was vividly revealed on 11th October when the commons of Beverley asked the legation from Lincolnshire "what they did with the suppressed abbeys" and received the disappointing reply: "they meddled with none".[102] The Beverley rebels were involved in the restoration of at least two dissolved houses. According to Stapulton, the men of Swanland called upon him to restrain the farmer of North Ferriby Priory from removing its goods. In response, Stapulton authorised them to place two brothers in the abbey to safeguard it until a further decision had been reached on all the houses so far dissolved.[103] In addition, the people showed concern for the goods already removed from the priory and deposited, along with the goods of Haltemprice Priory, in the house of Leonard Beckwith, receiver to the Court of Augmentations, at South Cave. Haltemprice was likewise restored; presumably by the Beverley rebels; and they may also have had a hand in the restoration of Nunburnholme Priory.[104]

The rebels' concern for religious houses is not surprising in view of

---

99 See below.
100 E36/119, f. 21 (L.P. XII{1}. 201).
101 E36/118, f. 118 (L.P. XII{1}. 29{2}).
102 SP1/109 (L.P. XI. 828/xii).
103 Stapulton, p. 104; Bateson, p. 342.
104 For Haltemprice, see Stapulton, p. 90 and Bateson, p. 342. For the restoration of Nunburnholme, see G.W.O. Woodward, The Dissolution of the Monasteries (London, 1966), p. 96. But there is no evidence to connect the rebels of the Beverley region with the actual restoration of this priory.

the number suppressed in the region. By October 1536 as many as four had been dissolved, all in the month of August.[105] As a result, a fair amount of the region's ecclesiastical wealth had passed to the Crown, now to be administered by the Court of Augmentations and the appointed farmers, Sir Ralph Ellerker the younger, Sir William Fairfax and William Hungate.[106] The exception was the estate of Warter Priory which was immediately alienated without survey to the Earl of Rutland.[107] What precisely offended the people about these dissolutions is not completely clear. The Lincolnshire articles had explicitly condemned the Dissolution on two grounds: because "the service of God is . . . minished" and because it was "a great hurt to the commonwealth" in reducing the amount of relief available to the poor.[108] That the Beverley rebels' attitude inclined towards the latter consideration is suggested by Stapulton's account of the restoration of North Ferriby. Here the consideration was primarily a material one. According to Stapulton, the commons' specific objection was to William Fairfax, the person appointed as farmer. Since he "neither would keep house nor men about him", the rebels thought him an unsuitable recipient for the lease of the abbey's site and demesne. Whilst starting his point with specific reference to North Ferriby, Stapulton finished it in more general terms, arguing that the commons objected to the suppression of religious houses because it resulted in their passing to men who provided the area with neither hospitality nor employment.[109] In presenting the objections to Dissolution, Stapulton said nothing of a threat to the faith. This does not rule it out as a concern of the Beverley rebels, but in all likelihood their religious concerns were connected not simply with the suppression of religious houses but with a related fear: the onslaught the government appeared to be planning upon parish churches.

This fear had been at the centre of the Lincolnshire uprising which had started in Louth as a means of defending the treasures of its church; which was prominently placed in the rebels' first communication to the government, the supplicatory letter of 3rd October from the captured subsidy commissioners; which featured explicitly in the

---

105 *V.C.H. Yorkshire*, III, p. 119 (Nunburnholme); p. 215 (Haltemprice); p. 242 (North Ferriby). For Warter, see n. 116.

106 For Ellerker's farm of Haltemprice, see P.R.O. SC6/Henry VIII/4505. For Fairfax's farm of North Ferriby, see ibid., 4509. The farm of Nunburnholme went to William Hungate (ibid., 4513).

107 *L.P.* XI. 519.

108 SP1/108 (*L.P.* XI. 705). For evidence that this is in part the text of the Lincolnshire articles, see Bush, "Up for the commonweal", p. 303.

109 Stapulton, p. 104.

Horncastle articles and, by implication, in the articles the Lincolnshire rebels sent to the king which deplored the suppression of religious houses because, as a result, "many parsons be put from their livings and left at large".[110] Its importance as a grievance was attested in Kyme's presentation to the Beverley rebels of the causes of the Lincolnshire uprising.[111] It also featured prominently in many of the eye–witness accounts of the rebellion.[112] For the Lincolnshire rebels, then, a major grievance was the fear that parish churches were under government threat, with all about to lose their treasures and some about to be demolished. There can be no doubt that the Stapulton host was moved in the same way: Hallom said as much; so did Ralph Sadler in his report on the causes of the Holderness uprising.[113] Furthermore, that the confiscation of church treasures was seriously feared north of the Humber was evident in the city of Hull's decision to sell its plate before the king's commissioners got their hands upon it, the news of which first inspired the Louth men to lock up their treasures.[114]

In his account of this grievance, Hallom connected it with the dissolution of the monasteries. In discussing the impact upon Yorkswold of Kyme and Dunne's warning that the government was about to remove all church treasures and some church buildings, he thought the news was made the more credible by what the government had already done to the lesser monasteries, arguing that "because people saw many abbeys pulled down, they believed all the rest to be true".[115] In the case of Beverley, the interconnexion was a fact. In being granted Warter Priory, the Earl of Rutland in September 1536 received the hospital and chapel of St. Giles in Beverley, attached to which was the rectory of St. Giles. Thus, in Beverley itself, a parish church came under direct threat of dissolution as a result of belonging to a suppressed monastery.[116] Since monasteries quite frequently owned parish churches, either because the monastery church acted as the parish church or because of appropriation, it was not unreasonably concluded that the dissolution of the one would lead to the dissolution

---

110 For the connexion with Louth, see Dodds, I, p. 92. For the letter of 3rd October, see ibid., pp. 98–9. For the Horncastle articles, see Bush, "Up for the commweal", p. 303. For the articles sent to the king, see SP1/108 (*L.P.* XI. 705).
111 For Kyme's declaration as it was recorded by Hallom, see *L.P.* XII{1}. 201/iv.
112 *L.P.* XI. 920, 967, 968, 973, 975, 828, 853, 854, 879 {2}; *L.P.* XII{1}. 70/i, ii and ix.
113 E36/119, fos. 27–27b (*L.P.* XII{1}. 201/iv); *L.P.* XII{1}. 200.
114 E36/119 (*L.P.* XII{1}. 70/i).
115 E36/119, f. 27b (*L.P.* XII{1}. 201/iv).
116 *V.C.H. Yorkshire*, III, p. 238; *L.P.* XI. 519 {1}; *V.C.H. East Riding*, VI, p. 77.

of the other. Furthermore, with the experience fresh in the mind of
royal commissioners arriving to confiscate the goods of the suppressed
religious houses, it was easy to believe, as Hallom suggested, the
rumours afloat that royal commissioners were about to expropriate
church goods as well. The threat to the parish churches, associated
as it was with the fate of the lesser monasteries, could therefore raise
the spectre of a loss of wealth. Moreover, since what was at stake were
treasures donated by parishioners, the wealth in question could be
regarded as a community possession rather than simply church property; and the laity could therefore regard the issue as an act of theft
perpetrated against itself.[117] The same issue, however, could also be
regarded as a matter of faith for associated with it, in all probability,
were fears that the confiscated treasures would reduce the efficacy of
church services and the removal of certain parish churches would
render church services less available.

That the religious changes of the time were for the rebels of the
Beverley region something more than a temporal issue was also made
evident in two other sources of grievance: the abrogation of holy days
and the Act of Supremacy. The holy day issue appeared in Stapulton's
list and was certainly present at the start of the Watton uprising when
the parishioners insisted upon the recognition of St. Wilfred's Day.[118]
The supremacy issue went unmentioned by Stapulton but was
declared in the deposition of Harry Gyll, the subprior of Watton.
According to him, the matter of the supreme head was "in everyman's mouth" and men said that "if that were not laid down it should
not do well".[119] Yet these two surviving instances of spiritual concern
were confined to Watton. The weight of the evidence, in fact, suggests
that the principal religious complaint concerned the wealth of the
church. This was made evident in the East Riding's perception of
the Lincolnshire uprising as being "up . . . for the commonweal",
threatened, it was thought, by the government's designs upon the
material possessions of both the church and the commonalty.[120]
With the focus of complaint in matters of religion upon "the wealth
of the church" or the "spoiling of holy church", rather than upon the

117 M. L. Bush, "Enhancements and importunate charges: an analysis of the tax
    complaints of October 1536", *Albion*, 22 (1990), p. 410.
118 Stapulton, p. 82; *L.P.* XII{1}. 201.
119 E36/119, f. 40 (*L.P.* XII{1}. 201 {3}). According to Thomas Lather, cellarer of
    Watton Priory, the house sent a letter, composed by Dr. Swinburn and delivered
    by Hallom, to the rebel convocation held in December at Pontefract on the
    subject of "the supreme head" (*L.P.* XII{1}. 201 {4}), and confirmed by the
    subprior (ibid., {3}).
120 E36/119, f. 35 (*L.P.* XII{1}. 201/vii).

issue of faith, the aim of the Stapulton host was to protect property against expropriation rather than to safeguard the spiritual efficacy of the church service. By its very nature, this grievance was popular or clerical rather than aristocratic, since the people and the clergy had nothing to gain from such expropriation whereas, through the dispensation of government patronage, the gentlemen could well become its beneficiaries.[121]

In general descriptions of the grievances held by the Beverley region two issues figured: first, the spoliation of the church and secondly, the exploitation of the commonwealth.[122] Characterising the Lincolnshire revolt was the prominence and variety of its tax grievances. Declared in its letter of the 3rd October which objected to "new enhancements and importunate charges", they dominated its articles of complaint. The uprising that inspired the Beverley region to take up arms was very much a tax revolt, objecting to a range of exactions, some of them real such as the fifteenth and tenth, the subsidy, first fruits and tenths and feudal dues and some of them imaginary, but nonetheless potent sources of agitation, such as taxes on beasts, ploughs, food and the sacraments.[123] How important tax grievances were to the Stapulton host, however, is quite impossible to work out and the actual nature of the tax grievance is not entirely clear. Sir Ralph Sadler in 1537 perceived the basic causes of revolt to be the imaginary taxes as well as the reduction in the number of churches. [124] But this was the view of a non–participant reporting well after the event. In listing the tax grievances, Hallom included the fifteenth and tenth, first fruits and tenths and "divers other payments", but it is not certain whether he was simply recalling the Lincolnshire articles or

121 The two canons from Lincolnshire had presented the cause of the Lincolnshire uprising as "the wealth of holy church". See above, p. 26. This was echoed by Dr. Pickering who allegedly claimed that the revolt was begun "for the wealth of the church" [P.R.O. SP1/118, f. 272 (L.P. XII{1}. 1019)] and by the peasant William Nicholson who saw the cause of revolt as "for spoiling of holy church and divers other things" [E36/119, f. 32 (L.P. XII{1}. 201/vii)]. The letter of 10th October, dispatched by the Beverley rebels into Lincolnshire made no mention of the faith but simply asserted the need to stop councillors from undoing "both the church and the commonalty" [P.R.O. SP1/107 (L.P. XI. 645)] and Wilson's proclamation of 8th October was a call "to maintain holy church and to take the commons' part" [SP1/109, f. 39b (L.P. XI. 841)]. The only report which specifically referred to "faith" was that of Marmaduke Neville who received, whilst in Durham, an account of the causes for which the Beverley rebels would "live and die" which mentioned "the right of God's faith and the church" [E36/118, f. 118(L.P. XII{1}. 29{2})].
122 See below.
123 Bush, "Up for the commonweal", pp. 302–3.
124 L.P. XII{1}. 200.

declaring that they were a concern north of the Humber.[125] Dr. Pickering composed a song based upon certain rhymes supplied to him by Hallom which complained of government exactions as well as "cursed heresy". When required at his examination to explain what was meant by "exactions", he replied: "I meant certain taxes, tenths, first fruits and suppression of monasteries".[126] But this simply substantiated Pickering's reported view that the revolt was begun for the wealth of the church and showed how the threat to it was seen as coming from taxation as well as Dissolution.[127] Nonetheless, in the Beverley region it was sincerely felt in October 1536 that the commonalty, as well as the church, was under attack. The point was made by the yeoman, William Horsekey, who claimed that Hallom raised Watton and beyond not only by complaining of suppressed abbeys but "other things touching the commonweal".[128] Moreover, the letter sent into Lincolnshire by the Beverley rebels on 10th October claimed that they were opposed to "unlawful demands" as well as "unlawful acts" and therefore were opposed to "all them that be councillors, inventors, procurers and their plan to undo not only the church but also the commonalty of this realm".[129] This complaint about the maltreatment of the commons, distinguished as it was from the maltreatment of the church, suggests that, in being moved by the grievances of the Lincolnshire rebels, the men of the Beverley region were likewise reacting against a process of governmental plunder which for them included not only exactions and expropriations made of the clergy but also taxes imposed upon the commons.

Because of its concern for both the church and the commonwealth, the Stapulton host had a strong animus against members of the council, especially Cromwell, but also against Lord Chancellor Audley, Richard Riche, the chancellor of the Court of Augmentations, Cranmer and Latimer. According to Hallom everyone cried out against them, for putting down abbeys, for exacting taxes, for attacks on the church, and for making new laws.[130] In spite of the impression given by Stapulton that the rebels were also moved against the landlords, the evidence presents a simple and straightforward hostility to the king's advisers for spoiling church and commonalty and for

125 E36/119, f. 27b (*L.P.* XII{1}. 201/iv).
126 *L.P.* XII{1}. 1021 {3}; SP1/118 (*L.P.* XII{1}. 1021 {5}).
127 See above, n. 121.
128 E36/119, f. 21 (*L.P.* XII{1}. 201).
129 SP1/107 (*L.P.* XI. 645).
130 E36/119, fos. 27–27b (*L.P.* XII{1}. 201/iv).

threatening Christ's faith and the commonwealth. This point was made by Pickering's song which presented the exactions and the heresy imposed upon the realm as an act of tyranny perpetrated by Thomas Cromwell, who true to his inappropriate background was behaving like a shearman, not a responsible minister to the king.[131] The popularity of the song, and the fact that it was based upon a number of rhymes composed by the rebels, expressed the general hostility shown in the region towards the king's advisers.[132]

In addition, certain companies within the Stapulton host, notably the woldsmen led by John Hallom and the townsmen of Beverley, had their own particular, local reasons for objecting to the government, its ministers and agents. Hallom himself detested Cromwell and collected together the rhymes composed against him.[133] This was because he held him responsible not only for the abrogation of holy days and for the plunder of the church but also for appointing Robert Holgate as Prior of Watton. Hallom had personal reasons for strongly disliking Holgate, quite apart from the fact that he was a Cromwellian placeman and had fled from the rebels.[134] According to the subprior of Watton, Hallom was "greatly incensed" with Holgate for evicting him from a farmhold.[135] Another source of alienation, as Hallom himself reported, was the prior's insistence that Hallom should pay him twenty marks rather than make a payment in corn "when God should send it": a reference to tithe farming, with Hallom, the lessee of the priory's tithes, claiming the right to collect them in return for a payment in kind which would vary according to the state of the harvest. This clashed with the prior's insistence upon a money payment which would remain constant no matter whether the harvest was good or bad.[136] In objecting to the prior's landlordship, Hallom spoke not only for himself but also for the rest of the tenantry, charging him with unnecessary severity in the manor court where he had rebuked the tenants "more like a judge than a religious".[137] So great was Hallom's hatred of the prior that sometime in October 1536, accompanied by a large company armed with bills and clubs, he invaded the priory,

131 SP1/118 (L.P. XII{1}. 1021 {5}).
132 According to the Prior of Bridlington, "many copies of the said rhyme [were] spread abroad as well about Bridlington as also about Pomfret and the same was also almost on everyman's mouth thereabouts" [SP1/118, f. 272 (L.P. XII{1}. 1019)].
133 L.P. XII{1}. 1021 {3}.
134 E36/119, f. 30 (L.P. XII{1}. 201/iv); Bateson, pp. 338–9.
135 E36/119, f. 39b (L.P. XII{1}. 201 {3}).
136 E36/119, f. 30 (L.P. XII{1}. 201/iv).
137 Ibid.

interrupted the brethren at dinner and commanded them to elect a new prior. When they objected, he threatened to vandalise the house if they failed to comply and decided on the spot to nominate in place of Holgate the Prior of Ellerton, who happened to be present, ordering the canons to accept him, even though he was unwilling to take on the office.[138] The local hostility to Holgate, then, provided further cause for anti–Cromwellian sentiment among the peasantry of Yorkswold. So great was Hallom's antipathy to, and fear of, Cromwell that he readily swallowed the rumour that, thanks to the Succession Act, the king would make Cromwell his heir to the throne. To prevent this from happening, Hallom advocated the legitimisation of Princess Mary.[139]

As in Yorkswold, so in the town of Beverley, a struggle with the lord of the manor sustained the local hostility towards Cromwell, again because he was seen as maintaining the offending party. In accounting for the uprising in Beverley of 8th October, a leading citizen of the town, Christopher Sanderson, opined that it was "to be principally revenged upon old grudges and quarrels one upon another, upon dissension amongst themselves by reason of a great suit betwixt the bishop of York and them for their liberties, wherein some took part with the bishop and some with the town".[140] This is misleading. Clearly, the extensive uprising that broke out in the Beverley region during the second week of October was much more than a local feud. Sparked off by the arrival of the articles from Lincolnshire and their appreciation by the Beverley burgesses, it undoubtedly developed into a sizeable revolt because the grievances motivating it were shared by surrounding areas which were not subjected to the archbishop's manorial lordship. Was the struggle between town and mitre, then, merely a complication present in the Beverley uprising? Did it do little more than incite conflict within the rebels' ranks, or was it an actual cause of revolt? The dispute between the archbishop and the town, largely over their respective privileges, was not in itself a sufficient motive for joining the pilgrimage of grace. However, arising from the attempt to resolve the differences over privilege, the archbishop was led to make several extraordinary interventions in the town's affairs, mainly to curtail the power Sir Ralph Ellerker the elder had acquired there. The consequent counteraction in the town persuaded him to enlist the support of Cromwell, whose willingness to support the

138 *L.P.* XII{1}. 201 {3} and {4}; Bateson, pp. 338–9.
139 *L.P.* XII{1}. 533.
140 Stapulton, p. 85.

archbishop's interventions politicised the conflict, turning it into a struggle for constitutional rights, with the town aggrieved against the king's council as well as against the archbishop.

The main events and issues of the town/mitre conflict were as follows. In late 1534 the archbishop agreed, as lord of the manor of Beverley, to concede certain commercial rights to the town, subject to the condition that the order of election traditionally used for choosing the twelve town governors should be respected and preserved.[141] Although the deputation of Beverley men who visited the archbishop at Cawood in December 1534 agreed with him, in practice the condition that the archbishop insisted upon could not be met, mainly because Sir Ralph Ellerker the elder had become one of the town governors that year and wished to remain in the office for a further twelve months. This breached the order that the governors should serve for no more than one year at a time.[142] In response, the archbishop made his first intervention. In January 1535 he nominated twenty–four men to the common council authorising them to have joint powers with the twelve governors. This was presented as a restoration of the traditional system which "within a few years past" had fallen into abeyance.[143] The twenty-four had been an important part of the old order of election, having served as the pool from which the new governors were taken and to which the serving governors were returned after their year in office.[144]

Yet the revival of the twenty-four by the archbishop breached tradition since these councillors were neither nominated by the governors nor elected by the commonalty but simply appointed by the archbishop. The archbishop was also breaching tradition by extending the powers of the twenty-four, for he required that they should have "joint authority" with the governors. Their revival was essentially a ploy to limit Ellerker's influence and to prevent his re-election. However, it failed. At the next election, held in April 1535, Ellerker and seven other governors managed to retain their offices for a further year.[145] In response, the archbishop intruded again, declaring the election void and withdrawing his offer to concede further rights to

---

141 See *L.P.* VIII. 721. *L.P.* confuses the sense of the letter. For the original, see SP1/ 92, fos. 182–3. Also see the indenture of 18th December 1534 between the town and the archbishop (H.R.O. BC/I/53). This has been sealed by the archbishop. It does not mention elections.

142 *L.P.* VIII. 721.

143 H.R.O. BC/I/54. There is an accurate translation in G. Poulson, *Beverlac* (Beverley, 1829), pp. 286–7.

144 *V.C.H. East Riding*, VI, pp. 20–22.

145 SP1/92, f. 182b (*L.P.* VIII. 721).

the town. Moreover, the violence shown by the Ellerker party in the election and afterwards caused the archbishop to enlist the support of the government, first by complaining to Cromwell and by requesting him to order Ellerker and his henchmen to dissociate themselves from Beverley; and secondly by exhibiting a bill of complaint to the council sitting in Star Chamber. Directed by Cromwell, the latter found for the plaintiff, confirmed the previous election null and void, banned Ellerker and his son-in-law Oswin Ogle from serving as governors ever again and authorised the archbishop to take full control of the town for the time being.[146] This decree was backed up by two injunctions, one obliging Ellerker, and the other obliging the townsmen, to comply with its terms. Ellerker was also forbidden from interfering in future elections of the governors. To enforce the injunctions, Ellerker was placed under the penalty of a fine of 500 marks and the townsmen, a fine of 1,000 marks.[147] The archbishop then appeared, in the eyes of the townsmen, to breach the Star Chamber decree himself with two further interventions, both of them denying the town "free election", the first in December 1535 when the twelve new governors were simply appointed by him; the second in April 1536 when he ordered his twelve placemen governors to remain in office.[148] Perversely, the archbishop's attempts to maintain the old order of election had resulted in its abandonment.

In the circumstances, the townsmen of Beverley were deeply offended. In the first place they felt that the group of them summoned before Star Chamber the previous November "had not been indifferently heard" and now wished to complain to the king for remedy against the decree.[149] Their other concern was that the archbishop had clearly contravened the decree of Star Chamber in taking upon himself such overriding powers and in using them to fill the town governorships with his own placemen. Adding insult to injury, one of the archbishop's appointees was the detested William Wise whom the townsmen had earlier dehoused in order to cancel his burgess rights and had come close to killing on the first day of the October uprising.[150] Faced by the archbishop's decision to avoid an election in April 1536, the townsmen

146 For correspondence with Cromwell, see *L.P.* VIII. 721 and 774; *L.P.* X. 18.
   For the bill of complaint, see *Star Ch. Yorkshire*, II, pp. 99ff. For the order, see
   R.F. Leach (ed.), *Beverley Town Documents*, Selden Society, 14(1900), pp. 64–5.
147 *Beverley Town Documents*, p. 65.
148 The order had explicitly required free election for December 1535 (ibid., p. 64).
   For the archbishop's contravention, see *Star Ch. Yorkshire*, III, pp. 109–10. For
   December 1535, see ibid., p. 114. For April 1536, see ibid., pp. 106–7.
149 Ibid., pp. 112–13.
150 See ibid., p. 114; Stapulton, p. 85.

conducted their own. The outcome was to re-establish the system of twelve governors elected by the burgesses for one year in office.[151] In response, the archbishop again resorted to Star Chamber which again ordered a cancellation of the election, with the result that the archbishop's placemen were restored to office and a free election once more denied.[152] The conflict was resolved only in November 1536, when the two parties, both of them now involved in the pilgrimage of grace, reached an agreement which restored the free election of both the twelve and the twenty-four, granted to the townsmen the additional privileges that they had sought in December 1534 and inserted into the borough's constitution certain safeguards to defend the custom that, in their struggle for power, both Ellerker and the archbishop had overridden.[153]

As a result of this conflict the Beverley uprising acquired yet another dimension: as well as a revolt against government exploitation and for the old religion, it became a revolt against government intervention and in support of the old custom. But the concern of the rebels was for the liberties of the townsmen, not the liberties of the archbishop and his officials. The custom defended was not the independence of the Liberty from royal government. Notably absent from the grievances articulated by the Beverley rebels was any objection to the statute abolishing the jurisdictional independence of franchises and liberties, an act which, in combination with the exclusion of papal authority, had, from 1st July 1536 transformed the polity to achieve a state of national sovereignty.[154] This profound political change appeared not to have alienated the inhabitants of the Beverley Liberty (i.e. the borough of Beverley and the water towns). The only possible suggestion that they were offended by it was the mention of "unlawful acts" in their letter of 10th October to the commons of Lincolnshire, but in all likelihood, the reference here was to the religious reforms of the government and the intrusion of Star Chamber.[155] For the Liberty inhabitants, the act had no practical drawback since all it did was to deprive the archbishop of certain powers: notably to pardon treasons and felonies and to serve in his own name writs cognisable in the king's courts. The one surviving objection came from Sir Robert Constable

151 *Star Ch. Yorkshire*, III, pp. 107–11.
152 Ibid., pp. 105ff.
153 *Beverley Town Documents*, pp. 66–72.
154 27 Henry VIII, c. 24.
155 *L.P.* XI. 645.

who submitted an article deploring the loss of the Liberty's powers to
the pilgrims' council at Pontefract when it was engaged in drafting
their December petition.[156] Probably as a result, the issue featured in
it.[157] But there is no reason to believe that, in submitting the article,
Constable was responding to pressure from the Beverley region.[158]

As for the agrarian grievances, specified by Stapulton but otherwise unmentioned in the evidence appertaining to the uprisings about
Beverley, three explanations are possible.[159] The first is that, in
identifying them, Stapulton was referring to the pilgrimage of grace
as a whole. The second possibility is that he had the Beverley region in
mind but was exclusively thinking of the yeoman captain, John
Hallom, and the differences that existed between him and his landlord, the prior and convent of Watton.[160] The third possibility is that
agrarian grievances were widespread in the region and stemmed from
the Percy family's decision in 1521 to apply to their Yorkshire estates a
custom found on their Cumberland estates: that is, the custom of the
Honour of Cockermouth.[161]

The adoption of this custom awarded some advantage to the
tenants, notably security of inheritance on tenures which in the law
were merely tenancies-at-will. But advantages undoubtedly accrued to
the lord as well, notably the right to exact a gressum not only upon a
change of tenant but also upon a change of lord, the second gressum
falling simultaneously upon all the customary tenants and therefore
yielding a considerable sum. If gressums had been nominal or unrevisable sums, no problem would have arisen. But for the lords they
were an essential compensation for fixed rents; and in periods of
inflation a vital safeguard against the devaluation of their landed
incomes. In border regions the military obligations associated with
tenant right served to restrain the raising of gressums, especially
when the increase weakened the tenant's capacity to serve in the
defence of the northern border with horse and harness and therefore
could be defined as unreasonable. But since in the East Riding border
service tenant right was not to be found, this criterion of reasonable-

---

156 See *L.P.* XII{1}. 851.
157 Article 19 (*L.P.* XI. 1246).
158 An extra political grievance concerned the fact that the borough of Beverley did
     not have an M.P. But this was expressed as a general objection to the under-
     representation of Yorkshire towns in parliament (See Bateson, p. 343), and there is
     nothing to suggest that it was articulated by the Beverley rebels.
159 Stapulton, p. 82.
160 See above, pp.49–50.
161 See Anthony Knowles, "Customary Tenures on the Northern Estates of the Percy
     Earls of Northumberland during the Sixteenth Century" (unpublished M.A.
     thesis, Manchester 1983), ch. 3. For a description of its operation in the lordship
     of Leconsfield, see P.R.O. E164/37, f. 249b.

ness was ruled out. Thus the application of the custom of Cockermouth to a region which lacked the protective argument of border
service could easily be seen to threaten an exploitation of the tenantry
through, as Stapulton put it, "the sore–taking of gressums".[162] Within
the region of the Beverley uprising were several large estates belonging
to the Percy family, all of them recently subjected to the custom of
Cockermouth: just north of Beverley was the lordship of Leconfield;
over to the west in the direction of York were the lordships of
Thornton and Pocklington; further north of Leconfield and close to
Great Driffield, and the region from which John Hallom drew some of
his support, were the lordships of Nafferton and Wansford. On none
of these estates had gressums increased all that much by 1536 but some
movement had occurred, making them at least equal to, or a small
multiple of, the annual rent rather than, as they had been, a fraction of
it; and now, following the change in custom, they were exactable at
twice the former frequency.[163]

Stapulton listed a wide range of agrarian grievance: besides the
exaction of oppressive gressums, he specified the raising of rents on
demesne leaseholds; deliberate depopulation through the destruction
of townships and farmsteads; enclosure of the commons; gentlemen
depriving the peasantry of land through leasing farms and of influence
through occupying the lowlier offices in local government.[164] Apart
from Hallom's complaint that he was deprived of a farmhold by the
Prior of Watton (which might have been awarded to a gentleman),
there is nothing to associate any of this directly with the revolts of the
Beverley region.[165] On the other hand, Sir Thomas Percy, whose
experience of the pilgrimage of grace was related to the northern
Yorkswold, agreed with Stapulton in presenting gressum-taking as a
cause of revolt.[166] In all likelihood, present at this time in Yorkswold
were agrarian fears. But there is no reason to believe that they were
as potent a cause of revolt in October 1536 as Stapulton suggests.
What is clear about the uprisings in the Beverley region is that, in
keeping with the other Yorkshire revolts, they were politically rather
than socially motivated and their grievances were socially unifying
rather than divisive. The rebels' benign attitude to the landlords
was evident in their willingness to recruit them as leaders. This
suggests that the agrarian grievance was a less potent cause of revolt

---

162 Stapulton, p. 82.
163 Knowles, op. cit., pp. 56–7; J. M. W. Bean, *The Estates of the Percy Family, 1416–
  1537* (Oxford, 1958), pp. 51–68.
164 Stapulton, p. 82.
165 See above, p. 49.
166 *L.P.* XII{1}. 393.

than, say, in Westmorland and Cumberland where the captured gentle-men were placed in tow rather than in command.[167] It also suggests that in the Beverley region the defence of the commonwealth was conceived as a struggle not with the landlords but with the govern-ment, and that the rebels' priority was to protect the wealth of the church and the commonalty from government expropriations and exactions.

The organisation of revolt

Having formed confederations bound by oath, the uprisings in the Beverley region quickly established military companies which soon came together to form the Stapulton host. In the process of mobilisa-tion the ringing of bells, the firing of beacons and the dispatch of muster summonses were all of vital importance. Having created the host, the next step was to link up with other rebel armies. The initial aim of the Stapulton host was to join the Lincolnshire rebels. Instead, it combined with the Aske host but then the two armies separated as the one went to take Hull and the other went to take York. Eventually, it joined with the other hosts as, in response to Robert Aske's summons, they converged in Pontefract to form the pilgrim host which went on to confront the army royal at Doncaster.

The Stapulton host, like the other rebel armies, was financed in three ways: by confiscating the goods of fleeing gentlemen, by taxing the clergy and by public subscription. Thus, Hallom's company requisitioned Edmund Copindale's sheep after his flight to Scarbor-ough Castle and Robert Creke's sheep after his flight to Cawood Castle. By selling them back to the owners enough money was raised to provide each member of Hallom's force with four shillings apiece.[168] The Holderness company, whilst engaged in the siege of Hull, sent out parties "to gather money of priests and abbots for their succour", according to William Nicolson.[169] The priors of Watton and Bridling-ton were approached for money, the former giving at least £10.[170] The Prior of Bridlington claimed that he gave the Holderness men £4 after they had threatened to drive away his cattle.[171] The religious houses of the region were approached not only for money but also for equipped

167 In parts an accommodation was probably reached between lord and tenant, as in the North Riding and in the wapentake of Dickering, see below, pp. 181 and 204.
168 E36/119, f. 28 (L.P. XII{1}. 201/iv).
169 E36/119, f. 32b (L.P. XII{1}. 201/v).
170 E36/119, f. 28b (L.P. XII{1}. 201/iv).
171 SP1/118, f. 271b (L.P. XII{1}. 1019).

and waged troops. Thus, the Prior of Watton was required to furnish six men with horse and harness and a week's wages at the rate of sixpence a day.[172] The priory also supplied the men with a quantity of bread and cheese.[173] The Prior of Bridlington was called upon to send eleven men, each horsed and harnessed and with twenty shillings of maintenance money.[174] The rebels made other demands of the religious houses. Watton, for example, was repeatedly called upon to supply horses.[175] In addition, the villages and townships of the region provided wages for the troops that they furnished.[176] On the other hand, it was forbidden to live off the countryside. Stapulton issued stern proclamations banning pillage and forbade the taking of victuals without payment.[177]

Although presented as an army of the commons, the Stapulton host was a sophisticated organisation. This was true not only of its financing but also of its behaviour in the field and the way it was equipped. In imitation of the Lincolnshire uprising, and given the need to move swiftly upon London, the emphasis was upon a horsed and harnessed army: that is, troops who were mounted and fully furnished in leather or resined-linen padded jackets, helmeted with a sallet, their arms protected by splints, and with bow or bill and occaasionally sword and buckler. This was the requirement made in the muster summonses to which there was some response: thus, the Prior of Bridlington sent mounted troops to the bailiff of Nafferton, and the servant sent by Richard Smytherly of Brantingham to the muster at Hunsley on 12th October was described as horsed and harnessed.[178] On the other hand, the army could not have consisted wholly or even predominantly of well-armed horsemen. Hallom stated that "everyone that was able to bear a staff" was eager to take part; and when his company burst upon the canons of Watton Priory as they were having their dinner, it was noticed that some had "bills and clubs".[179] Darcy

172 *L.P.* XII{1}. 201 {4}.
173 *L.P.* XII{1}. 201 {5}.
174 SP1/118, f. 271 (*L.P.* XII{1}. 1019).
175 *L.P.* XII{1}. 201 {4}.
176 SP1/115, f. 213 (*L.P.* XII{1}. 369).
177 Stapulton, p. 94.
178 Stapulton, p. 84 (the muster at Westwood Green on 9th Oct.); ibid., p. 89 (the muster at Hunsley on 12th Oct.). Kyme presented the Lincolnshire host as "horsed and harnessed" (Stapulton, p. 89). Hull was called upon to provide horse and harness on 14th Oct. (ibid., p. 93). For examples of the provision of horsed and harnessed troops, see SP1/118, f. 271 (*L.P.* XII{1}. 1019) and Stapulton, p. 90. The muster returns for 1539 show the two wapentakes of Harthill and Holderness possessing no more than 1284 horses in a total militia of 5734. See Appendix I.
179 E36/119, f. 27b (*L.P.* XII{1}. 201/iv) and *L.P.* XII{1}. 201{4}.

claimed that at the musters only "the best men" were allowed to join up.[180] Whether a process of selection operated in the Beverley region is not declared; but given the relatively small size of the host it is more than likely. The Stapulton host comprised about five hundred men from the Liberty of Beverley;[181] three hundred from Holderness;[182] four to five hundred from Yorkswold north of Beverley;[183] and perhaps 2,000 from the region south and west of the town.[184] Kyme estimated the total force at 3,000 on 12th October.[185] Aske put it, an absurd exaggeration, at 9,000 on 13th October. Richard Cromwell reckoned it at 6,000 on 19th October.[186] However, by the time it had joined the other hosts at Doncaster it was estimated at 2–3,000.[187] Since only the Holderness company had been left behind to guard Hull, it is likely that a weeding-out had occurred in order to create a well-furnished force.[188]

Of the hosts that came to join Aske, Stapulton's was the smallest. Compared with the 10,000 men from Durham and Cleveland led by Robert Bowes, the force of 5,000 men from the Malton region led by Sir Thomas Percy, and Robert Aske's own host of about 17,000 men, the Stapulton host must have seemed somewhat undermanned.[189] It formed but a very small fraction of an army which, according to Aske, numbered 34–35,000 troops.[190] The Stapulton host was also smaller than the other hosts which were formed in October – the force of 15,000 which besieged Carlisle, the force of 12,000 which besieged Skipton Castle, the two armies, each of 3,000, which confronted the Earl of Derby in Lancashire – and which brought the total force of rebels under arms, as reckoned at the time, to over 60,000 men.[191]

The uprisings around Beverley were undoubtedly a movement of

---

180 L.P. XI. 760 {2}.
181 Stapulton, p. 86.
182 Ibid., p. 94.
183 See above, n. 81.
184 Calculated as the difference between the given total of 3,000 for the whole host and the known totals for the Beverley, Holderness and north Yorkswold companies.
185 L.P. XI. 828/xii.
186 Bateson, p. 334 and L.P. XI. 789.
187 Bateson, p. 336.
188 Stapulton, p. 99. For this estimate's plausibility, see Appendix I.
189 For size, see below, p. 376.
190 Bateson, p. 336.
191 See below, p. 376. These figures were, no doubt, overestimations. A measure of their plausibility lies in the muster returns for 1535 and 1539. See Appendix I.

the commons. This was made explicit in the language of its letters and oaths, as well as in the way it was generally perceived and presented.[192] The original initiative, moreover, was distinctly popular, relying on the direction provided by Beverley burgesses, the yeoman John Hallom and the bailiffs of Holderness. In fact, the uprising had fully organised itself prior to the participation of the gentlemen. Yet moved by the example of the Lincolnshire uprising, whose organisation and aims were declared in the articles and letters brought across the Humber between 8th and 11th October, all of them declarations of the commons but signed by members of the Lincolnshire gentry, the Beverley rebels sought to construct their host in keeping with the society of orders. Thus, in the early stages a great deal of effort went into persuading gentlemen to pledge their allegiance to the commons' cause and then to assume the captaincy.

In the Beverley region the enlistment of the gentlemen had to be achieved by force, largely because so many of them took refuge in Hull and could only be recruited after the town had fallen to the rebels. Yet it would be misleading to conclude that the uprising was simply a popular movement with which the higher society was made to comply. In the development of the uprising both clerics and gentlemen had a vital part to play. This was not simply forced upon them by the commons but came of their own estrangement from the government, coupled with their own ability to share the basic grievances of the people, a compound of grudges against "evil ministers" for promoting policies perceived as threats to the faith, the church and the commonwealth. All three, moreover, could find agreement in the belief that the government was showing contempt for the society of orders through maltreating its component parts – the nobility, the clergy and the commonalty – and that therefore a rising of the commons was justified, all else having failed, to remind the government of its political and social obligations to the subjects of the realm.

Offended not only by the government's susceptibility to heresy but also by its onslaught upon the wealth of the church, a number of clerics, regular and secular, were easily persuaded to participate. Moving them to do so, in all likelihood, was a combination of spiritual and material grievances: alarm at the repudiation of the saints and the rejection of papal overlordship, dismay at the government's expropriations of church property and the extortionate exactions it imposed upon clerical incomes, the former achieved by a suppression of religious houses which threatened to include parish

192 See above, n. 1.

churches, the latter, resulting from the new taxes imposed upon the clergy in 1534 by the statute for first fruits and tenths. With such blatant causes for complaint, it is not surprising that a number of clerics became actively involved and used their literacy and authority to further a rising which started as a popular movement of traders, artisans and peasants. Several clerics helped to promote revolt by purveying in the Beverley region news of the Lincolnshire uprising. Thus Sir John Bowton and Sir William Mowde, variously described as canons and "poor religious men", crossed the Humber on 7th October, and then talked openly and approvingly in the Tabard Inn, Beverley, of the uprising across the water and its aims. To add weight to their tale, they made it known that their journey into the East Riding had been authorised by the gentlemen leading the Lincolnshire uprising;[193] and to prove it, they could show a signed letter of safe-conduct. Then there was the priest Sir John Tuvye who, on 8th October, along with Woodmancy and Wilson, informed the burgesses of Beverley of the Lincolnshire uprising and urged them to support it. On the very first day of the revolt he was a member of the small directional cadre which authorised Woodmancy to ring the common bell summoning the townsmen to the common hall where they were sworn and ordered to muster.[194] Also arousing the Beverley commons was Sir Thomas Bonaventura Johnson, friar and friend of Lady Stapulton and at the time resident at the Grey Friars in Beverley. Stapulton described him as a friar observant. If so, his order had been dissolved in 1534 for failing to accept the Divorce and the Royal Supremacy. However, in a list of friars observant for 1534 he was declared "an Augustine friar". Perhaps he had been a friar observant but to escape punishment had alleged otherwise. He came to Beverley via the Grey Friars of York and after a spell as chaplain in the Stapulton household at Wighill. On 9th October he joyously took the rebel oath and became so passionately attached to the cause that, forgetting his clerical vows, he joined the host as a soldier, accompanying it to Doncaster. Moreover, in the commons' initial search for captains cognisable to the society of orders, Johnson provided constructive help in advising them to choose William Stapulton and his nephew Brian.[195]

Another friar prominent in the opening stages of the uprising was

193 *L.P.* XI. 841; *L.P.* XI. App. 10.
194 *L.P.* XII{1}. 201/vii.
195 Stapulton, pp. 85–6; *L.P.* VII. 1607. For the fate of the friars observant, see Dom David Knowles, *The Religious Orders in England* (Cambridge, 1959), III, pp. 210–11.

Robert Esch. He was attached to the Trinitarian house of St. Robert's in Knaresborough, but had a licence to beg and preach within the town of Beverley.[196] In furthering the uprising he had two roles, both involving the composition, copying and circulation of bills. Having composed a letter telling of plans to pull down churches and to tax ploughs, beasts and sacraments, he distributed it in all three Ridings. In this way a motivating grievance of the Lincolnshire uprising became widely known in Yorkshire.[197] The friar preacher, Dr. John Pickering, singled him out as a "provoker" and "aider" of insurrection.[198] This was confirmed by William Stapulton. From him Esch sought on 10th October a licence "to raise them all" in the North Riding wapentakes of Ryedale and Pickering Lythe. Within the next week he did just that.[199] The Beverley townsmen were highly appreciative of his work and, when he returned to the town from his mission into the North Riding, they gave him twenty shillings to go upon another mission, this time into the Forest of Knaresborough.[200] The purpose of all these operations was to spread abroad the bills announcing the plucking down of churches and the exaction of new taxes. In addition, Esch assisted the Beverley uprising by composing a second bill which announced the muster on St. Wilfred's Day at Hunsley beacon and issued an order to attend it on pain of death in support of the Lincolnshire rebel cause.[201] Its effect was to transform an uprising which had so far been confined to the Liberty of Beverley into a regional revolt which encompassed the southern Yorkswold, Hullshire and Holderness.[202]

Two clerics are known to have served as leaders in the uprising about Beverley. Besides Tuvye who helped to start the revolt but, after the first day, went unmentioned, there was the vicar of Preston in Holderness who was probably Marmaduke Thomson. When the wapentake of Holderness first rose on 11th October, following the arrival of Anthony Curtis from Lincolnshire and the circulation of the friar of Knaresborough's bills, he administered the oath at the Nuthill assembly.[203] Yet thereafter he also failed to figure. In fact, in the Beverley uprising clerics are not much in evidence as leaders,

196 *V.C.H. Yorkshire*, III, p. 300; Dodds, I, p. 151; Stapulton, p. 88.
197 *L.P.* XII{1}. 1018; *L.P.* XI. 1047.
198 *L.P.* XII{1}. 1021.
199 Stapulton, pp. 88 and 96.
200 Ibid., p. 96.
201 *L.P.* XII{1}. 201/iv.
202 For wolds and Holderness, see above, pp. 34–7.
203 E36/119, f. 32b (*L.P.* XII{1}. 201/v). For his identification, see *V.E.*, 5, p. 119.
   The friar's bills were reported to Sadler, see *L.P.* XII{1}. 200.

delegates or policy-formulators. Furthermore, their ability to control
the uprising was very limited as Sir John Miller found out on 11th
October when his attempts to quieten things down came to nothing.[204]
Their main contribution lay in encouraging and spreading revolt. This
they did initially by disseminating news of the Lincolnshire rebellion
and its grievances in the East Riding. In composing the marching song
of the Pilgrimage, Dr. John Pickering, prior of the Dominican friary in
York but resident throughout October in Bridlington, played a part,
essentially one of provocative articulation, which closely resembled
that of the two friars and the two canons. Moreover, like them he
helped to cement the cause of the clerics with that of the commons by
proposing that rebellion was justified because the wealth of both
church and commonalty were equally under threat from a plundering
government.[205]

On 22nd October, having marched to Pontefract to join the rest of
the pilgrimage, the Stapulton host was appointed by the high command to wait upon Sir Thomas Percy under the leadership of Sir
Ralph Ellerker, the younger, of Risby, Sir William Constable of Great
Hatfield, Nicholas Rudston of Hayton and William and Brian Stapulton of Wighill.[206] By now the Beverley uprising had acquired the
semblance of a regional revolt properly led by gentlemen under the
command of a magnate, Sir Thomas Percy, who was acting for his
brother, the enfeebled 6th Earl of Northumberland. But this final
materialisation bore little resemblance to its original form: a popular
movement directed not by aristocrats but by news of a rising of the
commons in Lincolnshire. The one type of revolt was transmuted into
the other by a process of enlistment, the work of commoners desperate
to have gentlemen on their side. It did not happen overnight and was
only achieved by dint of perseverance and force.

The first gentlemen recruits were William Stapulton, along with
his young nephew, Brian. According to John Hallom, William (and the
same went for Brian), was "taken against his will by the commons".[207]
The purpose was to make him a captain and when he first joined the
rebel assembly, he was ecstatically welcomed.[208] As a stranger to the

204 Stapulton, p. 88. For his identity as a cleric, see *L.P.* XI. 841.
205 Dodds, I, pp. 280–81. The song had the catchy title "An exhortation to the nobles
    and commons of the north" [SP1/118, f. 292ff (*L.P.* XII{1}. 1021 {5})]. For its
    authorship, see *L.P.* XII{1}. 1019. For its use of rhymes collected by Hallom, see
    L.P. XII{1}. 1021 {3}. It was composed "when Norfolk first came to meet the
    rebels" (i.e. in late October) (ibid.).
206 Stapulton, p. 100.
207 E36/119, f. 28 (*L.P.* XII{1}. 201/iv).
208 See above, p. 30.

area and a younger son whose occupation was law not lordship, he was certainly not their first choice. But let down by Sir Ralph Ellerker the younger who refused to take the oath, and unable to rely on the head of the Stapulton family, who took the oath but was too ill to serve, the rebels fell back upon a combination of William and Brian.[209] Stapulton was not simply a lawyer but a leading estate official of the 6th Earl of Northumberland, having served since 1533 as his feodary.[210] In a region where the Percies remained the greatest private landowner, this may well have helped to recommend his captaincy. Stapulton remained their captain but not without friction which came to a head on 15th October when, having aroused the suspicion of the commons that he had fled, he offered his resignation only to be told that they would have no other captain.[211] As captain, Stapulton exercised a certain amount of control; but remained answerable to the commons who urged upon him the siege of Hull and, by refusing his request to go to York, obliged him to take part in the operation.[212]

Except for the Stapultons, no other gentlemen became involved until 12th October, four days after the start of the uprising. Then, within two days, Richard Smytherly of Brantingham, Robert Hotham of Scorborough, Sir Christopher Hilliard of Winestead, William Grymeston of Cottingham, Ralph Constable of Catfoss, John Wright of Danthorpe, Henry Newark of South Dalton, James Constable of Northcliffe, the Rudstons of Hayton and Philip Wardby were enlisted, largely under compulsion.[213] Most of these gentlemen acquired active roles in the uprising: Hilliard and Rudston as leaders in the siege of Hull; Rudston, Grymeston and Wright as delegates to the town of Hull and, in the case of Grymeston and Wright, as members of the rebel council formed on 20th October to draw up a set of articles;[214] Hotham, Rudston and Newark as captains of the

---

209 For Ellerker's non-cooperation, see Stapulton, p. 85. For the incapacity of Christopher Stapulton, see Stapulton, p. 83. Indicating the youth of his son and heir: in the winter of 1537, on the death of Christopher, special permission had to be sought to allow Brian to be declared of age in order to enter his patrimony (Bindoff, III, pp. 375–6).

210 Bindoff, III, pp. 375–6.

211 See above, p. 39.

212 See above, p. 39.

213 Stapulton, pp. 91–2.

214 For Sir Christopher Hilliard, see Stapulton, p. 95 and L.P. XII{1}. 380 (p. 178). For William Grymeston, see L.P. XI. 818 and Stapulton, p. 99. For John Wright, see Stapulton, pp. 97 and 99; L.P. XI. 818; L.P. XVII. 443 {14}. He is to be distinguished from John Wright, the Beverley burgess. For Nicholas and Robert Rudston, see Stapulton, pp. 92, 94–5 and 98; Bateson, p. 560; L.P. XI. 818. For Philip Wardby (also called Mawdeby by Stapulton), see Stapulton, p. 92.

woldsmen, with Hotham, along with Wardby, also placed on the council of four which met Aske on Weighton Hill and, along with Rudston, in the deputation sent to Hull to persuade it to yield. Moreover, Nicholas Rudston appeared to play a leading part in persuading the Stapulton host to go to Pontefract in response to Aske's summons on 20th October.[215] On the other hand, two of them, Hotham and Newark, quickly dissociated themselves by running away; and both Nicholas and Robert Rudston were, for some of the time, caught up with the Aske host.[216] The commons clearly longed for the leadership of gentlemen. This came of their belief in the society of orders as well as their need to follow the Lincolnshire example. Yet, apart from Hilliard, the ones so far recruited were minor gentlemen and not part of the county establishment.[217] The key families that the rebels needed to enlist were the Ellerkers and the Constables; but the two Sir Ralph Ellerkers had refused to swear and Sir Ralph the elder, along with Sir John Constable of Burton Constable and Sir William Constable of Great Hatfield had fled to Hull.[218] Moreover, Sir William's powerful brother, Sir Robert Constable of Flamborough, was out of reach as was Sir Marmaduke Constable of Everingham, the one in Pontefract Castle, the other in hiding.[219]

The Ellerker brothers, Sir Ralph the younger and Thomas, had been taken by 14th October. Ralph became a leader of the Yorkswold company that separated from the Stapulton host and on 15th October went to York.[220] Thomas served in the siege of Hull, in charge of a company from the lordship of Cottingham, the stewardship of which was held by his brother Ralph.[221] Then, with the fall of Hull on 19th October some of the major gentlemen were taken, including the elderly

---

215 For Newark, see *L.P.* XII{1}. 201/iv. For some intimation of his background, see P.R.O. E179/203/190 which revealed him as assessed for the subsidy on £20 of landed income in 1540. For Hotham, see *L.P.* XII{1}. 201/iv and Stapulton, p. 92. For his background, see above. For Rudston, see above, n. 214 and E36/119, f. 28 (*L.P.* XII{1}. 201/iv). The Rudstons appeared to join Aske on 15th October (Stapulton, p. 94) and became associated with Stapulton again only on 19th October (Stapulton, p. 98).

216 *L.P.* XII{1}. 201/iv.

217 Hilliard was a knight but a poor one, being assessed at only £13 in landed income in 1540 (see P.R.O. E179/203/222).

218 For not swearing, see Stapulton, pp. 85 and 89. For his flight to Hull, see ibid., p. 91.

219 For Marmaduke, see below, n. 264. For Robert, see below, p. 68.

220 For his capture, see Stapulton, p. 93. For his being in York by 16th October with the company from Yorkswold, see SP1/115, f. 164b (*L.P.* XII{1}. 306).

221 For his capture, see Stapulton, p. 93. For his part in the siege of Hull, see ibid., p. 95.

Ellerker, Sir William Constable and Sir John Constable.[222] Ellerker was placed in charge of Hunsley beacon; Sir John was left in charge of Hull and Sir William marched with the Stapulton host to Pontefract.[223]

However, the uprising was not converted into an aristocratic revolt. This was evident in the council formed at the Hunsley muster on 20th October to draft a petition to the government. The membership of the council was determined by the commons. Instead of appointing members of the county families, four minor gentlemen were chosen, two of them lawyers.[224] This probably did not express an unwillingness on the commons' part to follow the leadership of the higher gentry. Rather it reflected the conditions laid down by the Hull refugees for their submission: that they should not be obliged to swear the oath or to serve as captains. In this respect, the commons were thwarted in their aim. No matter how hard they tried to convert the uprising into an aristocratic revolt, it remained something else.[225]

The substantial gentlemen promoted the uprising not so much by taking part as by failing to proceed against it. If they had been resolved, they could have restrained the region, no matter how disaffected it was: as they proved during the November Truce and especially after the December Pardon. Moreover, normally the Ellerkers and Constables were powerful and assertive families, well prepared to get their way by physical force. However, in October 1536 they failed to counteract the rising. True, the most powerful resident in the region, Sir Robert Constable of Flamborough, was engaged in repressing the Lincolnshire uprising when the Beverley uprising began;[226] as was Sir Marmaduke Constable of Everingham[227]; and possibly long-standing feuds, notably between the Ellerkers and the Constables of Flamborough, reduced the capacity of the county families to take co-operative action. But why was Sir Ralph Ellerker the elder so passive when he attended the Westwood Green muster on 11th October?[228] In the Beverley area he was a highly respected figure. This was evident in the generosity shown towards him by the rebels on 11th October when they allowed him to come and go unsworn.[229]

222 Stapulton, p. 98.
223 Ibid., p. 99.
224 ibid., p. 98; and see above, p. 41.
225 Stapulton, pp. 97–8.
226 L.P. XII{1}. 1225.
227 Dodds, I, p. 109.
228 Stapulton, pp. 88–9.
229 Ibid.

Earlier, it was evident in the support he commanded in the town between 1534 and 1536, during its struggle with the lord of the manor, the Archbishop of York.[230]

To defend their interests against the archbishop, the townsmen over the years had formed special relationships with local lords. Once it had been with the Percies whose manor and seat of Leconfield was just north of the town.[231] Now it was with the Ellerkers whose nearest seat was at Risby, three miles to the west.[232] As steward of the royal lordships of Cottingham and Rise and of the seigniory of Holderness, the Ellerkers had considerable authority.[233] Their failure to use it in October 1536 can be explained in two ways. In generalising about the gentlemen's failure to suppress the uprisings, Lord Darcy attributed it to the popular nature of the uprising and its appeal to their tenants and servants, which deprived the lords of a trustworthy following and the means of imposing their will.[234] The other likely explanation is that some of the leading gentlemen held deep grudges against the government and therefore lacked the incentive to rescue it from an embarrassing situation, especially when the commons' revolt might pressure it to redress grievances that they shared.

The Ellerkers had good reasons for remaining loyal to Henry VIII. Over the previous fifteen years, he had rewarded them handsomely, both with stewardships of royal manors and with positions at Court.[235] Moreover, further rewards were in prospect, as Sir Ralph the younger was fully aware, having recently served as a commissioner for the Dissolution in the East Riding. Already he had acquired the lease to the site and demesnes of the dissolved priory of Haltemprice.[236] In this respect, they had a great deal to lose by going with the rebels. On the other hand, their association with the Court had brought them into the service of Catherine of Aragon;[237] and in the previous year they had been deeply offended by a Star Chamber decree, followed by an injunction issued in the same court, which had forbidden the family from holding office in the town of Beverley ever again and from

---

230 See above, pp. 50–3.
231 *V.C.H. East Riding*, VI, pp. 28 and 70.
232 This was the residence of Sir Ralph the younger. His father appears to have lived at Burstwick in Holderness. See *Index of Wills*, p. 217.
233 B. English, *The Great Landowners of East Yorkshire, 1530–1910* (New York, 1990), pp.18–19; Bindoff, II, pp. 89–90.
234 *L.P.* XI. 760 {2}. For relating the matter to the East Riding, see *L.P.* XI. 692.
235 Bindoff, II, pp. 89–90.
236 *L.P.* X. 980; SC6/Henry VIII/4505.
237 Bindoff, II, pp. 89–90.

meddling in its affairs.[238] In all likelihood, this had created a strong animus against the government if not against the king, and explains why Sir Ralph the younger, upon reaching York on 16th October with the Yorkswold contingent of the Beverley host, should say, in the company of the rebel leaders when dining with them at the house of Sir George Lawson, that Cromwell was "a traitor to the king's majesty which he would prove if the king would hear him".[239] A notable feature of the Ellerkers' behaviour during the uprising was not only their failure to oppose it but also their willingness to go and see the king on the rebels' behalf. On 14th October old Sir Ralph offered, in negotiating with the Beverley rebels from the safety of Hull, to deliver personally their articles to Henry VIII;[240] And young Sir Ralph realised both his own wish to speak to the king, as well as his father's offer to do so, when he took the pilgrims' five articles to Court on 28th October.[241] The Ellerker plan evidently was to obtain the king's ear in order to expose Cromwell who, among other things, was the recognised mastermind behind the Star Chamber decrees and injunctions issued against the Ellerkers in 1535/6.[242]

Another leading gentleman of the region with a deep grudge against the government was Sir Robert Constable of Flamborough. Like the Ellerkers his landed power in the region rested not simply upon family estates but also upon serving as steward for a number of lordships. However, by 1536 only one of these stewardships, that of the manor of Hotham, belonged to the Crown. Two appertained to the Percy lordships of Pocklington and Leconfield and the rest, to the religious houses of Bridlington, Watton and York St. Mary and to the bishopric of Durham.[243] Normally able to summon the manred of these estates, he was a powerful figure in the region, with seats at Flamborough and Holme-on-Spalding-Moor and a sphere of influence stretching into the West Riding, by virtue of his stewardship of the York St. Mary estate in Marshland, and enveloping Howden, the property of the Bishop of Durham.[244] All this made him a key figure in the control of north Humberside.

He was a violent figure, the defendant in a number of Star

238 See above, p. 52.
239 SP1/120, f. 225 (L.P. XII{1}. 1320). For indicating that it was on 16th October, see L.P. XII{1}. 306.
240 Stapulton, p. 95.
241 See above, n. 239; Dodds, I, pp. 267 and 274.
242 See above, p. 52.
243 L.P. XII{2}. 160–61.
244 English, op. cit., p. 17.

Chamber cases and locked in longstanding feuds with the Ellerkers and Sir William Percy of Bishop Burton. In view of Sir Robert's "troublous and dangerous" nature, Lord Darcy took the precaution of paying the dowry promptly following his daughter's marriage to Constable's son and heir.[245] Yet by 1536 Constable's star was on the wane; and, now in his sixties and troubled by sickness which included the gout, he was fighting a losing battle.[246] In the early 1530s he had suffered two humiliations at the hands of the government: first in 1531 when the stewardship of Sheriffhutton was transferred from him to the Cumberlander and Cromwellian client, Thomas Curwen; and secondly in 1532 when the stewardship of Holderness was transferred to his deadly rival, Sir Ralph Ellerker the younger.[247] In addition, he adhered to the old religion. In 1534 he had discussed with Lords Darcy and Hussey the heretical views of a priest in the service of Sir Francis Bigod which, when recollected in 1537, were encapsulated in a disturbing description of the virgin Mary as "a pudding when the meat was out". This tasteless remark had caused Darcy to exclaim: "I will be none heretic", a view with which Constable and Hussey had concurred.[248] Another indication of his religious conservatism was made evident in November 1536 when he took William Morland, a fleeing ex–monk, into his service, dressed him up in a pair of almain rivets and required him, in return for twenty shillings, to pray for all christian souls.[249] In all likelihood, he was against the government not only for depriving him of prestigious offices but also for embracing heresy. He was also against it for abolishing the Liberty of Beverley; and he had a strong dislike of Cromwell, so much so that he wished him dead.[250] However, these grudges and grievances did not cause him to join up immediately. His policy was to hold off for as long as he could. Although ordered by Shrewsbury and Suffolk in Nottingham to stay "the commons in the east part of Yorkshire", he proceeded no further than Pontefract Castle.[251] In fact, he only became a rebel when the castle yielded to Aske on 20th October, whereupon he became a committed and prominent leader of the Pilgrimage.[252] His brother, Sir William Constable of Great Hatfield in Holderness, and steward of

---

245 Bindoff, I, p. 686.
246 He was sixty-three, see *Star Ch. Yorkshire*, III, p. 112. For his poor physical state, see *L.P.* XII{1}. 146 and *Star Ch. Yorkshire*, III, p.110.
247 *L.P.* V. 506 (10); Bindoff, II, pp. 89–90.
248 SP1/118, f. 123 (*L.P.* XII{1}. 899).
249 *L.P.* XII{1}. 380 (pp. 178–9).
250 *L.P.* XII{1}. 851 and 891.
251 *L.P.* XII{1}. 1225.
252 Bateson, pp. 336–7; Stapulton, p. 100; *L.P.* XII{1}. 192, 393 and 1021.

the estates of Bridlington Priory, became a rebel in the same delayed and circuitous manner, fleeing in the first instance to Hull and, with the fall of this refuge, becoming a leader of the Stapulton host.[253]

Grudges, then, were borne by leading figures in the region and help to explain their failure to suppress the October uprisings. But several gentlemen became involved simply because they were taken captive and enforced to participate. This was true not only of minor gentlemen, such as Smytherly, Wright, Hotham, Newark and Grymeston, who had no hope individually of offering effective resistance and therefore could only chose between submission and flight, but also of significant local potentates, notably Sir John Constable of Burton Constable in Holderness.[254] Sir John was head of the leading landed family resident in the seigniory. According to all accounts, he made no attempt to stop the rebellion while, at the same time, refusing to participate. By the 12th October, within twenty–four hours of its outbreak in Holderness, he had fled to Hull, the rebels following close behind.[255] There he remained until 19th October when the town fell and he was compelled to attend the muster held the following day at Hunsley beacon.[256] During the siege he was more opposed to making a pact with the rebels than anyone else.[257] Then, when it was over he managed to avoid accompanying the host on its march to Pontefract and, with Sir Christopher Hilliard, was left in charge of Hull.[258] Throughout this period he appeared to be principally driven by a fear of the commons and of being compromised by them; and quite possibly his flight had sprung from his inability to trust his tenantry.

The gentlemen did not direct the uprising. The companies formed were not composed of the tenantry of the rebel leadership; nor were they financed from the donations of aristocratic supporters. The only financial contributions made by the gentlemen were the levies exacted by the rebels from those that fled.[259] In fact, in the organisation of the host, the gentlemen had no positive part to play since only later were they grafted onto it. In the early stages they were inclined to flee: to the Archbishop of York at Cawood Castle (as with William Babthorpe, former steward of Beverley, and Robert Creke, deputy to the absentee

253 Stapulton, pp. 91 and 100. For his stewardship, see V.E., 5, p. 121.
254 Bindoff, I, pp. 683–4.
255 Stapulton, p. 91; L.P. XI. 818.
256 Stapulton, p. 98; L.P. XII{1}. 201/iv.
257 Stapulton, p. 93.
258 L.P. XII{1}. 380 (p. 178)
259 See above, p. 56.

steward and receiver of Beverley, Richard Page);[260] to Scarborough (as with Ralph Eure, Edmund Copindale, George Conyers and Tristram Teshe);[261] to Hull (as with John Constable, William Constable, Edward Roos, Ralph Ellerker, John Hedge of Bilton and Walter Clifton);[262] and to Pontefract Castle where some fifty to sixty gentlemen were supposed to have taken refuge, some of whom, like the Archbishop of York, Robert Constable, Babthorpe and Creke, were drawn from the East Riding.[263] Then there were others in hiding, the most prominent of whom was Sir Marmaduke Constable of Everingham.[264]

The mass flight of the gentry was seen by Lancelot Collyns as "a cause of insurrection".[265] Chancellor Audley formed a similar impression, after receiving local information from Leonard Beckwith, Sir George Lawson and the mayor of York. On 17th October he was of the opinion that the rebellion in Beverley and other parts was by "some default of the gentlemen for that there was no good endeavour in the prime to repress them".[266] In this respect, the commons rose not because their lords commanded or encouraged them to do so but because, at the time, the lords made no attempt to stop them. With the leading gentlemen failing to set an example of opposition, there was no hope for the lesser gentry. A final factor was the absence of a resident territorial magnate capable of organising the gentlemen into a counter-insurgency force, as happened in Lancashire under the Earl of Derby and in Craven under the Earl of Cumberland. The great landowners of the region, the Percies and the Cliffords, lived in other parts.[267] If Sir Thomas Percy at Seamer had provided a strong lead against the uprising, he might have commanded some support but, after lying low, he became a rebel.[268] The intrusion of Lord Darcy might have helped; but ensconced in Pontefract Castle, he was inclined to believe that nothing could be done. Hoping that the uprisings beyond the Humber would strengthen the ability of the Lincolnshire

260 For their flight, see SP1/119, f. 2 (*L.P.* XII{1}. 1022). For their official connexion with the Liberty of Beverley, see *L.P.* V. 822.
261 Stapulton, p. 92.
262 Ibid., p. 91.
263 *L.P.* XI. App. 11; *L.P.* XI. 729.
264 Dodds, I. p. 283. Sir Marmaduke Constable, returned home following the Truce, but, threatened by the commons, had to flee to Lincolnshire (Bateson, p. 338). Also see, Bindoff, I, pp. 685–6.
265 *L.P.* XII{1}. 1018.
266 P.R.O. SP1/108, f. 151 (*L.P.* XI. 750).
267 English, op. cit., p. 14.
268 See below, ch. V.

rebels to extract remedy and pardon from the Crown, his policy was to do nothing but to emphasise and exaggerate the size and extent of the uprising in order to convince the government that it had no alternative but to yield to the rebels' demands. For this reason the instructions that the government issued to Ellerker, Constable and other gentlemen, ordering them to join with Lord Darcy in suppressing the uprising, stood no chance of success.[269]

In stirring up revolt, the contribution of the clergy and the gentlemen was quite peripheral, in the sense that initially the impetus and direction came from the commons, acting under the inspiration of the Lincolnshire rebellion. This was clearly evident in the town of Beverley where the outbreak of revolt on 8th October was directed by Richard Hendyke, Roger Kitchen, Richard Wilson and William Woodmancy, all of them exhilarated by the detailed news of the Lincolnshire rebellion which Woodmancy had brought across the Humber that very day.[270] Woodmancy was "a serving man", presumably one of the light or wild persons whose activities Stapulton deplored.[271] He was the first person to arrived with specific news of the midland uprising. He then rang the common bell which brought the town flocking to the market place.[272] Having done so, he delivered a letter written by the Beverley commons to the commons of Lincolnshire and on 11th October returned with the reply, accompanied by Kyme, Dunne and Curtis.[273] After that Woodmancy disappeared from view.

Of equal importance were the two Beverley burgesses, Richard Hendyke and Richard Wilson. Richard Wilson was a draper.[274] The previous April he had been involved in overthrowing the governors nominated by the archbishop and of replacing them with elected officers, one of whom was himself.[275] Prominent in this coup, he at one point gave a public reading of the Star Chamber decree in order to reveal that the archbishop had offended against it and to demonstrate that therefore the Beverley commons were entitled to proceed as if it

269 See *L.P.* XI. 729 and below, pp. 96–9. A letter of 13th October from the king instructed the gentlemen of the East Riding to join with the sheriff and Lord Darcy to put down the rebellion (*L.P.* XI. 688).
270 See above, pp. 26–9.
271 SP1/107, f. 56 (*L.P.* XI. 842 {4}). Evidently he was from Beverley. This is stated in the bill annexed to the proclamation of pardon of 24th July, 1537 (H.R.O. BC/I/55).
272 *L.P.* XII{1}. 201/vii.
273 Stapulton, pp. 84 and 88.
274 *Star Ch. Yorkshire*, II, pp. 107–8.
275 *V.C.H. East Riding*, VI, p. 72.

did not exist.[276] Hendyke had been involved in the same protest, although not so prominently.[277] Now in October the two resurfaced, if briefly. Wilson's role on the 8th was to bring in, along with Woodmancy, the news of the Lincolnshire uprising.[278] He authorised Woodmancy to ring the common bell and administered the oath to the responsive commons, the articles in one hand, a book, probably a missal, in the other.[279] It also seems that he read out the articles.[280] Finally he proclaimed, in the name of Robert Aske, a muster that evening on Westwood Green to meet Sir Ralph Ellerker the younger.[281] That he was not acting for Ellerker became evident both in Ellerker's failure to attend the muster and in the warning issued earlier by Wilson that, in the event of Ellerker's absence, "no man could do better service than to take him".[282] Thereafter, Wilson made two further appearances – as part of the deputation to take Stapulton on 9th October and as part of another deputation to the town of Hull on 12th October – before sinking without trace.[283] Hendyke also authorised the ringing of the common bell on 8th October.[284] On the same day he declared a proclamation in Beverley market place ordering every man to come and take an oath of allegiance to the commons on pain of death.[285] Both Wilson and he, moreover, must have had a hand in the letter that was composed that day and taken by Woodmancy to Lincolnshire.[286] Then he also fell out of sight. Between them Hendyke and Wilson organised the start of the Beverley uprising. But this was only made possible by the responsiveness of the commons, who flocked in with their arms even before the muster was announced.[287]

The other key figure was Roger Kitchen, a glover of the town.[288] On 8th October, intoxicated by the news from Lincolnshire, he became highly excited and, bent on some act of commitment, he had wished to ring the common bell before Woodmancy took the

276 *Star Ch. Yorkshire*, II, p. 108.
277 Ibid., p. 107. Hendyke and Newdyke are the same person.
278 *L.P.* XII{1}. 201/vii.
279 Stapulton, p. 84; *L.P.* XI. 841; *L.P.* XII{1}. 201/vii.
280 Ibid.
281 *L.P.* XI. 841.
282 SP1/109, f. 39b (*L.P.* XI. 841).
283 Stapulton, pp. 86 and 91.
284 *L.P.* XII{1}. 201/vii.
285 Stapulton, p. 84. According to Breyar, it was Wilson who made this proclamation. (*L.P.* XI. 841).
286 See above, p. 29.
287 SP1/109, f. 39 (*L.P.* XI. 841).
288 *L.P.* XII{1}. 201/vii.

matter in hand.[289] With Beverley up in arms, Kitchen was keen to raise the surrounding countryside; and on 9th October, after Stapulton had become the captain and was counselling against further action, Kitchen urged the people gathered on the green to go with him and raise the lordship of Cottingham and Hullshire.[290] That night, although not authorised by Stapulton, Hunsley beacon was lit and the region alerted, a realisation of Kitchen's wish and no doubt his handiwork.[291] Then he disappeared from view.

Several other burgesses of Beverley, notably John Webster and John Crowe, the latter probably an innkeeper, were recognised as leading agitators; but what they actually did to promote the uprising is unknown.[292] Finally, there were the two petty captains of the Beverley uprising, both of them commoners and appointed on 10th October to aid the two Stapultons in managing the commons: Richard Wharton, yeoman of Hull Bridge, one of the water towns within the Liberty of Beverley, who was appreciated by Stapulton for his honesty, substance, good age, gravity and diligence, and Nicholas Horncliffe, bailiff of the Liberty and an official of the Archbishop of York.[293] Stapulton presented them as having a sobering effect upon the rebels and, in this sense, of making his own policies more acceptable.[294] Essentially they were links between the gentlemen and the commons. Before they were made captains, they were used by the rebels to approach the Stapultons and Ellerkers in order to persuade them to join the uprising.[295]

Self-risen and self-directed, the commons took the initiative to spread their revolt into the surrounding areas. In response to the beacon unofficially lit on the night of 9th October, a certain Fober of Newbald and John Stakehouse of Cottingham came to Beverley to learn what to do; as did a messenger from North Cave.[296] As a result,

289 Stapulton, pp. 83–4.
290 Ibid., p. 87.
291 Ibid.
292 Webster and Crowe, along with Kitchen and Wilson, were all described by Hallom as "great doers in that time of the business" [E36/119, f. 27 (*L.P.* XII{1}. 201/iv)]. On 8th October the uprising was planned in Crowe's house (*L.P.* XII{1}. 201/vii). And on 11th October, the legation from Lincolnshire were entertained there (ibid./iv).
293 For Wharton, see *Index of Wills*, p. 195; Stapulton, p. 87. For Horncliffe, see Stapulton, pp. 86–7.
294 Stapulton, p. 87.
295 Stapulton, pp. 85, 86 and 87–8.
296 Stapulton, pp. 87–8. Fober was possibly John Fobery of Holme-on-Spalding-Moor who in the mid-1540s was assessed for the subsidy at £40 in goods (E179/203/222). John Stakehouse was another wealthy commoner with goods assessed at £40 in 1534 (E179/202/170).

these communities became incorporated in the uprising. John Smoothing, a burgess and governor of Beverley, and also involved in the disturbances of the previous April, travelled to Bridlington spreading the word.[297]

Holderness rose following the arrival of the gentleman lawyer, Anthony Curtis, but the rising was not simply his work.[298] Nor was it captained at the start by gentlemen. Initially, all the captains were commoners, although not ordinary folk for the three of them, William Barker, William Ombler and Richard Tenand, were bailiffs of the wapentake of Holderness.[299] Other commoners, notably Richard Kenny, Robert Lamyn and William Nicholson, were also prominent in the Holderness revolt.[300] Because the local gentlemen refused to take part, the Holderness uprising started as a hunting down of them, in the course of which Sir Christopher Hilliard was taken, made a captain and then played a positive part in taking Hull; but this was not to the complete exclusion of the original commoner captains who retained their leadership role.[301] Furthermore, as revolt spread into Yorkswold, it did so as a popular movement. This was clearly evident around Watton where the revolt began as a protest made by the congregation against the priest's failure to name a forthcoming holy day and was then directed by a peasant, the substantial yeoman John Hallom of Calkeld, not because the rebels wished to be directed by a commoner but because the gentlemen whom they elected as their captains let them down by fleeing at the first opportunity.[302]

William Horsekey presented Hallom as "ringleader and captain" of the area between Watton and Great Driffield.[303] Hugh Langdale saw the authority he exercised as stemming from his personal aggressiveness, describing him as "so cruel and fierce a man among his neighbours that no man durst disobey him".[304] He was undoubtedly belligerent. This was evident in his invasion of Watton Priory to dismiss the prior and in the letter he sent to the pilgrims' York council in late November which simply recited the articles that the rebels had already dispatched to the government with the addition "or else we are

297 P.R.O. SP1/118 (*L.P.* XII{1}. 1020 {2}); *V.C.H.East Riding*, VI, p. 200.
298 See above, p. 36.
299 Stapulton, p. 94; *L.P.* XII{1}. 201/iv and v.
300 *L.P.* XI. 818.
301 See above, pp. 36 and 38–9. For the leadership role that they retained, see Stapulton, pp. 95 and 100.
302 See above, p. 35.
303 E36/119, f. 21 (*L.P.* XII{1}. 201).
304 *L.P.* XII{1}. 201/ii.

fully determined to spend our lives and goods in battle".[305] But it seems that the commons obeyed him not simply because he was overbearing but also because they felt him to be a trustworthy and potent advocate of their cause.[306] The force he actually commanded amounted to no more than 230 men.[307] Moreover, it soon became absorbed into a larger force of woldsmen which by 15th October had fallen under the leadership of the gentleman, Robert Rudston.[308]

However, although his leadership was quickly subsumed, Hallom was undoubtedly a key figure in raising and organising the countryside above Beverley: not only by challenging the priest in the first instance over the recognition of a saint's day but also by returning from Beverley on 11th October with detailed information of the Lincolnshire uprising and with the friar of Knaresborough's summons to a muster at Hunsley beacon.[309] On 12th October, Hallom led the Watton men first to the Hunsley muster, where they met up with the Beverley men, and then to a muster at Arram where they joined the rebels from above Great Driffield and from northern Holderness.[310] As well as a convincing captain, Hallom also made his mark as a dynamic messenger: bringing home news of the Lincolnshire uprising, taking seditious rhymes to Dr. John Pickering in Bridlington, and eventually in early December delivering a letter from Watton Priory on the supreme headship of the church to the pilgrims' Pontefract council.[311] A combination of business, belligerence, commitment and credibility gave him, although no more than a rich peasant, a vital part to play both in arousing revolt in north Yorkswold and in linking it with the Stapulton host.[312]

Overall, the organisational aim of the uprisings in the Beverley region was to form a host captained by gentlemen. Eventually this was achieved; but that the aim took some time to realise indicates that these revolts comprised a popular uprising. What the movement sought to do was to don the disguise of the society of orders in the bid to gain some respectibility as well as to acquire some semblance of the

305 For his dismissal of the prior, see above, p. 50. For his letter to the York council, see R. W. Hoyle, "Thomas Master's narrative of the pilgrimage of grace", *Northern History*, 21 (1985), p. 73.
306 *L.P.* XII{1}. 201/iv.
307 See above, n. 49.
308 Stapulton, pp. 94–5.
309 See above, pp. 34–5.
310 E36/119, f. 28 (*L.P.* XII{1}. 201/iv).
311 *L.P.* XII{1}. 201 {4} and 1021 {3}.
312 In the subsidy assessment for 1524 he was reckoned to have £5 in goods (E179/202/170).

Lincolnshire rebellion. In this respect, the form that the uprising had taken by 22nd October, a host led by Ellerker, Rudston, Constable and Percy, was the creation of a rebellious commonalty rather than a demonstration that its claim to be a rising of the commons was merely a cloak to conceal an aristocratic conspiracy and a device concocted by rebel gentlemen to free themselves from blame.[313]

313 For the captaincy at this point in time, see Stapulton, p. 100 and *L.P.* XII{1}. 393.

III

✺▓▓▓▓▓▓▓▓▓▓▓▓▓▓▓▓▓▓▓▓▓▓▓▓✺

THE ASKE HOST

The uprising around Howden

The Lincolnshire connexion

This uprising affected the West Riding wapentakes of the Ainsty, Barkston and Osgoldcross as well as the East Riding wapentakes of Howdenshire, Ouse and Derwent and the western border of Harthill.[1] It was initially an offshoot of the Lincolnshire rebellion and with a combination of concern for the commonwealth and for the faith, it subscribed to roughly the same grievances. A confederation bound by oath, organised in a host and presented as a movement of the commons, it employed the same methods of protest. And in planning to present a petition to the king for a general pardon and the redress of specified grievances, to be enforced, if necessary, by a march on London, it had the same aim. Moreover, although a separate movement, it was very similar in organisation, complaint and purpose to the uprising around Beverley, another offshoot of the Lincolnshire rebellion.

Mainly responsible for its connexion with Lincolnshire were the midlander, Guy Kyme, and the northerner, Robert Aske. Kyme not only took news of the Lincolnshire rebellion to Beverley on 11th October, but he had also visited York on 6th October to drum up support, returning to Lincoln three days later with the encouraging news that the north was ready to meet up with the Lincolnshire rebels at Newark or Doncaster.[2] Likewise, Aske not only urged the Beverley

---

1 See map 3.
2 P.R.O. SP1/110 (*L.P.* XI. 972).

men to support the Lincolnshire rebellion but he also worked persistently to spread the movement into the wapentakes along the Ouse.[3]

Aske became a committed rebel on 4th and 5th October. Having been taken by the Caistor rebels and sworn "to be true to God and the king and the commonwealth", he was made, allegedly under compulsion, captain of the West Ancholme strand of the Lincolnshire uprising. In this capacity, he encountered the Louth host at Hambleton Hill near Market Rasen where he was told of its grievances, the supplicatory letter that it had already sent to the king and its plan to march on Lincoln.[4] The business of spreading the revolt into Yorkshire involved him in a frenzied shuttling to and fro between the two counties from 4th to 10th October, some of which he concealed in his Narrative (i.e. the account he eventually gave to the king in December) by claiming that between 7th and 10th October, the period in which the Beverley uprising began and the Howdenshire/Marshland revolt was germinating, he was stuck in Burton-upon-Stather, unable to cross the flooded waters of the Trent. His aim in making this point was to safeguard himself against the charge of being an instigator of revolt, whether it be in Howden or Beverley. This meant stressing the fact that, apart from his first crossing into Lincolnshire on 4th October, he had passed from one county to the other by crossing the Trent, thereby keeping well away from Beverley, rather than by crossing the Humber which would have brought him close to the town. The probable truth of the matter is that, having entered Lincolnshire by the Barton-Hessle ferry on 4th October, he returned to Yorkshire on 6th October via the Trent into Marshland, reaching Howden by the Whitgift ferry across the Ouse. Returning to Lincolnshire on 7th October, probably via Barton again, he was back in the East Riding on 8th October. On 9th October he made a third visit to Lincolnshire, returning at midnight via the Trent crossing.[5]

This close connexion between the two rebellions was manifest in the use the rebels of Marshland and Howdenshire made of the Lincolnshire articles of complaint, which had the same appeal for them as for

3 For Aske's part in raising Beverley, see above, pp. 28–9.
4 Bateson, pp. 331–3; *L.P.* XI. 971.
5 Bateson, pp. 331–4. That he was in Osgodby on 8th October is suggested by William Breyar who learned of the fact from two sources: Aske's brother Christopher and Raffles, the Beverley burgess (*L.P.* XI. 841). Several pieces of evidence suggest that he was at this time in the region of the Beverley uprising. John Dakyn described him as coming "over Hull" (*L.P.* XII{1}. 788). Both George Lumley and Ralph Sadler present him as going into Holderness (*L.P.* XII{1}. 200 and 369). John Hallom claimed that on 7th October Aske had been in the area bringing news of the Lincolnshire uprising [P.R.O. E36/119, f. 27b (*L.P.* XII{1}. 201/iv)].

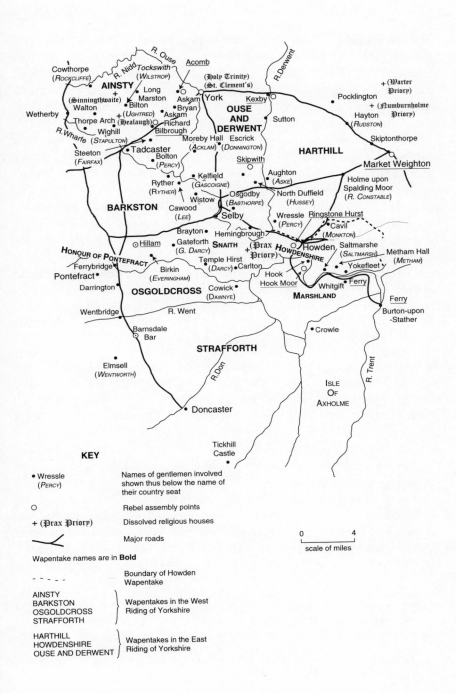

KEY

- **Wressle**
  (*Percy*)   Names of gentlemen involved shown thus below the name of their country seat

- ○   Rebel assembly points

- + (𝔓𝔯𝔞𝔵 𝔓𝔯𝔦𝔬𝔯𝔶)   Dissolved religious houses

- ⌐   Major roads

Wapentake names are in **Bold**

- - - -   Boundary of Howden Wapentake

AINSTY
BARKSTON
OSGOLDCROSS
STRAFFORTH
} Wapentakes in the West Riding of Yorkshire

HARTHILL
HOWDENSHIRE
OUSE AND DERWENT
} Wapentakes in the East Riding of Yorkshire

0   4
scale of miles

Map 3   The uprising around Howden

the Beverley rebels. Aske used them to declare the cause at the musters held on 11th October at Hook Moor and Ringstone Hurst, on 12th October at Skipwith Moor and on 15th October at Kexby Moor.[6] Taken to York, they also appeared to play a part in the city's submission on 16th October. According to Richard Bowier, a burgess of York, it was the arrival in the city on 15th October of "a fellow out of Lincolnshire with their articles" and three messengers from the Aske host with letters desiring permission for it to pass through, which caused York to yield.[7] Aske was so reliant upon the Lincolnshire articles that he referred to them in his first known proclamation and appended them to his second.[8] In fact, until he composed his oath on 17th/18th October, the Lincolnshire articles were his only formal statement of grievance.[9] The oath, moreover, was related to the articles in identifying roughly the same grievances.[10] The burden of complaint, then, was, as in Lincolnshire, concern for the faith of Christ assailed by heresy and concern for the commonwealth threatened by the government's exploitation of commonalty and church.

The outbreak of revolt

This happened on 10th October, with the ringing of the church and town bells alarum, first in Marshland and then in Howdenshire.[11] The particular cause was a letter from the incoming sheriff of Yorkshire, Sir Brian Hastings, ordering the gentlemen of Marshland to raise a force and to join him, presumably to resist the rebellion.[12] The prospect of reprisal triggered off the revolt. Also preparing the way was news of the Beverley uprising, conveyed by the lighting of Hunsley beacon on the night of 9th October.[13]

For at least the previous four days, however, the Ouse region south of York had been in an agitated state, aroused by tales of what was happening south of the Humber. Aske had found the inhabitants of Howdenshire and Marshland ready to ring the bells on 6th October.[14] And on the same day his two brothers, Christopher and John, had

6 See below.
7 P.R.O. SP1/115, f. 164b (*L.P.* XII{1}. 306).
8 SP1/107, f. 11b (*L.P.* XI. 622); *L.P.* XI. 705 {2}.
9 M. L. Bush, "Up for the commonweal: the significance of tax grievances in the English rebellions of 1536", *E.H.R.* 106 (1991), pp. 306–7.
10 Toller, pp. 50–1 (*L.P.* XI. 892 {1/3}) for the oath of the honourable men. For its composition, see below., pp. 91–2.
11 Bateson, p. 334.
12 Ibid.
13 Ibid.
14 Bateson, p. 333.

found "the people drawn out into the fields, preparing themselves forward and abiding the ringing of Howden great bell" as that evening the brothers had travelled from Hemingbrough, where they had been with the king's subsidy commissioners, to their home along the Derwent at Aughton.[15] Nothing happened at this point in time, according to Aske, because in both Howdenshire and Marshland he ingeniously dissuaded the commons from taking action by telling the people of each region only to ring the alarm after hearing the other do so first.[16] His concern, it seems, was to ensure that nothing was done until the king had replied to the supplicatory letter sent to him by the Lincolnshire rebels on 3rd October; and then to decide upon what to do in the light of the government's response.[17] His two brothers also claimed to have calmed things down.[18] A letter ordering obedience, sent into Howdenshire on 6th October by Lord Darcy, may also have had some effect.[19]

By 6th October Aske was already recognised as the rebel leader.[20] Besides being reputed in both Howdenshire and Marshland as a captain of the Lincolnshire uprising, he was a marked man. On the morning of 7th October, several commoners of Howden burst into his bedroom and urged him to leave since, if he did not, the sheriff, Sir George Darcy, would take him.[21] In response, Aske went again to Lincoln, hoping to learn of the king's reply.[22] But it had yet to arrive; and on 8th October he returned secretly to Yorkshire, staying with William Babthorpe in Osgodby where he met his two brothers.[23] The agitation in the region, however, was too much for Christopher and John who therefore resolved to go to Skipton with the money that Christopher had collected from the Clifford tenants in the East Riding.[24] In all likelihood, the commons at this time were already looking for gentlemen to serve as captains. On either the 9th or 10th they found one in Sir Thomas Metham who, taken from his bed, was forced into this role. However, he quickly fled and, in reprisal on 10th

15 SP1/120, fos. 58–58b (L.P. XII{1}. 1186).
16 Bateson, p. 333.
17 SP1/118, f. 92 (L.P. XII{1}. 946).
18 L.P. XII{1}. 1186.
19 See below, p. 96.
20 Bateson, p. 333.
21 L.P. XII{1}. 946.
22 Bateson, p. 333.
23 SP1/109, f. 39b (L.P. XI. 841).
24 SP1/120, fos. 58–58b (L.P. XII{1}. 1186). It looks as if they were disturbed on the night of 8th October, since the following day Christopher set out for Skipton amd was in Tadcaster on 9th October (L.P. XI. 841).

October, after the uprising had been formally announced with the peal alarum, Aske found them about to burn down his house. This he managed to stop, presumably because Metham's son and heir had now been recruited and made a rebel captain in his father's stead.[25]

Aske had returned to Lincolnshire on 9th October, but the king's reply had still not arrived and so around midnight he re-entered Yorkshire, crossing the Trent at Burton-upon-Stather, then the Ouse and so into Howdenshire via the ferry at Whitgift. At this point he was caught up in open revolt and immediately recognised as a captain by the Howden men.[26] The bellringing of 10th October was followed by a succession of musters, each of them held in a different wapentake. Two occurred on 11th October, the first at Ringstone Hurst in Howdenshire, the second at Hook Moor in Marshland. Aske was present at both.[27] At the Marshland muster the Lincolnshire articles, which had been finalised and dispatched to the king on 9th October, and had been brought into the West Riding by two serving men, were read out; just as, on the same day at Westwood Green, they were declared to the Beverley host by Kyme and Dunne.[28] Also by the 11th October Aske had assumed the title of chief captain and, in this capacity, he produced his first proclamation.[29] Its purpose was to summon the people of the wapentake of Ouse and Derwent to an assembly on Skipwith Moor for the following day. If the proclamation was stating the truth, the uprising had already acquired a command structure, consisting largely of gentlemen. Under Aske and designated as captains, were two of his relatives, his nephew Robert Aske and his brother-in-law William Monkton, Gervaise Cawood, the Bishop of Durham's bailiff of Howden, the cleric Sir Thomas Franke and representatives of two well-known Howdenshire families, Thomas Metham and Thomas Saltmarsh. The same proclamation also delineated the areas so far involved: Marshland in the West Riding, Howdenshire in the East Riding and the Isle of Axholme in Lincolnshire. There is nothing to corroborate that the latter area had actually

25 SP1/119, f. 2 (*L.P.* XII{1}. 1022); Bateson, p. 334; *L.P.* XI. 622. Stapulton calls him George (p. 92) but probably meant Thomas. For Sir Thomas' escape, see SP1/119, f. 3 (*L.P.* XII{1}. 1022).

26 Bateson, p. 334; *L.P.* XII{1}. 1018.

27 Bateson, p. 334. The Dodds confuse the assembly on Hook Moor of October 11th with the assembly on Skipwith Moor of October 12th (Dodds, I, p. 148).

28 Bateson, p. 334; *L.P.* XII(1). 852/ii; Stapulton, p. 89.

29 SP1/107, f. 116 (*L.P.* XI. 622). The Dodds claim that it was issued on 10th October (Dodds, I, p. 148); but since it referred to an assembly "on the morrow" which was held on 12th October (see *L.P.* XI. 1402), it must have been issued on 11th October.

risen at this time but Harry Lytherland, a cleric associated with the town of Crowle, later deposed how the commons of Yorkshire had approached them for support and, in response, he had sent to the Yorkshire host an unspecified number of well-harnessed men.[30]

Also set out in the proclamation were the procedure to be followed and the cause and intent of the uprising. Thus, after ringing the bells that night and the following morning, the people were instructed to assemble at Skipwith Moor and appoint as captains certain landlords of the region: i.e. "Mr. Hussey, Mr Babthorpe, Mr. Gascoigne and other gentlemen". Then the oath was to be administered *en masse* by calling upon everyone to be true "to the king's issue and the noble blood"; "to preserve the church of God from spoiling" and to safeguard "the commons and their wealths"; and by requiring the general assent of the assembled to these declared aims. The emphasis was upon defending the society of orders and stopping the government from plundering the church and the commonwealth. Presenting the government as a predator, which was utterly contemptuous of the principal constituents of the body politic, was very much in the idiom of the Lincolnshire uprising. So was the promise made in the same proclamation that, at the Skipwith Moor assembly, articles would be presented which would declare the cause of revolt and serve as "their petition to the king". In the absence of any other articles, there can be no doubt that those promised in the proclamation were the same (i.e. the Lincolnshire articles) as those read the same day to the Marshland assembly on Hook Moor.[31]

But at its inception the uprising was not simply a replica of the Lincolnshire rebellion. As directed by Aske, it quickly developed two distinctive features: its defence of "the noble blood" and its presentation as a pilgrimage. The former was declared in the first proclamation as a part of the oath in use at that time. Reasserted in Aske's second proclamation, it was also incorporated in the oath drawn up on 17th/18th October.[32] In the various statements of grievance produced by the Lincolnshire uprising there had been complaint specifically against

30 SP1/116, f. 171 (*L.P.* XII{1}. 537).

31 SP1/107, f. 116 (*L.P.* XI. 622). For Hook Moor, see above n. 28. For proof that the articles read at Skipwith Moor were the Lincolnshire articles, see Stapulton, p. 95.

32 The first proclamation mentioned being true "to the noble blood" [SP1/107, f. 116 (*L.P.* XI. 622)]. The second proclamation called for "the preservation of . . . the nobility" [*St.P.*, I, p. 467 (*L.P.* XI. 705 {2}]. Aske's oath required "the purifying of the nobility and to expulse all villein blood and evil councillors" [Toller, p. 50 (*L.P.* XI. 892 {1/3})].

ministers of low birth.[33] Now in Yorkshire the same complaint was differently articulated to emphasise the injustice done to the nobility by the present government.

Coupled with this new emphasis, and indicating the seriousness with which the grievance was held, the rebels of the region, in the very early stages of their revolt, made approaches to three powerful and disgruntled nobles. Thus they sent a letter, possibly as early as 8th October, to Lord Dacre, the border magnate who had been disgraced by the government in 1534 and deprived of his offices, and who had only been saved from complete ruin by the privilege of trial by peerage. He was resident at Hinderskelfe (now Castle Howard), north-east of York. They offered to join him in demanding "recompense of such injuries as you have sustained contrary to justice [in the matter] as was tried by your peers".[34] The rebels also approached the Percy family, possibly as early as 6th October, but probably on either 10th or 11th October.[35] The family was in a critical state, its future threatened by the government as Cromwell negotiated with the childless 6th Earl of Northumberland for the resumption of its whole estate.[36] Thus, a party from Howden led by Aske went to Wressle Castle and outside the gates emotionally shouted: "Thousands for a Percy".[37] Neither overture bore immediate fruit. Dacre refused to respond and soon afterwards left the East Riding for Cumberland, taking up residence in his border castle of Naworth.[38] Percy was not at home, although news of the rebels' visit to Wressle quickly reached the family seat at Seamer near Scarborough where the Earl's estranged brother and likely heir, Thomas Percy, was staying.[39] A third disgruntled peer, to whom the rebels were appealing through their show of concern for the noble blood, was Lord Darcy. On 12th

33 As in the articles submitted to the government [SP1/108 (*L.P.* XI. 705)] which simply objected to councillors "of low birth and small reputation". The noble cause, however, was mentioned by Brian Stanys on 8th October who proclaimed that the king should take noblemen into his council (*L.P.* XI. 828/v).

34 For Dacre's residence in the East Riding, see *L.P.* XI. 647. The letter has only survived in a summary of it made by Thomas Master [R.W. Hoyle, "Thomas Master's narrative of the pilgrimage of grace", *Northern History*, 21 (1985), p. 64].

35 The incident is mentioned in Thomas Percy's account of the uprising. According to him, news was brought of it to Seamer within three days of hearing of the Lincolnshire uprising [SP1/115, f. 258 (*L.P.* XII{1}. 393 {2})]. But everything depends on how long the news of Lincolnshire took to reach the North Riding. By 7th October details were reaching the Beverley area.

36 See below, p. 187.

37 SP1/115, f. 258 (*L.P.* XII{1}. 393 {2}).

38 See below, p. 344.

39 *L.P.* XII{1}. 393.

October a party was deputed to visit his house at Temple Hirst; yet he had already fled to Pontefract Castle.[40]

The same proclamation of 11th October ordered those assembled at Skipwith to spread the revolt "beyond the water", that is, across the Ouse, the border between the East and West Ridings, by warning the inhabitants of this region, the wapentake of Barkston, "to be ready (i.e. properly armed) upon pain of death for the commonwealth".[41] However, it is evident from the Archbishop of York's account of the uprising that this part of the West Riding was already up in revolt, although not yet organised as a military force. On 10th October three fleeing gentlemen sought refuge with the archbishop in Cawood Castle. They were John Aske, the brother of Robert and Christopher, Sir Thomas Metham, the impressed rebel captain who was fleeing from the Howdenshire rebels, and Thomas Portington of Barmby. In seeking to do so, they were following the example of other gentlemen, notably William Babthorpe and Robert Creke. After crossing the Ouse they were set upon by the archbishop's tenants, only making their escape, back across the Ouse rather than into the castle, because the archbishop's steward came to their rescue.

Then, on 11th October the commons of Selby, Wistow and Cawood sought to make the steward compromise himself by attending the Skipwith Moor assembly, but this he avoided by means of a bribe.[42] Thomas Maunsell, vicar of Brayton, revealed the part played by the Skipwith Moor assembly in raising revolt in Barkston and Osgoldcross. He was taken by the Howden commons on 10th October, sworn on 11th October and obliged to attend the Skipwith Moor assembly on the 12th. At the assembly he learned that the commons intended to cross the water in order to visit Lord Darcy's house at Temple Hirst and the Archbishop of York's house at Cawood. Accordingly, the following day a party of twenty-four commons crossed the Ouse, raised the town of Brayton by ringing its bell and required Maunsell to bring out all the communities in Lord Darcy's office: presumably in the lordship of Snaith and upon the estates of Selby Abbey, the stewardships of which were in Darcy's possession. Over the next three days this is what Maunsell did, reaching westwards as far as

---

40 SP1/113, f. 62 (*L.P.* XI. 1402).
41 SP1/107, f. 116 (*L.P.* XI. 622). The limited military capacity of Howdenshire (with no more than 605 troops) made it vitally important for the rebels to enlist better endowed regions: notably Ouse and Derwent (928 troops), Barkston (2155 troops), Harthill (2859 troops), York and Ainsty (1931 troops) and Osgoldcross (1494 troops). See Appendix I.
42 SP1/119, f. 3 (*L.P.* XII{1}. 1022).

the township of Hillam, and with no one to stop him.[43] By 11th
October the leading gentlemen of the region had taken refuge in the
castles of Pontefract or Skipton. Darcy from Temple Hirst and his son
from nearby Gateforth, went to Pontefract on 7th/8th October.[44] And
the archbishop, who had learned that the Beverley men were coming to
kill him and that the Marshlanders were coming to make him their
captain, followed on the troubled 10th, accompanied by the gentlemen
who had fled to Cawood.[45] The rising of the commons thus flourished
in a vacuum of authority, quickly enlisting armed support from the
wapentakes of Barkston, Ouse and Derwent, Howdenshire and
Osgoldcross.

Also set in motion by the Skipwith Moor assembly of 12th
October was a company led by William Edwyn, of Yokefleet in the
parish of Howden, a servant of Sir Robert Constable.This company
enlisted William Acklam of Moreby Hall, the son and heir of John
Acklam, sacked Leonard Beckwith's house at Stillingfleet, went to
Cawood to take the archbishop's servants and then travelled up the
Ouse towards York and into the Ainsty "stirring and moving the
people by the way".[46] They met no opposition and, as with Maunsell, were assisted by the flight of gentlemen, notably John Acklam,
William Babthorpe of Osgodby, Sir William Gascoigne of Gawthorpe
Hall, Sir William Fairfax of Steaton, Henry Ryther of Ryther and
Robert Ughtred of Bilton.[47] Like Maunsell, Edwyn and Acklam
appeared to act under instruction from Aske and on 16th October
they joined him at a muster outside York, the day of his triumphal
entry into the capital of the north.[48]

The march on York

From 9th October the authorities had expected a march on York to
take possession of the king's treasure deposited there.[49] On the 12th
October the rebels began to comply with this expectation. After

43 SP1/113, fos. 62–62b (*L.P.* XI. 1402).
44 The decision to go there was made on 6th October (*L.P.* XI. 563). Darcy was in
    the castle by 8th October (*L.P.* XI. 605). For his hope of a by-pass, see *L.P.* XI.
    762/ii; *L.P.* XII{1}. 1022.
45 SP1/119, fos. 2b–3 (*L.P.* XII{1}. 1022).
46 SP1/119, fos. 87–87b (*L.P.* XII{1}. 536). Also see Stapulton, p. 100. For Edwyn,
    see P.R.O. E179/203/222. For Acklam, see Tonge, p. 65.
47 Babthorpe and Gascoigne had fled by 10th October. Ryther and Ughtred had
    taken refuge in Pontefract Castle by 16th October. See below, pp. 129–30.
48 For Maunsell, see SP1/113, f. 62b (*L.P.* XI. 1402). For Acklam and Edwyn, see
    SP1/119, fos. 87–87b (*L.P.* XII{1}. 536).
49 See Darcy's warning to the mayor of that date (*L.P.* XI. 627).

mustering at Skipwith Moor, Aske's host went on a march led by priests and behind the cross of Howden Minster, a treasure the rebels feared the government was about to confiscate.[50] But its first aim was to join up with the Stapulton host. It therefore marched to Market Weighton, reaching it on the evening of 12th October and lodging there for the night.[51] The following day a conference was held between the leaders of the two hosts who, as professional lawyers practising in London and fellows of the same Inn of Court, must have known each other well.[52] Prior to the conference Aske met the legation from Lincolnshire, Guy Kyme and Robert Dunne, who since 11th October had kept company with the Stapulton host. Aske assured them of his familiarity with the Lincolnshire uprising and declared that he knew their articles as well as they did. In the same encounter he also revealed that by this time the uprising was seen, at least by Aske, as a pilgrimage, for he declared that, as pilgrims, there was a special journey upon which all of them had to go.[53]

At the Weighton conference a joint council was formed of four gentlemen from each host. It was far from socially impressive. Besides the two lawyers, Aske and Stapulton, there were two very young men, both of them sons and heirs of middling gentry (i.e. Brian Stapulton and Thomas Metham), Nicholas and Robert Rudston of nearby Hayton who had just joined Aske, Robert Hotham and Philip Wardby. Apart from Metham, none was of the county establishment; and nearly all of them had been compelled to serve.[54] The council's immediate problem was the unwillingness of the town of Hull to join the rebellion. Two days passed in fruitless negotiation. By 15th October the rebels had decided to lay siege to Hull and, at the same time, to march on York.[55] For the latter purpose Aske was joined by a contingent from the Stapulton host, the woldsmen from the Watton/Great Driffield area.[56]

Whilst awaiting a response from the commissioners sent to negotiate with the citizens of Hull, Aske and his army proceeded slowly

50 Aske in his Narrative stated that the commons of Howdenshire took "the cross of the church with them" on their march to Market Weighton (Bateson, p. 334)
51 Bateson, p. 334.
52 Ibid.; Stapulton, pp. 91–2.
53 Details are provided by Stapulton (Stapulton, p. 92) and Kyme (*L.P.* XI. 828).
54 Stapulton, p. 92. The composition of the delegation from the Aske host is assumed from Stapulton's remark, that when Aske met him at Weighton Hill, he was accompanied by the two Rudstons and Sir Thomas Metham's son and heir (see ibid.). Aske claimed that he met Nicholas Rudston for the first time on 13th October (Bateson, p. 560).
55 Stapulton, pp. 92–5.
56 Stapulton, pp. 94–5.

towards York, along the Roman road from Market Weighton, spending the night of the 13th October at Shiptonthorpe and travelled no further than Pocklington on 14th October.[57] Without a doubt, he was not only awaiting news from Hull but also recruiting support from the wapentake of Harthill. Perhaps when at Pocklington, he visited the dissolved monasteries of Warter and Nunburnholme. For the new recruits he held an assembly at Kexby Moor. This was on 15th October. To them he read out the Lincolnshire articles as a means of explaining why those who had already joined him had risen.[58]

York had been preparing its defences.[59] Aske had fears that the Ainsty, the wapentake to the west of the city which was part of the borough county and traditionally under obligation to provide the city with troops, would come to its aid under the leadership of Sir Oswald Wilstrop and would seek to stop the rebel host by destroying the bridges across the Derwent at Kexby and Sutton. To prevent this from happening, Aske on the 15th October placed a guard on both of them.[60] However, no opposition materialised, probably because of the rebels' success in raising support on the west bank of the Ouse and because the companies led by Maunsell, Acklam and Edwyn had already taken control of the Ainsty.[61] Making their task easy had been not only the flight of the gentlemen but also the considerable disaffection present in the wapentake and in York itself. Stapulton gave evidence of the former, connecting it with the rumours about the amalgamation of parishes and the destruction of churches. The suppression of Healaugh Priory was another matter of concern, so much so that the commons of the Ainsty restored it and reinstated its prior.[62] As for the commons of York, they were reported to be "up" on 11th October; and on 13th October Lord Darcy reported that the citizens "are highly disposed and favourable to the opinion of the rebels".[63]

With the ground prepared, Aske took the city without force,

57 Stapulton, p. 92.
58 Bateson, p 558. At the time it seems that he no longer had a copy of the articles and therefore sent to Stapulton for one, but Stapulton had misplaced his copy. Then, it seems, Aske secured a copy of the set sent from Lincolnshire to York (ibid.).
59 L.P. XII{1}. 306; L.P. XI. 750.
60 Stapulton, p. 95.
61 By 16th October Maunsell was stationed with his company at Bilburgh [SP1/113, fos. 62b–63 (L.P. XI. 1402)]. For Acklam and Edwyn, see above, n. 46. For their taking of Wilstrop, see Stapulton, p. 100.
62 Stapulton, p. 82; Yorkshire Chancery Proc., p. 63.
63 For 11th October, see L.P. XII{1}. 1018. For 13th October, see SP1/110, f. 44b (L.P. XI. 692).

simply by writing to the mayor to ask if the rebels might pass through.[64] Along with this request for free passage, a copy of the Lincolnshire articles was delivered to the mayor and a day or two earlier a copy of the oath used by the Beverley rebels, essentially an assurance to remain true to the Lincolnshire articles, had been delivered by two merchants.[65] Faced by threats of force, which he believed would come from Richmondshire as well as from the commons of Beverley, Cottingham, Howdenshire and Marshland, and subjected to the convincing propaganda of the articles and the oath, the mayor abandoned all thoughts of resistance and, without consulting the common council, agreed to let the rebels pass through on condition that no one was hurt, no pillage occurred and that the victuals taken were paid for at the specified rate of two pence a meal.[66] Aske was in full agreement with these terms and, to give the host a better chance of abiding by them, he banned the footmen from coming within the walls.[67]

Thus on 16th October a force of 4–5,000 troops came to York, led by Aske as chief captain and the petty captains, Rudston, Cawood, Monkton and Donnington. Entering the city at five p.m., Aske's first step was to go to the minster where he was received at the main door by the choir and by Lancelot Collyns, treasurer to the See, who welcomed him with a handshake. Taken in procession to the high altar, Aske offered his oblation and that night lodged with the alderman, Sir George Lawson.[68] However, he was too late to take possession of the king's treasure which had been moved to Tickhill Castle, south of Doncaster.[69]

Aske's army waited upon events for the next two days, hoping to hear of the fall of Hull, wondering what was happening in Lincolnshire where the uprising appeared to have evaporated (but had it?), and becoming aware of risings up-country, in the Yorkshire dales and moors and the palatinate of Durham.[70] In this time Aske was busy producing a number of policy statements, the chief of which were an

---

64 Bateson, p. 334; L.P. XII{1}. 306. According to the Dodds, Aske also sent his second proclamation (Dodds, I, p. 175). But there is no evidence for this; and it is highly unlikely that the second proclamation was composed before 17th October. See below, pp. 92–3.

65 SP1/115, f. 164b (L.P. XII{1}. 306); Stapulton, p. 97.

66 For the threat, see L.P. XI. 704. For the terms see SP1/115, f. 164b (L.P. XII{1}. 306).

67 Bateson, p. 334.

68 L.P. XI. 759; L.P. XII{1}. 306; L.P. XII{1}. 1018. For the petty captains, see below, pp. 124–6. The estimate of 4–5,000 men is only plausible if Aske had recruited considerable numbers from the West Riding wapentakes of Barkston and the Ainsty and the East Riding wapentake of Harthill. See Appendix I.

69 L.P. XII(1). 854. See map 11.

70 Bateson, p. 334.

order for suppressed religious houses, a written oath, his second proclamation (which was a letter of instruction to the gentlemen), and an order against the spoiling of property. He was also seeking resources for the host, especially by placing wealthy abbeys under obligation to support the uprising in return for granting them formal protection.[71]

Until its arrival in York, the Aske host did not appear to be especially concerned with the suppression of the monasteries. In Aske's first proclamation the preservation of the church of God from spoliation had been included in the terms of an oath, but this could have related to the rumours circulating about parish churches.[72] Neither in his written oath nor in his second proclamation was an objection explicitly made to the Dissolution, apart from its mention in the list of Lincolnshire articles appended to one surviving copy of the latter.[73] Nor does it feature in the account of the rebels' grievances which Aske presented to Lancaster Herald on 21st October; nor in the five articles which the pilgrims sent to the king on 27th October.[74] Furthermore, there is no evidence that Aske's army was involved in the restoration of any dissolved house prior to its arrival in York. The only evidence of this concern lies in Thomas Maunsell's account of the Skipwith Moor assembly which caused him to write to his brother William Maunsell and Leonard Beckwith warning them to "provide for themselves".[75] Both were beneficiaries of the Dissolution, notably of the two Benedictine monasteries situated in York, Holy Trinity and St. Clement's, which had been dissolved in July, leased to Maunsell and Beckwith, and restored by the rebels sometime in October.[76] Once in York, however, Aske, either on 16th or 17th October, declared his support for the restoration of suppressed houses by having an order nailed to the minster door. According to Aske, this order was a

71 For the policy statements, see below. For the protection offered York St. Mary Abbey, see *L.P.* XI. 784. In return the abbey had to place its goods and chattels at the disposal of the rebels. For the approaches made to Watton Priory, see E36/119, f. 28b (*L.P.* XII{1}. 201{iv}) and *L.P.* XII{1}. 201 {4}. For the approaches made to Bridlington Priory, see *L.P.* XII{1}. 1019. Also see *L.P.* XII{1}. 853.
72 P.R.O. SP1/107, f. 116 (*L.P.* XI. 622).
73 For the oath, see Toller, pp. 50–51 (*L.P.* XI. 892 {1/3}). For the second proclamation, see *St. P.*, I, p. 467 (*L.P.* XI. 705 {2}). This list is not appended to the two other surviving copies [P.R.O. SP1/108, f. 53 (*L.P.* XI. 705 {3}) and SP1/108, f. 55 (*L.P.* XI. 705 {4/ii})].
74 For Lancaster Herald, see *L.P.* XI. 826. For the five articles, see *L.P.* XI. 902 {2}.
75 SP1/113, f. 62 (*L.P.* XI. 1402).
76 For the leasing, see P.R.O. SC6/Henry VIII/4460 (Holy Trinity); SC6/Henry VIII/4466 (St. Clement's). For their restoration, see D. M. Palliser, *Tudor York* (Oxford, 1979), p. 50.

response to the wish of the commons to restore the monks.[77] Basically, it authorised the religious to re-enter their houses and proposed how they should conduct themselves until the matter was sorted out by the government: that is, "to such time our petition be granted".[78]

As yet, Aske's army had failed to submit a petition or even draw one up. It remained reliant upon the Lincolnshire articles, to which the government's reply was bound to be unfavourable since the Lincolnshire rebellion had submitted unconditionally. A fresh set of articles was a top priority, but it remained beyond the rebels' capacity. On 17th October, when Thomas Strangways asked for the articles and again on 21st October when Lancaster Herald requested them, the rebels were made to look foolish in not having any.[79] In the absence of articles they had to rely upon an elaborate oath to act as their formal complaint. This was produced hurriedly on the night of the 17th or the morning of 18th October, presumably to conveying to Strangways their grievances.[80]

As the steward of Lord Darcy, Strangways was an important figure. He claimed to have come to York on instruction from his master. Enticingly, he asked Aske and his companions if they wanted a head captain and suggested that one could be found "if the articles pleased his mind". Yet they suspected he had really come to spy out their strength and were none too keen to co-operate with him, so they insisted that he left the town before musters were held the following day.[81] However, keen to convince Darcy of their cause, although not able to agree that they needed a head captain, the rebels were eager to offer something.[82] That night, when Strangways had retired to his lodging, Monkton and Carwood delivered to him "the copy of the oath of Lincolnshire"; and the following morning Aske sent him his own freshly drafted oath.[83] What the former document was remains obscure: probably the Lincolnshire articles with a provision to remain

---

77 Bateson, p. 335. Aske justified the order "because the commons would needs put them in".
78 SP1/108, f. 210 (*L.P.* XI. 784/ii).
79 *L.P.* XI. 762 and *L.P.* XII{1}. 852/iii; St.P., I, p. 485 (*L.P.* XI. 826). The Dodds are wrong in stating that "the pilgrims' articles" were drawn up outside York on 15th October (Dodds, I, pp. 176-7). They overlook the fact that the articles to which they refer are the Lincolnshire articles (see Bush, "Up for the commonweal", pp. 303–5).
80 SP1/108, f. 171b (*L.P.* XI. 762) and *L.P.* XII{1}. 852/iii.
81 SP1/118, f. 47b(*L.P.* XII{1}. 852/iii).
82 Rudston and Cawood were against having a head captain (ibid.).
83 For the oath brought by Monkton and Cawood, see SP1/108 (*L.P.* XI. 762). For the oath brought by Aske, see *L.P.* XII{1}. 852/iii.

true to them (resembling, perhaps, the one that had come from Beverley).[84] But the latter document has survived. Aske presented it as composed wholly by himself, but also stated that it was the true declaration of the commons' grievances.[85] In all likelihood it was angled to appeal to Darcy and the other gentlemen in Pontefract Castle. Noticeably, it played down the issue of an exploited commonalty and emphasised as the major tenets of the rebel cause "the preservation of the king's person and his issue", "the purifying of nobility" coupled with the expulsion of "all villein blood and evil councillors from the privy council", "the restitution of the church" and "the suppression of these heretics and their opinions", all to be put right by taking "afore you the cross of Christ" and entering "this our pilgrimage of grace for the commonwealth".[86]

According to Aske, there was no problem in raising the commons. Nothing needed to be done because "they were already up in all parts of Yorkshire and the bishopric".[87] This was no doubt an exaggeration but the evidence does suggest that the commons did not require to be aroused, only directed; whereas, in contrast, the gentlemen needed to be both aroused and persuaded to take direction. The oath, according to Aske, was used specially for the purpose of involving the gentlemen.[88] So was the second proclamation which marked the first known instance of a rebel document addressed in the name of the baronage and commonalty.[89] For this reason it must have postdated "the order for religious houses suppressed" and a letter of protection for the abbey of York St Mary, both of which were authorised with the consent of "the headmen".[90] The text of the proclamation failed to

---

84 See above, n. 65.
85 *St.P.*, I, p. 485 (*L.P.* XI. 826); Bateson, p. 572.
86 For the two surviving versions, see SP1/108 (*L.P.* XI. 705 {4}). and Toller, pp. 50–51 (*L.P.* XI. 892 {1/3}). In his Examination Aske confessed that he composed it himself and with no one else's advice (Bateson, p. 572). The purpose of putting it into writing was, according to Aske, to swear the gentlemen and to have in writing something that incorporated the petition of the commons (ibid.). In one version, the one sent by Lord Darcy into Lancashire, it was called "the oath of the honourable men" (Toller, pp. 50–51). In the other surviving version it was called "oath of all men sworn to them" [SP1/108 (*L.P.* XI. 705 {4})]. In his Examination Aske referred to it as "the oath of the commons" (Bateson, p. 571).
87 Bateson, p. 560.
88 Bateson, p. 572.
89 *St.P.*, I, pp. 466–7 (*L.P.* XI. 705 {2}).
90 The order is authorised with the consent "of the headmen of this our pilgrimage for grace" [Toller p. 51 (*L.P.* XI. 784/ii)]. The letter is addressed from "all other the heads of the commonwealth" [SP1/110, f. 210b (*L.P.* XI. 784)].

refer explicitly to the Dissolution.[91] Rather it condemned "sundry new inventions" for which "simple and evil-disposed persons of the king's council" were held responsible, specifying only that they were contrary to the faith of God, the king's honour and the commonwealth and that their intention was "to destroy the church of England and the ministers of the same".

Then, having highlighted the threat to the church, it complained that the council "hath spoiled and robbed, and further intending utterly to spoil and rob, the whole body of the realm", and so word had been put about that the revolt was against "many impositions" had "of us" by the king. The proclamation stated the rebels were not objecting to having fiscal and service obligations to the Crown but, nonetheless, they were against the measures imposed and planned at present by the government, the ones imposed being specified in the appended articles, half of which dealt with matters fiscal and complained of the fifteenth and tenth, first fruits and feudal incidents, the ones planned being, it seems, the rumoured taxes on food, ploughs, sacraments and cattle. In emphasising the pilgrimage of grace as a tax revolt, this proclamation to the gentlemen complemented Aske's oath. Apart from stating the grievances of the uprising, it set out the purpose which was to make a pilgrimage with the grace of God for the favour of the king, and his acceptance of a petition "for the reformation of that which is amiss". Finally, it threatened the "lords, knights, masters, kinsmen and friends", to whom it was addressed, with a deadly struggle if they opposed the cause, and argued that, if they were successful in putting it down, they would not be gainers since, as a result, everyone would be placed "in bondage for ever" and they would earn for themselves the curse of Christ.

The proclamation was part of a campaign for bringing pressure upon the gentlemen to support the rebel cause. It reflected the rebels' lack of success so far in this respect; as well as their need to construct an uprising formed from the whole range of society and consonant with the society of orders. Whilst still in York, Aske had grounds for believing that such aims could be achieved, especially following the enlisting of Sir Oswald Wilstrop of the Ainsty (by Acklam and Edwyn) along with other gentlemen found in York, and Sir Ralph Ellerker the younger, taken by the Beverley host and found fraternising with Aske and his captains at Sir George Lawson's house on either

91 For the appended list of headings which begin "for the suppression of religious houses", see above, n. 73.

16th or 17th October.[92] On the other hand, it became clear that the organisation of the revolt as a community in action could not be completed until the various nests of refugee gentlefolk, notably at Skipton Castle and Pontefract Castle, had been smoked out. In all probability, it was in conjunction with this aim that the second proclamation was composed.

The yielding of Pontefract Castle

Having taken York, Aske's host proceeded to take Pontefract Castle. The key figure in this was Thomas Maunsell who, following his meeting with Aske on 16th October, had set out to raise the honours of Pontefract and Wakefield. Within a day or so, and assisted by a band of twenty men, he had sworn the townsmen of Pontefract and even of Doncaster.[93] Then on 18th October he returned to Aske in York to tell him of the support he had raised and to assure him that Pontefract Castle would have to yield.[94] Accompanied by Maunsell, Aske marched immediately to take possession. That night he threatened an assault and by eight o'clock on the morning of 20th October, the castle had yielded. Soon afterwards its prestigious inmates, among them Edmund Lee, Archbishop of York, Thomas Magnus, Archdeacon of the East Riding, Lord Darcy, Sir Robert Constable and Sir William Gascoigne, had taken the rebel oath.[95] No force was required: simply a letter from Aske setting out the grievances of the commons and their wish that the lords within the castle would be "the mean to the king by way of petition", followed by a visit to the castle the next morning from Aske when he lambasted the lords spiritual and temporal for neglecting their duty to the commons, especially by tolerating heresy and failing to declare to the king "the poverty of his realm and that part specially".[96] His message to them was essentially a secular one: the exactions and expropriations practised by the government would utterly impoverish the north by draining from it money and treasure, whilst the Dissolution would remove the poor relief provided by the abbeys at a time when impoverishment made it a vital necessity.

92 Stapulton, p. 100; Bateson, p. 560; L.P. XII{1}. 1320.
93 L.P. XI. 1402.
94 L.P. XII{1}. 852 {2}; ibid., 852/iii. In his own account (L.P. XI. 1402), Maunsell fails to mention that he returned to York. Also in his account he suggests that he raised the region under the direction of Strangways and Darcy. But, according to Henry Savile, his work in raising the West Riding was "under Aske" (L.P. XII{1}. 281), which is suggested by the way Maunsell reported back to Aske on 18th October.
95 Bateson, pp. 335-6; L.P. XII{1}. 1022.
96 Bateson, pp. 335–6.

Following this visit, the question was not whether to submit but when. Darcy insisted upon 21st October; Aske upon 20th October. Fearing that Darcy was providing the Earl of Shrewsbury with the chance to rescue him, Aske forced the issue by threatening action on the morning of the 20th. Abandoning his claim for a further respite, Darcy handed the castle over.[97]

Aske claimed to have taken the castle with three hundred men.[98] But in the vicinity of Pontefract at the time was a huge number of armed rebels, not organised in a host but, nonetheless, a formidable presence. Harry Sais put the number at 10,000.[99] Moreover, by now it was known that the uprising commanded massive support throughout much of the north and that large numbers of well armed men had gathered in hosts. On 15th October the lords in Pontefract Castle put the number at 20,000; on 17th October the loyalist Brian Hastings, a landowner of the southerly West Riding with a seat at Hatfield, put the number at 40,000.[100] It was also well known that over much of the north gentlemen had become drawn into the rebellion.[101] The question is not why the castle succumbed so easily on 20th October but why its inmates had not sought to crush the uprising in its infancy ten days earlier?

This was essentially because the crusty octogenarian Lord Darcy, the figure around which military resistance could have gathered, was, for various reasons, resolved to terminate the revolt by non-military means; and therefore had rebuffed the various schemes put forward, for example, by Brian Hastings on 10th October and by Richard Tempest on 13th October, for suppressing it with force.[102] He had several good reasons for following this policy. They included his sympathy for the rebels' grievances; the untrustworthiness of his tenants and the inhabitants of the areas he controlled as steward to the Crown, who appeared more ready to be directed by the commons than by himself; the success he had recently enjoyed with a non-military approach in dealing with the first outbreak of trouble in Howden; and Shrewsbury's non-violent pacification of Lincolnshire.

Darcy undoubtedly had grave reservations about the government, especially its policy of suppressing monasteries and its domination by

---

97 Bateson, p. 336; *L.P.* XI. 1086 (p. 436). The Dodds claim (Dodds, I, p. 190) that the castle yielded on 21st October is wrong.
98 Stapulton, p. 103.
99 SP1/109, f. 203b (*L.P.* XI. 879/ii). Aske in his Narrative talks of "proceeding forwards to the commons and gentlemen which were assembled before Pomfret Castle" (Bateson, p. 335).
100 *L.P.* XI. 729 and 759.
101 See *L.P.* XI. 760.
102 *L.P.* XI. 646 and 695.

the upstart heretic, Thomas Cromwell, who appeared to be against the nobility and the clergy.[103] He clearly believed that the grievances of the Lincolnshire rebels were justified; and he regarded the Yorkshire uprisings as moved by the same complaints.[104] His hope was that the government would take note and reform its policies accordingly. Such beliefs and aspirations led him to tolerate the revolts and to exaggerate their extent. But it did not seem part of his plan to raise revolt himself or to lead it. In order not to get caught up in the uprising as it first developed in Howdenshire, he quickly fled to Pontefract Castle; and, when it followed him, he lived in hope that the army of the commons would by-pass the castle on its march to London.[105] His eventual capture and enlistment by the rebels resulted from the failure, rather than the realisation, of his plans.

Several considerations encouraged Darcy to persist with a non-military policy. One was his success in settling the unrest which broke out in Howdenshire on 6th October following Aske's return from Lincolnshire with news of the rebellion there. According to Richard Tempest, in a letter of 9th October, Darcy stayed the unrest by dispatching a letter into the troubled region.[106] The letter in question was probably the one written on 6th October to Sir Thomas Metham.[107] It was sent unsealed, on the pretext of "for haste" but presumably to allow its contents to become common knowledge. It related that Darcy had sent his son, Sir Arthur Darcy to the king and that he expected in response "good and comfortable answers . . . for me and all his true and faithful subjects concerning the reasonable griefs that they grudge with". Arthur Darcy's mission is evident from the letter he took with him and the instructions he was given, to report on the uprisings breaking out in the north and the grievances that moved them.[108] Bearing his son's mission in mind, Darcy urged Metham "to beware and to eschew to enter into the hasty follies that others be ready assembled in" but rather "for a season to tarry for the return of Sir Arthur Darcy and to make them fast".[109] In all probability, similar letters were sent to other Howdenshire gentlemen;

103 For Darcy's grudges, see *L.P.* XII{1}. 783 (abbeys dissolved); *L.P.* XI. 1086 and *L.P.* XII{1}. 976 (Cromwell); *L.P.* XII{1}. 899 (heresy).
104 For Lincolnshire grievances, see *L.P.* XII{1}. 1200. For Yorkshire grievances, see ibid. and *L.P.* XI. 692.
105 See above, n. 44.
106 SP1/108, f. 131 (*L.P.* XI. 742).
107 SP1/110, f. 55b (*L.P.* XI. 566 and 929 {2}).
108 *L.P.* XI. 563 {1 and 2}.
109 SP1/110, f. 55b (*L.P.* XI. 566 and 929 {2}).

and the likelihood is that the action taken by William Babthorpe and the two Aske brothers proceeded under their direction.[110]

Evident in the letter to Metham is clear sympathy for the rebels' cause, tempered with the need to prevent disorder. Also present is the naïve belief that, with the king's eyes opened, by learning of the Lincolnshire uprising and the adherence to it of large parts of Yorkshire, he would put matters right. Darcy not only instructed the gentlemen to persuade the people to wait upon events but also sought to apprehend the ringleaders, notably Robert Aske. In a conversation with Somerset Herald on 14th November 1536 Darcy claimed that "at the first time that Aske raised the people hereabouts" (before Darcy had moved to Pontefract and therefore prior to 8th October) he sought to "take this fellow", but Aske evaded him by not keeping appointments and then disappearing from the region.[111] This was not concocted by Darcy; it is corroborated and dated by Aske's Narrative where he shows how, first thing on 7th October whilst still in bed, he was urged by a group of Howden men to leave the town quickly because Darcy's son, Sir George, was coming to apprehend him.[112] All this suggests that Darcy was against the disorders but, once they had become an insurrection, he hoped that they might have some persuasive effect upon the Crown. For this reason, he was inclined to believe that it was better to deal with them by policy rather than the sword.

Yet, although initially successful in staying revolt, Darcy felt sufficiently uneasy at Temple Hirst that, between 6th and 8th October, he took refuge in Pontefract Castle.[113] This was because the peace secured by his letter was fragile. It was also because of the very nature of the uprising: a general movement of the commons which, in drawing support or at least sympathy from those he ruled as landlord and steward, left him with limited means for taking forceful counteraction.[114] Archbishop Lee made a similar point to justify his flight to Pontefract Castle.[115] To proceed with any success, Darcy needed to recruit other gentlemen so that the combined forces of their household servants would give them sufficient manpower. This happened as, fleeing from the commons, the gentlemen gathered round Darcy in the castle. But then various factors prevented them from mounting a

---

110 *L.P.* XII(1). 1186; and see above, p. 81.
111 *L.P.* XI. 1086 (printed in full in Dodds, I, pp. 301–2).
112 SP1/118, f. 192 (*L.P.* XII{1}. 946).
113 See above, n. 44.
114 *L.P.* XI. 1086 and 692.
115 *L.P.* XI. 689. Also see *L.P.* XII{1}. 1022.

military expedition. One was the threats issued by the rebels to take reprisals against the properties the gentlemen had abandoned in their flight.[116] The other was the news, reaching them from 13th October, of the government's supposed accommodation with the Lincolnshire rebels, which raised the prospect of a similar arrangement with the pilgrimage of grace.

On 13th October Shrewsbury wrote to Darcy of his spectacular achievement in terminating the Lincolnshire uprising: simply with a threat of force conveyed in a proclamation of his own devising. According to Shrewsbury, the rebels were now prepared to disperse and only awaited word from the Duke of Suffolk. To show them how it could be done, he sent Darcy a copy of the proclamation.[117] The implication of Shrewsbury's letter was that the rebels had been won over by promises (why else await a response from Suffolk?), and, although completely untrue, this seemed to be confirmed in the following two days, first in a letter out of Lincolnshire which announced that the Lincolnshire rebels had been promised a pardon; and secondly, in a letter from Thomas Gryce, Darcy's servant, which declared that the king had granted to the Lincolnshire rebels not only his pardon but also "their reasonable desires" "especially concerning his churches".[118] How this information was received, interpreted and appreciated by Darcy is made evident in his reply to Shrewsbury of 15th October. This letter presented a pessimistic prospect of successful military counteraction, showing that 20,000 rebels were collected outside York and that, although the inhabitants of Darcy's more important stewardships, the honours of Pontefract and Knaresborough Fee, "sit still", they "favour the commons", refusing to proceed against them. It then remarked that the Lincolnshire rebels had been dispersed "upon certain comfort as by your letters we understand" and asserted: "we think it were right expedient that the like comfort should be sent hither".[119]

With the prospect of the revolt being terminated by governmental concessions, Darcy had no difficulty in rejecting the plan for military action which Sir Richard Tempest had sent him by 14th October.[120] He also had no incentive to comply with the impracticable instructions now reaching him from the government. Earlier it had proposed a non-military solution, largely because its own military resources were tied

116 E.g. against Darcy, see *L.P.* XI. 1086 (p. 436).
117 *L.P.* XI. 695.
118 *L.P.* XI. 706; SP1/108 (*L.P.* XI. 734).
119 SP1/110, fos. 47b-48 (*L.P.* XI. 729).
120 *L.P.* XI. 695.

up with the Lincolnshire uprising. Thus, on 8th and again on 9th October, it required Darcy to pacify the unrest in Yorkshire simply by dismissing the rumours and arresting those who complained of the suppression of abbeys, the taking of church treasures and "the new payments".[121] But as the government brought Lincolnshire to order, it adopted a more militant attitude towards Yorkshire, on 17th October ordering Shrewbury to advance into Yorkshire and Darcy to send his son with one thousand men to relieve the besieged city of York.[122]

However, these instructions were suspect since they overlooked the fact that the city had already fallen to the rebels. Any move by Arthur Darcy into the heart of the East Riding with no more than one thousand men could be judged suicidal. Moreover, with the castle deprived of so many men, it might fall to the commons, for by this time the rebels had taken the town of Pontefract, and had even sworn men in Doncaster.[123] In fact, by 18th October they had placed such a close blockade around the castle that the king's instructions could no longer get through.[124] The same blockade also excluded fresh provisions. For six days or so the town had refused to allow victuals to reach the castle.[125] Well before Aske's arrival the castle was in difficulties and had lost the capacity to take positive action. Darcy's choice was now between yielding or holding out. With the arrival of Aske, the presence to the north and south of large numbers of rebels and the inclination of the castle's inmates to flee or waver, he decided to succumb. Holding out a day or two longer, Shrewsbury might have had the chance to come to his relief. By 20th October he had brought his 6,000 troops from Southwell near Newark up to Scrooby near Doncaster. But quite probably, with their lines of communication cut, the inmates of the castle were unaware that their deliverance was nigh.[126]

As a result, the Aske host achieved one of its main aims: to enlist, in support of a rising of the commons, the whole range of society. With the lords, knights, esquires, gentlemen and clerics of Pontefract Castle now sworn to the cause, the uprising could take on the appearance of a revolt which complied with, rather than offended, the society of

121 For letter of 8th, see *L.P.* XI. 598. For letter of 9th, see *L.P.* XI. 611.
122 *L.P.* XI. 749.
123 SP1/108 (*L.P.* XI. 759); SP1/108 (*L.P.* XI. 774).
124 *L.P.* XI. 774.
125 SP1/119, f. 3b (*L.P.* XII{1}. 1022).
126 Lee claimed that of the 300 in the castle, there remained only 140 when Aske arrived and of those not all were trustworthy and some were inclining to the commons [SP1/119, f. 4b (*L.P.* XII{1}. 1022)]. Also see SP1/118, f. 192b (*L.P.* XII(1). 946) and SP1/118, f. 194 (*L.P.* XII{1}. 946 {2}). For Shrewsbury's march on Doncaster, see below, pp. 382–3.

orders; and even more so as the enlisted gentlemen did not serve merely as figureheads[127]. Once taken and committed, Darcy became a positive recruiter of support. It was he who dispatched the oath into Lancashire, urging the messenger to use it for raising the people.[128] He also sent out letters into the honours of Wakefield, Snaith and Pontefract summoning and organising armed assistance.[129] Essentially he acted out of fear that the Earl of Shrewsbury was about to fulfil an earlier threat. For when Arthur Darcy had told Shrewsbury, about 6th/7th October, that, if the Dissolution was undone, his father would provide him with 5,000 men for putting down the Lincolnshire rebels, Shrewsbury had claimed that, unless Darcy co-operated, he would switch his attention from Lincolnshire and sort him out.[130] Then with a chilling message delivered to Pontefract Castle on 21st October that "this night the earl of Shrewsbury intendeth to take you sleeper" and with Shrewsbury now at Scrooby and therefore in a realistic position to carry out the threat, Darcy became committed to the business of raising an army capable of keeping him at bay.[131]

Sir Robert Constable, another inmate of the castle, also became positively involved. Although there had been discord between him and Aske because the latter had acted so frequently as legal counsel to men bringing actions against Constable, they now worked together organising the host. Between the fall of the castle and the Doncaster appointment a week later, they sent out letters summoning support and took musters outside Pontefract on St. Thomas' Hill.[132] Other inmates of the castle helped to formulate policy: besides Darcy and Constable, Sir John Dawnye, Sir Robert Neville, Robert Chaloner and William Babthorpe became members of a council on 22nd October, which the other gentlemen joined as they arrived with their hosts.[133]

With the gentlemen enlisted, another aim could be concentrated upon: the presentation of the revolt as a unified movement embracing the whole north. This was done for a dual purpose: to add weight to the grievances that the pilgrims planned to declare by showing that they were the concern of at least half the realm; and also to bring the hosts together, partly to resist the oncoming Shrewsbury and partly to

127 See below, p. 128.
128 E36/122, f. 29 (L.P. XII{1}. 853).
129 SP1/115, f.131 (L.P. XII(1). 281). For Darcy's role as a military organiser in Snaith and Pontefract, see L.P. XI. 966.
130 L.P. XII{1}. 783.
131 L.P. XII{1}. 852/iv.
132 Bateson, p. 569.
133 Stapulton, p. 100.

form an army that might proceed to London without the likelihood of defeat. Thus, letters were sent to summon the Bowes, Stapulton and Percy hosts to Pontefract at the greatest possible speed.[134] Incited by the news imparted in the letters that Shrewsbury was about to attack the rebels at Pontefract, the three hosts quickly arrived. By 22nd October they were all in the Pontefract area and ready for action.[135]

That the intention was to march upon London was made evident on 21st October when Aske met Lancaster Herald in Pontefract Castle. After refusing to allow him to read a proclamation which told of the submission of the Lincolnshire rebels, Aske declared that the people were prepared to die in their cause, which was to march southwards and present their petition directly to the king.[136] Before this could be done, however, a petition had to be composed. On the 21st October Aske had to hand Lancaster Herald a copy of the oath when the herald asked for a copy of the articles simply because they had as yet to be formulated.[137] Then, over the next day or two, Aske sought to persuade the Archbishop of York to assist in drawing up a set of articles, but he refused.[138] In fact, the pilgrims were able to produce a written petition only at the last minute. This was on the command of the Duke of Norfolk who, having reached an agreement with the rebels on 27th October that two representatives, rather than the whole host, should take a petition to the king, required it to be written down rather than having it, as the pilgrims had planned, merely committed to the memory of Robert Bowes.[139]

Complaints and remedies

The grievances of the uprising are clearly set out in the various orders and declarations issued by Aske: notably in his first proclamation of 11th October and his second proclamation of 17th/18th October; in the oath that he composed on 17th/18th October; in the order for religious houses suppressed which was pinned to the door of York Minster on 16th October; in the letter he sent to the lords in Pontefract Castle on 18th October; and in the addresses that he made in Ponte-

134 For Bowes host, see *L.P.* XII{1}. 29. For Stapulton host, see Stapulton, p. 99. For Percy host, see *L.P.* XII{1}. 393.
135 *L.P.* XII{1}. 393; Stapulton, pp. 99-100; Bateson, pp. 336–7.
136 *L.P.* XI. 826.
137 Ibid.
138 SP1/119, fos. 6-6b (*L.P.* XII{1}. 1022).
139 SP1/119, f. 6b (*L.P.* XII{1}. 1022).

fract Castle, first to the clergy and gentlemen on 19th October and
then to Lancaster Herald on 21st October.[140] In view of the general
purpose of these statements, which was to drum up popular, genteel
and clerical support, and because of Aske's close association with the
uprisings in Howdenshire, Ouse and Derwent and Marshland, they
can be taken as a declaration of the grievances held in these parts.
Furthermore, there is the substantial evidence of Aske's Narrative,
composed by him in December to inform the king of the nature of
the pilgrimage of grace, and his Examination, compiled under inter-
rogation in April 1537, although both have the drawback of being
retrospective, exculpatory and, in presenting the causes, inclined to
generalise about the pilgrimage as a whole rather than to focus upon
this particular revolt.[141] In addition to these compositions of Robert
Aske, the grievances of this region were made evident in its appreciation of the Lincolnshire articles (with the same response here as in
Beverley) and in its susceptibility to rumours of new taxes and the
impending onslaught upon parish churches.[142]

   This evidence supports certain generalisations. As with the other
revolts, there was a deep concern, on the one hand, to protect the faith
from heresy and, on the other, to safeguard the commonwealth from
bad governance. However, this particular uprising had its own distinctive grievances. Thus, the complaint against the decay of the
commonwealth was presented exclusively as the work of a plundering
government. It did not object to greedy landlords. Moreover, the
complaint against the decay of the faith failed to specify the abrogation of holy days; and the government's maltreatment of the saints
received very little notice. It was mentioned but once: when Aske
addressed the clergy in Pontefract Castle on 19th October and complained of the contempt shown for relics by the commissioners
engaged in the suppression of the lesser monasteries.[143] Moreover, at
the time no complaint was made against the Act of Supremacy,

140 For the first proclamation, see SP1/107, f. 116 (*L.P.* XI. 622). For the second
    proclamation, see *St.P.*, I, pp. 466–7 (*L.P.* XI. 705 {2}). The Dodds misdate
    both, proposing that the first was issued on 10th (Dodds, I, p. 148) and the
    second on 15th (ibid., p. 175). For the true dating, see above, pp. 82, 92. For
    Aske's oath, see Toller, pp. 50-51 (*L.P.* XI. 892 {1/3}). For the order concerning
    religious house, see Toller, p. 51 (*L.P.* XI. 784/ii). For his letter to the lords in
    Pontefract Castle, see Bateson, p. 335. For his addresses to the clergy, the lords
    and Lancaster Herald in Pontefract Castle, see ibid., pp. 335–6; *L.P.* XI. 826.
141 For Narrative, see Bateson, pp. 331ff. For Examination, see Bateson, pp. 557ff.
142 For Lincolnshire articles, see above pp. 17–18. For rumours, see *L.P.* XI. 826, *L.P.*
    XII{1}.1018 and *L.P.* XI. 1047.
143 For the complaint about relics, see Bateson, p. 335.

although in his Examination Aske claimed that "all men much murmured at the same".[144] Instead, the complaint made in the region concerning the faith was inclined to be a general objection to the intrusion of heresy, and became specific only in condemning those held responsible, who were named as Cromwell, Audley, Cranmer, Latimer and Barnes, and in deploring the dissolution of the lesser monasteries for impairing "the divine service", notably by reducing the number of prayers offered for the dead and for making less available the holy sacrament.[145]

In the course of October the dissolution of the lesser monasteries emerged as a major grievance in the region but was presented very much as a temporal issue, affecting the commonwealth and resulting from government greed. At the heart of the complaint was alarm at an impending spoliation of the church, threatened not only by the suppression of monasteries but also by the new taxes imposed upon the clergy and the government's rumoured plans for parish churches, with some to be dissolved and others deprived of their treasures. A spoliation on this scale, it was objected, would do serious, material harm to the rest of society.[146] Finally, what characterised and co-ordinated the grievances of this particular uprising was the need to defend the society of orders. The policies and actions of the government were found intolerable because of the contempt they expressed for the basic components of this social theory: the royal family, the nobility, the clergy and the commonalty.

The rebels' concern for the royal family was found in Aske's first proclamation. In proposing an oath, it suggested that men should be true to "the king's issue". The same point was made in Aske's oath which required men to "enter the pilgrimage for the preservation of the king's person and his issue".[147] None of Aske's manifestos and orders were more specific than this; but behind this bland declaration of reverence for the royal family was undoubtedly an objection to the illegitimisation of Princess Mary, a grievance explicitly stated in the December articles which called for the repeal of the legislation that had denied her legitimacy and her right of succession to the throne.[148] That this article reflected what was in mind in October is made evident

144 Ibid., p. 565.
145 For divine service, see Bateson, p. 561 and SP1/111 (*L.P.* XI. 1069). For heresy, e.g. E36/122, f. 28 (*L.P.* XII{1}. 853).
146 See below, pp. 106–9.
147 SP1/107, f. 116 (*L.P.* XI. 622); Toller, pp. 50-51 (*L.P.* XI. 892{1/3}).
148 Article three (see *L.P.* XI. 1246). For Aske's commitment, see Bateson, p. 562.

in the reports of the imperial ambassador and of Dr. Ortiz.[149] Writing
in early November, they provided details of what Bowes and Ellerker
had been instructed to require, once they had presented the pilgrims'
October articles to the king.[150] Both accounts included the demand
that Mary be reinstated as the king's legitimate heir. This was not
simply the wishful thinking of the Spanish lobby since it was included
in the pilgrims' December articles and in a package of complaints,
reckoned to be the composition of Aske, that was found circulating in
the south in November 1536. It comprised a set of articles attached to
an oath – undoubtedly the October articles, which happened to take
this form – accompanied by a letter which contained the demand "to
have my lady Mary made legitimate".[151] The demand for Mary's
legitimisation was not unique to this uprising. But apart from its
association with the uprising around Beverley, it failed to figure
explicitly in the other revolts.[152]

Aske's first proclamation called upon men to be true to the noble
blood as well as to the king's issue.[153] A concern for the nobility also
featured in Aske's second proclamation, which declared that an aim of
the pilgrimage was to preserve the nobility; in his oath which called
upon men to support "the purifying of nobility"; and in the remarks
he made to Lancaster Herald on 21st October who was told that the
rebels wished "to exclude all vile blood from the king's council and all
noble blood set up again" and requiring him to inform the lords
leading the king's army that "it is for all their wealths that I do".[154]
Essentially, three issues featured in this complaint: one was that the
nobility should not be destroyed; another was that the traditional
system of government should be respected, with the nobility accepted
as the king's advisers and "all vile blood" excluded "from the king's
council".[155] The third issue concerned maintaining the nobility's
purity by excluding from the order men from lowly backgrounds.
All three represented objections to Thomas Cromwell: for his proceed-

---

149 *L.P.* XI. 1143 and 1204.
150 See below, pp. 392–3.
151 *L.P.* XI. 1405–6.
152 For Beverley, see above, p. 50. Aske in his Examination presented Mary's
    illegitimisation by statute as something "much grudged" not only by him but
    by "all the wise men of those parts" (Bateson, p. 562).
153 SP1/107, f. 116 (*L.P.* XI. 622).
154 *St.P.*,I, pp. 466-7 (*L.P.* XI. 705 {2})); Toller, pp. 50-51 (*L.P.* XI. 892{1/3});
    St.P., I, pp. 486-7 (*L.P.* XI. 826).
155 The other terms used by Aske are "villein blood" [Toller, p.50 (*L.P.* XI. 892 {1/
    3})]; "base councillors" and "simple and evil disposed persons" [*St.P.*, I, pp.
    466-7 (*L.P.* XI. 705 {2})]. The term used in the Lincolnshire articles was men
    "of low birth and small reputation" [SP1/108 (*L.P.* XI. 705)].

ings against Dacre and Percy; for his domination of the privy council; and for his recent admission to the peerage.[156] To put matters right, the king needed to ban Cromwell from the government and to take away his title. Making the complaint focus explicitly upon the nobility was part of Aske's plan to recruit the support of noblemen. It interlocked with the advances he had already made to Dacre, Percy and Darcy.[157] Yet there is no reason to dismiss it as just a tactic. Rather it was an integral part of a rising of the commons that typically explained bad governance in terms of the subversion of the natural social order and believed that remedy lay in returning to the system in operation on Henry VIII's succession when, in the words of the pilgrims' first petition to the government, "his nobles did order under his highness".[158]

Two pieces of evidence indicate that this was what the commonalty wanted. Early in November and shortly after the truce of 27th October, Percival Cresswell went to Temple Hirst to deliver letters to Lord Darcy. Encountering a group of commoners in the garden, he assured them that Cromwell had been absent from Court for the last two days and that the king was surrounded by nobles. In response the commoners exclaimed: "God save the king and them all" (i.e. the nobles) and elaborated: "for as long as such noblemen of the true noble blood may reign and rule about the king all shall be well". Then they declared that "what moves us to this (rebellion) is the faith we bear unto God, to the king's person and all his true noble blood and the commonwealth".[159] The commons' preference for noble rule was made evident again that month when Aske offered Darcy advice on how to deal with Norfolk, who had been deputed by the government to negotiate a final settlement with the rebels, and urged him "to have none but the nobility here to rule" on the grounds that "this the commonalty will have promised first".[160]

The various statements of complaint produced by Robert Aske were inclined to make a distinction between Christ's faith and Christ's church. Thus, in his address to Lancaster Herald on 21st October he declared the pilgrims' aim was, among other things, to ensure that the faith of Christ was kept and that there was "full restoration of Christ's

---

156 He was elevated in July 1536.

157 See above, pp. 84–5.

158 L.P. XI. 902 {2}. The same point was made in a copy of the oath picked up in the southerly West Riding by Brian Hastings [SP1/111 (L.P. XI. 1059/ii)].

159 Dodds, I, p. 290.

160 E36/122, fos. 65–65b (L.P. XI. 1128).

church" and remedy "of all wrongs to it".[161] In his oath the distinction was again made, with men being sworn to maintain "God's faith" as well as "the church militant" and urged to press for both the restitution of his church and the suppression of heretical opinions.[162] Whereas the faith was perceived as under attack from heresy and the deplored consequence was spiritual in nature, Christ's church was seen as under attack from a disrespectful and greedy government and the consequence deplored was an impoverished and humiliated institution whose servitors, the clergy, would be far less able than before to perform their spiritual and material obligations.

A central concern of the Aske host was the spoliation of the clergy. Thus Aske's first proclamation obliged men not only to be true to the king's issue, the noble blood and the commons but also "to prevent the church from spoiling" (i.e. being spoiled).[163] A blatant instance of "spoiling" was the suppression of religious houses. Although unspecified in Aske's first two proclamations and absent from his oath, it was undoubtedly a grievance of these parts: evident in the reverence shown towards the Lincolnshire articles, the first of which deplored "the suppression of so many religious houses"; in the order for religious houses suppressed which instructed "religious persons to enter their houses again", and in Aske's letter of 18th October to the inhabitants of Pontefract Castle which stated that the commons were "gnawn in their consciences with . . . suppression of houses of religion" – backed up the following day by the address delivered in the castle to the clergy which criticised them for failing to restrain the king in his suppression of the abbeys.[164] In the region of this revolt were a fair number of dissolved houses of religion: Drax, Healaugh and Sinningthwaite in the West Riding, Warter and Nunburnholme in the East Riding and Holy Trinity and St. Clement's within the city of York; but how many restorations occurred is unclear. Certainly Healaugh, Nunburnholme and the two houses in York, but how many more?[165] That the commons were moved by the issue was evident in attacks upon the property of men involved with the Dissolution, either as officials of the Court of Augmentations or as farmers of dissolved sites and demesnes.

161 St.P., I, p. 485 (L.P. XI. 826).
162 Toller, pp. 50–1 (L.P. XI. 892 {1/3}).
163 SP1/107, f. 116 (L.P. XI. 622).
164 L.P. XI. 705; Toller, p. 51 (L.P. XI. 784/ii); Bateson, p. 335; SP1/111 (L.P. XI. 1069).
165 For Healaugh, see Yorkshire Chancery Proc., pp. 62–4. For Holy Trinity and St. Clement's, see Palliser, Tudor York, p. 50.

In this way and for this reason, William Blitheman, William Maunsell and Leonard Beckwith were all victims of this particular revolt.[166]

Aske in his Examination claimed that the suppression of the abbeys was "the greatest cause which the hearts of the commons most grudged at".[167] But he believed that the church was being plundered in other ways as well: principally through the exaction of first fruits and the plans to proceed against parish churches. In his Narrative, when he was explaining the causes of complaint prior to the Truce, he singled out first fruits as well as the suppression of abbeys for special mention.[168] As far as he was concerned, and this was made evident in his Examination, his address to the clergy in Pontefract Castle on 19th October and in the final phrasing of the grievance in the December articles, first fruits represented another attack on religious houses, adversely affecting the interests of those houses that escaped the act of suppression.[169]

Furthermore, parish churches were also perceived by the rebels as threatened by the government's policies of expropriation. In his Examination Aske claimed that the rumours concerning the confiscation of church goods was "one of the greatest" causes of insurrection in the north, although he then proceeded to state that in Yorkshire such rumours were less important than they had been in Lincolnshire.[170] Moreover, nowhere does he state that the rumoured plan to reduce the number of churches was a cause of rebellion in Yorkshire. Yet in the opening stages, the uprising centring upon Aske, very much like the one centred upon William Stapulton, was moved by the rumours that had incited revolt in Lincolnshire. This was recognised by Aske in his address to the inmates of Pontefract Castle when he berated the clergy

---

166 SP1/113, f. 62 (L.P. XI. 1402). Beckwith was receiver for Yorkshire in the Court of Augmentations. Maunsell was agent to Sir Arthur Darcy who had already acquired a large part of the estate of Holy Trinity (see L.P. XI. 1047 and P.R.O. SC6/Henry VIII/4460). Maunsell farmed the site and demesne of St. Clement's (see SC6/Henry VIII/4466). Beckwith farmed the site and demesne of Holy Trinity (see SC6/Henry VIII/4460). For the sacking of Beckwith's house, see L.P. XII{1}.536. Blitheman was receiver for the archdeaconry of Richmond (see SC6/Henry VIII/7454). His house was sacked by Rudston (L.P. XII{1}. 1018). Maunsell had goods confiscated to value of one hundred marks [SP10/111, f. 74b (L.P. XI. 1047)].
167 Bateson, p. 558.
168 Bateson, pp. 342–3.
169 Bateson, pp. 562–3; ibid., p. 335. Also see M. L. Bush, "Enhancements and importunate charges: an analysis of the tax complaints of October 1536", Albion, 22 (1990), p. 414.
170 Bateson, pp. 558–9.

for failing to stop the royal plan to take "the ornaments of the church".[171] The impact of the same rumours was attested by the cleric Lancelot Collyns who believed that the revolt was caused partly by the flight of gentlemen and clerics to Pontefract Castle and partly by stories spread "among the commons" by the friar of Knaresborough about new sacramental taxes and plans "that churches should be pulled down".[172]

Although unmentioned by Aske, the rumoured plan to limit the number of parish churches was a major concern in the Ainsty, as William Stapulton's confession made clear. All his illustrations of the discontent caused by this plan were drawn from this wapentake, a region he knew well since the family's seat at Wighill was situated within it. According to him, the rumours that incited revolt involved a plan to abolish the tiny parishes of Wighill, Walton and Thorp Arch and include them either in the parish of Tadcaster or in that of Bolton Percy. The same rumours also proposed that the parishes of Askham Richard and Askham Bryan should disappear as separate entities through incorporation in the parish of Long Marston. Related to these fears was the apprehension that the treasures of the region's churches were about to be taken and, in preparation, replacement chalices of copper had been delivered. Giving substance to this fear was a commandment, supposedly issued to church wardens by Doctor Palmes, to bring to Tadcaster inventories of the goods belonging to their churches.[173] Furthermore, associated with Tadcaster church itself was the rumour that, with the suppression of Sawley Abbey, to which the church had been appropriated, it was under threat from Sir Arthur Darcy to whom the abbey and its landed and parochial possessions had been given. And certainly by 12th October tales had spread far and wide that the treasures of Tadcaster church were being removed and placed in Pontefract Castle.[174]

By government exploitation, then, Christ's church was being wronged. The concern of the rebels for the church, however, related not simply to the maltreatment of the clergy, both secular and regular, but to the effect the government's exploitation of the church would have upon the rest of society. On the one hand, the laity would be deprived of spiritual comfort, as religious services were withdrawn. On the other, it would be deprived of material assistance, and therefore the govern-

171 Bateson, p. 335.
172 SP1/118, f. 267 (*L.P.* XII{1}. 1018).
173 Stapulton, p. 82.
174 See below, pp. 222–3.

ment's policy of spoiling the church would be "to great detriment of the commonwealth".[175] This complaint was carried over from the Lincolnshire rebellion, the first of whose articles had objected to the suppression of religious houses on social as well as religious grounds.[176] A closely related point was made by Aske in his Examination where he presented the statutes for the suppression of religious houses and for first fruits and tenths as damaging the commonwealth of the north in reducing the availability of employment, charity and hospitality in the region and in causing a drain of money to other parts.[177] This was not a point that evolved retrospectively, for it was first made in the thick of the revolt. On 19th October, in his address to the lords of Pontefract Castle, Aske declared that "much relief of the commons" had been "by succour of abbeys" and that with the revenues of the suppressed abbeys and from first fruits going "out of these parts", "no money nor treasure" would be left "in those parts", thus preventing tenants from paying rents to their lords and leaving lords without the money to fulfil their services to the Crown. In this particular uprising, then, the rebel concern for the church was not simply a religious matter but one upon which the survival of the society of orders and the proper functioning of the body politic depended, since it was reasoned that, if the changes went ahead, the impoverished northerners would be forced either to ally with the Scots or to indulge in rebellion.[178]

The rebels' concern for the commonwealth focused upon the government's maltreatment of the commonalty, so much so that Aske's usage of the term implied the wealth of the commons.[179] The commons were seen as vulnerable to oppression not only as a material consequence of the government's attack on the church but also because of the government's exploitation of the laity. Again, this was a continuation of a prominent grievance of the Lincolnshire rebels against the government's fiscal policies, actual and rumoured.[180] In his first proclamation Aske called upon men "to be true to the commons and

175 For spiritual concern, see Bateson, 335 and 561; SP1/111 (*L.P.* XI. 1069). For material concern, see Bateson, p. 561, 563 and 571.
176 SP1/108 (*L.P.* XI. 705).
177 Bateson, pp. 561–6.
178 Bateson, p. 336.
179 The equation of the commonwealth with the interest of the commons was made by Aske in a letter to the Earl of Westmorland in which he accused him of not being "constant to the commonwealth". See the reply rebutting Aske's charge, SP1/110 (*L.P.* XI. 945). It is also evident in the language of his first proclamation [SP1/107, f. 116 (*L.P.* XI. 622)] where being true to the commonwealth is presented as being true to "the commons and their wealths".
180 As evident in letter of 3rd and articles of 9th (see Bush, "Up for the commonweal", pp. 302–5).

their wealths" and promised at the next assembly to give them not only "the articles and causes of your assembly" (i.e. the Lincolnshire articles) but also "all other of poor and commonwealth".[181] Furthermore, although beginning with a declaration that the rebels had no objection to paying taxes and serving the king, his second proclamation was essentially a complaint against the government's plan "utterly to spoil and rob the whole body of the realm" and professed the aim to preserve the commonalty as well as the king, the church and nobility.[182] His letter of 18th October to the lords in Pontefract Castle made it clear that the commons were enraged against the government not only for promoting heresy and suppressing abbeys but also for perpetrating "other matters touching the commonwealth to their impoverishment".[183] Finally, in his address to Lancaster Herald of 21st October Aske made the point that the rebels aimed not only to restore the nobility and the church to their former state but also to insist that "the commonty to be used as they should be".[184]

The complaint against lay taxation made in October 1536 concerned the subsidy due that year, the fifteenth and tenth due in 1537, the rumoured new taxes on sacraments, livestock and footstuffs and the feudal exactions the government was now free to make by virtue of the recently enacted Statute of Uses. All were probably sources of grievance in this particular uprising, although only one was explicit: the rumoured new taxes.[185] That they were a concern of the commons is vividly illustrated by Lancaster Herald who, close to Pontefract on 21st October, encountered a company of harnessed peasants. When asked why they were armed, they answered that they were "for the commonwealth" and asserted that if they failed to act "the commonty and the church should be destroyed". After the herald had asked how, they said that "no man should bury, nor christen nor wed nor have their beasts unmarked but that the king would have a certain sum of money for every such thing, and the beast unmarked to his own house, which had never been seen".[186]

A similar impression was given in a letter from Thomas Wriothesley to Cromwell of 18th October. After listing the rumours current in Yorkshire, including tributes on foodstuffs and sacraments as well as severe penalties for false declarations of wealth for tax purposes, he

181 SP1/107, f.116 (L.P. XI. 622).
182 St.P., I, pp. 466-7 (L.P. XI. 705 (2)).
183 Bateson, p. 335.
184 St.P., I, p. 485 (L.P. XI. 826).
185 Bush, "Enhancements and importunate charges", pp. 403ff.
186 St.P., I, p. 485 (L.P. XI. 826).

stated that, as a result of these rumours "throughout the country", "everyman thinketh that they shall be utterly undone for ever".[187] This impression was supported by William Maunsell, who was caught in York by the rebels. Writing to Sir Arthur Darcy early in November, he declared that "the people were most especially stirred" by the circulation of bills rumouring the imposition of new taxes, notably a tax on ploughs of 6s. 8d. per plough, a tribute of 6s. 8d. for every child baptised and a tax of fourpence for every beast. Lancelot Collyns, who became involved in the uprising when Aske took York, made a similar point, arguing that the uprising was provoked by rumoured exactions on christenings and marriages, as well as the rumoured demolition of certain parish churches.[188] Sacramental taxes, clearly, had religious as well as fiscal implications since if the services for baptism, marriage or burial were made dependent upon a tribute to the Crown, those unable to pay would have to go without the spiritual benefits the services were meant to confer. As it was presented by the rebels, however, the concern over the new taxes appeared to be materialistic rather than spiritual. The tributes on sacraments were objected to as sources of exploitation rather than devices for denying the poor their religious due. In this respect, the rebels appeared to regard them in the same light as the rumoured taxes on foodstuffs and livestock.[189]

The rebels' fiscal complaint could also have stemmed from a concern for the constitution since the subsidy and fifteenth-and-tenth, taxes normally levied for purposes of war, were being raised in peacetime, the latter tax without the usual rebate for poverty; the taxes on sacraments, food and livestock were unparliamentary as well as offending the principle that the poor should be fiscally exempt; and associated with the acts granted in 1534 for the subsidy and the clerical first fruits and tenths and in 1536 for uses was the belief that the process of enactment had been improper since parliament had been packed with government placemen.[190] There is no evidence to prove that the uprising along the Ouse saw its tax complaint in this light; but there can be no doubt that the rebels of the region were moved not only by the government's promotion of heresy and its contempt for the society of orders but also by a third objection: the breach of the constitution.

This complaint was put starkly in Aske's second proclamation

187 St.P., I, p. 482n (L.P. XI. 768 {2}).
188 For Maunsell, see SP1/111, f. 74 (L.P. XI. 1047). For Collyns, see SP1/118, f. 267 (L.P. XII{1}. 1018).
189 See Bush, "Enhancements and importunate charges", pp. 408–9.
190 Ibid., p. 418.

when it declared that the purpose of the protest was to punish not only heretics but also "subverters of the laws" and that, if the gentlemen successfully opposed the pilgrimage, "ye put both us and you in bondage for ever".[191] A matter for concern, according to Aske, was the way the government had recently managed parliament to force through a number of unacceptable statutes, notably the Act of Suppression, the Act of Supremacy, the Succession Acts declaring Mary illegitimate and allowing the king to will the succession, the Statute of Uses, the Statute for First Fruits and Tenths and the act that had made words a treasonable offence. Aske believed that these acts had been "passed by favour" – presumably as a result of the large number of M.P.s who were either pensioners or office-holders of the Crown.[192] Darcy also believed that, in the government interest and against that of the realm, certain parliamentary procedures had been recently altered.[193] Connected with the same acts, in Aske's version, were a number of technical irregularities which one would expect a lawyer to make much of.[194] In addition, according to Aske, the October rebels had a grudge against the Lord Chancellor for improperly granting and cancelling injunctions, clearly another common lawyer's complaint.[195] All this suggests that, within the ranks of Aske's host, was a grudge against the government for committing constitutional improprieties as well as for being heretical, sacrilegious and greedy.

The grudge, however, as Aske made clear, was not against the government as a whole, but against certain evil ministers who had

191 St.P., I, pp. 466–7 (L.P. XI. 705 (2)).
192 Bateson, pp. 559 and 569. Aske made it clear that these concerns were there before the first Doncaster appointment. Both Chapuys and Ortiz picked up information about them after Ellerker and Bowes had come to Court and made the same point that the rebels wanted parliament held in the old manner without pensioners and office-holders. See L.P. XI. 1143 and 1204.
193 Bateson, p. 568. All concerned departures from tradition in the Lords. Defended was the practice of dispatching spiritual matters to convocation rather than dealing with them in parliament; the practice of affirming in the Lords the first chapter of Magna Carta on the rights of the church (now stopped); the practice of allowing the Lords to have a preview of bills touching the king's prerogative (now stopped).
194 The act of first fruits and tenths had not been granted by the York convocation and therefore required annulment or qualification (see Bateson, p. 563). The suppression act was regarded as faulty for not specifying whether the lands affected were "in England or the seignories of the same" (see Bateson, p. 569). There was also objection to the statute of treasons for claiming that the king could convict for treason men denying verbally his headship of the church on the grounds that it contravened a law of God (see Bateson, p. 570).
195 Bateson, p. 342–3. The same point appears in the December petition (article 22) (L.P. XI. 1246).

introduced "new inventions" which offended the faith of God, the duties of the king and the interests of the commonwealth.[196] Excepted from the rebels' complaint, moreover, was not only Henry himself but also certain unnamed councillors whom "the commons never blamed but took them for honourable and good catholic men and willers of the commonwealth".[197] Aske affirmed that the burden of the rebels' hostility fell upon Cromwell, of whom, as the reputed destroyer of the commonwealth and the minister held responsible for "filling the realm with heresy", "there is no earthly man so evil believed . . . with the lords and the commons".[198]

Organisation

In the manner of the Lincolnshire and Beverley uprisings, the revolts along the Ouse first formed a confederation bound by oath and then created a host from this body of support. The aim was the same as in Lincolnshire: to present a petition from the commons to the king, calling for a general pardon and the redress of grievances.[199] Again, the petition was to be backed by a show of force and, in keeping with the risings of the commons of the late fourteenth and fifteenth centuries, the threat of a march upon London. Yet the uprising led by Aske was not merely a re-run of the Lincolnshire rebellion. Distinguishing it were partly the difficulties it had in producing the vitally important petition and partly its decision to cloak the movement in the conceit of a pilgrimage.

In the Lincolnshire and Beverley manner, the commons were first summoned by bells. Since the uprising had been in prospect for some time before it broke out, the sound of bells was a signal to assemble which the people had been awaiting. Thus, Christopher Aske had found the people between Howden and the family seat of Aughton out in the fields waiting for the great bell of Howden to ring;[200] and Aske's first known proclamation had ordered the people on the following morning "to ring your bells in every town", presumably to summon them to assemble at Skipwith Moor.[201] The ringing of

196 *St.P.*, I, pp. 466–7 (*L.P.* XI. 705(2)).
197 Bateson, p. 571.
198 Bateson, pp. 342–3; *L.P.* XII{1}. 853.
199 The keenness for a general pardon was evident in Aske's statement that he refused to allow Lancaster Herald to read his proclamation on 21st October because it did not promise one (Bateson, p. 336 and *L.P.* XI. 826).
200 SP1/120, f. 58 (*L.P.* XII{1}. 1186).
201 SP1/107, f. 116 (*L.P.* XI. 622).

bells determined the outbreak of the revolt. The revolt did not happen on 6th October when Aske persuaded both Howdenshire and Marshland to await the ringing of the other's bells; but it did happen on 10th October when a church bell was rung in Marshland, presumably at Whitgift, and this set off the bells in the surrounding marshland parishes and, across the Ouse, in the wapentake of Howdenshire.[202] The uprising was spread in the same manner. Thus, on 13th October a company of commons crossed the Ouse, probably at Selby, came to Brayton and raised the town by ringing its bell.[203] York yielded on 16th October with a peal of bells from York Minster; and, when a contingent of rebels penetrated as far south as Doncaster on 18th October, they achieved their purpose by ringing the common bell and by swearing the commons who assembled to the sound.[204]

The procedure of assembling in response to the ringing of bells allowed the commons to be sworn *en masse*, usually by means of the public recitation of an oath taken "upon a book".[205] The gentlemen, however, were less forthcoming and had to be enlisted and personally sworn. For this purpose, the rebel leadership produced three basic documents. One was Aske's second proclamation, a letter addressed to "lords, knights, masters, kinsmen and friends" and a cleverly intermixed compound of exhortation and threat.[206] The second was Aske's oath, the so-called oath of the honourable men, which presented the uprising as a "pilgrimage of grace for the commonwealth" and specified its basic causes.[207] The third was a so-called spoiling letter, designed to deal with those who refused to take the oath. These non-jurors were to lose their goods, but only if at least two of the rebel council approved and only if they were allowed twenty-four hours in which to change their mind.[208]

To encourage participation, the rebel leadership operated through companies of commons, which were authorised to raise townships by visiting them to ring their bells and to enlist the gentlemen by visiting their homes and subjecting the residents to the oath. One such

202 Bateson, pp. 333–4.
203 SP1/113, f. 62b (*L.P.* XI. 1402).
204 For York, see SP1/120, f. 175 (*L.P.* XII{1}. 1264). For Doncaster, see SP1/108 (*L.P.* XI. 774).
205 This is evident in the wording of Aske's oath which ends with "by all the holy contents of this book" [see Toller, p. 51 (*L.P.* XI. 892 {1/3})]. Henry Sais reported that the oath was sworn "upon a little book that one of them brought forth from his sleeve" [SP1/109, f. 203b (*L.P.* XI. 879/ ii)].
206 *St.P.*, I, pp. 466–7 (*L.P.* XI. 705 {2}).
207 Toller, pp. 50–51 (*L.P.* XI. 892 {1/3}).
208 Bateson, pp. 335 and 572.

company was a band of sixty armed men led by two of Aske's petty
captains, William Acklam and William Edwyn. Having raised the
region between Skipwith Moor and York, it concentrated upon raising
the Ainsty. In the process it took and swore the influential gentleman,
Sir Oswald Wilstrop.[209] A company with a similar mission was the
twenty commoners led by Thomas Maunsell who, having recruited
support within the wapentake of Barkston went first to Pontefract,
then to Wakefield and finally to Doncaster, stirring up the commons
and administering the oath.[210] Employing the same device, Aske rode
to Pontefract Castle on 18th October with a force of three hundred
men to persuade the gentlemen within to swear.[211] In each case success
relied upon the support of the region's commons which reduced the
gentry's means of resistance to a few unwilling household servants. A
second device for swearing gentlemen was to use the gentlemen already
sworn to persuade their friends to follow suit. In this manner Robert
Plumpton, of the barony of Spofforth, was enlisted, brought in by
Oswald Wilstrop; as was Brian Rokcliffe of Cowthorpe in the
Ainsty.[212] By these means, a revolt of the commons was converted
into a regional uprising.

In imitation of the Lincolnshire rebellion, the uprising led by Aske
was bent on presenting a petition to the king. This was its intention
from the very start. It said so in its first proclamation which promised
that, on the morrow, those who gathered on Skipwith Moor would be
shown "the articles and causes of your assembly and petition to the
king".[213] It said so in its second proclamation which declared the
intention "to make petition to the king for reformation of things
amiss".[214] The presentation of a petition was central to the order for
religious houses suppressed which recommended the monks to re-enter
their houses on a temporary arrangement until "such time as our
petition be granted".[215] It also featured in the letter sent by Aske to
the lords in Pontefract Castle calling upon them "to be the mean to the
king by way of petition".[216] And eventually, on 26th and 27th
October, and in conjunction with the other revolts, a petition of five

209 *L.P.* XII{1}. 536; Stapulton, p. 100.
210 *L.P.* XI. 1402.
211 See above, p. 94.
212 Bateson, p. 560 and Stapulton, p. 100. For Plumpton, see Tonge, p. 55. For
     Rokcliffe, see ibid., p. 58.
213 The Dodds in their transcription erroneously substitute "statute" for "articles"
     (Dodds, I, p. 148). See SP1/107, f. 116 (*L.P.* XI. 622).
214 *St.P.*, I, pp. 466–7 (*L.P.* XI. 705 {2}).
215 Toller, p. 51 (*L.P.* XI. 784 /ii).
216 Bateson, p. 335.

articles was produced and submitted to the king, a document that Aske referred to as "our petition on faith and commonwealth".[217]

The whole purpose of Aske's revolt was "for grace": that is, with the favour of God to secure the favour of the king. For this to be achieved, a supplication to Henry VIII had to be made. But the rebels were under no illusion that the king would grant it out of the kindness of his heart. The threat of military force was for them a vital element in its success. From the start they were prepared, in the event of the king's grace being withheld, to obtain redress "by sword and battle".[218] Aske explained in his Examination that military action has not occurred to him as a way of righting the wrongs of the commonwealth before he was taken by the Lincolnshire rebels; but afterwards, and when the people had assembled in Yorkshire, he thought that "because this intent was for grace by petition to the king's highness", and in view of the gravity of the cause – to safeguard the commonwealth and to secure "remedy for their faith" – a possible refusal by the king to grant their proposed reforms justified the military plans that they had made "for the succour of their lives and the country".[219]

A host, then, was a vital necessity; and much of the planning of the rebel leadership was devoted to raising troops and ensuring that they were properly equipped and adequately provisioned. For this purpose, a succession of musters was held: on Hook Moor in Marshland and at Ringstone Hurst in Howdenshire on 11th October; on Skipwith Moor in Ouse and Derwent on 12th October; at Hillam in Barkston wapentake and at Bilbrough and Acomb in the Ainsty between 13th and 15th October; on Kexby Moor in Harthill wapentake on 15th October; outside York on 16th and 18th October; at Barnsdale Bar, halfway between Pontefract and Doncaster, on 18th October; and on St. Thomas' Hill near Pontefract after taking the castle on the 20th.[220] The aim was to produce a well-trimmed force, preferably horsed and harnessed. By 16th October the host was reckoned to number 4–5,000 men. At the siege of Pontefract Castle were, according to Harry Sais, 10,000 men "the most part on horseback"; and on

217 SP1/111 (*L.P.* XI. 1079).
218 Bateson, p. 559.
219 Bateson, pp. 569 and 571.
220 For Howdenshire, Marshland, Skipwith and Kexby musters, see above, pp. 82, 85, 88. For the York musters, see *L.P.* XI. 1402 and SP1/108 (*L.P.* XI. 762). For Pontefract muster, see Bateson, p. 569 and P.R.O. STAC2/15/10. For Hillam muster, see *L.P.* XI. 1402. For Ainsty musters, see Stapulton, p. 100. For Barnsdale Bar muster, see *L.P.* XI. 759.

24th October Aske's host alone was thought to comprise 17,000 men "well tried on horseback".[221]

The troops appeared to be funded by the communities that provided them. The surviving evidence relates to the lordship of Carleton in the soke of Snaith and the manor of Dewsbury in the Honour of Pontefract.[222] In the latter the people were taxed in order to provide two soldiers, undoubtedly horsed and harnessed since there were so few of them. In Carleton the captain Edward Hungate ordered the whole lordship to rise "with horse and harness". Those that served received twenty shillings in wages for three days service, presumably raised by a tax on the inhabitants who stayed behind. Apart from this, an important source of provisions, weapons, money and men was the surviving religious houses and the high-ranking secular clergy. One device for milking the clergy was the letter of tuition, such as was addressed from Robert Aske and "all other the heads of the common-wealth" to the brethren of the tremendously wealthy priory of York St. Mary. The letter called for assistance with "victuals and other necessaries" in accordance with the monks' promise "to aid us in this our pilgrimage for grace" and in return it offered them protection of their goods and chattels.[223] Other letters, probably similar in form, were sent out: for example, Watton Priory received one requiring men with horse and harness and money.[224] Aske appointed Sir Richard Fisher, a cleric, to collect provisions from the abbots of Yorkshire.[225] The monastic support that Aske received came not simply from the region that he had personally raised: his host was provided with troops, for example, by the religious houses at Watton, Byland, Newburgh and Whitby.[226] In addition, Aske approached wealthy members of the secular clergy. Thus the dean and chapter of York cathedral were commanded to send armed men; and Lancelot Collyns was obliged to provide money, weapons and harness.[227] The understanding

---

221 For size on 16th October, see *L.P.* XII{1}. 1018. For size on 18/19th October, see SP1/109, f. 203b (*L.P.* XI. 879/ii). For size on 21st October, see Bateson, p. 336. Recruited from lowland Yorkshire, these forces could have included only a minority of horsemen. Nonetheless, the wapentakes of Barkston, Osgoldcross, Skyrack and the Ainsty were capable of providing considerable numbers of horse. See Appendix I.
222 For Dewsbury, see SP1/110 (*L.P.* XI. 960); SP1/111 (*L.P* XI. 1051). For Carleton, see SP1/120, f. 192 (*L.P.* XII{1}. 1271 {2}).
223 SP1/110, f. 210b (*L.P.* XI. 784).
224 E36/119, f. 41 (*L.P.* XII{1}. 201 {4}).
225 *L.P.* XII{1}. 853.
226 SP1/115, f. 213 (*L.P.* XII{1}. 369).
227 For dean and chapter, see SP1/115, f. 164b (*L.P.* XII{1}. 306). For Collyns, see *L.P.* XII{1}. 1018.

reached was that, in return, the clergy would receive not only protection but also exemption from military service.

A final source of income was drawn from those who fell foul of the spoiling order. For refusing to take the oath, they had their goods confiscated. £77, for example, were raised in this way from selling off the requisitioned effects of the unsworn Sir Brian Hastings and the dean of Darrington.[228] Having fled, Leonard Beckwith of Stillingfleet lost his cattle to the company led by Acklam and Edwyn.[229] In going to York the rebels had hoped to seize the king's treasure reputed to be lodged there; but this was spirited away by its keeper John Gostwick who took it out of the rebels' reach to the castle of Tickhill.[230]

As well as being a military force, Aske's host was regarded as a column of pilgrims in search of grace. This implied two things: a religious objective and a journey. The religious objective was shown not just in the rebels' profession of support for the faith but also in their requirement that the army should proceed behind the cross of Christ. Aske's oath had enjoined his supporters "to take afore you the cross of Christ" and, according to his Narrative, the host marched to Market Weighton on 12th October, taking with them the cross of Howden Minster.[231] This became the normal procedure. The lords in Pontefract Castle commented upon it on 15th October when they reported to Shrewsbury that the rebels "doth daily increase fast of every parish [and] the cross goeth afore them".[232] The crosses were carried by clerics.[233] For this purpose Lumley required of the religious houses he visited "two monks with the best crosses to come forward" and Wilstrop, in taking his force through York on 20th October, made the Abbot of York St. Mary bear a cross and lead the way. This the abbot was unwilling to do and afterwards fled, leaving his cross behind him.[234] Thus, although excused military service, several members of the clergy were required to attend the host in the capacity of cross-bearers.

In the eyes of its organisers, the uprising in Howdenshire, Ouse and Derwent and Marshland had taken the form of a pilgrimage by

228 L.P. XI. 1047.
229 L.P. XII{1}. 536.
230 L.P. XII{1}. 854. For the plan, see above, p. 86.
231 Toller, pp. 50–51 (L.P. XI. 892 {1/3}; Bateson, p. 334. According to Master the Aske host had "a company of priests that went before their army and the cross borne next them" (Hoyle, op. cit., p. 65).
232 SP1/110, f. 47b (L.P. XI. 729).
233 Hoyle, op. cit., p. 65.
234 For Lumley, see SP1/115, f. 212b (L.P. XII{1}. 369). For Wilstrop, see SP1/115, fos. 260b-261 (L.P. XII{1}. 393{2}).

13th October. By the 16th and 17th October the designation was firmly fixed and regularly used.[235] But as a pilgrimage the uprising was distinctly peculiar. This was not so much because of its military aspect. Pilgrimages as conceived included journeys of the armed, in the form of crusades aimed to secure the grace of God by defending holy places, as well as journeys of the unarmed, in the form of visits to shrines to seek the intercession of saints for the living and the dead by venerating their names, images and relics.[236] Little concerned with saints, organised as an army and not bent on invoking a miracle, Aske's uprising qualified to be a pilgrimage only as a crusade. For this purpose the badge it eventually adopted was appropriate. It was the one Lord Darcy had used when leading an expedition against the Moor in Spain. Representing the five wounds of Christ, centred upon the Eucharist and surmounted by the crown of thorns above the name of Christ (IHS), it was in keeping with the christocentric image imparted by the practice of heading the host with cross-bearers.[237] On the other hand, as a pilgrimage the uprising was most unusual in that the grace it sought was, first and foremost, not God's but the king's and its explicit concern was not so much atonement and the fate of souls in purgatory or the material benefit of individuals and communities – that is, the normal concerns of a pilgrimage – but the decay of a whole society. This was made evident in the uprising's full title: the pilgrimage of grace for the commonwealth.

In the manner of a pilgrimage, it involved a journey. Thus, on 21st October Aske told Lancaster Herald that "his company would go to London of pilgrimage to the king's highness". This was said in response to the herald's request to hear the articles with which Aske had stated that the people were "all of one accord". The journey to London was presented as the first article.[238] In the north, as earlier in Lincolnshire, there was a strong popular urge to "go forward".[239] This was made evident in the early stages of the Beverley uprising when talk in the town thought it a good idea to go to London and sort out the deceivers and it was believed, according to Kitchen, that the purpose of the oath was to oblige everyone "to go forward for reformation of the

---

235 See above, pp. 8–9.
236 See J. Sumption, *Pilgrimage, an Image of Medieval Religion* (New Jersey, 1975), passim.
237 Bateson, pp. 555 and 571–2.
238 *St.P.*, I, p. 486 (*L.P.* XI. 826).
239 In the Lincolnshire uprising, William Longbottom was alleged to have said: "Go forward, all is ours" [SP1/107 (*L.P.* XI. 842 {4})]; and according to Harry Childe, the priests had said in Louth market place: "Let us go forward" [SP1/110 (*L.P.* XI. 972)].

said articles".[240] It was also evident around Pontefract at the time that the castle was yielded, as Harry Sais reported. Having been taken by a band of commons when he was crossing the Aire at Ferrybridge, he heard them say "that they would forward towards London as far as they be suffered".[241] The same popular urge to speed south was made evident by Thomas Percy who during his examination told of "a common bruit . . . among the commons" that "they thought to have come towards London and to take up the country by the way and afterwards to have spoken with the king and to sue to his grace to have certain statutes revoked and to have them punished that were the causes of the making thereof".[242]

But whilst it was an urge of the commons, was a march on London the prime aim of the leadership? The petition had to be presented somehow but, clearly, there were simpler, safer and less disruptive ways of delivering it than by means of an army of the commons. The genteel leadership of the Lincolnshire rebellion had claimed it had sought to prevent such a march, by using the procedure of sending a petition and awaiting a reply as a device for staying the commons.[243] The Stapulton host, moreover, had planned to communicate its petition through the medium of the Duke of Suffolk; and Aske on 18th October appeared to be thinking of a petition delivered by the Archbishop of York and Lord Darcy.[244] The failure of the Lincolnshire petition caused no basic change in policy; and it was probably the fear that it might that made Aske prevent Lancaster Herald from publicly declaring the proclamation which he brought to Pontefract on 21st October and which announced the unconditional collapse of the Lincolnshire uprising.[245] It seems, then, that, whilst popular with the commons, the pilgrimage to London was but a last resort for its leadership which much preferred to present a petition through chosen representatives. Since this approach proved acceptable to the government, and was successful for the rebels first in realising the October Truce and then the December Pardon, the pilgrimage was not needed. On the other hand, the government's compliance with the rebels' demands, both on 27th October and 6th December, was due to the threat of a pilgrimage, coupled with the government's complete inability to form an army capable of matching the pilgrim host.[246]

240 L.P. XI. 841; SP1/107, f. 56 (L.P. XI. 842 {4}).
241 SP1/109, f. 203b (L.P. XI. 879/ii).
242 SP1/115, f. 261 (L.P. XII{1}. 393 {2}).
243 Hoyle, op. cit., pp. 65–6.
244 For Stapulton, see Stapulton, p. 99. For Aske, see Bateson, p. 335.
245 Ibid., p. 336.
246 See below, ch. X.

Central to the leadership of the revolts about Howden was Robert Aske. The knighthood held by his father and the fact that his mother was the daughter of the baron, John Clifford, indicated that the family was of some importance. As for Aske himself, a third son with a small estate in Hampshire and a little land at Bubwith, a village along the Derwent situated halfway between the family seat at Aughton and the Percy seat at Wressle, he was essentially a professional lawyer and, like William Stapulton, a socially peripheral figure in northern society, neither common nor genteel.[247] Since the whole direction of the uprising as well as its nomenclature, its proclamations, its orders and its dynamism appeared to stem from him, he can be regarded as its mastermind. But was he himself masterminded? Like Stapulton, he came from a family which belonged to the affinity of the Percy earls of Northumberland.[248] Moreover, in the late 1520s Robert Aske had served as secretary to the sixth Earl of Northumberland having, in the latter's words, "the keeping and conveyance" of all his letters.[249] But, as with Stapulton, there is no reason to believe that his involvement in the uprising had anything to do with the Percy family. Likewise, there is no reason to believe that he was the puppet of the other powerful figures of the region, Sir Robert Constable or Lord Thomas Darcy.

He first became leader of the uprising because of his first-hand experience of the Lincolnshire rebellion, as well as through his own keenness to raise support for it in Yorkshire. He was looked to for direction before the uprising broke out in Howdenshire and when it happened he was immediately appointed its captain.[250] By 11th October he had assumed the office of chief captain of Marshland, the Isle of Axholme and Howdenshire.[251] Moreover, although no lord, he remained the recognised captain in charge, even after the uprising had assumed the appearance of the society of orders by recruiting support from the whole social structure. From being chief captain on 11th October he had risen to "great" or "grand" captain by 20th October, a position he still held when the truce was declared a week later, even though the uprising was by now openly supported by

247 Tonge, p. 64; *L.P.* XII{1}. 1224.
248 R. B. Smith, *Land and Politics in the England of Henry VIII* (Oxford, 1970), p. 173; R. R. Reid, *The King's Council in the North* (London, 1921), pp. 133–4.
249. According to the sixth earl, this was when he first entered into his patrimony (i.e. 1527). See SP1/119, f. 49 (omitted from *L.P.* XII{1}.1062).
250 Evident in Aske's Narrative (Bateson, pp. 33–4). Also see Collyns' account [SP1/118, f. 267 (*L.P.* XII{1}. 1018)].
251 Declared in his first proclamation (*L.P.* XI. 622).

several peers and large numbers of substantial gentlemen.[252] His leadership did not go totally without question. By 16th October two gentlemen had fled the uprising, after serving as captains, because Aske was "taken above them".[253]

Furthermore, Aske's supreme headship was to some extent contrived. After taking Pontefract Castle, Aske had been prepared to hand in his white rod of office and his title of captain, out of respect for the society of orders and in keeping with the rebels' belief that the nobility should rule. But he was discouraged from doing so, on the grounds that if the office of grand captain were taken by any one noble it would create offence among the other noble rebels.[254] There were, in all likelihood, other considerations: preserving him as head captain upheld the image of the uprising as a movement of the commons, as well as preparing the way for setting him up as the eventual scapegoat. But this only explains why his captaincy was found acceptable, even though it contravened the social values normally associated with leadership. Essentially his pre-eminent role in directing the uprising sprang from the size of his own following, his popularity with the commons and a reputation for effectiveness which was boosted by his success in taking the inmates of Pontefract Castle in spite of their being, in his own words, "in degree far above" him.[255]

Sustained by the support of the commons and the tolerance of the lords, Aske's leadership rested upon the skill and ingenuity he showed in composing orders and declarations. All the letters issued by the rebel command, apart from the eventual five articles submitted to the government on 27th October, were his composition.[256] Yet at no point was he the one and only captain; and the orders issued were usually presented as co-operative efforts: composed by Aske but with the consent of the headmen or more generally the followers of the uprising.[257] Who were these headmen? By 11th October, that is, within one day of its out-

---

252 For 20th October, see *L.P.* XII{1}. 946. For 27th October, see the adapted oath to which the five articles are appended [SP1/109 (*L.P.* XI. 902 {2})].
253 Stapulton, p. 103.
254 Bateson, p. 343.
255 *L.P.* XII{1}. 946.
256 *L.P.* XII{1}. 369; Bateson, p. 572.
257 The first proclamation was from Aske and the other named captains (*L.P.* XI. 622). The order for religious houses was "by all the whole consent of the headmen of this our pilgrimage of grace" [Toller, p. 51 (*L.P.* XI. 784/ii)]. The letter of protection for York St. Mary was from Aske "and all other the heads of the commonwealth" [SP1/110, f. 210b (*L.P.* XI. 784)]. The second proclamation was from Aske "for the barony and the commonalty of the same" [*St.P.*, I, p. 467 (*L.P.* XI. 705 {2})]. And a letter sent to the brethren of Watton was from Aske "by assent of the baronage and commonalty" [SP1/118, f. 42 (*L.P.* XII{1}. 849 {54})].

break, the Howdenshire and Marshland uprising possessed a command structure consisting of Aske as chief captain and of Thomas Metham, Robert Aske the younger, Thomas Saltmarsh, William Monkton, Thomas Franke and Gervaise Cawood, all designated captains.[258] In reality, however, it seems that the distinction made at this stage between Aske and the other headmen was not very great since Metham and Saltmarsh dropped out of the revolt when, in York five days later, Aske was regarded as being above the others.[259] Moreover, the leadership appeared on 17th October to be against the idea of a head captain. When the idea was proposed, it was rejected as they "reasoned rather against any head captain than not".[260]

Of the original headmen, all but one were drawn from the Howdenshire gentry. The exception was the cleric, Thomas Franke, the parson of Loftus in the North Riding and dean of Cleveland. How he came to be involved is unknown and the actual extent of his involvement remains obscure. Later he was referred to as a head captain in Howdenshire, possibly by someone seeking to discredit him. Apart from being termed a captain in Aske's first proclamation, there is nothing to indicate the part he played. What is clear is that he quickly removed himself, not by flight but by travelling home in order to spread revolt in that quarter. This he did by establishing contact with Thomas Percy and by seeking, through the latter's agency, to raise the wapentake of Pickering Lythe.[261] In all likelihood, Franke took with him a letter from Aske and remained in the North Riding until he accompanied the Percy host to York on 20th October.[262]

Of the gentlemen captains, two were the eldest sons of leading gentry: Robert Aske the younger was heir to John Aske as well as nephew of the chief captain, whilst Thomas Metham was heir to Sir Thomas Metham of Metham Hall, whose mother was the daughter of Sir Robert Constable and who was addressed by Lord Darcy as cousin.[263] After Sir Thomas had fled to avoid being made a rebel captain, it seems that his son agreed to stand in his stead when the

258 *L.P.* XI. 622.
259 Stapulton, p. 103.
260 SP1/118 f. 47b (omitted from *L.P.* XII{1}. 852/ iii).
261 *L.P.* XI. 622; *L.P.* XII{1}. 1085; *L.P.* XII{2}. 12. For his deanship of Cleveland, see *Star Ch. Yorkshire*, I, p. 67.
262 Collyns implies that he came to York with Thomas Percy (*L.P.* XII{1}. 1018).
263 For Aske, see Tonge, p. 64. The Dodds present him as a "wild young law student" (Dodds, I, p. 149). For Metham, see Tonge, pp. 63-4; *Star Ch. Yorkshire*, II, p. 115 and *L.P.* XI. 566.

rebels threatened to burn down their house.[264] Robert Aske the
younger appeared to remain with the uprising, but, doubtless because
of his youth, he had no role apart from attending upon his uncle.[265] In
contrast, Metham seemed to play an important part, so much so that
John Hallom regarded him, along with Robert Aske and Nicholas
Rudston, as "chief captains overall".[266] In marching with the host
to Market Weighton to join up with the rebels from the Beverley
region, Metham was part of a deputation of four gentlemen which
met a similar deputation from the Stapulton host to discuss future
plans.[267] Then, for the next day or two, he was involved in persuading
the town of Hull to provide support.[268] Thereafter, he must have
marched with Aske on York, but he and another of the original
captains, Thomas Saltmarsh of Saltmarshe, a close relative of Metham
by marriage as well as neighbour and familiar, appear to have fled
before entering the city.[269]

By this time (i.e. 16th October) the captains had become, in the
terminology of the revolt, petty captains and the leadership had
changed in two respects: Saltmarsh and Metham had been replaced
by Nicholas Rudston and John Donnington.[270] Nonetheless, William
Monkton and Gervaise Cawood remained as headmen. Monkton was
Robert Aske's brother-in-law. He was a very minor gentleman of the
region, with an estate at Cavil and Portington which was assessed at £6
per annum in 1524.[271] Gervaise Cawood, another minor gentleman,
was receiver to the Bishop of Durham for his lordship of Howden and
was later dismissed from the office for his involvement in the uprising.[272] Both failed to feature in Aske's negotiations with the Stapulton
host on 13th October but were recognised as petty captains when the
Aske host entered York on 16th October; and during Aske's stay in the

---

264 *L.P.* XII{1}. 1022; Bateson, p. 334. Aske had previously acted as the Methams'
    solicitor, see *Star Ch. Yorkshire*, III, pp. 183–4; so there may be some truth in the
    allegation that he intervened to stop the commons from burning Metham Hall
    when Sir Thomas was found to have fled.
265 *L.P.* XII{1}. 1320.
266 *L.P.* XII{1}. 201/ iv.
267 Stapulton, p. 92.
268 Ibid. and *L.P.* XI. 818.
269 Metham and Saltmarsh were not included in the list of petty captains who
    accompanied Aske into York on 16th October (*L.P.* XII{1}. 306). Stapulton
    claimed that they left him at York (Stapulton, p. 103). When in York Aske
    claimed to have sent for them (Bateson, p. 560). For Saltmarsh, see Tonge, pp.
    xvii and 64. For his familiarity with Metham, see *L.P.* XII{1}. 1206.
270 For the reference to captains, see *L.P.* XI. 622. For the reference to petty captains,
    see *L.P.* XII{1}. 306. For the changes in membership, compare the two.
271 SP1/118, f. 47 (*L.P.* XII{1}. 852); *L.P.* XII{1}. 1175; P.R.O. E179/203/182.
272 *L.P.* XII{1}. 853 and *L.P.* XII{2}. 536.

city they were his close advisers and companions.[273] William Talbot described them as "the doers" under Aske. Collyns described them as "captains of the commons".[274]

Both newcomers to the captaincy, Nicholas Rudston, esquire, of Hayton in the wapentake of Harthill and John Donnington of Escrick in the wapentake of Ouse and Derwent, were recruited as Aske, having marched into the wolds to meet Stapulton, turned to take York. Rudston joined him on 13th October when Aske's force reached Market Weighton which is close by Hayton, the Rudstons' family seat. Immediately he assumed an important position, presumably because of his social status, and was admitted to the deputation of gentlemen which convened in council with the four gentlemen from the Stapulton host. By 16th October he was recognised as one of Aske's petty captains.[275] On 17th October he and Monkton were close at hand when Aske met Thomas Strangways, Lord Darcy's steward, and in the discussion Rudston made his mark, by accusing Strangways of coming to spy and by arguing against having a head captain.[276] George Lumley regarded Rudston as one of "the chief doers in the business"; John Pickering regarded him, along with Aske, as of outstanding importance in first stirring up revolt; John Hallom thought that he, with Aske and Metham, was "a chief captain".[277] With the retirement of Metham, he became second in command to Aske, his leadership assured by his part in taking Hull, just as Aske's leadership was assured by the taking of Pontefract Castle.[278] Between them they sorted out the fugitive gentlemen and ensured that the sworn supporters comprised the high as well as the low. By 22nd October his importance was fully recognised when he, as well as Aske, was admitted to the council that met in a window bay of Pontefract Castle to determine policy, the prestigious membership of which included Lords Darcy and Neville, Thomas Percy, Robert Bowes, Roger Lascelles, Robert Constable and Ralph Ellerker the younger.[279] Curiously, both Aske and Rudston were marked by an ocular defect, Aske having sight in only one eye and Rudston having "a pearl in his eye", perhaps a cataract.[280]

273 L.P. XII{1}. 306; L.P. XI. 762; L.P. XII{1}. 852/iv and 853.
274 SP1/118, f. 268b (L.P. XII{1}. 1018); L.P. XII{1}. 853.
275 Bateson, p. 560; Stapulton, pp. 92 and 99; L.P. XII{1}. 306.
276 SP1/118, f. 47b(L.P. XII{1}. 852/iii); L.P. XI. 762.
277 L.P. XII{1}. 369; L.P. XII{1}. 1021; L.P. XII{1} 201/iv.
278 Stapulton, p. 98.
279 SP1/115, fos. 259b-260 (L.P. XII{1}. 393 {2}).
280 For Aske, see L.P. XI. 1103. For Rudston, see L.P. XI. 818.

John Donnington, a minor gentlemen of Ouse and Derwent, with lands assessed in the 1540s at an annual income of £20, was recruited a little later, probably at the muster held on Kexby Moor on 15th October, possibly at the muster held outside York on 16th October, on which date he entered York as one of Aske's petty captains. Thereafter, like Monkton, Cawood and Rudston, he was companion and adviser to Aske.[281] His position of influence was acknowledged on 20th October when Lancelot Collyns, in a bid to avoid service in the host, offered a bribe to him as well as to Cawood and Monkton.[282] These men captained Aske's host and, as headmen, staffed the council of the commonwealth which was set up in York to formulate policy and to decide, in accordance with the spoiling order, whose goods to confiscate or destroy.[283]

In addition, there were three others who worked for Aske at a distance. Their function was to extend the revolt into the West Riding. William Acklam of Moreby Hall near Stillingfleet and William Edwyn of Yokefleet near Howden were both termed petty captains responsible to Aske. They played a vital part in raising the Ainsty.[284] The third figure was Thomas Maunsell, vicar of Brayton. Like Acklam, he claimed to have been taken in the first instance and compelled to participate.[285] But once involved he became a dynamic raiser of the commons, first in the wapentake of Barkston and then in the honour of Pontefract and the soke of Wakefield. Acklam and Maunsell joined Aske in his march to Pontefract Castle and, as evidence of their closeness to him and his trust in them, he selected them to deliver his letter of 18th October to the lords within, among whom was Acklam's father, John.[286]

Of these captains, headmen and agents, none was a commoner, apart from Edwyn. However, their credentials as gentlemen were not very impressive since, but for Metham and Robert Aske the younger, all were of the minor gentry; and neither Metham nor Aske had as yet entered into their patrimonies. For this reason, in social composition the captaincy of the Aske host when present at the Doncaster confrontation on 27th October bore no relationship to what it had been in

281 Tonge, p. 55; E179/203/222; *L.P.* XII{1}. 306; *L.P.* XII{1}. 1320.
282 *L.P.* XII{1}. 1018.
283 For its function in connexion with the spoiling order, see Bateson, p. 335. Aske's oath refers to it as "the council of the commonwealth" [Toller, p. 50 (*L.P.* XI. 892 {1/3})].
284 Stapulton, p. 100.
285 For Maunsell, see *L.P.* XI. 1402. For Acklam, see *L.P.* XII{1}. 536.
286 SP1/119, f. 4b (*L.P.* XII{1}. 1022).

the first week of revolt.[287] Bringing about the transformation was the capture of important gentlemen by the commons and their conversion into rebel leaders: first Sir John Wilstrop, taken by Acklam and Edwyn, and then the refugees in Pontefract Castle, taken by Aske.[288]

Besides being minor gentlemen, Aske's captains were, not, in all probability, acting as the clients of lords. In this respect, they resembled Aske himself. The possible but unlikely exceptions were Edwyn, Maunsell and Cawood. Both Edwyn and Cawood were answerable to Sir Robert Constable who was described as "a virtuous pilgrim of grace", Edwyn because he was Constable's servant and Cawood because, as the Bishop of Durham's receiver for Howden, he was under Constable as steward of the lordship. Moreover, Maunsell when examined claimed to have been directed by Lord Darcy.[289] However, there is nothing to suggest that Edwyn had acted upon his master's instructions in taking Acklam and in raising the region south and west of the city of York. Cawood, furthermore, had been daggers drawn with Constable rather than part of his affinity.[290] In Maunsell's case there is a strong suspicion that, by alleging he was Darcy's agent, he was seeking to free himself from blame. William Talbot presented Maunsell as "the most busy fellow that was among the commons" and Sir Henry Savile showed how Maunsell "visited under Aske in these parts".[291] Maunsell, like Edwyn and Cawood, appeared to be serving Aske rather than any lord.

By its very nature the uprising was the work of Aske. It came to include Darcy, Constable, Lee and others simply because Aske, in compliance with the commons, was bent on presenting the revolt as an enactment of the society of orders. This aim was evident in his first proclamation of 11th October when he called upon the commons of Ouse and Derwent to take three local gentlemen, Mr. Hussey of North Duffield, Mr. Babthorpe of Osgodby and Mr. Gascoigne of Kelfield,

---

287 The military leadership appeared to be Sir Richard Tempest (see Stapulton, p. 100), Robert Constable, Lord Darcy and Aske (see Bateson, pp. 336–7). The council of 22nd October which decided how the whole army should be ordered (as identified by Stapulton) had consisted of the peers, Neville, Latimer and Darcy, the knights, Robert Constable, James Strangways, John Bulmer, William Bulmer, John Dawnye, William Fairfax, Oswald Wilstrop and Robert Neville, and the gentlemen, Roger Lascelles, Robert Bowes, Robert Chaloner, Thomas Gryce and William Babthorpe (see Stapulton, p. 100).

288 See ibid.

289 For Edwyn, see *L.P.* XII{1}. 536. For Constable, see *L.P.* XII{1}. 192. For Cawood, see *L.P.* XII{1}. 853. For Maunsell, see *L.P.* XI. 1402.

290 *Star Ch.Yorkshire*, I, pp. 55–9.

291 E36/122, f. 28 (*L.P.* XII{1}. 853); SP1/115, f. 131 (*L.P.* XII{1}. 281).

and make them their captains.[292] This reflected the plan already attempted by the commons of Howden to make a captain of Sir Thomas Metham.[293] Aske's aim was expressed again in his second proclamation which, in a piece of wishful thinking, was addressed in the name of the baronage and the commons.[294] It was finally achieved with the taking of Pontefract Castle and the enlistment of its inmates. For this reason the yielding of the castle was a great victory for Robert Aske. It marked the realisation of a plan. Only later did it assume the appearance of a devious aristocratic ploy, as the lords used it to excuse their involvement in the rebellion and, by doing so, aroused the suspicions of the government.

The uprising was, in presentation, a rising of the commons. Designated "captain of the commons", Aske framed the cause of revolt in terms of "the griefs of the commons" and the need to safeguard "the commons and their wealths".[295] In the first instance he presented himself as obliged to act by the commons, suggesting as much by addressing them as "Masters" in his first proclamation.[296] But was this a fiction, devised to conceal a conspiracy, or did it denote a genuine popular movement? In the early stages there was a frenzy of popular activity as, moved by the Lincolnshire uprising, men wished to come forward and join it. This threw up commoner activists such as William Edwyn, Thomas Davy, the underbailey of Howden, and Ronald Consayte who, like the other two, was also of the parish of Howden. It was Davy who, "with other honest men of the town" (including Consayte and the cleric Richard Fisher), alerted Aske to the prospect of his capture by the sheriff and who, having taken Thomas Maunsell captive on 10th October, made him swear the oath on 11th October and attend the muster at Skipwith Moor on 12th October.[297]

The same popular impetus also led to the formation of self-activated companies of commons such as the Howden group which took Sir Thomas Metham on 10th October and threatened to burn his

292 SP1/107, f. 116 (*L.P.* XI. 622).
293 *L.P.* XII{1}. 1022.
294 *L.P.* XI. 705 {2}.
295 For "captain of the commons", see *L.P.* XII{1}. 854. The same term was applied to the petty captains [SP1/118, f. 268b (*L.P.* XII{1}. 1018)]. For "griefs of the commons", see Bateson, p. 335. For the "commons and their wealths", see SP1/107, f. 116 (*L.P.* XI. 622). Aske could refer to the oath that he composed as "the oath of the commons" (Bateson, p. 571).
296 Bateson, p. 334; SP1/107, f. 116 (*L.P.* XI. 622).
297 For Edwyn, see above. For Davy, see *L.P.* XII{2}. 536; *L.P.* XII{1}. 946; SP1/113, f. 62 (*L.P.* XI. 1402). He was assessed at £5 in goods in 1524 (E179/203/182) and £15 twenty years later (E179/203/222). For Consayte, see *L.P.* XI. 1402. He was assessed in mid-1540s at £18 in goods (E179/203/222).

house when he fled from them and the Cawood group which took
Metham again on 11th October when he sought refuge in Cawood
Castle.[298] With this strong pressure of protest from below there was no
problem in raising large assemblies of men. For Aske the problem was
to hold the people back until the time was ripe. It was a movement he
sought to use but because of its independence of spirit it was one that
he had to humour and respect. The force of the commons persisted.
Thus about 20th October in Ferrybridge, Henry Sais was taken by a
company of men "among whom he knew none to be superior over the
other". When made to take the oath, and Sais responded that he was
perfectly willing to swear to be true to God and the king, one of the
rebels truculently asked: "and not to us?". Sais demurred and was told:
"If ye do not swear thus, to be true to God and to the king and to the
commons, thou shalt lose thy head". And so Sais took the oath "upon
a little book that one of them brought from his sleeve".[299]

Central to the uprising, then, was an outraged, independent and
self-conscious commons urgently demanding redress. Their presence
influenced the behaviour of other aggrieved groups, clerical and
aristocratic. In turn, the course of the revolt was very much determined by the attitude that lords and clerics adopted towards it. In its
early development, an outstanding role was played by minor gentlemen from the wapentakes of Howdenshire and Ouse and Derwent, by
certain clerics, notably Sir Richard Fisher, Sir Thomas Franke, Sir
Thomas Maunsell, Sir Henry Lytherland and the friar of Knaresborough, and eventually by major gentlemen, notably Sir Oswald Wilstrop, Lord Darcy and Sir Robert Constable.[300] For this reason, to
regard the uprising as simply a popular revolt would overlook its true
character. Yet what was the vital function of the lords: to stimulate and
direct or merely to permit? Arguably their major contribution to the
uprising along the Ouse was to let it happen. This they did not by
passively waiting upon events but by actively removing themselves
from the scene. As significant as the upsurgence of the people in the
development of the uprising was the flight of the region's rulers.

The flight of the lords was well underway by 10th October when
John Aske, Thomas Metham and Thomas Portington, following the
example of Robert Creke and William Babthorpe, sought to join the
Archbishop of York at Cawood Castle, but had to return across the

298 L.P. XII{1}. 1022.
299 SP1/109, f. 203b (L.P. XI. 879/ii).
300 See above, pp. 123–7 (for minor gents); see below, p. 134 (for clerics); see above, p.
   100 (for major gents).

Ouse to avoid capture by the archbishop's tenants. The following day the archbishop, Babthorpe and Creke had become refugees, selecting Pontefract Castle as their retreat after deciding that the journey to Scarborough Castle was too long and hazardous.[301] They thus followed in the footsteps of Darcy and his household servants who had transferred from Temple Hirst to Pontefract Castle by 8th October.[302] Gentlemen in large numbers followed suit, so much so that when Aske arrived at the castle gates on 18th October there were fifty or sixty gentlemen within.[303] Besides the archbishop and Lord Darcy, they included Thomas Magnus, Archdeacon of the East Riding, and eight knights, the most significant of whom were Sir Robert Constable, a force in the region by virtue of being steward of the Bishop of Durham's lordship of Howden and of the York St Mary Abbey estates in Marshland, and Sir William Gascoigne, who along with the loyalist Sir Henry Savile, was the richest gentleman in the West Riding with a seat at Gawthorpe Hall in the parish of Harewood, which lies on the border of the wapentakes of Skyrack and the Ainsty.[304] Other important fugitives to the castle were the sheriff of Yorkshire, Sir George Darcy (whose seat, like that of Lord Darcy his father, was in Barkston wapentake), Sir Harry Everingham of Birkin in the same wapentake, Sir John Wentworth of Elmsall and Sir John Dawnye of Cowick, both in the adjacent wapentake of Osgold-cross, Sir Robert Neville of Liversage in Morley wapentake and Sir Robert Ughtred of Bilton in the Ainsty.[305] Lancelot Collyns thought the uprising was caused partly by the spread of various rumours but partly by the flight of leading figures such as the Archbishop of York, the Archdeacon of the East Riding and the steward of the Honour of

301 L.P. XII{1}. 1022.
302 At Temple Hirst on 6th October, but about to move to Pontefract (see L.P. XI. 563). At Pontefract on 8th October (see L.P. XI. 605).
303 L.P. XI. App. 11. This list of inmates cannot be later than 16th October since that day Arthur Darcy was sent to Court with the news that Aske had taken York (L.P. XII{1}. 1022). Another account, provided by Leonard Beckwith, claimed that on 17th October there were 120–140 gentlemen with Darcy in the castle [SP1/108, f. 150 (L.P. XI. 750)].
304 For Sir Robert Constable, see L.P. XI. App. 11; L.P. XII{2}. 160–1. For Sir William Gascoigne, see SP1/115, f. 164 (L.P. XII{1}. 306). He had been there since at least 9th October (ibid.). Also see Smith, op. cit., pp. 88, 135–6, 145–6.
305 For Sir George Darcy, see L.P. XI. App. 11; L.P. XI. 729; Smith, op. cit., p. 184. For Sir Harry Everington, see L.P. XI. App. 11; Tonge, p. 12. For Sir John Wentworth, Sir John Dawnye, Sir Robert Neville, Sir Robert Ughtred, see L.P. XI. App. 11; Smith, op. cit., p. 193. In addition, there was a middling gentry group consisting of Henry Ryther of Ryther in Barkston, William Babthorpe of Osgodby and John Acklam of Stillingfleet, both of Ouse and Derwent, and John Anne (see L.P. XI. App. 11).

Pontefract, Lord Darcy;[306] and this was undoubtedly true. With the leading gentlemen and major clerics in flight, chiefly to Pontefract Castle, the system of authority in the East Riding wapentakes of Howdenshire and of Ouse and Derwent and the West Riding wapentakes of Agbrigge, Morley, Barkston, Skyrack, the Ainsty and Osgoldcross crumbled. Moreover, every one of them was dramatically swept into the rebel camp when Aske took the castle on 20th October and subjected its inmates to the rebel oath.[307]

As for the gentlemen who failed to flee to the castle, they were left isolated and vulnerable. The most important of this group were Sir Oswald Wilstrop and Sir William Fairfax of the Ainsty, Sir Richard Tempest, steward of the lordships of Wakefield, Sowerbyshire and Bradford as well as a major officeholder and landowner in the deanery of Craven, and Sir Henry Savile of Thornhill in Agbrigge. Wilstrop and Fairfax were taken by the commons, the former at his home in the Ainsty by 17th October, the latter near Wakefield, presumably when in flight on 22nd October.[308] As for Sir Richard Tempest, his plans to organise an opposition flopped in the absence of support from Lord Darcy. All three had been incorporated in the uprising by 22nd October and were present in Pontefract when the incoming hosts were organised in one huge army.[309] Sir Henry Savile, after Tempest and Gascoigne the leading gentleman in the West Riding, escaped the clutches of the commons; but his flight to Rotherham was another contributory factor to the spread of the uprising.[310] The total inability of the local lords to mount an opposition to popular revolt contrasted sharply with their effective treatment of the agrarian revolts of 1535 which had been efficiently snuffed out by Tempest and others.[311]

306 L.P. XII{1}. 1018.
307 Bateson, p. 336.
308 For Wilstrop: Darcy claimed he had been taken by 17th October (L.P. XI. 760). Also see Stapulton, p. 100. For Fairfax, see L.P. XII{1}. 192. His capture is described in STAC2/15/10.
309 For Wilstrop and Fairfax, see Stapulton, p. 100. It is not certain how Tempest became a pilgrim. On 9th October and again on 17th October there is evidence that he was seeking to organise a military opposition to the rebellion [see L.P. XI. 741 (misdated) and L.P. XI. 747]; and on 23rd October Norfolk told the king that Tempest had taken a captain of the rebels and was formulating a plan to link up with Dacre, Scrope and Cumberland and to crush the uprising (L.P. XI. 846). But he was placed in charge of the middleward of the pilgrim's host, along with Darcy, on 22nd October (see Stapulton, p. 100) and about that time he was in Pontefract Castle with Darcy (see L.P. XII{1}. 192), and appeared to remain with Darcy for the rest of the month (see e.g. L.P. XI. 928). Neville called him "a guider of the people" (L.P. XII{1}. 29{2}).
310 Smith, op. cit., pp. 134, 136 and 193.
311 E.g. L.P. VIII. 994.

Their failure in 1536 is not to be explained in terms of their ineffectualness, but rather in terms of a deepseated opposition to the government which did not drive them to create a revolt but deprived them of any commitment to suppress the one that broke out. Thus, behind the revolt of the commons was an aristocratic conspiracy of inaction, one which was all the more remarkable because of the gains to be made, by acts of loyalism, from a Crown that was, thanks to the Dissolution, more flush with patronage than at any time since the Conquest.

Not all the gentlemen involved in the uprising subscribed to this conspiracy. For example, there is no reason to believe that Sir William Fairfax, a recent beneficiary of the suppression of North Ferriby Priory, sympathised with the commons' revolt. His involvement stemmed simply from his capture by the Wakefield commons.[312] Furthermore, there were certain gentlemen who became openly committed to the cause in its early stages: not just Aske's captains but also Thomas Strangways, Lord Darcy's steward; Thomas Gryce of Wakefield, Darcy's counsel; Gilbert Scott, the constable of Pontefract Castle; and John Lacy, brother-in-law to Sir Richard Tempest and his bailiff for the lordship of Halifax. Possibly they were acting for their masters; but the likelihood is that they were simply responding to the commons and the leadership of Aske whose cause they shared.[313] Sir Oswald Wilstrop, moreover, came out of the closet as soon as he had been taken and sworn, working actively to raise for Aske the Ainsty and, further west, the region around Wetherby and Spofforth. He was one of the jurors who, having acquitted William Wycliffe of murder earlier in the year, had been hauled before Star Chamber and heavily fined to the sum of £220. This was a *cause célèbre* and certainly a pilgrim grievance. Perhaps Wilstrop's commitment came of the grudge he must have borne as a result of it.[314]

312 He received the farm of the demesnes and site (P.R.O. SC6/Henry VIII/4509). See above, n. 308 for his enlistment.
313 For Strangways' involvement, see his meeting with Aske on 17th October (*L.P.* XII{1}. 852/iii) and his encouragement of Maunsell to raise Pontefract and Wakefield (*L.P.* XI. 1402). The information he imparted to Maunsell on how to take the castle by assault if it was not yielded suggests that he was not simply an agent of Darcy but had a policy of his own (*L.P.* XI. 1402) and bears out Aske's remark that he was encouraged to think that the castle would yield by the knowledge that certain serving men within favoured him (Bateson, p. 335). For Scott, who acted in conjunction with Strangways, see *L.P.* XI. 1402. For Gryce, see Smith, op. cit., pp. 89 and 189-90. For his commitment as a captain of the commons, see SC6/Henry VIII/4509; *L.P.* XI. 997 and 1042. For John Lacy, see Smith, op. cit., p. 189.
314 Stapulton, p. 100. For Wilstrops' fine, see SP1/104, f. 295 (*L.P.* X. 1257). It seems that he was allowed to pay in eight annual installments of £27. 10.0. That the pilgrimage was moved by the case, see Bateson, pp. 339-40, *L.P.* XI. 1244 and below, pp. 166-7.

However, they were the exceptions; that is, until the conspiracy of inaction collapsed with the fall of Pontefract Castle and the commons were now able to force upon the gentry a positive involvement. Then, protected by the excuse of impressment and by the belief that what they were doing was to serve the Crown by preventing the defeat of an army royal and a march on London, they worked openly and successfully, on the one hand, to organise the host and, on the other, to achieve a truce and to present a petition.[315] In this respect, the relationship of the lords with the uprising came in two phases: one in which they let it happen; the other in which, committed by their capture, they took charge. In neither phase did they seek to discourage the commons. In this respect their behaviour is to be contrasted with that of the rulers of Strafforth and Tickhill, the far southerly wapentakes of the West Riding, where Sir William Fitzwilliam, Sir Brian Hastings and the Earl of Shrewsbury came out positively on the side of the government and, as a result, the discontent evident in those parts in early October remained embryonic.[316]

Just as the lords were unwilling to become involved in a rising of the commons, so the clergy were unwilling to serve in a military operation. But, as with the lords, the clergy's detached attitude towards the uprising, did not mean that they lacked sympathy for the cause. It simply expressed an unwillingness to offend the values of the society of orders which emphasised obedience to the monarch and, in its allocation of duties, insisted that clerics should not fight and that commoners should not lead. William Fairfax sought to explain the uprising in terms of clerical rule, arguing that Howden and York were important centres of revolt simply because the former belonged to the Bishop of Durham and the latter was a Liberty of the Archbishop of York.[317] To prove his point he made comparison with two other notable foci of insurrection, Louth, a lordship belonging to the Bishop of Lincoln, and Beverley, another Liberty of the Archbishop of York. But this was no more than an outburst of ingenious anticlericalism. If anything, the Louth and Beverley uprisings were revolts against episcopal rule; and there is no reason to believe that the uprising in Howdenshire and the Liberty of York was stirred up by

---

315 This point was made by Constable (*L.P.* XI. 1300 and *L.P.* XII{1}. 1225) and by Aske (*L.P.* XII{1}. 1175, *L.P.* XI. 1047 and Bateson, p. 333). See below, chapter X.
316 Smith, op. cit., p. 197.
317 *L.P.* XII{1}. 192.

a bishop. In Howdenshire the Bishop of Durham's officials, notably his receiver Gervaise Cawood and his sub-bailiff, Thomas Davy, were leading rebels; but not because they were under instruction from their master who demonstrated no sympathy for the uprising whatsoever and escaped involvement by fleeing to the Scottish border castle of Norham.[318] Clearly the flight of the Archbishop to Pontefract Castle helped to create a vacuum of authority upon which the revolt thrived, but there is nothing to suggest that he provided encouragement or direction; and, in all likelihood, the uprising would have persisted even if he had remained at Cawood.

The role of the clergy in the development of the uprising was less decisive than Fairfax suggests, but nonetheless important. Clerics who acted as generators and disseminators of revolt were Thomas Franke, Thomas Maunsell and the friar of Knaresborough.[319] Another cleric, Richard Fisher, a chaplain of the college of Howden and priest in charge of the chantry of St. Cuthbert there, played an active and important part in enlisting Maunsell and in approaching various religious houses for funds and supplies.[320] The support the latter provided appeared to be given at the command of the commons but it was not grudgingly given, so much so that on occasions what was offered was in excess of what was demanded. For example, the Abbot of Rievaulx and a former Prior of Guisborough wanted to attend Aske's host in person, although it went against his orders. The ex-prior of Guisborough actually came to York and had to be ordered home again.[321] The religious houses were an important source of manpower, provisions, money, horses and carts. What they contributed, although made under order of the commons, came of their ability to share a cause which condemned the government's alliance with heresy and its seizure of church wealth. The same was true of the secular clergy, offended by the new clerical taxes and the rumoured threat that the Dissolution would be applied to parish churches.[322]

Moral as well as material support came from the clergy, both regular and secular, notably from those attached to the city of York. Thus, upon entering the city, Aske was well received by the cathedral

---

318 For Cawood, see above, pp. 124–5 For Thomas Davy, see above, n. 297. For Durham's flight, see Dodds, I, pp. 203–4.
319 For Franke, see above, n. 261. For Maunsell, see *L.P.* XI. 1402; *L.P.* XII{1}. 852 / iii, 852 {2} and 853; *L.P.* XII{1}. 1022. For friar of Knaresborough, see *L.P.* XI. 1047; *L.P.* XII{1}. 1018.
320 *L.P.* XI. 1402; *L.P.* XII{1}. 853. Also see *V.E.*, 5, p. 137.
321 SP1/115, fos. 212b-213 (*L.P.* XII{1}. 369).
322 See above, pp. 106–8 (for clerical grievances); pp. 117–18 (for clerical contribution).

chapter, his hand being taken by Lancelot Collyns at the minster door, and bells being rung as he was taken to the high altar.[323] Collyns later had him to dinner. John Aske, the prior of the Augustian Friary in York dined with him at Sir George Lawson's house on the day of his entry to the city.[324] Moreover, it was the prior of the city's other friary, the Dominican Dr. John Pickering who, from the distant retreat of Bridlington, produced his stirring marching song.[325] Although unwilling to serve as soldiers, the clergy played their part in furnishing the host, providing it with horsed and harnessed men and even with priests to carry the crosses before it.

The revolt, then, had as its starting point an uprising of the commons. For the organisers the commonalty presented no problem. "As for the commons", Aske admitted, little effort was required to raise them and by 16th October they were in revolt throughout Yorkshire and the palatinate of Durham.[326] This was achieved simply by bell-ringing and by holding a series of assemblies to which the people had flocked and at which the Lincolnshire articles were read, the oath was administered and musters organised. Much more of a problem lay in enlisting the other two orders, the clergy and the gentlemen. In practice, this was largely achieved by impressment. Nonetheless, the uprising was not without co-operation from lords and clerics, who had hopes that, in censuring the government for what it had done and in obliging it to abide by its duty of defending the commonwealth and the faith, a rising of the commons might succeed where parliament and convocation had failed.

323 *L.P.* XI. 759; *L.P.* XII{1}. 1018; SP1/120, f. 175 (*L.P.* XII{1}. 1264).
324 For Collyns, see *L.P.* XII{1}. 1018. For Aske, see SP1/115, f. 164b (*L.P.* XII{1}. 306).
325 D. M. Palliser, *The Reformation in York, 1534–1553* (Borthwick Papers, 40), p. 11.
326 Bateson, p. 560.

IV

▚▚▚▚▚▚▚▚▚▚▚▚▚▚▚▚▚▚▚▚▚▚▚▚▚▚▚▚▚

THE BOWES HOST

The Richmondshire uprising

This particular uprising had a major impact on the pilgrimage of grace. By co-ordinating revolts in the North Riding, the West Riding and the palatinate of Durham, it was responsible for creating two huge hosts, which came to form both the rearward and vanguard of the pilgrims' army when it confronted the government at Doncaster in the last week of October[1]. According to Aske, they furnished 22,000 troops out of a total force of 47,000.[2] The Richmondshire uprising also provided an outstanding leader and negotiator in the form of the lawyer/soldier, Robert Bowes. Moreover, it made its mark on the pilgrimage of grace by recruiting five of the six peers who took part; by providing the banner of St Cuthbert, behind which the pilgrim host was arrayed; by ensuring that the grievances submitted to the government should include the constitutional demand that the common law, and the practices associated with it, be restored to what was found in 1509; and by playing a vital part in bringing about the truce of 27th October.[3] The same uprising was also responsible for inciting the far north into open rebellion. It was the first revolt in the uplands to form

---

1 See Map 4.
2 Bateson, pp. 336–7. For the implausibility of these figures, see Appendix 1.
3 The participants from the peerage were Latimer, Westmorland and his son Lord Neville, and Lumley – all taken by 19th October (whereas Lord Darcy was only taken by Aske on 20th October) – Scrope, enlisted by 25th October, and Conyers, recruited by the end of November. For Conyers, see below, n. 9. For the others, see below, pp. 140 and 174(Latimer); pp. 150 and 176 (Lumley); p. 152 (Westmorland and son); pp. 175–6(Scrope). For the constitutional grievance, see below, p. 166–7.

a host. Then with its Captain Poverty letter, it produced as effective a rebel-rouser as the Lincolnshire articles, using the letter effectively to raise rebellion in the three border counties, the palatinate of Durham, the rest of the North Riding, north Lancashire and the northerly parts of the West Riding.[4] Of all the uprisings that comprised the pilgrimage of grace, it stood second in importance only to the one led by Aske; and as an inspiration for revolt it was equal to the Lincolnshire uprising.

Lord Darcy suggested that the Richmondshire uprising broke out before the insurrections of the East Riding. On 6th October he reported open sedition and confederations in Wensleydale. The source of his information was a neighbour, Thomas Hemsworth, who had witnessed oath-taking in Wensleydale by over five hundred men. As Darcy put it, they had been sworn "to certain unlawful articles".[5] But rather than proving that the Richmondshire uprising had started, Darcy's information belongs to a separate revolt which, having begun on 25th September in the lordship of Dent, affected the far westerly parts of Wensleydale and eventually materialised as the rebellion which, under the leadership of John Atkinson and supported by the barony of Kendal and the adjacent wapentakes of Ewcross in the West Riding and Lonsdale in Lancashire, took Lancaster on 28th October.[6] In contrast, the Richmondshire uprising began in the far east of Wensleydale and first came to notice on 11th October. In the evening a crowd of two to three hundred, recruited from the lordships of Masham in the North Riding and Kirkby Malzeard with Nidderdale in the West Riding, occupied Jervaulx Abbey and restored the dissolved Coverham Abbey where in celebration matins were sung late into the night.[7] For the next four days they came and went, travelling to Middleham; taking reprisals against those involved in suppressing Coverham; passing along Wensleydale and over to the town of Richmond. In that time they burned beacons at night and imposed oaths in the day. Support came in from Nidderdale, Colsterdale, Coverdale and Wensleydale, as well as from the Vale of Mowbray, notably the

---

4 M. L. Bush, "Captain Poverty and the pilgrimage of grace", *Historical Research*, 65 (1992), pp. 17–18.

5 P.R.O. SP1/110, f. 39 (*L.P.* XI. 564).

6 *L.P.* XII{1}. 841. A Monday is given as the starting day. That it was the 25th September and not the 2nd October, see below, ch. VII(n. 9).

7 The starting day is given as a Wednesday (*L.P.* XII{1}. 1035). That it was 11th and not 4th October is suggested by the chronology of events evident in the same document. For restoration of Coverham, see *L.P.* XI. 677 and *L.P.* XII{1}. 1035. For the singing, see SP1/118, f. 254b (*L.P.* XII{1}. 1011) and SP1/112, fos. 244–244b (*L.P.* XI. 1319).

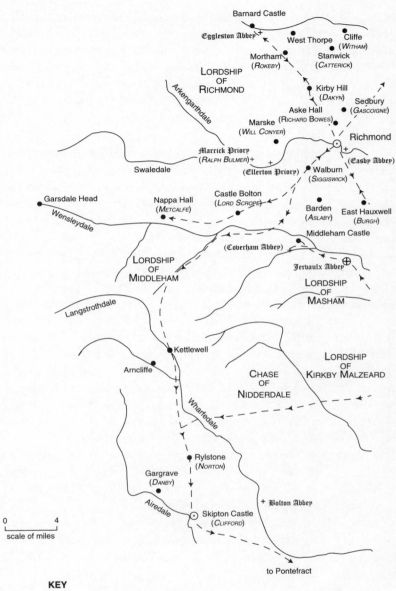

Barnard Castle

Eggleston Abbey +

West Thorpe

Cliffe
(*Witham*)

Mortham
(*Rokeby*)

Stanwick
(*Catterick*)

LORDSHIP
OF
RICHMOND

Kirby Hill
(*Dakyn*)

Sedbury
(*Gascoigne*)

Arkengarthdale

Aske Hall
(*Richard Bowes*)

Marske
(*Will Conyer*)

Richmond

Marrick Priory
(*Ralph Bulmer*) +

+

Walburn
(*Siggiswick*)

+ (*Easby Abbey*)

Swaledale

(*Ellerton Priory*)

Garsdale Head

Nappa Hall
(*Metcalfe*)

Castle Bolton
(*Lord Scrope*)

Barden
(*Aslaby*)

East Hauxwell
(*Burgh*)

Wensleydale

Middleham Castle

(*Coverham Abbey*)

Jervaulx Abbey ⊕

LORDSHIP
OF
MIDDLEHAM

LORDSHIP
OF
MASHAM

Langstrothdale

LORDSHIP
OF
KIRKBY MALZEARD

Kettlewell

Arncliffe

CHASE
OF
NIDDERDALE

Wharfedale

Rylstone
(*Norton*)

Gargrave
(*Danby*)

+ Bolton Abbey

Airedale

Skipton Castle
(*Clifford*)

0   4
scale of miles

to Pontefract

KEY

• Mortham
(*Rokeby*)

Names of gentlemen involved
shown thus below the name of
their country seat

○   Rebel assembly points

+ Jervaulx Abbey   Religious houses
(in brackets if dissolved)

– – ⟶ – ⟶   Rebel Movements

Map 4 The Richmondshire uprising

towns of Ripon and Bedale and their surrounding areas.[8] Unresisted, the uprising by 14th October had become a large-scale rebellion.

Sir Christopher Danby as lord of Masham, Lord Latimer as steward of the Liberty of Ripon, the Earl of Cumberland as steward of the lordship of Kirkby Malzeard, Lord Conyers as steward of the honours of Richmond and Middleham and Lord Scrope, the reversionary holder of Conyers' stewardship, had the responsibility for restoring order in the region. Only Lord Conyers was out of the country.[9] The others were at hand: the Earl of Cumberland at Skipton Castle and within marching distance of Nidderdale and Kirkby Malzeard; Danby at Thorpe Perrow, close to Masham; Lord Latimer at Snape Castle, within striking distance of Masham and Ripon; Lord Scrope at Castle Bolton in Wensleydale. But none of them proceeded against the uprising. Although warned by the Archbishop of York on 5th or 6th October to watch out for trouble in the Liberty of Ripon, Lord Latimer was apparently caught unprepared on 13th October. Along with Danby, his brother-in-law, he simply submitted.[10] As for the Earl of Cumberland, in response to the news of rebellion in the dales, he had decided by 12th October to disobey the king's orders to go to Hexham to deal with the insurrection there, but then, it seems, he was not prepared to do anything else without instruction from the government, apart from alerting his vassals, the Metcalfes of Nappa Hall in Wensleydale and the Middletons of Middleton, close to Dent.[11] Royal instructions then arrived and, following them, he raised some troops, but he still failed to march into Nidderdale and Kirkby Malzeard.[12] As for Scrope, he fled in a north-westerly direction to Hillbeck, which is close to Brough in the barony of Westmorland,

8 See *L.P.* XI. 677; *L.P.* XII{1}. 29{2}, 1035, 1326; SP1/118, f. 254b (*L.P.* XII{1}. 1011). In describing the Richmondshire host, Aske claimed that it included men from Ripon (Bateson, pp. 336–7). Possibly the uprising began at Ripon horse-fair, held from 10th October to 14th October (see below, p. 148).

9 Conyers was in London, under the restraint of an injunction not to pass beyond seven miles from the city (*L.P.* XI. 657). The restraint had been lifted, upon Norfolk's advice by late November (*L.P.* XII{2}. 14; Stapulton, p. 103). Returning to Richmondshire, Conyers broke his promise to the king (*L.P.* XII{2}. 14) and joined the rebellion (see Bateson, p. 340).

10 *L.P.* XI. 1022, p. 465. The plan to take them was concocted on 13th October [A. G. Dickens (ed.), *The Clifford Letters of the Sixteenth Century* (Surtees Society, 172 {London, 1962}), p. 112]. On 14th October they submissively attended the rebel assembly in Richmond (see *L.P.* XII{1}. 789).

11 P.R.O. E.36/118, fos. 170-170b (*L.P.* XI. 712); *L.P.* XI. 604.

12 R. W. Hoyle, "The first earl of Cumberland: a reputation reassessed", *Northern History*, 22 (1986), p. 83, n. 79.

and eventually joined his father-in-law, the Earl of Cumberland, in Skipton Castle.[13] Licensed in this way to flourish, the uprising did so.

At this stage the revolt was, in *genre*, a rising of the commons. The cause was that of the commons, as was evident in the oath "to be true to God, the king and the commonty" which the rebels imposed upon gentlemen and clerics.[14] And the initiative and momentum came from the commonalty. Thus, Robert Asporner, whom the rebels expelled from his house in the king's park of Cotescue beside Middleham and victimised because of his involvement with the dissolution of Coverham Abbey, complained to Cromwell "of the commoners of the said shire" for spoiling his goods and for depriving him of the office of park keeper.[15] On 12th October, a day after the outbreak of the revolt, Lord Scrope reported to the Earl of Cumberland: "the commons in Mashamshire and Nidderdale rose and came to Coverham Abbey and Middleham and burned beacons of fire yesternight". Fearing that they would come to Castle Bolton and either subject him to their oath "to be true unto them" or take him with them, he resolved to go into hiding.[16] Two days later he had gone, fleeing, according to his wife, in order to thwart "the commons of Richmondshire" and their plan to take the leading gentlemen of the region or their heirs. Her intention was to follow suit but, in the meantime, fearing that the commons would take her son in the absence of her husband, she hid him, along with his nurse, in a poor man's house.[17] This impression, reported at the time, adds some credibility to the evidence unearthed by the government in early 1537. Thus, when examined, Adam Sedber, the abbot of Jervaulx Abbey, told of a rampant commons who visited the abbey, presumably to requisition its horses, but also to subject him to the oath. As they arrived on 11th October he left by a back door and, accompanied by his father, took refuge on Witton Fell,

---

13 Dickens, *Clifford Letters*, p. 112.
14 Two variants have survived of the oath used by the Richmondshire uprising. The one quoted [see SP1/117, f. 216 (*L.P.* XII{1}. 789)] was put to John Dakyn; another, "to be true to God, to the faith of the church, to our sovereign lord the king and to the commonwealth of this realm", was proposed in the Captain Poverty letter [SP1/117, f. 54 (*L.P.* XII{1}. 687{2})]. Since the letter was perceived as "in the name of the commons" (ibid.), and since Lord Scrope feared on 12th October that the commons would make him swear an oath "to be true unto them"(see n. 16), it seems that, in this context, "commonty" and "commonwealth" meant the interest or cause of the commons.
15 SP1/120 (*L.P.* XII{1}. 1326).
16 SP1/110, f. 40b (*L.P.* XI. 677).
17 Dickens, *Clifford Letters*, p. 112.

a mile or so to the east. For doing so he was branded a traitor to the commons.[18] James Rokeby, a gentleman lawyer, official of the Court of Augmentations and would-be cleric, who allegedly sought to flee from trouble but continually landed in the thick of it, also presented the uprising as a movement of the commons. As a result of the bills issued by the Richmondshire rebels and nailed to church doors in neighbouring Cleveland, he claimed: "the commons arose in every part" whilst "the gentlemen did flee and hid them and was constrained to come unto them".[19]

In its earliest stages the revolt was led by commoners. On the first day, when the rebels came to Jervaulx and went on to restore Coverham Abbey, the captains were identified as three commoners of substance, all from the lordship of Masham: Ninian Staveley, Thomas Lobley and Edward Middleton.[20] However, they quickly disappeared from view as the revolt adopted gentry leaders, resurfacing as captains, however, when the revolt recommenced in January 1537.[21] By 15th October the rebels at Jervaulx, where they still awaited the return of Sedber, were under the leadership of two gentlemen. And when Sedber was persuaded to return to Jervaulx by the threat to burn it down, Leonard Burgh, whom Sedber described as one of the ringleaders, drew a dagger as the abbot entered the hall and had to be restained from attacking him.[22] He was a minor gentleman, aged twenty- seven, who probably lived at Leeming, two miles north-east of Bedale and part of a cluster of Coverham Abbey properties.[23] It was Burgh who administered to Sedber the oath.[24] Moreover, once Sedber was in the hall, William Aslaby (described by Sedber as chief captain of those parts) cried: "Whoreson traitor, where has thou been" and ordered: "Get a block

18 *L.P.* XII{1}. 1035.
19 SP1/118, f. 255 (*L.P.* XII{1}. 1011). The editors of *L. P.* failed to identify this deponent, but he was the younger brother of Thomas Rokeby of Mortham Tower, Richmondshire. As an auditor of the Court of Augmentations, James had been officially involved in the dissolution of Coverham Abbey (*L.P.* XII{1}. 1326). In late November he was appointed, along with Dakyn, to represent the Richmondshire commons at the York council (*L.P.* XII{1}. 1011).
20 *L.P.* XII{1}. 29{2}, 1011, 1035. Staveley was revealed in the 1535 muster returns for Hang East as coming from the town of Masham. He was represented as a horsed and harnessed billman. Lobley came from Healey within the Lordship of Masham, as did Middleton. Lobley was listed as a harnessed footman with bill; Middleton as a harnessed horseman with bow. See E36/44, fos. 15b and 17.
21 *L.P.* XII{1}. 1012.
22 *L.P.* XII{1}. 1035.
23 It seems that at the time he lived at Leeming and by 1544 had moved to East Hauxwell (see *Star Ch. Yorkshire*, III, p. 91 n. 2, 92 and 107).
24 *L.P.* XII{1}. 1035.

to strike off his head upon".[25] In behaving in this extreme fashion, Burgh and Aslaby were playing to the gallery of a very agitated commons. Sedber had annoyed the rebels not simply by fleeing but by failing to return until after the great assembly, held in Richmond on 15th October.[26] Aslaby was a minor gentleman from Barden in the parish of West Hauxwell, half way between Richmond and Middleham.[27]

How or why Burgh and Aslaby became involved is not clear; no evidence indicates that either was obliged to participate by the commons. Aslaby had been a member of the Yorkshire jury which earlier in the year acquitted William Wycliffe of the charge of murder and then, on the recommendation of Christopher Jennings, king's sergeant-at-law, was summoned to appear before the Council in Star Chamber and was heavily fined, an action which Aske alleged to be one of the grievances behind the pilgrimage of grace; but there is no good reason to believe that his involvement simply sprang from that fact. After all, eight of the twelve jurors did not become involved in the pilgrimage.[28] What is clear is that their leadership was soon subsumed under another level of captaincy, the result of the convergence of various strands of revolt; so much so that after 15th October this particular uprising appeared to be under the leadership of Lord Latimer of Snape Castle and Sir Christopher Danby, lord of Masham. Both had been impressed to participate following a decision to involve them, made by the rebels on 13th October.[29] Upon the order of the commons, they, along with other gentlemen and clerics, had come to Richmond on 14th October, probably after the rebels had visited their houses and

---

25 Ibid.
26 No mention is made of Sedber attending the Richmond assembly. His own account suggests that he was taken, via Richmond, from Jervaulx into the palatinate, catching up with the rebel host at Oxen-le-Fields (see *L.P.* XII{1}. 1035). Dakyn simply said that the Mashamshire men took him by force into the palatinate (see *L.P.* XII{1}. 786/ii{11}).
27 See SP1/104, f. 295 (*L.P.* X.1257/xii). In the muster returns for 1535, Aslaby was listed as horsed and harnessed with one horsed and harnessed servant; in contrast, Leonard Burgh was listed as being horsed and harnessed but without servants; whilst Lord Latimer was shown as providing forty servants horsed and harnessed, and Sir Christopher Danby supplied twenty-two servants horsed and harnessed. See E36/44, fos. 39 and 16–16b.
28 SP1/104, f. 295 (*L.P.* X. 1257/xii) and see below. Besides Aslaby, the jurors who became participants in the 1536 rebellion were George Lumley, Oswald Wilstrop, and Thomas de la River.
29 Dickens, *Clifford Letters*, p. 112.

had subjected them to the oath.[30] Within the next three days they emerged as leaders of the commons.[31]

Two other figures came to the fore in the opening stages of this revolt. One was Thomas Hutton. The government regarded him as such a major ringleader that it excepted him from its provisional pardon of 2nd November.[32] He came from either Bedale or Snape.[33] Like Staveley, Middleton and Lobley, he was a commoner who resurfaced as a rebel leader in 1537.[34] All that is known about his involvement in the rebellions of 1536 is that on 14th October he was very busy sticking exhortatory bills to church doors in the vicinity of Richmond.[35] Finally, there was Mr Soulby who made his mark on the revolt by taking charge at the Richmond assembly of 14th October and by persuading them to meet again the following day.[36] George Soulby, a minor gentleman, lived at Ellerton-on-Swale, leasing the manor from the Scropes of Castle Bolton.[37] He surfaced but this once, and no more is heard of him. In all likelihood he had come to Richmond on 14th, in response to the order of the commons. The 14th October was a day of extreme tension in Richmond. True Danby, Latimer and other gentlemen had come in, but the Bowes, whom a contingent of rebels had gone to fetch, failed to arrive and likewise the rebels, operating from Jervaulx and bent on taking the abbot, remained absent. In this fraught situation Soulby asserted himself, convincing the commons that it was best to postpone the great assembly until the following day.[38]

By this time another revolt had broken out in Richmondshire. Undoubtedly inspired by the Masham/Kirkby/Nidderdale revolt, the men of Swaledale, Arkengarthdale and the town of Richmond

30 The procedure is evident from Lady Clifford's account (ibid.); and from the depositions of Dakyn (*L.P.* XII{1}. 789), Lumley (*L.P.* XII{1}. 369), Percy (*L.P.* XII{1}. 393), Rokeby (*L.P.* XII{1}. 1011) and Neville (*L.P.* XII{1} 29). For Danby and Latimer, see SP1/118, f. 254b (*L.P.* XII{1}. 1011); SP1.'117, f. 216 (*L.P.* XII{1}. 789).
31 *L.P.* XII{1}. 29 {2}.
32 *L.P.* XI. 955.
33 For Bedale, see *L.P.* XII{1}. 786/ ii{8}. For Snape, see *L.P.* XI. 955. In the Hang East muster return for 1535, Hutton was listed as a harnessed billman for Snape but not as one of Lord Latimer's household servants. He may have been a Latimer tenant. See E36/44, f. 16.
34 *L.P.* XII{1}. 1012.
35 *L.P.* XII{1}. 786/ii{8}; SP1/117, f. 216 (*L.P.* XII{1}. 789).
36 SP1/117, f. 216 (*L.P.* XII{1}. 789).
37 *Yorkshire Chancery Proc.*, pp. 37–8. In the Gilling East muster return for 1535, George Soulby was recorded as being, like Aslaby, horsed and harnessed with one horsed and harnessed servant. See E36/44, f. 59.
38 SP1/117, f. 216 (*L.P.* XII{1}. 789).

rose on 13th October: that is, within two days of the occupation of Jervaulx Abbey.[39] Again, the revolt was a movement of the commons which enlisted support by obliging gentlemen and clergy to swear fidelity to God, the king and the commonalty and branded the non-cooperative as traitors to the commons.[40] However, its initial leader and stirrer was a minor gentleman, Henry Wycliffe, a servant and brother-in-law to Sir Ralph Bulmer of Marrick. Leland noticed him on his travels and identified him as "a mean gentleman", living a mile or so from Richmond along the Swale.[41] Apparently, Wycliffe "was the first riser within Swaledale and not past six or seven persons with him, and then went to Richmond when he had increased his numbers and was with Ralph Gower and they two raised Richmond and went towards Barne [Barnard Castle]".[42] Yet the revolt was not simply his work. In Richmond itself support was mustered by its bailiffs, Ralph Gower and Charles Johnson, both of them commoners of substance, and the revolt in Arkengarthdale was led by a yeoman, Anthony Peacock, bailiff of the lordship of Arkengarthdale, who was also involved in the rebels' march to Barnard Castle on the morning of 14th October.[43] As well as marching on Barnard Castle, this particular revolt restored Easby Abbey which, like Coverham, had been dissolved the previous June.[44]

The two revolts quickly merged: on 13th October a joint meeting was held in Richmond when the rebels decided to send out parties to bring in the gentlemen or their sons and heirs and otherwise to destroy their property; and the following day "a great multitude of Masham", along with the rebels from the Richmond area who had not gone to Barnard Castle, assembled in Richmond to receive the submitting gentlemen.[45] Also on 14th October the rebels composed their first formal statement of grievance, a letter condemning the dissolution

39 L.P. XII{1}. 786/ii{7}.
40 L.P. XII{1}. 788–9.
41 L. T. Smith (ed.), *The Itinerary of John Leland in or about the Years 1535–1543* (London, 1909), part VII, p. 28. The place of Wicliff that Leland mentioned is probably Whitcliffe-upon-Swale (see T. D. Whitaker, *A History of Richmondshire in the North Riding of the County of York* {London, 1823}, II, pp. 41–2). The 1535 muster returns for Gilling West presented Henry Wycliffe as Bulmer's servant and as an archer. No mention was made of horse or harness. See E36/44, f. 12.
42 B.L. Cottonian MS., Caligula B. I, f. 156 (*L.P.* XII{1}. 775).
43 *L.P.* XII{1}. 29{2}, 775, 786/ii{7}, 788, 789. For Johnson and Gower, see R. Fieldhouse and B. Jennings, *A History of Richmond and Swaledale* (London 1978), pp. 275–6. Peacock was listed in the 1535 muster returns for Gilling West as a horsed and harnessed archer. See E36/44, f. 12.
44 *L.P.* XII{1}. 29{2}, 491; P.R.O. SC6/Henry VIII/7454.
45 Dickens, *Clifford Letters*, p. 112; *L.P.* XII{1}. 789.

of the lesser monasteries and proclaiming that the rebels' cause was the defence of the commonwealth.[46] In the course of the day this letter was nailed to church doors and, responding to it, supporters poured in. Then on 15th October a third joint meeting was held, attended by 10,000 commons and the gentlemen of the region.[47] On this occasion the contingent that had gone to Barnard Castle returned with their spoils: three members of the Bowes family and Thomas Rokeby, the brother of James.[48] On the same day the rebels accepted as their chief captain Robert Bowes of East Cowton in Richmondshire who, as a lawyer and the younger son of a Yorkshire gentry family, was of similar standing to both Robert Aske and William Stapulton. But his family was more important than theirs and he was much more successful than either of them, having served as J.P. for the border counties, the palatinate and Yorkshire as well as on the Duke of Richmond's council. Unlike them he had also some military experience, from fighting on the northern border. Also unlike them he was a man of some reputation prior to the uprising. Early in 1537 Westmorland and Norfolk presented him as "not only much esteemed but . . . a wise, hardy man" who "both for war and peace hath not his fellow in these north parts of his degree" and therefore argued that it was vitally important that the king should seek to win him over.[49]

At the same assembly, having raised Richmondshire, the rebels decided to enlist the neighbouring regions. A letter was dispatched into Cleveland ordering its inhabitants to attend a muster just across the Tees at Oxen-le-Fields on 16th October.[50] About the same time, further letters were composed requiring support from the border counties of Northumberland, Westmorland and Cumberland and from the wapentake of Pickering Lythe.[51] These letters, each accompanied by a list of articles which the recipients were required to maintain on oath, were sent out under the signature of Captain Poverty and in the name of the commons, a procedure inspired partly

46 SP1/117, f. 204b (*L.P.* XII{1}. 786 /ii); *L.P.* XII{1}. 1011.
47 SP1/117, f. 212 (*L.P.* XII{1}. 788). Since at this stage the host could have been recruited only from the Richmondshire wapentakes of Gilling East and West, Hang East and West, and Hallikeld, and from the West Riding wapentake of Claro, this must have been a gross exaggeration. For the military capacity of the region, see Appendix I.
48 Cottonian MS. Caligula B. I, fos. 156–156b (*L.P.* XII{1}. 775).
49 SP1/117, f. 205 (*L.P.* XII{1}. 786/ii); Bindoff, I, pp. 471–83; SP1/118, fos. 155–155b (*L.P.* XII{1}. 919) and *L.P.* XII{2}. 100.
50 SP1/117, f. 218 (*L.P.* XII{1}. 789); *L.P.* XII{1}. 1011.
51 Bush, "Captain Poverty", p. 18. For the letter to Pickering Lythe, see below, p. 152.

by the appearance, presumably at the great Richmond assembly on the
15th October, of "a very simple poor man" whom the rebels named
Lord Poverty and who, Christ-like, declared that "he would die in the
matter", and partly by the popular literary tradition associated with
Piers Plowman, the dual embodiment of Christ and the commons.[52] In
addition, the Richmondshire host decided to march deep into the
palatinate of Durham in order to raise the bishopric men.

The two strands of revolt in Richmondshire clearly had much in
common. Each restored a dissolved abbey[53]. Moreover, whilst offending the society of orders in relying upon the initiative of the commonalty and by insisting that clerics should fight, both revolts were keen to
operate within its basic framework, drawing in the gentlemen, obliging
them to be "true to God, the king and the commonty" and employing
them as captains.[54] By this means the rebels secured a respectable
organisation and deprived the government of its normal means of
local control.

The Richmondshire rebels rose after learning that the rebellion of
the commons, having started in Lincolnshire, had crossed the Humber
into Yorkshire. This news passed quickly up through the North
Riding and into the bishopric of Durham.[55] Instrumental in bringing
it to Richmondshire was John Dakyn, rector of Kirby-by-Richmond
and the vicar general of the archdeaconry of Richmond, who fled to
York when he heard that Aske had crossed the Humber from Lincolnshire, probably on 8th October. Near York he met James Rokeby and
told him that the Yorkshire rebels were marching on the city. The two
of them fled northwards through Boroughbridge, Topcliffe and War-
laby to Yafforth, where Rokeby's mother lived, and on to Richmond.
This news followed that imparted by a letter from the Archbishop of
York who had dutifully alerted the officials of his Liberties of Beverley,
York and Ripon about the Lincolnshire uprising and the military
preparations being taken against it by the Earl of Shrewsbury, calling

---

52 Bush, op. cit., p. 17. The letters and articles must have been composed at one of
    the Richmond assemblies and, since Dakyn was excused the journey into
    Durham, then in all likelihood it was the one held on 15th October [see SP1/
    117, f. 218 (*L.P.* XII{1}. 789)]. Books 6 and 19 of Langland's poem provide a
    users' guide to the pilgrimage of grace, with book 6 proposing a pilgrimage led by
    the archetypal commoner, Piers Plowman, and book 19 presenting the allegorical
    figure of Grace counselling Piers "the commons to summon" and offering to give
    them "weapons to fight with that will never fail" for the battle against "the
    swarm of false prophets, flatterers and glib theologians" who "make themselves
    the confessors of kings and earls".
53 See above, p. 137 (Coverham) and p. 145 (Easby).
54 For the commonalty's attitude towards the clerics, see *L.P.* XII{1}. 789. For its
    attitude towards the gentlemen, see Dickens, *Clifford Letters*, p. 112.
55 *L.P.* XII{1}. 29 {2}.

upon them to see that order was maintained. Provocatively, he had
ordered the letter to be proclaimed at Ripon fair. This fair, one of the
major horse-fairs of the north, was held two days either side of St.
Wilfred's Day, that is, between the 10th October and 14th October.[56]
It is possible that the movement of Masham and Kirkby Malzeard
rebels which reached Jervaulx Abbey on the evening of 11th October
had its beginnings at the Minster fair in Ripon and was incited by the
news imparted in the archbishop's proclaimed letter.

Under examination in early 1537, Friar Pickering suggested that
the Richmondshire uprising was contrived by Aske, informing his
interrogators that "there were letters sent by Aske unto the far
parts, that is to say, unto Swaledale and Wensleydale to cause the
people to arise, the tenor whereof was that the people should appear
on a certain day in defensible array upon pain of death".[57] But this is
misleading since the letter in question, having been dispatched from
Pontefract, could only have reached its destination seven days or so
after the start of the Richmondshire uprising.[58] Whilst in York (i.e.
between 16th and 18th October), Aske had produced several manifestos which were spread abroad to raise support, but by this time the
Richmondshire rebels had already formed their host and marched into
the palatinate.[59] The first known communication to reach them from
Aske arrived about 20th October at Spennymoor.[60] However, by this
time the rebels had already worked out their plan of action to which
they stuck although it went contrary to Aske's instructions.[61] Whereas
he had ordered them to come as soon as possible to Pontefract, a
large contingent marched instead upon Skipton Castle.[62] Nonetheless, the Richmondshire uprising was undoubtedly fired by the
news of what was happening in south Yorkshire; and the timing of

56 For the news into Richmondshire, see *L.P.* XII{1}. 788 and SP1/118, f. 254 (*L.P.*
    XII{1}. 1011). For the archbishop's letter, see SP1/119, fos. 1–1b (*L.P.* XII{1}.
    1022). For the dating of the Ripon fair, see *Memorials of the Church of SS. Peter
    and Wilfred, Ripon*, I (Surtees Society, 74 {1881}), p. 53.
57 SP1/118, f. 280 (*L.P.* XII{1}. 1021).
58 Bateson, p. 569.
59 See above, pp. 101–2.
60 The letter was sent not before 20th October when Pontefract Castle was yielded,
    and, according to Aske, not until after his meeting with Lancaster Herald on 21st
    October (Bateson, p. 569). However, his summons to the Stapulton host reached
    it on 20th October (see Stapulton, p. 99); and the likelihood is that the letter to
    the Bowes host was sent at the same time. For its arrival in Spennymoor, see *L.P.*
    XII{1}. 29.
61 For evidence that their plans were worked out by 18th October, see SP1/117, f.
    218 (*L.P.* XII{1}. 789).
62 See below, p. 153.

the outbreak and the form the revolt took – a rising of the commons
bonded by an oath and organised as a host – were directed by it.

The raising of the palatinate

It made sense to push southwards, both to fulfil the basic aim of
confronting the government and to link up with the Aske host in its
march upon York. And this is what was expected: on 14th October the
mayor of York informed the king that the city was threatened not only
from the south but also by the commons of Richmondshire.[63] But
throughout the first week of the uprising, the Richmondshire rebels
marched northwards. The first stage of revolt, in which the men of
Mashamshire and Kirkbyshire marched the ten miles from Jervaulx to
Richmond and the men of Richmond marched the ten miles to
Barnard Castle, was followed by a second stage in which the rebels,
having mustered in Richmond on 15th October to form one large host,
now marched into the palatinate of Durham, where they held three
musters.

The first muster met at Oxen-le-Fields on 16th October with the
principal aim of joining up with the Clevelanders.[64] The second was
held in Bishop Auckland on the following day. As George Lumley
recorded, it was a huge gathering of 8–10,000, led by an impressive
array of gentlemen. Present were Lord Latimer, Sir Christopher
Danby, Robert Bowes, Sir Ralph Bulmer of Marrick with a company
from Swaledale, the adolescent George Bowes of Streatlam with a
company of a thousand from Stainmore, and Sir James Strangways
of West Harlsey with a company of a thousand from Cleveland.[65]
Whilst the bishop's palace was being sacked, presumably because he
had fled to Norham Castle the night before, bands of Richmondshire
rebels combed the surrounding countryside, visiting the seats of
leading families and persuading them, with threats to spoil their
property, to support the uprising. Thus George Lumley was visited
at Sedgefield, his father, Lord Lumley's house in the palatinate, by
"certain soldiers out of Richmondshire" and brought to be sworn at

---

63 *L.P.* XI. 704.
64 *L.P.* XII{1}. 789, 1035. See Map 5.
65 SP1/115, f. 212 (*L.P.* XII{1}. 369). The Yorkshire areas from which the
   Richmondshire host had been recruited (i.e. Birdforth and Allertonshire as well
   as the wapentakes listed above in n. 47) could have provided no more than 4,700
   troops (see Appendix I). If Lumley's figure was realistic, large numbers of troops
   must already have been raised from the palatinate.

Bishop Auckland, allegedly compelled by threats to spoil his father's property.[66] The third assembly was held at Spennymoor on 18th and 19th October.[67] By this time William Conyers of Marske in Swaledale had joined the revolt and further Clevelanders, accompanied possibly by men from the lordship of Topcliffe, had arrived led by Roger Lascelles of Breckenbrough Castle near Kirby Wiske and Roland Place of Hornby, as well as large numbers of palatinate men under Sir Thomas Hilton and Lord Lumley.[68] The reason for holding the assembly at Spennymoor was its proximity to the Neville seat of Brancepeth.

The journey north was in preparation for the journey south. Besides the recruitment of support, it had two other objectives. One was to ensure the defence of the frontier adjoining Scotland. For this purpose the rebels wrote to the inhabitants of Northumberland, Cumberland and Westmorland, ordering them to take the oath and to stop the Scots from seizing the opportunity, created by the insurrection, to ravage northern England.[69] Because of the need to defend the frontier against Scotland, the three border counties were not required by the Richmondshire rebels to provide recruits for their host.[70]

The other aim was to secure the support of the great border magnates. With the Percies this was no problem: Ingram Percy promptly complied with the letter sent to him, swore the oath and, after summoning the Northumberland gentry to Alnwick Castle, obliged them to follow suit. Simply in this manner the Percy interest in Northumberland had been attached to the rebellion by 21st October.[71] The compliance of the Nevilles was less immediate, presumably because much more was required of the Earl of Westmorland. Whereas the Northumbrian affinity of the Percy family was expected merely to keep watch on the frontier, the Nevilles and their following were required to join the march south. The Earl of Westmorland was first approached by Robert Bowes on 17th October, when the rebels

66 SP1/115, fos. 212 and 218 (L.P. XII{1}. 369).
67 L.P. XII{1}. 29.
68 This can be construed from George Lumley's account [see SP1/115, fos. 218-218b (L.P. XII{1}. 369)], and from Marmaduke Neville's account, see L.P. XII{1}. 29 and 29{2}. Lumley was present at the Bishop Auckland muster but not at the Spennymoor gathering, having returned home to the East Riding on 18th October (SP1/115, fos. 212–212b). For the possibility that Topcliffe men accompanied Lascelles, see below, p. 164, 195.
69 Bush, "Captain Poverty", pp. 18–19.
70 Thus the Cumbrians were required to send no more than four substantial gentlemen, see SP1/117, f. 54b (L.P. XII{1}. 687 {2}). For Northumberland, see below.
71 SP1/116, f. 81 (L.P. XII{1}. 467).

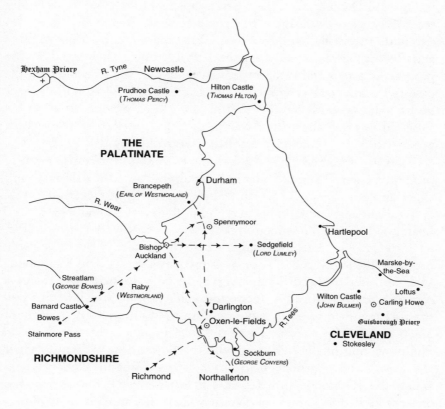

Hexham Priory   R. Tyne   Newcastle •

Prudhoe Castle •
(*Thomas Percy*)

Hilton Castle •
(*Thomas Hilton*)

**THE
PALATINATE**

Brancepeth
(*Earl of Westmorland*)

Durham •

R. Wear

⊙ Spennymoor

Bishop
Auckland ⊙

• Sedgefield
(*Lord Lumley*)

• Hartlepool

Streatlam
(*George Bowes*)

Raby •
(*Westmorland*)

Marske-by-
the-Sea •

Loftus •

Wilton Castle •
(*John Bulmer*)

⊙ Carling Howe

Barnard Castle •
Bowes •

Darlington •

Oxen-le-Fields ⊙

R. Tees

Guisborough Priory •

Stainmore Pass

CLEVELAND

• Stokesley

RICHMONDSHIRE

• Sockburn
(*George Conyers*)

Richmond •   Northallerton •

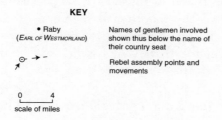
Map 5   The Durham uprising

from the North Riding were at Bishop Auckland but nothing came of it. On 18th October, with the rebels at Spennymoor, close to his family seat, the earl refused again to "come forth to them", in spite of a deputation from William Conyers, Christopher Danby, Roland Place and Robert Bowes. Finally, on the 19th October, when faced by the prospect of attack from an army of ten thousand, he came and took the oath to be true to the commons, but slipped out of serving in the host on its journey south by deputing his son, Lord Neville, to go in his stead. In this way, the host arrived in Pontefract on 22nd October with a leadership which included a thirteen-year-old boy.[72]

Between 15th and 20th October, the Richmondshire rebels actively promoted insurrection not only in Northumberland, the palatinate and Cleveland but also in the North Riding wapentake of Pickering Lythe, in Westmorland and Cumberland and in the West Riding lordships of Dent and Craven. Thus men in harness were sent to Pickering Lythe, on 16th October, reaching Seamer where the mother of the three Percy brothers lived and where Thomas Percy was staying. The Richmondshire outriders obliged Thomas Percy to take the oath, to become a captain and to attend a muster on the wolds beyong Spital. In this way the Richmondshire rebels had a hand in the formation of an army of 5,000 men which, under Thomas Percy, marched through York to Pontefract and finally joined up with the Bowes host to form together the van of the pilgrims' main army.[73] The Captain Poverty letter which the Richmondshire rebels sent across the Pennines inspired one revolt in the barony of Westmorland and another in Cumberland. Read at a succession of musters, it helped to raise a huge host which by the end of the month had marched on Carlisle.[74] Likewise, news of the Richmondshire uprising revived revolt in Dent, encouraged revolt in the barony of Kendal and helped to form the force which on 28th October took Lancaster.[75] In addition, the Richmondshire rebels contributed to revolt in Craven by their very presence: having marched into Durham to enlist the Earl of Westmorland and Lord Lumley, they marched on Skipton in an attempt to

72 *L.P.* XII{1}. 369; E36/118, f. 115 (*L.P.* XII{1}. 29); *L.P.* XII{1}. 849{17}. For the pressure upon the Earl of Westmorland and the requirement to send his son with St. Cuthbert's banner, see R. W. Hoyle, "Thomas Master's narrative of the pilgrimage of grace", *Northern History*, 21(1985), pp. 62–3 and 71.

73 That they were from the Richmondshire uprising is evident in the original MS, not in the *L.P.* summary [SP1/115, fos. 258b–259 (*L.P.* XII{1}. 393); *L.P.* XII{1}. 369; Bateson, pp. 336–7].

74 Bush, "Captain Poverty", p. 22. Also see below, pp. 328–9.

75 Bush, op. cit., p. 24. Also see below, pp. 251–3.

bring in two more peers, the Earl of Cumberland and his son-in-law, Lord Scrope of Bolton.

The march on Skipton Castle

On 18th October the Bowes host was divided into two separate armies.[76] One largely consisted of Clevelanders and Durham men; the other was composed of men from Richmondshire, Kirkby Malzeard, Nidderdale and Ripon.[77] The latter force, an army of 12,000 men, was led by the knights Christopher Danby, William Mallory and Ralph Bulmer, the gentlemen John and Richard Norton, Richard Bowes, Christopher Metcalf, Thomas Markenfield, William Ingilby and Christopher Wandesford and two burgesses of Richmond, Ralph Gower and Charles Johnson.[78] Whereas the first host responded to Aske and marched to Pontefract, the second host disobeyed him and laid siege to Skipton Castle. Given the time needed to get there from Spennymoor, via Wensleydale and along Bishopdale, it could not have reached Skipton before the 21st October.[79] The siege, which it started, either on 21st or 22nd October, continued until 27th October, when, in response to overtures from Aske, it marched to join the pilgrim host outside Doncaster but was stopped at Pontefract by news of the Truce.[80]

Why did this host direct itself against Skipton Castle? In one sense it derived from the rebels' policy of seeking to bind the magnates to the cause and of punishing the ones who refused to comply.[81] In all likelihood, the general hostility generated by the Earl of Cumberland resembled that shown towards the less accessible Earl of Derby. In springing from their failure to join the rebellion, it was political rather than social in motive.

76 See n. 61 for the division.
77 For the inclusion of Ripon men, see Bateson, pp. 336–7. Unless this army picked up recruits from other regions on its journey south, it must have been considerably smaller. See Appendix I.
78 *L.P.* XII{1}. 29{2}; *L.P.* XI. 928; Stapulton, p. 100; Bateson, op. cit., p. 337.
79 For the route, see *L.P.* XII{1}. 789 and Stapulton, p. 100.
80 Aske reckoned that on 25th October the host was "then coming forward" and was "at or nigh Pontefract" (see Bateson, p. 337). But on 26th October Cumberland suggested that the host was still besieging his castle (see Hoyle, "Thomas Master's narrative", p. 70). By 28th October the host had reached Pontefract (see *L.P.* XI. 928 and 1045). But that it had just arrived is evident in its absence from the front and in the failure of Lord Scrope, who accompanied the host from Skipton to Pontefract, to serve in the deputation which met Norfolk on Doncaster bridge late on 27th October (see Bateson, op. cit., p. 337).
81 Hoyle, "The first earl of Cumberland", p. 86.

The Earl of Cumberland had little connexion, landed or official, with Richmondshire, and, in the very early stages of the revolt, he admitted that Wensleydale was beyond his rule.[82] However, it was the rebels from Richmondshire rather than from Cleveland or Durham who were deputed to deal with him, probably because it was felt that, living closer to Skipton and being dalesmen familiar with the terrain, they were better qualified to root him out. But something else gave the Richmondshire men a special incentive for going to Skipton. This had nothing to do with Cumberland and everything to do with Scrope. Lord Scrope of Bolton, the leading aristocrat in Wensleydale, was known to have fled to Skipton Castle.[83] The plan for bringing in gentlemen, as formulated in Richmond on 13th October, had entailed a visit to Castle Bolton to take him.[84] The march on Skipton which aimed, according to John Dakyn, "to bring in" Cumberland and Scrope, seemed to be, from the Richmondshire men's point of view, an attempt to make up for the failure of this earlier plan.[85] Having taken the two peers, the rebels intended, according to William Stapulton, "after to repair to the host": that is, to join the pilgrims' army which, between 20th and 23rd, assembled at Pontefract and, between 23rd and 25th October, closed on Doncaster in order to confront the royal forces under Norfolk and Shrewsbury.[86]

Just as the men of Wensleydale and Swaledale had their own special reason for marching on Skipton, so had the rebels from the countryside north and west of Ripon. In these parts a hostility towards the Earl of Cumberland predated the rebellions of 1536. It derived from the conflicting claims of the Nortons and Cliffords to the stewardship of Kirkby Malzeard, from disputes between the same parties over the extent of the Cliffords' deer park, the forest of Barden, and from the rough treatment of Norton's tenants in the Craven manor of Rylstone by Cumberland, its overlord. Enmity, then, sprang from a feud between the Norton affinity and the Clifford family that had been underway for perhaps a decade prior to 1536, and originated in John Norton's marriage to the heiress of the Ratcliffe family which had brought into his possession a number of fiefs held of

---

82 L.P. XI. 604. For the repudiation of the Dodds' view that it was a social movement of tenants against an evil landlord (Dodds, I, p. 192), see Smith, *Land and Politics in the England of Henry VIII* (Oxford, 1970), pp. 200-202 and Hoyle, op. cit., pp. 78ff.
83 For evidence of his whereabouts, see Hoyle, op. cit., pp. 83–4 and n. 83.
84 Dickens, *Clifford Letters*, p. 112.
85 SP1/117, f. 218 (L.P. XII{1}. 789).
86 Stapulton, p. 100. Also see below, ch. X.

the Clifford family and located close to Skipton.[87] Intensifying the
enmity was the inexorable aggrandisement of the house of Clifford.
The family's traditional sphere of influence had been the barony of
Westmorland and the parts of Craven incorporated in the Honour of
Skipton.[88] Now, having secured the reversion of the stewardship of
Knaresborough Fee and possession of the stewardship of Kirkby
Malzeard with Nidderdale, the Clifford power base in the West Riding
was being considerably extended eastwards at a time when the family's
hold on Craven was much enlarged by its acquisition of the Percy Fee
and its political position had been spectacularly raised by the marriage
in 1535 of Cumberland's son and heir to a member of the royal family,
Eleanor Brandon, the daughter of Mary Tudor, the king's sister.[89]

The eastward expansion of the house of Clifford, coupled with the
westward expansion of the Nortons, had already led to battles between
the two families (the Nortons aided by their in-laws, the Mallorys and
the Wandesfords), notably on 17th April 1531 when sixty Clifford
supporters clashed with ninety Norton supporters in the vicinity of the
township of Kirkby Malzeard.[90] The siege of Skipton Castle in
October 1536 was for them a continuation of the struggle. On the
other hand, there is no reason to believe that the Nortons and their
followers joined the rebellion to continue their feud with the Cliffords.
Norton and Mallory, like Danby, were taken by the commons and
travelled north into the palatinate before descending upon Skipton.[91]
Moreover, Cumberland in his brief account of the siege presented it as
the work of the commons.[92] In going to Skipton rather than Pontefract,
the leadership, which seemed to lie with Ralph Bulmer, Richard Bowes
and Christopher Danby, was, in all likelihood, complying with the

87 Evident in a number of Star Chamber cases: see P.R.O. STAC2/27/35 and 143
   for the deer park; STAC2/18/164 and 27/135 for the stewardship of Kirkby
   Malzeard cum Nidderdale. All are partially printed in Star Ch. Yorkshire, II, pp.
   48–50 and ibid., III, pp. 200–202. For the reprisals taken against Norton's tenants
   in Rylstone, see ibid., IV, pp. 24–6. The disputes are discussed, so as to exculpate
   Cumberland, by Hoyle in "The first earl of Cumberland", pp. 73–4 and 80–1.
88 M. E. James, "The first earl of Cumberland (1493–1542) and the decline of
   northern feudalism", Northern History, 1 (1966), p. 44.
89 For the eastward expansion, see Hoyle, op. cit., pp. 71-2. In 1538 it proceeded a
   step further when Cumberland obtained the reversion of the stewardship of the
   Liberty of Ripon. For the marriage, see James, op. cit., p. 45.
90 The extent of the Norton following, with the names and locations of those
   involved in the fray, is given in P.R.O. KB9/516 m. 27 and 28.
91 Darcy reported that they were taken on 17th October (see L.P. XI. 760{2}). That
   they went to Spennymoor is suggested by Stapulton's remark that they came to
   Skipton via Wensleydale with Danby (Stapulton, p. 100). If they had gone to
   Skipton straight from home they would have travelled via Pateley Bridge.
92 L.P. XI. 927.

rank and file rather than placing 12,000 men at the disposal of the Nortons for the pursuit of a private vendetta.[93]

The siege of Skipton was a mixture of success and failure. The castle proved impregnable. Cumberland remained untaken, unsworn and unpunished. The rebels only managed to prevent him operating as a military threat behind the rebel lines and to rob his parks, take his cattle, sack his houses at Barden and Carleton and to destroy some of his estate records.[94] On the other hand, the rebels succeeded in persuading Lord Scrope to switch sides. In his Narrative Aske indicated that Scrope had joined the pilgrimage by 25th October.[95] This was confirmed by Darcy in a letter of 31st October which, in relating what had happened in Pontefract on 28th October, denoted Lord Scrope as a leader of the Richmondshire host.[96] In all likelihood, other gentlemen followed suit. Cumberland found that, after raising forces for the king as he was commissioned to do, many deserted him upon the approach of the rebel army.[97] Within the ranks of the Richmondshire host were men who normally would have served the Cliffords but who joined the opposition not because of any animus against the earl but to save their own persons and property. The presence in the Richmondshire host of Thomas Markenfield is perhaps to be explained in this way.[98] In addition,whilst besieging Skipton Castle, the Richmondshire host undoubtedly enlarged itself, picking up support from the Craven region and possibly from the barony of Westmorland, so much so that although reckoned at 12,000 when it left Spennymoor, it was calculated at 20,000 when it reached Pontefract.[99]

93 Of these leaders, Bowes was a brother-in-law of Cumberland. Moreover, like Norton, Danby had become a Clifford vassal, holding a fief of the earl at Gargrave, close to Skipton, as a result of marriage (see James, op. cit., p. 51). But in Danby's case there is no evidence of a feuding relationship. The acquisition of Clifford fiefs by Danby and Norton marked an erosion of the Cliffords' feudal power base since both were from outside the Clifford affinity, and remained so.

94 L.P. XI. 927.

95 Bateson, p. 337.

96 L.P. XI. 928.

97 Hoyle, "The first earl of Cumberland", p. 83 n. 79 and pp. 86–7.

98 Markenfield, a Clifford relative, took the Clifford side in the earlier Norton/ Clifford conflict (see Hoyle, op. cit., pp. 72 and 80–81). Ingilby might have switched sides also, since, as with Markenfield, there is no evidence of his being involved in the Richmondshire uprising prior to the siege of Skipton. For their involvement in the siege, see Stapulton, p. 100.

99 The figure of 12,000 is given by Marmaduke Neville (see L.P. XII{1}. 29), presumably based on his experience of the Spennymoor assembly, and by Aske for 25th October (see Bateson, op. cit., p. 336). The figure of 20,000 is given by Darcy for the force that he encountered on 28th Oct. (L.P. XI. 928). The same host claimed to be 30,000 strong [see SP1/110 (L.P. XII. 928)]. Norfolk accepted this estimate (see Hoyle, "Thomas Master's narrative", p. 71). For the possibility of the presence of the Westmorlanders, see below, p. 302.

The march to Pontefract

The other host was mainly composed of men from the palatinate and from the Cleveland wapentakes of Allertonshire and Langbaurgh.[100] Whilst incited and directed by the Richmondshire uprising there is no reason to believe that revolt in these two regions was simply ordered into existence by outsiders. Nor was it simply created by the gentlemen who served as its captains. Like the revolts along the Swale and Ure, those in Durham and Cleveland were sustained by a strong popular impetus.

In the palatinate this was made evident in the adventures of James Rokeby, George Lumley and his father, and Francis Bigod, between 15th and 20th October. Having been driven by a storm at sea to take refuge in Hartlepool, Bigod was disturbed that night by the ringing of the common bell and an assembly of commons bent on taking him captive; and so he fled.[101] Rokeby, in seeking to escape rebellion in the North Riding planned to travel overland to Newcastle but as the palatinate rose in revolt he was obliged to remain in Yorkshire.[102] In fleeing from the rebels around Sedgefield in the palatinate, the Lumleys managed to reach Newcastle but, finding the commons of that town sympathetic of revolt, they left, the father to stay with Sir Thomas Hilton at Hilton Castle, the son returning to his father's house at Sedgefield. There he was taken by Richmondshire rebels and brought to the muster at Bishop Auckland.[103] As in Richmondshire, helping to generate revolt was the passivity of the county establishment whose members either fled or did nothing to resist the commons. Of the largest landlords, the Bishop of Durham fled to Norham Castle and the Earl of Westmorland remained inactive at Brancepeth until 19th October when he submitted and took the oath.[104] Of the county families, Lord Lumley and Hilton fled and then succumbed, in all likelihood at Spennymoor on 19th October, while the Bowes of Streatlam, having been taken by the Richmondshire men in Barnard Castle, became rebel captains.[105] As for Sir George Conyers of Sockburn, he fled at the first opportunity to the sanctity of Scarborough Castle.[106]

---

100 Bateson, p. 336. For Cleveland, see below, pp. 158–9.
101 SP1/116, f. 199 (L.P. XII{1}. 578).
102 SP1/118 f. 255 (L.P. XII{1}. 1011).
103 SP1/115, fos. 212 and 218–218b (L.P. XII{1}. 369).
104 The bishop fled on the night of 16th October [SP1/115, f. 218 (L.P. XII{1}. 369)]. For Westmorland, see above, p. 150–2.
105 For Lumley and Hilton, see above, n. 68. For the Bowes, see above, p. 146.
106 Stapulton, p. 92. The composition of the county establishment is given by M. E. James, Family, Lineage and Civil Society: a Study of Society, Politics and Mentality in the Durham Region, 1500–1640 (Oxford, 1974), p. 30.

Undoubtedly several of the recruited families held grudges against the government.[107] But their involvement largely came of the pressure brought upon them by the army out of Richmondshire.

Support for the uprising poured in from the palatinate at the musters held on 17th October at Bishop Auckland and 18th/19th October at Spennymoor.[108] The extent of this support, and its responsiveness, coupled with the initial unwillingness of the leading families, suggest a popular movement liberated by the presence of the host from Richmondshire. As with other revolts, the uprising in Durham had as one of its leaders a commoner – Henry Coke of Durham, shoemaker – but what part he played in the uprising is unknown.[109] Although a popular movement, it was keen to abide by the traditional social order. By 19th October, and with the help of the Richmondshire rebels this had been achieved: a rising of the commons led by the peers, Lord Neville and Lord Lumley and the gentlemen Sir Thomas Hilton and George Bowes.[110] That Lord Neville was no more than thirteen and George Bowes nineteen simply indicates the ascriptive code of values to which the rebels adhered. In practice, however, the leadership of the Durham men fell upon George's uncle, the experienced soldier Robert Bowes, and upon Lord Latimer, a close blood relative of Lord Neville.

In Cleveland, a movement of the commons was more evident than in the palatinate simply because the Richmondshire rebels impressed themselves upon the region not by sending in an army but by means of proclamations nailed to church doors and delivered by outriders.[111] Its progress can be discerned through the adventures of Bigod and Rokeby. In fleeing the commons of Hartlepool, Bigod returned in secret to Cleveland, "keeping now the waters, now the woods", only to be taken by a band of commons when he reached his home at Mulgrave Castle, near Whitby.[112] James Rokeby also encountered a rebellious commons in Cleveland. Fleeing from Richmond to the east coast, he stopped at his mother's home in Yafforth, on the Richmondshire/Cleveland border. Thereabouts he found nailed to the church doors "a letter to the commonwealth" at the sight of which "the commons rose in every part" and "the gentlemen did flee and hid

107 See below, pp. 174–6.
108 See above, p. 149–50.
109 *L.P.* XI. 955.
110 *L.P.* XII{1}. 29 {2}; Stapulton, p. 100; Bateson, pp. 336–7; *L.P.* XII{1}. 393.
111 See below.
112 SP1/116, f. 199 (*L.P.* XII{1}. 578).

them and were constrained to come to them".[113] Without a doubt, the
letter was the one composed by the Richmondshire rebels and stuck to
church doors across the Vale of Mowbray by Thomas Hutton on 14th
October. It included a complaint about "the pulling down of
abbeys".[114] Rokeby then travelled on to Marske-by-the-Sea, where
his uncle William Rokeby lived. Finding it impossible to escape,
either by sea or by travelling overland to Newcastle, James returned
to Guisborough on 16th October where he met a man from Stokesley
with a letter which he wished the bailiff of the town to proclaim. When
the bailiff refused, the townspeople of Guisborough took the matter
into their own hands, overruled the bailiff and required the messenger
who had brought the letter to read it out.[115] The letter may have been
the one already encountered at Yafforth. In all probability, however, it
was the one composed by the Richmondshire rebels on 15th October
and sent into Cleveland ordering a meeting with "their neighbours of
Richmond" at Oxen-le-Fields, just across the Tees, on 16th October.[116]

At this point Rokeby tried to make his escape but was captured
and told of the rebels' plan to enlist both his uncle William and Sir
John Bulmer of Wilton Castle. At Marske-by-the-Sea they threatened
to burn down William's house causing him to submit. At Wilton
Castle the bailiff told them that Sir John Bulmer was not at home.
In response, they collected together a great deal of wood. Faced with
the prospect of his house going up in flames, Bulmer, along with his
brother, Sir William, gave in and met the rebels at Carling Howe, close
to Guisborough on 17th October. This meeting was clearly a muster.
At it Rokeby was required to serve as a soldier. When he ingeniously
sought to excuse himself on the grounds that, although he was not a
priest, he was about to become one and therefore should not be
expected to fight, the rebels gave vent to their grievances calling him
a Lollard, a "puller down of abbeys" and Cromwell's servant. At the
same muster a message came from the rebels in Durham counter-
manding the order summoning them to march into the palatinate
(which had arrived too late in the Guisborough area to be obeyed)
and ordering them instead to await further instruction. This had
arrived by 20th October, leading to a muster on that day at Northallerton where the commons of the wapentake of Langbaurgh, accompanied by the captured gentlemen – the two Bulmers, the two Rokebys

113 SP1/118, f. 255(*L.P.* XII{1}. 1011).
114 See above, p. 144.
115 SP1/118 f. 255 (*L.P.* XII{1}. 1011). See Map 5.
116 SP1/117, f. 218 (*L.P.* XII{1}. 789); *L.P.* XII{1}. 1011.

and possibly Sir Francis Bigod – joined the host of Clevelanders and bishopric men which, in response to Aske's orders, speedily covered the ninety miles from Spennymoor to Pontefract between 20th and 22nd of October, riding behind the miraculous banner of St. Cuthbert.[117]

Essentially this force consisted of three contingents of Clevelanders: the one from Allertonshire and Birdforth under Sir James Strangways which had arrived for the Oxen-le-Fields muster on 16th October; another, also drawn from the same two wapentakes and led by Roland Place and Roger Lascelles which had turned up in Spennymoor on 18th or 19th October; and the Bulmer company from Langbaurgh.[118] Nothing is known of how Lascelles, Place and Strangways became involved, apart from Darcy's report that the commons had taken Lascelles by 17th October.[119] However, Rokeby's account of what was happening around Yafforth on 14th and 15th October and of what happened to Bulmer on 17th and 18th October suggested that their enlistment was the achievement of an active and forceful commons.[120] In addition, the same host comprised several companies drawn from Durham: the thousand men from Stainmore led by George Bowes with the assistance of his uncle, which turned up to the Bishop Auckland muster of 17th October, and the forces led by Lord Neville, Lord Lumley and Sir Thomas Hilton which had been recruited by 19th October.[121] Within this force Richmondshire men formed a minute component: no more than four or five townships recruited from the estates of Lord Latimer and captained by his brother, Marmaduke Neville.[122] Aske put this army at 10,000 strong; Stapulton, at 5000 and Thomas Percy, at 3–4,000.[123]

The conjunction of this host with the forces led by Aske was troubled by tension and disagreement. Shortly after its arrival in Pontefract on 22nd October, Lord Darcy ordered the Durham/Cleveland host to the front, requiring it, in the company of Thomas Percy and his force, to guard the crossing at Wentbridge, in preparation for moving the whole army to Doncaster. Bowes objected because their horses were exhausted. As a result the order was countermanded. His

---

117 For Rokeby's adventures and the Northallerton muster, see SP1/118, fos. 255–256b (*L.P.* XII{1}. 1011). For the journey from Spennymoor to Pontefract, see ibid.; Stapulton, p. 100. Also see Map 4.
118 See above, pp. 149–50.
119 *L.P.* XI. 760 {2}.
120 See above, pp. 158–9.
121 See above, pp. 149–50.
122 *L.P.* XII{1}. 29 and 29{2}.
123 Bateson, p. 336; Stapulton, p. 100; *L.P.* XII{1}. 393. For a consideration of these estimates, see Appendix I.

host, however, was not averse to battle and on 23rd October it took up the vanguard position close to Doncaster at Hampole Nunnery.[124] Then, on 25th October, excited by a skirmish and a rout of government cavalry, the commons from Durham and Cleveland wanted to take Doncaster immediately and were only restrained with some difficulty.[125] Further disagreements occurred with Lord Darcy between 24th and 26th October. Part of the problem was the commons' hostility to Darcy because he had ordered them to the front so soon after their arrival in Pontefract and, adding insult to injury, now lingered himself in the comfort of Pontefract Castle while the pilgrim host was taking up battle positions near Doncaster.[126] On 24th October Lancaster Herald arrived with the Duke of Norfolk's negotiating terms and Robert Aske raced back to Pontefract to consult with Lord Darcy. Returning the following day, he indiscreetly answered the herald without seeking the advice of the lords and gentlemen of the North Riding and the bishopric, an act of high-handedness which caused "ill-pleasure" in the Durham/Cleveland camp.

A basic difference over policy developed between the Durham/Cleveland host keen on military action and the high command of Darcy and Aske keen on a peaceful settlement. Yet this was resolved in return for allowing the leaders of the Durham/Cleveland host a prominent part in negotiating the Truce.[127] Robert Bowes and Thomas Hilton were two of the four delegates authorised to present the rebels' five articles to Norfolk on 27th October; and because they were not written down it was left to Bowes to recite the articles to the royal party. Later the same day, Hilton and Bowes, along with Lords Latimer, Darcy and Lumley and the knights John Bulmer and Robert Constable, discussed the five articles on Doncaster bridge with Norfolk and his party; and Robert Bowes was deputed with Sir Ralph Ellerker to take them to the king.[128] Prominently placed in the five articles was the demand concocted by the Richmondshire uprising: that the laws and practices of the realm should remain as they were on the accession of Henry VIII.[129]

124 See Marmaduke Neville's account, *L.P.* XII{1}. 29 and Thomas Percy's account, SP1/115, fos. 259b–260 (*L.P.* XII{1}. 393{2}).
125 For the commons' keenness to set on Doncaster and the problem of staying them, see Stapulton, p. 101. That the event described related to the Durham/Cleveland host: see Bateson, pp. 571–2; SP1/120, f. 35b (*L.P.* XII{1}. 1175).
126 Stapulton, p. 101; *L.P.* XII{1}. 29.
127 E36/118, f. 118 (*L.P.* XII{1}. 29{2}); and for the course of events, see Bateson, pp. 336–7; Stapulton, p. 101. Also see below, ch. X.
128 Bateson, p. 337; *L.P.* XII{1}. 1022.
129 SP1/109 (*L.P.* XI. 902{2}).

More of a problem for the pilgrim high command was the other contingent of the Bowes host which, in going first to Skipton instead of straight to Pontefract, took so long to join the pilgrim host that it missed the grand *dénouement* of 27th October.[130] When the battle plans were drawn up by Aske, Darcy, Bowes and others, in a window of Pontefract Castle on 22nd October, this particular host was designated the rearward and therefore conceived as a vital part of the main army.[131] However, its preoccupation with taking Skipton Castle meant that the rebel army assembled before Doncaster on 26th October was not fully formed, but consisted only of the van and the middleward. This may well have dissuaded the rebels from resorting to battle, essentially by providing the gentlemen with the opportunity to impose instead a policy of negotiation, although it was clear at the time that, because of its superior numbers, morale and horsemen, the pilgrim host enjoyed the military advantage over the confronting army royal.[132]

Further problems arose for the pilgrim high command when the Richmondshire host finally arrived in Pontefract, probably on 27th October, and was infuriated to learn that the battle was off. Its unwillingness to accept the Truce caused its members to oppose the order to disperse. Darcy found them "wild people evil to order". This, he claimed, was due to the fact that there were "nothing like so many of worship" in that host as in each of the other two wards.[133] Yet the rearward had its men of worship: a peer, three knights and seven gentlemen.[134] Its fury stemmed from the *fait accompli* that it encountered upon reaching Pontefract and probably from a commoner feeling that the advantage had been foolishly thrown away by the gentlemen who, in the Lincolnshire manner, were too ready to submit to the king.

130 Aske, it seems, had called upon John Norton "to come to Pontefract to host upon the duke of Norfolk", perhaps on 22nd October [SP1/117, f. 84 (*L.P.* XII{1}. 698{3}). But this had no effect in drawing the Richmondshire rebels from Skipton to Doncaster.
131 For the council in the window, see SP1/115, f. 259b (*L.P.* XII{1}. 393). For the battle order, see Bateson, pp. 336–7.
132 The rebel advantage was not only spelled out by Aske, see *L.P.* XII{1}. 1175 , but also admitted at the time by Norfolk, see Hoyle, "Thomas Master's narrative", pp. 70–71.
133 SP1/110 (*L.P.* XI. 928); *L.P.* XI. 1045.
134 The rearward included Lord Scrope; Danby, Mallory and Bulmer (knights);and the two Nortons, Richard Bowes, Metcalfe, Markenfield, Ingliby and Wandesford (gents) (see above, n. 78).

The grievances of the rebels

The rebels' grievances were declared in word and deed. With lesser
monasteries and their properties thick on the ground – Egglestone,
Marrick, Easby, the Cell of St. Martins, Coverham, Ellerton, Nun
Monkton – and a considerable amount of land owned by the great
houses of Jervaulx, Rievaulx, Byland, Bridlington and Fountains, the
Dissolution not surprisingly was a foremost concern. One of the earliest
acts of the rebels was to restore the abbeys of Coverham and Easby,
and much support was recruited from the regions where the estates of
these two abbeys were located. The rebels attached so much importance to the restoration of Easby that a monk fom Sawley Abbey was
told in December when he visited Richmond: "Rather than our house
of St. Agatha [i.e. Easby Abbey] should go down, we shall all die".[135]
Moreover, the letter composed by the Richmondshire rebels on 14th
October and fixed to church doors in the region and which was a major
source of recruitment, objected to "the pulling down of abbeys".[136]
Likewise the Captain Poverty letter composed by the same rebels on
15th October stated: "And where abbeys were suppressed we have
restored them again and put the religious men into their houses;
wherefore we exhort you to do the same".[137] The concern was not
confined to Richmondshire as can be seen, for example, in the accusation brought by the Clevelanders against James Rokeby that he was a
suppressor of monasteries and, in the palatinate, Marmaduke Neville's
proud declaration: "Mary, for all abbeys in England be beholden to us
for we have set up all the abbeys in our country and though it were
never so late they sang matins the same night"; and in Thomas
Hilton's support for the restoration of the Friars Observant in Newcastle.[138] Some indication of the nature of the concern in Richmondshire was given by the cleric John Dakyn. As he and others saw it, the
suppression of the abbeys imperilled the "estate of the church" and
was lamented for this reason not only by "religious persons" but also
"such as had living by their houses".[139] The case against suppression was thus presented as a material issue: a loss of wealth which

---

135 *L.P.* XII{1}. 491.
136 SP1/117, f. 204b (*L.P.* XII{1}. 786/ii).
137 The text of this letter has only partially survived. It is given in Barnard Townley's
     account of the letter addressed to Westmorland and Cumberland [SP1/117, f. 50
     (*L.P.* XII{1}. 687, p. 301)].
138 For Cleveland, see SP1/118, f. 256 (*L.P.* XII{1}. 1011). For the palatinate, see
     L.P. XI. 1372 and SP1/112, fos. 244–244b (*L.P.* XI. 1319).
139 SP1/117, f. 206 (*L.P.* XII{1}. 786).

would harm not only the church as an organisation but also its lay employees and dependants.

But religious houses were not the only worry. Also agitating the Richmondshire rebels was the fear that the government's policy of Dissolution would be applied to parish churches as well, through a plan to reduce their number and confiscate their treasures. James Rokeby, who was present in Richmond on 14th October, deposed that at the time "there was a common noise in Richmondshire that Drs. Layton and Leigh would come down avisiting into the country and would pull down all chapels dependent and many parish churches leaving but one in every ten miles and take away all silver chalices, leaving tin ones in their place". According to Rokeby, it was rumoured that they were about to arrive in Topcliffe "to rob its church" and that plans to resist them had been made by Mr. Tankard, a lawyer, and other gentlemen of that town.[140] It was well known that close to Topcliffe was a family seat of the Percies. This knowledge probably gave the rumoured resistance greater credibility.

Another major grievance came to light on 15th October when John Dakyn arrived in Richmond to attend the third of the rebel meetings held in that town. He had been enlisted and sworn the day before by a band of five hundred commons as they had passed through his parish of Kirby-by-Richmond on the way to Barnard Castle. In the throng Dakyn found himself threatened physically by a certain Thomlynson of Bedale as a "putter down of the holidays" which "the people did also murmur at": in other words, there was opposition to the royal injunction for reducing the number of holy days, issued the previous August as part of a campaign to stamp out belief in the power of saints to intercede with God for the grace of the living and the dead.[141] Clearly, the cause of rebellion embraced much more than the annexation of church wealth. Another spiritual matter that moved the commons was "the alteration of the power of the Bishop of Rome" which was thought to be "not good and should not stand".[142] Dakyn picked up such remarks from his parishioners and felt the force of their concern after Christmas when he exhorted the parishioners of Richmond against believing in the pope and in response they threatened to eject him from the church.[143]

Thomlynson of Bedale also took exception to Dakyn for being a

140 SP1/118, f. 254 (L.P. XII{1}. 1011).
141 L.P. XII{1}. 788; SP1/117, f. 216 (L.P. XII{1}. 789).
142 SP1/117, f. 205b (L.P. XII{1}. 786/ii).
143 L.P. XII{1}. 788.

"maker of the new laws".[144] Since this charge was brought against a cleric who, as vicar general of the archdeaconry of Richmond, was a member of convocation but not of parliament, the reference was, in all likelihood, to the Ten Articles which convocation had sanctioned on 11th July 1536. Without a doubt the religious grievances of the Richmondshire rebels incorporated not simply the onslaught upon religious houses and parish churches but also the range of government measures which in the previous two years had dramatically challenged the old religion and which had been publicly declared, in July and August 1536, in four explicitly heretical policy statements: the Ten Articles, the royal injunctions directing the clergy on the enforcement of the Ten Articles, the royal injunction reducing the number of holy days and a new order of prayer. Hence the opening of the letter which the Richmondshire rebels dispatched into the north-west: "Well beloved brother in God, we greet you well, signifying unto you that we, your brethren in Christ, have assembled us together and put us in readiness for the maintenance of the faith of God, his laws and his church".[145] The threat of heresy agitated not only the Richmondshire rebels. At the Cleveland muster of 17th October on Carling Howe, James Rokeby was abusively called a Lollard.[146] Moreover, reflecting the views of the Durham/Cleveland host that he accompanied from Spennymoor to Pontefract, Marmaduke Neville declared that the objection made against the government centred upon heresies "the which . . . they would have reformed in any wise".[147]

These grievances against the government created certain hate figures: notably William Blitheman for his part in dissolving Coverham Abbey and as receiver in the Court of Augmentations for the Richmond archdeaconry; Leigh and Layton for allegedly overseeing the dissolution of monasteries and parish churches; William Maunsell for administering the granges of Coverham Abbey which the king had granted to Sir Arthur Darcy; and Thomas Cromwell for misusing his authority to promote heresy.[148] Yet in this former Yorkist enclave Henry VIII was not opposed for being the son of, and successor to, a Lancastrian usurper. Only Abbot Sedber stated as much, in a letter

144 SP1/117, f. 216 (*L.P.* XII{1}. 789).
145 *L.P.* XII{1}. 687, p. 301.
146 SP1/118, f. 256 (*L.P.* XII{1}. 1011).
147 SP1/112, f. 244b (*L.P.* XI. 1319).
148 For Blitheman, see *L.P.* XII{1}. 788, 1326. For Leigh and Layton, see *L.P.* XII{1}. 788. For Cromwell, see ibid., and SP1/118, f. 256 (*L.P.* XII{1}. 1011) and *L.P.* XI. 1319. For William Maunsell, see SP1/111, f. 74b (*L.P.* XI. 1047) and Sir Arthur Darcy, see P.R.O. SC6/Henry VIII/7454.

to Thomas Cromwell of May 1537, and, in making the point, he was probably seeking to suggest that responsibility for the rebellion should not be attributed solely to the monks.[149] As for the supporters of the Richmondshire uprising, they were not against the Tudor dynasty itself; they were only against the government of Henry VIII for departing from the revered ways of Henry VII.

The cause, then, was not just a defence of the old religion. According to Dakyn, "they would have all laws removed made in the King Henry's reign putting no difference".[150] The same point was picked up by James Rokeby at Northallerton when the Cleve-landers from around Guisborough met up with the Bowes host on "its great ride" to Pontefract and he heard it cried that "they would have all the governance of the realm in like estate as it was in the latter end of Henry VII's day".[151] The grievance applied not only to new laws but also to new practices in the law. As Aske recorded, another reason for detesting Cromwell, and one that moved the commons of the Bowes host with a consuming passion – so much so that they could eat him – was Cromwell's extreme behaviour in hauling a Yorkshire jury of arraignment before the Council in Star Chamber at Westminster because it acquitted William Wycliffe of murder, and in punishing it with a heavy fine for refusing to alter its opinion (i.e. in rebel eyes, for refusing to perjure itself).[152] The acquittal occurred in late March, 1536; the summons to London, on 20th May.[153] Although the victim was from Newcastle-upon-Tyne, it was very much a Richmondshire affair: the murder was committed at West Thorpe, a small village on the south bank of the Tees three miles or so south-east of Barnard Castle; the murderer and his accomplices came from nearby Wycliffe; and five members of the jury were Richmondshire men.[154] Two other members of this jury were also from the North Riding, leaving only

149 *L.P.* XII{1}. 1269.
150 SP1/117, f. 207 (*L.P.* XII{1}. 786/ii).
151 SP1/118, f. 256b (*L.P.* XII{1}. 1011).
152 See Bateson, pp. 339–40. The issue was raised with Lancaster Herald when he came to the rebel army on 24th October positioned close to Doncaster. Since only the vanguard was in this area at the time, Aske must have been making reference to the Bowes host of which the van was mainly composed. The fine amounted to £1,036.13.4 and was paid in several annual instalments (*L.P.* X. 1257).
153 *L.P.* VIII. 457 (wrongly attributed to 1535). The point about the jury being pressed to commit perjury was made by Thomas Tempest [SP1/112 (*L.P.* XI. 1244)].
154 P.R.O. KB9/976, mm. 129-132. The Richmondshire jurors were Nicholas Girlington, William Barningham, Ralph Spence, William Aslaby and John Warde: see *L.P.* X. 1257. Only Aslaby is known to have joined this revolt.

three from the West Riding and two from the East Riding.[155] Besides
the weight of the fine, the rebels were aggrieved at the pressures brought
by Cromwell's servants upon the legal process to have, in Sir Thomas
Tempest's words, "the law . . . ordered at their commandment" for it
seemed that they "will take upon them to command sheriff, justices of
the peace, coram and of sessions in their master's name at their
pleasure".[156] In other words, they had a constitutional complaint
against what appeared to be a tyrannical extension of the government's authority. The same grievance also stemmed from the belief
that subjects north of the Trent should not be summoned by subpoena
to make a personal appearance anywhere else but in York unless the
offence was specifically against the king; that is, equitable jurisdiction
should not normally have the power to summon northerners to Westminster, a point made in the pilgrimage's December articles.[157]

The complaints moving the Bowes host were declared in a statement of grievance put to the pilgrims' Pontefract council in the first
week of December, without a doubt by Sir Thomas Tempest, yet
another lawyer and younger son, who in his own words was "born
to no lands and of mean substance" but who by the 1530s possessed
estates in both the bishopric of Durham and Richmondshire, was
closely connected with the region by virtue of service in the house-
holds of the bishops of Durham and the Duke of Richmond, as J.P.
and M.P. and as steward of the extensive lordship of Northallerton.[158]
Too ill, or so he claimed, to attend the Pontefract council, the result of
a drenching he had received when returning home from the pilgrims'
York council in late November, he composed his complaint "in the
great causes of the country" and sent it to his friend and cousin,
Robert Bowes, to deliver to Aske.[159] The grievances it identified
centred upon Thomas Cromwell who was charged with being a
Lollard and traitor. The solution it proposed was to expel him and

155 They were Sir George Conyers, whose manor of Sockburn lay astride the Tees
and was in the palatinate as well as in the North Riding, and Thomas de la River,
who resided in Bulmer wapentake (see *L.P.* X. 1257).
156 SP1/112 (*L.P.* XI. 1244, p. 505). That the Wycliffe case is being quoted is evident
in the reference to Sir George Conyers and Sir Oswald Wilstrop "and their
fellows" and to "the extreme fines" that they were subjected to by Cromwell.
For their involvement in the Wycliffe case, see *L.P.* X. 1257.
157 *L.P.* XI. 1246 {23}.
158 SP1/112 (*L.P.* XI. 1244); Bindoff, III, pp. 432-3. The statement is not directly
attributable. But that it was his, see SP1/112 (*L.P.* XI. 1211), which appears to be
in the same hand.
159 SP1/112 (*L.P.* XI. 1211).

his creatures from the realm. Cromwell's treachery lay in his maltreatment of the commonwealth, which came of promoting the royal interest before that of his subjects and of creating a tyrannical and plundering government.

The statement of grievance revealed that the constitutional complaint was a considerable one and concerned not only the pressures brought upon the king's officers to comply with what Cromwell wanted but also the pressure brought upon parliament to become simply a servitor of the Crown. Thus, it complained that parliament no longer represented the realm. As parliament was packed with government agents, it should be called a council "of the king's appointment". The term "parliament" was no longer appropriate for a parliament "ought to have the knights of the shire and burgesses for the towns at their own election that could reason for the wealth of the shire or town" and "not such men [Sir Francis Bryan was named] as the king will appoint for his private lucre". Developing the point, the statement condemned as improper the acts for the suppression of religious houses and for making words treason since the parliaments that had passed them were "of neither authority nor virtue". With the constitution offended in this manner, the statement deplored that "whatsoever Cromwell sayeth is right and none but that" and that consequently "whatsoever they will have done must be lawful" (i.e. they twisted the law to suit their needs). Led astray by his evil minister, the king was accused of having broken his coronation oath. Although it was not mentioned in Tempest's complaint, a related constitutional concern of the Bowes host was over the recent Succession Act 28 Henry VIII, c. 7 which allowed the king, in the absence of direct heirs, to will his Crown to anyone he chose. This was raised by Bowes at the Pontefract council in December and, perhaps as a result, it was included in the December petition where its repeal was called for. The act could be seen not only as irregular in itself but also as another indication that, having become a puppet of the government, parliament had lost it ability to defend the constitution and to serve the realm.[160]

The same statement also declared a deep concern for the wealth of the realm, believing that the government was bent on pillaging it to please the king and to serve itself. It picked up a remark of Cromwell that "he shall make the king the richest prince in Christendom", rejoining "a man can have no more of the cat but the skin". It argued

160 SP1/112 (*L.P.* XI. 1244). For the Succession Act, see Bateson, p. 570; *L.P.* XI.1246 (article 16). For Aske's comments, see Bateson, p. 559.

that the king had already made heavy exactions of his people, presumably a reference to the heavy taxation of the 1520s, and urged that if he wanted to be rich "let him follow the trade of his noble and wise father". The commonwealth, then was presented as under threat from a greedy as well as a tyrannical government. The letters the rebels had composed and dispatched on 14th and 15th October in Richmond had likewise asserted a concern for the commonwealth, as did the Richmondshire outriders who called upon Thomas Percy at Seamer, near Scarborough, and declared that they rose "for the weal of us all".[161]

This concern was probably aroused, as it was in other parts, by government taxation. On 6th October Lord Darcy claimed that in Wensleydale, "with other dales and countries", there was objection to paying more money to the government, as well as to the suppression of abbeys and parish churches and to the confiscation of jewels and ornaments, because it was felt "such acts against God, the king and his commons' wealth is not his grace's pleasure"; and George Lumley and Thomas Percy, both of whom were visited by Richmondshire rebels and obliged to take the oath, reckoned that a major cause of revolt in October 1536 was new taxes on food and sacraments which the government was rumoured to be about to impose.[162] James Rokeby in his account of the Richmondshire uprising identified new taxes as a grievance, notably the 6s. 8d. tax on baptisms and the groat tax on cattle.[163] Marmaduke Neville instanced another tax grievance when he declared that the rebels wished to secure the repeal of the Statute of Uses. Enacted that year, this statute had left the aristocracy exposed to the full force of the government's fiscal feudalism.[164] However, the supporters of the Richmondshire uprising were not simply aggrieved at the government. Their concern for the commonwealth was directed against the landlords as well. In their eyes the commonwealth of the

---

161 For Tempest's complaint, see L.P. XI. 1244. For letter of 14th October, see SP1/118, f. 255 (L.P. XII{1}. 1011). For letter of 15th October, see SP1/118, f. 54b (L.P. XII{1}. 687 {2}, pp. 302–3). Thompson claimed that it was "for the maintenance of certain articles as well concerning the christian faith as the commonweal" and said that it closed with the threat that, if the Cumbrians did not co-operate, they would be regarded as "enemies to the Christian faith and to the commonwealth". For the visit to Thomas Percy, see SP1/115, f. 258 (L.P. XI{1}. 393 {2}).

162 SP1/106 (L.P. XI. 563{2}); L.P. XII{1}. 393 and 369. For the nature and the extent of the tax complaint see M. L. Bush, "Enhancements and importunate charges: an analysis of the tax complaints of October 1536", Albion, 22 (1990), pp. 403ff.

163 This is just distinguishable in a badly mutilated document [see SP1/118, f. 254b (L.P. XII{1}. 1011)].

164 L.P. XI. 1319; and Bush, op. cit., pp. 415–18.

north was threatened by lords who were overriding the custom of
tenant right and, in doing so, were weakening the border defences
and rendering the region more prone to looting and pillaging by
invading Scots.

The charge against the landlords was first declared in the Captain
Poverty letters which the Bowes host dispatched "in the name of the
commons" to the border counties where tenant right prevailed. It was
made again in a letter found circulating in the North Riding in January
1537.[165] In this respect, the oath to be true to the commons had a dual
purpose for the followers of the Richmondshire uprising: on the one
hand, it obliged gentlemen to commit themselves openly and explicitly
to a "rising of the commons"; on the other, it obliged them to respect
the rights of the tenantry.

The letters of October 1536 have not survived; but their character
and content are evident from comments made by their recipients.
They dealt with matters of commonwealth as well as religion. Their
concern for the commonwealth centred upon the exaction of gressums.
Attached to these letters was a set of articles. Their form and content,
and the rebel practice in Richmondshire and Cumbria of taking
gentlemen and obliging them to swear the oath, suggest that the
Captain Poverty letters of October 1536 resembled the letter with
articles attached which circulated in the Richmond area in January
1537 when attempts were made to revive revolt. The 1537 articles
ordered the commons to "take all lords and gentlemen and make them
swear on the mass book to these articles" which included the agrarian
demand that "no lord nor gentlemen take nothing of their tenants but
only their rents".[166] The agrarian issue rested upon how much
peasants should pay for tenancies which required unpaid military
service on the northern border. To defend their position against the
landlords, the Richmondshire rebels were asserting the custom of the
honours of Richmond and Middleham which confined tenurial obligation to military service at the warden's calling, a rent perpetually fixed
by custom and, whenever a change of tenant or lord occurred, the
payment not of the usual gressum but of a God's penny, a small,
unchanging and notional sum that by the sixteenth century had

---

165 See Bush, "Captain Poverty", p. 18.
166 For the 1536 letter and articles, see *L.P.* XII{1}. 687 {1} and {2}. For the 1537
     letter and articles, see SP1/114 (*L.P.* XII{1}. 163).

symbolic rather than monetary value, thereby preventing the landlord from compensating for the fixed rent with a revisable due.[167]

The agrarian grievances of the Richmondshire rebels, however, were much more complicated than this. What the Captain Poverty letter demanded is different from the article on tenant right which the pilgrims submitted to the government in December. Of the regions directly involved in the Richmondshire uprising, the pilgrims' article specified only the lordships of Masham and Kirkby Malzeard and in these parts its complaint was confined to tenant right on the abbey lands.[168] Monastic property was not especially extensive in the Lordship of Masham but very extensive in Kirkby Malzeard, whilst the attached Chase of Nidderdale was virtually owned by either Fountains Abbey or Byland Abbey.[169] However, since the larger abbeys owned most of the monastic property in the two lordships and the lesser monasteries no more than a very small fraction, this particular agrarian grievance could only be seen as generated by the Dissolution if the fear was held that it would be extended to all religious houses.[170] Furthermore, the article proposed a different system of tenant right from what appeared in the Captain Poverty letters: one that allowed gressums for a change of tenant or lord but required them to be fixed at double the rent. In all likelihood, within the ranks of the Richmondshire rebels were two complaints concerning tenant right, the one seeking to preserve the custom of Swaledale and Wensleydale which substituted for gressums the God's penny. A related complaint was also found in Cleveland. It became evident early in 1537 when a bill was brought to Sir John Bulmer by a man who presented himself as coming from the commons. The bill demanded that "men should pay

167 See J. S. Willan and E. W. Crossley, "Three seventeenth-century Yorkshire surveys", in Y.A.S.R.S., 104, pp. 147 and 149. There is nothing to support Rachel Reid's point that the rebels of Richmondshire were made desperate by the dues imposed on them as a result of the death of the Duke of Richmond, see R. R. Reid, The King's Council in the North (London, 1921), pp. 135–6.
168 L.P. XI. 1246 {9}.
169 The abbey lands consisted of nine separate properties in Masham Lordship with a gross annual rental of £15.8.4d and twenty-one separate properties in Kirkby Malzeard Lordship with a gross annual rental of £135.17.8d. They were owned by Coverham (V. E., 5, p. 243), Easby (ibid. p. 235), Jervaulx (ibid p. 241), Newburgh (ibid. p. 92), Mount Grace (ibid. p. 84) and Fountains (ibid. p. 253 and List of the Lands of Dissolved Religious Houses, Lists and Indexes, Supplementary Series no. 3, vol. 4, pp. 147, 149 and 150). For the Chase of Nidderdale, see B. Jennings, A History of Nidderdale (Huddersfield, 1976), chs. 3 and 5 and especially the map on p. 88.
170 Easby had possessed land with a gross annual rental of £4 in the Lordship of Kirkby Malzeard; Coverham had possessed land with a gross annual rental of 26s. 8d. in the Lordship of Masham. See SC6/Henry VIII/7454.

no gressums".[171] The other complaint over tenant right insisted upon
the custom of Nidderdale which allowed a gressum but one restricted,
in accordance with the December article, to twice the rent.[172] The
custom of Swaledale and Wensleydale, moreover, concerned customary
tenures which were under obligation of border service with horse and
harness, whilst the custom of Nidderdale concerned demesne leaseholds, and made no explicit mention of military service. The issue in
dispute in Swaledale and Wensleydale was whether or not the lord had
the right to impose gressums; whereas in Nidderdale the issue was
whether or not leaseholders had the right of hereditary possession and
if so, how much the lord could exact of them through the gressums
they were obliged to pay for this right.[173] When the pilgrims came to
draw up their detailed demands in December, it was clearly difficult to
draft a form that incorporated these differing and conflicting claims;
and for the gentlemen rebels it was difficult to sympathise with the
God's penny which went so much against the landlord's interest. That
this claim was seen as socially divisive was made evident in Barnard
Townley's belief that it was meant to "undo the gentlemen" and in Sir
John Bulmer's exclamation upon reading the Cleveland bill: "this will
make the gentlemen and the commons fall forth".[174] For this reason
the less radical proposal was preferred, especially as it was made by the
rebels not only of Kirkby Malzeard but also of Cumberland, Westmorland, North Lancashire and the lordship of Dent. Thus, in the
formulation of the pilgrims' demand for agrarian reform, the tenant
right areas which found its terms acceptable were named whereas the
areas which found them unacceptable went unmentioned.[175] In all
likelihood, the agrarian movement of January 1537, with its insistence

171 SP1/119, f. 63b (L.P. XII{1}. 1083).
172 The custom is evident in a series of actions brought before the courts of equity:
    P.R.O. C1/734/1 (Yorkshire Chancery Proc., pp. 29–30); STAC2/19/114 (Star
    Ch. Yorkshire, II, pp. 90–1); STAC2/26/341 (Star Ch. Yorkshire, III, pp. 158–9);
    STAC2/30/127 (Star Ch. Yorkshire, IV, pp. 68–70); P.R.O. Req2/5/276. The
    custom was not always presented as confined to Kirkby Malzeard cum Nidder-
    dale. In Req2/5/276, for example, it is presented as the custom of the county of
    York.
173 Such leaseholds existed profusely in Nidderdale and Kirkby Malzeard because of
    the prevalence of monastic granges: nine in Kirkby Malzeard, against one in
    Masham, and virtually nothing but granges in the Chase of Nidderdale.
174 L.P. XII{1}. 687; SP1/119, f. 63b (L.P. XII{1}. 1083).
175 Mentioned in article nine of the twenty-four articles, see L.P. XI. 1246. For the
    Westmorlanders, see L.P. XI. 1080. Also see A. Knowles, "Customary tenure on
    the northern estates of the Percy earls of Northumberland during the sixteenth
    century" (unpublished University of Manchester M.A. thesis, 1983), pp. 5 and
    85.

on the abolition of gressums, was a reaction to the way tenant right had been presented to the government in the December articles.[176]

The agrarian complaint of the Richmondshire rebels was not confined to the custom of tenant right. If Barnard Townley's account of the Captain Poverty letter is correct, the rebels were also concerned with the manner in which rent was paid, requiring that the tenant should have the right to choose whether to pay in money or in kind. This requirement also applied to tithes, awarding parishioners the right to make a money payment, if they so wished. In addition, the tithe payment was to be voluntary in the sense that the size of the contribution which each parishioner made was to be determined by himself.[177] Such demands represented a rejection of the basic tenets of the predial tithe: that it should be a payment in kind fixed at one tenth of the yearly produce. The complaint against tithes, as presented by Townley in his account of the Captain Poverty letter, was corroborated by John Dakyn's account of the Richmondshire revolt. Under examination he alleged that he was obliged to humour his parishioners "lest they should treat me like some neighbouring parsons: of some they took half the profits of the benefice and of some the third".[178] Moreover, so concerned were the people of Richmondshire with the tithe that, after the renewal of revolt in early 1537, they sought to hold a council "for the commons' weal" in Richmond on 5th February, with the matter of tithes placed prominently on the agenda.[179] The Durham men appeared to share the same grievance: as the bishop reported, during the commotions many priests had lost their corn when it was taken from barns.[180]

Procedures of revolt

Why was there so little aristocratic resistance to the rebellion, especially when so many gentlemen lived in castles or fortified houses, and had earlier demonstrated their military prowess either on the border or in the local affrays recorded in the proceedings of Star Chamber? Lord Darcy explained it in terms of the commons favouring the revolt as an order. After listing the gentlemen taken by the Richmondshire rebels he informed the king on 17th October that the rebels could not be

---

176 It declared itself in several circulated bills and proclamations (see *L.P.* XII{1}. 163 and 163 {2} and. 1083).
177 For Townley's remarks on rents and tithes, see SP1/117, f. 50(*L.P.* XII{1}. 687).
178 SP1/117, f. 220 (*L.P.* XII{1}. 789).
179 SP1/118 (*L.P.* XII{1}. 959); *L.P.* XII{1}. 362, 671/iii , 914{2}, 959, 965.
180 *L.P.* XII{1}. 568.

resisted "for as much as all the whole commons openly favour them
that do arise . . . so that no man dare trust his tenants and that scant
were may trust their own household servants and they say plainly they
will not fight against them".[181] Another reason may have been the
absence of a figure around which resistance might have collected,
caused principally by the passivity of Latimer and Westmorland, the
flight of Lord Scrope and the absence of Lord Conyers.

Moreover, why was flight so infrequent? Lord Scrope fled to
Skipton, James Rokeby to Cleveland, the Lumleys to Newcastle,
William Asporner fled south to join the king's army, and Sir George
Conyers fled to Scarborough Castle; but compared with what happened in the East and West Ridings, it was of limited extent.[182] In the
same letter Darcy explained this in terms of the speed at which the
commons acted: "They make such speed and come so suddenly . . .
that they have surprised many gentlemen of the most worshipful in
their own houses". Perhaps the absence of impregnable refuges in the
region was the reason; or perhaps it was the threats made by the rebels
either to destroy the property of the uncooperative or to take their heirs
captive. Furthermore, after being taken why did the gentlemen not
seek to escape? According to Marmaduke Neville, this was because
"the commons had always the noblemen and gentlemen in jealousy
that they would deceive them", the implication being they kept them
under close surveillance. The other reason he offered was that the
gentlemen involved had no clear idea of how they would be received
if they did escape and therefore desisted from making the attempt.[183]

These may have been good reasons or, at least, persuasive pretexts,
but what cannot be overlooked is that the gentlemen of Richmondshire
appeared to be willing conscripts, submitting quickly to the commons,
compliantly taking the oath, even providing leadership. Lord Latimer
and Christopher Danby came forward, it seems, as soon as they were
approached; and Barnard Castle, although "well furnished with men
and victuals" was "yielded without any business, assault or tarrying"
when confronted by a band of five hundred rebels, and its residents,
the three Bowes and Thomas Rokeby, "joined immediately with the
commons". Lord Conyers, moreover, promptly became a pilgrim
when the king released him from his confinement to the verge of the

181 SP1/108, ff. 168b–169 (L.P. XI. 760 {2}).
182 For Scrope, see Dickens, Clifford Letters, p. 112; L.P. XI. 760 {2}. For Rokeby, see
       L.P. XII{1}. 1011. For Asporner, see L.P. XII{1}. 1326. For Conyers, see
       Stapulton, p. 92.
183 E36/118, f. 119 (L.P. XII{1}. 29).

Court in November and he made his return to Richmondshire.[184] This responsiveness must have been because, like the commons, they held strong grievances against the government. Some were presumably personal grudges, while some rested upon principled objections to government policy. In the absence of better evidence, the nature of the objection can only be guessed at.

In January 1537, Lord Latimer admitted that some of the "desires of the people" were "reasonable" and for this reason should be respected by the government.[185] Thomas Hilton had supported the restoration of a house of Friars Observant in Newcastle; and Marmaduke Neville had felt that the Statute of Uses should be repealed.[186] Neville, moreover, was also a keen supporter of restoring the dissolved monasteries and recovering the old religion, answering the question "how do the traitors in the north?" that was put to him in December as he passed through Colchester on his way to London with the retort: "No traitors, for if ye call us traitors we will call you heretics". Elaborating on this point he said the main objection was to Cromwell and Riche and two or three bishops "for they were the causes of all these mischiefs and heresies".[187] As for Robert Bowes he seemed alarmed as a lawyer at changes in the law which appeared to be altering the constitution, as was Thomas Tempest, and he probably was against the Dissolution, having personally approved of the restoration of Easby Abbey in December 1536 by putting out the canons and then by reinstalling them in the king's name, a procedure concocted earlier in the month as a legitimate means of preserving the abbeys restored, without offending the pardon, until the promised free parliament had decided their fate. Robert Aske applied the same procedure at Haltemprice and North Ferriby, and Hilton may have acted likewise in Newcastle.[188]

Among the nobility, it is possible that Lord Conyers had been moved to oppose the government because of the favours it had bestowed, at his expense, on his enemy Lord Scrope. As for Lord Scrope, the favours he had received in recent months (having been granted the reversion of the stewardship of the honours of Richmond

---

184 For Danby and Latimer, see Dickens, *Clifford Letters*, p. 112 and *L.P.* XII{1}. 789. For Bowes, see Cottonian MSS Calig. B. I, fos. 156–156b(*L.P.* XII{1}. 775). For Conyers, see above, n. 9.
185 *L.P.* XII{1}. 131.
186 For Thomas Hilton, see *L.P.* XI. 1372.
187 SP/112, fos. 244–244b (*L.P.* XI. 1319).
188 For constitutional complaints, see above, pp. 166–8. For monastic complaints, see E36/118, f. 173b (*L.P.* XII{1}. 787)(Bowes); *L.P.* XI. 1372 (Hilton); Bateson, p. 342 (Aske).

and Middleham and the lease of the demesnes and site of Easby
Abbey) might explain his flight from the rebels of 12th October; but
how is one to account for his submission at Skipton Castle on 25th
October? There is nothing to suggest that he had any grudges,
personal or ideological, against the government. In all likelihood,
faced by what appeared to be a hopeless situation, he simply submitted to the pressures brought upon him by the Richmondshire men,
even though he was within the impregnable walls of Skipton Castle:
perhaps to safeguard his property against the rebels, perhaps doing so
on the calculation that he had already safeguarded himself against
government reprisal by his earlier action in fleeing from the
rebels.[189] Lord Lumley, although impressed by the rebels, was
undoubtedly a deeply committed pilgrim, as was made evident in
the way he hung out of the window his banner of the five wounds
when in Pontefract on 30th November to attend the pilgrims' Pontefract council, and as was declared by the expectations held of him early
in 1537 when as "the cock of the north" he was seen as doing "great
adventures" once he "calls his chickens together". But what bound
him to the pilgrims' cause? Possibly, a grudge against the government
for depriving him in the early 1530s of Lumley Fee in the barony of
Westmorland when it was constructing for the king's illegitimate son a
liberty in Westmorland? In the absence of further evidence nothing
more can be said.[190]

By complying with the commons, lords could not only safeguard
themselves and their property against violation but also criticise the
government, without having to commit the blatant treason of aristocratic revolt. This device of making a protest indirectly through the
medium of a rising of the commons was explicitly admitted in early
1537 when the Cleveland knight, Sir John Bulmer – who had been
forcibly enlisted in 1536 by threats to burn his house – had said that, if
the king was against him, "he would flee to Wilton Castle there to be

189 For the favours received by Scrope, see SC6/Henry VIII/7454 and L.P. X.
775{17}. For the feuding between Scrope and Conyers, see L.P. VI. 920; L.P.
VII. 1317; L.P. XII{2}. 741. For his flight from the rebels, see above. For the
hopeless situation on 26th October, as recorded by the Earl of Cumberland, with
a large number of gentlemen leaving the castle to submit to the rebels, see Hoyle,
"Thomas Master's narrative", p. 70.
190 Aske described him as taken by the Richmondshire rebels (Bateson, p. 335). For
his commitment, see L.P. XI. 1253, L.P. XII{1}. 1083 and L.P. XII{2}. 1212. For
the Crown's acquisition of Lumley Fee in 1532, see J. Nicolson and R. Burn,
History and Antiquities of the Counties of Westmorland and Cumberland (London,
1777), I, p. 63.

taken of the commons of Guisborough and suddenly go and take the duke".[191] The gentlemen, for the most part, were not innocents swept against their will by the tide of commons revolt. Rarely were they made captives and forced to participate.[192] On the other hand, it could not be said that they were the cunning instigators of revolt. Usually they became rebels upon the order of the commons; and participated under threat of compulsion.[193] Moreover, rather than bringing revolt into being, they allowed it to develop and endure, largely through failing to offer any opposition and through permitting themselves or their heirs to be taken. This point was made by Adam Sedber, Abbot of Jervaulx: "if any gentlemen had done their parts at the beginning this matter had never gone so far"; but, as John Dakyn explained, the gentlemen "could have done little . . . the commons being so set".[194]

The procedure of revolt in Richmondshire, then, was as follows: a rising of the commons bent on enlisting gentlemen to support their cause. Enlistment involved securing their agreement both to respect tenant right – a lot to ask when tenant right was conceived as relieving the tenantry of the need to pay entry fines – and to support the rebellion. This support had to be formalised by taking an oath to be true to the commons. In addition, the gentlemen were expected to provide leadership; and when they offered to serve as captains of the commons or, to use Marmaduke Neville's term, "guiders of the people", they received an enthusiastic, if not deferential, reception and regained some of the social control that, thanks to the society of orders, they normally possessed.[195]

A turning point in the relationship between the commons and the gentlemen occurred on 15th October when Robert Bowes arrived in Richmond. On the previous day Lord Latimer, Sir Christopher Danby, James Rokeby and Anthony Brackenbury had been present in the town but were subdued, passive and fearful of sounding "contrary to the insurgents".[196] The following day, however, "after

---

191 For the threat to Bulmer's house, see SP1/118, f. 256 (L.P. XII{1}.1011). For Bulmer's admission, see SP1/119, f. 74 (L.P. XII{1}. 1087).
192 Rokeby was held captive in Cleveland but this was because he had tried to escape [see SP1/118, f. 255b (L.P. XII{1}. 1011)].
193 As a result, a number of gentlemen participated who had very good reasons for not doing so: age in the case of Siggiswick, Caterick and Witham; and, in the case of Sir Henry Gascoigne, the fact that, when summoned by the commons, he was busy burying his mother-in-law (see L.P. XII{1}. 789, p. 345). For the manner in which gentlemen were recruited, see L.P. XII{1}. 29{2}, 369, 393, 1011.
194 SP1/119, f. 21b (L.P. XII{1}. 1035); S.P.1/117, f. 205 (L.P. XII{1}. 786/ii).
195 L.P. XII{1}. 29{2}.
196 L.P. XII{1}. 788, 789; SP1/117, f. 205 (L.P. XII{1}. 786/ii).

Bowes was come", according to John Dakyn, "the people was greatly glad . . . and whatever he said amongst them they in manner took it for authority".[197] Moreover, Dakyn noticed that "because he is greatly esteemed . . . as soon as he come in amongst them all things that he devised to the going forward took effect".[198] Thus, at the great Richmond assembly on 15th October he created an organisation for revolt, dividing the rebels into their respective parishes and requiring each parish to appoint four captains. On the same day he had a hand in producing the letter which ordered the Clevelanders to join the Richmondshire men at Oxen-le-Fields. According to Dakyn, Bowes read the letter to the assembled rebels in Richmond and then gave it to Lucas Metcalfe to write out. The following day Bowes imposed order upon the rebel army by threatening that "he would not meddle with them" if they continued to take reprisals against each other in the settlement of old scores.[199] He also persuaded the commons to abandon their insistence that the clerics, if young and able, should serve in the rebel host, arguing that the clergy's duty was to pray, not to fight.[200] According to Dakyn, Bowes "did most and spake most of any man at that time" and so impressed himself as the leader. Moreover, on the 15th October, he persuaded the Richmondshire rebels to take their first major step: the march into the bishopric of Durham, perhaps as a device to stop them from immediately marching south.[201] On this journey northwards Lord Latimer emerged as another principal leader, playing a positive part in ordering gentlemen to join the rebellion and in subjecting them to the oath.[202]

Nonetheless, both Latimer and Bowes remained answerable to the lower orders, having to seek their consent, not always having their way, and taking charge only because it seemed that they were serving the commons. As Dakyn observed, however, there was no assurance that the commons would have accepted his orders "if he had persuaded the contrary". They could not prevent the commons from sacking the Bishop of Durham's palace at Bishop Auckland on 17th October when it was discovered that he had fled to Norham Castle: the proclamation they issued forbidding this action went ignored.[203] Moreover, their bid

197 SP1/117, f. 218 (*L.P.* XII{1}. 789).
198 SP1/117, f. 205 (*L.P.* XII{1}. 786/ii).
199 SP1/117, f. 218 (*L.P.* XII{1}. 789).
200 Ibid.; *L.P.* XII{1}. 786/ii(11).
201 SP1/117, f. 205 (*L.P.* XII{1}. 786/ii).
202 *L.P.* XII{1}. 29{2}, 369, p. 164.
203 SP1/117, f.205 (*L.P.* XII{1}. 786/ii); *L.P.* XII{1}. 369, p. 166; *L.P.* XII{1}. 789.

to persuade the commons at Oxen-le-Fields to allow the Abbot of Jervaulx to go home failed. Only at the Spennymoor assembly, held two days later, were they able to secure the commons' consent for Sedber's return and this was given on condition that he served within a secretariat stationed at Jervaulx Abbey for dispatching letters between the two armies into which the Richmondshire rebels and their allies from Cleveland and Durham were now divided.[204] These letters were described as "from the commons".[205] In practice, the ones recorded as passing through the secretariat's hands were from gentlemen: Christopher Danby, Ralph Bulmer, William Conyers and Robert Bowes.[206]

The relationship between the two orders, then, was a symbiosis brought about as the one sought to operate through the other; but, even after the rebellion had assumed an aristocratic leadership, it remained a movement of the commons. Moreover, this movement, according to Marmaduke Neville, was always suspicious of the nobility and gentry and ever fearful that they would betray the commons' cause. These suspicions were proved to be justified when the Richmondshire host eventually got to Pontefract and found that the leadership of the pilgrimage had reached an accommodation with the government; and proved again in December when the agrarian grievance was presented in the twenty-four articles in such a way as not to offend the aristocratic interest; and yet again in January when the Richmondshire aristocracy resolutely stuck by the December agreement and the commons of the region found themselves rebelling alone.[207]

Likewise, the clergy of Richmondshire did not join the revolt simply upon rebel orders. Abbot Sedber alleged that, after being taken in Jervaulx Abbey, he was made to ride bare-back through Richmond and north into the palatinate of Durham.[208] But the impression he gave that his participation was wholly enforced is questioned by George Lumley's account of the muster at Bishop Auckland where "there was an abbot, a tall lusty man . . . which said that I hearsay that the king doth cry thirteen pence a day and I trust we shall have as many men for eight pence a day; and, as he troweth, it was the abbot of Jervaulx, and his chaplain had a bow and

204 L.P. XII{1}. 789, 1035.
205 SP1/119, f. 21b (L.P. XII{1}. 1035).
206 L.P. XII{1}. 789, 1035.
207 For Neville, see E36/118, f.119 (L.P. XII{1}. 29{2}). For the October truce, see L.P. XI. 928, 1045. For the post-pardon revolts, see Dodds, II, pp. 105–108.
208 L.P. XII{1}. 1035. Also see L.P. XII{1}. 786/ii{11}.

sheaf of arrows".[209] The abbot not only provisioned the rebels but also appointed the servants of the abbey and two of the brethren to join the rebel army.[210] In view of the rebels' grievances, the clergy, secular and regular, had a compulsive reason for sympathising with their cause. In Sedber's case, he clearly sought to avoid direct involvement but, when forced to take part and assured by the recruitment of leading gentlemen, he was prepared to support the rebels with exhortation and encouragement. His resistance was limited to the initial outbreak of revolt and to opposing the commons' desire that the clergy fully commit themselves to the rebellion by taking up arms. The latter requirement clearly offended the allocation of functions as set out in the notion of the society of orders.

Other clerics, notably John Dakyn, were also initially resistant whilst generally sympathetic. Like Sedber, John Dakyn fled to begin with: first from the revolts raised by Aske, and then from the Richmondshire rebels. As with Sedber, the commons consequently declared him a traitor to their cause.[211] But Dakyn was a firm opponent of the Henrician Reformation. Although in his examination he claimed to be a supporter of the royal supremacy and the abrogation of holy days, other evidence, especially of his activities as commissary to the archdeaconry of Richmond show him to be a firm believer in intercession and the payments and practices associated with it. The same evidence reveals him as a friend of the papacy, accepting indulgences and opposing a sermon which declared papal authority in England as usurped.[212] Dakyn was a firm opponent of the Dissolution, so much so that later, in early December, he wrote letters to the canons of the restored Cartmel Priory urging them to remain for the time being in possession of their house.[213] Prior to the revolt he had pleaded in vain for the preservation of Nun Monkton Nunnery; and after it he declared to the government: "no abbey should have been suppressed".[214] The archdeaconry of Richmond had suffered a large number of Dissolutions, eight in all.[215] It also experienced a large number of restorations in association with the pilgrimage of grace: five out of the twelve

209 SP1/115, f. 213 (*L.P.* XII{1}. 369).
210 *L.P.* XII{1}. 1035.
211 *L.P.* XII{1}. 788.
212 SP1/118, fos. 9–9b (*L.P.* XII{1}. 842). The commissary mentioned is Dakyn.
213 *L.P.* XII{1}. 787.
214 *L.P.* XII{1}. 786 /ii{15}; SP1/117, f. 210 (*L.P.* XII{1}. 788).
215 Nun Monkton; Easby; Coverham; Ellerton; Calder; Seton; Conishead; Cartmel. See SC6/Henry VIII/7454 and P.R.O. DL41/11/497.

known to have occurred.[216] As vicar general to the archdeaconry, Dakyn's concern at the Dissolution, and his involvement in the revolt against it, are not surprising. Like Sedber, Dakyn could not be said to have raised revolt; but once caught in its flood he was prepared to promote the cause. However, this had to done in a manner appropriate to the clergy: that is, by prayer and by serving in the Jervaulx secretariat.[217] His attitude towards the rebels was clearly evident in the protest he made to Robert Bowes on 15th October when the commons were insisting that the priests should attend the host, readily armed for military action.[218] It was also firmly declared in a letter of reproof that he wrote to William Tristram, a chantry priest, for donning harness and for offering to fight: "Withdraw yourself from this warfare", he ordered. "We all ought to be warriors but not in this fashion" – even though it might curry "favour of the parishioners" – since it was "disobedient to God's laws".[219]

Clerics, gentlemen and commons all believed in the cause of rebellion because for roughly the same reasons they found the government's policy obnoxious. But, for the clergy and the gentlemen, actual involvement in the Richmondshire uprising was not the direct outcome of this belief. For them the manner of their involvement was determined by the fact that the uprising began from below as a movement of the commons which got out of hand because it was not initially resisted and then could only be controlled by means of their own participation. A rising of the commons with agrarian grievances would naturally incite aristocratic reprisal and clerical disapproval; but on this occasion the prominence of grievances against the government allowed gentlemen and clerics not only to tolerate the revolt but also to use it as the medium for their own protest. In the process of accommodation, issues that were socially divisive came to be buried under others that were socially cohesive.

The outstanding achievement of the Richmondshire uprising was to raise two large armies of its own, and, through its Captain Poverty

---

216 I.e. Easby; Coverham; Seton, Conishead and Cartmel. See G. W. O. Woodward, *The Dissolution of the Monasteries* (London, 1966), pp. 94-6. Woodward's figure of sixteen restorations is an exaggeration, caused by counting instances of resistance to Dissolution (Lanercost, Hexham and Norton) as restorations. On the other hand, he overlooks the restoration of Seton Nunnery.
217 *L.P.* XII{1}. 787, 1035.
218 *L.P.* XII{1}. 788 and 789.
219 SP1/112 (*L.P.* XI. 1284).

letters, to inspire the creation of at least four more.[220] In spite of their size (with one reckoned at 12,000 and the other between 4,000 and 10,000 strong) the two parts of the Bowes host were well-equipped fighting forces rather than rebellious rabbles.[221] Each contained a large contingent of horsed and harnessed troops, with a good supply of mounts provided by the horse-rearing abbeys of Jervaulx and Fountains.[222] Trained in the methods of border warfare, they were led not only by the young figureheads, George Bowes and Lord Neville, but also by men experienced in military matters. Although lacking artillery and therefore ill-equipped for siege warfare, as was made evident in the failure to take Skipton Castle, they were well suited to penetrate the south in a quick ride upon London once the royal army on the Don had been defeated. The distinguishing marks were the banner of St. Cuthbert, formerly in the custody of the Earl of Westmorland and blessed with the power of victory, and the badge of the black cross. The banner was brought to the front by the Durham and Cleveland men and served as the flag behind which the pilgrims' army was arrayed.[223] The black cross was worn by the Bowes host until an unfortunate accident occurred. The problem was its close resemblance to the red cross worn by the army royal. In a scrimmage between Bowes and Norfolk's men shortly before the Truce, the rebels killed one of their own, mistaking the black cross for the red and causing the only death committed by the pilgrimage of grace. As a result, the badge of the black cross ceased to be worn and the order was issued that everyone should wear either the badge of the five wounds or the badge of Christ's name (i.e. IHS) "both before and behind".[224]

In the first instance one host was raised. This happened between 13th and 15th October by means of letters nailed to church doors, bands of rebels visiting the houses of the gentry and leading clergy, and summonses to muster in the town of Richmond. There was undoubtedly an enthusiastic response throughout the North Riding and the

220 The armies inspired were: the host of the four captains from Cumberland, the Atkinson host from Dent and Kendal, the Pulleyn/Musgrave host from the barony of Westmorland and the Percy host from Pickering Lythe, Blackamore, Buckrose and Dickering, and possibly the Hamerton/Tempest host from Percy Fee.
221 For size of the Durham/Cleveland host, see above, n. 123. For size of Richmondshire host, see above, n. 99.
222 Aske described the rearward as "on horseback, well harnessed" (Bateson, p. 337). He described the van and middleward as "well-tried on horseback" (ibid., 336). The muster returns for the North Riding reveal large numbers of horsed and harnessed men: 4,000 out of a total of 10,000. See Appendix I.
223 Ibid., p. 337; Hoyle, "Thomas Master's narrative", p. 71.
224 Bateson, pp. 571–2.

palatinate of Durham. But operative at each stage in recruiting support was the persuasiveness of a military presence: the company from the lordships of Masham and Kirkby Malzeard, which between 11th and 14th October marched up to Richmond, and the Bowes host, formed in Richmond on 15th October, which marched into the palatinate. By 18th October the decision had been made to divide the forces raised into two separate armies, a consequence of having two objectives: one, to join with Aske in Pontefract; the other, to deal with the Earl of Cumberland at Skipton.[225] This led to the creation of a secretariat at Jervaulx, given the task of passing letters from the one force to the other and staffed by a group who had been excused military service because either they were clerics or elderly gentlemen. Besides John Dakyn and Adam Sedber, Abbot of Jervaulx, it consisted of the two gentlemen, Richard Siggiswick of Walburn in Lower Swaledale and Matthew Witham of Cliffe in Teesdale, the former, after falling ill, being replaced by William Catterick of Stanwick.[226]

The organisation of the hosts probably followed a procedure of selection identified on 17th October by Lord Darcy. Commenting on the risings in the Dales, he wrote: "the commons swear every man, priest and other and charge them to repair to a certain place to muster themselves on pain of death; and there they choose out such as they best like of the most likely and the best harnessed".[227] The two armies, it seems, were organised in companies, each centred upon a gentleman prominent in the area from which the force was recruited. This was made evident by the musters held in the palatinate where the attendance was noted of one thousand men from Stainmore under George Bowes; a thousand from Allertonshire under Sir James Strangways; a company from Swaledale led by Sir Ralph Bulmer; a company from Mashamshire led by Sir Christopher Danby; further companies from Allertonshire led by Roger Lascelles and Roland Place; the four or five townships from the estate of Lord Latimer placed under his brother Marmaduke Neville.[228] In contrast to the hosts of the East Riding, which were first captained by minor gentlemen or socially limitrophic figures, such as the lawyers Stapulton and Aske, and which recruited the county establishment only by means of taking the refuges to which its members had resorted, the hosts formed by the Richmondshire

225 See above, n. 61.
226 *L.P.* XII{1}. 788 and 789.
227 SP1/108, f. 168b (*L.P.* XII{1}. 760).
228 SP1/115, f. 212 (*L.P.* XII{1}. 369) and *L.P.* XII{1}. 29 and 29{2}.

uprising were captained virtually from the start by the lords of the region.

Yet the two hosts were not a composition of "feudal" armies. From at least the Richmond muster of 15th October, every company was divided into parishes with the inhabitants of each parish electing four captains to direct the rest. This followed an idea proposed by Robert Bowes, but it was one which presented the army as a popular force with a command structure resting upon the consent of the partici- pants.[229] The manner of appointing the head captains of each com- pany upheld this popular image. As was evident with, for example, Danby, Latimer and John Bulmer, the captaincy complied with the expectations of the society of orders; but rather than being simply assumed by the appointee, the captaincy was imposed from below.[230] When Marmaduke Neville was placed in charge of the four or five townships from his brother's estate, he claimed to have been appointed not only by Latimer but also by "the commons".[231] As for his office, he presented it as having the guiding of certain townships. Similarly, the captains as he listed them were referred to as "the guiders of the people".[232] Notably at the musters held in the palatinate, the instruc- tions to assemble were not simply passed to the gentlemen, on the understanding that they would turn up with their servants and tenants, but were sent directly to the townships which were "bidden to get them together" and "likewise [to] all men's servants".[233] In keeping with this immediate and answerable structure, the high command was determined by popular choice, with Robert Bowes enthusiastically selected by the assembled commons on 15th October. Thereafter his leadership was respected by the commons but not unquestionably and rested upon persuading them that what was done was in their best interest.[234]

As they were deployed, the hosts fulfilled two roles. One was to enlist the lords. Thus the host assembled in Richmond on 13th October was divided into three companies, each with the same task of visiting a locality to bring in its gentlemen. One band concentrated upon Wensleydale and visited the houses of Scrope at Bolton, Siggis- wick at Walburn and Metcalfe at Nappa Hall; another marched out

229 SP1/117, f. 218 (*L.P.* XII{1}. 789).
230 For Danby and Latimer, see above, n. 10, pp. 143 and 178–9. For Bulmer, see
     above, p. 159.
231. E36/118, f. 115 (*L.P.* XII{1}. 29).
232 E36/118, f. 118 (*L.P.* XII{1}. 29 {2}).
233 E36/118, f. 115 (*L.P.* XII{1}. 29).
234 See above, pp. 177–9.

into the Vale of Mowbray to visit Latimer at Snape and Danby at nearby Thorpe Perrow; yet another marched northwards towards the Tees returning with three members of the Bowes family, Henry Gascoigne of Sedbury and Thomas Rokeby of Mortham; a fourth band concentrated upon recruiting the Abbot of Jervaulx.[235] This use of the host continued with the march into Durham on 16th October and then the march to Skipton Castle four days later. The other role was to link up with the pilgrimage of grace. This had been decided upon before the arrival of Aske's summons to join him at Pontefract.[236] It had been accomplished by 22nd October.[237] As a military force the hosts were highly successful, achieving their goals by inspiring confidence and by intimidation. In the only military incident that occurred between the government's troops and the pilgrims, the Bowes host came off best.[238] Even the march on Skipton Castle was successful; for, although Cumberland stood firm, Scrope was persuaded to switch sides.[239]

Moreover, it was the placing of the Durham and Cleveland host in the van of the pilgrims' army which convinced the leaders of the army royal that the pilgrim host was a formidable force with which it was best to treat rather than to do battle.[240] In this respect, the Truce agreed on 27th October owed something to the negotiating skills of Robert Bowes but also something to the impressiveness of the force that he had brought down from the uplands. The Truce depended on its acceptance by both sides. Just as the presence of one part of the Bowes host helped to persuade the government to follow a policy of concession rather than suppression, the absence of the other part helped to persuade the pilgrims to negotiate even though they possessed the military advantage. In this respect the Richmondshire uprising had a decisive impact upon the course of events.[241]

In studying the Richmondshire uprising the Dodds underestimated its importance and misrepresented its character. Tucked away in one chapter entitled "The extent of the uprising", which deals with all the revolts outside the East Riding and Lincolnshire, the Rich-

235 Dickens, *Clifford Letters*, p. 112. For Bowes, see *L.P.* XII{1}. 775. For Gascoigne, see *L.P.* XII{1}. 789, p. 345. For Jervaulx, see *L.P.* XII{1}. 1035.
236 See above, p. 148.
237 Stapulton, p. 100.
238 Stapulton, p. 101; Bateson, pp. 571–2; *L.P.* XII{1}. 1175.
239 Bateson, p. 337.
240 Hoyle, "Thomas Master's narrative", pp. 70–71.
241 See below, pp. 376–7 and 389.

mondshire uprising gets overlooked for what it was.[242] Moreover, the Dodds identified the presence of two movements in the pilgrimage of grace: a religious movement directed by gentlemen and a social movement directed against gentlemen. According to them the revolts, of which it was composed, were either of the one or the other. And so they presented the Richmondshire uprising as "chiefly social" and "directed against the Earl of Cumberland", and therefore different in kind from the uprising in Lancashire where, according to them, discontent was "caused chiefly" by the royal supremacy and the suppression of the monasteries.[243] But the Richmondshire uprising was much more complicated; and even more complicated than Fieldhouse and Jennings suggest in stating that it was "partly opposed to the religious changes" but was "more broadly a revolt against hard social and economic conditions".[244]

A movement of the commons led by Captain Poverty, it arrived in Pontefract under the leadership of peers and gentlemen. Whilst very much concerned with the commonwealth, including an objection to harsh landlordship as well as to changes in the tax system and threats to the constitution, it was also a religious movement deeply offended by the dissolution of the monasteries and the religious changes imposed by the government. Moreover, its agrarian complaint was not simply against exploitation but also the infringement of tenurial rights. The cohesive forces of anti-government sentiment struggled against the divisive force of agrarian complaint. But what promoted social cohesion was not just the strength of the shared complaint against the government but also certain acts of compliance: the apparent willingness of the gentlemen to agree to an agrarian settlement in the peasant interest and the willingness of the commons to be directed by the gentlemen. As a result the Richmondshire uprising of October 1536 was able to operate through the society of orders; whereas in 1537 the capacity of the society of orders to act as the vehicle of protest had broken down as the rebellious commons now mistrusted both gentlemen and government. That the gentlemen did not initiate insurrection in October 1536 is proposed by its continuation without them in 1537; that they had been important in enabling it to develop in 1536 as a considerable force was evident in its speedy termination in 1537, when it had become a revolt solely of the commons.[245]

242 Dodds, I, ch. 9.
243 Ibid., pp. 225–6. Also see ibid., pp. 192 and 212.
244 Fieldhouse and Jennings, *History of Richmond*, p. 80.
245 Ibid., pp. 84–5.

V

THE PERCY HOST

Revolts around Malton

With the government manipulating the ailing, deranged and childless sixth Earl of Northumberland in order to acquire the Percy patrimony, his two brothers, Ingram and Thomas, had strong reasons for joining the uprisings of October 1536.[1] Realising as much, the rebels sought their support.[2] Without difficulty, both were sworn to the cause. Whilst Ingram remained in Northumberland, swearing the county's gentlemen to the rebels' cause but uninvolved militarily with the pilgrimage, Thomas Percy led a host of 5,000 men, recruited from the Yorkshire Moors, the northern Yorkswold and the intervening vale.[3] By 20th October it had reached York. A day later it joined Aske at Pontefract, and was then directed to the front at Doncaster, forming, along with the host from Durham and Cleveland, the vanguard of the pilgrims' army.[4]

The course taken by this particular uprising is obscure in its early

---

1 For the designs of the government, see J.M.W. Bean, *The Estates of the Percy Family, 1416–1537* (Oxford, 1957), pp. 144ff and R.W. Hoyle, "Henry Percy, sixth earl of Northumberland and the fall of the house of Percy, 1527–1537" in G.W. Bernard (ed.), *The Tudor Nobility* (Manchester, 1992), ch. 4.

2 For the rebels' dealings with Thomas Percy, see below. For their dealings with Ingram Percy, see M. L. Bush, "Captain Poverty and the pilgrimage of grace", *Historical Research*, 65 (1992), p. 19.

3 See Map 6. For Ingram, see P.R.O. SP1/116, f. 81 (*L.P.* XII{1}. 467). Since the host was recruited from the wapentakes of Ryedale, Pickering Lythe, Whitby, Strand, Dickering, Buckrose and probably Bulmer, this figure would appear realistic in the light of the muster returns for 1539. See Appendix I.

4 For Thomas, see below, p. 196.

stages, largely because the surviving evidence is imprecisely dated.[5] The basic chronology, however, appears to be as follows: the commons had risen by 10th October around Malton, taking captive two leading officials of the Archbishop of York, his chancellor and his registrar. For this reason the archbishop chose to flee to Pontefract, rather than Scarborough, Castle. At this point Ralph Eure, a leading gentleman of the region intervened, rescuing the two officials from the commons' clutches; but by the 13th October he was no longer prepared to resist and had sought refuge in Scarborough Castle.[6] Furthermore, about 10th October the friar of Knaresborough travelled up from Beverley with the aim of raising the North Riding wapentakes of Ryedale and Pickering Lythe, principally by spreading the rumour that the government was about to impose new taxes and plunder the parish churches. A week later he had returned to Beverley with the assurance that he had "raised at Malton all that quarter".[7]

This was a reference to an assembly held at Malton, probably on 16th October. Thomas Percy allegedly learned of it as he was seeking incognito to leave his mother's house at Seamer, close to Scarborough, where he had been staying after a spell of hunting in Lincolnshire, in order to rejoin his wife and children at Prudhoe Castle, situated close to Newcastle. Disguised as a servant and with a small entourage of three companions, he was stopped by two men after having travelled two or three miles in the direction of Pickering.[8] One of them was the distinctly red-faced and excitable William Percehay, lord of the manor of Ryton, a village close to Malton, and a keen activist who on 21st October was encountered by William Stapulton in the vicinity of York crying "forward every man" after receiving the false news that the government's defence of Doncaster bridge had been breached.[9] The two men had been deputed by the rebels assembled at Malton to enlist Thomas Percy and, unaware to whom they were talking, they told him that if they had not succeeded by midday the rebels would plunder the Percy house at Seamer. Without declaring his identity,

5   The two main eye-witness accounts, by Thomas Percy and George Lumley, are inadequate in failing to relate events to specified weekdays (see *L.P.* XII{1}. 393 and 369). The brief account provided by Thomas Percy's servant, Gerald Rede (*L.P.* XII{1}. 467) helpfully corroborates Thomas Percy's account but is just as unspecific as to the actual days upon which the related events occurred.

6   *L.P.* XII{1}. 1022 and Stapulton, p. 92.

7   Stapulton, pp. 88 and 96.

8   SP1/115, fos. 258–258b (*L.P.* XII{1}. 393 {2}); SP/116, f. 81 (*L.P.* XII{1}. 467).

9   SP1/115, f. 258 (*L.P.* XII{1}. 393 {2}; Stapulton, p. 99. For Percehay's background, see *V.C.H. North Riding*, II, p. 448. The other was William (not Thomas as *L.P.* would have it) Muddleton [SP1/116, f. 81 (*L.P.* XII{1}. 467)].

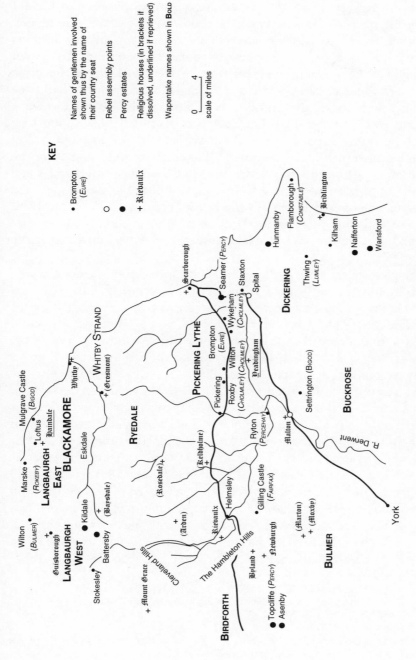

Map 6 The uprising around Malton

Thomas Percy returned to Seamer. According to his servant Gerald
Rede, his plan was to slip away the following day across the moors.
However, at two o'clock that afternoon a large company of commons
arrived, led by a certain Preston, Nicholas Howborne and William
Burwell, all of them minor gentlemen. Meeting them in the great
chamber, Thomas Percy learned that the Malton assembly had con-
nections with the Richmondshire rebellion which, having formed a
host on 15th October, had then sought to recruit further support by
marching into the palatinate of Durham and by sending out letters
summoning support for the cause.[10] These letters were written in the
name of the commons and addressed from Captain Poverty or some
variant of this title.[11] Some were simply taken by messengers: for
example, the ones delivered to the border counties of Westmorland,
Cumberland and Northumberland. But others, notably those dispatched to Durham and Ryedale were accompanied by contingents
of troops.

Having described the Richmondshire uprising as a great army of
the commons properly led by Lord Latimer, Lord Neville, Christopher Danby and Robert Bowes, and having presented it as fighting for
"a thing that should be for the weal of us all", Preston, the chief
captain, told Percy that they had come to take him to it.[12] This,
however, never happened. In all likelihood the plan was for Thomas
Percy to join this army when it marched south, in the manner of the
rebels recruited in Cleveland who joined it at Northallerton around
20th October.[13] But before that could happen pressure was brought
upon him to join with the Aske host. This had initially come through
Sir Thomas Franke, rector of Loftus in the North Riding and dean of
Cleveland. Franke had been declared a captain by Aske's first proclamation, but soon left Aske to join Thomas Percy as his chief counsel
and factotum.[14] In all likelihood he switched revolts after taking a
letter from Aske to Thomas Percy calling upon him to join the planned
siege of York and encouraging him to do so with the news that the men
of Howden had shouted "thousands for a Percy" outside the main gate
of Wressle Castle.[15] Without a doubt Percy had received this advance

10 SP1/115, f. 258b (*L.P.* XII{1}. 393 {2}); *L.P.* XII{1}. 467.
11 See above, pp. 146–7; and Bush, "Captain Poverty", pp. 17–18.
12 SP1/115, f. 258b (*L.P.* XII{1}. 393 {2}).
13 See above, pp. 159–60.
14 For Franke, see above, p. 123. For Franke's association with Thomas Percy, see
   L.P. XII{1}. 1018 and 1085 and *L.P.* XII{2}. 12.
15 For the letter from Aske that Franke probably delivered, see SP/115, f. 259 (*L.P.*
   XII{1}. 393 {2}). One account presented him as going from Howdenshire to
   Pickering Lythe and causing Thomas Percy to rise (*L.P.* XII{1}. 1085).

from Aske several days before he was sworn by the men from Richmondshire. It was but one of several communications that Aske sent him. Thus, when York had fallen, a further letter urged Percy to participate in the siege of Hull; and, with the fall of Hull, another of Aske's letters urged him to join the siege of Pontefract Castle.[16] Responding to this third letter, Percy had moved to York by the time that the Bowes host, having shifted into the palatinate, turned and made its southerly journey.[17]

The surviving evidence of this uprising is limited not only by temporal vagueness but also by inherent contradictions. What is known rests principally upon the eye-witness accounts of Thomas Percy and George Lumley. The one account clashes with the other, in the sense that Percy presented himself, in exoneration, as initially the victim of a headstrong commons and then as the puppet of Robert Aske; whereas Lumley accused Percy of being, along with Nicholas Rudston, "next Aske the chief doers of that business" and "the lock, keys and wards of this matter".[18] But certain facts and a certain chronological order appear to be indisputable. Thus, having been sworn on 16th October at Seamer, on 17th October Thomas Percy attended an assembly on the wold beyond Spital (that is, near Staxton) with an entourage of at least sixteen men. This assembly was well attended: put at 3–4,000 men according to Thomas Percy and 4–5,000 by his servant Gerald Rede. There can be no doubt that it was a muster of armed men, raised as the next step after the Malton assembly of the previous day when the cause had been declared and the oath sworn.[19] At this muster Thomas Percy was, in all likelihood, elected captain.[20] The army's first appointed task was probably to provide assistance for Aske in the siege of York, but this was made redundant by the news that York had submitted.[21] Instead, it con-

16 SP1/115, fos. 259–259b (L.P. XII{1}. 393 {2}).
17 By 20th October. See below, p. 195.
18 For the Percy point of view, see SP1/115, fos. 258–259b (L.P. XII{1}. 393 {2}). For the Lumley point of view, see SP1/115, fos. 213 and 218b–219 (L.P. XII{1}. 369).
19 SP1/115, fos. 258b–259 (L.P. XII{1}. 393 {2}); L.P. XII{1}. 467. The dating of the events can only be determined by working back from 19th October, the date upon which Thomas Percy is known to have been at Seamer (see L.P. XI. 792).
20 He was certainly captain on 18th October and was presumably appointed the day before when the force was first mustered. See SP1/115, f. 259 (L.P. XII{1}. 393 {2}).
21 This is suggested by Percy's claim that he had started to make his way towards York in response to Aske's order to join the siege there and was then stopped by Aske's order that he should instead join the siege of Hull. See SP1/115, f. 259 (L.P. XII{1}. 393 {2}).

centrated upon plundering a house belonging to the Cholmley family as a punishment for its failure to join the uprising.[22] There were three houses in the area to choose from: at Ruston in the parish of Wykeham, at Roxby in the parish of Thornton Dale and at Wilton. All were situated on the road between Seamer and Pickering, just below the moors and on the edge of the flood plain of the Derwent.[23] The fact that the operation took place on two separate days (17th and 18th October) suggests that more than one of these houses came under attack.

In all likelihood the rebels were not moved simply by the need to punish a family for remaining loyal to the government and for having Cromwellian affiliations.[24] Their animus against it also came of a longstanding conflict between the abbey of Rievaulx as lords of the Waste in the Honour of Pickering and certain communities and families subjected to this lordship, notably the village of Ryton and the Percehay clan. The Cholmleys were implicated as chief officers of the honour. Evident in a series of actions brought before Star Chamber, the conflict had gone on for over a decade, featuring the distraint of goods for the nonpayment of rents and fines and culminating in the recent dispossession of Robert Percehay from the manor of Hildenley.[25] But to explain the uprising in terms of this dispute would be just as simplistic as to explain it in terms of the Percy family's differences with the government. The two antagonisms merely fuelled the revolt. They did not generate it in the first instance.

Besides forming an army and using it to take reprisals against the uncooperative Cholmley, the rebels of the region may also have started a siege of Scarborough Castle where several gentlemen had taken refuge. Darcy reported on 17th October that there were "great

22 Ibid. and *L.P.* XII{1}. 467.
23 For the houses at Roxby and Wilton, see L. T. Smith, *The Itinerary of John Leland in or about the years 1535–1543* (London, 1907–9), pt. I, pp. 62–3 and *V.C.H. North Riding*, II, pp. 492–3 and 495–6. For the house at Ruston, see *Star Ch. Yorkshire*, IV, p. 67n.
24 The surviving evidence refers to Mr. Cholmley's house (see. n. 22). Resident in the area was Sir Roger Cholmley who probably lived at Roxby and his twenty-year-old married son, Richard, who probably lived close by at Wilton. For the two of them, see Bindoff, I, pp. 642–3. Richard was in Cromwell's service, see *L.P.* XII{2}. App. I.
25 For the abbey's lordship of the Waste, see *V.C.H. North Riding*, II, p. 470. The Cholmleys held office in their own right and as deputies of the Earl of Rutland. For over forty years they had exercised the offices of steward, bailiff, receiver and master forester of the Honour. See *V.C.H. North Riding*, II, pp. 495–6; Leland, pt. I, pp. 62–3; *L.P.* XII{2}. 583 and App. I. For the conflicts, see *Star Ch. Yorkshire*, II, pp. 180–84; ibid., III, pp. 99–100; ibid., IV, pp. 62–8.

numbers before . . . Scarborough Castle". However, neither Percy nor Lumley made reference to it. Moreover, all the surviving evidence specifying a siege, apart from Darcy's distant observation, appertains to a siege started in mid-November. This was organised by John Hallom, the yeoman from the lordship of Watton, and was provoked by the taking of a ship *en route* to Scarborough which was found to contain money, provisions, gunpowder and a letter suggesting that it was the government's intention to establish in the castle a garrison for the repression of the region. In all likelihood, no serious attempt was made in October to take the castle. The Percy host, it seemed, was deployed for other purposes. Rather, a watch was kept to see that the gentlemen there remained immured and harmless.[26]

According to his own account, Thomas Percy's relations with the commons were not entirely smooth. Thus, when he sought to stop them from sacking Cholmley's house they reacted angrily, accusing him of planning their betrayal. They even called for his head and required him to be replaced as captain. But it would be naïve to take his account at its face value and accept that his involvement was totally enforced. The commons, in fact, were very trusting of him, allowing him to return to his mother on 18th October and to remain at Seamer for the whole of 19th October.[27] According to Lumley "the people were more glad to rise with him than with any other" and showed more affection towards him than any other leader.[28] This partly reflected his social standing and his personal charisma but it also came of his commitment to the cause. He took the oath without complaint, willingly attended the muster on 17th October, and without demur became the captain. He failed to march on Hull, although Aske instructed him to do so, but this was because he thought he could better achieve its submission by sending a message to Sir Ralph Ellerker, one of the gentlemen refugees in the town who were persuading it to hold out.[29] By 19th October his support for the uprising was fully declared in a letter that he wrote to the subprior of Watton. Evidently preparing for some great expedition,

---

26 For Darcy's report, see SP1/108 (*L.P.* XI. 760/ii). For the November siege, see SP1/118, f. 271b (*L.P.* XI. 1019), *L.P.* XI. 1088, 1116, 1128, 1162. Lord Herbert's claim that the siege lasted twenty days makes sense if related to November rather than October [see his *Life and Reign of Henry VIII* (London, 1672), p. 478]. Government plans were being made by 27th October and accomplished within the next week to supply the castle with victuals and gunpowder, implying that a watch was being kept but no sustained siege (see *L.P.* XI. 883 and 989). For the gents within, see below, n. 109.

27 SP1/115, f. 259 (*L.P.* XII{1}. 393 {2}) and the corroborative letter, *L.P.* XI. 792.

28 SP1/115, f. 218b (*L.P.* XII{1}. 369).

29 Stapulton, p. 96.

he asked the subprior for two geldings and to send "some great trotting bay" that he had heard about. In the same letter he admitted that he was "in the king's business and (that of) his commonalty and for your sake and the wealth of this realm of England".[30] Then, on 20th October, having received Aske's summons to go to Pontefract Castle rather than Hull, he attended a muster of 10,000 at Malton, held presumably to comply with this order.[31]

Percy failed to identify the localities which furnished this force. When it reached Pontefract, Aske described it as the band from Pickering Lythe and Blackamore.[32] Pickering Lythe was a huge wapentake stretching from Pickering to the coast. It included the Derwent valley north of the river as well as a very large tract of moorland. In identifying the Blackamore region, a problem is set by the fact that two different areas in the region went under this name: one was situated in Upper Ryedale and located between the Hambleton Hills and Rievaulx Abbey; the other lay north of the wapentake of Pickering Lythe in the Cleveland wapentake of East Langbaurgh. Both areas were associated with the uprising: the former was close to the residence of a leading participant, Sir Nicholas Fairfax of Gilling Castle; situated in the latter was Mulgrave Castle, the North Riding seat of the rebel, Sir Francis Bigod.[33] Both were likely areas of support for the Percy host.[34]

30 SP1/108 (*L.P.* XI. 792).
31 SP1/115, fos. 259–259b (*L.P.* XII{1}. 393 {2}). For the implausibility of this figure, see Appendix I. The militia returns for Pickering Lythe, Ryedale, Dickering, Buckrose and Whitby Strand produced a force totalling no more than 5,002 men. It is distinctly possible that the revolt also recruited from Bulmer wapentake, for which no muster return has survived, but highly improbable that Bulmer alone could have made up the difference.
32 Bateson, p. 336.
33 Only one is located by the English Place Name Society which places it in the parish of Old Byland, east of the Hambleton Hills. See *The Place-Names of the North Riding of Yorkshire*, English Place-Name Society, V (Cambridge, 1928), p. 197. The other is located in two documents relating to the pilgrimage of grace: the examination of John Smyth, servant to Sir Francis Bigod, who placed Mulgrave Castle in Blackamore when giving an account of an uprising of the commons there which enlisted Bigod (see *L.P.* XII{1}. 578) and Sir John Bulmer's account of the disturbances of 1537 which suggested that Blackamore was between Cleveland and Pickering Lythe [SP1/119, f. 63b (*L.P.* XII{1}. 1083)]. Nicholas Saxton's map of Yorkshire placed it between Mulgrave and Pickering Lythe [see William Ravenhill (ed.), *Christopher Saxton's Sixteenth-century Maps* (Shrewsbury, 1992), pp. 76–7]. For Fairfax, see Bindoff, II, pp. 114–15. For Bigod, see A. G. Dickens, *Lollards and Protestants in the Diocese of York, 1509–1558* (Oxford, 1959), ch. 3.
34 Rather than being involved with the Percy host, it is possible that Bigod and the commons around Mulgrave formed part of an uprising in the wapentake of East Langbaurgh that also enlisted William Rokeby of Marske and John Bulmer of Wilton Castle and then joined up with the Bowes host at Northallerton. See SP1/118, fos. 255b–256 (*L.P.* XII{1}. 1011).

In view of the mustering point at Malton and the evidence provided by George Lumley, it is clear that Aske's identification of the region from which the uprising recruited support was far from adequate since it also included the north Yorkswold between Malton and Bridlington: that is, a part of the East Riding comprising the wapentakes of Dickering and Buckrose. When at Seamer on 18th and 19th October, Thomas Percy had not been simply comforting his mother but was engaged in raising this region. Returning to his house at Thwing, after unsuccessfully seeking to evade the Bowes host in the palatinate of Durham, Lumley learned that Percy had recruited and mustered "all the people of that quarter of Yorkswold".[35] As well as from Yorkswold, the Malton assembly of 20th October may also have recruited men from the Percy territory around Topcliffe in the Vale of Mowbray. James Rokeby revealed that this region was in a state of agitation in early October. On the other hand the Topcliffe men may have accompanied its steward, Roger Lascelles, when he joined up with the Bowes host.[36]

How the force was actually raised is evident in the work of the bailiffs of Kilham and Nafferton who, as recognised captains of the commons, ordered the Prior of Bridlington to send men and in response received eleven horsed and harnessed troops, each with twenty shillings in his purse, and two brethren, presumably to carry the crosses.[37] Percy's involvement in this operation is evident in his commendation of the prior for being so co-operative.[38] Otherwise, it seems that the various communities provided a certain number of men and clubbed together to ensure that they were sufficiently waged.[39] Then, at the Malton muster of 20th October, the best were selected and, as a result, the assembly of 10,000 was reduced to a well-equipped host of, at most, 5,000 which, according to Stapulton, was "a goodly band of men" when on 21st October it passed through York on its way to Pontefract.[40]

In York Thomas Percy was welcomed by the commons who openly called him to his face "Lord Percy", thus recognising him as the sixth earl's heir.[41] So important was his arrival that Robert Aske who had just taken Pontefract Castle travelled back to York in order to greet

35 SP1/115, f. 217 (L.P. XII{1}. 369).
36 For Topcliffe, see above, p. 164. For Lascelles, see above, p. 150.
37 SP1/118, f. 271 (L.P. XII{1}. 1019).
38 L.P. XII{1}. 369.
39 See below, p. 212.
40 SP1/115, f. 259 (L.P. XII{1}. 393); Bateson, p. 336; Stapulton, p. 99.
41 SP1/115, f. 261b (L.P. XII{1}. 393{2}).

him and, after they had dined together, he returned that afternoon to Pontefract.[42] Aske's evident gratitude was understandable, for Percy's arrival realised his plan to enlist the Percy interest. It also brought in the first of the outlying hosts to join the main pilgrimage: neither the Bowes host nor the Stapulton host arrived until a day later. For Percy his stay in York allowed him to meet up with the forces raised in another Percy sphere of influence: the lordship of Spofforth. Originally recruited by Sir Oswald Wilstrop, the Percy affinity and tenantry from this lordship, along with the commons of the Ainsty, were incorporated with the Percy host as, led by Percy, Sir Nicholas Fairfax, who by virtue of his estate at Walton was a lord of the Ainsty as well as of the North Riding, and Sir Oswald Wilstrop, it marched in triumphant procession through York, led by the Abbot of York St. Mary bearing a cross, and then on to Pontefract, but no longer with the abbot who, at the cost of abandoning his cross, made his escape.[43]

After arriving in Pontefract, the Percy host was joined by the troops drawn from yet another Percy sphere of influence, the lordship of Leconfield, as the Stapulton host was placed under Percy's command and together on 22nd October the two forces set out to defend Wentbridge against the likelihood of a sudden advance from the army royal under the Earl of Shrewsbury. This conjunction was not in keeping with the order of battle decided by the rebel council at Pontefract on 22nd October which had linked the Percy host with the one led by Bowes, placing them together as the two components of the van, an arrangement which came unstuck because the host from the North Riding and Durham needed, in the first instance, to take a rest following its long ride from Spennymoor.[44] As a result, it seemed on 23rd October as if Thomas Percy, by virtue of his leadership of the van, headed the pilgrimage of grace and that the uprising was essentially a materialisation of the earlier cry "thousands for a Percy", and that its aim was to reclaim the family's patrimony from the clutches of the government.[45]

Grievances and aims

A problem with identifying the grievances of this uprising lies in not being able to ascertain the contents of the oath that was taken. Thomas

42 *L.P.* XII{1}. 1018.
43 Stapulton, pp. 99–100; *L.P.* XII{1}. 369; SP1/115, fos. 260b–261 (*L.P.* XII{1}. 393 {2}); *L.P.* XII{1}. 1090/i.
44 See below, p. 377.
45 *L.P.* XI. 714.

Percy said it was written out, implying that it was something substantial: thus, when he asked what the oath was, Preston, the rebel
leader, "read unto him the same oath".[46] Two things are certain about
it: first, it was not Aske's so-called oath to the honourable men since
this had yet to be composed; second, its provenance was the Richmondshire uprising. In proposing that Percy should take the oath,
Preston stated: "we are come to fetch you unto them" – that is, to
the Richmondshire host – and that "we are come . . . to swear you to
take such part as we do".[47] In all likelihood, the oath was the same one
that the Richmondshire rebels had drawn up and dispatched to other
regions; and that what was sworn in Northumberland by Ingram
Percy, and also in Westmorland and Cumberland, was the same oath
that was taken by Thomas.[48] If this was so, its content, if not its actual
wording, can be educed.

   Associated with the oath was a letter addressed from Captain
Poverty which, declaring that the Richmondshire commons had
restored suppressed abbeys, exhorted others to follow suit. The same
letter also urged the maintenance of certain articles which concerned
both the faith and the commonwealth, requiring an oath to be taken
which consisted of agreeing to accept and promote these articles. The
articles have failed to survive, yet surviving descriptions of their
content suggest some resemblance to a set found circulating in the
Richmondshire area in 1537 which ordered the commons to take all
lords and gentlemen and make them swear "on the mass book" to
"maintain the profit of holy church" as the means of "upholding . . .
the christian faith" and to suppress the heretics who, led by Lord
Cromwell, "made the king put down praying and fasting". Besides
these two religious grievances, both of them objections against the
government, the articles contained a purely secular complaint, against
the landlords and ordering them to exact of their tenants no more than
the rent. Thus, in taking the oath the gentlemen were obliging
themselves to respect an order which outlawed the taking of
gressums.[49]

   In addition to the oath, several other statements of grievance
moved the region. One was a letter, written in the name of Chief
Captain Aske and nailed to church doors. It declared that the people

46 SP/115, f. 258b (*L.P.* XII{1}. 393 {2})
47 Ibid., f. 258b (*L.P.* XII{1}. 393 {2}).
48 Bush, "Captain Poverty", pp. 18–19.
49 SP1/114 (*L.P.* XII{1}. 163); Bush, op. cit., pp. 18–21.

should rise to oppose heresy and the decay of the commonwealth.[50] Another was the bill composed by the friar of Knaresborough, complaining of new taxes and the robbing of churches.[51] Both are now lost. What has survived is the song of Friar Pickering, composed at Bridlington in late October and popular within the region. Generally it blamed the government, especially Cromwell, for favouring heretics, for plundering the church and the commons, and for planning the destruction of the nobility. Then, it called upon the commons "these heretics to suppress and tyranny restrain", in order to maintain the faith and "the rights of this land".[52] Finally, both Thomas Percy and George Lumley were obliged by their examiners to list the causes of revolt. Thomas managed to recall six grievances: the rights of the church, the suppression of religious houses, old usages and customs, the Statute of Uses, the taking of gressums and rumoured taxes on christenings and ploughs.[53] George identified two: the pulling down of abbeys and rumoured taxes on sacraments and bread.[54]

As in other parts, the complaint was a varied one, applying to both the faith and the commonwealth. Characterising it was the emphasis placed upon preserving the wealth of the realm, chiefly against the greed of the government. In fact, when the rebels first told Thomas Percy that the cause of the uprising was for "the weal of us all", they offered a theme which incorporated most of the complaints made.[55] In this respect, the grievances fall into the following categories: concern for the wealth of the church; concern for the wealth of the commonalty; and concern for the wealth of the baronage. However, there were other important grievances which failed to fall into these categories, notably the objection to heresy and a complaint against the infringement of constitutional rights.

Elsewhere the wealth of the church tended to be seen, in keeping with fears generated by the Lincolnshire rising, as under threat not only from the dissolution of religious houses but also from government plans to confiscate church treasures and to reduce the number of the parish churches and from the new taxes imposed on the clergy, the first fruits and tenths. This was probably true of this uprising,

---

50 *L.P.* XII{1}. 1021. This is misrepresented by *L.P.* which summarises the letter in such a way as to suggest that the commonwealth was decayed because of certain heresies (see SP1/118, f. 280).
51 For the friar's effect in the region, see Stapulton, p. 96. For the nature of his letters, see *L.P.* XII{1}. 1018 and 1047.
52 SP1/118, fos. 292ff (*L.P.* XII{1}. 1021 {5}).
53 SP1/115, fos. 260–260b (*L.P.* XII{1}. 393 {2}.).
54 SP1/115, f. 213 (*L.P.* XII{1}. 369).
55 SP1/115, f. 258b (*L.P.* XII{1}. 393 {2}).

although in the surviving evidence no complaint is made against the planned onslaught upon the parish churches, in spite of the rumour-mongering of the friar of Knaresborough, and the complaint evidently articulated against the new clerical taxes is found only in an explanation offered by Pickering at his examination of what was meant by a line in his song.[56] The focus of complaint was simply upon the suppression of religious houses, with Percy specifying that a cause of revolt was "for holding up of abbeys that should be suppressed", and with Lumley attributing the revolt to "the pulling down of abbeys".[57]

Within or very close to the region of the uprising eight Dissolutions had occurred. Of these, five were very small nunneries (Rosedale, Arden, Moxby, Keldholme and Baysdale) The remaining three were the minute house of Grosmont (worth no more than £12 p.a. and with five brethren) the hospital of St. Nicholas in Scarborough, affected by the dissolution of Holy Trinity in York, and the relatively substantial Marton Abbey, worth £151 p.a. and with sixteen canons.[58] Furthermore, within the same region were three nunneries rescued from suppression: Wykeham and Yedingham, both of them situated in the Carrs between Seamer and Malton, and the more distant moorland nunnery of Handale, located in Sir Thomas Franke's parish of Loftus in Cleveland. Clearly, the region had suffered the direct experience of suppression whilst also witnessing the provocative anomaly of some houses reprieved and others condemned, with no obvious justification for either.

Yet no reference was made to any of these suppressed houses by the rebels and none appeared to be restored. A further possibility is that the concern for suppression was especially aroused not by what had gone but what might go next. Pickering's song proposed that, as a result of the combined effects of heresy and tyranny, "Christ's church very like is spoiled to be/ And all abbeys suppressed"; and Percy in his letter to the subprior of Watton said he rose, among other things, "for

---

56 When questioned about what he meant by "exaction" in the poem, Pickering replied: "I meant certain taxes, tenths, first fruits and the suppression of monasteries" [SPl/118 (*L.P.* XII{1}. 1021 {3})]. Only if the Topcliffe region became involved with this revolt (for the possibility, see above, p. 150) does the complaint about the plundering of churches become associated with the Malton uprising. See SP1/118, f. 254 (*L.P.* XII{1}. 1011).

57 SP1/115, f. 260 (*L.P.* XII{1}. 393 {3}); SP1/115, f. 213 (*L.P.* XII{1}. 369).

58 See D. Knowles and R. N. Hadcock, *Medieval Religious Houses, England and Wales* (London, 1953), passim. They misdate both the dissolution of Holy Trinity, York and the suppression of the dependent hospital of St. Nicholas, Scarborough (see pp. 82 and 304).

your sake".[59] Bordering the region was an impressive array of wealthy houses, notably Mount Grace, Rievaulx, Byland, Newburgh, Malton, Whitby, Scarborough, Bridlington and Watton, most of them providing willing participants.[60] Sustaining the monastic issue, then, was the fear that a further stage of Dissolution was imminent. As for the rebels' reasons for opposing the suppression of religious houses, they concerned either the maintenance of church wealth as proposed, according to the Prior of Bridlington, by Friar Pickering as the original cause of revolt, or the defence of the faith against the encroachment of heresy as proposed by Sir Nicholas Fairfax.[61] The likelihood is that, in the rebels' mind, the two issues, although quite separate in themselves, were present in the interconnected form posited by the Richmondshire articles of 1537 which justified protecting "the profit of holy church" in terms of "the upholding of the christian faith".[62]

What is clear, however, is that the rebels' fears in matters of religion were not confined to religious houses or the wealth of the church. Sir Nicholas Fairfax was reported as saying that since "they rose . . . for the defence of the faith", their cause ought to be pleasing not just to the priors and abbots but also to "other men of the church".[63] Moreover, in listing the main grievances, Thomas Percy chose to place either side of the complaint against the suppression of abbeys "maintaining the rights of the church" and "maintaining old usages and customs".[64] The reference to rights implied a constitutional grievance, the need to preserve the privileges traditionally enjoyed by the clerical order and the church in relation to the laity and the state. The reference to old usages was a liturgical complaint, an objection to the abolition of practices which the government had associated with saint-worship and intercession. Neither had anything to do directly with the government's expropriation of church wealth. On the other hand, the failure of the evidence to specify which rights and usages had to be defended might suggest that, although genuinely felt, these grievances were not as important to the rebels as the spoliation of the church.

Foremost among the grievances associated with the wealth of the

59 SP1/118, f. 292 (L.P. XII{1}. 1021 {5}); SP1/108 (L.P. XI. 792).
60 See below, pp. 213–14.
61 For Friar Pickering's comment, as reported by the Prior of Bridlington, see SP1/118, f. 272 (L.P. XII{1}. 1019). For Fairfax's comment, see SP1/115, f. 212b (L.P. XII{1}. 369).
62 SP1/114 (L.P. XII{1}. 163).
63 SP1/115, f. 212b (L.P. XII{1}. 369).
64 SP1/115, f. 260 (L.P. XII{1}. 393 {2}).

commons was a fiscal complaint, not explicitly against the subsidy or the fifteenth and tenth but certainly against the new taxes rumoured to be imminent and considered to be especially onerous for the poor. In the complaints made by the Lincolnshire and Yorkshire uprisings of October 1536 a great range of new taxes can be identified: taxes on gold, on cattle, on food, on sacraments and on ploughs.[65] Of these taxes, the evidence associated with the Percy host failed to mention the first two. However, it specifically objected to paying the last three. Between them Lumley and Percy identified as a cause of revolt a complaint against a tax on christenings and marriages.[66] Rumour had it that a noble (i.e. 6s. 8d.) would be due to the Crown for every baptism, marriage and burial. This was readily seen as a major threat to the material well-being of the commons; but from the way it was presented it could also be taken as a threat to their spiritual welfare. These rumours were circulated through bills nailed to church doors.[67] The only surviving bill declared that "no enfant shall receive the blessed sacrament of baptism unless a tribute be paid to the king", the implication being that the right to baptism and its benefits would only be extended to those who could afford this tribute and that, for those who could not, their children would be condemned to limbo and denied the chance of salvation.[68] It was also implied, but perhaps not grasped, that, if such a tax was introduced, the ministration of a sacrament would no longer be simply a matter for the congregation and its priest but would become something determined by the government.

Lumley also identified a grievance against a tax on bread.[69] This related to the rumour that a tribute was due to the king from all men whose goods and chattels were assessed at less than £20 whenever they wished to eat wheaten bread, chicken, goose or pork.[70] The reference to £20 specified the threshold of the 1534 subsidy, the second part of which was due.[71] The meaning imparted by the rumour was that all those who had been exempted from this subsidy would not escape the fiscal net since they would now have to pay taxes for what they ate. The size of the tribute went unmentioned; but in itself and by virtue of

65 M. L. Bush "'Enhancements and importunate charges': an analysis of the tax complaints of October 1536", *Albion* 22 (1990), pp. 408–10.
66 SP1/115, f. 213 (*L.P.* XII{1}. 369); SP1/115, fos. 260–260b (*L.P.* XII{1}. 393 {2}).
67 See n. 65.
68 The one surviving set of articles, see Toller, p. 49–50 (*L.P.* XI. 892).
69 SP1/115, f. 213 (*L.P.* XII{1}. 369).
70 As indicated in n. 68.
71 Bush, "Enhancements and importunate charges", p. 406.

its presentation it was an obviously offensive levy. Unfairly, it breached the convention that the poor should not pay government taxes and, turning the tables, proposed that in future they should either be heavily taxed or severely curtailed in their diet. Like the tax on sacraments, this consumer tax was presented as a device which would deny a basic right to those unable to pay. That it was taken in this manner by the rebels was evident in how the complaint came to Lumley who consequently presented it as: "that no poor man should eat white bread".[72] Percy failed to identify this particular grievance but instead named a tax on ploughs.[73] In the only surviving bill that complained of the new taxes, it was claimed that "every ploughland shall pay a tribute".[74] Elsewhere the rumour proposed a tribute 6s. 8d. on every plough.[75] However, no matter how this rumour was interpreted, and no matter whether it was seen as a tax on ploughs or ploughlands, the message was the same: a burdensome tax upon the commons and sufficiently novel to offend traditional rights.

Such taxes were concoctions, far removed from the actual tax policy of the government. They belonged to a traditional armoury of exactions upon the poor which governments had studiously avoided but which opponents in a bid to raise the commons had occasionally accused them of introducing.[76] For spreading them to the region of this particular uprising the friar of Knaresborough was mainly responsible, receiving a licence to go there from William Stapulton on 10th October and returning a week later to declare his mission completed and successful.[77] That the friar had good cause for self-congratulation was made evident by Lumley who listed the complaint against the new taxes as the only cause of revolt he could recall apart from the suppression of religious houses, and by Percy who included it in his list of the six basic causes of revolt.[78]

The only mention of an agrarian grievance in the evidence associated with this uprising was made by Thomas Percy. Without elaboration, he included "ingressum-taking" in his causes of revolt: that is, the exaction of dues which, within the manorial system, were payable upon a change of tenant or lord.[79] In doing so, he echoed

72 SP1/115, f. 213 (*L.P.* XII{1}. 369).
73 SP1/115, f. 260b (*L.P.* XII{1}. 393 {2}).
74 See n. 68.
75 Bush, "Enhancements and importunate charges", p. 408.
76 See M. L. Bush, "Tax reform and rebellion in early Tudor England", *History*, 76 (1991), p. 395.
77 See above, pp. 60–1.
78 *L.P.* XII{1}. 369; *L.P.* XII{1}. 393.
79 Ibid.

William Stapulton who regarded "the sore-taking of gressums" as a major grievance of the commons and he raised an issue which seriously affected the rebels of Westmorland and Cumberland; which appeared to be present, if not prominently, in the Richmondshire uprising; and which was eventually ensconced as item nine in the December articles.[80] Although there is nothing to link the grievance for certain with this particular revolt, pieces of evidence suggest that gressums were an issue in the region and that what was in contention was whether tenants claiming to hold their farms by tenant right should be burdened with gressums. One source of evidence are the rebel bills, manifestos and articles which circulated in the north in late 1536 and in early 1537. On gressums they adopted a extreme position calling either for their complete abolition or their restriction to a nominal sum.

Such proposals infiltrated the region in the form of the oath brought by the Richmondshire outriders on 16th October or by means of letters like the one brought to Sir John Bulmer early in 1537 which asserted that "men should pay no gressums" and that "they should ever have with them the old lord or the new": that is, they should not be obliged to pay an acknowledgement for any change of lord.[81] Quite possibly such ideas were imported and had little effect upon the region apart from horrifying the gentlemen who in reaction overemphasised their importance. However, the tenant concerns of the Percy family at this time and the policies of estate management they were adopting and adapting, and the effect these policies could have in setting an example for other lords to follow, suggest that gressums were a grievance in the region and that the bills and articles brought in from other parts preached to the converted.

On their Yorkshire estates the Percies introduced a major innovation in 1521 when, in subjecting them to the custom of the Honour of Cockermouth, they ensured that their Yorkshire tenantry, like that of Cumberland, would be subjected to a gressum not simply upon a change of tenant, as had normally happened in the past, but also upon a change of lord.[82] If the gressums had remained a nominal sum, there would have been no problem for the tenant. However, the custom of Cockermouth defined them as arbitrary dues limited only by the requirement that they should appear to be, in the light of what else was required of the tenant, reasonable. And in the 1520s and

80 Stapulton, p. 82; Bush, "Captain Poverty", passim.; *L.P.* XI. 1246.
81 *L.P.* XII{1}. 1083.
82 Bean, *The Estates of the Percy Family*, p. 63.

1530s, pressed by inflation and permitted by the custom, the Percies, along with other lords, began to enlarge their gressums so that they became a multiple rather than a fraction of the rent.[83] By 1536 the concern of the tenantry had enlisted the sympathy of the Crown. A problem for the Percies was not simply tenant unrest but also the opportunity it provided the Crown to establish a special relationship with this tenantry and thus to ease its take-over of the Percy inheritance.[84] For this reason a change in estate management was forced upon the Percy family, with the result that early in 1537 the sixth earl conceded to his Yorkshire tenants twenty-one year leases, thus excusing them from paying another gressum until the lease had terminated and which in practice substituted for the Cockermouth system one in which a gressum was taken only at twenty-one year intervals.[85] Its effect was recorded by the Earl of Northumberland in a letter to Cromwell which declared "what love I have among my own tenants since my repair into the country, as well in Yorkshire as in Northumberland".[86]

Such was the agrarian context in which this uprising occurred. In taking the Richmondshire oath which obliged them to reform the system of tenancy by abolishing the gressum, Thomas and Ingram ensured that this rising of the commons was directed against the government rather than against themselves and that it should be a political rather than a social movement. Moreover, because of the promises of agrarian reform that the lords were prepared to make to establish cohesion with the commons, agrarian grievances could not be said to have directed the uprising. As in the Richmondshire uprising, then, they were played down.[87] Nonetheless, they were of prime importance in determining the character of the revolt in the sense that its organisation – an uprising of the commons that remained true to the society of orders in having a ·leadership appropriately composed of gentlemen – was reliant upon the understanding lord and tenant were able to reach on the agrarian question; and that the general character the revolt assumed, a political movement protesting against misgovernance and directed at curing the body politic, relied upon a prior agreement to settle an agrarian problem.

---

83 Bean, op. cit., pp. 51–68. For a description of the custom of Cockermouth, see SP1/124, f. 67 (L.P. XII{2}. 548).
84 See Bush, "Captain Poverty", pp. 18–19.
85 See Robert Southwell's account of the Percy estate's liability to fines in 1537 [SP1/124, f. 67b (L.P. XII{2}. 548)].
86 SP1/113 (L.P. XI. 1368).
87 See above, p. 181.

Picking up what was said in, and close to, the Court, the nephew of Eustace Chapuys, the imperial ambassador, reported that on 23rd October Thomas Percy had brought 30,000 men to join the commons in revenge for the wrong the king had inflicted upon him by denying his wish to be heir to the earldom of Northumberland.[88] The details are untrue but the inaccuracies can be explained away as the impression readily formed by the government's forces when, in first encountering the pilgrim host, they witnessed at the head of it, by virtue of his leadership of the van, the sixth earl of Northumberland's brother.[89] Both Ingram and Thomas undoubtedly were enraged by the government's plans to annex the family's patrimony and to leave it landless. For them, the rebel aim of preserving "the weal of us all" and "the wealth of the realm" meant, first and foremost, safeguarding the family estate from the machinations of Thomas Cromwell, against whom both were recorded as fulminating during the course of the revolt.[90] But how important was this issue for the rank and file?

The retention of the Percy inheritance was not a concern that moved only the family. As Lumley put it, "the people were more glad to rise with him than with any other man" and "proclaimed him twice as Lord Percy, and showed such affection towards him as they showed towards none other man that he knew; and because he was the best of the Percies that were left next to my lord of Northumberland" – that is, the helpless sixth earl who was in the north at the time of the uprising but played no part in it, apart from submitting, and in late October lay low and presumably sworn in its midst at Selby.[91] The pilgrimage generally took on the appearance of a Percy uprising because so many of its captains were attached to the family by present or former service: e.g. Aske, Monkton, Stapulton, Lascelles, Hamerton, Robert Constable, Norton and Gilbert Wedell; and also because among the rebels was the firm belief that, like the lesser monasteries, the family deserved to survive, both with its possessions

---

88 *L.P.* XI. 714.
89 See below, pp. 377–8.
90 For "the weal of all", see SP1/115, f. 258b (*L.P.* XII{1}. 393 {2}). For "the wealth of this realm", see SP1/108 (*L.P.* XI. 792). For the anti-Cromwellian sentiments uttered by Thomas Percy, see *L.P.* XII{1}. 1018. For those of Ingram Percy, see *L.P.* XII{1}. 1090 (23).
91 SP1/115, fos. 218b–219 (*L.P.* XII{1}. 369). Lumley's account is confirmed by Thomas Percy who stated that the two occasions were at York and at Pontefract. See SP1/115, f. 261 (*L.P.* XII{1}. 393 {2}). For Northumberland's whereabouts during the course of the Pilgrimage and for his involvement with it, see *L.P.* XI. 774 and 1402; SP1/119, f. 49 (*L.P.* XII{1}. 1062); Stapulton, p. 99.

intact and with Thomas Percy as the childless sixth earl's heir.[92] At the time, it is true, the rebels were contemptuous of the present earl for failing to participate, for submitting to the government's wishes and (a point made by Sir Thomas Hilton) for offending the society of orders by making gentlemen of knaves through granting them lands. But this caused no antipathy to the family; and, according to Stapulton, it was frequently said by the rebels: "Strike off the head of the earl and make Sir Thomas earl".[93] The cry "thousands for a Percy" then, as it was uttered by the Howdenshire rebels at the very start of their uprising, probably expressed not simply a ploy to enlist the family's support but genuine sympathy for the Percy cause.

Only a small proportion of the rebels, however, could have been the family's tenants, servants and friends. This was as true of the regions that provided the Percy host as it was of the pilgrimage as a whole. In the region was a substantial Percy estate around Seamer, Hunmanby, Nafferton and Wansford, all of it the dower lands of Thomas Percy's mother, the Countess of Northumberland; and on the western edge of the region was the Percy estate in the Vale of Mowbray, at Catton, Asenby and Topcliffe; and on the northern edge was Thomas Percy's own estate at Kildale.[94] There is no means of telling if the manred of these peripheral estates contributed troops to the Percy host or if they attended the two Malton assemblies. But even if they did, large-scale recruitment from the estates of other lords would still have been necessary to make up the numbers.[95] For this reason, the Percy cause probably enlisted sympathy and support, in this particular revolt as in the rest of the pilgrimage, not simply because of reverence for the Percy name but because it was seen as part of a general attack upon the noble order. As well as being made in the declarations of complaint produced by Aske, this point was linked with the northern Yorkswold, a region which provided support for the Percy host, through the evidence of Pickering's song which complained

92 See R. R. Reid, *The King's Council in the North* (London, 1921), pp. 133–4. For Gilbert Wedell, the bailiff of Nafferton, see *L.P.* XII{1}.201/iv and 1019. For Monkton, see Hoyle, "Henry Percy, sixth earl of Northumberland". p. 198. Hoyle is wrong in declaring (p. 198) that there is nothing to indicate that Aske had been a servant of the sixth earl. Northumberland himself in early 1537 declared that when he first succeeded his father Aske had been responsible for "the keeping and conveyance of all my letters" [SP1/119, f. 49 (*L.P.* XII{1}. 1062)].

93 Stapulton, p. 102.

94 See P.R.O. SC11/959 and Bean, op. cit., p. 147.

95 The Malton assemblies were of 4,000 and 10,000 men. The size of the host was 5,000 troops.

that "The nobility of the realm [was] brought to confusion" and predicted that if Cromwell were to remain in power "Our nobles for their boldness shortly should be shut/ Their heads to be lost and that was great pity/ This country to be desolate of so noble progeny".[96]

The wealth of the lords was regarded as threatened not only by the impending annexation of the Percy estate but also by the recent Statute of Uses. This statute was condemned both in the Lincolnshire articles and in the pilgrims' December articles, but it rarely featured in the rest of the evidence. Robert Aske commented upon it in his Examination, suggesting at one point that it had little meaning in Yorkshire and at another that it was one of those recently enacted statutes especially "grudged at" by the pilgrims.[97] Otherwise, there exist only two pieces of evidence. One related to the Richmondshire and Durham uprising and was presented in December by Marmaduke Neville, brother of Lord Latimer and servant of the Earl of Westmorland, who named "especially the act of uses" as one of the statutes the king had promised to reform as a result of the agreement reached between him and the pilgrims.[98] The other piece of evidence waas provided by Thomas Percy who included the Statute of Uses as item four in his list of the causes of revolt.[99] It would seem that, although the grievance had a fairly narrow geographical appeal, it was nonetheless present in this particular revolt as well as in the uprisings of Richmondshire, Durham and Howdenshire.

In repudiating the complaint against the Statute of Uses, the government pointed out that it was a matter for the lords not the commons; and Marmaduke Neville suggested that it was especially offensive to younger sons of the landed order.[100] This was undoubtedly true and, in order to overcome the limitation of its appeal and to convert it into a grievance that the commonalty could share, the rebels presented the statute as adversely affecting all with landed rights.[101] Quintessentially, however, the complaint was a tax matter since the statute in question sought to destroy the efficacy of a device (i.e. the Use) developed and employed by landlords to evade feudal dues. What is more, it was the exclusive concern of the fiefholders who alone had

96 For Aske's declarations, see above, p. 104. For Pickering's song, see SP1/118 (*L.P.* XII{1}. 1021 (5)). For its connexion with the wapentake of Dickering, see *L.P.* XII{1}. 1019.
97 See Bush, "Enhancements and importunate charges", pp. 415–18.
98 *L.P.* XI. 1319.
99 *L.P.* XII{1}. 393.
100 See Bush, op. cit., p. 415 and *L.P.* XI. 1319.
101 Bush, op. cit., pp. 415–16.

benefited from it. The complaint, then, was closely associated with the need to protect the wealth of the baronage against a government which was now liberated by the Statute of Uses to enjoy fully, for the first time in centuries, the feudal rights accruing, by virtue of its suzerainty, to the Crown.[102]

In the typical manner, the rebels of the region appeared to hold no grudge against the king. Thomas Percy explained in a letter to the subprior of Watton that, in participating in the revolt, "I am in the king's business".[103] Friar Pickering claimed under examination that, whilst he had hoped "for mutation and reform of divers laws lately made", he had held no expectation "concerning the mutation of the prince's estate"; and he closed his song with the firm statement that the rebel cause was "not against our prince". On the other hand, he had hoped "for a mutation . . . of his council".[104] For the rebels, high and low, the key to the problem was Thomas Cromwell. Pickering in his song presented him as "the cruel Haman", "the cursed Cromwell" who was one of "those southern Turks perverting our laws and spoiling Christ's church": that is, a tyrant who, "the wealth of the realm regarding not one straw" and true to his origins, practised the art of the shearman by imposing "intolerable exactions", and who had proved to be an arch enemy of the faith by promoting heresy and heretics. For the rebels, the solution was simple:

> If this Haman was hanged, then dare I will say
> This realm then redressed full soon should be.

To bring it about, the song urged "the faithful people of the boreal region" to "boldly go forward in our peregrinage".[105] The rancour in the region against Cromwell was not solely expressed in Pickering's song. When Thomas Percy and Aske met for the first time after the outbreak of the revolt, in York on 20th October, they did little more than rail against him.[106] Anti-Cromwellian sentiments also moved the commons. This was made evident in the hostility shown towards Sir Francis Bigod, who as lord of Settrington was a considerable land-owner in the wapentake of Buckrose and, following his capture by the commons, was with the Percy host at Pontefract. According to his own account, his known association with "such a lewd one", (i.e. Crom-well), left him hated by the commons, the reason being that Cromwell

102 Ibid., pp. 417–18.
103 SP1/108 (*L.P.* XI. 792).
104 For his examination, see SP1/118, f. 280b (*L.P.* XII{1}. 1021).
105 For his song, see SP1/118(*L.P.* XII{1}. 1021 {5}).
106 *L.P.* XII{1}. 1018.

was regarded as an enemy of "Christ's church, the faith thereof and the commonwealth".[107]

According to Thomas Percy, the rebels who followed him had a clear idea of how to right what was wrong. Their aim was to march on London, enlisting the support of "the country by the way". Then they would sue the king to have certain statutes repealed, to punish their perpetrators, especially Cromwell, and to grant the rebels a general pardon. This plan of action, he thought, was the common expectation. It was not formulated in any council but was "a common bruit that went abroad among the commons".[108]

Organisation of revolt

In the usual manner, the uprising was transformed into something more than a popular revolt as prominent gentlemen were enlisted and converted into captains. The Aske and Stapulton hosts were able to recruit important gentlemen by taking the strongholds to which they had retreated, especially Pontefract Castle and the newly walled town of Kingston upon Hull. From the 13th October another nest of fugitive gentlefolk was to be found in Scarborough Castle. Possibly an attempt was made by the rebels of the region to take them. However, the castle did not yield; and no concentrated attempt was made to bring it to submission.[109] The Percy host therefore had to enlist its gentlemen piecemeal. This it did by taking them captive, as with Francis Bigod, or by threatening to spoil their houses, as with Lumley and Percy, or through the persuasions of gentlemen already enlisted, as with Fairfax. By the time it reached Pontefract the host included within its ranks the knights, Sir Thomas Percy, Sir Oswald Wilstrop, Sir Nicholas Fairfax and Sir Francis Bigod as well as George Lumley of Thwing, the son and heir of Lord Lumley. But the recruitment of prestigious gentlemen did not transform the uprising from one type of revolt to another. From the very start, minor gentlemen were very much involved: notably William Percehay, lord of Ryton, George Bawne of Kilham, Gilbert Wedell of Nafferton and

---

107 Dickens, Lollards and Protestants in the Diocese of York, p. 90.
108 SP1/115, f. 261 (L.P. XII{1}. 393 {2}).
109 For the gentlemen in the refuge of Scarborough Castle, see Stapulton, p. 92. They were George Conyers, Ralph Eure, Tristram Teshe and Edmund Copindale. For the rebels' treatment of it, see above, pp. 192–3.

the four gentlemen who led the Richmondshire outriders.[110] The only change was that a leadership of minor gentlemen gave way to a command structure of major gentlemen. Moreover, there is no reason to believe that the uprising ceased to be a movement of the commons. A rising of the commons had simply succeeded in clothing itself properly in the society of orders.

As far as it is known, the host marched to join the other hosts as one co-ordinated force led by gentlemen. However, there is no reason to believe that it was an aristocratic uprising, stirred up by lords and manned by their tenants. A central feature of the uprising was the late point at which the region's leading families joined up. In the person of Thomas Percy, the Percy family was the first to join; but that was on the 16th October, almost a week after the start of the disturbances in those parts.[111] The host's second in command, Sir Nicholas Fairfax of Gilling Castle in Ryedale and of Walton in the Ainsty, did not join until 20th October when he came to the Malton assembly on the request of his friend and kinsman, Sir Thomas Percy.[112] The third in command, Sir Oswald Wilstrop, joined the Percy host only when it reached York.[113] George Lumley and Francis Bigod, the two other prominent gentlemen known to have served in the Percy host were also late arrivals. George was in Durham until the 18th October when he was taken and sworn by the Richmondshire rebels, allowed to return to his house at Thwing in the wapentake of Dickering, presumably in return for the promise that he would assist the uprising there, and then agreed to join the Percy host after threats were issued against his property.[114] Bigod at the start of the uprising was absent from Settrington and resident on his estate at Mulgrave in Cleveland. The pattern of his involvement followed that of Lumley, with an attempt to flee thwarted, capture by the Blackamore commons, permission granted to return to Settrington and a latterday enlistment in the

---

110 For Percehay, see *V.C.H. North Riding*, II, p. 448 and above. For George Bawne and Gilbert Wedell, see *L.P.* XII{1}. 201/iv and Stapulton, p. 92. For the Richmondshire outriders, described by Percy as led by three to four gentlemen, see SP1/115, f. 258b (*L.P.* XII{1}. 393 {2}).

111 *L.P.* XII{1}. 393.

112 Bindoff, II, pp. 114–15 and R. B. Smith, *Land and Politics in the England of Henry VIII* (Oxford, 1970), p. 186. For his involvement with the Percy host, see *L.P.* XII{1}. 393 and 369; Stapulton, p. 99.

113 Stapulton, p. 100. For his association with Percy in York, see *L.P.* XII{1}. 393. Wilstrop was originally impressed by the commons of Ouse and Derwent under orders from Robert Aske and then became a keen organiser of revolt in the Ainsty and Skyrack (Stapulton, p. 100).

114 *L.P.* XII{1}. 369.

Percy host.[115] Rather than by leadership, the crucial contribution of the prominent gentlemen to the development of the uprising in its early stages was to offer no resistance. Under examination, Friar Pickering supposed that the gentlemen could have stopped the October insurrection as they did the one that broke out the following January.[116] Responsible for the uprising was not only the group that stood back and then joined up but also another group which went into retreat and remained there. This included Cholmley of Roxby in Pickering Lythe, who fled and for his pains had his house plundered, and Sir Ralph Eure of Brompton, also in Pickering Lythe, who by the 13th October had taken refuge in Scarborough Castle where he remained for the rest of the month.[117] Finally, with Sir Robert Constable of Flamborough, engaged elsewhere, first in taking action against the Lincolnshire rebels and then in refuge with Lord Darcy at Pontefract Castle, an uprising of the commons in the wapentake of Dickering was allowed a free rein.[118]

Another organisational feature of the uprising, which further questions the thesis that it was the creation of a regional aristocracy, was the way it fell under the influence of revolts in other regions. Thus from the west came the Richmondshire outriders who played a prominent part in organising the first assembly at Malton and in recruiting Thomas Percy.[119] From the south came the rebels of the Beverley region, led by John Hallom who raised the region as far as Great Driffield and, through the bailiffs of Kilham and Nafferton, raised the wapentake of Dickering.[120] Lumley, who was keen to present Sir Thomas Percy as a decisive force in this uprising, claimed that when he returned to Thwing he was led to understand that it was Sir Thomas Percy who had "raised and mustered all the people of that quarter of Yorkswold".[121] However, Lumley who had not been present at the start, was simply commenting upon what Percy had done once compelled to take part. Lumley's account offered no explanation for the large assembly held at Malton on 16th October which resulted from outside influences, brought not only from the rebels of Beverley and Richmondshire but also by the friar of Knaresborough with the

115 Dickens, *Lollards and Protestants in the Diocese of York*, p. 90.
116 *L.P.* XII{1}. 1021.
117 For Cholmley, see n. 24; For Eure, see Stapulton, p. 92 and for family's standing, see Bindoff, II, pp. 109–10.
118 See above, pp. 67–9.
119 *L.P.* XII{1}. 393.
120 P.R.O. E36/119, f. 21 (*L.P.* XII{1}. 201); *L.P.* XII{1}. 201 {iv}; SP1/118, f. 271 (*L.P.* XII{1}. 1019).
121 SP1/115, f. 212 (*L.P.* XII{1}. 369).

explosive letters that he nailed to church doors and by Thomas Franke, parson of Loftus, who was dispatched to the region by Robert Aske.[122]

Before Percy became committed to revolt, an uprising of the commons occurred which, for its own advantage, first latched upon him and which he then appreciated as a device for achieving his ambition to save the Percy patrimony and to become the next earl. Whereas the major gentry were recruited with some effort, the commons, and certain members of the lesser gentry, appeared eager to rise, as was evident in the large numbers that attended the Malton assemblies on 16th and 20th October. It was also evident in the way each township organised its contribution to the host, imposing a tax upon the inhabitants to provide the wages of those chosen to serve. Thus, according to Thomas Percy, "every town found certain men"; and according to George Lumley, "every township delivered to such soldiers as went out from them twenty shillings to a piece which served them for so long as they went forth"; and according to John Pickering, "every township bore their own charges by a gathering and a taxation among themselves".[123] As for the gentlemen, according to both Lumley and Percy, they "had no wages" and "went of their own cost".[124] Nor did it seem that the gentlemen participants paid out wages unless to their own servants. For this purpose it seems that Thomas Percy, who was, in his own words, "forth of my own country" and short of cash, sought twenty nobles from the Abbot of York St. Mary's, presumably to provide for the sixteen men he first brought to the assembly on the wolds beyond Spital on 17th October.[125] In contrast, the bulk of the troops were financed by the communities they represented.

In the early days of the uprising certain clerics had an important part to play, especially in conveying to it a spirit of revolt from other regions, with the friar of Knaresborough coming to raise Ryedale and Pickering Lythe and with Sir Thomas Franke providing the link between the revolts in Howdenshire and Pickering Lythe. Franke remained as chief adviser to Thomas Percy at least until his host reached York on 20th October when he persuaded Lancelot Collyns to act as surety for Thomas Percy so that he could purchase four pounds of velvet and be fitted out like a lord.[126] Finally, Friar

122 See below, n. 126.
123 SP1/115, f. 260b (L.P. XII{1}. 393 {2}); SP1/115, f. 213 (L.P. XII{1}. 369); SP1/118, f. 280 (L.P. XII{1}. 1021).
124 L.P. XII{1}. 369; SP1/115, f. 260b (L.P. XII{1}. 393 {2}).
125 SP1/108 (L.P. XI. 792); SP1/115, f. 260b (L.P. XII{1}. 393 {2}).
126 For the friar, see Stapulton, p. 88. For Franke, see Stapulton, p. 88; L.P. XII{1}. 1018 and 1035.

Pickering from his adopted base in Bridlington Priory played his part by articulating the grievances of the rebels in a song which was soon on everyone's lips.[127] Yet, apart from these examples, the role of the clergy was not to lead or to influence or to incite. Rather it was to comply with the rebels' demands for money, horses and carts; for properly furnished troops; and for clerical cross-bearers. All this the clergy appeared willingly to do, although under examination they alleged that their contributions had been enforced. The Prior of Bridlington responded to the request from the bailiffs of Kilham and Nafferton "to help the commons" by providing eleven men horsed and harnessed, each with twenty shillings apiece and also by dispatching two of his brethren to act as crossbearers; the Prior of Malton sent a servant and a cart; the Abbot of Whitby sent five marks and "an ambling nag", stating that he did so because "their going forth was for their cause"; the Abbot of York St. Mary contributed twenty nobles to Thomas Percy; the Prior of Watton contributed horses.[128]

Yet the laity, especially the gentry leadership, felt that the clergy were not doing enough. On 20th October Sir Nicholas Fairfax argued that since the cause was the defence of the faith, the clergy should do more to support it; asserting that clerics, both regulars and seculars, should be prepared not only to send aid but also to "go forth in their own person". In holding this view, he was strongly supported by Sir Oswald Wilstrop and Sir Thomas Percy.[129] Visits were paid to a range of religious houses to make this point known. Fairfax himself went to the Abbot of York St. Mary whilst Lumley or his servant approached a succession of abbeys (Newburgh, Rievaulx, Whitby, Malton, Kirkham, Mount Grace, Bridlington, Guisborough) to persuade their heads, along with two monks from each house, "with their best crosses to come forward in their best array".[130] In addition, Wilstrop and Fairfax visited Lancelot Collyns, urging him to go with the commons; and Sir Oswald obliged the Abbot of York St. Mary "to come forward with his cross before the commons" as they passed through the city of York *en route* to Pontefract.[131]

Whilst the religious were appreciated for their horses, carts, ready

---

127 *L.P.* XII{1}. 1021 {5} and *L.P.* XII{1}. 1019.
128 For Bridlington, see SP/118, f. 271 (*L.P.* XII{1}. 1019). For Malton, see *L.P.* XII{1}. 534. For Whitby, see SP1/115, f. 261 (*L.P.* XII{1}. 393 {2}). For York, see above, n. 125. For Watton, see SP1/115, f. 261 (*L.P.* XII{1}. 393 {2}).
129 SP1/115, f. 212b (*L.P.* XII{1}. 369)
130 Ibid.
131 For Collyns, see SP1/118, f. 268b (*L.P.* XII{1}. 1018). For the abbot, see SP1/115, fos. 260b–261 (*L.P.* XII{1}. 393 {2}).

cash, tenants and servants, they were especially appreciated for the effect of their presence. To give the proper impression of a pilgrimage, it was essential that the host should be led by monks with crosses, the more high-ranking the better. To give a convincing impression that the uprising was the society of orders in action, it was as important to have clerical, as to have gentry, participants on show. To convince the government that its religious policy was wrong, it was vital that clerics should be visible as committed rebels, especially since they had authorised it both in parliament and in convocation. The insistence upon personal attendance created differences between the gentry and clergy. The normal response received from the abbeys by Lumley was that the abbots and priors could not attend themselves, but would send "all the furtherance and aid they could"; and the Abbot of York St Mary had to be forced by Wilstrop to carry his cross before the Percy host as it passed through York.[132] Nonetheless, this did not mean a lack of commitment to the rebels' cause. In fact, certain exceptional monks, like the Abbot of Rievaulx and the Quondam of Guisborough, were prepared to attend.[133] Each of the religious houses made its contribution in money, men and horses; and, although opposed to his own personal attendance of the rebels' army, Collyns gave Aske an enthusiastic welcome when, upon first entering York, he came to the minister door. As treasurer of the see, he was also generous in providing the rebels with funds and military equipment.[134] The discord that developed only expressed a difference in perception of how the clergy ought to participate. They sought to do so in the discreet manner that they considered appropriate to their order, whilst the gentlemen felt that, in comparison with their own commitment, the participation of the clergy was too indirect and low key.

The uprising of October 1536 occurred because, in contrast to the revolts that briefly erupted in January and February 1537, when the commons rose the gentlemen failed to stay them. But this offers only a part explanation of the uprising. It identifies the vital role played by Eure, Cholmley, Bigod and Lumley, but not the contribution made by Thomas Percy, Sir Nicholas Fairfax and Sir Oswald Wilstrop. Vital to the later organisation of this uprising was undoubtedly their commitment. Moreover, what it achieved was due to the leadership that Thomas Percy provided, the drawing power of his name and his

132 SP1/115, fos. 212b–213 (*L.P.* XII{1}. 369); SP1/115, ff. 260b–261 (*L.P.* XII{1}. 393 {2}).
133 SP1/115, fos. 212b–213 (*L.P.* XII{1}. 369).
134 *L.P.* XII{1}. 1018.

popularity with the commons. The host's eagerness for the fray reflected the disgruntlement of the commons; but its efficiency and dynamism, evident in the speed at which it responded to Aske's summons of 20th October and in the fact that it was largely manned by well-equipped troops, reflected Percy's determination to support and organise this disgruntlement, ostensibly for the weal of all, in reality to preserve the house of Percy.

VI

THE HAMERTON/ TEMPEST HOST

The hosts in Craven

Between 20th October and the end of the month, two rebel hosts operated in the deanery of Craven: the one in Percy Fee, to resist the Earl of Derby and to defend Sawley Abbey; the other in the honour of Skipton, to confront the Earl of Cumberland and to besiege Skipton Castle[1]. Neither was simply a native movement. In fact, the uprising in the Honour of Skipton was largely the work of a rebel host from Richmondshire. The revolt in Percy Fee was genuinely indigenous, but developed under the influence of the Richmondshire uprising and of Robert Aske and reached outward both to enlist support in Lancashire and to ally with the uprising in Kendal and Dent.

The two hosts failed to connect with each other. After an early attempt to persuade the Earl of Cumberland to provide his support, the rebels of Percy Fee fell under the threat of the Earl of Derby and directed their activities towards Lancashire. They provided no aid for the siege of Skipton Castle. However, their opposition to the Earl of Derby was intended not only to defend Sawley Abbey but also to prevent him from relieving the Earl of Cumberland. As for the other host, it remained singlemindedly concentrated upon Skipton Castle until 27th October when it marched to Pontefract to join Robert Aske.

The grievances and aims of the two hosts were very similar. Just as the Percy Fee rebels were concerned with the Dissolution, the revolt having begun with the restoration of Sawley Abbey, so were most of the rebels active in the Honour of Skipton, having earlier restored the

1 See Map 7.

abbeys of Easby and Coverham in Richmondshire And since Sir Arthur Darcy had been the recipient of property from both Sawley and Coverham Abbeys, the hostility of the two hosts towards the Dissolution focused upon the same person[2]. In addition, both hosts were moved by purely secular grievances. These centred upon the fear that the government was threatening the well-being of the common-wealth. Neither revolt, however, marked a continuation of the agrarian revolts that had affected Craven in 1535.[3] They were not principally against harsh landlordship. Although it expressed itself in the refusal to pay rent, the animus shown towards Arthur Darcy was simply because he had acquired the Sawley Abbey estate. The animus shown towards the earls of Derby and Cumberland came of their loyalty to the government. Both were self-proclaimed risings of the commons, but this did not mean they were just popular movements. Active in both were clerics and gentlemen. The two hosts had the same aim: to withstand two great magnates of the north who had remained true to the government. For the pilgrimage of grace as a whole, they had the same strategic importance of preventing a magnate alliance behind its front line. For this reason both were appreciated, respected and cultivated by Robert Aske and the rest of the pilgrim high command.

The revolt in Percy Fee

The restoration of Sawley Abbey

The Percy Fee uprising occurred in two phases. It began as a move-ment of the commons to restore Sawley Abbey. Then a week later it mobilised an army whose principal tasks were to recruit support for the uprising and to defend the restoration. The army moved twice into Lancashire: on 23rd of October to swear the commons in the hundred of Blackburn and on 30th October to confront the army raised by the Earl of Derby.

Sawley Abbey was not dissolved in the normal manner. Following the Act of Suppression of March 1536, the other lesser monasteries of Yorkshire had undergone in May and June a process of supervision, entailing a survey of their possessions and an inquiry into whether or not their brethren wished to remain regulars. Dissolution had followed in August. Both stages had been administered by commissioners for

2 See below.
3 R. B. Manning, *Village Revolts: Social Protest and Popular Disturbances in England, 1509–1640* (Oxford, 1988), p. 49.

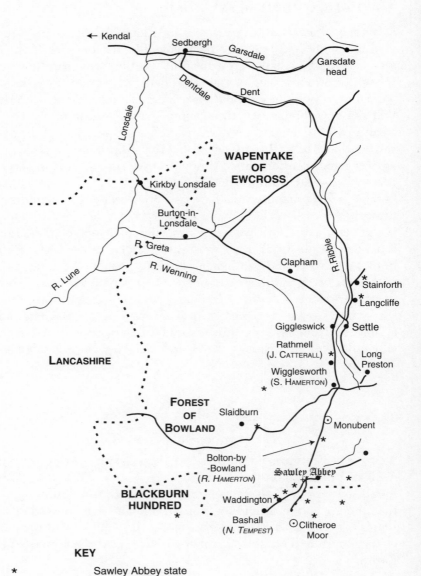

← Kendal

Sedbergh

Garsdale

Garsdate head

Dentdale

Dent

WAPENTAKE OF EWCROSS

Lonsdale

Kirkby Lonsdale

Burton-in-Lonsdale

R. Greta

R.Ribble

Clapham

* Stainforth

* Langcliffe

R. Lune

R. Wenning

Giggleswick

Settle

Rathmell (*J. Catterall*) *

Long Preston

Lancashire

Wigglesworth (*S. Hamerton*) *

Forest of Bowland

Slaidburn *

⊙ Monubent

→ *

Bolton-by -Bowland (*R. Hamerton*)

Sawley Abbey + *

*

Blackburn Hundred

Waddington * *

*

*

Bashall (*N. Tempest*)

⊙ Clitheroe Moor *

*

KEY

⋆	Sawley Abbey state
West Halton (*A. Talbot*)	Names of gentlemen involved shown below names of country seats
▪ ▪ ▪ ▪	County
- - - -	Barony } Boundaries
⌇	Major roads
⊙	Rebel assembly points

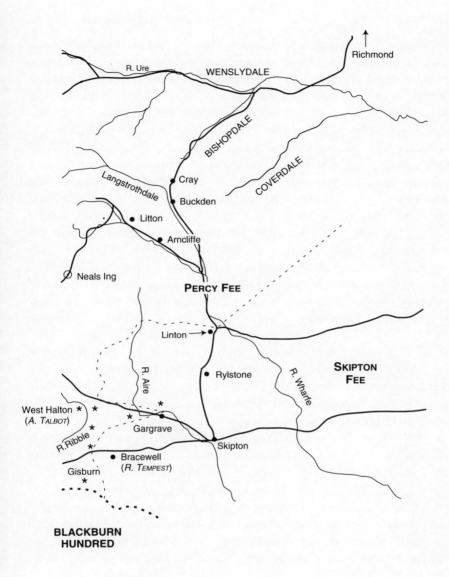

Map 7   The Percy Fee uprising

suppression, operating through the newly formed Court of Augmentations. In the interval between supervision and suppression a month or
so had elapsed allowing the threatened houses the opportunity to sue
for their reprieve.[4] Moreover, in spite of the initial flush of suits for
monastic property, the lands and goods of the suppressed houses
tended not to be granted away immediately.[5] Most of it remained in
the possession of the Crown, administered by the Court of Augmentations. The dissolution of Sawley Abbey followed a very
different course since without survey and before the monks had
been evicted, it was alienated to the younger son of Lord Darcy,
the up-and-coming courtier, Sir Arthur. In the parliamentary session
that enacted the suppression of the lesser monasteries, an act was
passed assuring certain lands to him and his heirs.[6] This act made
reference to an indenture of bargain and sale dated 28th March in
which the king had granted to Darcy the site, estate, advowsons and
goods of Sawley Abbey as well as portions of the estate formerly
belonging to Coverham Abbey and the Priory of Holy Trinity in
York.[7]

The purpose of the act was to confirm the indenture. In doing so, it
presumed that the three houses had already been suppressed and that
their possessions were now the Crown's. This was perfectly in keeping
with the Act of Suppression which simply laid down that the king
should have all religious houses which were recorded in the Exchequer
(i.e. in the Valor Ecclesiasticus of 1535) as having landed incomes not
in excess of £200 p.a. and that he should have the lawful right of
disposal "at his will and pleasure . . . without further inquisition to be
had".[8] On the other hand, the matter was not totally above board. For
this estate Darcy had exchanged a considerable property in Northamptonshire. This transaction was not declared in the act, although it
was made evident in the indenture of 28th March; nor was it made
explicit in another act of the same session which conveyed Darcy's

4 G. W. O. Woodward, "Exemption from suppression of certain Yorkshire pri-
    ories", E.H.R. 76 (1961), pp. 388–9; S. Jack, "Dissolution dates for the mon-
    asteries dissolved under the act of 1536", Bulletin of the Institute of Historical
    Research, 43 (1970), pp. 161–180; D. Knowles, Religious Orders in England
    (Cambridge, 1959), III, p. 305.
5 See Knowles, pp. 292–3; R. B. Smith, Land and Politics in the England of Henry
    VIII (Oxford, 1970), p. 229.
6 27 Henry VIII, c. 28.
7 P.R.O. C54/407, m. 2.
8 27 Henry VIII, c. 54.

Northamptonshire estate to the king.[9] It only came formally to light in letters patent of May 1538.[10] The reason for this secrecy was that the exchange had been agreed on 1st January 1536, that is, in anticipation of the passing of the Suppression Act.[11] For the goods of the abbey, Darcy agreed to pay something like £373, but by February 1537 he had paid no more than £160 and was asking to be released of the remainder.[12]

With the abbey granted away in this manner, the suppression commissioners had no need to survey its estates. This meant that the only valuation made was that of the Valor Ecclesiasticus which grossly underestimated the abbey's worth.[13] It also seems that the house was suppressed in one stage, on 13th May, when the commissioners assessed the value of the goods awarded to Darcy and removed the monks.[14] Of the monks, three went to Furness Abbey and then returned for the restoration.[15] The others probably went the few miles downstream to join the neighbouring Cistercian monastery of Whalley.

Darcy, it seems, did not act immediately to take possession of what he had been granted.[16] Yet the exceptional procedure of suppression must have created a great deal of resentment, at Court as well as in the country: partly because it effected the earliest Dissolution in the north,

9 27 Henry VIII, c. 29.

10 *L.P.* XIII{1}. 1115 {13}. Earlier it was made evident in a letter from Darcy to Cromwell of June 1537 (see *L.P.* XII{2}. 59). The Northants estate was purchased by Darcy on 24th December 1535 from Lord Harrowden. See P.R.O. E305/7/D62.

11 See the indenture of 1st January 1536 mentioned in the statute 27 Henry VIII, c. 29 which states that the king made payment with "great and notable sums of money" and "for divers manors . . . to a great yearly value" which the king by the same indenture granted to Darcy. The indenture (E305/7/D62) is not as explicit as the act suggests that it is. It does not mention what the king has agreed to pay and basically states that Darcy is under obligation of a surety of £3,000 to sell the Harrowden estate to the king within the next two years. The indenture of 28th March (C54/407, m. 2) reveals that the king paid Darcy £1,000 plus Sawley etc.

12 P.R.O. SC6/Henry VIII/4641, m. 5; *L.P.* XII{1}. 506.

13 In June 1537 Darcy informed Cromwell that the king "gave me my lands unsurveyed": see T. Wright (ed.), *Three Chapters of Letters relating to the Suppression of the Monasteries*, Camden Society, 26 (1843), pp. 158–9 (*L.P.* XII{2}. 59) . The reference to the first survey in the same letter denotes the Valor Ecclesiasticus of 1535. For the latter's valuation, see *V.E.*, 5, p.144 (£147. 3. 10d.).

14 See Jacks, op. cit., p. 178. But not until 25th June was the abbot pensioned off. See W. S. Weeks, "Abbot Paslew and the pilgrimage of grace", *Transactions of the Lancashire and Cheshire Antiquarian Societies*, 47 (1930–31), pp. 199–223.

15 *L.P.* XII{1}. 841 {3}.

16 See below, p. 223.

partly because the *modus operandi* denied Sawley all chance of reprieve, and partly because Darcy's acquisition of the estate before any survey could be carried out by the suppression commissioners created the impression that he had deceived the king as well as the monks. Technically disqualifying Sawley Abbey from dissolution was the fact it was not a lesser monastery. With twenty two religious in residence and an annual income of at least £467, drawn from an extensive estate in Ribblesdale and the Forest of Bowland, it fell well outside the terms of the Suppression Act.[17] Yet because of the *fait accompli*, this evidence could not be deployed to save it. That members of the government were aggrieved came to light in 1537 when allegations were made to the Chancellor of Augmentations that, thanks to the undervaluation of the Sawley Abbey estate, Darcy had secured a magnificent bargain.[18] In response, the king authorised a special survey. Fortunately for Darcy, this was cursorily conducted by Robert Southwell who found, in spite of clear evidence to the contrary, that the transaction of March 1536 between Darcy and the king had been fair.[19] Nonetheless, throughout the period of the pilgrimage of grace doubts must have lingered, condemning the dissolution of Sawley Abbey not simply as an heretical act but as the quick killing made by an unscrupulous courtier.

Sawley Abbey was restored on 12th October. As the monks reported to Robert Aske, on that day they were "by the good and loving commons of the country there assigned, admitted and entered into their house by virtue of the said commons"; and something like forty servants were re-employed.[20] What provoked the restoration is unknown. One possibility was news that Coverham Abbey, another victim of Sir Arthur Darcy, had been restored the day before.[21] Another sprang from Darcy's belated action in taking possession of

17 For the estimation of its value, see *L.P.* XII{2}. 205. For the number of monks, see *L.P.* XI. 784. The act declared that houses with lands worth no more than £200 p.a. were to be suppressed and in the preamble condemned religious houses with under twelve persons as worthy of suppression, see 27 Henry VIII, c. 28.
18 *L.P.* XII{2}. 59.
19 *L.P.* XII{2}. 205. Darcy had certainly secured a bargain since, in exchange for the Northants estate, valued at between £300 and £400 p.a. (27 Henry VIII, c. 29 and *L.P.* XII{2}. 59), he received an estate estimated at between £467 and £600 p.a. (L.P. XII{2}. 205); and in addition £1,000 (see C54/407, m. 2).
20 P.R.O. SP1/108, fos. 209–209b (*L.P.* XI. 784). Another account was provided by the government when in a letter of 19th October it reported that an assembly lately attempted on the borders of Lancashire had restored the monks (*L.P.* XI. 783). For the abbey servants, see SP1/109 (*L.P.* XI. 872).
21 Darcy was granted the granges of the abbey for an annual rent of £25 (SC6/ Henry VIII/7454).

what he had acquired the previous March. On 8th October, or so it was reported in Percy Fee, he had confiscated the tithe corn and church ornaments of Tadcaster parsonage, which previously had been the possession of Sawley Abbey and now belonged to him.[22] By this time he had not as yet annexed the goods of Sawley since he later claimed that they had gone missing; and as for the lands of the abbey, William Maunsell, the lawyer he was employing to administer the Sawley estate, had, on his own admission, not got very far in surveying them by November.[23] In all likelihood, then, the act of restoration resulted from local fears, especially aroused by the Tadcaster incident, that the new proprietor was about to impose himself, as well from hearing that extensive revolts against the Dissolution had broken out north and south of the Humber. Although the monks presented the restoration as the work of the commons and the abbot even claimed that it happened against his will, in reality the monks were artful accomplices.[24] Nor was the movement that restored them simply a popular one. Alienated by the way the suppression of Sawley Abbey had inserted into the region an outsider and with no incentive to accept it since all the benefits had gone to Darcy, the gentlemen of Percy Fee offered support, encouraging the abbey's restoration and organising its defence when the government summoned the Earl of Derby to put it down.[25]

The mobilisation of the host

A rebel army, at least three hundred strong, had been formed in Percy Fee by 20th October. The following day it amounted to one thousand men. A day later it was reckoned to be three thousand strong.[26] The location of its first muster – at Neals Ing above the Sawley Abbey manors of Great Stainforth and Langcliffe and on the road crossing Fountain Fell to Littondale – coupled with Hamerton's account of how the people and the priests of Giggleswick were involved and how the leadership was provided by Jacks from Buckden and Fawcett from

22 L.P. XI. 784.
23 For goods, see SP1/116 (L.P. XII{1}. 506). For lands, see L.P. XI. 1047. The half year rents, presumably for the period Easter to Michaelmas 1536, had not been paid by January/February 1537 (see L.P. XII{1}. 218 and 506).
24 See L.P. XI.784 and L.P. XII{1}. 506.
25 See below, pp. 241–4.
26 For the 300, see L.P. XII {1}. 1034. For the 1,000, see L.P. XII {1}. 1014. For the 3,000, see L.P. XI. 807. But this is to be doubted in the light of the fact that on the 23rd, when the host was divided between Tempest and Hamerton for the first march into Lancashire, Tempest found himself with no more than 500 men (see L.P. XII {1}. 1014). In the light of the muster returns for Staincliffe and Bowland, the figure of 3,000 would appear a gross exaggeration at this stage of the revolt, whereas the other figures would appear realistic. See Appendix I.

Litton, reveals that it was initially recruited from the far northerly parts of the Honour, attracting support not just from upper Ribblesdale but also from Langstrothdale and Littondale.[27]

As yet the restored abbey of Sawley had not been threatened.[28] The decision to mobilise, therefore, must have come from news of revolts in other parts, notably in the dales to the north of Craven. In the lordship of Dent there had been disturbances in late September; and by 6th October the infected area included upper Wensleydale and much of the wapentake of Ewcross.[29] Then, with the outbreak of the Richmondshire uprising between 11th and 13th October, and with its deliberate and vigorous incitement of revolt in other regions, the movement spread to much of the far north. The Richmondshire revolt had been dispatching exhortatory letters across the Pennines from the 15th October.[30] By reviving revolt in Dent and upper Wensleydale, it probably helped to agitate the northerly parts of Percy Fee as well. On 18th and 19th October men from Dent were busy raising the barony of Kendal and also the southerly parts of the wapentake of Ewcross, which were very close to the starting point of the Percy Fee uprising.[31] Quite probably at the time they were seeking to raise revolt in Percy Fee. Moreover, as the Percy Fee uprising was getting under way, news must have reached the area of the approaching host from Richmondshire. Just as Percy Fee was organising its first muster on 20th October, a huge force was in the vicinity, snaking down into Craven from Richmondshire, via Wensleydale and Bishopdale.[32]

Although there was no sign of bell-ringing, the rebel army in Percy Fee was raised in the familiar manner: by bills nailed to church doors, by oath-swearing ceremonies and by musters which required, in the manner of the militia, all between the ages of sixteen and sixty to attend the summons appropriately armed. Thus, on 19th October a bill appeared on Giggleswick church door, announcing for the following day the muster at Neals Ing.[33] Within the next ten days, further

27 The only account of the Neals Ing muster is provided by Hamerton (*L.P.* XII {1}. 1034) who was absent from it. It is quite possible that organised revolt began before 20th October. On 17th October Darcy reported that the commons had risen in Langstrothdale and Craven (*L.P.* XI. 760 {2}), but this might have been a reference to the restoration of Sawley.

28 The government had instructed Derby to take action against Sawley Abbey on 19th October, but the letter did not reach him until 23rd October (see below, n. 67), several days after the mobilisation of Percy Fee.

29 See below, pp. 249–50.

30 See above, pp. 146–7.

31 See below, pp. 251–2.

32 See above, p. 153.

33 *L.P.* XII {1}. 1034.

musters were held, at Monubent in the southerly part of the Fee (on 22nd October and again on 27th October); and across the Lancashire border at Clitheroe Moor on 30th October.[34]

At least two bills were associated with these assemblies. The first ordered the muster at Neals Ing; the second ordered the muster on Clitheroe Moor. The latter has survived.[35] It commanded all between sixteen and sixty to be present upon Clitheroe Moor on 30th October "in all best array" (i.e. properly armed) by nine o'clock. As well as summoning the muster, the bill forbade anyone to aid the Earl of Derby or anyone else who was not "sworn to and for the common-wealth". In addition, it included a statement of grievance which was heavily influenced by Robert Aske and which, in one variant of the bill, appeared to come from the pilgrim high command, in declaring itself to be "by all the whole consent of the headmen in this our pilgrimage for grace to the commonalty".[36]

By this time the host from Percy Fee had clearly fallen under the spell of Aske. But when did this first occur? It had happened by 23rd October when Aske's oath was put by the host to the monks of Whalley;[37] and it was certainly evident in the following week when the host presented itself as part of the pilgrimage of grace not only by calling upon Aske for aid against the approaching Earl of Derby but also by employing the causes, terminology and authority of Robert Aske to summon the muster on Clitheroe Moor.[38] But was the bill found nailed to the church door in Giggleswick on 19th October,

---

34 For first Monubent muster (22nd October), see *L.P.* XII {1}. 1034. For second Monubent muster (27th October), see SP1/119, f.19b (*L.P.* XII {1}. 1034). For Clitheroe Moor muster, see *L.P.* XI. 892 and 947. A reasonably accurate chronology of events was worked out long ago by Mrs. Arthur Cecil Tempest in "Nicholas Tempest, a sufferer in the pilgrimage of grace", *Yorkshire Archaeological Journal*, 11 (1890–91), pp. 251ff and confirmed by J. E. W. Wallis in his "The narrative of the indictment of the traitors of Whalley and Cartmell, 1536–7" in *Chetham Miscellanies*, 5 [Chetham Society n.s. 90 (1931)], pp. 1–3. However, a succession of historians, notably the Dodds [Dodds, I, pp. 209–10], Smith [Smith, op. cit., pp. 200–201] and Hoyle [*Northern History*, 22(1986), p. 84] have got it wrong, mainly through assuming that the chain of events began on 18th and not 19th October. The only event remaining in doubt is the second Monubent muster. According to Hamerton it happened within a week of the first muster of 22nd [SP1/119 (*L.P.* XII 1. 1034]. Wallis dates it the 25th October (p. 2). I date it 27th October. For my dating of it, see below, n. 73.

35 Toller, pp. 51–52 (*L.P.* XI. 892); *L.P.* XI. 892 {2}.

36 *L.P.* XI. 892 {2}. The original, reckoned by *L.P.* to be located in P.R.O., is missing.

37 SP/118, f. 265 (*L.P.* XII {1}. 1014).

38 Bateson, p. 338 and *L.P.* XI. 892 {2}.

which turned the Percy Fee revolt into an armed rising, an Aske composition?[39] By this time, the Sawley monks had, in all likelihood, written to Aske; and his reply may well have reached them. But this reply was not an order to muster but an oath to be sworn.[40] Moreover, the orders that Aske dispatched into the dales calling upon the commons to muster and join the pilgrimage were not sent out until, at the earliest, the 20th October.[41]

In all probability, the bill of the 19th October had another provenance. It was briefly described by Stephen Hamerton who, having heard that it was fixed to the church door, went to Giggleswick to view it on the following day only to find that it had been removed. Hamerton claimed that it had summoned every man on pain of death to the assembly point by nine o'clock. He also indicated that it had been highly effective. In Giggleswick he was told that "all the people . . . and the priests of the church" had gone to the appointed place, taking the bill with them.[42] Rather than the work of Robert Aske, this bill could have been a Captain Poverty composition, several of which were circulating in the north west in late October.[43] One was picked up by the Earl of Derby and presented by him to the government as having been nailed to church doors by the Dent and Kendal rebels and other rebel movements in the region.[44] Addressed from "Master Poverty, the conductor, protector and maintainer of the whole commonalty", it excoriated heretics both for proceeding against the Church and for procuring new laws harmful to the commonwealth. It also ordered "all in general from sixteen years and above, on pain of death and forfeiture of goods, to be in a readiness to aid us in maintaining of the said faith of Christ and his church, of the most

---

39 As alleged by Dodds and Smith: see Dodds, I, p. 209 and Smith, op. cit., p. 200.
40 SP1/108, fos. 209–209b (*L.P.* XI. 784); SP1/109, f. 110b (*L.P.* XI. 872). The letter to Aske was addressed to him as captain of the city of York which suggests that it was not written before 16th October.
41 Aske claimed that it was sent on 21st October. See Bateson, p. 560 and R. W. Hoyle, "Thomas Master's narrative of the pilgrimage of grace", *Northern History*, 21 (1985), p. 69. However the communication with the Beverley uprising was sent on 20th October (see Stapulton, p. 99), suggesting that Aske may have been a day out. Likewise, his communication with the Bowes host must have proceeded the 21st October (see above, p. 160); similarly, with the Percy host (see above, p. 194).
42 SP1/119 f. 19 (*L.P.* XII {1}. 1034).
43 See M. L. Bush, "Captain Poverty and the pilgrimage of grace", *Historical Research*, 65 (1992), pp. 20–26.
44 It was included in a batch of bills that Derby dispatched at the end of October to the government, see Toller, p. 42 (*L.P.* XI. 947).

high honour of our sovereign lord the king and of the common-wealth".[45] It was possibly this type of bill, deriving from the insurrec-tions of northern rather than southern Yorkshire, and filtering down into Percy Fee from Dentdale, that first moved the people of the honour to muster and host.

There were several forms of oath associated with the uprising in Percy Fee. One bound the recipient to be true to God, the king "and for the maintaining of the faith". As administered by Jacks to Hamer-ton on 20th October, this oath was pledged with a raising of the hand.[46] Another bound the recipient "to be true to the commons". On 21st October this was administered by John Catterall to Nicholas Tempest with a holding of the hand as the promise was made.[47] Another oath used in Percy Fee was the one composed by Aske specifically for Sawley Abbey and in response to a supplication from its monks. Reflecting Aske's general oath, it was to be taken "on a book" and required a promise to maintain the faith and the church, to expel all villein blood from the king's privy council and to suppress all heresy. Then, focusing upon the concerns of Sawley Abbey itself, it required the tenantry to pay their dues to the abbot rather than to Sir Arthur Darcy and "to maintain this house of prayer".[48] Besides providing an answer to the monks' supplication and a relevant oath that combined a general statement of the pilgrims' cause with a statement specially suited to the rebels of Percy Fee, it offered for the benefit of the monks a revision of the order already issued by Aske for religious houses suppressed. In assuming that the dissolved houses were in the hands of farmers, the original order was not applicable to Sawley Abbey which had been alienated rather than leased out.[49]

This oath may have reached the region by 20th October; and it may have been the oath that Hamerton was made to swear.[50] It was certainly the oath the host imposed upon the monks of Whalley Abbey

45 Toller, pp. 47–9 (*L.P.* XI. 892).
46 SP1/119, f. 19 (*L.P.* XII {1}. 1034). It is likely that Hamerton curtailed the actual oath, perhaps to conceal the fact that he had sworn to be true to the commons or the commonwealth. If the oath had been "to be true to God, the king, the maintaining of the faith and the commonwealth", it would have been identical with one used by the Richmondshire rebels [see above, ch. IV(n. 14)].
47 SP1/118, f. 265 (*L.P.* XII {1}. 1014). Without a doubt the oath was more complicated than this and probably duplicated the one taken by Hamerton with the addition of "to be true to the commons/commonwealth".
48 SP1/109 (*L.P.* XI. 872) in response to *L.P.* XI. 784. For Aske's general oath – the oath of the honourable men – see Toller, pp. 50–51.
49 See SP1/108, f. 210 (*L.P.* XI. 784 {2}). A variant is printed in Toller, p. 51.
50 It must have been composed after 17th October, the day upon which Aske's general oath was composed (see above, pp. 91–2).

on 23rd October and may well have been the oath that it put to the commons of Whalley, Colne and Burnley on the same day.[51] These oaths were taken *en masse* by the commons at the various assemblies and sworn individually by the gentlemen and clerics. By means of these devices and, as a result of its keenness to recruit further support, the host by the end of October had become a considerable force, of at least one thousand and possibly up to three thousand armed men, drawn not simply from Percy Fee but also from the Forest of Bowland and the Lancashire hundred of Blackburn.[52]

Although the uprising was perceived and presented as a movement of the commons, the rebels sought to operate though the medium of the society of orders.[53] Having summoned the commons, the next step was to enlist the gentlemen, principally by pressing upon them oaths of allegiance. Sir Stephen Hamerton, the most influential gentleman in Percy Fee, by virtue of being its steward, was taken by a band of armed men who, it seems, had been deputed at the Neals Ing assembly to visit his house at Wigglesworth. Having subjected him to the oath, they made him a captain.[54] A day later the rebels sought to enlist Nicholas Tempest of Bashall in Bowland who was especially influential on the Yorkshire/Lancashire border as deputy to his brother Sir Richard Tempest, steward of Blackburnshire and Forester of Bowland.[55] When a thousand rebels visited his house, he at first resisted by absenting himself but was called to order as they began to spoil his possessions and threatened to execute his son. Within three hours of

---

51 Tempest refers to Aske's oath being used to swear the monks of the abbey, see SP1/108, f. 265 (*L.P.* XII {1}. 1014). He also refers to the swearing of the commons on the same day but does not specify the form of oath. However, it would make sense to subject the commons to Aske's oath especially if they were tenants of the abbey since it bound them to pay their rents to the monks and not to Darcy. Another possibility is that the oath used for the monks was the other oath devised by Aske, his oath of the honourable men (Toller, pp. 50–51) which a servant of Derby, who had been taken by the rebels, brought to Lancashire on 21st October. See Hoyle, "Thomas Master's narrative", p. 69 and Bateson, p. 560.

52 That the Forest of Bowland had become a rebel area is evident in William Singleton's unwillingness to go there in November on the grounds that "the persons of the rebellion were lodged thereabouts". He was fearful that they would subject him to the rebels' oath. See SP1/116, f. 128b (*L.P.* XII {1}. 518). In Blackburn hundred, the area around Chippendale was presented by Singleton as safe (see ibid.). And so it seems as if the part that fell under rebel control was the parish of Whalley. For the size of the army, see above, n. 26.

53 For its presentation as a rising of the commons, see below, p. 236.

54 *L.P.* XII{1}. 1034. For his stewardship, see *L.P.* VIII. 991 and 995 and M. E. James, "The first earl of Cumberland (1493–1542) and the decline of northern feudalism", *Northern History*, 1 (1966), p. 62.

55 Smith, op. cit., p. 201.

their arrival, he had bound himself to the rebel cause with an oath of allegiance to the commons.[56] A factor in his submission was a letter he had seen, written by the Earl of Derby to Lord Darcy, which had caused him to believe that it was pointless holding out since Derby "would do little to the matter when it should come to the point". Without any assurance of Derby's support, the local gentry, he felt, had no choice but to join the commons. If they did not, "their house would have been pulled down and their goods spoiled".[57] Taken and sworn, however, he became, like Hamerton, an earnest rebel, essentially because he was strongly moved by similar grievances to those of the commons. Both gentlemen, it seems, had supported the restoration of Sawley Abbey. Tempest, a neighbour of the abbey, had provided the monks upon their return with an ox, a sheep and some geese; and Hamerton later helped the monks by writing a letter, at their request, to Robert Aske. Rather than to support an alien cause, the summons from the commons to join up only caused them to articulate their grievances in open revolt.[58]

As part of the same policy of recruiting the leading figures of the region, a deputation of nine men, including Hamerton, went to Skipton Castle. This was on 21st October. Admitted to the castle, they were granted an audience with the Earl of Cumberland, presumably because Hamerton was with them. At the time they must have known that the Richmondshire host was marching down Bishopdale and rapidly approaching Skipton. To lever Cumberland into joining the rebellion, they used the threat posed by this force, telling him to his face that "they were afraid of Bishopdale, Wensleydale and other quarters lest they would come upon them and spoil them".[59] But Cumberland refused to be drawn in; and the meeting ended with Cumberland declaring: "I defy you and do your worst, for I will not

---

56 *L.P.* XII {1}. 1014. His confession tallies with the account he gave in November to a servant of Sir Richard Hoghton. See SP1/116, fos. 129–129b (*L.P.* XII {1}. 518). Suggesting that there was some truth in his allegation is the fact that, as a result of the delay in taking him, the contingent appointed to this task failed to arrive at Monubent on 21st October as previously planned. See *L.P.* XII {1}. 1034.

57 SP1/116, f. 129b (*L.P.* XII {1}. 518).

58 For Tempest, see SP1/118, f. 265b (*L.P.* XII{1}. 1014). According to the chaplain of Sawley, Richard Eastgate, he was "at the first . . . one of their great favourers" [see SP1/117 (*L.P.* XII {1}. 695)]. There is no evidence that Hamerton helped to restore the monks. It seems from his own account that he had no knowledge of the assembly of commons that had restored the monks on 12th October, referring to the assembly at Neals Ing on 20th October as "the first commotion in Craven" [SP1/119, f. 19 (*L.P.* XII {1}. 1034)]. For his part in writing letters to Aske, see *L.P.* XII {1}. 491.

59 SP1/119, f. 19 (*L.P.* XII{1}. 1034).

meddle with you".[60] Leaving Skipton before the host from Richmond-shire and Claro arrived, the deputation met their own host not at Monubent as planned – because of the delay in taking Tempest – but between Bolton-by-Bowland and Sawley Abbey. Upon hearing of Cumberland's defiant stand, the host angrily resolved that "they would have him" or die in the attempt.[61]

Yet from then onwards the host from Percy Fee directed all its activities in the opposite direction, aiming to enlist support in Lanca-shire and to stop the Earl of Derby. It was obliged to do so by Derby's aggressiveness; it was free to do so because, besieged by the Rich-mondshire host, Cumberland was a prisoner in his own castle. Thus, at the muster held on 22nd October at Monubent, the rebels decided to "fetch . . . unto them" and swear the commons of Lancashire, speci-fically the people living in the extensive parish of Whalley, which comprised the eastern half of the hundred of Blackburn, in the belief that if they won over one quarter of the county the rest would follow.[62] Tempest was deputed to convert the region around the town of Whalley whilst Hamerton was required to raise Colne and Burnley. Dividing the host between them, they set about their task on 23rd October. The only resistance came from the monks of Whalley Abbey who at first refused to admit Tempest but after two hours of resistance submitted when he threatened to burn the house down. With the great gate opened, the abbot and eight of his brethren took the oath composed by Aske. Of Hamerton's activities in Lancashire little is known since he failed to discuss them in his confession.[63] With a force of some five hundred he impressed himself upon Colne and Burnley; and, as well as enlisting the support of the commons, he probably obliged Sir John Towneley to take the oath.[64] The operation took one day. After meeting that evening to discuss

60 SP1/119, f. 19b (L.P. XII{1}. 1034).
61 Ibid.
62 See SP1/118, f. 265 (L.P. XII{1}. 1014) and SP1/108 (L.P. XI. 807).
63 The details are exclusively provided by Tempest's account (see L.P. XII{1}. 1014). The other surviving narrative of the Percy Fee rising, Hamerton's account, states that after the first muster the rebels simply went home (see L.P. XII{1}. 1034).
64 The letter L.P. XI. 804 suggests that, of the two Towneley brothers, both of them named John, one had been sworn but not the other. Derby thought that Sir John had been sworn because he failed to respond to his summons for troops and had been consorting with the commons [see SP1/112, f. 157b (L.P. XI. 1251)]. Aske implied that this Towneley had collaborated with the commons when he instructed the king that the best way to secure the support of the commons was to send letters to certain named gentlemen who presumably had their trust because of an earlier involvement. In his list of gentlemen Towneley was named. See Bateson, pp. 343–4.

what had been done, the host disbanded with orders to remain ready for action at one hour's warning.[65]

On 19th October the government called off its plans to use Derby against the Humberside rebellions and sent him strict instructions to crush the Craven revolt and to have the monks of Sawley Abbey publicly hanged in their habits. For the purpose, he was commissioned to levy Lancashire.[66] Receiving the instructions on 23rd October, he sought to carry them out, but this was not easy because of the time of year, the general barrenness of the region and the adversity of weather and terrain, especially after the heavy rains of 25th October.[67] In addition, the apparent sympathy of the Lancashire commons for the pilgrims' cause created difficulties in raising an army. As Thomas Stanley reported to Lord Darcy, probably on 22nd October, "the people are wholly with the commonalty till it come to his (Derby's) very household servants" and, according to him, it was felt that "the most part of his company will not stick with him but turn to the commons".[68] On 24th October Derby was planning to be at Sawley by 28th October, but on 25th October, the day of the rains, the schedule had to be revised, with his arrival at Whalley now planned for the evening of 30th October.[69]

But there can be no doubt as to Derby's intentions. As Stanley informed Darcy, Derby was "fully determined to be against the commons" and that whilst the people were "with the commonalty" "he himself is very stiff in the contrary"; and, in all, he managed to raise a force of over 7,000 men.[70] Moreover, because of the strong lead given by Derby in organising military resistance, made possible by the government's firm and clear instructions which told him precisely what to do, the commons in much of Lancashire could not enlist the support of the gentry. As a result actual insurrection was arrested and confined to the border regions – Lonsdale hundred in the north and Blackburnshire in the east – where it was generated and sustained by

65 SP1/118, f. 265 (*L.P.* XII{1}. 1014).
66 Toller, pp. 28-31 (*L.P.* XI. 783).
67 For receipt of letter, see *L.P.* XI. 856. For heavy rains, see *L.P.* XII{1}. 1175. For barrenness, see SP1/109 (*L.P.* XI. 856). For the difficulty of the way to Whalley and Sawley, see Toller, p. 42 (*L.P.* XI. 947).
68 SP1/108 (*L.P.* XI. 807). The dating of this letter can be assumed from his knowledge of the plan to arouse support in Lancashire, which was determined at the Monubent muster of 22nd October.
69 *L.P.* XI. 856; *L.P.* XI. 872 {3}.
70 SP1/108 (*L.P.* XI. 807). For forces raised, see SP1/112, fos. 159–60 (*L.P.* XI. 1251 {2}).

direct contact with hosts from across the county boundary: that is, from the West Riding and Westmorland.[71]

In reaction to Derby, the Hamerton/Tempest host arranged a second assembly at Monubent.[72] This happened within a week of the first assembly, in all likelihood on either 27th or 28th October, in response to learning of Derby's plan to be at Whalley on 30th October.[73] At this assembly the host was informed, by a letter from Sawley Abbey, that Derby intended to destroy both Whalley and Sawley Abbeys as well as the houses of Sir Stephen Hamerton and Sir Richard Tempest.[74] A counterplan was created. The rebels wrote to Atkinson, captain of the Dent/Kendal uprising, to enlist his support. They also wrote to Aske to tell him of Derby's designs and to seek his aid. Plans were made to join up with the inhabitants of Blackburnshire on Clitheroe Moor in order to do battle with Derby at Whalley.[75]

The muster on Clitheroe Moor was timed to coincide with Derby's plan to move from Preston to Whalley.[76] But as matters reached a climax they were suddenly deflated by news of the truce agreed at Doncaster between the government and the rebel high command. Faced by two armies, the Atkinson host which had already taken Lancaster and was threatening to march south and the Hamerton/ Tempest host at Clitheroe which was threatening to march west,

71 Derby's various dispatches connect the rebellion of the commons in Lancashire with these two regions. See Toller, p. 46 (*L.P.* XI. 947 {2}); SP1/111 (*L.P.* XI. 1118); SP1/112 (*L.P.* XI. 1251).

72 In contrast with the first Monubent muster which is detailed by Tempest but by-passed by Hamerton, the second Monubent muster is detailed by Hamerton and passes unmentioned in Tempest's account. See *L.P.* XII{1}. 1014 and 1034.

73 For the second meeting occurring within a week of the first, see SP1/119, f. 19b (*L.P.* XII{1}. 1034). The date depends upon when the rebels came into possession of Derby's letter of 25th October since all the plans made at the second Monubent assembly were a reaction to the contents of this letter. For the letter's contents, see SP1/109 (*L.P.* XI. 872). It must have been known for some time that Derby meant business and by 28th he had made the move from Lathom to Preston (see *L.P.* XI. 901). But until the letter revealed all, it was not clear what his plan was: to proceed against the Craveners or against the Kendal rebels who had marched into Lancashire [see Toller, pp. 44–5 (*L.P.* XI. 947 {2})]. It is unlikely that the letter reached Whalley before the 26th, having been sent from Lathom. On the other hand a copy of the same letter, sent to Aske by the Percy Fee rebels, had reached him in Pontefract by 28th October (see Bateson, p. 338 and E36/118, f. 88b (*L.P.* XI. 1046{3}). Abbot Paslew of Whalley was noted to have committed a treasonable act on 28th October (Wallis, op. cit., p. 2). This may have been to hand over the letter to the rebels. All this points to the Monubent meeting occurring on the 28th October at the latest and on 27th October at the earliest.

74 *L.P.* XII{1}. 1034.

75 SP1/119, f. 19b (*L.P.* XII{1}. 1034). For the letters to Aske, see Bateson, p. 338 and *L.P.* XI. 1046 {3}.

76 SP1/119, f. 19b (*L.P.* XII{1}. 1034); *L.P.* XI. 901.

Derby complied readily with the Earl of Shrewsbury's order to disperse and return home.[77] Moved by the same news, imparted to them by letters from Aske and Darcy, the two rebel hosts followed suit, but not before the Hamerton/Tempest host had subjected Whalley Abbey to a second occupation and not without making preparations to rise again at an hour's warning.[78] Aske's letter of 28th encouraged the latter by indicating that, in spite of the Truce and the agreement to demobilise, the king had retained an army in the field: the troops garrisoned at Lincoln under the Duke of Suffolk.[79]

Grievances

Although the revolt began with the restoration of Sawley Abbey and continued as a defence of it against the designs of the Earl of Derby, it would be wrong to assume that the rebels of Percy Fee were only concerned with the dissolution. The oath put to Hamerton, which was "for maintaining of the faith" suggested that the rebels were agitated by the onset of heresy and its effect upon the practices of the English church.[80] This was made evident in a bill that was nailed to the door of Arncliffe church in Littondale when the commons resumed their revolt in January 1537.[81] The bill presented itself as being "by the whole assent of the parishioners and tenants of my lord of Northumberland": that is, the people of Percy Fee. It was addressed to the rural dean of Craven who happened to be vicar of Arncliffe. Similar bills were sent to the priests of other parishes. Basically it objected to changes in the church service and the expulsion of the pope from the headship of the English church. In this respect, the bill mostly defended the traditional order of prayer which had been altered

77 For the Atkinson host, see below, ch. VII. For Shrewsbury's letter and its effect, see *L.P.* XI. 901.

78 *L.P.* XI. 947 and SP1/119, f.19b (*L.P.* XII{1}.1034). For Aske's intervention, see Bateson, p. 338. For Darcy's intervention, see *L.P.* XI. 912. Whereas Derby claimed that the rebels took Whalley after receiving news of the Truce (*L.P.* XI. 947), and this is also suggested by Hamerton [SP1/119, f. 19b (*L.P.* XII{1}. 1034)], Aske claimed that they reached Whalley before the news of the Truce had arrived (Bateson, p. 338).

79 *L.P.* XI. 1046 {3}.

80 SP/1/119, f. 19 (*L.P.* XII{1}. 1034).

81 For the bill, see SP1/107 (*L.P.* XI. 655). For further details, see *L.P.* XII{1}. 792. The bill can be dated from the whereabouts of Lord Clifford to whom it was sent by the Clifford servant, Thomas Jolye. Jolye at the time assumed that Lord Clifford was at Court. This was not the case until mid-January 1537 when he went south after a long spell of service in Carlisle Castle. See Chatsworth Trustees, Clifford Letter Book, f. 6b.

in the previous year. Its especial concern was the absence in the church service of a prayer for "the pope of Rome, the head of our mother church". Its other concern was the omission from the church service of cursing: that is, the practice of publicly listing the offences for which damnation was the penalty, prominent among which was heresy.[82]

Moreover it would be wrong to assume that the uprising was only moved by religious grievances. The Percy Fee rebels were notable for echoing the phrase "the pilgrimage of grace for the commonwealth" which first appeared in Aske's general oath.[83] Thus, the Clitheroe proclamation of late October referred to "our pilgrimage for grace to the commonwealth" and the petition the monks of Sawley Abbey addressed to Sir Thomas Percy in December mentioned "the pilgrimage of Christ's faith and the commonwealth". Moreover, in replying to a letter (now lost) from the monks of Sawley in the same month, Aske appeared to reflect a phrase in it when he termed them "special brethren of this our pilgrimage of grace for the commonwealth".[84] Whilst the commonwealth was a matter of concern, however, it did not cause the Percy Fee rebels to complain specifically of either taxation or rent.[85] As articulated by them, the threat to the commonwealth came from the government's expropriation of the wealth of the church.

This was made evident in the Sawley ballad, a poem in the first person plural and presented as voiced by the commons, although probably composed by a monk.[86] It proposed that, guided by Christ, the commons were on a pilgrimage that aimed "through God's grace" to secure for the spirituality "old wealth and peace". This was necessary because the church, in contravention of God's law as set out in Deuteronomy, had been "robbed, spoiled and shorn" of its cattle, corn, houses and lands. In being responsible, the government had breached natural limits and had therefore acted tyrannically. As a result, "God's woeful ire" had been aroused with a consequent loss of grace and goodness. In the circumstances, the commons had no choice but "to mell/ to make redress". The second half of the ballad urged the poor commons to come to the church's rescue since its decay would affect them materially. Succoured with bread and ale, the poor had

---

82 C. S. L. Davies, "Popular religion and the pilgrimage of grace", in A. Fletcher and J. Stevenson (eds.), *Order and Disorder in Early Modern England* (Cambridge, 1985), p. 74.

83 Toller, pp. 50–1.

84 *L.P.* XI. 892 {2}; SP1/108 (*L.P.* XI. 785); SP1/112, f. 66 (*L.P.* XI. 1218).

85 But for the possibility of a tax grievance present, see below, p. 236.

86 SP1/108 (*L.P.* XI. 786 {3}). It is printed but with a few obscuring inaccuracies by Bateson (see Bateson, pp. 344–5).

never been denied "good bait/ At churchmen's gate", but now, oppressed by the government, the church was less able to dispense charity and hospitality. Then the ballad invoked God to "Again make free" all "that is [in] thrall" through the medium of this pilgrimage, calling upon him to reward the pilgrims with "wealth, health and speed" and, by releasing them from sin, with "joy endless/When they be dead". Finally, the ballad exposed the source of the problem, the evil ministers Cromwell, Cranmer and Riche and the three Ls (Hells), Layton, Leigh and Latimer, and showed how it could all be put right: that is by allowing Aske "Without delay/ Here make a stay/ And well to end".

The ballad proposed a thesis consisting of two intertwined themes: the church's vital role in offering intercessory prayers for the living and the dead and its necessary role in providing physical relief for the poor. Both functions were seen as threatened by the tyranny and greed of the government, so much so that Christ's faith was threatened and the commonwealth impaired. The emphasis upon the abbey's temporal function was made not simply in the ballad but on two other occasions: in the letter written by the men of worship to Aske at the second Monubent muster which reached him on 28th October and in the petition addressed by the monks of Sawley to Thomas Percy in December. In the former, according to Aske, Sawley Abbey was presented as worth preserving because it provided "the charitable relief of those parts and standing in a mountain country and amongst three forests". [87] The letter to Percy elaborated this point, alleging that the effect of the suppression was to deny provision not only for prayer but also for alms and hospitality "with other deeds and works of charity and man's relief there to be had and maintained", the latter being especially necessary because of the situation in "a barren country betwixt the king's forests", so much so that "the inhabitants and whole country" support its continuation.[88] Thus behind the Craveners' support for the restoration of Sawley were emphatic temporal and material, as well as spiritual, considerations. In this sense the arguments proposed by the Percy Fee rebels for the defence of Sawley Abbey were in close accord with the case that Aske made against the Dissolution in general.[89]

The rebels' grievances, however, was not conceived simply in terms of the government's attack on the traditional practices of the

87 Bateson, p. 338.
88 SP1/108 (L.P. XI. 785).
89 Bateson, p. 561.

church and its wealth. This is made evident in the Clitheroe proclamation which highlighted the concern for both the commonwealth and the church and, influenced by the declarations of grievance issued by Aske, blamed the repudiation of the society of orders, proposing that remedy would lie not only in the suppression of heresy but also in the exclusion of "villein blood" from the king's presence and from his privy council. In this way the commonwealth would be safeguarded and the king's person and his issue, another clause taken from Aske, would be preserved.[90]

A final possible source of evidence for the grievances of the Percy Fee rebels lies in a muster bill addressed from "Master Poverty" which circulated in the north-west in late October 1536 and may have been the letter attached to Giggleswick church door on 19th October.[91] It complained of heretics who, on the one hand, had suppressed or spoiled abbeys, churches and minsters; had shown contempt for the laws of the church and had blasphemed the saints, and who, on the other, had secured the passage of certain acts of parliament which were thought to be against the interests of the commonwealth in that, if enforced, they would prove to be unbearable to "the estate of poverty". Although nothing is specified, implied here is an objection to the tax measures which had helped to raise revolt in other parts of the north as well as in Lincolnshire.[92]

A rising of the commons?

At the time the Hamerton/Tempest host was perceived, by both its supporters and opponents, as representing a rising of the commons. Its grievances were offered as "the commons' causes"; its oath obliged men to be true to the commons; the regions that fell under its control were described as having been "sworn to the commons"; and, to describe its demobilisation, it was said that "the commons were disparpled to their houses".[93] Achievements associated with the Percy

90 Toller, pp. 51–52 (*L.P.* XI. 892).

91 Toller, pp. 47–9.

92 As part of the wapentake of Staincliffe, Percy Fee had been notorious earlier in the reign for its resistance to taxation. See *Early Tudor Craven: Subsidies and Assessments, 1510-1547*, ed. R. W. Hoyle, in *Y.A.S.R.S.*,145 (1987), pp. xxv–xxvi. So had the adjacent wapentake of Ewcross, from which the bill had probably come. See ibid., pp. xxviii–xxix. According to Darcy there had been a protest there by 6th October against paying more money to the government (*L.P.* XI. 563).

93 SP1/116, f. 129b (*L.P.* XII{1}. 518); *L.P.* XII{1}. 1014; e.g. SP1/112 (*L.P.* XI. 1251); SP1/116, f. 128 (*L.P.* XII{1}. 518).

Fee revolt were attributed to the commons, notably the restoration of Sawley Abbey, the enlistment of Hamerton and Tempest, the second march into Lancashire and the taking of Whalley Abbey on 30th October.[94] Much of this evidence for a movement of the commons might be dismissed as a cover-up, designed either to conceal or to exonerate clerical and aristocratic involvement. Yet not all of it was produced by parties seeking to free themselves from blame. Loyalist as well as rebel gentlemen alleged a rising of the commons. The Earl of Derby, for example, saw himself as warring against the commons, reporting on 1st November that Whalley Abbey had been taken two days before by "the commons of the borders of Yorkshire near to Sawley with some of the borders of Lancashire next to them".[95] The picture he presented in his dispatches to the government was of a rebellious commons and a loyalist gentry.[96] A similar impression was given by Sir Thomas Southworth of Salmesbury and Sir Richard Hoghton of Hoghton who suddenly found themselves close to the front line at the end of October when the rebels marched down the Ribble into Lancashire to confront the Earl of Derby. According to their servants, both saw themselves as serving the king against the commons and bragged that, but for the Truce, they would have had them for breakfast.[97]

The driving force behind the host was the energy of a discontented commons, made militant not by local aristocrats and clergy but by hearing of uprisings in other parts. This was discernible in the bands that descended upon Hamerton on 20th October and on Tempest a day later. The three hundred armed men that took Hamerton were led by two commoners, Fawcett and Jacks, whom Hamerton described as "most lusty in that insurrection".[98] According to the tax records of the period, both were relatively wealthy men. In all probability Jacks was John Jacks of Cray in the manor of Buckden. He may also have had some connexion with Giggleswick. He appeared to be a tenant of the Percy earls of Northumberland. His goods were valued at £5 in 1525 and £4 in 1543.[99] Judged by the tax band in which he was placed he

94 For the restoration of Sawley, see SP1/112, f. 6b (*L.P.* XI. 1218). For the enlistment of Hamerton, see *L.P.* XII{1}. 1034 and *L.P.* XI. 807. For the enlistment of Tempest, see *L.P.* XII{1}. 518 and 1014. For the second march into Lancashire, see *L.P.* XII{1}. 1034. For the second taking of Whalley Abbey, see ibid.

95 Toller, p. 41 (*L.P.* XI. 947).

96 E.g. SP1/112, f. 157b (*L.P.* XI. 1251).

97 SP1/116, f. 128b (*L.P.* XII{1}. 518).

98 SP1/119, f. 19 (*L.P.* XII{1}. 1034).

99 Hoyle, *Early Tudor Craven*, pp. 13, 62 and 86.

was well-off. As assessed in 1525, in the whole wapentake of Stain-cliffe, which included the Percy Fee and the Honour of Skipton, only 4.7 per cent of tax payers were in this band and only 13.8 per cent in higher bands. In 1543, 7.1 per cent were in the same band and 11.4 per cent in higher bands. Moreover, in the manor of Buckden, no one was in a higher tax band in 1525. In 1543 four of the Buckden taxpayers assessed on goods were in a higher tax band but sixty-three were in lower tax bands.[100] Fawcett was, in all probability, Richard Fawcett of Litton, a tenant of Fountains Abbey. His goods were valued at forty shillings in the early twenties and at £7 in 1543.[101] At the later date there is no doubt about his affluence. At the earlier date he seemed of average wealth relative to the other taxpayers of Staincliffe: in 1524, 34 per cent were in the same category and 30.6 per cent in higher tax bands. Yet within the community of Litton no one was in a higher tax band either in 1524/5 or in 1543.[102] Neither of the two men were of the gentry. Since they were assessed on the value of goods and chattels rather than upon landed income and in view of their rural residence, they were undoubtedly peasants; but, judged by their tax assessments, they were men of substance. In meeting up with Hamerton they told him that they were pleased to take him "for before he had ruled them and now they would rule him".[103] This was probably a comment on the powers that he had possessed as steward of Percy Fee, but it also signified a rising of the commons, implying that since the rulers had failed, the ruled now needed to take charge, temporarily, to put matters right. In other words, a rising of the commons was required as the cure for bad governance.

The force of one thousand men that took Tempest was led by John Catterall of Rathmell, Anthony Talbot of West Halton and Richard Hamerton of Bolton-by-Bowland.[104] All three had gentry connexions: Catterall was lord of the manor of Rathmell; Talbot and Hamerton were scions of landed families well established in, and long-connected with, Percy Fee and the Forest of Bowland. Richard Hamerton was the brother of Sir Stephen Hamerton of Wigglesworth; Anthony Talbot was directly connected to Sir Thomas Talbot of Bashall.[105] At what

100 For 1525: ibid., p. 125. For 1543: ibid., p. 127.
101 Ibid., pp. 36, 49, 60 and 84.
102 For 1524: ibid., p. 123. For 1543: ibid., p. 127.
103 SP1/119, f. 19 (*L.P.* XII{1}. 1034).
104 See SP1/118, f. 265 (*L.P.* XII{1}. 1014). For Catterall, see Hoyle, *Early Tudor Craven*, p. 36. For Hamerton, see ibid., pp. 32 and 89. For Talbot, see ibid., pp. 11–12.
105 For Hamerton, see T. D. Whitaker, *History and Antiquities of the Deanery of Craven* (3rd edition, Leeds, 1878), p. 150. For Talbot, see ibid., p. 157n.

point they joined the revolt is unknown. What is known is that the force that took Hamerton was led by peasants and the force that took Tempest a day later was led by gentlemen. Conceivably the three gentlemen were taken by the rebel host as it marched down the Ribble valley from the assembly point at Neals Ing, since the residences of all three were *en route*. Taken and sworn, the gentlemen were converted into captains. Superimposed upon the peasant leadership of Fawcett and Jacks, they in turn yielded rank to Hamerton and Tempest. However, the captaincy of gentlemen did not appear to alter the basic nature of the revolt. The force that descended upon Tempest's house was, like the one that took Hamerton, a movement of the commons.

Idiomatically a rising of the commons, the uprising undoubtedly gave expression to a popular protest. On the other hand, because of the part played by clerics, notably the monks of Sawley Abbey, and the gentlemen of Percy Fee, notably the Tempest and Hamerton families, to describe it as a popular revolt would conceal its social complexity.

Early in 1537 the Abbot of Sawley told Sir Arthur Darcy that the responsibility for restoring the abbey had lain with "the commons that put him in contrary his will".[106] In October 1536 the monks of Sawley told Robert Aske that the restoration was the work of the "good and loving commons" and in December they wrote to Thomas Percy to show him that they had been "set in by the commons" and that "the commons were keen that the monks should stay and were willing to proceed in the said pilgrimage if this were disallowed"[107] The reality was more complicated. For one thing, the restoration was not simply the work of the commons since, as Richard Estgate, the abbey's chaplain, revealed under examination, the gentleman Nicholas Tempest "at the first was one of their great favourers". On his own admission, Tempest generously supplied the abbey with provisions when it was first restored.[108] Furthermore, evidence for the monks' active involvement in the revolt itself questions their alleged passivity in the abbey's restoration. In promoting and directing the revolt, the monks proved to be extremely adept and persistent. Thus, in its early stages they wrote to Robert Aske, reporting on the revolt so far and requiring his protection against Sir Arthur Darcy, the new owner.[109] At the second Monubent assembly they furnished hair-raising information of the Earl of Derby's plans, claiming that he was bent on

106 SP1/116 (*L.P.* XII{1}. 506).
107 SP1/108 (*L.P.* XI. 785); SP1/119, f. 20 (*L.P.* XII{1}. 1034).
108 SP1/117 (*L.P.* XII{1}. 695).
109 *L.P.* XI. 784.

pulling down not only Sawley Abbey but also Whalley Abbey, along with the houses of the Tempests and Hamertons.[110] In November, it was the Abbot of Sawley who informed Tempest and Hamerton, when they were attending the pilgrims' York council, that the border between Lancashire and Yorkshire was again rising to resist the Earl of Derby, causing the two to hasten home in order to manage the commons.[111]

Then, still active in December, in spite of the peace and the pardon, the monks wrote to Thomas Percy supplicating his support. Moved by the rumour that Aske had "discharged himself from the captainship", and that a new order for the restored religious houses had been issued which authorised their lessees to evict the monks until parliament had deliberated, they told Percy of their fears that "our most sinister back friend Sir Arthur Darcy" would seize the opportunity to commit "great enormities" against the people of the region as well as the monks, thus making the matter the concern of the whole community.[112] At the same time, through the agency of Hamerton, they wrote to Aske, seeking his advice on what to do. In response, both Percy and Aske told them to wait upon events.[113] The letter to Aske was delivered to the family home at Aughton by Shuttleworth, a servant of the abbey. *En route* he passed through Tadcaster, whose parsonage the Sawley monks had formerly owned. After he had gone, a seditious bill was found nailed to the church door.[114] In addition, among the surviving papers associated with the abbey, and probably produced by its monks, was the Sawley ballad and some notes for a sermon that supported rebellion when faith and country were in danger on the following grounds: that, whilst injuries to the self were acceptable, those committed against God and one's neighbours were not.[115] Thus, once reinstalled the monks became active proponents of revolt. In all likelihood, before their restoration they were instrumental in persuading the commons and gentry of the surrounding parts to take action against Sir Arthur Darcy. Under examination a tenant of Sawley revealed in February 1537 that "the religious persons stirred this pestilent sedition".[116]

---

110 See above, p. 232.
111 SP1/118, f. 265b (*L.P.* XII{1}. 1014).
112 SP1/108 (*L.P.* XI. 785).
113 For Aske, see Bateson, p. 338. For Percy, see *L.P.* XII{1}. 490–91.
114 *L.P.* XII{1}. 491 and 490.
115 For ballad, see above, pp. 234–5. For sermon, see SP1/108, f. 214 (*L.P.* XI. 786 {2}).
116 SP1/116 (*L.P.* XII{1}. 506).

Apart from the monks of Sawley, however, it could not be said that the clergy featured with any prominence in this uprising. Nonetheless, as Hamerton revealed, the assembly at Neals Ing of 20th October was attended not only by the people of Giggleswick but also by the priests attached to its parish church.[117] Moreover, Ralph Lynney, vicar of Blackburn and a monk from Whalley, was alleged to have said after the Truce that "if the commons come again into Lancashire he would bear the cross afore them", suggesting that he might have been of assistance in October on the two occasions that the Hamerton/Tempest host marched into Lancashire.[118] As for the other monks of Whalley Abbey, apart from the accusations brought by the government against them, there is little evidence of active support. On the two occasions that the abbey was occupied, the entry of the rebels was due to the forcefulness of the host rather than the complicity of the monks. However, it seems that Abbot Paslew contributed to the rebel cause by passing on to the rebels a letter of 25th October from the Earl of Derby which set out his military plans.[119]

Although contemporaries unanimously presented it as a rising of the commons, the key figures in the uprising were the esquire Nicholas Tempest and the knight Stephen Hamerton. Both were responsible for ordering the host and for leading it twice into Lancashire, the first time to swear the commons in Blackburnshire, the second time to confront the Earl of Derby. They were the delegates from Percy Fee that attended the pilgrims' York council in November and, in Hamerton's case, the Pontefract council in December.[120] They were the two special friends of Sawley Abbey, singled out for commendation in the monks' letter of December to Sir Thomas Percy.[121] In the eyes of the outside world they were the leaders of the revolt and the captains of its host.

In both cases the authority they possessed as rebel leaders stemmed from their social position. Nicholas was the brother of Sir Richard Tempest. Although the latter had shifted his residence from Craven to Bradford and Wakefield, following his marriage to Rosemund, the daughter and heiress of Tristram Bolling of Bolling, he retained a position of great influence in the region of the Percy Fee revolt with seats at Waddington and Bracewell, manors at Hebden, Bracewell, Horton, Paythorne and Conistone cum Kilney, the steward-

117 SP1/119, f. 19 (*L.P.* XII{1}. 1034).
118 *L.P.* XII{1}. 853.
119 For letter, see SP1/109, f. 110 (*L.P.* XI. 872) and Weeks, op. cit., pp. 202–7.
120 *L.P.* XII{1}. 785; Bateson, p. 340.
121 *L.P.* XI. 785.

ship of the manors of Malham, Barnoldswick and Thornton, the forestership of Bowland and the East Lancashire stewardships of Rochdale and the hundred of Blackburn.[122] It was in his name that John Lacy, his son-in-law, was alleged to have commanded the men of Halifax to arm themselves and carry the church cross into Lancashire raising the commons.[123] It was he that Derby suspected in October, so much so that he planned to destroy his house at Waddington near Whalley and blamed him in early 1537 not for being directly involved in the uprising but because he "was neither good first nor last" and because, if he had wanted, he could "have stayed his brother Nicholas".[124] There was probably some truth in this.

Sir Richard played no direct part, either for or against, in the Percy Fee revolt, largely because he was engaged in coping with the commons of Wakefield and Sowerbyshire and when, eventually enlisted as a pilgrim, he remained close to Lord Darcy and, as one of the leaders of the middleward, involved in organising the army that confronted the government on the Don in the last week of October.[125] However, he made his mark on the Percy Fee revolt, partly through tolerating it. His behaviour in October 1536 contrasted sharply with the swift and effective action that he took against the Craven riots of 1535.[126] He also made an indirect contribution to the revolt through the men who employed his authority in the rebel cause: besides his brother Nicholas, several of his servants were involved, notably Edmund Lawde, a gentleman of Gisburn, William Smythies and Richard Core who, under Nicholas, led the force which on 23rd October sought to persuade the commons around Whalley and the monks of the abbey to support the cause.[127] For this reason, the Percy Fee revolt was to some extent a Tempest rising. For the Tempests, especially for

---

122 R. W. Hoyle, "The first earl of Cumberland: a reputation reassessed", *Northern History*, 22 (1986), pp. 67–8; Tempest, op. cit., p. 248; Whitaker, *Craven* (3rd ed.), pp. 98–9; Bindoff III, p. 430–31 and Hoyle, *Early Tudor Craven*, pp. 7, 8, 9(bis), 20 and 22–3.

123 *L.P.* XII{1}. 784.

124 SP1/116, f. 253b (*L.P.* XII{1}. 632). The location of the threatened house was not specified, but it was presumably the more accessible Waddington rather than Bracewell in Skipton Fee.

125 See *L.P.* XI. 702, 733-4; Smith, op. cit., pp. 189–90. For his association with Darcy, see Stapulton, p. 100 and *L.P.* XI. 928.

126 *L.P.* Add. 996; *L.P.* VIII. 946, 992, 993.

127 For Nicholas, see Tempest, op. cit., pp. 247ff. For his servants and the part they played, see SP1/116, f. 253b (*L.P.* XII{1}. 632). For Lawde, see the note on the verso of the order taken at York, SP1/111, f. 236b (*L.P.* XI. 1155). He was assessed at £4 on lands and fees in the 1543 subsidy (see Hoyle, *Early Tudor Craven*, p. 83).

Nicholas as his brother's lieutenant in the region, the problem was the position that Sir Arthur Darcy would establish in Percy Fee as a result of acquiring the Sawley Abbey estate. The Tempest animus against him became evident in 1537 when the task of repossessing the house was given to Richard since Darcy was engaged in serving the Duke of Norfolk as he travelled the north restoring order. It was given to Tempest presumably to test his loyalty, but the plan backfired against the owner. When Darcy eventually arrived to take possession he found that the three servants of Richard Tempest, who had been left in charge of the abbey, had wasted his goods, cattle and sheep and had taken all his rents for the last half year.[128]

As for Hamerton, he was clearly important to the rebels not only by virtue of being a considerable landowner in the region, with the manor of Hamerton in the Forest of Bowland, the manor of Wigglesworth in Percy Fee and land leased in Hellifield from the Cliffords and in Settle from the Percies, but also as an official of the Percy family, serving as steward of Percy Fee and steward of the Percy manor of Long Preston.[129] Given his local importance, Hamerton, like the Tempests, must have been moved by the sudden intrusion of Sir Arthur Darcy. Like them, he clearly had no incentive to oppose an uprising which was seeking to exclude this man. Was he acting for the Percies? They had good reasons for aiding and abetting this revolt, partly because of the government's plans to annex the Percy patrimony upon the death of the sixth earl, partly because Sawley Abbey was a Percy foundation and, following its suppression, the lease had not been granted to the family. But, whilst active as rebels in Northumberland and in the North and East Ridings, the family appeared to have no involvement with the uprising in Percy Fee, in spite of the fact that it was initially led by John Jacks, a Percy tenant, and captained by Stephen Hamerton, a Percy officer. There is nothing to suggest that either became involved because of instructions from the Percy family

---

128 SP1/116 (*L.P.* XII{1}. 506). Tempest was part of the Darcy affinity, by kinship and service, as he stated in October 1536 when he told Sir George Darcy, "I am of your blood and would take part with you against any lord in England" [see SP1/108 (*L.P.* XI. 741); *L.P.* XII{1}. 849 (9)]. But by this time the Darcy family was deeply divided between Lord Darcy who opposed the Dissolution and Sir Arthur Darcy, his son, who had been its very first beneficiary.

129 For landownership, see Whitaker, *Craven*, pp. 41–2 and 154. Also see Hoyle, *Early Tudor Craven*, pp. 14–15, 41–2. In 1524 he was assessed at a landed income of £40 p.a. (ibid., pp. 51 and 58). For stewardship, see Hoyle, "The first earl of Cumberland", p. 85 and his *Early Tudor Craven*, p. 18. On 5th July 1535 the earl of Northumberland described him as his cousin and "mine officer there [i.e. in Craven]" [SP1/93, f. 239 (*L.P.* VIII. 991)].

to raise the manred. In fact, contact with the Percy family did not appear to be made before December 1536 when, after receiving a disappointing answer from Robert Aske, the monks of Sawley sent a letter to Thomas Percy, then lodged close to Newcastle-upon-Tyne, and in response were told to comply with the king.[130] For this reason, then, it seems that Hamerton became involved not under instruction from his lord but because he was taken by the commons and had grievances of his own.

The rebel host in Percy Fee, then, after being given its initial impetus by the commons, was not simply directed by any one part of society, but involved elements from all three orders. It was a movement which, although ostensibly a rising of the commons, was in reality a conjunction of aristocratic, clerical and popular revolt; and permitting it to develop was the failure of the families who normally exercised authority in the region – the Percies, the Cliffords, the Tempests – to take counteraction. In all three cases this was because they were preoccupied with revolts elsewhere. But, even if they had not been, it is unlikely that, in view of their rebel sympathies, the Percies or the Tempests would have come to the government's rescue.

130 SP1/116 (*L.P.* XII{1}. 490); *L.P.* XII{1}. 491.

VII

▪▪▪

THE ATKINSON
HOST

Mobilisation

As with the revolt in Percy Fee, the uprising in Dent and Kendal began
with the traditionally emotive claim that a defence was needed against
invaders from the north.[1] The two revolts also resembled each other in
declaring, in the early stages, that to put matters right society needed
to be upturned, with the traditional rulers directed by the ruled.[2] Both
subscribed, therefore, to the conceit of being risings of the commons.
Both formed armies which in the last week of October confronted the
Earl of Derby, only avoiding a battle with him because of the truce
reached with the government on 27th October. On the other hand, the
two hosts, although in communication with each other, failed to unite.
Nor did either join up with any other rebel army. Distinguishing the
two uprisings from each other were the agrarian grievances of the Dent
and Kendal rebels. These centred upon the preservation of customs
appertaining to tenancy and tithes.

Yet the Dent and Kendal uprising was not simply a revolt of
peasants against lords. Politicising it were the complaints it held against
the government for dissolving holy places, for making heretical changes
in religion and for imposing new taxes. It was more obviously a popular
revolt than most of the other October uprisings; yet this was only
because it chose not to convert the gentlemen it enlisted into captains.

The Atkinson host was recruited from a very extensive area: the
barony of Kendal, much of the Yorkshire wapentake of Ewcross and

---

1 No longer invading Scots, but invading commons. For Percy Fee, see above, pp.
  229. For Dent and Kendal, see below, p. 251.
2 For Percy Fee, see above, p. 238. For Dent and Kendal, see below, p. 253.

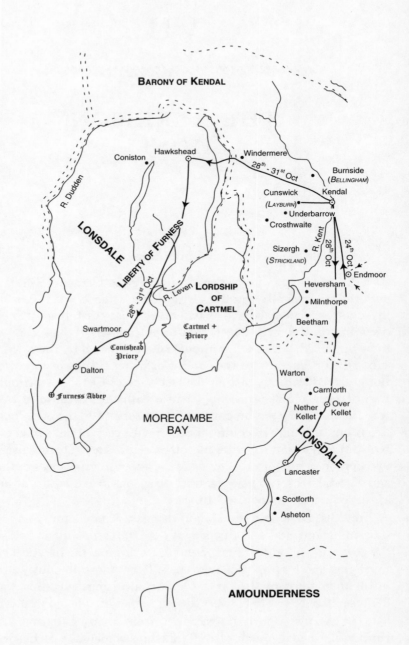

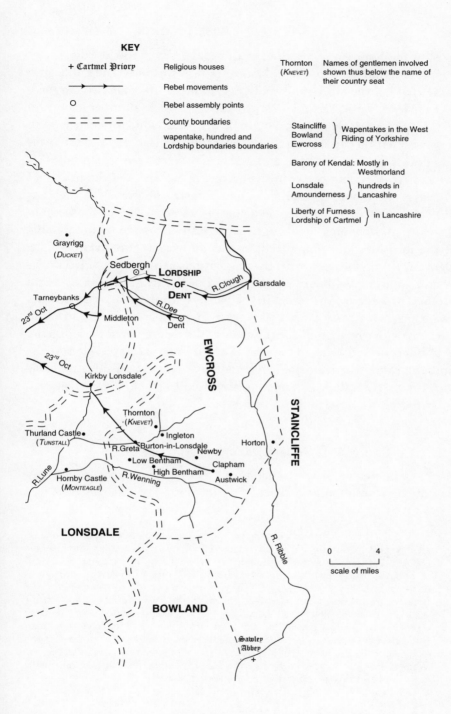

Map 8   The Dent and Kendal uprising

most of the Lancashire hundred of Lonsdale. Given the low density of population that came of the upland terrain, it was of considerable size: somewhat between three and six thousand men.[3] Its main driving force was the lordship of Dent which provided the original impetus both to confederate and then to take up arms, and which selected John Atkinson as the captain-in-chief.[4] Most of the leadership, moreover, was drawn from this region; and it was men from Dent that played an active part in raising revolt in the barony of Kendal and the liberty of Furness.[5] However, to establish the character of the Dent revolt is difficult since the surviving evidence is meagre, especially because there are no surviving confessions or depositions made by inhabitants of the lordship, and prejudiced, especially because the details of the Dent revolt rely heavily upon the tendentious account, provided under examination, of William Collyns, bailiff of the town of Kendal and a prominent leader of the revolt in the barony.[6] Collyns' account arouses suspicion for stressing that the men of Kendal were enforced to participate by the men of Dent, whereas the former were undoubtedly less innocent and passive than he claimed. Yet his impression of the uprising cannot be dismissed as a complete fabrication. The momentum for confederation and hosting appeared to stem, as he suggested, from the north-westerly tip of the West Riding.

In the lordship of Dent

A host was created in the lordship of Dent on 21st October, within a day of the formation of a rebel army in Percy Fee.[7] It was recruited

3 See Map 8. These figures were given by the Earl of Derby [see Toller, p. 43 (*L.P.* XI. 947 {2}], for the force that marched to Lancaster on 28th October. He claimed that it was first thought to number 5–6,000 but "by examination thereof made since" it was now thought to have been 3,000 strong. However, these figures do not account for the total military support received by this uprising since at the time the troops raised in Lancashire Oversands had not joined the main army. Another figure, of 10,000 (see *L.P.* XII{1}. 914), was associated with the Dent rebels' threat, made between 20th and 23rd October, to spoil the town of Kendal. But this figure was either wild exaggeration or it referred to support from elsewhere: i.e. the huge Richmondshire host which in this time marched via Wensleydale into Craven to besiege the Earl of Cumberland in Skipton Castle. For the plausibility of a figure of 3,000, see Appendix I.

4 P.R.O. SP1/118, f. 140b (*L.P.* XII{1}. 914{2}).

5 See below.

6 *L.P.* XII{1}. 914.

7 SP1/118, f. 139 (*L.P.* XII{1}. 914{2}). That they rose on the Saturday is concealed in the *L.P.* version of the document which presents "on the Saturday

from the extensive parish of Sedbergh which included Dentdale and Garsdale.[8] There had been rumblings of revolt in the lordship for almost a month, with confederations bound by oath forming in the last week of September, a week before the first disturbances in Lincolnshire and a fortnight before the Aske uprising got underway. This was discovered by William Breyar who, after being assaulted in the town of Dent by a small crowd for wearing the king's livery, fled to Kirkby Lonsdale where he was told that the men of Dent and the residents of "three other parishes thereabouts" had been sworn on the 25th September.[9] From the crowd in Dent, Breyar learned of the fear that the churches of the region (i.e. the parish church of Sedbergh and its chapels dependent at Garsdale and Dent) were about to be dissolved.[10] Generating the fear was a rumour prevailing in the north at the time, but it is likely that the people of Dent specifically feared that they would lose their churches because they were appropriated to the recently dissolved Coverham Abbey.[11] A young smith thought the

next after, they of Dent and Sedbergh were up" as "on the Saturday next, after they of Dent and Sedbergh were up". The Saturday mentioned can be identified as the 21st October by working backwards in Collyn's day-to-day account of the uprising from the known date of 28th October for the march on Lancaster. Reports from Darcy (see *L.P.* XI. 692 {2} and 760) claimed that the commons of Dent and Sedbergh were "up" on 13th and 17th October, but he was confusing confederation with armed revolt.

8 SP1/118, f. 139 (*L.P.* XII{1}. 914{2}.
9 The oath was taken on a Monday: that is, either on 25th September or 2nd of October. It can be identified as occurring on 25th September by working back from known dates in Breyar's chronology of events. See SP1/109, f. 37b (*L.P.* XI. 841). The other parishes confederating can only be guessed at. To the north of Dent were two parishes in the same position, their churches having been appropriated to religious houses which were now dissolved: Orton, formerly of Conishead Priory and Barton, of Warter Priory. Both were in the barony of Westmorland. Other possibilities are the parish of Kirkby Stephen which became the epicentre of the Westmorland uprising, Aysgarth in upper Wensleydale or the south Ewcross parishes of Thornton-in-Lonsdale and Clapham. Thornton was reported as confederating in the first week of October; Clapham became involved, though its vicar in the Dent revolt. The likelihood is that the three parishes referred to were Orton, Barton and Thornton.
10 SP1/109, f. 37b (*L.P.* XI. 841).
11 T. D. Whitaker, *A History of Richmondshire in the North Riding of the County of York* (London, 1823), II, pp. 355, 357 and 362. Also creating anxiety was probably the fact that with the recent death of its vicar, Roger Horseman, they were awaiting the next presentation which, with the dissolution of Coverham Abbey, now lay with the king who on 1st October appointed Richard Corney to the office. See *L.P.* XI. 943 {16}. The Garsdale part of the parish must also have been concerned with the dissolution of Easby Abbey which had maintained a small chapel there as well as having been lord of the manor of Garsdale. See Whitaker, op. cit., pp. 480–81.

king was to blame and accused him of being a thief. But the rest of the crowd asserted: "it is not the king's deed but the deed of Cromwell", declaring that if they could get their hands upon him "we would crum him that he was never as crummed'. As for the king, if they could take charge of him, they would do no more than "new crown him", presumably to remind him of his coronation oath.[12]

These rumblings of revolt continued into the first week of October. They affected the valley of the Greta, in southern Ewcross and across the border in the Lancashire hundred of Lonsdale, with pressures brought upon gentlemen to take the rebel oath. Thus in the first week of October Marmaduke Tunstall of Thurland was approached by the men of Dent, according to William Breyar; and, according to Harry Sais, William Knevet of Thornton-in-Lonsdale, having fled in the direction of Kendal when he found that "all the townships about . . . were up", was taken and sworn. In the same week upper Wensley- dale was affected as well, with five hundred Wensleydalers having taking the oath by 6th October and with the range of reported grievances now including the suppression of abbeys, the confiscation of church treasures and the payment of taxes.[13] The tax complaint, as reported by Lord Darcy, expressed an unwillingness to pay any more money to commissioners, presumably an objection to paying a subsidy in 1536 and a fifteenth and tenth in 1537, and also a refusal to pay new taxes on baptisms, foodstuffs and ploughlands which, according to Darcy, were set out in "certain unlawful articles".[14] The revolt in Dent, then, was initially a protest against the government's plunder- ing of the realm. Inciting it to take action was a corpus of rumour that affected Lincolnshire and much of the North and which alleged that the Dissolution would apply to parish churches as well as religious houses and that the government planned to impose new taxes which would fall heavily upon the poor.[15]

In the first three weeks of October, before the movement became an army, it spread not only into upper Wensleydale and the southerly

12 SP1/109, f. 37b (L.P. XI. 841).
13 For upper Wensleydale, see L.P. XI. 563 {2}; L.P. XI. 564. For the valley of the Greta, see SP1/109, f. 37b (L.P. XI. 841); L.P. XI. 879 /ii.
14 See SP1/106 (L.P. XI. 563{2}); SP1/110, f. 39 (L.P. XI. 564). For the content of the articles, see Toller, p. 50.
15 Cumberland (as was made evident in Henry VIII reply of 14th October) had reported on 9th October of confederations in Dent, Sedbergh and Wensleydale "by the mean and reporture of such false and untrue matters as was never by us or any or any of council purposed or intended" (i.e. the plunder of the churches and new taxes). See Chatsworth Trustees, Clifford Letter Book, f. 3b.

parts of Ewcross but also into the barony of Kendal.[16] The evangelising process, and the dynamic role played by the Dent men in promoting it, is best illustrated by what happened around the town of Kendal. On 18th October two men from Dent entered the town.[17] One was George Willan, the other, William Garnet.[18] Both were prominent in the leadership of the Dent uprising.[19] In a manner reflecting the Percy Fee rebels' deputation to the Earl of Cumberland on 21st October, the two men visited Sir James Layburn, the leading gentleman resident in the region by virtue of being deputy to the absentee steward of the barony, William Parr, and of having an estate in the barony and north Lancashire worth £100 p.a.[20] Since Parr also held the lordship of Dent, Layburn was undoubtedly known there as well.[21] The two Dent men told him that word had come from the commons of Westmorland, Cumberland and Richmondshire that they were up in arms and ready, if the people of Dent, Sedbergh and Kendal failed to co-operate, to take action against them. The two men asked Layburn how these rebels could be best resisted and he advised them

16 Darcy identified the area of confederation as not only Dent, Sedbergh and Wensleydale but also "other dales and countries" [SP1/106 (*L.P.* XI. 563)] which in another letter written on the same day were presented as "other their neighbours" [SP1/110, f. 39 (*L.P.* XI. 564)].

17 These events and dates rely solely on the account of William Collyns. See SP1/118 (*L.P.* XII{1}. 914 {2}). In declaring that the day was a Saturday and that their arrival occurred "ten days or thereabouts afore any insurrection was in Kendal" (f. 138), Collyns infers that they came to Kendal on 14th October. But there is reason to believe that Collyns was providing misinformation on this point and that the actual date of arrival was Wednesday 18th October. According to Collyns, the two men claimed to be acting under threat from movements of the commons in Westmorland, Cumberland and Richmondshire. This was in all likelihood true but 14th October is too early for it to have happened. By this time the Richmondshire revolt had yet to compose the letter that it sent westwards to rouse revolt in the West March and by this time there seemed to be no armed rebellion in either Westmorland and Cumberland. In contrast, by 18th October the Richmondshire letter had been dispatched across the Pennines and the barony of Westmorland was organising itself in response. Moreover, that the date was the 18th October can be established by working back from known dates in Collyns' account. If Collyns is to be trusted and the 14th October is accepted as the day upon which the two Dent men arrived in Kendal, a strange gap of four days is left, between Sunday 15th October and Friday 20th October (f. 139) in which nothing happens. However, if 18th October is taken as the true date, Collyns' account then provides a continuous day-by-day narrative of events over the next ten days.

18 *L.P.* XII{1}. 914.

19 See below, p. 285.

20 *L.P.* VII. 432; *L.P.* XII{1}. 825.

21 *L.P.* XII{1}. 362. For Parr's estate in northern Ewcross, see below, p. 291.

to do nothing.[22] They next approached the bailiff of Kendal, the wealthy merchant William Collyns. According to him, he also advised inaction, adding that they had no cause to rise unless they were deprived of their "old ancient customs", a reference to the barony's system of land tenure and tithe payment.[23]

Learning from this exchange how best to recruit the men of the barony, the two that evening met a number of townsmen who, presumably as a result of this meeting, assembled the residents of North Street at daybreak in a croft and persuaded them to swear an oath which conventionally was "to be true to God and the king" but then, in place of the usual pledges to be true to the commons or to the commonwealth or to the maintenance of Christ's church, substituted a pledge to be true to their "ancient laudable customs".[24] This revised oath did the trick. By the close of day the whole town, including bailiff Collyns, had been assembled and sworn, not in the town itself but at Tarneybank which is five or so miles away in the direction of Dent.[25]

The next step taken by the Dent men was to form an army and then to use it for persuading men to become rebels. Thus, when the townsmen of Kendal, having taken the advice of two local gentlemen (William Knevet and Richard Ducket), informed the Dent men that they were not prepared to join their rebellion, the Dent men threatened that if they failed to attend a muster at Endmoor on 23rd October, Kendal would be ravaged by a force of 10,000 men. The townsmen, according to Collyns, first planned to resist this threat but were let down by the gentlemen who either failed to turn up, as with Nicholas Layburn, or, as with Richard Ducket, Walter Strickland and William Knevet, came to the town but lingered on its edge, declining to join in. And so on 23rd October five hundred townsmen met the Dent host at Endmoor. Since this was not on the road to Dent but six or so miles south of Kendal, the choice of venue suggests that a purpose of the muster was also to join up with supporters from the barony and from other parts of the wapentake of Ewcross.[26] That this host from the West Riding was recruited not simply from the lordship of Dent is evident in its leadership at this point in time which comprised, besides three townsmen from Sedbergh and two from Dent, the vicar of Clapham and James Buskell of Middleton.[27] This, taken with the

22 SP1/118, f. 138 (*L.P.* XII{1}. 914 {2}).
23 Ibid.
24 Ibid., f. 138b.
25 Ibid.
26 Ibid., fos. 139–139b.
27 For the leadership as it existed on 23rd October, see ibid., f. 140.

very size of the Dent host, suggests that, prior to enlisting the townsmen of Kendal, the uprising had already recruited the inhabitants of
the eastern border of the barony and the southerly parts of the
wapentake of Ewcross.[28]

The next pressure the men of Dent brought upon the barony of
Kendal was to recruit its gentlemen. At Endmoor on 23rd October
they had noticed and questioned their absence. When the townsmen of
Kendal admitted that the gentlemen "would not come with them", the
men of Dent rejoined: "if ye cannot rule them, we shall rule them",
meaning that if the commons of Kendal could not persuade the
gentlemen to follow their lead, the men of Dent would have to do it
for them.[29] With this in mind the Dent army, led by Captain
Atkinson, decided to hold a meeting in Kendal on 24th October.
Following the example of the Richmondshire uprising, it produced a
proclamation "in the name of Lord Poverty" which ordered every man
upon pain of death to meet the next day in Kendal "to know the Lord
Poverty's pleasure".[30] When the gentlemen failed to turn up, the Dent
host took action. For the next three days they targeted Sir James
Layburn, hoping to enlist his support and, through his example, to
draw in the other gentlemen. As a result, his house was visited and his
property spoiled. That the Dent men were very much to the fore in
this campaign was made evident on 27th October when Layburn's
brother bought a temporary reprieve for Sir James by paying the men
of Dent £20 to put off further reprisals until the following day.[31] That
their policy of seeking to control the gentlemen through proceeding
against Layburn had worked was demonstrated on 27th October
when, along with Layburn, the gentlemen of the barony came to
Kendal town and, in the tolbooth, were sworn to the rebel cause.[32]

Then, having raised considerable support, having bound the
leading gentlemen to the cause, and after making further provision
to recruit support in Lancashire Oversands by sending into the lordships of Cartmel and Furness companies of commons and rousing
proclamations, the Atkinson host marched on Lancaster, accompa-

28 There is no good reason to believe in the figure of 10,000 (see n. 3), but the
    implications of the threat made and its acceptance by the townsmen of Kendal are
    that the host was already a large one.
29 SP1/118, fos. 139b–140.
30 SP1/118, f. 140.
31 Ibid.
32 Ibid., f. 140b.

nied by Sir James Layburn, Sir Robert Bellingham, Nicholas Layburn, William Lancaster, Richard Ducket and Walter Strickland.[33] Taking it without difficulty, the rebels subjected its inhabitants to the oath.[34] Here they learned of the impending battle for Sawley Abbey between the Hamerton/Tempest host and the Earl of Derby.[35] They were approached from both sides. Hamerton told them how Percy Fee and the Forest of Bowland had been sworn and "made sure" to the rebel cause.[36] The Earl of Derby, who was busy mustering troops at Preston, sent a challenge to Atkinson for a battle of equal strengths on Bentham Moor. In the exchange of words that followed Captain Atkinson declared that "they had a pilgrimage to do for the common-wealth". For this cause, according to Atkinson, they were prepared to die but they nonetheless rejected Derby's challenge to arms stating that they would only do battle with him "if he interrupted them of their pilgrimage".[37] By this time the Dent and Kendal uprising was clearly falling under the influence of Robert Aske. However, this does not mean that, in its earlier stages, it was free from outside influences. They came notably from the Richmondshire uprising. It was later observed that a leader of the revolt, Walter Rawlinson of Milnthorpe, was bailiff to Lord Latimer; and another leading figure in the Richmondshire revolt, John Dakyn, was charged with being the instigator of the Kendal uprising.[38] Neither charge can be corrobo-rated. However, the revolt was clearly inspired by news of revolt in the North Riding, sharing with it, in all probability, concern for the dissolution of Coverham and Easby Abbeys and contracting from it the language and cause of Captain Poverty.[39]

Fears were held that the Atkinson host planned to march through Lancashire. This may well have been the case in November, but its main aim in October was simply to establish a huge confederation that included Lancashire from Lancaster northwards, the wapentake of Ewcross and the barony of Kendal. The formation of a host and its march on Kendal and then onto Lancaster had this aim basically in mind. For this reason, having achieved it with the taking of Lancaster on 28th October, the host ignored the pleas for assistance from Percy Fee. Overlooking the fact that Sawley Abbey was in extreme peril from

33 For the raising of Lancashire Oversands, see below, pp. 270–2.
34 SP1/118, f. 140b.
35 See above, p. 232.
36 SP1/118, f. 140b.
37 Toller, pp. 44–5.
38 For Latimer, see *L.P.* XII{1}. 632. For Dakyn, see *L.P.* XII{1}. 788.
39 See below, pp. 283–5.

the Earl of Derby it disbanded and went home. On the other hand, bearing the Earl of Derby in mind and the reprisals that he might take if, having defeated the Percy Fee host, he turned his attentions northwards, the captaincy issued a proclamation ordering a meeting on Bentham Moor three days later to work out what to do next.[40] But, before that meeting was held, news of the Truce and the disbandment of Derby's army had made it unnecessary.

In the barony of Kendal

Whilst the initiative, leadership, general policy and direction was provided by the Dent men, the Kendal rebels were undoubtedly a dynamic force in their own right. The picture presented by Collyns, of the reluctant accomplice drawn into the fray by external compulsion, is untrue. After all, the town of Kendal was not difficult to arouse; and the day following the arrival of the men from Dent, and well before the threat of an attack by 10,000 men had been issued, its inhabitants had formed a confederation bound by oath.[41] Directing the Kendal revolt were its own grievances and, in the person of William Collyns, its own leader. Its alliance with the Dent men, moreover, was not due simply to intimidation but came of shared discontents and agreed plans.

Before the arrival of the emissaries from Dent, there had been trouble in the barony, especially because of friction between Sir James Layburn and the peasantry, so much so that on 11th October Sir Thomas Wharton had informed Cromwell that towards Layburn the barony's inhabitants "be very troublous".[42] The source of the friction, it seems, was the custom of tenant right which obliged the landlords to make reasonable exactions of their tenants. The criterion of reasonableness was determined by the military services required of the tenantry for defending the northern border. Within the scheme of things, the exactions had to be low enough to permit the tenantry to carry out their military duties in an adequate manner: that is, to turn up, horsed and harnessed, whenever summoned by the warden of the marches and to serve him without charge for as long as was necessary. Offending the tenantry in Kendal, and probably in parts of north Lancashire,[43] was the estate management of Layburn himself who

40 SP1/118, f. 140b (*L.P.* XII{1}. 914 {2}).
41 SP1/118, f. 138b.
42 SP1/107 (*L.P.* XI. 666).
43 Ibid. Wharton referred to his being held in contempt in Lancashire. For the extension of the barony of Kendal and its custom into north Lancashire, see below, n. 152.

was allegedly raising gressums – the payments that fell due upon change of either tenant or lord – to unprecedented levels and, if so, was breaching custom by acting unreasonably.[44]

Offended were not only his own tenants but also the rest of the barony's tenantry since tenant right was the prevalent tenure and it was felt that, given his influential position as deputy steward of the barony, he was well placed to determine the management of not only the royal estate but also the holdings of other landlords, both by setting a bad example and by failing to prosecute those who were offending the custom.[45] At the time, the tenantry holding directly of the Crown was vulnerable, having become liable that year to a gressum with the death in July of the king's son, Henry Fizroy, Duke of Richmond and holder of the barony; that is, shortly after having paid another gressum on the occasion of his receiving possession of the barony, which was as recently as 1534 for the part called Marquis Fee, 1532 for the part called Lumley Fee and 1531 for the part called Richmond Fee. Treasurer Gostwick reported in July 1536 that the half year's revenues from the barony had not been paid the previous March suggesting that there was agrarian friction between the duke and his tenants prior to his death.[46]

The custom of tenant right, then, was felt to be at stake throughout the barony; and prior to the revolt, the Kendalers of both town and country had already petitioned Layburn to change his ways, arguing that his demand for a £40 gressum was unreasonable when his father had only taken four marks (£2. 13. 4d.), especially in view of the tenantry's obligation to serve the lord warden of the marches without wages whenever summoned by his proclamation or beacon.[47] So important was this grievance that, after the arrival of the men from Dent and for the next few days, the Kendalers were intent on sorting it out. Its overriding importance, at least at the start of the revolt, was made explicit by William Collyns, the bailiff of Kendal, when he told the men from Dent that the preservation of "our old ancient customs here" was the prime concern; and also in the oath which, refashioned

44 SP1/118, fos. 138b–139 (*L.P.* XII{1}. 914 {2}).
45 Ibid. As an indication of its prevalence in the barony, see the Johnson Survey of 1607 (B.L. Lansdowne MS 169, fos. 107b–8) in which 863 tenants held by custom as against 103 freeholders and 18 leaseholders.
46 For his receipt of the barony, see below, n. 55. For Gostwick's statement, see *L.P.* XI. 174.
47 Collyns claimed that "both before the insurrection and after [he] and divers others of the town and country of Kendal came to [Layburn] and desired him, by way of petition, to be good unto them for their ancient customs" [SP1/118, f. 139 (*L.P.* XII{1}. 914 {2}].

to suit the barony, pledged support for "their ancient, laudable customs";[48] and in a visit paid on 19th October by the Kendalers to Sir James Layburn's house at Cunswick, a mile or so west of Kendal town, when they required him not only to defend them "against all enemies that would come upon them" but also "to be good unto them concerning their laudable customs".

When they put to him their oath with its pledge to maintain tenant right, Layburn refused to swear, but he did place his seal in the custody of his brother Nicholas, on the understanding that, if other gentlemen agreed formally to warrant the custom, he would do likewise; and that evening his seal, along with the seal of Walter Strickland, was applied to a declaration of the custom drawn up by the tenantry.[49] The following day six men from the town of Kendal went again to his house, presumably to secure his personal approval of what had happened the previous evening; but they found him gone, in all probability to his house at Ashton in Lancashire.[50] Further visits to his Kendal residence occurred between 24th and 27th October when, backed by the Dent host, further demands were made of him to respect the custom. The rebels finally had their way. On 27th October Layburn came to Kendal and, along with the other gentlemen of the barony, took the oath with its requirement that they remain true to the "ancient, laudable custom".[51] At this stage an agrarian movement in the barony had succeeded in obtaining what it wanted: an assurance from the gentlemen that, in the management of their estates, they would abide by the custom.

The custom, as elaborated upon in Collyns' account, specified tenant right. But the custom of Kendal, as quoted at the time, also appeared to include a certain procedure for the payment of tithes. This was made evident in several proceedings that came before the courts of equity in the 1520s and 1530s. In them the claim was made that "a laudable and prescribed custom" used "time out of mind" permitted "all persons holding land" in the barony of Kendal to acquit their tithes in the form of a money rent rather than to pay it in kind.[52] There is nothing to suggest that the rebels were referring to tithes when they quoted custom in October 1536; but there is the action taken in January and February 1537 by the parishioners of Heversham who in mid-January obliged Richard Redman to swear the oath "to the

48 Ibid., f. 138.
49 Ibid., ff. 138b–139.
50 Ibid., f. 139.
51 Ibid., fos. 140–140b.
52 E.g. P.R.O. C1/845/16–17; C1/856/16.

custom of Kendal" and then, in February, refused to allow the tithe farmers the tithe corn that they had leased from the Abbot of York St. Mary, presumably because it was customarily commuted to the payment of money rent.[53] The barony also showed its concern for tithes by sending delegates to the Richmond council, an assembly of commons and their captains, summoned in February 1537 to deal with this matter.[54] In all probability, then, the campaign waged by the Kendal rebels in October to preserve custom related to tithes as well as tenant right, with the latter having the priority.

In the early 1530s the custom of Kendal was used in another context and given another meaning. By 1534 the barony of Kendal had been granted as a franchise to the king's illegitimate son, the Duke of Richmond, whose officials subsequently clashed with those of the Earl of Cumberland, the hereditary sheriff of the county of Westmorland.[55] The issue in contention was whether the powers of Cumberland's office extended to the barony or whether the latter was to be administered, in the manner appropriate to a franchise, by its own officials.[56] The parliamentary act that created the franchise for the Duke of Richmond had appeared to respect Cumberland's right to hold sheriff's tourns in the barony, but an order from the Crown, followed by two amendments of the original act, seemed to rule it out.[57] The case made for Richmond in 1534 by his own officials, Sir James Layburn and William Parr, stressed that freedom from the sheriff of Westmorland's interference was the ancient and laudable

53 *L.P.* XII{1}. 671 {2/ii} and {2/iii}.
54 SP1/117, f. 32 (*L.P.* XII{1}. 671).
55 22 Henry VIII c. 17 granted him Richmond Fee (i.e. in 1531); 23 Henry VIII, c. 28 granted him Lumley Fee (i.e. in 1532); and 26 Henry VIII c. 21 granted him Marquis Fee (i.e. in 1534). In this way he gained possession of the whole of the barony of Kendal.
56 SP1/69 (*L.P.* V. 966) – the date is 1531, not 1532; SP1/75 (*L.P.* VI. 306) – the date is 1532, not 1533; SP1/81 (*L.P.* VI. 1620) – the date is 1532, not 1533; SP1/69 (*L.P.* V. 951) – the date is 1534, not 1532; A. G. Dickens (ed.), *Clifford Letters of the Sixteenth Century*, Surtees Society, 172 (1962), p. 81.
57 For the exception, see *Statutes of the Realm*, III, p. 341 which lays down that what is granted by the act should be not prejudicial to the Earl of Cumberland "of, for or in the offices of sheriffwick of the county of Westmorland". For the statutory amendments and their effect, see 23 Henry VIII, c. 28 which laid down that the duke should hold his lands in Westmorland "without disturbance . . . of any sheriffs, escheators, bailiffs or other officers of his highness" (see *Statutes of the Realm*, III, p. 409); and 26 Henry VIII, c. 21 (iv) which enacted that he should enjoy the same rights as had been enjoyed by Edmund, Earl of Richmond (the king's grandfather) (see *Statutes of the Realm*, III, p. 526) and "without any manner of account . . . to be yielden (to the Crown)" (see ibid., p. 527). For the royal order, see Chatsworth Trustees, Clifford Letter Book, f. 12.

custom of Kendal.[58] In making their case, they argued that the preservation of the custom safeguarded the interest of the poor by protecting their tenant right and enabled them to fulfil the obligations attendant upon this tenurial privilege.[59] That tenant right was closely associated with the defence of the custom in 1534 was also made evident in a letter to Sir James Layburn from his servant of the same name who told him how Cumberland's officials had been prevented from holding a sheriff's tourn in the barony and, following their departure, the barony's officials had panelled the constables to conduct an inquest to consider the complaints of tenants against some of the barony's leading landlords.[60] But it remains clear that the custom as it was perceived and presented in 1534 was first and foremost a matter of autonomy.[61]

The question is: how did the custom and the issues associated with it differ between 1534 and 1536? By October 1536 Richmond had died without heirs; and so the franchise had reverted to the Crown, never again to be alienated. Moreover, the two accounts for the Clifford family that have survived for this period, one of 1533/4, the other for 1540/1, show Cumberland holding tourns in the barony; and it is also clear that he was holding another in 1536.[62] This raises two possibilities: one, that he ignored the royal order of 1531 and the acts of amendment; the other, that he was liberated from the statutory restraints imposed upon his shrievalty in the early 1530s when the franchise was resumed upon Richmond's death. In other words, Cumberland's intervention in the barony could have been a source of friction in both 1534 and 1536, although evident only in the former year. On the other hand, the villain of the piece in 1536, as exposed by the complaints made, was not Cumberland but Sir James Layburn. In

58 Layburn claimed that the action taken against the Duke of Richmond and his tenants was aimed "to undo . . . the good ancient laudable customs used time out of mind" in the barony. See SP1/83, f. 65b (*L.P.* VII. 432). Also see *L.P.* VI. 306 and 1620. His master, William Parr, informed Cromwell that "the ancient custom of the barony of Kendal time out of mind" had been for the stewards of the barony to settle disputes within it without "resort to London" [SP1/69, f. 263b (*L.P.* V. 951)]. That he was being critical of Cumberland is made evident in the same letter.

59 SP1/69, fos. 263b–264 (*L.P.* V. 951); SP1/81, f. 78 (*L.P.* VI. 1620).

60 SP1/69 (*L.P.* V. 966).

61 This is made clear in Parr's letter to Cromwell (*L.P.* V. 951). In 1532 the case for autonomy was made by Layburn (*L.P.* VI. 306 and 1620).

62 Cumbria Record Office (Kendal), WD/Hoth Box 48, estate account roll 32/33 Henry VIII; Chatsworth Trustees, Bolton Abbey MS, vol. 10, fos. 19b and 20b; B.L. Althorpe Papers, B. I, f. 53 (Letter from Sir John Lowther to Earl of Cumberland, 5th October, 1536).

1536 the custom was being protected not against the aggressor of 1534 but the man who in that year had been its defender. It seems that whereas the conflict over the custom in 1534 was principally waged between the officials of the two parties and the basic concern was the profits to be made from holding courts, serving writs, imposing fines, taking amercements and confiscating strays and felons' goods, in 1536 the conflict was essentially between payers and payee of dues and tithes. However, it is quite possible, given the short interval between them, that the earlier conflict with its emphasis upon safeguarding the custom, provided the language of protest for the later one and, picked up and adapted in 1536, was then used to resist the barony's own officials especially when they appeared to be as obnoxiously favourable to the landlords as Westmorland's hereditary sheriff had been.

What the episode of 1534 demonstrates is that tenant right did not suddenly surface as a problem in 1536 and that responsible for this problem was not simply Layburn's oppressive estate management. As it was presented in the early 1530s, the concern for preserving the barony's custom of autonomy derived not only from a struggle between the Earl of Cumberland and the Duke of Richmond for the profits of office but also from the need to protect the system of tenant right from certain landlords, namely Sir Roger Bellingham, Walter Strickland, Sir Richard Weston, Geoffrey Middleton and a Mr Redmayn (probably Richard), who, assisted by the county sheriff, had allegedly gained their way by violent seizures of property and by bringing private actions against the tenantry in the courts at Westminster which were unanswerable since the defendants could not afford the trip to London.[63]

Thus, although confederated and militarised by the men of Dent, the movement in Kendal possessed a life of its own. This stemmed not only from the force of its agrarian grievances but also from the leadership of William Collyns. According to his own account, he urged caution and inaction in the very early stages of the revolt;[64] and when a letter was sent to Kendal from the priory of Conishead on 16th October urging him and other townsmen to come to the assistance of the restored monks, he did not respond.[65] But once sworn on

63 For the gentlemen's names, see *L.P.* V. 966. For actions against property, see *L.P.* VII. 432. For actions at Westminster, see the allegation of William Parr [SP1/69, f. 264 (*L.P.* V. 951)].
64 *L.P.* XII{1}. 914.
65 *L.P.* Add. 1112 and *L.P.* XII{1}. 849 (29). His documented dealings with Conishead relate to December and happened after the Pardon. See SP1/118, f. 214 (*L.P.* XII{1}. 965{2}) and *L.P.* XII{1}. 878.

19th October, he became a changed man, regarding himself as sworn to the commons and therefore obliged "to be true to them".[66] John Ayrey of Patton, part of the estate of the dissolved Conishead Priory, deposed in April 1537 that Collyns was "the principal doer in all the insurrection from the beginning" in that he "did make writings and harboured and lodged the said Atkinson and them of Dent and Sedbergh with other of his retinue", presumably when they came to Kendal on the 24th October and stayed for two or three nights in order to help the Kendalers enlist the support of the gentlemen.[67] Not surprisingly, this is concealed in Collyns' own account.

Moreover, later, in December 1536 and February 1537, Collyns was responsible for a number of initiatives. One concerned Cartmel Priory and involved persuading its canons to stay put until the Dissolution issue had been reconsidered by parliament.[68] He was also responsible for circulating the bills that reached Kendal around 3rd February from Westmorland and Dent announcing a council to be held at Richmond to consider the ills of the commonwealth and ordering each parish to send two delegates.[69] He was again responsible for circulating on 12 February a letter written under the name of the Captain of Poverty summoning an assembly at Kendal for the following day to support the rebels of the barony of Westmorland in the struggle with the Cliffords.[70] Collyns was thought to be the author of this letter,[71] but, in all likelihood, his essential role was to have copies made and to ensure that it received proper publicity.[72] In commenting on the uprising and its leadership, Sussex and Derby described Collyns as "chief counsel . . . in Kendal" to Captain Atkinson; and this appeared to be his function: of seeing that the lead provided by the Dent men gained the backing of the Kendalers.[73]

Also maintaining the close alliance between the rebels in Dent and Kendal were the grievances that they shared. Binding them together in a common cause was the custom of tenant right and the fear that it was under threat from the landlords.[74] They also had in common the rule of William Parr, lord of Dent as well as steward of the barony of

---

66 *L.P.* XII{1}. 965.

67 SP1/118 (*L.P.* XII{1}. 959). For the connexion with Conishead, see *V.E.*, 5, p. 271.

68 *L.P.* XII{1}. 787; *L.P.* XII{1}. 965 {2}. Also see below, p. 267.

69 E.g. *L.P.* XII{1}. 849 {30}. Also see *L.P.* XII{1}. 965 and 671.

70 *L.P.* XII{1}. 671 and 878. For the letter itself, see *L.P.* XII{1}. 411.

71 *L.P.* XII{1}. 849 {27} and *L.P.* XII{1}. 411.

72 See *L.P.* XII{1}. 959.

73 SP1/116, f. 253b (*L.P.* XII{1}. 632).

74 See below, pp. 276–7.

Kendal, which was delegated in his absence (for he resided in Essex) to his kinsman, Sir James Layburn.[75] Moreover, it seems that at his examination Collyns was bent on concealing in his account of the events of October not only his leadership of the Kendal uprising but also some of its anti-government sentiments. Like the Dent men they bore strong grudges against the government. They came to light in early 1537 when two attacks were made on the clergy in Kendal church for failing to conduct the church service in the traditional manner; and in early 1538 when a minstrel from Cartmel was attacked in Windermere for refusing to sing an anti-Cromwellian ditty entitled "Crummock" which had been sung in Crosthwaite "in the time of the rebellion".[76]

In the hundred of Lonsdale

The Dent and Kendal uprising eventually involved the hundred of Lonsdale: that is, Lancashire Oversands and the part of Lancashire situated between Lancaster and the Westmorland border. In both areas the intrusion of the Atkinson host was a vital factor in raising revolt. The region north of Lancaster was simply recruited by the rebel army as it marched from Kendal to Lancaster on 28th October. In Lancashire Oversands signs of native resistance were evident in the restoration of the two dissolved priories, Conishead and Cartmel, but there appeared to be no organised revolt until the Dent and Kendal rebels sent into the region contingents of armed men to swear the populace and to recruit troops.

Since little evidence has survived for the two restorations, little of certainty can be said about them. What is clear, however, is that in both houses the canons returned shortly after their eviction; and what is probable is that, rather than put in by the commons, they simply reoccupied the premises, perhaps inspired to do so by the three monks from Sawley Abbey as they passed by on their way home from Furness Abbey; perhaps incited to do so by the reprieve granted in July to the other priory of the Morecambe Bay area, Cockersand.[77] In neither

---

75 See below, pp. 291.
76 For the incidents in Kendal church, see *L.P.* XII{1}. 914 and *L.P.* XII{1}. 384. For the Windermere incident, see *L.P.* XIII{1}. 1346 and 1370.
77 According to Robert Legate, the three monks "went home to Sawley Abbey and took possession against our grace's act of parliament" [SP1/118, f. 4b (*L.P.* XII{1}. 841 {3})]. If they had taken the short-cut across Cartmel sands their route would have taken them via Conishead and Cartmel. For Cockersand's reprieve, see C. Haigh, *The Last Days of the Lancashire Monasteries and the Pilgrimage of Grace*, Chetham Society, 3rd series 17 (1969) p. 44.

restoration is there is any evidence that the canons were put in by the mob.[78]

Dissolved on 15th September, Conishead Priory had been restored by 16th October when it appealed to the townsmen of Kendal to help in its defence,[79] perhaps approaching them because close to the town was the hospital of St Leonard, a foundation of the priory and beyond it, in the barony of Westmorland, was the extensive parish of Orton, an advowson appropriated to Conishead whose prior was its vicar, with one of its canons serving as curate.[80] With dissolution and restoration happening in such a short period of time, it is likely that the five canons who wished to remain at the priory, having been ejected from the regular clergy and left, apart from the prior and the quondam, pensionless,[81] simply took the practical step, with winter coming on, of re-entering (or perhaps of remaining in) their house once the commissioners and Lord Monteagle, the lessee, had moved out of the area and before the latter had been able to start the work of demolition.[82] Three were especially committed to the restoration, having informed the commissioners that their preference to remain as regulars depended upon the survival of the house, while the prior in August had made two attempts to redeem Conishead, undoubtedly moved by the success of Cockersand in purchasing its own reprieve.[83]

But were the canons restored by the commons? No such claim was ever made at the time. And perhaps the commons had little cause to defend a convent, five of whose seven religious residents had been charged with having sexual relations with women, two of whom the visitors had found to be grossly incontinent, and whose prior had, within the previous three years fallen under suspicion of complicity to murder.[84] After all, since much of its estate was leased to Monteagle before the suppression, just as it was afterwards, a continuity in its

78 As is suggested by Haigh, see ibid., p. 53.
79 For date of dissolution, see P.R.O. DL41/11/49, f. 3b. For the letter, see *L.P.* Add. 1112. This document is now virtually unreadable, even under ultra-violet light. Fortunately a contemporary summary of it has survived (*L.P.* XII{1}. 849 {29}).
80 *V.C.H. Lancashire*, II, p. 142. When an attempt was made to suppress Conishead in 1525, the Duke of Suffolk had come to its rescue declaring it to be "of great succour to the king's subjects" (ibid.). For Orton's connexion with Conishead, see below n. 172.
81 See C. Haigh, *Reformation and Resistance in Tudor Lancashire* (Cambridge, 1975), pp. 127–8; and Haigh, *Last Days*, p. 48.
82 He visited on 19th September [see SP1/120, f. 257(*L.P.* XII{1}. 1321)]. On 15th September he agreed to pay £100 for the fittings (see P.R.O. DL41/11/49, f. 3b).
83 Haigh, *Last Days*, p. 36; DL41/11/59, items 8 and 9.
84 Haigh, *Last Days*, p. 22.

management was assured, and its dissolution imposed no stranger upon the region.[85] Moreover, apart from maintaining a warning bell and guides for people crossing Morecambe Bay, apart from providing £9 p.a. in alms to seven poor men and waged employment for thirty-nine servants, and apart from possessing the girdle of St Mary which was reckoned good for pregnant women (and a saving grace given the high incidence of canonical incontinence), the priory appeared to do little for the community.[86] The priory church was not a parish church and so the dissolution did not threaten the area with a loss of religious service; and the hostelry at Conishead was leased out rather than directly operated by the priory's servants.[87] As the Dissolution commissioners had made provision for maintaining the warning bell and the guides across the sands, the attitude of the commonalty towards the priory's suppression hinged on its appreciation of the alms and wages dispensed by the house and its regard for the efficacy of the girdle.[88] Instructively, when the prior put the argument for redemption, he could only recommend its work in finding a "carter" to lead the people across the treacherous sandbanks and washes, a task which could be performed just as readily in the priory's absence.[89]

What is clear is that the restoration of Conishead occurred before the commons of the region had risen; and the letter which the canons dispatched to Kendal on 16th October, calling for assistance and requiring Collyns and others to issue a proclamation exhorting men to come to the priory's aid and "the preservation of its goods", suggested not only that the canons felt in danger but also that they had received little local support.[90] The government later regarded the letter as "a great cause" of the rebellion in Kendal.[91] But this revolt received its impetus and direction from movements to the east rather than to the west of the barony.[92] Furthermore, the letter's request that help should be sent that night or the following day went ignored. Not until the very end of October was any response forthcoming; and this only happened when Captain Gilpin and a company of commons

85 P.R.O. DL29/143/2273. Monteagle also bought the goods of the priory (see DL41/11/ 49 f. 3b).
86 V.C.H. Lancashire, II, p. 142; Haigh, Last Days, p. 48; L.P. X. 364, p. 140. For the warning bell, see DL41/12/11 f. 3.
87 DL29/143/2273.
88 For provision of a warning bell and guider, see DL41/12/11 f. 3.
89 DL41/11/59, item 9.
90 L.P. Add. 1112.
91 SP1/118, f. 24 (L.P. XII{1}. 849 {29}).
92 See above, pp. 250–4.

drawn from the Atkinson host arrived in the Furness peninsula to swear its inhabitants and recruit its manred.[93]

Even less is known about the restoration of Cartmel Priory. According to the Earl of Derby, "the commons of Cartmel . . . put the prior in to the late priory of Cartmel . . . against his will". Then the prior "stole away" to join the earl at Preston, doing so after the truce of 27th October but before the news of it had reached him.[94] He presumably took flight, as did the Abbot of Furness, upon hearing of the approach of Gilpin and his company and did so partly because his heart was not in the restoration – after all he had asked earlier to be relieved of his monastic vows – and partly because, like the Abbot of Furness, he wished to avoid taking the rebels' oath.[95] Derby's information helps to date the restoration as having occurred some time before 27th October. It also suggests the involvement of the commons of Cartmel in the priory's act of resistance. But his account does not present the actual restoration of the priory as the work of the commons. It only states how they had brought pressure upon an unwilling Richard Preston, the prior, to join his former brethren. Again, it is possible that the canons, having received similar treatment to the canons of Conishead – suffering a very recent dissolution (9th September) which gave them no chance to remain as regulars, although all but the prior wished to do so, and which made no provision for a pension[96] – simply crept back (or alternatively never left) and were able to remain there unmolested because the Atkinson host prevented reprisals from being taken against them.

From the commons' point of view Cartmel Priory must have seemed a worthier cause to fight for than Conishead. The lessee, Thomas Holcroft, was a stranger to that area, a social upstart and a creature of Cromwell's.[97] Furthermore, the priory church acted as the parish church in which the community of Cartmel felt that it had a vested interest, not only because of the religious services the church provided but also because of the treasures it contained – part of the cross, a chalice, a suit of copes, other vestments, a mass-book – which it declared a wish to retain, partly because they were necessary to the

---

93 See below, p. 271.
94 Toller, p. 45. For dating, Derby was at Preston between 28th and 30th October. See ibid., pp. 42 and 43.
95 See below, p. 273. For his wish to leave the order, see Haigh, *Last Days*, p. 35.
96 Haigh, *Reformation and Resistance*, p. 128.
97 Bindoff, II, pp. 373–4.

church service and partly because they had been donated by the congregation.[98] What is more, certainly in comparison with Conishead, the canons of Cartmel were relatively pure. Only two out of ten had been charged with sexual lapse.[99] On the other hand, the commissioners, upon instruction from the chancellor of the duchy of Lancaster, had made several concessions to the parishioners of Cartmel, ordering that, since the church was a parish as well as a priory church, it should be allowed to "stand unplucked". The commissioners also allowed the suit of copes that had been donated to the church by a parishioner to remain with it.[100] However, not all the wishes of the parish had been respected. No reassurance was given concerning the chalice, the mass-book and the vestments. As for the relic of the holy cross, it and its tabernacle were taken and sold.[101] The community, then, kept its church but probably was left with a grievance over the confiscation of its treasures. This may have caused it to be receptive to the Dent and Kendal uprising but, as with the community around Conishead, it did not persuade it to confederate. Prior to the arrival of Gilpin, there is no suggestion of oath-swearing or assemblies or attempts to form a host.

The bulk of the surviving evidence, in fact, related not to the restoration of the two priories but to the struggle of the canons to remain in possession. It belonged not to the month of October but to the period following the second appointment at Doncaster, December 1536 to February 1537. What light does this later evidence throw on how the two restorations were accomplished? A key supporter of the canons at this later time was William Collyns, leader of the Kendal revolt. Their main adversaries were the lessees, Lord Monteagle for Conishead and Sir Thomas Holcroft for Cartmel.[102] The rebel aim was to preserve the canons in occupation until parliament had judged the matter. The issue in dispute was how, in the mean time, the resources of each priory were to be allocated between lessee and brethren. In December the lessees were annoyed when the brethren took what they felt to be their corn.[103] And in early February the struggle between the two parties created a commotion in Cartmel when

98 Made evident in a list of queries produced by the Lancashire commissioners (see DL41/12/11, items 11,12 and 21).
99 Haigh, *Last Days*, pp. 21–2.
100 See the answers to queries 11 and 12 (DL41/12/11).
101 DL41/11/49, fos. 4b–5.
102 Haigh, *Last Days*, pp. 48–9.
103 *L.P.* XII{1}. 914.

the canons, supported by a small number of peasants, took some sort of riotous action.[104]

As for Collyns, he did his best to maintain the occupation of the priory. At Pontefract he approached John Dakyn, vicar-general of the archdeaconry of Richmond, of which Lancashire Oversands was a part. Since Dakyn had been chief visitor of the two priories, Collyns asked him to send them a letter of advice.[105] This Dakyn was unwilling to do, but he was prepared to write to the Prior of Cartmel who, after his flight in late October, had still to return to the priory, advising him to rejoin his canons and comforting him with the misinformation that "all religious persons in the north parts had entered their houses by putting in of the commons".[106] Picking up the letter in York, Collyns had it delivered.[107] Then, returning to Kendal he intervened a second time in the priories' favour. It happened when a royal herald was in town proclaiming the December pardon. After being pressured by the lessees of Cartmel and Conishead, the herald ordered, ambiguously, that the possession of tithes, lands and leases should remain, for the moment, as it was at the time of the second Doncaster appointment.[108] But what did this mean? For the lessees, it meant that the right of possession lay with them; for the occupying canons, it meant that the right was theirs. Collyns sought to settle the matter, in such a way that it complied with Robert Aske's order for religious houses, allowing the lessees, as a temporary arrangement, the right of administration and receipt and the religious the right to receive sufficient provisions for their needs.

He acted in response to a request from two of the Cartmel canons for the order to be put in writing, a task which the herald deputed to him. And so he composed a letter which, according to his own account, simply added to the herald's order the phrase "except ye will of your charity help the brethren there somewhat towards their board". According to his account this letter was addressed and sent to "the neighbours" of the two priories.[109] In reality, his letter was not so mild or innocuous as he later alleged; and for this reason he retrieved the one sent to Cartmel after the commotions of early February for which the letter could be held to blame; and in his confession he said nothing

104 Ibid.; Haigh, *Last Days*, pp. 78–9. As a result the nine canons and sixteen peasants were tried for treason. The manred of the lordship amounted to 300. See Haigh, *Last Days*, p. 58. According to Collyns, there was also a commotion in Conishead at this time but the government took no action against it.
105 *L.P.* XII{1}. 914.
106 P.R.O. E36/118, fos. 173–173b (*L.P.* XII{1}. 787).
107 *L.P.* XII{1}. 787; *L.P.* XII{1}. 965 {2}.
108 *L.P.* XII{1}. 914.
109 Ibid. For Aske's order, see Toller p. 51.

of the letter to Conishead.[110] In all likelihood, as was later testified by others, the content of the letter was to the effect "that the canons might enter their house again and to be found of the king's cost at the farmers' hands or else to take afore record as much as would serve them", a proposal which tallied with rebel policy, as specifically set out in Aske's order for religious houses.[111]

All this clearly reveals lay sympathy and support for the regular clergy. But, connected as it is with the later stages of revolt, its actual concern is not the issue of restoring the canons but of allowing them to stay put and to hold out. By now the restored religious houses were a pawn in the power struggle between the Crown and the pilgrims. It was of vital strategic importance to the rebels that the religious remained in occupation until the matter had been determined by the York parliament because, arguably, if the restored religious abandoned their houses beforehand, the rebels' bargaining position would be seriously weakened. Hence the rebels determination that "the abbeys should stand until the next parliament".[112] The evidence of December 1536 and February 1537 therefore offers inadequate proof of what the commons actually did to restore the two houses in October and how they felt at the time about their suppression. On the other hand, for the region the general issue of Dissolution was undoubtedly a matter of concern and a cause for revolt. This is firmly declared in the two surviving manifestos produced by the Dent and Kendal revolt: the one associated with Lancashire Oversands failing to mention priories but specifying as the rebels' aim "the re-formation of such abbeys and monasteries now dissolved and suppressed without any just cause".[113] Within the purview of the uprising were five dissolved houses – Coverham, Sawley, Easby, Conishead, Cartmel – all of them restored in October. Without a doubt the rebels' concern was intensified by restoration and the need to prevent it from being undone.

The mobilisation of Lancashire Oversands, however, was also due to two other factors: firstly, discontent against the government among the monks of Furness Abbey and secondly, and more importantly, the efforts made by the Atkinson host to raise the region. The two factors interacted as the Dent and Kendal rebels sought to operate through the authority exercised by Furness Abbey and, in so doing, received positive support from the monks. But until the instruction to rebel

110 For its retrieval, see SP1/118, f. 214 (*L.P.* XII{1}. 965). That a letter was written to Conishead as well, see ibid. and SP1/118, f. 93 (*L.P.* XII{1}. 878).
111 SP1/118, f. 214 (*L.P.* XII{1}. 965).
112 As made evident by Dakyn (*L.P.* XII{1}. 787).
113 Toller, pp. 48–9; ibid., pp. 49–50.

came from the Atkinson host nothing had happened in the region, apart from rumblings of seditious talk within Furness Abbey and the peacefully achieved restoration of the two priories. In this respect, actual revolt was imported by invading rebels rather than internally generated.

The grievance of the Furness Abbey monks did not spring specifically from the dissolution of neighbouring religious houses. There were four in all – Seton and Calder in Cumberland as well as Conishead and Cartmel – three of them restored.[114] None was mentioned in the monks' recorded talk. As it was articulated, their concern was the Crown's assumed headship of the Anglican church. This offended them partly because it had terminated the papal supremacy and partly because it had placed the Church under the rule of laymen. Especially incensed were Henry Salley, John Broughton and John Green. Loosened by ale, Henry Salley had railed on one occasion: "no secular knave should be head of church nor should have anything to do with them" (i.e. the monks), and on another: "it was never good world with us since that secular men and knaves had rule upon us and they made the king head of the church".[115] John Broughton elaborated on the same theme saying that "the bishop of Rome was unjustly put down".[116] John Green thought that abbots should not be made by the king's appointment but should be selected by the monks themselves.[117] The hostility aroused in them by the issue of the king's headship, and the wishful thinking that it generated, found expression in predictions. Broughton, aided by the monk John Harrington, explained the prophecy that the red rose should die in his mother's womb in terms of the king's assassination by clerics.[118] Broughton also predicted that within three years the bishop of Rome would be restored and "all the new laws that the king's grace had made" would be undone.[119] The same hostility caused the monks to question the king's right to any rule. Because "his father came in by the sword", the monks reasoned, Henry VIII had no right to inherit the crown.[120]

In addition, the monks of Furness were enraged at having had imposed upon them the friar and reformer, Robert Legate. Following

---

114 For Calder and Seton, see P.R.O. SC6/Henry VIII/7454. Seton was restored (see below, p. 334).
115 SP1/118, f. 5 (*L.P.* XII{1}. 841 {3}); SP1/118, f. 7 (*L.P.* XII{1}. 841 {3/ii}).
116 SP1/118, f. 4b (*L.P.* XII{1}. 841 {3}).
117 *L.P.* XII{1}. 841 {3}.
118 SP1/118, f. 4b (*L.P.* XII{1}. 841 {3}); SP1/118, f. 7 (*L.P.* XII{1}. 841 {3/ii}).
119 SP1/118, f. 4b (*L.P.* XII{1}. 841 {3}).
120 SP1/118, f. 7b (*L.P.* XII{1}. 841 {3/ii}).

the visitation, he was appointed to read and interpret the Scriptures to the monks. As an outsider, heretic and government sympathiser, his presence caused extreme friction within the abbey, and led to his revealing all, probably more than all, when he was eventually examined by government officials.[121] As a supporter of the government's religious changes, Legate was not alone in the Liberty of Furness. There was also Sir William Rede, priest and schoolmaster, and the monk Roger Waller, vicar of Dalton.[122] Creating tension in the area over the previous twelve months had been clashes between the devotees of the old religion and this reformist group. In this respect, the religious conflict within the region was generated not simply by a government campaign to impose new ways in religion but also by an internal struggle between supporters of the old and new religions.[123] This struggle, moreover, centred not upon Dissolution but the basic issues of the remission of sin and the headship of the church.

These discontents did not in themselves cause a revolt since Furness was drawn into rebellion by outside intervention. Vital to the Furness uprising, such as it was, were two initiatives taken by the Atkinson host. Having organised itself on 24th October as an army drawn from the barony of Kendal and the West Riding wapentake of Ewcross, it sought to enlist the Liberty of Furness as part of a campaign to raise north Lancashire. This is evident in a surviving proclamation addressed to the bailiffs and constables of the manor of Furness Fells.[124] Essentially it ordered a muster at Hawkshead on 28th October. Its opening presented the picture of an active alliance between the commons and the convent of Furness – "and whereas our brother poverty [i.e. the leader of the commons] and our brother Rogers [i.e. Roger Pyle, Abbot of Furness and lord of the manor of Furness Fells] goeth forward" – and then stated that "the said brotherhood [i.e. brother poverty and the abbot] . . . hath sent to us [i.e. the risen commons] for aid and help". To entice support it not only suggested that the abbey had joined the revolt but also listed the grievances – the decayed faith, the dissolved monasteries, the threat to tenant right, the imposition of new taxes – and warned that non-attendance of the

---

121 Haigh, *Last Days*, pp. 28 and 96. For Legate's evidence, see *L.P.* XII{1}. 841 {3} and *L.P.* XII{1}. 842.

122 See *L.P.* XII{1}. 841 {2}; SP1/118, fos. 9–10b (*L.P.* XII{1}. 842) and Haigh, *Last Days*, p. 52.

123 It was recorded in a letter from Legate to the king (see *L.P.* XII{1}. 842).

124 Toller, pp. 49–50. Haigh suggests that the proclamation came from the rebels engaged in defending Sawley Abbey against the Earl of Derby, but there is no supporting evidence. See *Last Days*, pp. 65–6.

muster would be punished with loss of life, the destruction of property and damnation. Its use of the poverty idiom, and the secular grievances it specified, suggest that the proclamation came from the Dent and Kendal uprising; and its threat of hell-fire for noncompliancy, "the pain of deadly sin", for which they "will make answer before the high judge at the dreadful day of doom", suggests a clerical author, in all likelihood Christopher Howden, the vicar of Clapham. As one of Captain Atkinson's chief advisers, he was called "steward of the commons"; earlier he had promised that those who died for the cause would go to heaven and had been associated with the missing Lord Poverty proclamation issued at Endmoor on 23rd October.[125]

As well as ordering musters in Furness, the Atkinson host sent into the Liberty companies of commons to inspire and enforce support. One of these companies was led by a certain Gilpin who was later described as a petty captain to John Atkinson, the main leader of the Dent and Kendal uprising.[126] Like Atkinson he appeared to come from the West Riding hundred of Ewcross rather than the barony of Kendal and was part and parcel of the Dent uprising.[127] His role as a leading agitator was declared by Collyns who alleged that, after the pardon, Atkinson and Gilpin made several attempts to raise the town of Kendal.[128] In late October he was described as a "captain of the commons" who arrived at Furness Abbey "with his company".[129] His evident purpose was to swear the monks and their tenantry to be true to the commons' cause and to raise an armed following by holding musters to which each peasant was ordered to attend "horsed and harnessed and in his best array".[130] He failed to reach the abbey until the very end of October, perhaps because he had been dis-

125 *L.P.* XII{1}. 632 and 914. The vicar read the proclamation out.
126 SP1/118, f. 142 (*L.P.* XII{1}. 914 {2}).
127 At least eight, and possibly nine, came from the parish of Sedbergh: two Willans, two Cowpers, Middleton, Hebblethwaite, Robinson, Garnet and perhaps Atkinson. One came from Middleton close by: Buskell. One, and possibly two, came from South Ewcross: Howden and perhaps Atkinson. Three came from the barony of Kendal: Rawlinson, Collyns and Sadler. Gilpin's home is unknown. The name in the sixteenth century was associated with Kentmere in Kendal, this family becoming armigerous (Nicolson and Burn, op. cit., I, pp. 136–7). By 1540 a William Gilpin was listed as an esquire (*L.P.* XIV{1}. 653) and, as a gentleman of Westmorland, was required to provide six horses in 1543 for border service (Nicolson and Burn, I, p. l). But Collyns' apparent ignorance of Gilpin's christian name coupled with Gilpin's association with Atkinson [SP1/118, f. 142 (*L.P.* XII{1}. 914{2})] rather suggest that he derived not from around Kendal but from the wapentake of Ewcross.
128 SP1/118, f. 142 (*L.P.* XII{1}. 914 {2}).
129 *L.P.* XII{1}. 652.
130 SP1/117, f. 7 (*L.P.* XII{1}. 652).

patched to raise support only after the return of the Atkinson host from Lancaster or, more probably, because he had been busy earlier recruiting support in the lordship of Cartmel, or enforcing the proclamation in Furness Fells.[131]

The task of raising Furness was made easier by the positive co-operation of the monks. Upon his arrival in the peninsula on 31st October, Gilpin was met by four monks from Furness Abbey at Swartmoor, a mile outside Ulverston and two miles from Conishead Priory.[132] Rather than acting upon their own initiative, they were a welcoming party sent with the consent of their brethren.[133] From Swartmoor they accompanied the rebels to Dalton and on to Furness Abbey.[134] Not only did they oblige the rebels by taking the oath but they also donated two sums of money: £23 at Swartmoor "to save the house" and a further £20 at the abbey "to maintain the rebellion".[135] Either at Swartmoor or Dalton the four offered encouragement to the visiting rebels, exhorting Gilpin and his company of commons: "Now must they stick to it or else never, for if they sit down both you [the commons] and holy church is undone". They also told them that "if they lack company [i.e. if the rebels did not possess sufficient support] we will go with them to defend their most godly pilgrimage".[136] In addition, the monks sought to bind their tenantry to the rebel cause. In Dalton, on their journey with Gilpin from Swartmoor to Furness Abbey, the four monks were consulted by abbey tenants on what to do and responded unequivocally: "agree with them [i.e., take the oath] as we have done".[137] The monks also helped in the raising of troops. They had considerable forces at their disposal, thanks to the system of tenant right and the obligations of military service that it placed upon the region's peasantry.[138] Putting it at the rebels' disposal was a magnificent gift. Thus, following Gilpin's arrival, the prior, Brian Garner, and John Green sent servants to their tenantry in Dalton, Walney and Stank ordering them to come to the abbey on the morrow

---

131 He arrived on All Hallows Eve (31st October) (see *L.P.* XII{1}. 841 {3}). The vicar of Dalton suggested it was either the 30th or 31st October (ibid., 841 {2}), but the latter date fits better into the chronology supplied by the surviving evidence.

132 SP1/117, f. 7 (*L.P.* XII{1}. 652) and Haigh, *Last Days*, p. 95.

133 For the consent of the brethren, see SP1/118, f. 4b (*L.P.* XII{1}. 841 {3}).

134 *L.P.* XII{1}. 841 {2}; *L.P.* XII{1}. 652.

135 SP1/117, f. 7 (*L.P.* XII{1}. 652); SP1/118, f. 4b (*L.P.* XII{1}. 841{3}).

136 SP1/118, f. 4b (*L.P.* XII{1}. 841 {3}).

137 SP1/118, f. 2 (*L.P.* XII{1}. 841 {2}).

138 The lordship of Lower Furness alone was obliged by tenant right to provide sixty horsed and harnessed men. See T. A. Beck, *Annales Furnesienses* (London, 1844), pp. 304 and 308.

(i.e. 1st November) "horsed and harnessed" or else to die and to have their houses pulled down.[139] Not all, however, responded, perhaps because the authority of the abbey had been eroded by the improving policies it has adopted in the management of its estates.[140] What happened to the force that was assembled on 1st November is unknown. In all likelihood, it was quickly disbanded as the news of the Truce, agreed as long ago as 27th October, reached this isolated world. The only outcome of Gilpin's missionary effort was to ensure that Lancashire Oversands was sworn to the commons' cause and, if needed in the future, would be ready to join the Atkinson host.[141]

Among the monks of Furness Abbey was a party of enthusiastic supporters for a rising of the commons.[142] This group was able to take charge, under the direction of the prior, Brian Garner, when, upon hearing of the approaching Gilpin, the abbot fled by sea to the Earl of Derby's manor of Lathom. With him went the acting steward of the monastery, William Fitton, leaving the monastery and its resources completely in control of the pro-rebellion faction.[143] Ironically, the abbot's flight coincided with the proclamation sent to Furness Fells by the Atkinson host, which had declared the abbot to be a promoter of the commons' cause.[144] His flight, however, did not mean that he was totally against the pilgrimage of grace. He fled not to organise counter-action but to avoid swearing the commons' oath.[145] Just before leaving, he suggestively ordered the monks to "stick altogether and serve God truly" and to "do their best that they can do to the commons" whilst he would "do the best he can doeth with the king".[146] His basic concern was to avoid commitment to either side and in this way, hopefully to save the abbey from reprisal. He explained this policy to the monks in a letter written from Lathom sometime in November.

139 SP1/118, f. 2 (L.P. XII{1}. 841 {2}); SP1/113, f. 7 (L.P. XII{1}. 652). These three communities were normally obliged at this time to find the following numbers of horsed and harnessed men: Dalton (6), Walney (9) and Stank (4). See Beck, op. cit., pp. 304–5.

140 L.P. XII{1}. 652; S. M. Harrison, The Pilgrimage of Grace in the Lake Counties, 1536–7 (London, 1981), pp. 19–20.

141 That the lordships of Cartmel and Furness had been sworn and made ready for further military action was suggested by a letter from the Earl of Derby, written in late November to the gentlemen of Furness, in which he informed them that the commons of the barony of Kendal were planning to mobilise the inhabitants of the two lordships who were sworn to them. See Toller, pp. 61–2 (L.P. XI. 1092).

142 Haigh, Last Days, p. 95.

143 Toller, pp. 45–6.

144 See above, p. 270.

145 For his own account, see SP1/118, f. 7 (L.P. XII{1}. 841 {3/ii}).

146 Ibid.; SP1/118, f. 23b (L.P. XII{1}. 849 {24}).

It told them "to be of good cheer for he had taken such a way that he was sure enough both from the king and also from the commons".[147] This was not enough for the monks. Upon his return to the convent in late November he found them deeply committed to the rebel cause, so much so that "all the convent came to me and would have had me to set my hand, and promised them to observe and keep certain articles by them made"; and it is probable that, deeply hostile towards him for not complying with the commons, the monks were planning to replace him with an abbot of their own choosing.[148]

Rebellion, then, eventually developed in Lancashire Oversands, but so belatedly that it was terminated by news of the Truce almost before it had started. Moreover, because the recruitment of the region took place latterly, between 28th October and 1st November, there is little chance that the rebel army which marched to Lancaster on 28th October included troops drawn from it.[149] On the other hand, there is no reason to believe that the Atkinson host was simply recruited from the West Riding wapentake of Ewcross and Westmorland. Without a doubt, in marching towards Lancaster, it was joined by Lancastrians. They were permitted to enlist by the decision of the leading lords of the region, Lord Monteagle of Hornby Castle and Marmaduke Tunstall of Thurland, to join the Earl of Derby at Preston, pressed, as they were, to do so by the proximity of the rebel host and the threats it made against the lives and property of those who refused to be sworn.[150] As the host stopped at Kellet Moor and when it reached Lancaster, the inhabitants of this part of the hundred of Lonsdale joined the cause.[151] Many undoubtedly acted because they were part of the barony of Kendal which, although mostly situated in Westmorland, overlapped into Lancashire and Yorkshire, and therefore could

---

147 SP1/117, f. 7 (L.P. XII{1}. 652).

148 SP/118, f. 7b (L.P. XII{1}. 841 {3/ii}). On 17th November John Green had remarked that their abbot should be chosen by the monks rather than appointed by the king (L.P. XII{1}. 841 {3}).

149 It is just possible that men from Cartmel crossed the sands and joined the march to Lancaster of 28th October. But, if Cartmel was like Furness raised by Gilpin, this is highly unlikely since it could not have happened before 29th October in view of the fact that he did not reach Furness before 30th October. Moreover, given the distance and the terrain, it is improbable that the Hawkshead muster of 28th October furnished any troops for the march on Lancaster either. Gilpin's mission might have been to raise further troops for the assembly at Bentham Moor, planned for 31st October (see L.P. XII{1}. 914)

150 According to Derby men came from north Lancashire to join him at Preston "for fear of being taken with force by the said rebels" (Toller, pp. 46–7). For instances of impressment, see Toller, p. 44 and L.P. XI. 1232.

151 L.P. XII{1}. 914.

readily find a common cause with the Westmorlanders, especially on the issue of preserving the custom of Kendal.[152]

Evidence of the venture's success in ensuring that Lancashire north of Lancaster was bound to the cause lies in the complaints, made by the Earl of Derby in November and December, that the inhabitants of this region were sworn to the commons and not to be trusted.[153] However, this was but an impression formed at a distance. Writing from Hornby Castle in early December, Lord Monteagle painted a rosier picture, admitting that "divers of my servants and tenants . . . be sworn to the said rebellion" but claiming that they were ready to serve the king nonetheless, and indicating that there were others, friends, servants and tenants, who had remained unsworn and were his trustworthy supporters.[154] But these men were, in all likelihood, those who had served in the retinue of 616 troops which had accompanied him to Preston. Another sixty-one had gone with Tunstall.[155] Limiting the impact of Atkinson's host upon the region were the large numbers who escaped it by serving in the army raised by the Earl of Derby to crush the restored Sawley Abbey. Otherwise, it seems as if the Atkinson host had effectively recruited north Lancashire.

Causes of revolt

Distinguishing the uprising as a whole was the dynamic role of the men from Ewcross, especially those drawn from its northern lordship of Dent. Although on a smaller scale, their part in raising the north-west was as remarkable an achievement as the part played by the men of Richmondshire in raising the north-east. Three other distinctive features characterised the uprising: the predominance of the agrarian grievance; the frequent use of Captain Poverty to declare and authorise policy; and the equation of a rising of the commons with a popular rebellion. Whereas the claim made for the revolts so far studied to be risings of the commons appears contrived because the leadership was aristocratic or clerical, in this case (and the same applies to the

---

152 The fact that the barony was not confined to Westmorland is made evident in the act 22 Henry VIII, c. 17 (*Statutes of the Realm*, III, p. 339). The Lancashire manors of Warton, Scotforth and Whittington were all part of the barony, as was the West Riding manor of Thornton. See J. Nicolson and R. Burn, *History and Antiquities of the Counties of Westmorland and Cumberland* (London, 1777), I, p. 39.

153 SP1/112, f. 157b (*L.P.* XI. 1251); Toller, p. 46 (*L.P.* XI. 947 {2}; SP1/111 (*L.P.* XI. 1118).

154 SP1/112, f. 114 (*L.P.* XI. 1232).

155 SP1/112, f. 159 (*L.P.* XI. 1251 {2}).

uprisings in the barony of Westmorland and in Cumberland) it seems genuine.

The nature and importance of the agrarian grievance was declared in the oath to be true to God, the king and the ancient laudable customs; the procedure of obliging landlords to seal agreements on tenant right; the Hawkshead proclamation of October mobilising men "for the good and laudable customs of the country"; the stick-ye-together manifesto of early 1537 which, in advocating the preservation of tenant right, argued that it would ensure such harmony between lords and commons that the former could go undistractedly on pilgrimages for the defence of the faith.[156] The agrarian grievance was not confined to the barony of Kendal. In fact, all the component revolts of the Dent and Kendal uprising appeared to be moved by agrarian discontent; and this discontent had a common source. It sprang from the system of tenant right, which prevailed not only in Kendal and Dent but also in Lancashire Oversands, in Lancashire between Lancaster and Westmorland, and in much of Ewcross.[157] At issue was the defence of tenant right, as it was threatened by lords who needed to raise their landed incomes in accordance with price rises and as it appeared to be threatened by the prospect of massive land transfers, brought about by the Dissolution.

The extent of agrarian concern, and its association with the Dent and Kendal uprising, was made evident in the pilgrims' December petition to the king; in Cromwell's instructions to Sir Marmaduke Tunstall on the management of the lordship of Newby and to John Lamplugh on the management of the lordship of Furness; in the king's instructions to the earls of Sussex and Derby on how to restore order in north Lancashire; and in the region's response to the Richmond council of February 1537. Thus, the December petition mentioned not only Kendal (which also included manors in north Lancashire and the West Riding as well as in Westmorland) but also Dent, Sedbergh

---

156 For oath and sealing, see *L.P.* XII{1}. 914. For Hawkshead proclamation, see Toller, p. 49. For the stick-ye-together proclamation, see *L.P.* XII{1}. 163{2}.

157 For Kendal, see above, pp. 255–7. For north Lancashire, see for example, P.R.O. DL1/5/H2; DL1/8/T4 and P.R.O. DL5/10, fos. 202b–203. For Lancashire Oversands, see the custom of Furness (Beck, op. cit., pp. 303–4 and 307–8); and the custom of Cartmel [H. Fishwick (ed.), *Pleadings and Depositions in the Duchy Court of Lancashire*, Record Society for Lancashire and Cheshire (1896–9), II, 69–70 and 72–3]. For Ewcross, see the custom of Newby (DL41/13/5 and DL29/159/2505) and the custom of Dent [R. W. Hoyle, "An ancient and laudable custom: the definition and development of tenant right in north-western England in the sixteenth century", *Past and Present*, 116 (1987), p. 32].

and Furness, requiring that the lands in these areas "may be by tenant right".[158] Cromwell's instructions to Tunstall indicated that the Furness Abbey estate in Ewcross – an extensive congregation of properties centred on Newby and situated in Upper Ribblesdale, Dentdale and the valleys of the Lune tributaries, the Greta and the Wenning – had an agrarian problem.[159] To allay fears of what would happen now that the estate had passed completely into lay hands, he ordered that, as the king's tenants, they will be "as well, or better, used, than under the abbots"; that only accustomed dues would be exacted; that extraordinary gressums and other unlawful burdens should not be charged; and that, while mounted military service was still required, no man needed to provide what was beyond his means. In this way, the tenants "may have cause rather to rejoice that they be now tenants of the king than to lament".

The instructions Cromwell issued to John Lamplugh for the lordship of Furness made similar points and inferences, imparting the impression of an agrarian problem arising from the abuse of tenant right.[160] The government's instructions issued to Sussex and Derby were even more specific in diagnosing agrarian ills and in prescribing remedy.[161] They identified two matters which "have been thought a great occasion of the late rebellions": "commons taken into several" (i.e. commoning rights denied by enclosure) and the exaction of "excessive fines" (i.e. gressums). The commission which received these instructions was confined to those parts of Lancashire that had been involved in the 1536 rebellion. This meant that they related either to the far eastern hundred of Blackburn or to the far northern hundred of Lonsdale. The East Lancashire revolt was an appendage of the Percy Fee uprising whose grievances were without agrarian foundation. This leaves the north Lancashire revolt, an appendage of the Dent and Kendal uprising, as the focus of the government's agrarian concern. There in early October Sir James Layburn was "disdained much", presumably because, as a landlord, he was adopting towards his Lancashire estates, which were likewise part of the barony of Kendal and subject to its custom, the same improving management that he had adopted towards his estates in

158 L.P. XI. 1246 (art. 9).
159 SP1/118 (L.P. XII{1}. 881). The reference in the letter is to the lordship of Lonsdale. What was meant was the large collection of Furness Abbey properties in the deanery of Kirkby Lonsdale which centred upon the lordship of Newby. See below, n. 226.
160 SP1/118 (L.P. XII{1}. 881); L.P. XII{2}. 1216.
161 SP1/115, f. 157 (L.P. XII{1}. 302).

Westmorland.[162] In singling out these two grievances, excessive gressums and the loss of commoning through enclosure, the government was clearly responding to the pilgrims' December petition.[163] But at no point did the Dent and Kendal rebellion explicitly condemn enclosure. On the other hand, enclosure was a frequent complaint in the region; and it is likely that the laudable customs for which the rebels fought included commoning rights which, along with low rents and dues, were normally regarded as the perquisite of tenant right.

The concept of laudable custom in 1536 was not exclusively confined to tenant right but also included the belief that tithes should be paid in money, not in kind. This again was not spelled out by the rebels in 1536; but that tithes were a matter for concern was made evident in early 1537 when a council was convoked in the Grey Friars at Richmond to deal with "the commons' weal", and when, in its letter summoning parochial delegates to the meeting on 5th February, it appeared to place the tithe on the agenda.[164] The Richmond council was presented as another meeting with the Duke of Norfolk, presumably to deal with matters not treated at the previous meeting in December.[165] The barony of Kendal was responsive to the summons; and this was not surprising since its custom embraced tithes as well as tenant right, not only in its Westmorland parishes but also in its Lancashire parish of Warton where, upon receiving the letter, Edmund Laurence of Yeland addressed the parishioners at the choir door in the parish church: "Sirs, let us draw together. Here is a letter come for the wealth of the parish for that oath that I am sworn to [i.e. obliging him to maintain the ancient custom] I will to stick".[166] The grievance over tithes was stirred by the same preconditions that affected the issue of tenant right: inflation that made the receivers of tithes prefer to take them in kind rather than as a fixed rent, coupled

---

162 Layburn leased several manors from William Parr: Ashton, Carnforth and Scotforth. For his disdain, see SP1/107 (*L.P.* XI. 666).

163 *L.P.* XII{1}. 1246 (arts. 9 and 13).

164 For the Richmond council, see *L.P.* XII{1}. 671, 914, 959 and 965. The phrase "for the commons' weal" was allegedly used by William Collyns when he asked John Ayrey to go to Richmond and to find out from the commons there "what they would conclude upon for the commons' weal" [SP1/118 (*L.P.* XII{1}. 959)]. That tithes were on the agenda, see SP1/117, f. 32 (*L.P.* XII{1}. 671).

165 Ibid. and *L.P.* XII{1}. 671 {iii}.

166 For tithe custom of Kendal, see above. For its response to the Richmond council, see *L.P.* XII{1}. 959 and 671. For Dent's response, see *L.P.* XII{1}. 959 and 965. For Warton's response, see *L.P.* XII{1}. 671. The lordship of Furness had the same tithe custom as Kendal (Beck, op. cit., pp. 307–8); but there is no evidence of either a receipt of the summons or a response to one.

with anxieties, aroused by the Dissolution, that innovatory changes with dire consequences were afoot.

The rebels' insistence upon preserving custom, however, did not mean that they were totally averse to change. Within the region of the uprising several forms of tenant right were practised, some of them more advantageous than others. The rebels' temptation was to opt for the more beneficial system rather than to insist on maintaining what was already in operation. Thus, the December petition proposed a system that was more lenient to the tenant than the custom of Kendal, substituting a fixed fine for an arbitrary one.[167] The stick-ye-together manifesto of early 1537, which explicitly associated itself with Kendal by offering approval of the Kendalers' practice of obliging lords to warrant custumals drawn up by the tenantry, went even further and advocated a tenant right system that, in the manner found in Wensleydale and here and there in the wapentake of Ewcross (i.e. Garsdale and Ingleton), substituted for the fine no more than the payment of a God's penny.[168]

Although bound together by their reverence for tenant right, the component uprisings were far more than an agrarian movement. All of them were driven by a variety of complaints. Their compelling force, in fact, was an accumulation of grievances rather than the priority achieved by any one of them. As well as objecting to improving landlords, the rebels were aggrieved at the government, partly for repudiating the old religion and partly for threatening the commonwealth. Their hostility towards it is made evident in two muster proclamations, both of them issued before the end of October; in the recorded talk of disaffected monks in Furness Abbey, and in the troubles in Kendal church of December 1536 and January 1537.[169] The "religious" complaint against the government concerned the rejection of the pope as head of the anglican church; the removal of holy places – churches and minsters as well as monasteries – and the government's denial of the efficacy of the saints as a means of interceding with God. In this respect the

---

167 *L.P.* XI. 1246 (art. 9).

168 *L.P.* XII{1}. 163 {2}. For Garsdale and Ingleton, see Hoyle, op. cit., p. 32.

169 For the two proclamations, see Toller, pp. 48–50. That they were composed by the Dent and Kendal rebels is made evident in Derby's letter to the king of 1st November. See ibid., pp. 38–43. He described them as letters and devices "that hath been feigned by that assembly and others": that is the host which eventually marched on Lancaster (ibid., p. 42). Along with an account of the Dent and Kendal rebels' march, he sent the two proclamations to the king accompanied by his letter of 1st November. For the talk of the monks, see above, pp. 269–70. For the troubles in the church, see below, p. 281.

religious objection was not simply to the Dissolution Act, but also to the Act of Supremacy, the order for prayer and the Ten Articles. The "commonwealth" complaint against the government concerned the material effects of confiscating the wealth of religious houses and parish churches and the rumoured plans to impose new taxes that would oppress the poor. Since it was an objection on both spiritual and material grounds, the complaint against the Dissolution was especially important.

That the Dissolution was found offensive not simply because religious houses were appreciated as social institutions but also because they were regarded as an integral part of the revered religion, was firmly declared in two proclamations produced by this rebellion. The one, an order to muster at Hawkshead, presented the movement's aim as "for the reformation of such abbeys and monasteries now dissolved and suppressed without any just cause" and to aid your "faith and holy church" by taking "further direction concerning our faith so sore decayed".[170] The other, an order to be in readiness to fulfil the oath to be true to God, the king and the commonwealth, presented the rebel aim as "principally" "the defence . . . of the faith of our Saviour Christ Jesu" which, in spite of the king's title of defender of the faith, had been "abominably confounded" by "certain heretics" through, among other things, the "spoiling and suppression of holy places as abbeys, churches and minsters of the same".[171]

Especially worrying was the prospect that certain parish churches would be either spoiled or completely suppressed. This was generated by rumours sweeping the north in early October, rumours substantiated by the proceedings of the Dissolution commissioners against the buildings and possessions of the condemned religious houses. Fears for the churches led to several protests in the north west, notably against the rumoured dissolution of Manchester parish church, the church attached to Holland Priory, the church attached to Burscough Priory, the church attached to Cartmel Priory, and against the feared dissolution of parish churches appropriated to dissolved monasteries, notably Sedbergh with its chapels dependent at Garsdale and Dent, feared threatened by the dissolution of Coverham Abbey, and possibly the parish church of Orton, under threat as a possession of Conishead.[172]

170 Toller, p. 49.
171 Ibid., pp. 48–9.
172 For Manchester college, see L.P. XI. 635. For Holland, see DL41/12/11 (it. 10), f. 1b. For Burscough, see L.P. XI. 1118 and Toller, p. 128. For Cartmel, see above, pp. 265–6. For Conishead and Orton parish church, see V.E., 5, p. 271. For Coverham and Sedbergh, see Whitaker, op. cit., pp. 355 and 362 and V.E., 5, p. 259.

In several instances, the government backed down when faced by these protests. Generally it sought to scotch the rumours but it also made a number of concessions, notably at Cartmel, Holland and Burscough, where in each case the church was permitted to survive the suppression of the religious house to which it was attached on account of its parochial function. Arguably such concessions helped to safeguard against revolt, notably in south Lancashire. Elsewhere, fears that the Dissolution would affect not only the monasteries but also the churches was a potent source of disobedience, for example in the lordship of Dent and also in the lordship of Cartmel where the church was saved but its treasures were plundered.

In the eyes of the rebels, the government was confounding the faith of Christ in two other ways: first, by "vilipending and despising the laws and ordinances of our Mother Holy Church".[173] That this included the termination of papal rule in England was made evident in December and January when disturbances occurred in Kendal parish church after the congregation had demanded the old service, specifically the bidding of the beads in the ancient manner.[174] The issue in contention was whether the church service should include prayers for the pope and the cardinals. In this respect, and this is supported by the reported talk of the Furness Abbey monks, the rebels were against the exclusion of the pope and the transference of his ecclesiastical authority in England to a layman.[175] The second objection to the Henrician settlement centred upon "blaspheming the honour of our lord God" and "blaspheming our Lady and all other saints in Heaven", a reaction against the government's onslaught upon intercession as it was expressed in the Ten Articles and in the royal injunctions issued for abrogating holy days and for instructing the clergy on how to apply the Ten Articles.[176] At the core of this obviously heretical onslaught was a disbelief in the existence of purgatory and the traditional practice of invoking the saints to intercede with God in favour of the living and the dead. What the rebels objected to was the heretical view that God could not be swayed either by words or deeds; that the church was to no avail in determining the health, wealth and fate of its members; and that the veneration of saints was a pointless and vulgar exercise. The outcome, as conceived by the rebels, was that "our faith [is] so sore decayed" and that the

173 Toller, p. 48.
174 *L.P.* XII{1}. 7, 384, 671 {iii}, 914.
175 See above, p. 269.
176 See Toller, p. 48.

responsibility for it lay with the heretics who had taken charge of the king.[177]

Upholding the revolt as a religious movement intent on preserving the old intercessory ways was its self-conception as a pilgrimage. The idea was taken from Aske and the revolts of the East Riding, but it was dear to the leadership of the Dent and Kendal uprising: Atkinson used it to typify the revolt in his communications with the Earl of Derby on 28th October and in a letter to John Towneley of the following month.[178] Yet it was far from being a conventional pilgrimage. Not only did it lack a specific destination but, in the Aske manner, it was seen as "a pilgrimage to do for the commonwealth", a term with material and temporal implications.[179] The rebels' proclamations presented their quarrel in terms of "the utter undoing of the commonwealth" and condemned the actions and deeds that were "purposed against the commonwealth".[180] Spelt out, this referred not only to exploitative landlords who were destroying tenurial rights but also to an exploitative government which was imposing new taxes.

The taxes were listed in a set of articles appended to the Hawkshead muster proclamation which stated that they were "accepted and admitted" and likely to be imposed "if our said brethren be subdued".[181] The first article presented a baptism tax. It did so in such a way as to imply that unless a tribute was paid to the king "no infant shall receive the blessed sacrament", raising the horrendous prospect of the children of the very poor being condemned, by virtue of their parents' poverty, to spend eternity in limbo. It thus made a spiritual as well as a material point. The second article, as presented, was also highly provocative, proposing that men exempted from paying the subsidy because their goods and chattels were worth less than £20 would now be taxed on their consumption of wheaten bread, chicken, goose and pig. Failure to pay a tribute to the king would deprive them of the right to eat such basic foodstuffs. The third article proposed yet another emotive tribute, one that would fall upon every piece of plough land. For the Westmorlanders, these tax proposals raised the prospect of losing the fiscal exemption traditionally allowed them as inhabitants of a border shire. For the Yorkshire and Lancashire men

---

177 A point made in both of the October muster proclamations. See ibid., pp. 48–9. For the matter of intercession and saint-worship, see R. Whiting, *The Blind Devotion of the People* (Cambridge, 1989), passim.
178 Toller, p. 44; SP1/108 (*L.P.* XI. 804).
179 Toller, p. 44.
180 Ibid., pp. 48–9.
181 Ibid., pp. 49–50.

involved in this revolt it threatened a major increase in their tax burden and for the poor the loss of the exemption licensed by the high tax thresholds normally attached to the parliamentary subsidies. For the rebels the real grievance was not simply economic but also concerned the loss of rights. The defence of the commonwealth was equated with the grinding down of the poor; but, in reality, its defence was a means of upholding rights which ensured that the people remained either free of taxation, as in the border shires; or no more than lightly taxed, as with the poor; and that, thanks to the custom of tenant right, their properties remained leniently rented.

Whilst the religious and commonwealth grievances were presented in separate categories, they were linked by the rebels' belief that both were the work of the same malefactors: the heretics leading the onslaught upon Christ's church were also thought to have designs against the commonwealth. For this reason, the solution was simple enough. As one of the muster proclamations put it: "God save the king and send him good counsel".[182] In effect, this meant getting rid of Cromwell. For the various strands of revolt that furnished the Atkinson host, Cromwell was the enemy: the lay knave unjustly placed in charge of the Church, as the monks of Furness Abbey complained; the man responsible for demolishing holy places according to the men of Dent; the minister lampooned in the poem entitled "Crummock" that was composed and sung by a Cartmel minstrel in the Windermere area of the barony of Kendal in late 1536.[183]

Characterising the Dent and Kendal revolt was the Captain Poverty idiom.[184] This was employed in all its known declarations of grievance and intent. Thus, in October 1536 the proclamation summoning support from all aged sixteen and above was addressed from "Master Poverty, the conductor, protector and maintainer of the whole commonalty".[185] In the same month, following the conjunction of the Dent and Kendal rebels at Endmoor, a muster was announced "in the name of Lord Poverty", to be held at Kendal "to know the Lord Poverty's pleasure".[186] A few days later the proclamation ordering a muster at Hawkshead was issued, requiring assistance for "our

---

182 See Toller, pp. 48–9.
183 For Furness, see above, p. 269. For Dent, see above, pp. 249–50. For the lampoon, see SP1/134, f. 131 (*L.P.* XIII{1}. 1346); *L.P.* XIII{1}. 1370.
184 M. L. Bush, "Captain Poverty and the pilgrimage of grace" *Historical Research*, 156 (1992), pp. 17–29.
185 Toller, p. 48.
186 The text has not survived. For all that is known about it, see SP1/118, f. 140 (*L.P.* XII{1}. 914 {2}).

brother Poverty" who "goeth forward openly".[187] Then in early 1537
a further two letters were issued in the same idiom, the first addressed
from the Captain of Poverty and ordering a muster at Kendal on 13th
February to provide "help according to your oaths", especially for the
defeated Westmorlanders; and the second calling upon the commons
"to stick . . . together" ready armed to "claim old customs and tenant
right". Whilst making no mention of Poverty, it signed off with the
suggestive jingle:

> Maker of this letter, pray Jesu be his speed,
> He shall be your captain when that ye have need.[188]

The actual authorship of these letters is a matter for speculation.
Associated with their composition, or at least their copying out and
publication, were Atkinson, Collyns and Howden.[189] What is clear is
that Poverty was no particular rebel. Essentially, he was an embodiment of Christ and the Commons and derived from a literary tradition
centring upon Piers Plowman.[190] The implication of the idiom was
that the body politic was out of joint and that to put matters right the
society of orders needed to be temporarily upturned. The idiom as
used by the Atkinson host was derived from the Richmondshire
uprising, reaching the north-west by means of a letter dispatched to
Cumbria from Richmond.[191] The connexion is evident in the language
used. Thus the letter from Richmond began: "Wellbeloved brethren in
God, we greet you well".[192] Likewise, one of Atkinson's muster
proclamations of October was from master Poverty who "sendeth
you all greeting" and the other began: "Wellbeloved, we greet you
well" and then proceeded to address its recipients as "good brethren".

---

187 Toller, p. 49.
188 For the Kendal muster proclamation, see *L.P.* XII{1}. 411. For the stick-ye-
     together manifesto, see *L.P.* XII{1}. 163 {2}.
189 For Howden and his connexion with the Kendal muster proclamation of 23rd
     October, see *L.P.* XII{1}. 914 and for his possible authorship of the proclamation
     sent to Hawkshead, see above, p. 271. For Atkinson's involvement with the
     Kendal muster proclamation of 12th February 1537, see SP1/118, f. 143–143b
     (*L.P.* XII{1}. 914 {2}). Without a doubt he was also involved in the muster
     proclamation of 23rd October. See *L.P.* XII{1}. 914. For Collyns' involvement
     with the muster proclamation of 12th February and the attribution of its author-
     ship to him, see *L.P.* XII{1}. 849 {27}. This Collyns denies in his own account.
     See SP1/118, fos. 143–143b (*L.P.* XII{1}. 914 {2}).
190 Bush, "Captain Poverty", p. 17.
191 Ibid., pp. 17–18.
192 SP1/117, f. 50 (*L.P.* XII{1}. 687).

Furthermore, the muster proclamation of February 1537 addressed itself to the "wellbeloved brethren in God".[193]

The frequent use made of the idiom by the Dent and Kendal rebels meant a firm declaration of the uprising as a rising of the commons since, within the jargon of the revolt, "the commons" and "poverty" were interchangeable terms and "the estate of poverty" was equivalent to "the commonalty".[194] This is how the uprising was seen; this is how it presented itself; and this is how it was. Yet involved with it were a number of gentlemen.

The social framework of revolt

The actual leadership was listed on two occasions: in the very early stages of the revolt by William Collyns who identified it at the Endmoor muster on 23rd October as consisting of Christopher Howden, vicar of Clapham, James Cowper, John Middleton and John Hebblethwaite, all of Sedbergh, the Dent men, William Garnet and George Willan, plus James Buskell from Middleton. Collyns described them as "the most notable doers and stirrers of that business" and as the advisers to the captain, John Atkinson.[195] Later in 1537, the earls of Derby and Sussex also produced a list. Atkinson they named as "the principal captain of these parts". Then they identified his "chief counsel in Kendal" as Walter Rawlinson of Milnthorpe, William Collyns and Christopher Sadler of Kendal town, John Hebblethwaite, Richard Cowper and John Robinson of Sedbergh, Brian Willan of Dent and Christopher Howden, vicar of Clapham.[196] The differences between the two lists lie in the fact that Collyns was describing the uprising prior to the full engagement of the Kendal men and when it was still essentially the Dent revolt, whereas the Derby/Sussex list indicates how the barony's involvement in an uprising started in Dent was followed by the inclusion of Kendal men in the high command. The lists do not provide a complete tally of known activists, omitting, for example, Gilpin who was described as petty captain to Atkinson and who took the cause to the Liberty of Furness.[197] But apart from this omission, and the failure to take note of the rebel activities in Lancashire Oversands, they provide an adequate account.

193 Toller, p. 48; ibid., p. 49; *L.P.* XII{1}. 411.
194 Bush, op. cit., p. 27.
195 SP1/118, f. 140 (*L.P.* XII{1}. 914 {2}).
196 SP1/116, fos. 253–253b (*L.P.* XII{1}. 632).
197 *L.P.* XII{1}. 914.

Both Atkinson and Hebblethwaite were probably gentlemen, but neither was more than a minor one and Hebblethwaite was relatively poor, with goods and chattels valued at £6 for the 1547 subsidy.[198] As for Atkinson, his background is obscure. In all likelihood he came from the Yorkshire wapentake of Ewcross, from Sedbergh or Austwick.[199] Collyns assumed that he was a gentleman and he claimed to be related to the Towneleys of Burnley. More substantial and *bona fide* gentlemen became involved in the revolt – notably the knights Sir James Layburn and Sir Robert Bellingham, and the esquires William Lancaster, Richard Ducket and Walter Strickland – but none became captains of the commons and all were essentially passive participants. Recruited with some effort, they accompanied the march on Lancaster rather than leading it, and Bellingham used the excuse of a poorly leg to slip away at Kellet Moor and join the Earl of Derby at Preston.[200]

The uprising, then, was not organised through the society of orders. On the other hand, it was far from being the movement of the poor that is suggested by its employment of the Captain Poverty idiom and by the reference made in one of its proclamations to "the estate of poverty".[201] Whilst the gentlemen leaders were, relative to their order, poor and of low status, the leaders from the commonalty were wealthy and, within their communities, important personages. John Middleton of Sedbergh was assessed at £60 for his goods and chattels in 1547.[202] In the same tax assessment, James Cowper who

---

198 Derby and Sussex described Hebblethwaite as a gentleman [see SP/116, f. 253b (*L.P.* XII{1}. 632)]. For his subsidy assessment, see R. W. Hoyle (ed.), *Early Tudor Craven* [*Y.A.S.R.S.*, 145 (1985)], p. 102.

199 There is no certainty that Atkinson was a gentleman. Collyns suggested that he was when he recorded: "And there were of gentlemen most notable, Sir James Layburn, parson Layburn, William Lancaster, Richard Ducket, Walter Strickland and one Atkinson was their captain, and Sir Robert Bellingham went with them" [E36/119, f. 126b (*L.P.* XII {1}. 914)]. Another suggestion lies in his letter to the gentleman John Towneley of Burnley whom he described as his cousin. See *L.P.* XI. 804. He was clearly not known before the revolt in the barony of Kendal, being given no christian name. Collyns presents him as being made captain by the rebels of Dent and Sedbergh (see SP1/118, f. 140b). It is possible that he came from the town of Sedbergh where several Atkinsons lived. See Hoyle, op. cit., pp. 102–3. Another possibility is that, like the vicar of Clapham, he was drawn from further south in the Ewcross wapentake, for in 1522 a John Atkinson of Austwick was recorded in the loan book of that year. See Hoyle, op. cit., p. 45. The Dodds are wrong in associating him with Gisburn in Craven (Dodds, I, p. 213). The document in question relates to Guisborough in Cleveland as they reveal elsewhere in their book (see ibid., p. 73).

200 *L.P.* XII{1}. 914 and Toller, p. 45.

201 Toller, p. 49.

202 Hoyle, op. cit., p. 102.

lived two miles east of the town had his goods and chattels valued at £100.[203] John Robinson, also of Sedbergh, was it seems another wealthy man, his widow in 1547 paying more in tax than most of the townsmen.[204] Also prominent in the leadership were a number of important officeholders, especially bailiffs: Collyns, bailiff of Kendal, Willan, bailiff of Dent and Rawlinson, bailiff of Milnthorpe.[205] All three were undoubtedly well-off, Collyns especially so since, as a merchant, he had been engaged in recent years in importing wine from abroad to Liverpool and Foulney, a haven at the tip of the Furness peninsula.[206] In addition, several clerics had a dynamic role in the uprising: notably the four monks of Furness Abbey who greeted Gilpin and his company at Swartmoor, the three canons of Cartmel, executed for their activities between December 1536 and February 1537, the vicar of Clapham, Christopher Howden, and Nicholas Layburn, brother to Sir James Layburn, although, in all likelihood, the intention of his involvement was merely to safeguard Sir James from the commons' reprisals.[207] As for the lay leadership of the revolt, it was predominantly drawn from the sprawling parish of Sedbergh.[208]

Atkinson, Collins, Gilpin and Howden stand out as the major activists. Atkinson was undoubtedly the chief captain. Appointed by the rebels of Dent and Sedbergh as their leader, he led the host which brought pressure upon the Kendalers to appear at Endmoor on 23rd October, commanded the force that on 28th October marched into Lancashire and confronted, at a distance, the Earl of Derby.[209] He was also the activist who, during the Truce, with Aske's encouragement, sought to revive revolt both in the barony of Kendal and in Lancashire.[210] Gilpin was his petty captain, undoubtedly an important figure in the operation to raise Lancashire Oversands and Atkinson's accomplice in the attempt to revive revolt in the barony of Kendal in November and December.[211] Collyns was also described as a captain and was a leading activist in October 1536, as well as in January and

203 SP1/116, f. 253b (*L.P.* XII{1}. 632); Hoyle, op. cit., p. 103.
204 Ibid., pp. 102–3.
205 *L.P.* XII{1}. 632.
206 DL1/9/R2.
207 For monks of Furness, see above, pp. 272–3. The three canons of Cartmel were James Estrigge, John Riddley and Thomas Person. See Haigh, *Last Days*, p. 90, n. 8. Sussex and Derby in March 1537 described the three as "the principal leaders of all the mischievous" [SP1/116, f. 253 (*L.P.* XII{1}. 632)].
208 See above, n. 127.
209 SP1/118, f. 140b (*L.P.* XII{1}. 914 {2}); Toller, p. 44.
210 For his attempts to raise Kendal, see SP1/118, f. 142 (*L.P.* XII{1}. 914 {2}). For his attempts to raise Lancashire, see *L.P.* XI. 804; *L.P.* XI. 1060.
211 For Oversands, see above, p. 271. For Kendal, see SP1/118, f. 142 (*L.P.* XII{1}. 914 {2}).

February 1537.[212] Howden was the fourth member of the main command. Sussex and Derby in their report to the government claimed that he was styled by the rebels "steward of the commons" and they regarded him as one of the "chief counsel" to Atkinson.[213] This was confirmed by Collyns who vividly portrayed the vicar of Clapham as the man who swore the commons to the cause at the Endmoor meeting of 23rd October, who was "the counsellor in all that business", presumably to the high command, who read the proclamation at Endmoor that summoned everyone to Kendal on 24th October and who incited the commons to action by promising Heaven for those who perished in the struggle.[214]

The strong impression given by the surviving evidence is of a movement from below, with upward pressure applied at several levels. There was first the pressure brought by the commons upon the gentlemen to support their cause.[215] Then, if one can believe Collyns, there was the popular pressure brought upon the rebel leadership. He gave two instances. He mentioned "the light persons of the town" who, responding to the ambassadors from Dent on 18th October, proceeded to assemble and swear the other townsmen. Collyns named the ringleaders of this movement as Thomas Dockwray and Brian Jobson.[216] The second instance of popular pressure occurred on 31st December when, according to Collyns, "certain of the lewd persons of Kendal town that were most busy in the first insurrection" (Thomas Dockwray was mentioned again, but others surfaced for the first time such as William Harrison, the shoemaker, James Tailor, Oliver Ydell and Peter Warrener), objected to the failure of the parish priest to offer prayers for the pope and turned on Collyns when he sought to persuade them to respect the terms of the pardon with the words: "Come down, carl, thou art false to the commons". Corroborating this account was Sir James Layburn who described the disturbance as something "done by light persons against the minds of the ancient men of Kendal" and suggested that the "busiest in the commotion" were "the poorest of them".[217]

As well as a movement from below, the uprising was clearly a

---

212 *L.P.* XII{1}. 1089 and see above, pp. 260–1 and 266–8.
213 SP1/116, f. 253b (*L.P.* XII{1}. 632).
214 SP/118, f. 140 (*L.P.* XII{1}. 914 {2}).
215 See above, pp. 253 and 256–7.
216 SP1/118, f. 138b (*L.P.* XII{1}. 914 {2}).
217 SP1/118, fos. 142–142b; SP1/117 (*L.P.* XII{1}. 671 {iii}). Yet a further corroboration was provided by Edmund Parker who misnamed Collyns as Wilson (*L.P.* XII{1}. 7).

movement from outside, with invasions into adjacent regions and pressure brought by companies of armed men upon the inhabitants to support the cause. This was especially the case in Lancashire between Westmorland and Lancaster. It also happened in the barony of Kendal with the Dent host appearing on the scene and commanding allegiance. What the revolt clearly was not was an aristocratic conspiracy. The rebel cry was not "a Dacre, a Dacre" but "Commons".[218] The uprising, moreover, began in Dent, a region so lacking in resident gentlemen that when the pilgrims' York council in late November drew up the party of three hundred deputed to assemble for the December meeting with the Duke of Norfolk at Doncaster, it could only propose for Dent and Sedbergh "four of the tallest yeomen . . . well horsed and harnessed".[219] The council named a number of gentlemen to represent the barony of Kendal, drawn from those who had taken the oath; but, in recognition of the movement from below, it proposed that the barony should also be represented by "six of the most tallest and wisest men, well horsed and harnessed, of the commons to be chosen by election".[220]

Generally, the gentlemen's contribution to this revolt was to submit or flee, not to lead or manipulate. In this way they promoted revolt by allowing a movement of the commons to have a free rein. Arguably, the leading resident gentlemen of north Lancashire and the adjacent parts of the West Riding, Marmaduke Tunstall and Lord Monteagle, played a major part in its development first of all through failing to co-operate in its counteraction, probably because of the feud between them, and secondly, by leaving the region to join the Earl of Derby at Preston.[221] The surviving evidence gives two contradictory reasons for their move to Preston, presenting it either as a flight from the approaching rebels or as a response to the Earl of Derby's mobilisation of an army to suppress Sawley Abbey and to crush the uprising in Percy Fee.[222] In all likelihood, having received Derby's

218 Used by Atkinson and Gilpin in their attempt to raise Kendal after the Truce. See SP1/118, f. 142 (*L.P.* XII{1}. 914 {2}).
219 SP1/111, f. 244b (*L.P.* XI. 1155 {2}).
220 Ibid.
221 For the feud, see Haigh, *Last Days*, p. 50; J. B. Watson, "The Lancashire gentry and the public service, 1529–58", *Transactions of the Lancashire and Cheshire Antiquarian Society*, 73 (1963), pp. 29–30; *V.C.H. Lancashire*, II, p. 217.
222 Derby claimed that they came "from their houses . . . for fear of being taken with force by the said rebels and came to me to Preston" (Toller, p. 46). On 25th October Derby wrote to the Lancashire gentry asking them to meet him at Whalley on 31st October (Toller, pp. 35–6). That Tunstall and Monteagle were in the list of gentlemen summoned, see SP1/112, f. 159 (*L.P.* XI. 1251 {2}). In Monteagle's case it seems as if there was an earlier summons from Derby

summons to join his army, which was issued probably before news had reached him of the Dent uprising and before Kendal and North Lancashire were up in arms, the two men obeyed. Unlike the refugees from the Dent and Kendal uprising – Bellingham, Fitton, the Abbot of Furness and the Prior of Cartmel – Monteagle and Tunstall took with them large contingents of troops, suggesting that they went to Preston in response to Derby rather than simply in flight from the rebels.[223] If this is so, the development of the Dent and Kendal uprising owed a great deal to Derby's military preparations against the troubles in Percy Fee and to the government's instructions that he was diligently carrying out.[224]

Much, then, had depended upon a stand being made by Monteagle and Tunstall. For doing so they had considerable resources. Their power in the region, both as office-holders and landlords, was considerable. Tunstall was steward of the hundred of Lonsdale with a castle at Thurland on the Lune and a large estate in the Lune valley between Lancaster and the Westmorland border. Lord Monteagle also had a castle on the Lune, at Horning, and a large estate in the same area. Between them they virtually owned the Lune valley between Lancaster and Kirkby Lonsdale. In addition, Monteagle owned sizeable estates in the adjacent parts of Westmorland (at Farleton in Kendal, Burton-in-Kendal, Monsergh and Staveley) and the West Riding (at Over Bentham, Nether Bentham, Greystonegill, Lenacre in Dentdale and Sedbergh). He was also well placed to control the south Ewcross region as steward of the Earl of Derby's lordship of Burton-in-Lonsdale, as steward of the Earl of Wiltshire's lordship of Austwick and as steward of the Pickering family's lordship of Ingleton.[225] Monteagle was clearly a key figure not only in Lonsdale but also in Ewcross.

The other major landowners of the region were the Abbot of Furness and William Parr. The former had property concentrated both in the Liberty of Furness and in Ewcross. Centred upon Newby

to join him (on 25th October) to meet up with Shrewbury. This was issued in response to the government's instruction of 15th October, which reached Derby on 19th, and was countermanded in a further government letter of 19th October, which reached Derby on 23rd October. See *L.P.* XI. 807.

223 Derby listed the refugees in the articles he attached to his letter of 1st November. See Toller, pp. 44–6. For the contingents brought by Monteagle (616) and Tunstall (61), see above, n. 155.
224 See above, pp. 230–3.
225 For Tunstall, see Watson, op. cit., p. 19 and *Ducatus Lancs*, I, p. 11. For Monteagle, see *Ducatus Lancs*, I, pp. 24 and 40–41; P.R.O. C142/40/2; *IPM Henry VII*, III, pp. 373–4; Hoyle, op. cit., pp. 41, 43 and 45.

and Clapham in the Wenning valley, the Ewcross estate extended along both banks of the Ribble above Horton and over towards Langstrothdale and Dentdale.[226] Parr's estate was now concentrated in north Lancashire, with lands at Asheton, Scotforth and Carnforth, and in the West Riding wapentake of Ewcross, where he owned the manors of Dent, Sedbergh and Ingleton. Until as recently as 1534 he had owned Marquis Fee, a quarter of the barony of Kendal. In addition, he was a major office-holder in the region, as steward of the barony of Kendal whose authority encompassed not only half of Westmorland but also extended into the West Riding and north Lancashire, well south of Lancaster.[227]

The abbey, however, was disaffected; and Parr was an absentee landlord. Having married the only child of Henry Bourchier, Earl of Essex, he resided in the south east, at Stanstead.[228] To be effective any resistance to the uprising needed to depend upon Monteagle and Parr's deputy, Sir James Layburn. Whereas Monteagle marched his manred to Preston, Layburn remained in the area, but acted equivocally, probably because he had no choice, having in recent years alienated both the peasantry and the lesser gentry of the barony, the former as an improving landlord on his own estates, the latter as a result of the conflict between the Earl of Cumberland and the Duke of Richmond, into which he had been drawn, along with Parr, as a leading official of the duke.[229] Also weakening his position was the fact that he was an agent of Cromwell.[230] Since he chose not to flee, he was obliged to play a procrastinating and concessionary game. When this was no longer possible, he took the oath and joined the rebellion, but not as a captain.[231] In this manner, then, with Monteagle absent in Preston and Layburn impotently present in the barony, there was nothing in the region to stop the formation of the Atkinson host.

---

226 For the Furness estate in Ewcross, see *V.E.*, 5, p. 270 where it is described as "rents in Lonsdale". In DL29/159/2505 m. 19 it is described as "Newby lordship in Lonsdale". Cromwell referred to it as the lordship of Lonsdale (*L.P.* XII{1}. 881).

227 Bindoff, II, pp. 531–2; P.R.O. C142/33/107; C142/54/59; *L.P.* V. 951. For transference of Marquis Fee, see above, n. 55

228 *G.E.C.*, XI, pp. 669–74.

229 See above, pp. 258–60.

230 *L.P.* XI. 427.

231 See above, p. 257.

VIII

‣▪▪▪‣

THE PULLEYN/
MUSGRAVE HOST

Revolt in the barony of Westmorland

Mobilisation

The formation of the host and its initial activities were set out in detail by Robert Thompson, the vicar of Brough. Interrogated in the Tower on 20th March 1537, he provided two related accounts, one entitled his "examination", the other his "answers", the latter a response to questions arising from the former.[1] However, since he was seeking a pardon, he was obliged to play down his own complicity. Thus, in keeping with the typical allegation of enforced participation, he showed how, at the start of the uprising, he sought to escape to Penrith where his mother lived, but was prevented from doing so by five men, armed with spears and bows, who insisted that he attend an assembly of the commons. Made to take an oath at this assembly, he was then allowed to visit his mother on condition he rejoined the rebels the following day.[2]

Yet there is no good reason to disbelieve some of the basic facts that he associated with the outbreak of the revolt: for example, on 15th October at Sunday service in Kirkby Stephen church, the curate, faithful to the government order abrogating holy days, failed to announce the forthcoming St. Luke's Day. When this omission caused "a great murmur" among the congregation, he knuckled

---

1 For the "examination", see P.R.O. *L.P.* XII{1}. 687 {2}. For the "answers", see *L.P.* XII{1}. 687 {4}. Both need to be consulted in the original since the *L.P.* summary omits a great deal of important matter: i.e. P.R.O. SP1/117 for the first and P.R.O. E36/119 for the second.
2 SP1/117, fos. 53-53b.

under, rang the sacring bell and bade it.[3] Again according to Thompson, on the 16th October a muster was summoned for the same day at Sandford Moor, on the initiative of the townsmen of Kirkby Stephen, and was attended by the parishioners of both Kirkby Stephen and Brough.[4] Each parish was a sprawling one, containing several villages as well as a substantial township.[5] Sandford Moor was chosen as the meeting point,[6] probably to allow the enlistment of further communities along the River Eden but also because it was the recognised muster point for those inhabitants of the East Ward who were under obligation to provide military service on the border, and who normally assembled there, horsed and harnessed, in response to the lord warden's calling.[7]

Thompson's account is suspect, not because of what he included but because of what it left out. He said, for example, nothing of what happened on 15th October in his own church of Brough. Did he announce the holy day in breach of the royal injunction and, if not, did he have to face the congregation's protest? Furthermore, there is no good reason to believe that the muster of 16th October was held because of the protest made in Kirkby Stephen church the day before. After all, St. Luke's Day had been announced, in keeping with the parishioners' wishes. In all probability, the muster was held because of a letter from Richmondshire. If so, Thompson failed to declare this fact. He merely stated that the Sandford Moor muster was summoned because of rumours current that "they were up in Richmondshire, Yorkshire and Durham".[8] He also failed to mention two other matters, which suggests that he was bent on concealing the connexion between the muster held and the letter from the North Riding. In his "examination" he did not specify the actual oath to which he was subjected, which only emerged in his "answers".[9] It happened to be the very same oath that was set out in the Richmondshire letter: a pledge to be true to God, the faith of the church, the king and the commonwealth.[10]

Nor in his "examination" did he mention that the Sandford Moor

3 Ibid., f. 53.
4 Ibid.
5 See map 9.
6 SP1/117, f. 53.
7 See B.L. Althorpe Papers, B. I, f. 37.
8 SP1/117, f. 53.
9 E36/119, f. 78.
10 For the oath in the letter, see SP1/117, f. 54b. According to Barnard Townley, Thompson used the very same oath to swear Cumberland [see SP1/117, f. 47 (*L.P.* XII{1}. 687)].

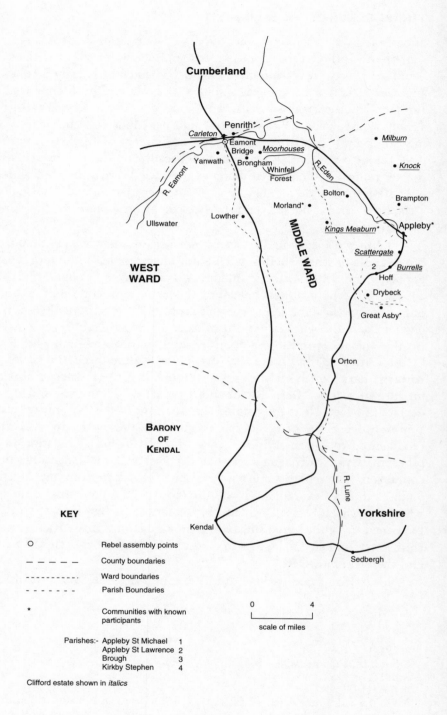

Cumberland

Penrith*

Milburn

Carleton
Eamont
Bridge
Moorhouses
Yanwath
Brongham
Whinfell
Forest
Knock

R. Eamont

Bolton

Brampton

Morland*

*Appleby**

Lowther
*Kings Meaburn**

R. Eden

MIDDLE WARD

Ullswater

Scattergate

2
Burrells

WEST
WARD
Hoff

Drybeck

Great Asby*

Orton

BARONY
OF
KENDAL

R. Lune

Yorkshire

Kendal

Sedbergh

KEY

○   Rebel assembly points

– – – – –   County boundaries

·········   Ward boundaries

- - - - -   Parish Boundaries

*   Communities with known
          participants

Parishes:- Appleby St Michael   1
          Appleby St Lawrence 2
          Brough   3
          Kirkby Stephen   4

Clifford estate shown in *italics*

0   4

scale of miles

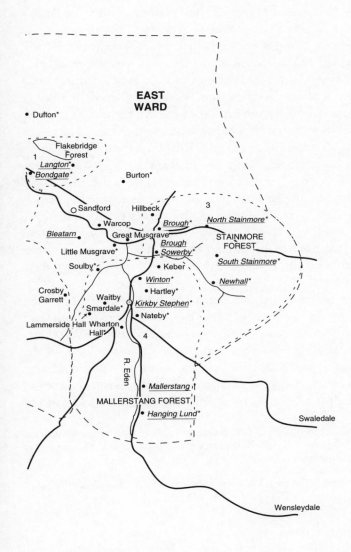

Map 9   The uprising in the barony of Westmorland

muster recruited not only from the parishes of Brough and Kirkby Stephen but also from the parish of Warcop.[11] The manor of Warcop belonged to Lord Latimer, a leader of the Richmondshire uprising.[12] Quite possibly it had served as a staging post for the messengers as they brought the letter along the Stainmore Pass.[13] Thompson, in fact, eventually recognised the existence of the letter in his "examination" but only in a situation which absolved him from having anything to do with its introduction to the West March. Thus, he alleged that revolt in Penrith was sparked off by the arrival of the Richmondshire letter, but he was careful to add that this happened before the 20th October, the date of his involvement with this particular uprising.[14] Without a doubt, the letter, having been composed in Richmond on 15th October, was dispatched to Cumbria on that or the following day.[15] Brought along the Stainmore Pass, it must have entered the barony of Westmorland at its north-easterly tip, the parish of Brough where Thompson was resident vicar. Barnard Townley later alleged that Thompson was instrumental in making the letter known in Cumberland.[16] In all likelihood, he first became associated with it a few days earlier in Westmorland.

The letter has failed to survive but it can be reconstructed, from the descriptions of its contents offered by Thompson himself and Barnard Townley.[17] It was addressed to the inhabitants of Westmorland and Cumberland.[18] It was regarded as written in the name of the commons and was signed Captain Poverty, or some variant of this title.[19] It declared that "we your brethren in Christ" have assembled and "put us in readiness" (i.e. formed a host) to maintain "the faith of

---

11 Sandford was in Warcop parish. Robert Hilton, one of the four captains was from this parish. See J. Nicolson and R. Burn, *History and Antiquities of the Counties of Westmorland and Cumberland* (London, 1777), I, p. 612.
12 Nicolson and Burn, op. cit., I, p. 600.
13 Thompson indicated the route taken by the letter in stating that it was "received from beyond Stainmore" (SP1/117, f. 54b).
14 SP1/117, f. 54b.
15 For composition, see above, pp. 146–7.
16 SP1/117, f. 50 (*L.P.* XII{1}. 687).
17 The opening of the letter was given verbatim by Townley (see SP1/117, f. 50). The rest of the letter was summarised in some detail by Thompson. See ibid., f. 54b.
18 Ibid.
19 Thompson declared that it was written "in the name of the commons" (ibid.). That it was a Captain Poverty letter was revealed by Townley who stated that, in reading the letter in Cumberland, Thompson presented himself as "Poverty's chaplain and secretary" (ibid., f. 50). For the Captain Poverty idiom, see M. L. Bush, "Captain Poverty and the pilgrimage of grace", *Historical Research*, 156 (1992), pp. 17-29.

God, his laws and his church", and had already restored some suppressed abbeys (i.e. Easby and Coverham).[20] Having declared what it had done and why, it exhorted the Cumbrians to follow suit, with precise instructions on how to do so. They were told to assemble "for the maintenance of certain articles concerning the christian faith and the commonwealth".[21] These articles are now lost but they were probably appended to the letter and contained an agrarian complaint concerning rents, gressums and tithes.[22] Once assembled, the Cumbrians were ordered by the letter to take the oath to be true to God, the faith, the king and the commonwealth which involved abiding by the articles. Then they were called upon to "restore all abbeys suppressed" and to ensure that these abbeys regained all their confiscated goods. In addition, they were told to maintain good relations with the Scots, so that their campaign was not distracted by foreign war. Finally they were required to send four gentlemen to the commons of Yorkshire: that is, to the rebels of Richmondshire. Failure to comply with the letter, it was threatened, would cause "they of Yorkshire" to regard the Cumbrians "as enemies to the christian faith and the commonwealth".[23]

No deputation of gentlemen was sent into Yorkshire, but otherwise the letter was taken to heart by the Westmorlanders who, as instructed, assembled, swore the oath and formed a host. Thompson was not very forthcoming about the host. He gave no information on its size or how it was armed. That it was substantial was evident in the impudence with which it invaded the homes of the leading gentlemen, Wharton, Warcop and Lowther.[24] That it was well armed, and probably manned by horsed and harnessed men familiar with war, is more than likely given the region's role in the defence of the northern border and the prevalence of tenures which, thanks to cornage and tenant right, were obliged to maintain mounted troops.[25] Thompson also provided little information on how the host was financed, apart from mentioning the confiscation of the goods of commoners who failed to join the uprising, a tax imposed upon beneficed clerics resident in the barony "for the maintenance of the commons and the cost of their captains" and a plan to take the "fruits of the benefices" of absentee clerics.[26] However, as

20 SP1/117, f. 50.
21 Ibid., f. 54b.
22 Evident in Townley's account (see ibid., f. 50).
23 Ibid., f. 54b.
24 See below.
25 See below, pp. 309 (tenant right) and 315 (cornage).
26 SP1/117, fos. 58b–59.

the freeholders and tenant right tenants were normally required to provide free service, it is likely that participants were expected to serve at their own charge. On the other hand, Thompson did provide details about the captaincy of the host, its initial activities and how it was inclined to operate in two companies, the one led by Pulleyn, the other by Musgrave. He also indicated its basic function: to persuade the county families to take the oath by threats of force.

At the muster on Sandford Moor four captains were chosen. Two were minor gentlemen: Robert Pulleyn of Ormside and Robert Hilton of Burton. The former was so minor that on occasions he was termed a commoner; the latter was a lord of the manor, but a very insubstantial one: in 1543 he was only required to provide two horsemen for the lord warden, an obligation equalling that required of Pulleyn but which was far less than what was expected of the great majority of gentlemen in Westmorland, who were called upon individually to provide at least twice that number. The other two captains, Nicholas Musgrave and Christopher Blenkinsop, were substantial yeomen, the one from Kirkby Stephen, the other from Brough. Blenkinsop and Hilton quickly fell out of sight. Since no further captains were appointed, the host fell under the command of Pulleyn and Musgrave.[27]

On the following two days, the 17th and 18th October, the host concentrated on enlisting those who had failed so far to attend. They were principally the substantial gentlemen of the region. Thus, having met again at Sandford Moor on 17th October, the rebels went to swear or spoil Sir Thomas Wharton who had already been in communication with them but without any agreement.[28] As steward to the Earl of Cumberland, the seigneur of the barony, Wharton was as important a local figure as Hamerton in Percy Fee or Layburn in Kendal.[29] His house was on the banks of the Eden, a mile and a half south of Kirkby Stephen. Finding him absent, the rebels took his son and heir and brought him back to Kirkby Stephen.[30] Then in anger they took charge of Wharton Hall, spent the night there and even considered

27 Ibid., 53b. The captains are dealt with below, see nn. 125–6 and 136. For Pulleyn's and Hilton's military obligations in 1543, see Nicolson and Burn, I, p. li. For the military obligations of the Westmorland gentry, see ibid., pp. l–li.
28 According to the "examination", the communication was by message (SP1/117, f. 53b). According to the "answers", Wharton had already "been with them" but "could not agree" (E36/119, f. 78).
29 A Clifford account of 1534 revealed him as steward and forester of Mallerstang (Chatsworth Trustees, Bolton Abbey MSS, 10, f. 23b). For his stewardship of the Clifford estates, see B.L. Althorpe Papers, B I, f. 48.
30 E36/119, f. 78; SP1/117, f. 53b.

burning it down.[31] Also on 18th October they threatened to take action against the Musgraves of Hartley, another leading family of the barony, with a castle half a mile east of Kirkby Stephen. But the family was, for the time being, safely resident in Cumberland at Edenhall and Bewcastle.[32]

On the 18th October, St. Luke's Day, the rebels assembled in the town of Kirkby Stephen, having openly proclaimed on the previous day at Wharton Hall that they would do so. The rebel host was now directed to Lammerside Hall, the family seat of the Warcops. In all probability, this was not the peel tower by that name that is situated a mile or two south of Wharton Hall along the Eden, but what became Smardale Hall, a mile or so west of Kirkby Stephen. They hoped to find there and swear Warcop, Wharton and other gentlemen; however, they found only servants. Taking charge of the house, Pulleyn set a day for both Wharton and Warcop to join up, failing which their properties would be spoiled.[33] For the rest of the day they used the Warcops' house as a requisitioning base, sending out two-man parties under oath to bring in the goods of commoners who had yet to assemble, the smallness of these parties suggesting that the commoners who had as yet to join were the exceptional few. All that day the parties came and went, great cries going up whenever confiscated goods were brought in.[34]

Having recruited the far eastern part of the barony, on 19th October the host, under Musgrave and Pulleyn, marched along the Eden towards Penrith, Pulleyn on the right bank, Musgrave on the left. Musgrave visited Lowther Hall, hoping to recruit Sir John Lowther, deputy sheriff to the Earl of Cumberland for the county of Westmorland and a leading gentleman in the Clifford service. But he also had fled. In reaching Penrith Pulleyn found it already in revolt. Returning on 20th October, he held a further assembly at Eamont Bridge, presumably to meet up with Musgrave and to swear and arm the region. At last the host succeeded in recruiting some gentlemen. The big fish had as yet evaded them, apart from the son and heir of Wharton, but at the Eamont meeting, Thomas Dudley, an esquire of Yanwath came in, along with several unnamed, minor gentlemen.[35]

In this manner, aided by the presence of the host, the uprising was

31 E36/119, f. 78.
32 Ibid. For Musgrave family, see Bindoff, II, pp. 646-7. For whereabouts of Sir Edward and Sir William, see below, pp. 346, 349.
33 SP1/117, fos. 53b–54.
34 Ibid., f. 54.
35 SP1/117, f. 53b. For Thomas Dudley, see Nicholson and Burn, op cit., I, pp. 412–13 and 348.

spread throughout the East Ward and into the northerly parts of the
Middle and West Wards. Untouched were the southerly parts of the
Middle and West Wards. Mainly affected was the East Ward which
followed the Eden from below Kirkby Stephen to above Appleby.
Although not exclusively, the host was mostly recruited from the
estates directly held by the Cliffords, the Earl of Cumberland and
his son Lord Clifford.[36]

At the Eamont Bridge gathering Thompson was openly proclaimed
by Robert Pulleyn as adviser to the Penrith uprising. Thompson alleged
he had no choice in the matter. The Penrith rebels wanted him because
he was the brother-in-law of one of their captains, Gilbert Whelpdale;
and Pulleyn ordered him to go. His task was to advise the Penrith "in the
business of the commons".[37] Detached in this way from the Westmorland uprising, Thompson's account of events for the rest of October
concentrated upon Cumberland. However, the Westmorland revolt
continued as a separate entity. It did not become completely fused
with the Cumberland uprising.[38] In this respect, the Cumbrian region
produced three separate revolts in October 1536: one in the barony of
Kendal, another in the barony of Westmorland and a third in the county
of Cumberland, each with its own host and its own leaders.

The connexion with Robert Aske

Although in Thompson's absence the Pulleyn/Musgrave host went out
of sight, certain details indicate a continuing revolt in the barony. What
is clear is that, of the three Cumbrian uprisings, the one in the barony of
Westmorland was the most closely associated with the main pilgrimage
of grace: it had the most influence upon the pilgrim high command and
was the best informed of the struggle ensuing between the pilgrims and
the government. This association was due to three visits paid by Robert
Pulleyn to the high command; to the dispatch from the barony's commons of at least two letters to the high command; and to the barony's
receipt of several instructions from Robert Aske himself, along with
copies of the two petitions that the pilgrims sent to Henry VIII.[39]

36 See map 9.
37 SP1/117, f. 54.
38 In running the two together to form the "northern movement", Harrison is
     wrong [S. M. Harrison, *The Pilgrimage of Grace in the Lake Counties* (London,
     1981), pp. 92–3].
39 For Pulleyn's visits to the high command, see SP1/117, f. 58b. His first visit was
     on 28th October; his second was in late November for the York council; his third
     was for the second Doncaster meeting in early December. For the correspondence
     with Aske, see below. For the first petition, see E36/119, f. 81b and SP1/117, f.
     58. For the second petition, see SP1/117, f. 58b.

A connexion with Aske was first established when the commons of the barony composed an answer to the Richmondshire letter and sent it to him. This is a detail left vague in Thompson's "examination" but clarified in his "answers".[40] The actual content of the letter is unknown since it has not survived but, according to Thompson, it was delivered by Robert Pulleyn. Lord Darcy revealed that Aske had received from the Cumbrian region, sometime before mid-November, a letter urging him not to "shrink in this business" and offering to send him 30,000 men with a month's wages, as well as to provide another 30,000 for the defence of the Scottish border.[41] In all likelihood, then, the Westmorlanders had been moved by the Richmondshire letter not only to swear the region and form a host but also to compose a letter of ecstatic support for the rebellion as a whole. Thompson claimed that Pulleyn had reached Aske by the time of the first Doncaster meeting (27th October), but this is contradicted by Aske who declared that he met "one of the heads of the commons at Westmorland" (i.e. Pulleyn) a day later at Pontefract. At this meeting Aske informed Pulleyn of "the order taken at Doncaster", suggesting that Pulleyn had only just arrived. Furthermore, in defence of Thomas Wharton, Aske told him not to mistreat the gentlemen of the barony and to allow Wharton to pass into Yorkshire if he so wished, the result, it seems, of some special pleading by William Stapulton, captain of the Beverley host and Wharton's brother-in-law.[42] In return, Aske was handed the letter composed by the Westmorland commons.[43]

All this suggests that, *en route* to deliver the letter, Pulleyn had encountered the Richmondshire host which, since 21st October, had been engaged in the siege of Skipton and that together they had ridden to Pontefract only to be told of the Truce. According to Darcy, this force upon reaching Pontefract was a massive gathering of 20,000,

---

40 See SP1/117, f. 58. In his "examination" Thompson made it clear that a letter was sent to Robert Aske from the commons of Westmorland, but he ambiguously claimed that it was an answer to a letter from the commons of Yorkshire and failed to specify a date. Clarification comes in his "answers" which declared the answer to be to the letter "that was first sent into the country" (i.e. the Captain Poverty letter from Richmondshire) and that Pulleyn took this answer with him to his first meeting with Aske and that it was composed when Thompson was in Cumberland (i.e. between 20th and 31st October) and was drawn up at the Appleby council (see E36/119, f. 81b).

41 Dodds, I, p. 304 (*L.P.* XI. 1086).

42 For Thompson's account, see SP1/117, f. 58 and E36/118, f. 81b. For Aske's account, see E36/118, f. 90b (*L.P.* XI. 1046 {3}). For Stapulton's account, see Stapulton, p. 103.

43 This is not made evident by Aske but can be construed from Thompson's account. See above, n. 40.

whereas the original Richmondshire host was reckoned at 12,000.[44] Whilst besieging the Earl of Cumberland in Skipton Castle, it in all likelihood received assistance from other quarters, one of which could have been the barony of Westmorland. The rebels of the barony held grudges against the Clifford family, both as official overlords (in connexion with the exaction of noutgeld and sergeant corn) and as landlords (in connexion with gressums and intakes).[45] For this reason, they possessed a strong affinity with an anti-Clifford element in the Richmondshire host.[46] Whether or not Pulleyn took an army with him is unknown, but it is improbable that he went unaccompanied. Whether or not he went to Skipton is unascertainable, but, given that it was on the most obvious and direct route to Pontefract, and given the earl's intimate and fractious association with the parts of the barony that were foremost in the uprising, it is unlikely that Pulleyn could have passed him by.

The letter from the commons of Westmorland which Pulleyn took to Aske was drawn up by a council established at Appleby. It consisted of the two captains, Robert Pulleyn and Nicholas Musgrave, aided, like a manorial court, by twenty-four quests.[47] In its proceedings it consulted village constables and other commoners.[48] Its function was to determine "all matters there".[49] From late October and throughout early November it met frequently to formulate policy and even to make "new laws".[50] In returning to Westmorland after his first meeting with Aske, Pulleyn showed the Appleby council the petition of five articles that had just been taken to the king. What especially moved the council was the article requiring the laws of the realm and of the church to be returned to what they were on Henry VIII's accession, causing it to demand the restoration of holy days, along with the traditional order of prayer, and to have it openly proclaimed in Appleby that every curate should "bid the holy days and beads after the old manner on pain of death".[51]

44 See above, ch. IV(n. 99).
45 See below, pp. 309–20.
46 See above, pp. 153–5.
47 This is made evident, if not fully clear, in Thompson's "answers" where he states that the letter was composed by Pulleyn "with the quests and their council" (E36/119, f. 81b). That this was the Appleby council, see SP1/117, f. 58.
48 E36/119, f. 81b.
49 SP1/117, f. 58.
50 SP1/117, f. 58 and E36/119, f. 81b. Its earliest known meeting was to compose the reply to the Richmondshire letter which was delivered to Aske on 28th October. Its last known meeting was to compose the letter of 19th November.
51 SP1/117, f. 58 and E36/119, f. 81b.

Besides opposing new laws, the Appleby council made them. Its own new laws had been formulated by 19th November when they were set out in a supplicatory letter addressed to Lord Darcy and taken to York by Pulleyn, Musgrave, the vicars of Morland and Brough and six commoners.[52] They were substantially of an agrarian nature, proposing innovations in the payment of gressums (to be fixed rather than arbitrary), noutgeld and sergeant corn (to be abolished) and enclosures (to be pulled down if "noisome").[53] In addition, they also proposed a number of innovations in the relationship between the laity and the clergy, requiring for the Appleby council the right to tax benefices for the purpose of funding the uprising and the right to replace benefice-holders who were either laymen or heretics by others who would "serve God" and "keep hospitality"; as well as requiring for the laity the right to pay tithes as a voluntary contribution rather than as a compulsory tenth.[54] The letter impressed the high command and Aske found most of it acceptable, so much so that its proposals led to the inclusion of two agrarian grievances in the December petition.[55]

The Westmorland commons not only pressed innovations upon the high command but also imposed them upon the gentlemen of the barony who, in the manner of the Dent and Kendal revolt, were obliged to apply their seals to warranties drawn up by the rebels, authorising certain gressums and a benefice tax.[56] Undoubtedly, the Appleby council, in its capacity as chancellery and court, had a hand in this operation.

52 The letter is printed in Harrison's *The Pilgrimage of Grace in the Lake Counties*, Appendix I. For the deputation to York, see SP1/117, fos. 58–58b.

53 For their analysis, see below.

54 In proposing the right to tax the clergy, the letter simply refers to "taxes casten among the beneficed men . . . for the commonwealth" (Harrison, op. cit., App. I). That the taxes were meant to support the commons and their captains during the rebellion is made known by Thompson (SP1/117, fos. 58b–59).

55 As alleged by Thompson (SP1/117, f. 58b). The articles were no. 9 on tenant right and no. 13 on enclosure (*L.P.* XI. 1246). However, what was formally allowed was a great deal less than what was asked for. Nothing was done about tithes, the right to dismiss clerics or noutgeld and sergeant corn. And the items admitted to the December petition did so in an altered form, with gressums pitched at double the rate required by the Westmorlanders and their request for a limitation upon intaking met by an order for the enforcement of the tillage laws which had no relevance to the enclosure problem as it existed in the uplands. For a discussion of these grievances and their presentation by the Westmorlanders, see below.

56 SP1/117, f. 59.

The Cumberland connexion

The evidence so far has suggested that, after Pulleyn's march to Penrith on 19th October, his followers withdrew into the barony and concentrated their efforts upon linking up with Aske. The Earl of Cumberland, however, reported on 31st October that the commons of both Westmorland and Cumberland were engaged in the siege of Carlisle; and eventually in February 1537 a huge combination of Westmorland and Cumberland men marched, in pursuit of the bastard Clifford, upon that border town.[57] The two uprisings had a great deal in common. Their discontents, in matters of faith and commonweal, were similar. Both were strongly moved by agrarian grievances, notably unreasonable gressums and tithes. Both had the same *bêtes noires*: especially Sir Thomas Wharton, who, as sheriff of the county, as agent of the Cliffords and as landlord and steward in the Percy Honour of Cockermouth, was as important and as abrasive a figure in Cumberland as his position as landlord and steward of the Clifford interest had made him in Westmorland.[58] The Earl of Cumberland, moreover, was as unsatisfactory a ruler in Cumberland as in Westmorland, annoying the Cumberlanders, however, as an incompetent and absentee warden of the West March rather than as an extortionate lord.[59]

Both regions were ignited by the Captain Poverty letter from Richmondshire; and also connecting them was the involvement of Robert Thompson. Whilst remaining prominent in the Westmorland uprising, so much so that he was part of the barony's deputation to the pilgrims' York council in late November, Thompson also became a chief organiser of revolt in Cumberland during the last ten days of October.[60] Both counties, moreover, followed a similar pattern of revolt, hosting in the third week of October, remaining disorderly during the period of the Truce and breaking out in a fresh rebellion in February, 1537.[61] Initially, their hosts even had a similar system of command, with each led by a quartet of captains.[62] The question is: how involved were the Westmorlanders in the activities of the Cumberland commons? Did the Westmorland host project itself towards

---

57 For the October attack, see *L.P.* XI. 927. For the February attack, see *L.P.* XII{1}. 415, 426 and 427.
58 For Westmorland, see Stapulton, p. 103 and *L.P.* XI. 1046{3}. For Cumberland see ibid., *L.P.* XII{1}. 185 and SP1/124, f. 67b (*L.P.* XII{2}. 548).
59 See below, p. 369.
60 See below, p. 356.
61 For disorders during the Truce, see *L.P.* XII{1}. 946 (p. 431); *L.P.* XI. 993, 1045, 1064{2}, 1086; Dodds, I, p. 304. For fresh outbreaks in 1537, see above, n. 57.
62 For Westmorland, see above, p. 298. For Cumberland, see below, p. 332.

the northern border? Thompson gave nothing away. He made no mention of any Westmorland involvement in the raising of Cumberland, and his account of the October march on Carlisle gave no intimation that Westmorlanders were a part of it.[63] Several hints remain, however, to suggest that they participated in October 1536, both in swearing and mobilising the Cumberlanders and in the attempt to take Carlisle.

Writing from faraway Skipton, but in touch with the West March through his heir Lord Clifford and his bastard son Thomas, both of whom were in Carlisle in late October and throughout November, the Earl of Cumberland referred twice to the October activities of Westmorlanders in Cumberland: first in his report of 31st October to the king on the siege of Carlisle and secondly in his report of 6th November to Sir William Fitzwilliam, claiming that "the commons in Westmorland sent unto Sir William Musgrave, and Jack his deputy, at Bewcastle and would have had them sworn".[64] In all probability, the Westmorland host divided its activities in October, with a contingent from the south-east, under Pulleyn linking up with the Yorkshire rebels, and a contingent from the north-west of the barony, perhaps led by Nicholas Musgrave, assisting the Cumberlanders in the planned siege of Carlisle and in the defence of the region against attack from the loyalist mosstroopers of the border. Connecting the two contingents was the council conveniently placed in Appleby.

Grievances

The only surviving declaration of the Westmorlanders' grievances, the letter addressed to Darcy of 19th November, fails to dwell upon matters of religion.[65] It is largely a statement of agrarian discontent. Nevertheless, as with the other revolts, the uprising in the barony was moved by a variety of complaint, so much so that the Dodds are wrong to regard it as "essentially a rising of the poor against the rich" and "almost entirely directed against unpopular landlords".[66] Religious grievances were declared in the oath which obliged men to be true to God and the faith of the church.[67] They were also made evident in the actions and reactions of people associated with the uprising: especially the pressures brought upon local clergy to uphold the traditional

63 *L.P.* XII{1}. 687{2}.
64 *L.P.* XI. 927; SP1/110 (*L.P.* XI. 993).
65 Harrison, op. cit., App. I.
66 Dodds, I, pp. 192 and 225.
67 SP1/117, f. 54b.

church service, notably by the congregations of Kirkby Stephen and Brough and in the proclamation issued by the Appleby council at the end of October ordering, upon pain of death, holy days and prayers to be conducted "after the old manner".[68] The proclamation emphasised the importance of the religious grievance to the Westmorland rebels, revealing that they appreciated the pilgrims' article for the repeal of all laws made since 1509 essentially as a means to restore the traditional church service.[69]

In addition, religious grievances were implied by the reception given to the Captain Poverty letter from Richmondshire which advocated the defence of the christian faith as well as the commonwealth.[70] Moreover, the letter of 19th November made an explicit objection to heretics in proposing that the rebels should have the power to depose benefice-holders who could be identified as "Cromwell's chaplains".[71] The strength of lay feeling in religious matters, as well as the ambivalence of the clergy, was revealed in November when Aske required the clergy of Westmorland and Cumberland to state their opinion on the two basic issues of Dissolution and Headship, giving them the choice either of declaring their views directly or of authorising the Archbishop of York to speak in their stead. The Cumbrian clergy, weakly, opted for the second course since it excused them of the need to commit themselves to any particular opinion. In angry response, Pulleyn stopped their letter to the archbishop, believing that, on such important matters, they ought to make their views known.[72]

A broad range of religious discontent was thus associated with the uprising in the barony of Westmorland, including the dissolution of religious houses; abrogated holy days; the revised order of prayer; the expulsion of the papacy; the tenure of clerical office by absentees, laymen and heretics. Generally at fault in the rebels' eyes were the new laws in religion: that is, the articles, injunctions and statutes through which the government had formulated its religious policies. But, among the religious grievances, some appeared to be more important than others. Whilst welcoming the Richmondshire letter with its order to restore suppressed abbeys, the Westmorland rebels failed to object explicitly to the Dissolution. This was noticed by Aske who, after reading their letter of 19th November, expressed his

68 For congregational pressures, see *L.P.* XII{1}. 687{2}. For the proclamation, see SP1/117, f. 58.
69 Made clear in Thompson's "answers" (E36/119, f. 81b).
70 See above, pp. 296–7.
71 Harrison, op. cit., App. I.
72 SP1/117, f. 58b; E36/119, f. 81b.

concern at their failure to do so.[73] But this omission is not surprising since, apart from the abbey of Shap, none of the lesser monasteries were situated in the barony; and Shap was reprieved. It is true that most parishes in the barony were appropriated to religious houses, but only two, both situated in the far westerly part (i.e. Orton and Barton), were appropriated to houses that had been dissolved (i.e. Warter and Conishead). The parts of the barony which provided the uprising with its driving force (notably the communities within the parishes of Kirkby Stephen, Brough, Appleby and Morland), were all unaffected so far by the Dissolution. In response to Aske, the rebels sought to make amends; and, when he instructed them to enquire and report on the visitation of Doctors Leigh and Layton, they responded. As a result according to Aske, there came to be included in the December petition article eleven, which accused the two doctors of taking money, horses, advowsons and leases as bribes.[74]

Of greater import to the Westmorland rebels were changes in the church service. This issue was raised on three occasions: on 15th October when the curate of Kirkby Stephen omitted to announce St. Luke's Day; at the close of October when, in accordance with the order of Captain Pulleyn and the commons, it was proclaimed that beads should be bidden and holy days announced "after the old manner"; and on 29th January 1537 when Robert Thompson, the vicar of Brough, was obliged by his parishioners to incorporate in his order of prayer some of the traditional elements, notably a prayer for the pope and his college of cardinals.[75] In his examination Thompson set out the order of prayer that he followed that day:

Ye shall pray for the good estate of our mother the holy church, for the peace and tranquillity of all christian realms and on this part for the realm of England and our sovereign lord the king, supreme head of the church of the same next under God like as he is proclaimed by act of parliament. And, as I am commanded by the church's wardens which said it was the parishioners' mind, ye should also pray for the pope of Rome with his college of cardinals, and so forth in the common form.[76]

This is without doubt a twisting of reality, brought about by Thompson's bid to secure a pardon which caused him to present himself as remaining loyal to the king whilst having to respond to

---

73 Ibid. The account in his "examination" fails to make the point about reporting back to Aske. See SP1/117, f. 58b.
74 SP1/120, f. 36b (*L.P.* XII{1}. 1175).
75 SP1/117, f. 53; ibid., f. 58; ibid., fos. 59b–60.
76 SP1/117, fos. 59b–60.

his flock. But why should he make the whole thing up? In all probability, some popular pressure was brought upon him to acknowledge the pope and cardinals in the bidding of the beads and thus safeguard a central feature of the old religion. What is probably not true is Thompson's suggestion that, in praying for the pope, he only acted under duress. Two concerns moved these attempts to preserve the traditional service: the need to recognise the papacy as part of the christian faith and the need to preserve the belief that the saints were efficacious intermediaries between man and God. The former was to be achieved by restoring the traditional order of prayer; the latter, by restoring the banished holy days.

Also of some importance to the Westmorland rebels was their objection to benefices held by absentees, laymen and heretics. This particular grievance came to light in the letter of 19th November. It was aroused by certain local events and featured a struggle against the plans of Thomas Cromwell. It concerned the two parishes of Kirkby Stephen and Musgrave, both of them appropriated to the abbey of York St. Mary, although the patronage of Musgrave had fallen to the bishops of Carlisle.[77] At the start of the year the parishioners of Musgrave had objected to having Sir John Knollys as their rector because he was one of Cromwell's chaplains. To express their opposition they had withheld their tithes.[78] Moreover, the year before some disquiet was caused when Cromwell persuaded York St. Mary to appoint the layman, Sir Thomas Wharton, as vicar of Kirkby Stephen. On this occasion, the king intervened and ordered the abbey to confer the benefice instead upon his Latin secretary, the cleric Sir Peter Vannes, thus substituting for a layman as vicar an absentee priest.[79] It was in this context that the religious complaint, evident in the letter of 19th November, was made. The radical remedy, as conceived by the rebels, was to establish the parishioner's right to depose vicars who, through being absentees, laymen or heretics, could not provide a satisfactory service, either in ministering to the spiritual needs of the parish or in dispensing hospitality and charity. Alternatively, they wished parishioners to have the power to persuade the unsatisfactory vicar to mend his ways through imparting to them the right to withhold tithes.[80]

77 For Musgrave, see Nicolson and Burn, op. cit., I, pp. 587–8. For Kirkby Stephen, see ibid., p. 535.
78 SP1/101, f. 91 (*L.P.* X. 96). That the reference was to Musgrave, see *V.E.*, 5, p. 294.
79 *L.P.* VIII. 167.
80 Harrison, op. cit., App. I.

The grievances of the Westmorland rebels were unusual, especially in a religious sense, since they contained no demand for the restoration of suppressed monasteries. Nor did they express any opposition to the spoiling and dissolution of parish churches.[81] They were also out of the ordinary in failing to object to the government's fiscal policies. Nor was there any complaint of misgovernment on grounds of unconstitutional conduct. The pilgrim article that called for a return to the government practice of 1509 was not seen by the Westmorland rebels as a defence of political rights but as a means of restoring the old religion.[82] On the other hand, their grievances were conventional in expressing anti-Cromwellian sentiments and, for a rising of the upland north, in making agrarian complaints.

Distinguishing the Westmorland uprising was the extent of its agrarian grievances. They encompassed gressums, enclosures, noutgeld, sergeant corn and tithes. All were noticed in the letter of 19th November which complained that, as a result, "the wealth of our country and the profit of the commonalty" were impaired.[83] Most of these grievances were complaints against the Clifford family. But were they simply reactions against its loyalty to the government at the time of the rebellion; or did they express genuine criticism of the way it had conducted itself as landlord, overlord and sheriff? The fact that the rebels of the barony produced a programme of agrarian reform suggests the latter, although, couched as it was in general terms, the same programme also suggests that, from the rebels' point of view, the estate management of the Cliffords was not at fault alone but that the improvements of other landlords was a target of the same objection.

As with the barony of Kendal, the barony of Westmorland was predominantly a region of tenant right in which a system of tenure, upheld by custom, conferred benefits upon the tenantry in return for certain service obligations, the chief of which was to provide, free of charge, mounted military service, at the warden's calling, for the defence of the marches against Scotland. At this time in Westmorland, the tenants' benefits were safeguarded by no more than a concept of reasonableness which required the landlord's exactions to be sufficiently lenient to enable them to fulfil adequately their service obligations. Since rents were fixed by custom, landlords had to raise their *rentier* income by increasing the gressum, the fine which fell due both

---

81 However, for the possibility that the parishes of Orton and Barton were involved, along with Sedbergh, in the September confederations which were concerned with the destruction of churches, see above, ch. VII(n. 9).
82 See above, p. 302.
83 Harrison, op. cit., App. I.

upon change of lord or upon change of tenant. Perhaps setting the
scene for the agrarian discontent in the barony, although there is no
surviving evidence to prove as much, was the general fine that had
fallen due in 1536 on part of the Clifford estate as a result of the lands
conveyed by the Earl of Cumberland to his son and heir, Lord
Clifford, in celebration of the latter's marriage to the blue-blooded
daughter of the Duke of Suffolk, Eleanor Brandon. [84]

Pressed by inflation, lords were undoubtedly raising gressums, the
Earl of Cumberland setting an example to his gentlemen vassals.[85] The
question is: were they raising them to unreasonable heights? Sustaining
the rebels' grievance against gressums was the feeling that the concept
of reasonableness was ceasing to protect the tenant against harsh
landlordship and therefore a change in the system was required.
Unlike the men of Kendal who simply demanded that the custom be
respected, the rebels of the barony of Westmorland required the
custom to be revised, so that the arbitrary gressum was replaced by
one fixed in accordance with the level of rent. Thus the "new law"
proposed in the letter of 19th November required "gressums for poor
men to be laid apart but only penny farm, penny gressum".[86] In other
words, it ordered each gressum to be equal to one annual rent. Since
the rent was unalterable, the rebels were asking for a great deal. In
effect, they were demanding that the gressum should remain fixed for
ever more. As well as requiring captured gentlemen to seal their
approval of this revision of custom, the rebels inserted it into the
deliberations of the pilgrims' high command, from which it emerged
in a somewhat modified form; as was evident in article nine of the
December petition which respected the principle of an unalterable
gressum but doubled its value, proposing that it should be twice,
rather than equal to, the value of the annual rent.[87]

The struggle over the gressum was presented as a battle of the poor
against the rich; but in reality this was not the case.[88] As in Kendal,
Cumberland and the North Riding, it was mostly a struggle of the
privileged peasantry to retain rights which ensured that they were

84 For the transfer of Clifford property, see table, p. 319. For the system of
   gressums, see M. L. Bush, "Tenant right under the Tudors: a revision
   revised", *Bulletin of the John Rylands Library*, 77 (1995), pp. 161–8.
85 See R. W. Hoyle, "An Ancient and laudable custom: the definition and development of tenant right in north-western England in the sixteenth century", *Past and
   Present*, 116 (1987), pp. 39–42. For the Earl of Cumberland, see remarks by
   Darcy (Dodds, p. 305) and Norfolk (*L.P.* XII{1}. 319, 478, 919).
86 For the "new laws", see Harrison, op. cit., App. I; SP1/117, f. 58.
87 *L.P.* XI. 1246.
88 See above, n. 86.

under-rented. The same struggle by the privileged to maintain rights was also a feature of the complaint against enclosure, even though this was also framed within an allegation of impoverishment, the letter of 19th November proposing that the enclosures which needed to be levelled were specifically those which worked against the interests of the poor.[89]

Besides the reasonable gressum, another perquisite of tenant right was access to the waste for the grazing of livestock and estovers – the collecting of firewood, timber, nuts, berries, fungi and bracken. In defence of this commoning right the rebels of the Westmorland barony opposed new enclosures. Landlords constrained by tenant right had two basic devices for increasing their rentals: one was to raise gressums; the other was, by enclosing parts of the waste, either to create new farmsteads whose rents were not fixed by custom or to found leases of the herbage on the newly enclosed land. In the technical jargon of the time, lords created intakes as a means of approvement and by doing so realised "new rents". The new farms could be of benefit to the local peasant community, but objection was made because they worked against its interest in establishing new levels of rent and in curtailing highly appreciated free commoning rights. Moreover, as a result of intaking, what was left of the waste was subjected to greater usage, with an increased number of farmsteads obliged to rely upon a decreased amount of common, thus reducing its value to the individual user.

The Westmorlanders declared their grievance against enclosures not only in their letter of 19th November but also taking militant action. One instance of militancy occurred on the eve of the uprising when two men and three women broke down a house in the Kirkby Stephen area. This was presumably a new farmstead created by intaking waste.[90] But most instances of anti-enclosure action followed in January 1537.[91] They cannot be dismissed simply as a reprisal taken against the Cliffords for seeking to capture the rebel leader Nicholas Musgrave since, long before this event, the letter of 19th November had proposed "all the intakes that [are] noisome for poor men to be laid down".[92] Apart from the letter, the surviving evidence of the Westmorlanders' attitudes towards enclosure consists of Thomas Curwen's report to Norfolk that "a great number of people were up

89 See below.
90 B. L. Althorpe B. I, f. 53 (Letter of 5th October 1536, John Lowther to the Earl of Cumberland).
91 SP1/117, fos. 59–59b.
92 Harrison, op. cit., App. I.

and have thrown down many enclosures of my lord of Cumberland";
Robert Thompson's account of the enclosure riot against "new
intakes" of January 1537 which began in the parish of Kirkby Stephen
and spread to neighbouring parishes including the parish of Brough;
and Norfolk's comment that the process of enclosure was oppressive in
Cumbria because it caused an increase in rents as well as a curtailment
of commoning.[93]

Although a Cumberland gentleman without landed connexions in
the barony, Curwen was well placed to make informed comment on the
Westmorland enclosure riots of January 1537, having travelled along
the Stainmore Pass at this time as he fled to Richmond from the rebels
of Cockermouth.[94] As a resident of Brough, so was Robert Thompson.
He made no mention of the Earl of Cumberland but told of anti-
enclosure movements in a part of the barony dominated by Cumberland's landlordship. According to Thompson, the riots occurred in two
phases. Sometime after 6th January 1537, and provoked by news that
Sir Thomas Clifford was descending upon the barony from Carlisle to
take Nicholas Musgrave captive, the parishioners of Kirkby Stephen
pulled down all the new intakes in the parish. Showing that this was
not simply a reprisal against the Cliffords is the fact that it followed,
and was fuelled by, an earlier incident in which, during the Christmas
holidays, the young men of Kirkby Stephen had accused Robert
Pulleyn of admitting men to the possession of lands in return for
bribes. These lands were, in all likelihood, farmholds created by the
new intakes. The matter was defused when certain locals agreed to
stand surety for Pulleyn's cooperation. But, according to Thompson, it
"stirred the country and put it out of order". Finally, on 28th January
the parishioners of Brough responded to encouragement from the
men of Kirkby Stephen and pulled down the new enclosures in
their parish.

What neither Curwen nor Thompson revealed was the extent of
the anti-enclosure action, for, in all likelihood, enclosures were
wrecked in the forests of Whinfell, close to Penrith, and of Flakebridge, to the north of Appleby, as well as in the forests of Mallerstang (the work of the parishioners of Kirkby Stephen) and of
Stainmore (the work of the parishioners of Brough). All were areas

---

93 For Curwen, see SP1/115, f. 178b (*L.P.* XII{1}. 319). For Thompson, see SP1/
   117, f. 59b. For Norfolk, see *L.P.* XII{1}. 478.
94 *L.P.* XII{1}. 185.

in which the Cliffords had been recently active as intakers.[95] On the other hand, what they do make clear is that the objection was to certain enclosures, rather than enclosures in general. This is not surprising given the important role of the intake in establishing and developing the region as a farming community. Certain enclosures, then, were targeted, all of them the recent work of the Cliffords, and they were presented as deserving destruction because they were "noisome to poor men".[96] However, their harmfulness to poor men takes some believing for intaking, by creating new farmsteads, provided the genuinely poor, the landless, with a greater chance of acquiring a small holding. Moreover, the amount of waste in the region was, and is, enormous.

The issue, then, was not so much actual oppression as the infringement of rights coupled with the prospect of exploitation; and at the heart of the matter was the fact that the enclosures had been constructed without the consent of the tenantry and therefore improperly.[97] In this context, the term "poor men" was probably a synonym for the commons, and the genuinely poor were not the beneficiaries of the action taken against enclosures but the victims since it destroyed the farms that the process of enclosure had created for them. This point was made by Thompson. After the parishioners of Brough had acted against the new Stainmore intakes on 28th January 1537, he questioned their actions, presumably at the Sunday service, on the grounds that "some of them had no other living": in other words, because intaking was providing opportunities for the poor.[98] However, there is no mistaking the hostility shown to the new intakes, not only among the villagers and townsmen of the Eden valley but also among the inhabitants of isolated hillside settle-

---

95 This can be gleaned from an incomplete account roll for 1540–41 which is still dealing with costs accrued "at after the commotion time" and records payments for enclosure repairs in Flakebridge, Whinfell and Newhall (Stainmore). See C.R.O. (Kendal), WD/Hoth Box 45. That a great deal of approvement was taking place through enclosure in this period is evident in the surviving Clifford account for 1533–4 (Chatsworth Trustees, Bolton Abbey MSS, vol. 10) and for 1540–41 (WD/Hoth Box 45). Both accounts are similarly and suspiciously incomplete, each having lost their section for Kirkby Stephen and Mallerstang. But suggestive of what was happening in this part of the barony is a fragment of an account for 1543, now found attached to a receiver's survey of free rent for 1527, which suggests that new tenements had been created in Mallerstang, as well as in Stainmore, by the first earl, presumably by intaking. See C. R.O. (Kendal), WD/Hoth Box 48.

96 Harrison, op. cit., App. I.

97 A. W. B. Simpson, *An Introduction to the History of the Land Law* (Oxford, 1961), p. 107.

98 E36/119, f. 79.

ments which had been recently created by intaking waste. Highly significant is the high number of executed rebels coming from the minute settlements of Hanging Lund in Mallerstang Forest and from Newhall in Stainmore Forest. The tally for the one was nine and for the other five. In comparison the number of executions for the substantial townships of Kirkby Stephen and Brough was five and one respectively.[99] Activating these tiny communities was the challenge posed to one phase of intaking, and the gains made from it, by a further phase which now restricted their opportunities for free grazing and threatened to overstock the adjacent waste.

Finally, Norfolk's comments on the problem of enclosure underline its connexion with tenant right and assert, if by overstatement, its importance as a source of rebel discontent. In discussing agrarian developments in the border region and "specially Westmorland", by which he appeared to mean the barony, he deplored not only the increase in gressums but also the extension of enclosure. He connected both with tenant right, stating that between them the two developments had weakened the border defences. For him their importance was such that they were "the only cause of this rebellion".[100]

Whereas the complaint against gressums helped to shape article nine of the December petition, the Westmorlanders' complaint against enclosure had some part to play in the formulation of article thirteen.[101] However, the latter simply proposed the enforcement of tillage laws, which were designed to solve the problems of a lowland, arable peasantry under threat of depopulation from the extension of pastoral farming. They therefore offered to the upland, pastoral Westmorlanders a remedy which was totally irrelevant to their needs, as it was to any other upland community where enclosures in the form of intakes were a problem because they increased rather than decreased the number of farms, and where the peasantry's major concern was not depopulation but a contraction of the waste. No wonder the rebels of the barony remained mistrustful of gentlemen and continued their revolt into the new year.

In demanding the abolition of noutgeld and sergeant corn, the letter of 19th November identified two further agrarian grievances, both of them closely associated with the Clifford family. Abolition, the letter argued, would be "great wealth for all the country", but since the

99 Harrison, op. cit., App II.
100 SP1/116, f. 89 (L.P. XII{1}. 478).
101 L.P. XI. 1246.

amount exacted for the whole barony was less than £50, this is difficult
to believe. Moreover, because the receipts from the two levies in the
1530s were no more than had been exacted for a very long time, the call
for abolition could not be seen as a reaction to a loss of rights or a
safeguard against exploitation.[102] Both payments were owed to the
Earl of Cumberland and the demand for their abolition expressed an
antipathy towards him. This demand was undoubtedly occasioned by
his stand against the pilgrimage of grace but it would be simplistic to
explain it away as just a reprisal for his loyalism. After all, the proposal
was for abolition, not for suspending payment until he reformed his
ways. Its roots went deeper and probably formed part of a campaign
whereby the peasants of the barony were seeking to protect their
surplus from the landlord.

Noutgeld was an annual levy originally paid to the Crown by
freeholders who held their land in cornage; but centuries ago it had
been alienated to the Cliffords, the overlords of the barony. Normally
it fell upon freeholders who did not hold in socage: that is, it applied to
free tenements with a military obligation of border service, but in
certain manors, notably Brough and Winton, it fell upon customary
tenants as well. Sergeant corn, another annual levy, had once provided
sustenance for the horses of the local officials who assisted the sheriff;
and so it was another exaction extrinsic of landlordship and originally
a perquisite of the Crown. It fell into Clifford hands by virtue of their
hereditary tenure of the sheriffdom of Westmorland. It differed from
noutgeld in being paid in kind. Reflecting its origin, payment was
measured in oats which were no longer used to feed the sergeants'
horses but were sold off by the earls' officials who appeared to keep the
difference between what was raised from their sale and the fixed sum of
money received by the earl.[103] Moreover, whereas noutgeld was
normally paid only by the freeholders, sergeant corn fell upon the
customary tenants as well. Noutgeld and sergeant corn allowed the
Cliffords to make exactions of manors which they no longer directly
held.

The Cliffords kept a careful check on the liability to noutgeld.

102 For the letter, see Harrison, op. cit., App I. For receipts, see the accounts for 1482:
W. Ragg, "The feoffees of the Cliffords from 1283 to 1482", *C.W.A.A.S.*, new
ser. 13 (1908), pp. 268–91; 1527: C.R.O. (Kendal) WD/Hoth Box 48; 1533–4:
Chatsworth Trustees, Bolton Abbey MSS, vol 10, fos. 14 and 16–17b; 1540–41:
WD/Hoth Box 45. Usually the amount for cornage included the white rent of
£7.11.4 which has to be subtracted to obtain the actual income from noutgeld and
sergeant corn.
103 Implied by the fact that, although paid in kind, the amount received was recorded
in the Clifford accounts as an unchanging sum of money.

Eventually they increased its amount, principally by converting socage to cornage tenures; but by 1536 no reform had taken place and the revenue received and the communities liable remained the same as in the late fifteenth century. [104] Yet the rebels were clearly agitated by such payments. They made Robert Pulleyn promise to secure their abolition; they made a new law in early November to abolish both noutgeld and sergeant corn, including this new law in their letter of 19th November; and the young men of the parish of Kirkby Stephen eventually attacked Robert Pulleyn when he broke rank and paid his noutgeld in late December 1536. [105] Yet the protest was not against cornage tenure itself. No demand was made for the abolition of the other exactions associated with it: relief, wardship and marriage and unpaid military service on the border. The grievance against cornage was confined to noutgeld.

Given the nature of noutgeld in the barony, there were three possible sources of opposition to it: the mesne lords, free tenants and customary tenants. The first can probably be ruled out, simply because they could pass the payment on to their freehold tenants. Although Robert Hilton, mesne lord of Burton, was one of the original leaders, a characteristic of the uprising is that it was not promoted or actively supported by the Cliffords' vassals. [106] In this respect, it contrasted sharply with the uprising in Craven where vassals of the Honour of Skipton, such as Christopher Danby and John Norton, led the revolt against the Earl of Cumberland. [107] A possible exception in the barony was Lord Dacre, a deadly enemy of Cumberland with manors held of the Cliffords at Orton, Dufton, Yanwath, Brampton and Hoff, all of them liable to noutgeld. But the protest against noutgeld cannot be presented as his work since there is no evidence of his involvement in the uprising. As for the free tenants, those liable to noutgeld held land either directly of the Cliffords or on the estates of the mesne lords, as a result of the latter's practice of passing it down to the free tenures. Perhaps the mesne lords were exacting a higher noutgeld of their own tenants whilst paying the Cliffords the traditional amount. For this there is no evidence.

104 Evident from a comparison of the freeholder survey of 1527 [C.R.O.(Kendal),WD/Hoth Box 48] with the cornage account of 1572 (same box).
105 According to Thompson (SP1/117, fos. 58 and 59). For its inclusion in the letter of 19th November, see Harrison, op. cit., App. I.
106 For Hilton, see C.R.O.(Kendal), WD/Hoth Box 48, Christopher Aske's freeholder survey for the barony of 1527.
107 See above, pp. 154-5.

Perhaps the free tenants were alienated against noutgeld because, with annual payments as well as military service, it was heavier than the freeholds associated with enfeoffment or socage. However, why should they find it objectionable to the point of wishing its abolition now and not earlier? Only one freeholder, Robert Pulleyn, is known to have been involved in the demand for abolition; but he did so under pressure from others. Furthermore, so uncommitted was he to the demand for abolition that he had paid his noutgeld before the year was out. That this should spark off another insurrection suggests that it was a deeply moving issue but for whom? Pulleyn's breach of promise over the payment of noutgeld caused a band of young men from Kirkby Stephen to go to his house in a great rage and threaten his ejection and the seizure his goods.[108]

This incident suggests that it was a contentious issue for many people in the area and implies that involved in the protest against noutgeld were not just freeholders but also customary tenants. As the Clifford surveys of cornage and socage show for 1482 and 1527, on two of the Clifford manors noutgeld was exceptionally demanded of customary as well as of free tenants. In Brough it was a relatively small amount of ten shillings; but in Winton it was a relatively large amount of over one pound.[109] In these communities noutgeld could be seen as part and parcel of landlordism and easily linked with such issues as raised entry fines and curtailed commoning. The pressure for abolition, then, may well have come from these communities motivated by the need to protect themselves against the aggressive estate management of the Earl of Cumberland. What is not so certain is that the town of Kirkby Stephen itself was directly involved in the noutgeld protest. As part of the manor of Brough it may have been liable, but there is no evidence of payment.[110] Moreover, if there was liability, sharing the payment of ten shillings with Brough could not have been onerous. In all likelihood, some pressure for reform came from Winton, a community free of sergeant corn but saddled with a high noutgeld which fell upon the whole community of tenants.

A final possibility is that noutgeld was found objectionable when it coincided with sergeant corn. Whereas noutgeld was evidently spread across the barony, sergeant corn was confined to a limited number of

108 At Christmas 1536 (see SP1/117, f. 59). Payment normally fell due on St. Andrews Day (i.e. 30th November).
109 For 1482, see Ragg, op. cit., p. 291. For 1527, see Christopher Aske's survey [C.R.O.(Kendal), WD/Hoth Box 48].
110 For Kirkby Stephen and its being held by the Cliffords as part of the manor of Brough, see Nicolson and Burn, op. cit., I, p. 544.

communities: of the forty-eight that paid noutgeld only fifteen paid sergeant corn. However, eight of these fifteen communities were in the East Ward, six concentrated in the parishes of Kirkby Stephen and Brough and the other two in the adjacent parish of Crosby Garrett. What is more, 9/16ths of the oats exacted from the barony were taken from these three parishes. Thus, although a light charge overall, amounting to £16–£17 for the whole barony, it fell heavily upon the parts where the uprising originated.[111] In this region sergeant corn and noutgeld frequently coincided: of the thirteen communities that paid noutgeld, eight of them were liable to sergeant corn. Since it was a payment in kind and exacted at a fixed rate of one bushel per oxgang, rather than a fixed cash payment as with noutgeld or the payment of a fixed proportion of the crop as with the tithe, sergeant corn became especially onerous in times of dearth.

The poor harvests of the mid-1530s, coupled with the demands made for oats by the horsed and harnessed hosts of October 1536, must have rendered it especially excessive and perhaps especially objectionable because, in the period of famine, the Cliffords had allowed no rebate. Moreover, since it fell upon customary tenants as well as freeholders it must have been a matter of concern for virtually the whole community. Two types of community were likely to have been especially moved. First, there was the manor of Brough and possibly the attached township of Kirkby Stephen. Uniquely within this manor, customary as well as free tenants were subjected to both noutgeld and sergeant corn. Although neither exaction was heavy (twenty-seven bushels for sergeant corn and ten shillings for noutgeld), the whole landed community had the incentive to object. The other type of community which had cause for complaint was the one subjected to a heavy imposition of sergeant corn. Soulby, Kaber and Crosby were heavily charged, two of them paying sixty-three bushels apiece and the third paying fifty-five bushels. They were also subjected to relatively high noutgeld payments of 13s. 8d., 17s. 8d. and 10s. 2d. respectively.[112] On these manors the conjunction of sergeant corn with delegated payments of noutgeld may have aroused freeholders to oppose both.

How did these two grievances relate to the rebels' other agrarian complaints? Taking into account the known participants – that is, the named leaders and the individuals executed in 1537 – it is clear that

111 For location of sergeant corn, see Nicolson and Burn, I, pp. 292–4. For its total weight, see above, n. 102.
112 For sergeant corn, see Nicolson and Burn, I, pp. 292-4. For noutgeld, see C.R.O.(Kendal) WD/Hoth Box 48.

Manors forming the Clifford Estate
in the barony of Westmorland:
incidence of noutgeld and sergeant corn

manor	noutgeld[⊗]	sergeant corn[⊕]
Mallerstang		
Kirkby Stephen⁺	?	?
Winton	20s.	
Sowerby		
Stainmore		
Blentarn		
Brough	10s.	27 bushels
Langton		
Bondgate*		
Scattergate		
Burrells*		
Kings Meaburn*		
Milburn Fell*	21s. 8d.	
Knock	3s. 4d.	
Brougham	13s. 6d.	
Moorhouses		
Whynfell		
Carleton and *Penrith**		

Blank entries indicate no payment.

Communities shown in italics are those known to have provided rebels in 1536/7; see Harrison, op. cit., Appendix II.

* The estate that the earl granted to his son in 1536 as a result of the latter's marriage [C.R.O. (Kendal) WD/Hoth Box 45 (account roll of estate income and expenditure 32/33 Henry VIII)].

⁺ Kirkby Stephen may have been liable as an attachment of the manor of Brough (see above, p. 317).

[⊗] For noutgeld payments, see Christopher Aske's freeholder survey for 1527 [C.R.O. (Kendal) WD/Hoth Box 48 for a clear copy; the original is in WD/Hoth Box 45].

[⊕] For sergeant corn payments, the earliest surviving detailed evidence is connected with a Chancery dispute of 1629–34: see Nicolson and Burn, op. cit., I, pp. 292–4 and C.R.O. (Kendal) WD/Hoth Box 48.

the rebels were predominantly the tenantry of the Cliffords. Six of the eight known leaders and thirty-nine of the fifty-three victims were drawn from the Clifford estate; and the three epicentres of revolt, Kirkby Stephen, Brough and Appleby, were all part of it.[113] How-

---

113 Harrison, op. cit. App II (for victims minus the Penrith group). The leaders Musgrave, Pulleyn, Tibby, Thompson, Blenkinsop and Taylor were all from the Clifford estate. The other two, Blythe and Hilton were from Morland and Burton. For the Clifford estate, see map 9.

ever, the Clifford estates were remarkably free of noutgeld and sergeant corn. Of the eleven Clifford estates which furnished known
participants only one (i.e. Brough) owed sergeant corn and only two
(i.e. Winton and Brough) paid noutgeld.[114] In Brough which paid both
and in Winton which paid noutgeld alone but in a relatively large
amount, it is likely that hostility to the Cliffords was connected with
such grievances and that it was felt by whole communities rather than
just the freeholders, especially because they were being pressured by
other demands, notably for raised gressums and curtailed commons.
Elsewhere in the East Ward the objection to noutgeld and sergeant
corn probably came from the freehold tenants who had to pay both
and perhaps from customary tenants whose sergeant corn obligations
were becoming intolerable because, in the circumstances of a famine,
the Cliffords were offering no concessions and perhaps because their
own lords, inspired by Clifford example and permissiveness, were
raising gressums and reducing wastes.

It seems, then, that the objection to paying sergeant corn and
noutgeld interlocked with the agrarian complaints mentioned above,
producing a hostility to the Cliffords which may have been influenced
by their loyalty to the government but which had developed of its own
accord as a genuine agrarian complaint against a family that was using
its powers as sheriff, overlord and landowner to exact profit rather than
to exercise virtue. In reaction the rebels produced a programme of
reform distinguished by its resort to innovation.[115] As with the
hostility to intaking and the insistence upon fixed gressums, the call
for the abolition of noutgeld and sergeant corn proposed remedies
which blatantly disposed of tradition. What was proposed, moreover, coupled with the remark in the letter of the 19th November
that the rebels were not prepared to admit gentlemen to the Appleby
council, suggests that the uprising was not simply directed against the
Cliffords but against the other landlords of the barony as well, and that
this resulted not simply from their loyalty to the government but also
from the improvements they were making in the management of their
estates.[116]

A final complaint with agrarian implications concerned the exaction of tithes. The letter of 19th November, after making its point
about gressums, required "all the tithes to remain to everyman his own
doing . . . according to their duty". As proposed above, this may well

114 See table, p. 319.
115 Set out in the letter of 19th November (Harrison, op. cit., App. I).
116 For letter, see ibid. For approvements, see Hoyle, op. cit., pp. 39-42.

have been a device to control the incumbents of benefices. On the other hand, as in Cumberland and Kendal, it may also have expressed objection to paying the tithe as a literal tenth in kind since, as formulated in the letter, it required that the method and amount of payment should be left to the discretion of the payer. This point in the letter was suggestively interpreted by Thompson as "that every man should have his own tithe corn".[117] As with the opposition to sergeant corn, it may have expressed hostility to a payment whose value had soared in accordance with the inflated price of corn.

The Westmorlanders were concerned with tithes in their own right. This was evident in their keenness to raise support for the Richmond council of February 1537. Generally, the aim of the council was to deal with the commonwealth, but specifically it was to deal with the matter of tithes. Associated with the council was the plan to arrange a third meeting with the Duke of Norfolk, presumably to treat issues such as tithes which had been omitted from the December petition. The barony's involvement in organising the council was evident in a letter sent from the commons of Westmorland into the barony of Kendal calling upon every parish to send two delegates to Richmond on Monday next.[118] In all likelihood, then, the complaint against tithes in the barony raised an agrarian issue. Where it differed from the other agrarian complaints, however, lies in its failure to implicate the Clifford family whose tithe income, although exacted in kind, was limited in extent and insubstantial in amount.[119]

Organisation

Characterising the uprising in the barony of Westmorland was both its popular dynamism and its hostility to clerics and gentlemen. Its social hostility sprang not from any disbelief in the society of orders, but from its religious and agrarian grievances which rendered its supporters, for specific and temporary reasons, critical of the divinely ordained ruling element. Thus, the clergy were held in contempt for being heretics; or for not exercising sufficient pastoral care; or for

117 Ibid. and SP1/117, f. 58.
118 SP1/118, f. 213 (*L.P.* XII{1}. 965); SP1/117, f. 31b (*L.P.* XII{1}. 671).
119 For 1533–4, see Chatsworth Trustees, Bolton Abbey MSS, vol. 10, f. 18. For 1540–41, see C.R.O.(Kendal), WD/Hoth Box 45, when it was worth 7s. 5d. The Earl of Cumberland also farmed the tithes of Kirkland on the Westmorland/Cumberland border for the Prior of Carlisle [see *L.P.* XII. 1345 and A. G. Dickens, *Clifford Letters of the Sixteenth Century* (Surtees Society, 172 {London, 1962}, no. 2)] and possibly the tithe of Bolton for the Abbot of York St. Mary (see ibid., nos. 13-14).

failing to defend the old religion against the government's plans for its destruction.[120] The gentry were held in mistrust because of their unwillingness to side with the rebels and because of their disregard for the privileges of tenant right. As a result, the rebels pressured them not only to take an oath of allegiance to the uprising but also to seal their agreement to the rebels' demand for fixed gressums.[121] The rebels' letter of 19th November stated: "we do accept no gentlemen of our council" (i.e. the Appleby council) and then gave the reason: "because we be afraid of them as yet", implying that the present dysfunction was a temporary arrangement, to be terminated when the gentry had mended its ways and justified its leadership.[122] The letter of 12th February, which the men of the barony sent to summon support in the barony of Kendal, presented the gentlemen as the enemy: the recent fray in Kirkby Stephen was emotively described in the letter as the work of "our enemies the captain of Carlisle and gentlemen of our country of Westmorland", presumably because it was thought that, following the Cliffords, they had decided to side with the government. The way the rebels pitted themselves against the gentlemen was noted by the Earl of Cumberland in a letter of 12th November to the gentlemen of the barony in which he observed how "the commons within Westmorland" had not only resorted to rebellion but had "also done sundry displeasures to you . . . which were minded to live in peace and quietness".[123] Aske formed the same impression and, through Pulleyn, urged the Westmorland commons "to make no spoils nor to maltreat gentlemen".[124] Stemming from agrarian and religious grievances, the hostility of the commons to clerics and gentlemen was intensified by the latter's unwillingness to support the uprising.

Yet it was by no means a popular uprising, pure and simple. Within the leadership were gentlemen and clerics. Of the four captains that were quickly appointed on 16th October, Robert Hilton was a gentlemen and so probably was Robert Pulleyn. As lord of the manor of Burton, north-west of Brough, Hilton was a vassal of the Clifford family.[125] Whilst no lord of the manor and regarded by the vicar of Brough as a commoner, Robert Pulleyn was designated a gentleman in

---

120 See Harrison, op.cit., App. I; SP1/117, ff.53, 58b and 59b.
121 SP1/117, fos. 58b–59.
122 Harrison misses out the "yet" (Harrison, op. cit., App I; SP1/111 (*L.P.* XI. 1080).
123 Dodds, II, p. 113 (*L.P.* XII{1}. 411).
124 For Clifford, see Althorpe Papers B I, f. 47. For Aske, see E36/118, f. 90b (*L.P.* XI. 1046 {3}).
125 Nicolson and Burn, I, pp. 612–13.

1537/8 and again in 1539/40.[126] Furthermore, although distracted for a time by his involvement with the Cumberland uprising, Robert Thompson, the vicar of Brough, remained a key figure in the Westmorland uprising, serving as one of its delegates to the pilgrims' York council in November.[127] Another of the delegates was John Blythe, vicar of Morland; and a third clergymen surfaced as an activist in February 1537 when the letter sent by the Westmorlanders to raise the barony of Kendal was delivered by Sir Michael Nuthead.[128]

Rather than to exclude the gentlemen, the original aim of the rebels was to swear them to the cause. This plan came unstuck when leading gentlemen – notably John Warcop of Lammerside Hall, Edward Musgrave of Hartley Castle, Thomas Wharton of Wharton Hall and John Lowther of Lowther Castle – responded to the rebels' summons by absenting themselves from the region. In disgust, the rebels contemptuously occupied, and probably soiled, their houses.[129] Some gentlemen, however, were quickly implicated. Wharton may have fled, but his son was taken and, along with the family servants, was sworn. And when Pulleyn assembled his host on 20th October at Eamont Bridge, several gentlemen came in, including Thomas Dudley from nearby Yanwath.[130] It is also likely that, before the end of October, Wharton had been sworn, the result of pressures brought upon him by the capture of his son and the threat to sack his property. Sir John Leigh charged him in April 1537 of being "the first that was sworn in Westmorland". Whilst he was clearly not the first to take the oath, it is probable that, faced by the deadline set by the rebels for his submission and to safeguard his property, he had abjured by the end of October and, as a result, was able to visit the Appleby council on 29th October to learn the news brought back from Pontefract by Robert Pulleyn.[131]

---

126 For his designation as a commoner, see SP1/117, fos. 58–58b. For his designation as a gentleman, see Nicolson and Burn, I, p. 516 and *L.P.* XIV {1}. 653.

127 For involvement in Cumberland, see *L.P.* XII{1}. 687 {2}. For the York council, see SP1/117, f. 58b.

128 For Blythe, see ibid. and Nicolson and Burn, op. cit., I, p. 445. For Nuthead, see SP1/118, fos. 143–143b (*L.P.* XII{1}. 914 {2}).

129 See Thompson's account, SP1/117, fos. 53b–54.

130 See above, n.35.

131 For the claim that Wharton had been sworn, see *L.P.* XII{1}. 904. For his visit to the rebels at Sandford Moor on 17th October, see E36/119, f. 78. However, in his "examination", Thompson merely claimed that Wharton sent a message to this assembly (SP1/117, f. 53b). For his visit to the rebels in Appleby on 29th October, when Pulleyn returned with the pilgrims' five articles, see E36/119, f. 81b. The same point, however, is not made in Thompson's "examination", and in his "answers" the name of Wharton, along with that of Lowther, are smudged

Eventually, both Lowther and Musgrave were sworn, if not by the rebels of Cumberland then by the rebels of Westmorland.[132] It also seems that a number of unnamed gentlemen sealed agreements on taxing the clergy and safeguarding the custom of tenant right.[133] However, in keeping with the uprisings in Dent, Kendal and Cumberland, the enlisted gentlemen were not, for the most part, turned into captains. The two exceptions were Robert Hilton, and he ceased to figure after the first assembly at Sandford Moor, and Robert Pulleyn and he was so minor that he could be taken for a commoner. Moreover, the rebels remained suspicious of gentlemen, consciously excluding them from their Appleby council and also from the delegation they sent to York and Pontefract. Elsewhere the aim was to enact the society of orders in revolt. The high command of the pilgrimage of grace proposed as much when it suggested that the Westmorland delegation should consist of the barony's leading gentlemen (i.e. Wharton, Lowther, Musgrave and Lancaster) as well as eight commoners to be selected by the "captains of the commonalty" (i.e. Nicholas Musgrave and Robert Pulleyn). But in the barony of Westmorland the aim of the rebels was simply to compel the local gentry and clergy to comply with the commons' plans for agrarian and religious reform; and, as a result of the mistrust of the commons and the gentry for each other, the delegation that was dispatched to York failed to include gentlemen, apart from the socially peripheral Pulleyn, and consisted of two clerics and seven commoners.[134] Undoubtedly the manner in which the uprising was organised stemmed from the strength of the rebels' agrarian grievances which made it impossible for gentlemen and commons to reach an accord, causing the gentlemen to distance themselves from the uprising and causing the commons to hold the gentlemen in contempt for their lack of commitment and to exclude them from having any direction of the uprising.

through, as if to delete them. For the rebel threat to spoil his goods and chattels if he failed to take the oath by an unspecified date, see SP1/117, f. 53b. Stapulton and Aske presented Wharton as under threat from the commons of Westmorland but this might have stemmed from his refusal to participate rather than offering proof that he had not taken the oath (Stapulton, p. 103 and *L.P.* XI. 1046 {3}). The fact that Aske granted Wharton a safe-conduct to leave Westmorland for Yorkshire might also suggest that Wharton had taken the oath (see *L.P.* XI. 1045).

132 See below, pp. 355(Musgrave) and 348(Lowther).
133 SP1/117, f. 58b–59.
134 For the proposal from the high command, see SP1/111, f. 245 (*L.P.* XI. 1155 {2}). For the membership of the actual delegation, see SP1/117, f. 58–58b.

On the other hand, although a peasant revolt and self-conceived as an uprising of the poor, it was not a movement of the impoverished.[135] Robert Pulleyn was clearly a man of substance, probably a freehold tenant and on the brink of becoming a gentleman. Nothing is known of Nicholas Musgrave, but the authority he commanded suggests that he was of similar background.[136] Christopher Blenkinsop, the third leader, was another man of substance, serving as rent collector for the Clifford manor of Stainmore and as churchwarden of the parish church of Brough.[137] Several of the participants were estate officials of the Cliffords: e.g. Edmund Playce, approver in Stainmore, Richard Waller, bailiff of Winton and Kaber; William Wylkyne, reeve of Sowerby, Hugh Beyle, bailiff of Langton and forester of Flakebridge and William Waterman, reeve of Langton.[138]

As with the Dent and Kendal revolt, the uprising in the barony of Westmorland was not simply drawn along by its leaders but pushed from below, so much so that the established rebel leadership was pressured by its followers to pursue certain courses. Thus, Robert

135 See the letter of 19th November (Harrison, op. cit., App. I); and for its relationship with Captain Poverty, see above, pp. 296–7.

136 Neither Musgrave nor Pulleyn are designated officials in the Clifford accounts, but perhaps this is because in the surviving accounts [Chatsworth Trustees, Bolton Abbey MSS, vol. 10 (1533–4)) and C.R.O. (Kendal), WD/Hoth Box 45 (1540–41)] the sections relating to Kirkby Stephen and Mallerstang Forest have been removed. The accusation made against Pulleyn by the people of Kirkby Stephen that he was receiving bribes at Christmas 1536 and giving men "possession of lands" suggests that he was a Clifford official. See Thompson's account, E36/119, f. 79 and SP1/117, f. 59. Pulleyn appears but once in the Clifford accounts (Bolton Abbey MSS, vol. 10, f. 24b). Harrison claimed that it was connected with his paying "comensale" which he proposes was a "subsidiary payment of sergeant corn" (Harrison, op. cit., p. 70). But Pulleyn was the payee, not the payer. Thus, in 1533–4 he received from Thomas Birkbeck, receiver for the Cliffords' Westmorland estate, twenty-six shillings for the "commonsale" of William Butterfield, warrener of Ketland, suggesting that Pulleyn had had a hand in paying the warrener for the Cliffords and was being recompensed for this service. Ketland was near Great Ormside, with which Pulleyn was associated by 1538 as a result of a release of lands to him and his fellow rebel, Robert Hilton, lord of Burton (see Nicolson and Burn, I, p. 516). Harrison suggests that both were freeholders (Harrison, op. cit., p. 101), Pulleyn because he was a payer of noutgeld (ibid., p. 70). Normally this was the case but in Brough with Kirkby Stephen and in Winton the obligation fell also upon customary tenants. The evidence therefore does not actually prove his freehold status.

137 For Blenkinsop's office as collector, see Bolton Abbey MSS, vol. 10, f. 4b (for which he received an annual fee of twenty shillings). For his position as church warden, see SP1/117, f. 59b–60.

138 Evidence for their participation lies in their execution. See Harrison, op. cit., App. II. For Playce, see Bolton Abbey MSS, vol. 10, f. 5. For Waller, see ibid., f. 2. For Wylkyne, see ibid., f. 22. For Beyle, see ibid., fos. 7b and 22. For Waterman, see ibid., f. 22.

Pulleyn was made to promise that he would seek the abolition of
noutgeld and lost all credibility when it was discovered that he had
paid up and was also accepting bribes. Morever, Thompson's authority
as leader was eventually challenged by his congregation who, through
the advocacy of the church wardens, Thomas Taylor, Christopher
Blenkinsop and Anthony Wharton, obliged him on 29th January to
pray for the pope.[139]

In organisation, the uprising followed the usual course. It was seen
as a rising of the commons; it referred to itself as a rising of the
commons; its captains were regarded as captains of the commons
and it acted in the commons' name.[140] Moreover, it proceeded by
holding a series of assemblies at strategic points in the barony –
Sandford Moor, Kirkby Stephen, Lammerside Hall, Eamont Bridge
– to draw in the people of the surrounding areas. Their function was
twofold: to form confederations bound by oath and to create an armed
force which was marched across the barony from Kirkby Stephen to
Penrith with the purpose of persuading and encouraging men to join up.
All this was in keeping with what happened elsewhere in the north.
Exceptionally, the rebels of the barony of Westmorland formed a
council which, sitting at Appleby, met regularly from late October
until late November to define policy and to make laws. Rebel policy
was announced locally by "crying out" rather than in writing.[141] But
written statements were used to enforce policy, in the forms of new
agrarian laws, to which the gentry were obliged to seal their agreement,
and four known letters: the reply to the letter from Richmondshire, the
letter of 19th November to the pilgrim high command and two letters
written to the Kendal commons in February 1537, the one announcing

---

139 For pressures upon Pulleyn, see SP1/117, f. 59. For pressures upon Thompson,
   see SP1/117, f. 59b.
140 See Cumberland's description of the rising (B.L. Althorpe Papers, B. I, f. 57).
   The letter of 19th November was addressed from the captains and the commonalty of Westmorland (Harrison, op. cit., App. I). Thompson's account repeatedly
   refers to the uprising as a movement of the commons. Thus he mentions how the
   commons assembled at Sandford Moor (SP1/117, f. 53); how the gentlemen were
   brought to the commons at Eamont Bridge (ibid., f. 54); how he was ordered to
   help the Cumberland rebels "in the business of the commons" (ibid.); how the
   letter taken to Robert Aske in late October was from "the commons of Westmorland" (ibid., f. 58); how the plan to tax the clergy was for the maintenance of "the
   commons and their captains" (ibid., f. 58b) and how the arrival of the Captain of
   Carlisle to take Musgrave in 1537 "stirred the commons greatly"(ibid., f. 59b).
141 At Kirkby Stephen on 17th October, they "made a cry" (E36/119, f. 78); at
   Lammerside Hall on 18th October they made "many cries" (SP1/117, f. 54); at
   Eamont Bridge on 20th October Pulleyn made "an open cry" (ibid.); at Appleby
   on 29th October "they cried openly" (E36/119, f. 81b).

the forthcoming Richmond council and the other summoning help in resisting the border mosstroopers.[142]

Thus, although conventional in organisation, in being presented as a rising of the commons reliant upon confederation bound by oath and the holding of assemblies to extend the confederation and to raise an army; and although conventional in grievance, with the usual binary emphasis upon defending the faith and the commonwealth, the uprising in the barony possessed certain distinctive features. Its religious complaints failed to specify the Dissolution, concentrating instead upon restoring holy days and the pope. Its commonwealth complaints ignored governmental extortion and constitutional irregularity, identifying instead a very wide range of agrarian problems. As a rising of the commons it was genuinely popular. It was not manipulated by aristocratic hands, overt or covert. Yet it was remarkably sophisticated, formulating new laws in a specially formed council and securing recognition of these laws by obliging local gentlemen to accept them and by impressing them upon the high command, so much so that the Westmorland rebels were able to ensure that, in accordance with their wishes if not their precise demands, the December petition recognised an agrarian problem.

142 For sealing, see SP1/117, f. 59. For letters, see E36/119, f. 81b (October); Harrison, op. cit. App. I (November); L.P. XII{1}. 411 (February) and L.P. XII{1}. 671 (February).

IX

╼▓▓▓▓▓▓▓▓▓▓▓▓▓▓▓▓▓▓▓▓▓▓▓▓▓▓▓▓▓▓▓▓▓╾

THE HOST OF THE
FOUR CAPTAINS

Captain Poverty in Cumberland

The Cumberland uprising was another insurrection sparked off by the Captain Poverty letter from Richmondshire. The two surviving accounts of the uprising – the depositions of Robert Thompson, vicar of Brough, and of Barnard Townley, rector of Caldbeck – agree on this point.[1] According to Thompson there was a gathering in Penrith on Thursday 19th October because of a letter "from beyond Stainmore", which had been sent from "Yorkshire, Richmondshire and the Bishopric in the name of the commons", ordering "all of Westmorland and Cumberland" to assemble for "the maintenance of certain articles as well concerning the christian faith as the commonwealth".[2] This impression is corroborated by Townley who supposed "the cause of the insurrection" to be "certain letters which was sent unto them . . . forth of Richmondshire". But he attributed to Thompson himself their delivery.[3] Thompson may have concealed his role in introducing the letter to Cumberland; and a question remains over what he did when visiting his mother in Penrith on 16th October after hearing of the uprising in Richmondshire and after knowing of its effect in raising the people of the parishes of Kirkby Stephen and Brough.[4] On the other hand, Townley may have been commenting upon the letter's introduction to the parish of Caldbeck rather than to Penrith, for his account

1 For Townley's account, see P.R.O. SP1/117, fos. 47-51 (L.P. XII{1}. 687). For Thompson's account, see SP1/117, fos. 53-60 (L.P. XII{1}. 787{2}) and P.R.O. E36/119, fos. 78-81b (L.P. XII(1). 687{4}).
2 SP1/117, f. 54b.
3 Ibid., f. 50.
4 Ibid., f. 53; and see above, pp. 292–6.

begins with his own involvement in the revolt. This was not until 23rd October when the commons of Caldbeck received their order from the commons of Penrith to take part.[5] Without further evidence there is no means of proving which account is correct.

However, two matters are made clear: one is that the Captain Poverty letter was employed not simply to start the Cumberland uprising but also to spread it throughout the northerly parts of the county; and the other is that the vicar of Brough was prominent in circulating the letter and in publicising its contents. Townley provided a picture of Thompson reading the letter "among the commons, calling himself Poverty's chaplain and secretary".[6] And Thompson revealed that one of the first acts of the Penrith rebels was to send a copy of the letter to Sir Edward Musgrave at Edenhall, with the order that he, along with other inhabitants of the parish, should swear the oath contained in it, obliging them to be true to God, the faith, the king and the commonwealth.[7]

Incited by the Captain Poverty letter, the Cumberland uprising had the same genesis as the uprisings in Westmorland and Dent and probably those in Percy Fee and the easterly parts of the North Riding.[8] The Cumberland uprising, moreover, must also have received some of its original impetus from the Westmorland rebels who had risen three days earlier, whose host arrived in Penrith on the very day that the Cumberland uprising started, who stayed the night and, after returning to Westmorland, deputed Robert Thompson to remain with the Cumberland rebels as adviser "in the business of the commons".[9] However, the Cumberland uprising quickly acquired a life and character of its own; and before the Westmorland host arrived in Penrith, the Cumberland rebels had probably formed an army of their own; they had certainly established a system of captaincy.[10] Although similar in motivation and procedure, the two uprisings went their different ways, the Westmorlanders orientated towards the main pilgrimage of grace, the Cumberlanders drawn northwards in the bid to take Carlisle.

Like the Westmorland rebels, the Cumberlanders in the first instance chose four captains. Appointed on 19th October, the opening

5 SP1/117, f. 47.
6 Ibid., f. 50.
7 Ibid., f. 55.
8 See above, pp. 296–7(Westmorland); pp. 283–4(Dent); p. 227(Percy Fee); pp. 146–7 and 197(North Riding).
9 SP1/117, f. 54; and see above, pp. 299–300.
10 SP1/117, fos. 54–54b.

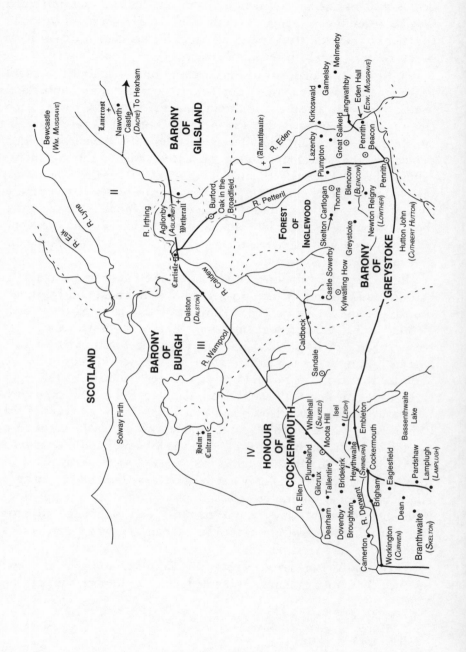

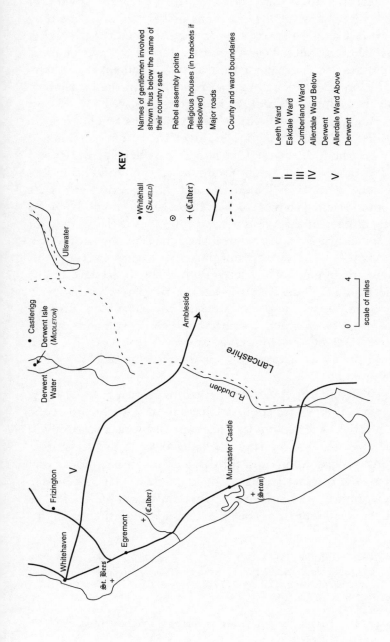

Map 10 The Cumberland uprising

day of the uprising, they were called either "the four captains of Penrith" or "the captains of the commons of Penrith".[11] In keeping with the spirit of Captain Poverty's letter, they adopted the allegorical pseudonyms, Charity, Faith, Poverty and Pity.[12] All were residents of the lordship of Penrith. To begin with, one was a gentleman, Anthony Hutton of Hutton Hall, a small mesne manor within the lordship of Penrith, but by 23rd October he had been replaced by Robert Mownsey because, in his own words, "the commons would have no gentlemen to be their captains".[13] The three other captains remained unchanged throughout the revolt. One was Gilbert Whelpdale, Robert Thompson's brother-in-law, and no doubt a commoner of some substance.[14] The other two, John Beck and Thomas Burbeck, were probably from the same yeoman stock as Robert Pulleyn and Nicholas Musgrave, the leaders of the Westmorland commons.[15] Turning up at all the musters and directing its course, the four captains kept a firm hold on the revolt.[16] But they were not the only captains. As the revolt spread beyond the bounds of the lordship of Penrith, lesser captains came to be appointed. Thus, on 23rd October, the parish of Caldbeck, the barony of Greystoke, the parishes east of the River Eden and the huge forest of Inglewood which stretched between Penrith and Carlisle chose two captains of the commons apiece.[17] Likewise, on 28th October two captains were appointed for the lordship of Holm when it joined the uprising.[18]

Assisting the four captains to organise the uprising was Robert Thompson, whose official function as Chaplain of Poverty and as the captains' secretary was to present the four captains at each assembly in their allegorical guise, to administer the oath, to see to the declaration of the captains' proclamations and the dispatch of their letters as well as to publicise the original Captain Poverty letter.[19] He acquired a dominant role, rather like Christopher Howden, vicar of Clapham, in the Dent and Kendal uprising, as the captains and the commons

11 Ibid., fos. 47 and 55.
12 Ibid., fos. 54b–55 and E36/119, f. 78b; SP1/117, fos. 47 and 49b.
13 SP1/117, f. 55; J. Nicolson and R. Burn, *History and Antiquities of the Counties of Westmorland and Cumberland* (London, 1777), II, pp. 401–2.
14 E36/119, f. 81; SP1/117, f. 54.
15 Named: ibid., f. 55.
16 See below, pp. 345. Townley presents them as being at each muster (see SP1/117, f. 49b).
17 Ibid., f. 56. Also see Map 10.
18 Ibid., f. 57.
19 For presenting captains, see ibid., f. 49b. For oaths, letters and proclamations, see ibid., f. 55. For reading the Captain Poverty letter, see SP1/117, f. 50.

came to regard him as a prophet.[20] In addition, the uprising possessed an official crossbearer, Sir Edward Penrith, who carried the cross before the four captains, presumably when they attended the various musters. There was also an official crier, Thomas Berwick, who shouted out the captains' proclamations to the various assemblies.[21] Added to the uprisings' officialdom were the four chaplains of Poverty who were appointed on 25th October. They were all eminent clerics: Barnard Townley, chancellor to the Bishop of Carlisle as well as rector of Caldbeck; Christopher Blenkow, vicar of Edenhall; the recently deposed Prior of Carlisle, Christopher Slee, now vicar of Castle Sowerby; and the pluralist, Roland Threlkeld – and their appointment appeared to stem from this fact rather than from their commitment to the cause. The latter was so weak that the rebels found it necessary to threaten them with execution if they failed in their duty. This was to instruct the commons "concerning faith", and presumably to provide religious services at the musters.[22] In addition, the organisation of the revolt featured a council, attended by the captains and the gentlemen, and a specially devised religious ceremony entitled the captains' mass.[23] The mass was performed on Wednesday 25th October and on the following day in Penrith church, with Thompson acting as the officiating priest, but because a priest objected to the display of naked swords in church, never again. It began with a procession of the four captains holding drawn swords, led by Thompson. Passing through the church to the door of the chapel, the captains then sheathed their swords and Thompson conducted the service, interspersing a recitation of the ten commandments with remarks which made the point that "the breaking of all these was the cause of all that great trouble".[24] In this respect, the movement was very much infused with the spirit of Captain Poverty which provided it with an organisation and a ceremony as well as a programme of action. Elsewhere Captain

20 Ibid., f. 50b. For Howden, see above, p. 288.
21 For Penrith, see SP1/117, f. 55. For Berwick, see ibid., f. 57b.
22 SP1/117, f. 56; ibid., f. 47. Three of the chaplains were appointed when present. Threlkeld was appointed in his absence and did not join the uprising until 30th October. See ibid., f. 58. For Christopher Blenkow as vicar of Edenhall, see V.E., 5, p. 288. For Christopher Slee as vicar of Castle Sowerby, see V.C.H. Cumberland, II, pp. 148–9. For Roland Threlkeld, see below, pp. 360–1.
23 For the council, there is but one mention. On 28th October at Moota Hill Thompson recorded that "the captains and gentlemen of the council took order for Carlisle" (ibid., f. 57).
24 Ibid., f. 56b. Townley also provided an account which tallies with Thompson's. See ibid., f. 50b.

Poverty made his mark simply as the signatory of an inflammatory letter.[25]

The Captain Poverty letter was followed in Cumberland, to the extent that oaths were sworn and musters held. But two of its instructions went ignored.[26] The Cumberland rebels did not send gentlemen to Richmond to confer with the rebels who had sent the letter. Nor did they restore any religious houses. Unlike the barony of Westmorland, Cumberland had several houses which had been recently condemned: Calder, Seton and Armathwaite had been suppressed; and Lanercost was about to be.[27] However, the parts of the county with suppressed or threatened religious houses, its southerly and north-easterly regions, were, with one exception, not involved in the uprising. The exception appertained to the nunnery of Armathwaite which remained unrestored. Of the four houses, Seton was restored and the attempt to suppress Lanercost was successfully resisted. But this was not the work of the Cumberland uprising. In both cases, it came of local initiative and was carried out by men who had no part to play in the host of the four captains and who acted independently of the instruction from Richmondshire.[28] The rebels of Cumberland, then, like those of the barony of Westmorland, had a somewhat different perception of what needed to be done to defend the faith from that held by the rebels of Richmondshire.[29] This was made evident in the proclamation produced by the Cumberland rebels on 20th October.[30] Composed by Anthony Hutton, the one gentleman among the four captains, it was put into writing by the priest Sir George Corney and proclaimed by Thomas Berwick, the crier.[31]

According to Thompson, the proclamation closely resembled the Captain Poverty letter; but there were glaring differences since the proclamation made no mention of oath-taking or of restoring sup-

---

25 See M. L. Bush, "Captain Poverty and the pilgrimage of grace", *Historical Research*, 65 (1992), pp. 20–26.
26 Thompson summarises the content (SP1/117, f. 54b).
27 For Lanercost, see below, p. 344. For Calder and Seton, see P.R.O. SC6/Henry VIII/7454. For Armathwaite, see ibid., 7346, m.6b.
28 For the restoration of Seton, see the complaint of its farmer, Hugh Ascue which is printed in *V.C.H. Cumberland*, II, p. 194. For the resistance at Lanercost, see below, pp. 342ff.
29 The two regions had in common the fact that their dissolved religious houses mostly belonged to the archdeaconry of Richmond and so were suppressed by the same commissioners. See above, ch. IV(n. 215).
30 Provided verbatim by Thompson (SP1/117, fos. 55–55b).
31 Ibid., f. 55.

pressed abbeys.[32] Like the letter, it was concerned with the Scots but, whereas the letter stressed the need to maintain peaceful relations with them, the proclamation urged the people to organise themselves to resist "when the thieves or Scots would rob or invade us". Instead of ordering the restoration of monasteries, the proclamation ordered that priests should "bid holy days and beads after the old custom", suggesting that, as in the barony of Westmorland, the main religious concern was the changes in the church service brought about by the royal injunction on holy days and the new order of prayer, and that what was demanded in matters of religion was quintessentially the right to venerate saints and recognise papal authority. Rather than a replacement for the letter, the proclamation was a supplement to it. Its role was to declare the general purpose of the uprising, to justify the measures so far taken and to raise a host. Mustering a host, then, was presented as necessary "for the maintenance of the faith" and also "for the maintenance of this country".[33] Then it went on to say that the commons were obliged to see to the latter "because the rulers of this country do not come among us and defend us", a reference possibly to Lord Dacre who, after his fall in 1534, had resided first in London and then in the North Riding at Hinderskelfe, but probably to the Earl of Cumberland who, although lord warden of the west marches since 1534, tended to reside in faraway Skipton or at Court.[34] In being anti-Clifford, the Cumberland uprising resembled the uprising in the barony of Westmorland, with the difference that, whereas the one was principally concerned with the Cliffords' harsh lordship, the other was mainly agitated by their ineffectiveness as border officials. In the proclamation the need to defend against invading Scots and border thieves was presented as the justification for appointing the four captains and their host and for urging upon the region unity and co-operation, a reflection of the disorder incited in recent years by the feud waged between the Clifford and Dacre interests.[35] Eventually, having set out the means of preserving "this country", the commonweal of which was perceived as under threat from a badly controlled border,

32 Thompson said that it was "made much part after the letter that was sent into the country" (E36/119, f. 80). For purposes of comparing letter and proclamation, the Captain Poverty letter has to be reconstructed from the fragment of text provided by Townley (SP1/117, f. 50), plus the description of its contents provided by Townley (ibid.) and by Thompson (ibid., f. 54b).
33 SP1/117, f. 55.
34 Ibid., fos. 55–55b. For Dacre's residence away from the border, see *L.P.* IX. App. 1; A. G. Dickens (ed.), *Clifford Letters of the Sixteenth Century*, Surtees Society, 172 (1962), no. 28 (misdated - it should be 1536); *L.P.* XI. 477 and 647.
35 SP1/117, f. 55b. For the feud, see below, pp. 364ff.

the proclamation focused on matters of religion. In doing so, it implied that the maintenance of the old religion and its customs would be good for the commonwealth since it would encourage everyone to beseech God in their prayers "that we may have quietness and peace". For the same purpose it also desired priests "to go with daily processions" and to conduct the traditional church service.[36]

Both letter and proclamation firmly proposed a defence not only of the faith but also of the commonwealth; the letter ending with the warning that those who refused to co-operate would be taken "as enemies to the christian faith and to the commonwealth", the proclamation ending with "God save the king and the commonwealth".[37] In doing so, they reflected the oath employed by the Cumberlanders to swear support for the uprising which had the commonwealth as one of the things to which men were to be true.[38] It would therefore be quite wrong to assume that the matter of spiritual welfare was the top priority. Central to their grievance was not just the fate of souls in purgatory but also the well-being of bodies close to the border. Man's physical well-being, however, was seen not simply as threatened by the sacking and pillage caused by an ineffectual and absent lord warden. Also to blame was exploitation by tithe farmers and landlords. This is not made evident in the proclamation. Nor is it declared in the surviving fragments of the Captain Poverty letter.

However, the fact that the rebels' concern for the commonwealth stemmed from an agrarian problem was revealed in Barnard Townley's account. In seeking to identify the purpose of the Captain Poverty letter, he hair-raisingly conjectured that it could be no other than "to have [de]stroyed nobles and gentlemen, for they [i.e. the rebels] would have made that no man shall have paid any ingressums to his landlord and [i.e. but for] a small rent for his tenement and several places to have paid no rent nor tithe but in money at their pleasure".[39] Townley was basically saying that the Captain Poverty letter had inspired men to demand so much protection as tenants and tithe payers that the landlords and owners of benefices would be impoverished, as their capacity to tap the surplus product of agriculture was reduced to a minimum. He was also alarmed by the innovatory nature of the demands, which conjured up revolutionary fantasies. Thus, he believed that, if the rebels had their way over rents and tithes, it

36 SP1/117, f. 55b.
37 Ibid., fos. 54b and 55b.
38 "To be true to God, to the faith of the church, to our sovereign lord the king and to the commonwealth of this realm" (ibid., 54b).
39 SP1/117, f. 50.

would bring "all to common", or alternatively create another hierarchy chosen by the commons.[40] For the Cumberlanders, as for the rebels of the baronies of Kendal and Westmorland, the agrarian issue was associated with the system of tenant right. Since this system was a vital part of the border defences, the agrarian complaint was closely connected with the fear that marauding Scots and reivers would destroy their country. In safeguarding their right to be leniently charged in rents and dues, the Cumberland rebels were proposing that the major device at the landlord's disposal for raising his landed revenues – the gressum due upon change of lord and tenant – should be abolished. What is more, in some quarters it seems the demand was made, presumably to limit new rents since the old ones were fixed by custom, that the rent should be low and in cash with the amount paid to be determined by the tenant. Unlike the rebels of Kendal and the barony of Westmorland, the rebels of Cumberland failed to produce an explicit statement of their agrarian concerns.

That Cumberland had an agrarian problem in the 1530s, and one created by the raising of gressums and the enclosure of the waste, was declared in two reports of the region, the one made by the Duke of Norfolk, the other by Robert Southwell, after they had visited it early in 1537.[41] Both were concerned at the effect of this agrarian problem upon the defence of the border: that is, upon the capacity of the tenantry to fulfil the military obligation towards the lord warden. Norfolk's report emphasised the damage done by "gressing" and by "enclosing". He associated the latter with "increasing of lords' rents" rather than the curtailment of common grazing. His meaning was that lords were establishing additional farms on the waste, by a process of intaking, and were charging for them a level of rent well above that taken of the customary tenures. Southwell raised the same two matters, with direct reference to the custom of tenant right. He was specifically referring to the Honour of Cockermouth which had just passed into the king's hands following the death of the Earl of Northumberland and which the king had deputed him to survey for the purpose of exacting of the tenantry the gressum owed the new lord. As he described it, the custom obliged the tenants to serve the king "at their own charge" and at the lord warden's command, with horse and harness. They also had to pay an annual rent and a gressum falling due upon every death of either lord or tenant. The lord's obligation, as

40 Ibid.
41 For Norfolk, see *L.P.* XII{1}. 478. For Southwell, see SP1/124, fos. 67–67b and 68b (*L.P.* XII{2}. 548).

described by Southwell, was to exact gressums not too frequently nor excessively. To preserve the tenant's ability to perform his military obligations, then, the custom laid down that the payments demanded of him should be lenient and reasonable. According to Southwell, to uphold the principle of reasonableness the amount of each new gressum needed to be determined with the consent of the tenants. It also needed to be closely related to the amount exacted in annual rent. The system, however, was breaking down. High gressums were being charged by "the more part" of the landlords, Sir Thomas Wharton included, often in return for exemption from border service.[42]

Thus, the complaint made by Southwell focused upon a problem of border defence created by an abuse of the tenant right system. But in making it he was implying that the tenantry had cause for concern since the resulting decay of the border's defences was exposing the region to outside attack. Without being as specific as Norfolk, he also identified enclosure as a problem, remarking that the "approvement of the commons accustomably used here . . ." had, along with the increase in gressums, "done much more hurt than good". Whilst failing to raise the issue of rents, Southwell was proposing that the intaking of the commons was working against the tenant's interest. Whether this came of limiting the amount of land available for free grazing or whether it came of raising the level of rent, he did not specify. However, the general import of his remark is clear: that the tenantry had cause for alarm because of what was happening to the dues and commoning rights associated with their tenures; and that for them, as for the government, the arising problem was the increased difficulties they were having in fulfilling their military obligations to the Crown.

It was also made evident in one particular incident associated with the Cumberland uprising of late 1536 that concerned Peter Middleton, farmer of the manors of Derwentwater, Castlerigg and Tallentire and of the deer park of Derwent. It came to light in a bill of complaint exhibited by Middleton against his tenantry in Star Chamber in which he complained that "in this great insurrection" the tenants of the three manors, assisted by rebels from the Cumberland uprising, tried to force him "to take their part" (i.e. to take the oath).[43] Middleton

42 Evident in Southwell's remark that, associated with the raising of gressums, the tenant right system of military service had become "almost by the covetousness of them that hath been lords here and negligence of the officers . . . converted from an honest laudable custom into corruption, whereby it is thought . . . that the king is far underpeopled of the number of men armed to serve" than formerly. See ibid., f. 68b.
43 P.R.O. C1/859/50.

refused but, instead of fleeing to Carlisle as other gentlemen did, he and some friends took refuge on an island "upon one of the said manors". Although he presented this retreat as "nigh . . . adjoining Carlisle", it must have been one of the islands on Derwent Water. The full name of one of his manors was the Isle of Derwentwater.[44] There he claimed to have defended himself for fifteen weeks until liberated by the Duke of Norfolk, suggesting that the siege began at the start of November rather than at the very beginning of the uprising, probably with the aid of the rebel company from the Honour of Cockermouth after it had separated itself from the host engaged in besieging Carlisle. As a result of his refusal to participate in the rebellion he was robbed of goods to the value of £100, mainly by his own tenants.[45]

Quite possibly his tenantry were motivated by the same aims as the rebels that joined them. Perhaps, then, they proceeded against him simply because of his refusal to participate in the Cumberland uprising. But the antagonism evident between Middleton and his tenants was not simply the result of the uprising, but belonged to a saga of agrarian conflict which had gone on for at least five years. This is vividly told in the complaints exhibited in the equity courts: from the tenants objecting to Middleton's estate management; from the lady of the manor complaining of Middleton's behaviour towards both her and the tenantry; and from Middleton complaining of both his tenants and the person from whom he leased his rights.[46] Without a doubt there were no angels in this can of worms; and it is unlikely that any of the three parties were innocent. But clearly revealed is the fact that for some time Middleton's relationship with his tenantry had been far from harmonious and that moving the tenantry against him were three issues, all of them connected with the system of tenant right: the right of succession; the payment of gressums; and free commoning on the waste. In all likelihood, then, for Middleton's tenantry their involvement in the Cumberland uprising, which must have entailed taking the oath, was moved by agrarian grievances. This is confirmed by further disturbances in January 1537, against Middleton and Thomas Wharton as well. These disturbances included attacks upon their tithe barns,

---

44 C. R. O. (Carlisle), Transcript of Survey of 1578.
45 C1/859/50. That is, the company which assembled close to Carlisle at the Broadfield on 30th October but failed to attend the next meeting there, held on 3rd November.
46 Middleton filed four complaints: C1/853/43; C1/859/50; P.R.O. STAC2/27/ 147 and 154. Alice Ratcliffe, lady of the manor, filed one complaint: C1/878/6. The tenants filed four complaints: C1/727/12; C1/802/24; C1/923/8; C1/926/ 26.

and showed that the Cumberland uprising was moved not only against the government but also against local landlords.[47] But there is nothing to corroborate Townley's allegation that the Cumberland peasantry were demanding the termination of gressums and a rent decided by the tenantry. Middleton's tenantry, it is true, refused to pay gressums to him, but their refusal did not spring from an objection to gressums but rested on the belief that, having agreed to pay a gressum to the lady of the manor upon her entry to the estate "after the custom of the country", they had no need to pay another gressum to him.[48] The only proposal made at the time for terminating rent came from one of the Graemes of Eskdale and that was requested in reward for his loyalty during the uprising and his part in putting it down, and because it was claimed to be in keeping with a right his forbears had enjoyed in return for border service.[49] In all likelihood, horrified by the prospect of innovation, Townley either picked upon the more extreme proposals that were put forward or he was inclined to accept the rumours circulating that justified his worst fears.

In contrast with Townley on rent, Townley on tithes is corroborated. In Cumberland an extensive spoiling of tithe barns occurred shortly afterwards, between 30th December and the end of January. It happened in the vicinity of Cockermouth and affected the parishes of Bridekirk and Camerton to the north of the Derwent, and Brigham and Dean to the south of it. It began in Broughton, Tallentire, Camerton and Eaglesfield, the work of the tenants of Thomas Wharton and Peter Middleton who appeared to be the tithe-farmers. Initially the corn was not taken. The community leaders simply cleared out Wharton's and Middleton's threshers and, fitting their own locks alongside those of the tithe-farmers on the barn doors, they insisted upon a truce, during which new terms could be negotiated between payer and payee.[50] But further disturbances occurred. By 4th January the locks had been removed, the people confiscating the corn and dividing it among themselves. A further spate of barn-raiding occurred on 18th January. According to Thomas Curwen, all the tithe barns were spoiled to the west of the River Derwent, with 800 rioters drawn from the parishes of Dean and Brigham, and notably involving the communities of Branthwaite, Pardshaw, Embleton, Cockermouth

47 L.P. XII{1}. 319.
48 For Townley's allegation, see SP1/117, f. 50. For Middleton's tenantry, see C1/853/43.
49 L.P. XII{1}. 1217.
50 SP1/114, f. 259 (L.P. XII{1}. 18).

and Brigham.[51] The raiding expressed an animus against Sir Thomas Wharton, who not only farmed the tithe of Broughton but was also impropriator of the parish of Dean, and against Peter Middleton, farmer of the tithe of Tallentire.

Yet the action taken was not simply to punish two men who had failed to join the Cumberland uprising, since communities took part in the action from the extensive parish of Brigham, which owed tithes to neither.[52] Essentially it was to assert a principle; and this was in accordance with Townley's account of the tithe grievance held by the Cumberland host in October. Townley had claimed that for tithes the rebels wished "to pay. . . money. . . at their pleasure".[53] That this was the wish of the parishioners of Brigham had been made evident in a bill of complaint exhibited in Chancery, within the period 1533 and 1537, by the tithe-farmers of that parish. The bill alleged that, contrary to former practice, the parishioners had refused to deliver their tithe corn and instead proposed to "pay. . . money for the same at their own pleasure".[54] That this was the wish of the rioters of January 1537 was made evident in Sir Thomas Curwen's account of the disturbances occurring in the parishes of Brigham and Dean. According to him large numbers from these two parishes congregated in Cockermouth and "made their quarrel to take every man his corn that he had tilled and would have the same for their money"; in other words, their preference was to pay in money rather than corn and to have the right to decide how much to pay.[55]

The tithe grievances of the Cumberland rebels thus bore some affinity with the grievances of the rebels in the baronies of Kendal and Westmorland. As in Kendal, the objection was to paying in kind; and as in the barony of Westmorland, the objection was to paying a sum determined by someone other than the payer.[56] Giving rise to the grievance was the insistence of tithe-farmers upon payments in

---

51 SP1/114 (*L.P.* XII{1}. 185) and *L.P.* XII{1}. 319. The communities can be identified from the surviving lists of Cumberlanders executed for their part in the 1537 revolts. See S. M. Harrison, *The Pilgrimage of Grace in the Lake Counties, 1536–7* (London, 1981), App. II, p. 140. Branthwaite and Pardshaw belong to the parish of Dean and the other three belong to the parish of Brigham.

52 For the farm of Broughton and Tallentire, see *L.P.* XII{1}. 18. For Wharton's impropriation of Dean, see Nicolson and Burn, op. cit., II, p. 57. Brigham was farmed by Richard Wynder and Robert and Peter Hudson (see C1/924/70).

53 SP1/117, f. 50.

54 C1/924/70. The date can be determined from the fact that the bill was addressed to Sir Thomas Audley as Lord Chancellor, who did not enter the office before 1533. Also, among the defendants named is John Wilson who was executed for his part in the uprising of January/February 1537 (see Harrison, op. cit., p. 140).

55 *L.P.* XII{1}. 319.

56 See above, pp. 278–9(Kendal); pp. 320–1(barony of Westmorland).

kind to enable them to benefit from the inflation of food prices; and
the need of parishioners to prevent an increase in value of their tithe
payments as well as to have some means of action against absentee
or heretical clerics. What the rebels wanted was the abolition of the
literal tenth and to substitute in its place a payment of cash determined
by the payer. In Cumberland the tithe complaint was not presented as
a defence of custom, as it was in Kendal. But, in all likelihood, the
conversion to cash had occurred in the recession of the fifteenth
century; whilst in the sixteenth century there was a reversion to
payments in kind as the inflation of foodstuffs gave lessees of the
tithe the incentive to pay high rents for the right of collection in
return for the opportunity to receive marketable produce. It was this
reversion to an older custom that the Cumberland rebels were determined to stop. Their tithe complaint failed to gain admission to the
December petition. Moreover, although the complaint about gressums
was included in the petition it was only in a bowdlerised and inappropriate form, with a demand for the abolition of gressums turned
into a demand for their preservation fixed at twice the rent.

As in the lordship of Dent, the barony of Kendal, the Lonsdale
hundred of Lancashire and the barony of Westmorland, the presence of
agrarian grievance helped to shape the character of the uprising and its
relationship with the society of orders. Presented as an uprising of the
commons, its organisation and source of momentum in Cumberland
allowed it to live up to its name. The two higher orders sought to keep
away, not because they lacked grievances against the government but
because they feared that the success of the uprising would deny them
their basic means of income and radically challenge their way of life.
And yet large numbers of gentlemen and clerics were drawn in, sworn
and given roles to play. The success of the uprising was to enlist the
apparent support of so many prominent inhabitants of the county; its
failure was to take Carlisle. Having secured this goal, the rebels would
have been free to direct themselves against the real enemy, the government. But with Carlisle unsworn and therefore lacking the assurance
that the reivers of the Debateable Lands could be checked, the rebels
had no alternative but to look north; and for this reason, from late
October 1536 to February 1537, their cause became the conquest of
Carlisle and its castle.

The Lanercost prelude

Although the Cumberland uprising broke out specifically in response
to the arrival of the Captain Poverty letter from Richmondshire, it had

a mysterious prelude. In the previous two years the northern parts of
the county had been troubled by disorders caused by a family feud
between the Dacres and the Cliffords. This had been intensified by the
government's decision to transfer the rule of the West March from the
one to the other. These disorders continued in 1536.[57] But in early
October disturbances of a different nature occurred. At the time, in a
letter of 9th October the Earl of Cumberland reported "the misdemeanours of Gilsland", linking them with the confederations which had
formed in Dent, Sedbergh and Wensleydale, and explaining them as
caused "by the mean and reporture of such false and untrue matters as
was never by us or any of council purposed".[58] Because Clifford was so
economical with his information, the Gilsland disturbances can only
be pieced together conjecturally. The reference to rumour related to
the stories circulating at the time throughout much of the north, some
alleging that the government was bent upon robbing the poor through
the introduction of new taxes on food, ploughs, cattle and sacramental
services; others, that the government planned the dissolution of
certain parish churches and the confiscation of treasures from the
ones allowed to survive.[59] Just as in the lordship of Dent, where it
was feared that Sedbergh church might be abolished because it had
belonged to the suppressed abbey of Coverham, it is possible that a
similar fear was activated in Gilsland where the as yet undissolved but
imminently threatened priory of Lanercost put into question the
future not only of Lanercost parish church and the chapel dependent
of Walton, which had always belonged to the priory, but in addition
the large number of rectories which had been appropriated to it: i.e.
Brampton, Carlatton, Denton, Irthington, Grinsdale, Farlam, Mitford
and Lazonby.[60]

The limited surviving evidence suggests that some resistance to the
government came from the canons of Lanercost. This was revealed in a
letter from Henry VIII to the Duke of Norfolk. Written in February
1537 it instructed him to tie up a number of monks and canons
specifically of Lanercost "for as much as all these troubles have
ensured by the solicitation and traitorous conspiracies of the monks
and canons of those parts".[61] Unlike some of the other religious houses
specified as trouble-spots in the letter (i.e. Sawley, Newminster and

57 Harrison, op. cit., ch. 3.
58 Chatsworth Trustees, Clifford Letter Book, f. 3b.
59 For a list of such rumours, see *L.P.* XI. 768{2}.
60 For Dent, see above, p. 249. For Gilsland, see *V.C.H. Cumberland*, II, p. 152 and
   the Dissolution survey for 29/30 Henry VIII (SC6/Henry VIII/7348).
61 *St.P.*, I, pp. 539–40 (*L.P.* XII{1}. 479).

Easby), Lanercost had not been dissolved by October 1536.[62] The protest, then, did not feature the restoration of a religious house but rather an attempt to prevent its suppression. At the time, having been defined as a lesser monastery, it was clearly under threat.[63] In this respect, it was in the same position as its fellow Augustinian house at Hexham and was probably inspired by the latter's resistance. The Dissolution commissioners were still at work on the borders at this late date, although elsewhere in the north they had by this time completed their business. On 15th September they dissolved Newminster, and on 28th September they proceeded to Hexham.[64] Presumably, after suppressing Hexham, their plan was to deal with Lanercost. Reaching Hexham they found themselves shut out.[65] In all probability, the effective resistance offered at Hexham inspired a restoration at Newminster and led to preparations for resistance at Lanercost, the canons arousing local support by playing on the people's fears about the introduction of new taxes and what would be done to the parish churches.

But it seemed that the Lanercost protest came to a sudden end, the result of the failure of the commissioners to arrive and perhaps the arrival instead of Lord William Dacre, who was at his Yorkshire seat of Hinderskelfe as late as 10th October but who must have returned to Naworth Castle shortly afterwards in response to news of the Gilsland troubles.[66] He clearly had ambitions to take possession of the priory, which was a Dacre foundation, and was probably embarrassed by the protest associated with it.[67] A notable feature of the Cumberland uprising is that it did not directly involve either Lord Dacre or his barony of Gilsland. Unlike the other Dacre baronies, Gilsland remained unsworn to the rebel cause and its warriors played a vital part in routing the rebels when they sought to take Carlisle in February 1537.[68] In this respect, the defence of Lanercost did not form an integral part of the Cumberland uprising and, in return, it received

62 This is made clear at the end of the survey of border monasteries for the year Michaelmas 1535 to Michaelmas 1536 (SC6/Henry VIII/7346, m. 7).

63 L.P. X. 1238.

64 See SC6/Henry VIII/7346.

65 For Hexham, see L.P. XI. 504.

66 For his residence in Yorkshire, see L.P. XI. 647. He must have left soon afterwards to have avoided capture, either by the commons in that region who had risen by 15th October or by the Richmondshire rebels. He was at Naworth by 30th October (L.P. XI. 1331) and had been there, it seems, for some time.

67 This became evident in his dealings with the farmer. See L.P. X. 260 (misdated - it should be 1538); L.P. XIII{1}. 304 and 522.

68 See Harrison, op. cit., pp. 123–4. Also see L.P. XI. 1331 which reveals that Gilsland held out even when Dacre had left the area.

a reprieve. Whereas Hexham was dissolved in February 1537, Lanercost Priory survived until January 1538.[69]

Forming the host

The uprising largely consisted of a series of musters, each held at a well recognised vantage point, a hill top which served as a beacon, such as Penrith Fell and Moota Hill, or an ancient meeting or mustering place, such as Cartlogan Thorns and Burford Oak in the Broadfield.[70] Their general purpose was to introduce the four captains and enable them to enlist the country about. To begin with, the musters were held on a daily basis; but as the leadership moved further away from its base in Penrith, they were held every other day, simply because each night the commons and their captains went home, reappearing at the next muster, the date of which was announced at the previous meeting.[71] The practice of reassembling indicates that the function of the musters was partly to bring pressure upon a region to take the oath and partly, by a process of accumulation, to recruit and maintain a large host. Each muster followed the same formula, with a summons for everyone in the vicinity to join the company of those already sworn. At each muster Thompson acted as master of ceremonies, presenting the four captains of Penrith, making public the Captain Poverty letter and the Cumberland rebels' own proclamation, administering the oath to all that came in – en masse for the commons and individually for the clergy and gentlemen.[72] In addition, petty captains of the commons were appointed for the newly recruited areas, another indication that the general purpose of all this activity was to create a military organisation capable of ordering a large army.

Between 19th and 21st October three musters were held in the vicinity of Penrith. At the first, a gathering in the town of Penrith, the four captains were chosen after the Captain Poverty letter had been read and the oath sworn.[73] At the second, a meeting of 20th October held on Penrith Fell for the communities about, Robert Thompson, in

69 For its eventual suppression, see SC6/ HenVIII/7348. It was leased to William Penyson on 10th March. For the dissolution of Hexham Priory, see L.P. XII{1}. 546.

70 See Map 10.

71 Thompson made this general point (SP1/117, f. 55b).

72 For introducing the captains, see ibid., f. 49b. For instructing the crier over the proclamation and captains' letters, see ibid., fos. 47 and 47b. For administering the oath, see ibid., f. 47 and 55. For declaring the Captain Poverty letter, see ibid., f. 50.

73 Ibid., f. 56 and 57.

his capacity as chaplain of Poverty and secretary to the captains, not only declared the Captain Poverty letter and administered the oath but also sent out copies of the letter to the communities which had failed to attend. Thus a copy was sent to Edenhall. According to Thompson, it was simply taken by messengers. In response Sir Edward Musgrave took the oath and the whole parish of Edenhall followed suit.[74] Sir Edward was no ordinary gentleman. A son-in-law was Lord Latimer, leader of the Richmondshire uprising. Musgrave's estates were situated not only at Edenhall but also at the epicentre of the uprising in the barony of Westmorland, at Hartley, Soulby and Musgrave. Although now elderly and retired, he had served the county as sheriff on three occasions.[75] His son, Sir William, a Cromwellian and instrumental in the downfall of Dacre in 1534, was a powerful and fractious figure in the region, having also served as sheriff of Cumberland and having held since 1531 the keepership of the border lordship of Bewcastle with command of its mosstroopers.[76] Sir Edward did not play an active part in the uprising; but his acceptance of the cause was a useful asset to the rebels, allowing them an uncomplicated control of Edenhall and perhaps some leverage over his son, although at the time the two were estranged.[77] A feature of the uprising was the failure of William to proceed against it, although he had the military means, in the form of the loyalist borderers of Bewcastle, at his command.[78]

At the same muster on Penrith Fell the rebels produced their own statement of grievance and instruction, the proclamation, and established a procedure of presentation consisting of an official crier to declare the proclamation and a crossbearer to lead the host and to give it the appearance of a religious procession or pilgrimage.[79] The third of these early musters, held on 21st October, took place on the fells six miles north-east from Penrith, close to the River Eden and, in all probability, near Great Salkeld. Having already enlisted the communities around Penrith and between Penrith and the Eden, the plan on the third day was to involve the parishes across the river. This was accomplished without difficulty. According to Thompson "the commons and townships beyond Eden" – that is, from the smallish, under-

---

74 For Thompson's declaration of the letter at these early musters, see ibid., f. 50. For his administration of the oath, see ibid., fos. 54b-55. For Edenhall, see ibid., f. 55.

75 *Lists and Indexes P.R.O.*, IX, pp. 27–8; M. E. James, *Society, Politics and Culture* (Cambridge, 1986), p. 100; Nicolson and Burn, op. cit. I, pp. 546–7 and 553.

76 Bindoff, II, pp. 646–7; Harrison, op. cit., pp. 32–6.

77 SP1/117, f. 55. For his relations with his son, see below, p. 371.

78 See ibid.

79 SP1/117, fos. 54b–55b.

populated parishes of Kirkoswald, Langwathby, Melmerby, Adding-
ham, Ousby, and possibly of Ainstable, Croglin and Renwick – "came
and took the oath".[80]

Having involved the Cumberland communities to the north-east of
Penrith by 21st October, the rebel command now concentrated upon
bringing in the north-west of the county. By the 25th October, the
whole of Leeth Ward had been enlisted. This was achieved by holding
two further musters, the first at Cartlogan Thorns. Situated probably
at Thornbarrow north of Catteren, this was a recognised meeting place
for the inhabitants of Inglewood Forest.[81] The second muster was held
at Kylwatling How (or Kenwathen How) near Castle Sowerby, a
beacon and gathering point for the barony of Greystoke. At the
Cartlogan Thorns muster, held on 23rd October, support came in
from the parish of Caldbeck, on the edge of the Honour of Cockermouth, the barony of Greystoke and the lordships of Castle Sowerby,
Hutton and Skelton, joining up, under the command of the four
captains, with those recruited from the lordship of Penrith and from
along the Eden.[82] This meeting was important, partly for the changes
it brought about in the system of captaincy and partly for its recruitment of important gentlemen and clerics.

At the muster it was decided both to establish a lesser command,
with captains of the commons chosen for the various regions (i.e. two for
Caldbeck, two for Inglewood Forest and two for Greystoke) and to alter
the high command, the gentleman Anthony Hutton being replaced by
the commoner Robert Mownsey.[83] Although the reason given was that
the commons were against having gentlemen as captains (which echoed
the Westmorlanders' claim that they would have no gentlemen to be of
their council), the Cumberland uprising did not become a war against
them.[84] As in Westmorland, the rebels remained keen to enlist their
support. At the Cartlogan Thorns meeting, according to Thompson,
the "gentlemen dwelling thereabouts" were sworn, with Thompson
administering the oath "in the name of the whole commons".[85] Two

---

80 SP1/117, f. 55b.
81 Cartlogan Thorns is not exactly locatable. It was probably the open-air spot
where the forest court for Inglewood (called the Court-thorn) had traditionally
held its annual meetings. See S. Jefferson, *History of Leath Ward* (Carlisle, 1840),
pp. 205–6.
82 SP1/117, fos. 55b–56; ibid., f. 47.
83 For regional captains, see ibid., f. 56. For captains of Penrith, see E36/119, f. 81.
84 As Tawney suggests: see R. H. Tawney, *The Agrarian Problem in the Sixteenth
Century* (London, 1912), p. 319. For the antipathy of the Westmorlanders, see
above, p. 322.
85 SP1/117, f. 55b; ibid., f. 47.

were named: Richard Bewley and Richard Vachell, both of them, according to Townley, brought in by the commons of Caldbeck upon the command of the captains and commons of Penrith.[86] Nor was the uprising, a war against clerics, in spite of its occasional outbursts of anticlericalism. Along with the two gentlemen, the commons of Caldbeck brought in their rector, Barnard Townley, who was a former chancellor to the Bishop of Carlisle.[87] The same gathering was also attended by Sir John Lowther, a leading knight of Cumberland and Westmorland and deputy to the Earl of Cumberland both as sheriff of Westmorland and as warden of the West March. He was also lord of Newton Reigny, a manor close to Cartlogan Thorns.[88] Since no attempt was made to subject him to the oath, it can be assumed that he was already sworn, probably by the Westmorland rebels under Nicholas Musgrave.[89] He attended the assembly not to offer his service but to call upon the men from the parish of Castle Sowerby to fulfil the military obligations of their tenant right in order to serve him in his wardenship duties. Having put his request to the captains of Penrith, he was allowed to proceed to Carlisle where he remained for the rest of the uprising.[90]

Further gentlemen were recruited two days later at the muster on Kylwatling How.[91] In terms of status or power, none measured up to Lowther or Musgrave, but Cuthbert Hutton of Hutton John in the Dacre lordship of Greystoke was a notable catch, having served, although a minor landowner, as sheriff of Cumberland in 1534–5.[92] The purpose of the Kylwatling How assembly, it seems, was to draw in the inhabitants from the southerly parts of the Greystoke barony and to bring pressure upon the adjacent Honour of Cockermouth. Its other purpose was to commit several important clerics to the cause by obliging them to serve as chaplains of Poverty. Just as the petty

86 Ibid., f. 47.
87 Ibid.
88 Ibid., f. 56. For Lowther, see Nicolson and Burn, op. cit., II, p. 393.
89 Led by Nicholas Musgrave, they visited his house on 19th October and found he was out. Possibly they caught up with him later.
90 SP1/117, f. 56. For his being at Carlisle, see ibid., f. 57. Thompson claimed that at the end of the month he was with the Westmorland rebels in Appleby (ibid., f. 58).
91 SP1/117, fos. 47 and 56. It is called Kylwatling How by both Thompson (Kylwatling Howe) and Townley (Kylwatlynhow) and Waytlyng Howe by the monk Graeme [B.L. Cottonian MSS, Calig. B. III, f. 287 (L.P. XII{1}. 1259 {3})]. Neither is locatable. In all likelihood the meeting place was How Hill, which in early descriptions of the bounds of Inglewood Forest was called Kenwathen Hill. See Jefferson, op. cit., p. 492.
92 Bindoff, II, pp. 429–30; Nicolson and Burn, op. cit., II, pp. 366–7.

captains appointed two days earlier were intended to be local equivalents of the captains of Penrith, the chaplains appointed at Kylwatling How were meant to be local delegates of Robert Thompson. Three of the four chaplains appointed (the rector of Caldbeck, and the vicars of Edenhall and Sowerby) were already present and sworn, but Roland Threlkeld, the parson of Melmerby, had yet to come in. The importance attached to having the rector of Caldbeck and the parson of Melmerby positively and openly engaged in the uprising was made evident in the threat, declared at the same muster, to have both of them executed if they failed to attend the host, with their heads displayed on the highest point in the diocese, and in the proclamation issued specifically to command Threlkeld to come in and take up his duties.[93]

The remaining musters were all concerned with binding Carlisle to the rebel cause. As the town resisted, this aim took charge of the uprising, becoming its major goal. The support of Carlisle was important not simply because of its position as a border bastion but also because the frontier regions, Cumberland Ward and Eskdale Ward, remained unsworn. Sir William Musgrave, commander of the mosstroopers from Bewcastle, held out; likewise, Lord Dacre and his uncle Sir Christopher Dacre, along with their far northern baronies of Burgh and Gilsland, stood aloof.[94] The support of Carlisle, and of the royal officers and troops lodged within its castle, therefore became vitally important to defend the uprising from a reprisal which, it was feared, would be unleashed from the warrior societies of the frontier and would take the form of pillaging by the reivers of Eskdale against the regions which had taken the oath. For the rebels, the enlistment of Carlisle was necessary not only to comfort those who had already committed themselves to the rebel cause but also to assure others that it was safe to participate. The submission of Carlisle was also important because of the Clifford interest lodged within it.[95] The Cumberlanders' attempt to take Carlisle was therefore akin to the Richmondshire rebels' attempt to take Skipton Castle, with both attempting to destroy the loyalism of the same magnate family. Moreover, with Carlisle resistant, the role of the host was defined as an instrument for browbeating it into submission and a means of defend-

93 SP1/117, f. 56; ibid., f. 47.
94 For William Musgrave, see SP1/110 (*L.P.* XI. 993). For Dacre, see *L.P.* XI. 1331.
95 That is, Lord Clifford, the earl's son and heir and Sir Thomas Clifford, his bastard son. See below, p. 370.

ing the rebel areas from the expected onslaught of the defiantly loyalist border mosstroopers.[96]

Returning to the field on 27th October, after two days spent invoking God's grace through the ceremony of the captains' mass, the captains of Penrith and Thompson led the commons of Leeth Ward to Sandale Hill.[97] This was in keeping with an arrangement made at the last meeting. Its aim was to enlarge the host by recruiting more of the Percy Honour of Cockermouth as well as by reaching into Cumberland Ward. At Sandale Hill the rebels were joined by a delegation from Carlisle who declared that, whilst agreeing with the rebels' cause, the commons of Carlisle would not take the oath.[98] This news raised the fear, already declared in the rebels' first proclamation, that the reivers of Eskdale would use the uprising as a pretext to rob the region. And that day the same fear was substantiated when reports came in from the barony of Burgh that the inhabitants of Carlisle had already permitted a number of robberies to occur. It became clear that if the region was to become fully committed to the cause, Carlisle had to be persuaded to change its mind. The rebels therefore ordered that no victuals should be taken into the town. That the uprising was already recruiting from the frontier was made evident in the permission granted at the muster for several men there to return home so that they could protect their goods against the reivers.[99]

With matters unsettled in the far north of the county, and because they were now so far from home, the captains of Penrith broke their habit of returning nightly to their houses and ordered another muster at Moota Hill on the morrow. The purpose was both to draw in the full extent of the Honour of Cockermouth, not only north of the Derwent but also south of the river, and also to recruit the lordship of Holm. That night Thompson, the captains of Penrith and sixteen others rode, in heavy rain, to the town of Cockermouth and the following day (28th October), probably accompanied by a company from it, came to the beacon of Moota Hill.[100] At this muster gathered an impressive display of gentlemen and clerics, including John Leigh of Isel in the Honour of Cockermouth and of Frizington in the Honour of Egremont, a former constable of Carlisle Castle, a deputy to the warden of the West March, an M.P. for Cumberland and father of the detested

96 For the fear of the mosstroopers, see Thompson's account (SP1/117, fos. 55–55b, 56b and 57); *L.P.* XI. 993 and 1331.
97 SP1/117, f. 56b.
98 Ibid.; SP1/117, f. 47b.
99 Ibid., f. 56b; E36/119, f. 80.
100 SP1/117, f. 56b; E36/119, f. 80b; SP1/117, f. 47b.

visitor, Dr Leigh.[101] He was accompanied by Sir John Lamplugh, a former lieutenant of the Honour of Cockermouth.[102] Both, it seems, had been sworn earlier at Penrith.[103] In addition, John Skelton of Branthwaite was present, another gentleman from the Honour of Cockermouth who had also been sworn prior to the Moota Hill muster, probably the day before at Cockermouth.[104] Their attendance reveals clearly that the uprising was now supported south of the Derwent.[105] Another important gentleman present was Thomas Dalston of Dalston, sworn that very day, and providing further evidence that Cumberland Ward had become involved.[106] In addition, Richard Blenkow of Little and Great Blencow in the barony of Greystoke was named as present, although he must have been sworn at a previous gathering.[107] And by now the lordship of Holm was fully involved, with its abbot present and sworn and with two petty captains appointed to lead the company it had provided.[108]

At Moota with its spectacular views of the Solway Firth, Carlisle and the Debateable Lands beyond, a council sat. In spite of the earlier antipathy towards gentlemen, it consisted of the captains of Penrith and the gentlemen. Its purpose was to work out what to do about Carlisle.[109] Its solution was to establish a commission, appointed by the captains of Penrith and Robert Thompson and consisting of the two clerics, Townley and Abbot Carter of Holm Cultram and two gentlemen, one a Dacre client, Richard Blenkow, the other a Clifford client, Thomas Dalston. The commission's instruction was to go to Carlisle and, in conjunction with Sir John Lowther who was already in the town, to ask the mayor and brethren to protect the commons from the attacks of thieves and Scots and to require the town to take the oath.[110] The commissioners, however, were unwilling to go, probably because they feared being taken into custody. This caused an explosion

101 SP1/117, f. 47b. For John Leigh, see Bindoff, II, pp. 508–9. That he was Dr. Leigh's father, see L.P. VIII. 1133 and L.P. XII{1}. 904.
102 SP1/117, f. 47b and James, op. cit., p. 100, n. 40. That his relationship with the Percies had soured, see the sixth earl's complaint against him in C1/866/40 and Lamplugh's answer, C1/866/41.
103 SP1/118, f. 129 (L.P. XII{1}. 904).
104 SP1/117, f. 47b; Nicolson and Burn, op. cit., II, pp. 58–9.
105 That is, the Ward of Allerdale above Derwent. See Map 10.
106 SP1/117, f. 57; Bindoff, I, pp. 7–8. The latter suggests that the Thomas of Dalston mentioned as present at this meeting was the vicar of Dalston, but the vicar of Dalston was George Bewley.
107 SP1/117, f. 57; Nicolson and Burn, op. cit., II, pp. 375–6.
108 SP1/117, f. 57.
109 Ibid.
110 SP1/117, fos. 47b and 57.

of anger and exasperation among the commons which Percy Simpson expressed with the anti-clerical words: "they should never be well till they had stricken off all the priests' heads, saying they would but deceive them".[111] The deadlock was broken by the crier Thomas Berwick who, upon his own initiative, simply ordered the commons to reassemble at Burford Oak in the Broadfield on Monday 30th October, that is, at a well recognised meeting place to the south of Carlisle, and well positioned, if necessary, to assault the town, on the understanding that in the meantime the commission would seek to persuade the mayor and two of his brethren to attend the Burford Oak meeting, to take the oath and then to apply it to the rest of the citizenry.[112]

Before this meeting was held, news of the Truce arrived, reaching Carlisle before it reached Penrith. It was imparted to Townley and Abbot Carter by the Carlisle citizens; then through Thompson, who had remained at Dalston, it was conveyed to Penrith; but without effect.[113] Dismissing it as "but craft and falsehood", the Cumberlanders persisted in rebellion, holding a massive muster at Burford Oak on 30th October, with some 15,000 men present, and another at the same place on 3rd November.[114] At the first Burford Oak muster Thompson inexplicably retired from the fray and "went no more to the commons".[115] Townley took over his function as swearer and administered the oath to two canons from Carlisle Priory and to the parson of Melmerby who had at last joined the uprising.[116] Adding to the numbers present was a huge host from the Honour of Cockermouth

---

111 Ibid., f. 57b.
112 Ibid. This was called Burford Oak in the Broadfield by Thompson (ibid., f. 57b) and Burntwich Oak and Brunsfield Oak beside Carlisle by Townley (ibid., fos. 48 and 49). In an anonymous account, the meeting of 3rd November was described as being within three miles of Carlisle [SP1/112, f. 263 (L.P. XI. 1331)]. The place must be close to present day Burthwaite. Jefferson claims that there was an old oak at Wragmire Moss which fell down in 1823 (Jefferson, op. cit., pp. 206–7). This was close to Broadfield but about five miles from Carlisle. For the commissioners' task, see SP1/117, f. 47b.
113 SP1/117, f. 57b; ibid., f. 48.
114 Ibid., f. 57b (30th October); ibid., f. 49 (3rd November). The estimate of 15,000 would appear to be a gross exaggeration (see Appendix I). But the muster returns for Cumberland in 1535 would suggest that the county was capable of raising a very large and well equipped force; and in addition, in all likelihood, there was some support from the barony of Westmorland. For the muster returns, see E101/61/33 and E101/549/13.
115 SP1/117, f. 58; E36/119, f. 80b.
116 SP1/117, f. 58.

which "brought all the country with them, both gentlemen and others of the whole commons".[117]

Another commission was appointed by the captains of Penrith, consisting of two clerics (Townley and Threlkeld) and four gentlemen (two from Leeth Ward, Richard Bewley and Richard Blenkow, and two from the Honour of Cockermouth, Lancelot Salkeld and John Swynburn the younger). But, when ordered to go to Carlisle to ask the mayor to come to the commons and take the oath, the commission again stalled. Instead it sought to operate through the two recently sworn canons from Carlisle Priory, Sir Richard Huttwyth and Sir William Florens.[118] In response two townsmen appeared with a copy of the proclamation declaring the Truce and forbidding further assemblies, which the four gentlemen took to the commons hoping that it might restrain them, whilst Townley and Threlkeld persisted in seeking to persuade the mayor to take the oath. The four gentlemen presented the proclamation as a genuine document so convincingly that when Townley and Threlkeld returned with the mayor's request for more time to make up his mind about taking the oath, they found that the commons had disbanded and retired.[119]

Thus, within ten days, a huge host came into being recruited from Leeth Ward, the two Allerdale Wards (i.e. above and below Derwent), Cumberland Ward and possibly from the barony of Westmorland. Although gentlemen were present, they did not have a leadership role, and the army was commanded by four commoners, the captains of Penrith. The host itself was divided up into companies, each drawn from a different region and led by its own two petty captains. About the host was an extraneous religiosity, expressed in the allegorical pose of its captains, the ceremony of the captains' mass, the chaplains of Poverty and the crossbearer. But this did not mean that it was simply pursuing a religious cause or that it was simply a religious procession reliant upon God's grace. Essentially, it was an army of experienced warriors, mounted and well-armed in accordance with tenant right, seeking not only to reject heresy but to defend the military system of which they were a part, and from which their tenurial privileges stemmed, and upon which the order and security of the border depended.

---

117 Ibid., f. 48.
118 Ibid.
119 Ibid., f. 48b. For contents of proclamation, see ibid., f. 57b.

The assault on Carlisle

In a letter of 31st October the Earl of Cumberland suggested that the failure of the rebels to take Carlisle was due to his son and heir, Lord Clifford, whose presence in the town steeled its inhabitants to resist the rebels' overtures.[120] But the matter was not so simple. Lord Clifford had fled to Carlisle in late October when rebels had blocked his route to Berwick. On his father's admission he had entered the town in secret. Unknown to the townsmen, he appears to have taken up residence in the castle. Eventually he declared himself, offering to act as his father's deputy, but when?[121] In all probability, not until the 30th, the day that the host gathered at the Broadfield and appeared to be bent on attacking the town if the mayor failed to guarantee its support for the uprising. The threat from the Broadfield gathering shifted the other key figures of the border. The same day, a message came from Lord Dacre at Naworth proposing to Clifford a reciprocity of support if either was attacked; and Sir William Musgrave came from Bewcastle to the defence of the town with a company of troops.[122]

By this time, however, the citizens had already held out for several days. Sustaining them in their resistance before 30th October was probably the same factor that had persuaded the rebels of the urgent need to take Carlisle: the knowledge not only that Lord Dacre and his tenants in Gilsland and Burgh remained unsworn but also that the keeper of the royal lordship and castle of Bewcastle, and the warrior clans inhabiting it, remained free of the oath. Whilst the violent inhabitants of these territories retained their loyalty to the government, the prospect of counteraction remained very real; so much so that swearing the oath could be seen as the best means not of safeguarding goods and chattels but of losing them. Furthermore, the uprising did not terminate on 30th October as a result of Lord Clifford's self-declaration. The rebels made a further attempt to take Carlisle on 3rd November, having concluded, after considering the matter in the meantime, that they had been duped into dispersing. Again, they mustered on the Broadfield, the force, according to Townley, recruited "from the commons of most parts of the country", but

120 *L.P.* XI. 927.
121 Ibid.
122 For Dacre, see SP1/112, f. 263 (*L.P.* XI. 1331). For Musgrave, see *L.P.* XI. 993.

without the force from the Honour of Cockermouth.[123] Having lost patience with the mayor, their intent was to besiege the town.

This plan was scuttled not by Lord Clifford but by Lord Dacre's uncle and right-hand man, the influential Sir Christopher Dacre, who came to the rebels under safe conduct – that is, unsworn – persuaded the rebels to call off the siege and, aided by Townley, Parson Threlkeld, Richard Bewley and Cuthbert Hutton, arranged a truce, the terms of which obliged the commons to disband and to end the embargo placed on Carlisle market. In return the mayor agreed to keep the gates of the town open and Lord Clifford agreed that the garrison troops should not "ride on the commons".[124] Also persuading the rebels to cease hostilities against Carlisle were two startling changes in the border situation, both occurring in the first week of November. The first came when Lord Dacre suddenly left the the region. Following his departure, his Honour of Burgh but not of Gilsland, joined the rebellion with five hundred of its inhabitants taking the oath.[125] The second change resulted from the sudden decision of Sir William Musgrave to follow his father's example and to become sworn. He presented this submission as a ruse for allowing him to travel unimpeded to Skipton. But it may have resulted from pressures brought upon him by the rebels of the barony of Westmorland who had approached him over the matter and perhaps had obliged him to take the oath after capturing him as he travelled through the barony to join the Earl of Cumberland.[126]

Enlisting the orders

The clerics

Although a revolt that professed itself to be, and was perceived as, a movement of the commons led by commoners, the Cumberland uprising contained a substantial following of gentlemen and clerics. How did they become involved? How important were they to the uprising? At least twelve members of the clergy took part.[127] The

---

123 The meeting place on 3rd November had been announced in the usual way at the previous meeting of 30th October. See SP1/117, f. 48b. For the meeting of 3rd November, see ibid., f. 49.

124 Ibid., fos. 49–49b. For Sir Christopher Dacre, see Bindoff, II, p. 102.

125 SP1/112, f. 263 (*L.P.* XI. 1331).

126 *L.P.* XI. 993 and 1242.

127 I.e. Robert Thompson, vicar of Brough, Edward Penrith, George Corney, Barnard Townley, rector of Caldbeck, Roland Threlkeld, rector of Melmerby, Christopher Slee, vicar of Sowerby, Thomas Carter, Abbot of Holm, George Bewley, vicar of Dalston, William Robin, Christopher Blenkow, vicar of Edenhall, William Florens, canon of Carlisle, Richard Huttwythe, canon of Carlisle.

majority were seculars, at least six holding benefices. Of the four known regulars, all were drawn from the largish houses of Holm Cultram and Carlisle Priory and included the abbot of the former and the ex-prior of the latter.[128] None was from a religious house dissolved or threatened with dissolution.[129]

Besides being sworn, most of these clerics were appointed to specific functions, usually of an administrative or ceremonial nature: thus Sir George Corney acted as scribe; Sir Edward Penrith served as crossbearer; Townley, Thompson, Slee, Threlkeld and Bewley acted as chaplains of Poverty, with the duty of instructing, and ministering to, the commons; the Abbot of Holm Cultram, Threlkeld and Towneley served as commissioners to treat with the city of Carlisle and two canons of Carlisle, Sir William Florens and Sir Richard Hutwith, and Sir William Robin acted as their messengers.[130] Since the clergy were appreciated as a vital part of the uprising, the commons were incensed by any sign of clerical deceit.[131] Yet only one cleric for certain, and possibly one other, played any part in directing the uprising. In his capacity as the captains' secretary and Chaplain of Poverty and because of his reputation as a prophet, and on account of his presence as swearer and proclamation-instructor at all the assemblies held between 20th and 30th October, Robert Thompson had a central part to play.[132]

Acting in conjunction with the four captains, Thompson undoubtedly had a hand in the making of policy. Although professing that his participation was enforced, he had no difficulty in leaving the uprising at the crucial Broadfield meeting of 30th October; and Barnard Townley provided detailed evidence of his key role in the unfolding of revolt in the previous ten days.[133] As for Barnard Townley, he was the other cleric with a likely leadership role. In his own deposition he was keen to declare that "I have come among the commons but against my will" and to present all his actions as designed to "put them to silence and quiet".[134] However, he showed no signs of flight and provided only

---

128 Carter, Slee, Forens, Huttswythe. Slee was an ex-prior.
129 See above, p. 334.
130 For the scribe, see SP1/117, f. 55; for the crossbearer, see ibid.; for the chaplains of Poverty, see ibid., f. 56; for the commissioners, see ibid., f. 57; for the messengers, see ibid., f. 48.
131 Thompson and Townley's remarks (SP1/117, fos. 47, 56 and 57b).
132 According to his own account (SP1/117, fos. 55–58).
133 He was, according to his own account, ordered by Pulleyn with the threat of death to participate in the Cumberland uprising (ibid., f. 54). Also see ibid., f. 58; E36/119, f. 80b; SP1/117, fos. 47–50b.
134 Ibid., f. 49b.

one instance of resistance: that is, when required to take the oath "in the name of the whole commons", he allegedly declared that he had no need as he had already sworn along similar lines to the king. Yet, as he admitted, this led only to "divers deferments" and before the day was over he had submitted to the commons, receiving their oath from Robert Thompson.[135] Townley, as with Robert Thompson, was quickly involved. Once the captains of Penrith had concentrated upon recruiting the north-west of the county, Townley came in to their very first assembly although it was held at Cartlogan Thorns, a considerable distance from Caldbeck, and was designed to raise the forest of Inglewood and the barony of Greystoke, not the Honour of Cockermouth, of which his parish was a part.[136] In fact, two further assemblies had to be held, at Kylwatling How and Sandale, before the rest of the Honour of Cockermouth north of the Derwent was recruited.[137] Townley alleged that his involvement happened under compulsion from the commons who, in response to instructions from the commons of Penrith, assembled, "brought unto them" Townley and the two gentlemen, Richard Bewley and Richard Vachall, and took them to meet the Penrith commons at Cartlogan Thorns. There may be some truth in this. Yet once recruited, Townley became an important rebel, present at all the assemblies, acting as a chaplain of Poverty (allegedly under compulsion), and eventually as commissioner to Carlisle (allegedly to restore peace).[138] Moreover, once Thompson left the rebellion, Townley's role became even more important since he took over his function of swearing in the new recruits.[139]

Although he played no part in the general organisation of the revolt, another leading clerical participant was Thomas Carter, the Abbot of Holm Cultram. Evidence of his involvement is found not only in the accounts of Townley and Thompson but also in the depositions brought against him in May 1537. The former presented him as sworn to the commons at Moota Hill on 28th October and, following his appointment as a commissioner to Carlisle, they show him travelling, in the company of Townley, to the city with a message from the commons to the mayor and of being refused entry.[140] Whereas this evidence provides no proof that he took voluntarily a

135 Ibid., f. 47.
136 Ibid. Also see above, pp. 347–8.
137 See above, pp. 348–50.
138 For his impressment, see SP1/117, f. 47. For his rebel activities, see SP1/117, fos. 56–58; ibid., fos. 47–49b.
139 Ibid., fos. 57b–58.
140 Ibid., f. 57; ibid., f. 57b; ibid., f. 48.

positive part in the uprising, the depositions propose that his participation owed much to his own initiative.[141] The problem with the
evidence drawn from the depositions is that, for October 1536, it is
heavily reliant on the testimony of Thomas Graym which was prejudiced by the fact that in August 1536 he and Carter had been rivals
for the office of abbot following the death of Abbot Ireby. Backing
Carter had been the monks of Holm; backing Graym had been Sir
Thomas Wharton. In spite of Graym's offer of 400 marks over and
above first fruits for the office, Carter was appointed. Graym clearly
had a strong incentive to damage Carter.[142] But the evidence he
brought against him was not totally fabricated. In fact, his account
of Carter's involvement in the insurrection of February 1537 is
corroborated by the depositions of the abbey officials, James Perkyng
and Cuthbert Musgrave and of the abbey tenant, John Austan.[143]
Moreover, Graym's account of Carter as commissioner to Carlisle
tallies with the account provided by Thompson/Townley.[144]

The basic point made by Graym was that "all the stirrings of the
tenants within the Holm lordship was ever by the commandment of the
abbot both at the first insurrection and also at the last".[145] He gave two
instances: thus, the tenantry were instructed by the abbot to meet the
Cumberland commons at Castle Sowerby on 25th October; likewise,
he instructed them to attend another muster at the Broadfield on 16th
February 1537.[146] Neither instruction had much effect. The lordship
of Holm only became involved in the October uprising on the 28th of
the month; whilst in February 1537 the tenantry, led by officer
Musgrave, simply refused to accept the abbot's instruction and said
that they would be prepared to participate only if he accompanied
them: in other words, they were not prepared to take part unless the
abbot made explicit his commitment to the cause.[147] On the other
hand, his instructions to the tenantry suggested that the abbot was an
active proponent of revolt. As well as revealing Carter's attempts to
raise his tenantry long before the rebellion had become a close physical
threat, Graym's deposition also showed him riding all the way to
Penrith in late November to give the delegates, chosen to represent

141 L.P. XII{1}. 1259 {3}.
142 V.C.H. Cumberland, II, pp. 170–71.
143 L.P. XII{1}. 1259 {4}.
144 L.P. XII{1}. 1259 {3}.
145 B.L. Cottonian MS Calig. B. III, f. 287b (L.P. XII{1}. 1259 {3}).
146 L.P. XII{1}. 1259 {3}.
147 Cottonian MS Calig. B. III, f. 287b (L.P. XII{1}. 1259 {3}) and Calig. B. III, fos.
      288–288b (L.P. XII{1}. 1259 {4}).

the county at Doncaster, forty shillings to cover their expenses.[148] The abbot's active involvement in the uprising may have had something to do with the abbey's embroilment in the feud between Dacre and Clifford. This was essentially caused by the government which at first transferred the stewardship of the abbey lands from Dacre to Clifford, then granted it back to Dacre and then restored it to Clifford. All this happened between August 1534 and July 1536. It led to a fray in December 1534 in which, soon after Dacre had been awarded repossession, a force of his men, drawn from the adjacent barony of Burgh and aided by abbey servants, physically expelled Clifford's acting steward, the gentleman Thomas Dalston, from his office. Moreover, in the election of a new abbot that occurred in 1536, the Clifford interest failed to back Carter's candidacy.[149] All this may have encouraged Carter's positive support for the uprising. However, at the same time Carter was clearly moved by other concerns, especially the fear that if the rebellion failed "this abbey is lost".[150]

Monastic support for the Cumberland uprising came from not simply the abbey of Holm but also the priory of Carlisle, whose ex-prior, Christopher Slee, was made a chaplain of Poverty on 25th October. He had been deposed from the office of prior in the previous year and replaced by Lancelot Salkeld.[151] Also involved in the October uprising were two canons of the priory, Sir William Florens and Sir Richard Huttwythe, both of them sworn on 30th October and used that day as messengers by the rebel commissioners in their dealings with the mayor of Carlisle.[152] Sir William Florens had been a contender for the office vacated by Slee and was recommended as a worthy candidate to Cromwell, having proved his worth both in providing the monastic visitors with information on the priory and in his willingness to pay one hundred marks for the office, although, on the debit side, he had been declared incontinent by the visitors, but so had Slee; and Salkeld, along with six others in the house, was a sodomite.[153] Yet to explain their involvement simply in terms of career disappointment would overlook the priory's stolid adherence to the old ways: particularly the veneration of saints, especially St. Thomas Becket whose sword was one of their relics, and the recognition of papal overlord-

---

148 Calig. B. III, f. 287 (*L.P.* XII{1}. 1259 {3/i}).
149 Dickens, *Clifford Letters*, no. 4 (pp. 61–2); *L.P.* VIII. 310; *L.P.* VIII. 1041. For the fray, see SP1/48, fos. 238b–239 (*L.P.* VIII. 310) and *L.P.* VII. 1588–9.
150 *L.P.* XII{1}. 1259 {3/i}.
151 *V.C.H. Cumberland*, II, pp. 148–9.
152 SP1/117, f. 58; ibid. f. 48.
153 *V.C.H. Cumberland*, II, p. 149 and SP1/102, f. 99b (*L.P.* X. 364).

ship. This came to light in May 1540 when it was discovered that the
canons still had in daily use a book of legends in which a service
dedicated to Thomas Becket had yet to be removed and in which
references to the pope remained unerased. Moreover, Sir William
Florens became involved in an attempt to safeguard the book from
correction; for when another canon sought to remove the service to
Becket, Florens took the book from him and gave instructions to the
clerk of the choir to hide it away. And when news of the criminous
book was leaked and the justices of the peace set up a commission to
look into the matter, Florens left the priory, went to Sir Christopher
Dacre for advice and funds, then on to the parson of Melmerby for a
letter of favour to Dr. Bellisis, and then on to London.[154] Florens'
flight suggested his complicity and guilt. Another member of the
house, the steward Sir John Austane nonchalantly commented when
he learned that the book was in the commissioner's hands: "Tush, it is
but for a book. It will be dispatched well enough for money". Lancelot
Salkeld, once prior and now guardian of the house, was less sure and
sought to persuade the commissioners to place the book in his hands,
but this was not allowed and, uncorrected and incriminating, it was
sent to the king.[155] Whilst the clergy had a variety of motives for
participating in the uprising, one was fidelity to the old religion.

Finally, among the clerical participants of importance, there was
Roland Threlkeld, referred to as the parson of Melmerby, but an
outstanding figure in the region by virtue of the clerical offices he
held: as well as rector of Melmerby he was vicar of Lazonby, rector of
Dufton in Westmorland and, possibly by this time, master of the
college of Kirkoswald.[156] His local importance also stemmed from
his Dacre connexions. Although a cleric, he was Lord Dacre's general
receiver, responsible for administering his landed revenues.[157]
Upholding his local standing was his considerable wealth some of
which he put to public use: he funded the reconstruction of the choir
in the church of Kirkoswald when, under Dacre patronage in 1523, it
was converted into a college with twelve secular priests; and he built a
bridge across the Eden to connect his two benefices of Melmerby and
Lazonby.[158] His all-male household and retinue of twelve to sixteen
men gave him a powerful physical presence.[159] His standing in the

154 Ibid.; *L.P.* XV. 619 and 633 and *V.C.H. Cumberland*, II, pp. 149–50.
155 *L.P.* XV. 633; ibid. 619.
156 Jefferson, *History of Leath Ward*, p. 311.
157 *L.P.* VII. 281 and 676/i.
158 Jefferson, op. cit., pp. 278 and 307.
159 Ibid., p. 307.

region was recognised when on 25th October 1536 he was appointed, in his absence, a chaplain of Poverty.[160] A notable feature of the Cumberland uprising was his failure to participate before 30th October. This was in keeping with Dacre policy. It followed the course adopted by Lord William Dacre and Sir Christopher Dacre. All three remained close by but uninvolved, taking no part on either side until 30th October. On that day Lord Dacre committed himself to supporting Lord Clifford in the defence of Carlisle and Threlkeld finally joined the rebellion, attending the massive assembly at Burford Oak where he took the oath.[161] What game he was playing is not entirely clear, but, in all likelihood, his sudden commitment, like that of Lord Dacre, was caused by the fear that the rebels were about to take Carlisle. Immediately, he was placed in the commission of two clerics and four gentlemen deputed to negotiate with the mayor of Carlisle and played a part in heading off an assault of the town.[162]

No doubt the rebels appreciated this clerical support; and the anti-clerical sentiments uttered were aroused not by a basic hostility to clergymen but by the suspicion that they would betray the commons, if given the chance.[163] Since central to the uprising was a ritual of religious service, involving processions, prayers and masses, their participation became of vital importance, both to legitimise the revolt and to confer upon it the blessing of God's grace.[164]

The gentlemen

The number of gentlemen involved in the uprising was at least fourteen: something like one eighth of the county's gentry families.[165] In addition, mention was made of other gentlemen attending the various assemblies who were neither counted nor identified.[166] Among the

160 SP1/117, f. 56; ibid., f. 47.
161 For Threlkeld, see ibid., f. 58. For Dacre, see above, p. 354.
162 See above, p. 353.
163 For anti-clericalism, see above, pp. 349 and 352.
164 For processions and prayers, as ordered in the proclamation, see SP1/117, f. 55b. The importance attached to procession was evident in the appointment of a crossbearer. A procession also figured in the captains' mass (ibid., f. 56b). The Abbot of Holm also ordered processions to assist the 1537 uprising (see L.P. XII{1}. 1259 {3/i}). For masses, see SP1/117, f. 56b
165 The gentlemen involved in the uprising were Anthony Hutton, Edward Musgrave, Richard Bewley, Richard Vachall, John Lowther, Cuthbert Hutton, John Leigh of Isel, John Lamplugh, John Skelton, Thomas Dalston, Richard Blenkow, Lancelot Salkeld, John Swynburn the younger and William Musgrave. A full list of the gentlemen of Cumberland is provided for 1539/40 in L.P. XIV {1}. 653. It contains 113 names.
166 At Cartlogan Thorns (SP1/117, f. 55b); at Kylwatling How (ibid., f. 56) and at Burford Oak on 30th October (ibid., f. 48).

named participants were important county figures, notably the knights
Sir Edward Musgrave, Sir John Lamplugh, Sir John Lowther and
eventually Sir William Musgrave; and the esquires Cuthbert Hutton, John Skelton of Branthwaite, John Leigh of Isel, Thomas Dalston
and Lancelot Salkeld, son of the esquire Thomas Salkeld.[167] All were
sworn but none was obliged to serve as captains.[168] In fact, of the
fourteen identifiable gentlemen only one is known to have served as a
leader and then for no more than a very short time. Thus, Anthony
Hutton of Hutton Hall, a minor gentleman from the lordship of
Penrith, was made one of the four captains of the commons of Penrith
on 19th October. However, by 23rd October he had either withdrawn
from the office or had been dismissed, the commons having impressed
upon him, as he informed Robert Thompson, "that they would have
no gentlemen to be their captains".[169]

Yet the gentlemen were not merely bystanders, doing no more than
take the oath and attend the musters. They were called upon, for
example, to provide advice to the four captains. Thus, on 20th
October, they helped Hutton and the other captains to devise the
proclamation, the main declaration of the rebellion's aims and grievances;[170] and eight days later at Moota Hill the captains and the
gentlemen formed a council to work out a policy for taking Carlisle.[171]
They were also required to serve as commissioners in the commons'
negotiations with the city of Carlisle. Richard Blenkow and Thomas
Dalston were appointed to this role at the Moota Hill muster; and at
the Broadfield muster of 30th October Blenkow was appointed again,
along with Richard Bewley, Lancelot Salkeld and John Swynburn.[172]
As commissioners, the gentlemen played a vital part in staying the
commons. Thus, returning to the host on 30th October with a copy of
the proclamation declaring the Truce, the four gentlemanly members
of the commission persuaded the commons to go home; and, when the

167 Musgrave eventually took the oath. See above, p. 355.
168 It is possible that gentlemen served as the petty captains, who throughout were
     never named. However, this is unlikely in view of Anthony Hutton's remark on
     the same day that these petty captains were first appointed that the commons were
     opposed to having gentlemen as captains. See SP1/117, f. 56 and E36/119, f. 81.
169 SP1/117, f. 55; E36/119, f. 81.
170 SP1/117, f. 55. Who the gentlemen giving advice were is not made evident.
     Moreover, Thompson's account makes no mention of any gentlemen having
     joined at this point apart from Musgrave (who took the oath but did not
     attend) and Captain Hutton. Later John Leigh of Isel told how he and Sir John
     Lamplugh were "ordered at Penrith" [ibid., f. 129 (L.P. XII{1}. 904)]. Possibly
     these two were sworn at the start of the revolt and had a hand in the composition
     of the proclamation.
171 SP1/117, f. 57.
172 Ibid. and SP1/117, f. 48.

commons reassembled on 3rd November to besiege Carlisle, Richard
Bewley and Cuthbert Hutton, acting with Sir Christopher Dacre and
the two clerics, Townley and Threlkeld, succeeded again in avoiding
military conflict, persuading the commons to end the siege of Carlisle
and to await the king's response to the articles submitted by the
pilgrim high command.[173]

The general impression given by the two surviving narratives of
the uprising, the one by Townley, the other by Thompson, was that
the inhabitants of each region joined the uprising as a complete society.
Thus, according to Thompson, "all the parish of Edenhall" was sworn
on 20th October along with its lord, Sir Edward Musgrave and its
vicar, Christopher Blenkow.[174] At the Cartlogan Thorns' muster on
23rd October the gentlemen "dwelling thereabouts", as well as the
commons, were presented as in attendance and taking the oath; and
with Sir John Lowther arriving to raise troops to assist him on the
border as deputy warden, the assembly at Cartlogan Thorns took on
the appearance of a normal muster, to which the customary tenants by
virtue of tenant right and the freehold tenants by virtue of cornage
were summoned, for the defence of the border rather than for a rising
of the commons.[175] Likewise, at the Kylwatling How muster on 25th
October, Thompson described how Cuthbert Hutton and the gentlemen and commons "thereabouts" turned up and took the oath.[176]
Townley described the same assembly as one "where all the country
was gathered".[177] Finally, at the Broadfield on 30th October, Townley
described how the rebels were joined by the inhabitants of the Honour
of Cockermouth which "brought all the country with them, both
gentlemen and others of the whole commons".[178]

Whereas the uprising seemed to be supported by the whole range
of society and therefore assumed the character of a regional revolt, it
was also clear that, in opposition to the expectations of the society of
orders, the gentlemen were brought in by the commons and were
without a leadership role. This picture undoubtedly owed something
to Thompson's and Townley's need to provide a narrative which freed
themselves from blame for having taken part. After all, it was very
much in their interest, especially as both were seeking pardon, to
present the uprising as a popular force, surging upward from below

173 Ibid., f. 48b and 49.
174 Ibid., f. 55.
175 SP1/117, fos. 55b–56.
176 Ibid., f. 56.
177 Ibid., f. 47.
178 Ibid., f. 48.

to sweep everyone along in its track. Moreover, to emphasise examples of resistance, apart from their own, would infer that their submission had not been inevitable. Yet there was resistance from both gentry and clerics. Just as Parson Threlkeld ignored the threats to execute him and failed to take up his duties as a chaplain of Poverty until the 30th October, so a number of gentlemen ignored, at least for a time, the commons' call.[179] Lord Dacre, Sir Christopher Dacre, the incoming sheriff Sir Thomas Curwen, possibly the outgoing sheriff, Sir Thomas Wharton and Sir William Musgrave remained aloof.[180] Thomas Dalston took the oath at Moota Hill and was entrusted, as one of the commissioners, to negotiate with Carlisle, yet two days later he had fled, taking refuge in the town.[181]

As for those that joined the uprising and remained with it, what made them act? There is little evidence of enforcement. The siege of Middleton at Derwentwater is exceptional; and he held out. The other surviving example of a visit to a gentleman's house was the one to Sir Edward Musgrave in Edenhall on 20th October; but, as presented, this involved not the despatch of an armed company but merely messengers; and simply in response to the delivery of their message, Sir Edward and the rest of the parish complied.[182] On the other hand, but for a rising of the commons that, having been stirred by news of the uprising in Richmondshire and encouraged by the arrival in Penrith of the Westmorlanders on 19th October, then reached out eastwards, westwards and northwards in search of support, the gentlemen of Cumberland would have done nothing. Yet this does not mean that they were without grudge or grievance. In the circumstances, two ways were open to the gentlemen for obtaining revenge or remedy. One was to be swept along by the rebellious host; the other was to step aside, allowing a rising of the commons its head.

The Cumberland/Dacre feud

The Cumberland uprising was not an aristocratic revolt. The Dacres stood aside. Nor can it be said that the gentlemen of the region became involved because they were Dacre clients. Of those with Dacre connexions (Anthony Hutton, Cuthbert Hutton, Lancelot Salkeld, Sir Edward Musgrave, John Leigh, Parson Melmerby, the Abbot of

---

179 For Threlkeld's appointment as a chaplain on 25th October, see ibid., f. 56, and
       for his being sworn on 30th October, see ibid., f. 58.
180 See below.
181 SP1/117, f. 57. By 29th October he was in Carlisle (ibid., f. 48).
182 Ibid., f. 55. For Middleton, see above, pp. 338–9.

Holm), none participated out of support for the Dacre cause.[183] In joining the revolt they were going against Dacre policy which was to stand aside from the fray. For this reason it would be misleading even to term the revolt an aristocratic conspiracy. Nonetheless, aristocratic discontent undoubtedly permitted its development, much of it stemming from the events of 1534 when the government sought to bring the Dacre family down, but succeeded only in dismissing it from office, not in destroying its power base in the West March.[184] Although neither a Dacre revolt nor a Dacre conspiracy, the Cumberland uprising certainly benefited from the deliberate inactivity of the aggrieved Dacre interest, especially because, at the time, the government's representative in the region, the Earl of Cumberland, was pinned down in Skipton Castle by the Richmondshire host and therefore could do little to restore order in the West March.

In accounting for the revolts in the north-west, the government emphasised the disruptiveness of aristocratic feuds. In January 1537 Henry VIII explained to the Earl of Cumberland the relationship that existed between the society of orders and the body politic, pointing out that just as the king was head of the realm, "our nobles, officers and ministers", in representing the king, were "head and governor of the multitude every in his quarter and country". He then went on to say that, bearing in mind the "division, hatred and enmity between you and others being of our nobility and worship as the lord Dacre, the Parrs and the Musgraves", the king had to conclude "that if you would have conformed yourselves to an honest unity and agreement being there, in the lieu of heads for the direction of that part of our said politic body, the same could not have grown to that trouble and discord it is now in". The proposed solution was that Cumberland should patch up his differences with Dacre and "to cause all your friends, tenants and servants to do the semblable".[185] Earlier on 30th November, and moved by a letter from Sir William Musgrave which provided information at first hand on the situation in Cumberland, the Duke of Suffolk made a similar point, arguing that, because Dacre and

---

183 Anthony Hutton's mother was a bastard Dacre. See Nicolson and Burn, op. cit., II, pp. 401–2. Cuthbert Hutton was a Greystoke vassal, but was made sheriff in the year of Dacre's downfall. See ibid., p. 366; Bindoff, II, pp. 429–30. Lancelot Salkeld's family had a history of Dacre connexion (see James, op. cit., p. 142); likewise, Sir Edward Musgrave (see ibid., p. 100) and John Leigh (see ibid., p. 142 and Harrison, op. cit., p. 62). Roland Threlkeld was receiver-general to Lord Dacre (James, op. cit., p. 142). The Abbot of Holm may also have had a Dacre allegiance. See above, p. 359.

184 Harrison, op. cit., pp. 36–8 and 41–2.

185 Chatsworth Trustees, Clifford Letter Book, fos. 5b–6.

Cumberland were unable to pool their resources in one counter-insurgency effort, the commons were out of control not only in Cumberland and the barony of Westmorland but also in the barony of Kendal, Sedbergh and Lonsdale.[186] This explanation, however, was but another version of the truth. As with the importance the government was inclined to attach to agrarian grievances in causing the uprising, its emphasis upon the feud was moved by an attempt to free itself of blame. Besides their feuding, there were other reasons why the great lords of the far north-west failed to deal with the rebellious commons, the chief of which was the government's own alienation of the house of Dacre.

The House of Lords, exercising the privilege of trial by peerage, acquitted Dacre of the charge of treason. However, denied the opportunity to confiscate his estates, the government proceeded to deprive him of the wardenship of the West March and the considerable perquisites accompanying this office: notably the stewardship of the Queen's Hames (i.e. the Crown lands in the Honour of Penrith, and its attendant manors of Carleton, Langwathby, Penrith, Great Salkeld and Scotby); the stewardship of further Crown lands in the lordships of Castle Sowerby, Gamblesby and Plumpton; the stewardships of church lands, notably the Cumberland estates of the bishopric of Carlisle, the priory of Carlisle, the abbey of Holm, the priory of Wetheral and the abbey of York St Mary; the stewardship of the city of Carlisle with the captaincy of its castle; and the right to receive the tithes of Penrith, Langwathby, Rickerby, Crosby, Orton, Stainton and Kirkland. To add insult to injury, the wardenship and its perquisites were handed to Dacre's arch-enemy, the Earl of Cumberland, who had served on the commission which had brought Dacre down.[187] Not surprisingly, the Dacre interest was thereafter bent on revenge. Its members sought to get their own back by maintaining men indicted by the Cliffords for March Treason; by seizing the tithe corn which the Crown had transferred from Dacre to Clifford hands; by attacking Clifford officers; by reclaiming sheep and cattle allegedly confiscated by the Cliffords; by showing contempt for the warden's authority as, for example, when at a meeting of the Scottish and English wardens, each with a retinue of borderers, the Dacre affinity chose their moment, all three hundred of them suddenly leaving without the warden's permission.[188] To settle the discord, Cromwell, with the

186 *L.P.* XI. 1207.
187 *L.P.* VII. 1018, 1217, 1549 (misdated).
188 See *L.P.* VII. 1588–9, *L.P.* VIII. 310 and 1030 {2}.

consent of both parties, made an award in July 1535.[189] But this only incited further fury. Throughout 1536 the Earl of Cumberland was charged by the Dacres with dishonouring its terms.[190] Since they retained a considerable estate and following in Cumberland, the Dacres were strongly placed, as well as highly motivated, to create maximum inconvenience for the Cliffords in the running of the West March.[191] It was in their interest to avoid being blamed for the uprising of October 1536 but not to crush a movement which usefully demonstrated the insufficiency of the Cliffords as rulers of the West March and offered, by implication, criticism of the government for its treatment of Lord Dacre and his uncle, Sir Christopher Dacre.

In this anarchic situation the uprising of October 1536 flourished. The vital part played by the Dacres was not to direct the revolt but to permit its development, in spite of having the military resources (as was revealed in February 1537) to bring it to an abrupt end.[192] In October 1536 William Lord Dacre and Sir Christopher Dacre remained unsworn. They also remained out of the way, presumably at Naworth Castle, until the rebels addressed themselves to the task of taking Carlisle. Then they took action, with Lord Dacre stiffening the resistance of the town by offering troops for its defence, and with Christopher Dacre appearing, under safe-conduct, at the Broadfield to persuade the commons that it was best to disband.[193]

The only evidence of direct participation by the family occurred in November and December, and none of it involved Lord William or Sir Christopher. On 15th November a Richard Dacre appeared at a muster in Caldbeck, took the oath and proposed to serve as "grand captain of all Cumberland". With him were three Dacre clients, Christopher Lee, William Porter and Alex Appleby, all gentlemen and prepared to serve as Richard Dacre's petty captains. Then, on 9th December the same Richard Dacre came to Carlisle with a company of Lord Dacre's tenants and, in the course of that day, insulted Lord Clifford by giving him a haughty look and by failing to doff his bonnet when they met outside the church. Shortly after-

189 *L.P.* VII. 1549 {2}. This is misdated by *L.P.* as 1534 instead of 1535. For its true dating, see *L.P.* VIII. 1041/ ii.
190 Dickens, *Clifford Letters*, no. 28; *L.P.* XI. 477.
191 See S. G. Ellis, "A border baron and the Tudor state: the rise and fall of Lord Dacre of the North", *Historical Journal*, 35 (1992), pp. 259–61. For their relative power, see *L.P.* VII. 829 and *L.P.* XII{2}. 203.
192 See *L.P.* XII{1}. 479.
193 See above, pp. 354–5.

wards, he drew a dagger on Sir William Musgrave as he left the church and then sought to raise revolt, in the aristocratic way, by shouting in the market place "a Dacre, a Dacre". This caused "a great company of Lord Dacre's tenants to assemble" and obliged Lord Clifford and the rest of his retinue to take refuge in the castle. Finally, on 17th December Richard Dacre came to Carlisle with twenty men from Gilsland, all of them Lord Dacre's tenants, but was stopped by the sight of the company attendant upon Lord Clifford.[194] However, these disturbances appeared to be the actions of a maverick Dacre acting in the manner expected of the Dacres prior to the uprising but out of keeping with the policy followed by the family during it. None succeeded as a summons to arms; and all three failed to revive revolt in the county. Furthermore, Lord Clifford admitted that, as far as he knew, the affair on 9th December was not "prepensed" by Lord William or Sir Christopher and none of the evidence incriminated either of them. What is more, the surviving evidence for all three incidents was of Clifford provenance and, whilst not necessarily untrue, is suspect.[195]

As for the Dacre tenantry, they submitted quickly in the more accessible barony of Greystoke but held out in the frontier baronies of Burgh and Gilsland, where they were undoubtedly directed by the example and near presence of William and Christopher Dacre. This became evident in the first week of November when Lord William left the region and the barony of Burgh immediately went the way of Greystoke, with five hundred of its menfolk taking the oath.[196] That Burgh should submit whilst Gilsland held out suggests that its submission came not of Dacre contrivance but tenant initiative.

If Dacre was well placed, but poorly motivated, to crush the host of the four captains, the Earl of Cumberland was well motivated but poorly placed. Essentially, the uprising was yet another anti-Clifford protest, resembling the objection made by the Kendalers to his intrusions as sheriff of Westmorland and the reaction in the West Riding lordships of Kirkby Malzeard and Winterburn against his appoint-

---

194 SP1/112, fos. 263b–264 (*L.P.* XI. 1331). How closely related he was to Lord Dacre is unknown. He appeared to be a military freebooter. Earlier in the year he had been imprisoned in irons in Dublin. See *L.P.* X. 30 and *L.P.* XI. 1249.
195 The evidence rests upon a letter from Lord Clifford to the Earl of Cumberland of 9th December 1536 (misdated 1531). See Cottonian MS Calig. B. VIII, fos. 148ff (*L.P.* V. 573). It also rests upon a document compiled after 17th December 1536 entitled "articles to be remembered concerning the demeanour of the Dacres in Cumberland since the beginning of the insurrection of the commons" [see SP1/112 fos. 263ff (*L.P.* XI. 1331)].
196 SP1/112, f. 263 (*L.P.* XI. 1331).

ment as their steward.[197] As in the barony of Westmorland, the
uprising in Cumberland first developed in the parts of the county
held by the Cliffords. Penrith, Great Salkeld, Langwathby, Castle
Sowerby and Plumpton were all under Clifford control, not by right
of proprietorship but thanks to the stewardships recently granted to
the earl by the Crown.[198] Some of the hostility to the family may have
stemmed from the fear that, as steward of extensive Crown and church
properties, Cumberland would promote a raising of rents and dues and
offend the system of tenant right; but at the heart of the rebels' cause
was the earl's position as the Crown's representative in the region and
his key role as the warden of the West March. The proclamation issued
by the rebels on 20th October defined the grievances of the country as
not only the changes in religion but also the incapacity of its rulers to
defend it "from robbing of the thieves and Scots".[199] One target of
this criticism was the Earl of Cumberland whose task was made
insuperable, as it had been a decade earlier when for two years he
had also held the same office, partly because he was an alien without
much land or connexion of his own in Cumberland, and partly because
in taking on the office he had displaced the reigning magnate family,
the Dacres of Greystoke, Burgh and Gilsland.[200]

In the circumstances, the Earl of Cumberland needed to make
himself felt with a forceful presence. But at the time problems faced
him from other quarters. Hearing of unrest on the borders in early
October, and under instructions from the Crown, he had planned to go
to Hexham and Carlisle, essentially to crush the opposition shown to
the commissioners charged with the suppression of Lanercost and
Hexham Priories.[201] But other events got in his way, notably the
uprisings that broke out first in upper Wensleydale and Dent, then
in Kirkby Malzeard, Masham and Richmond, then in Percy Fee and

197 See above, pp. 258–9 (barony of Kendal); pp. 154–6 (Kirkby Malzeard); and for
   Winterburn in Craven, see Dickens, *Clifford Letters*, no. 43 and *Star Ch.
   Yorkshire*, IV, pp. 52 and 136–8.
198 See above, n. 187.
199 SP1/117, fos. 55–55b.
200 See M. L. Bush, "The problem of the far north: a study of the crisis of 1537 and
   its consequences", *Northern History*, 6 (1971), p. 43; Harrison, op. cit., pp. 35–8.
   Quite posssibly, the complaint against the failings of the rulers of the region was
   also pointed at Dacre who, after his disgrace in 1534, had lived well away from the
   West March, either in London or at Hinderskelfe in the North Riding. See above,
   n. 34.
201 The government directed the Earl of Cumberland to Hexham on 5th October
   (Chatsworth, Clifford Letter Book, f. 8). On 9th October it seems that, in
   response to news of misdemeanours in Gilsland (ibid., f. 3b), he had plans to
   go to Carlisle. See *L.P.* XI. 742 (misdated as 16th October).

finally in his own barony of Westmorland. And ruling out completely
any chance of counteraction was the siege of Skipton Castle by the
Richmondshire host. In his stead his son Lord Clifford reached
Carlisle in late October but circuitously and secretly and presumably
with little military support. Creeping into Carlisle Castle, he remained
there in secret probably until the rebels confronted the town on 30th
October.[202] In the Clifford absence, the responsibility for taking action
fell upon the Clifford clients in the region – Sir Thomas Clifford, the
earl's bastard son and captain of Carlisle Castle, Aglionby, Curwen,
Wharton, Lowther, Sir William Musgrave and Dalston of Dalston.
But individually they were impotent and collectively they were rent by
feuds between themselves as well as with the Dacres.

Wharton had established himself in the country through his
connexion with both the Percies and the Cliffords. As steward, he
exercised the authority of the Percies in the Honour of Cockermouth.
As sheriff and as one of the lord warden's deputies, he exercised the
authority of the Crown.[203] But within the Honour of Cockermouth
there was considerable hostility towards him because of his improving
estate management, his attitude towards tithes and his general asser-
tiveness; and it seems as if he was a source not only of peasant
disaffection, of the sort that erupted in January 1537, but also of
gentry discontent, evident, for example, in the antipathy shown
towards him by two of the participants in the October uprising,
John Leigh and Sir John Lamplugh.[204] Elsewhere in the county he
was handicapped by feuds between him and both the Musgraves and
the Dacres. In October 1536 a bill circulated in Cumberland ordering
Wharton's death on account of "old displeasures" between him and
Lord Dacre. He had been another accomplice in the downfall of the
Dacres.[205] Moreover, in 1537 Norfolk commented on Wharton that
"the Musgraves love him not".[206] Intensifying the latter's enmity
towards him was the recent murder of one of Sir Edward Musgrave's
servants by the servants and tenants of Sir Thomas Wharton in a

202 As revealed by his father on 31st October (*L.P.* XI. 927).
203 Bindoff, III, p. 597; P.R.O. SC11/959; *L.P.* XI. 666.
204 For Wharton's harsh landlordship, see Southwell's comments [SP1/124, f. 67b
    (*L.P.* XII{2}. 548)]. For tenant hostility towards him in early 1537, see *L.P.*
    XII{1}. 18. For gentry hostility towards him, see *L.P.* XII{1}. 904. Lamplugh
    had been replaced by Wharton as lieutenant of the Honour of Cockermouth
    (James, op. cit., p. 100, n. 40), and probably for this reason bore him a grudge.
    That Lamplugh was aggrieved by the mid-1530s on the grounds that the office
    had been granted to him for life, see C1/866/40–41.
205 *L.P.* XI. 1046 {3}.
206 *St.P.*, V, p. 97 (*L.P.* XII{2}. 422).

quarrel over rights to the hunting of deer.[207] Furthermore, Wharton's position had been compromised by the rumour that he had taken the rebels' oath.[208] Rather than seeking to make a stand, he went into hiding and then appeared to be taken by the rebels of the barony of Westmorland.[209]

The other key figure of the region, and another stalwart of the Clifford clientage, was Sir William Musgrave. His strength in the county lay in his family's possessions at Edenhall and its longstanding connexion with the royal manor of Bewcastle, situated on the border in Eskdale Ward.[210] Throughout late October 1536 he was resident in Bewcastle, although normally a man of the Court. Called upon by the rebels to take the oath, he held out and was backed in his stand by those of the Graeme surname.[211] In fact, supported by the mosstroopers of Eskdale who, it seems, in October were prepared to harry "all Cumberland and Westmorland" if authorised to do so, Musgrave had the means to defeat the rebels, as was made evident in February, 1537.[212] But weakening his position were differences with his own family, especially his mother and father. These derived from his part in the downfall of the Dacres – he had provided the vital evidence upon which the charge of treason had rested – and also from his unwillingness to participate in the family's vendetta against Wharton.[213] In addition, there was no prospect of his working in collaboration with Lord Dacre, his neighbour in Eskdale Ward. Like Dacre he remained throughout much of October in his border castle unsworn but failing to direct his manred of warriors drawn from the clan society of the border highlands against the uprising; that is, until 30th October when, in response to the news that Lord Clifford was in Carlisle Castle and the commons were without Carlisle's walls, Musgrave came to the town with a company of men; but with the dispersal of the commons he was not needed.[214] Shortly afterwards, as

---

207 St.P. V, p. 28 (L.P. VIII. 1030 {2}) and L.P. VIII. 1046.
208 L.P. XII{1}. 904.
209 Wharton was in Carlisle on 11th October (L.P. XI. 666), preparing for a Day of March, for which Lowther also seemed to be preparing on 23rd October (see SP1/117, f. 56). Then it seems that he was at Wharton Hall on 17th October, but left smartly to avoid the rebels, leaving his son behind. According to Thompson he appeared in Appleby at the end of the month, suggesting that, as with Lowther, he had submitted and had taken the oath. See above, p. 323.
210 Bindoff, II, pp. 646–7. For a recent account, see Ellis, "A border baron and the Tudor state", pp. 273–5.
211 L.P. XI. 993.
212 Ibid. For 1537, see L.P. XII{1}. 1217.
213 L.P. VII. 829 and 1647.
214 See above, p. 354.

he sought to escape the region and report to the Earl of Cumberland in Skipton Castle, he was taken and sworn.[215] But this did not prevent him from returning to Carlisle and assisting Lord Clifford from holding the town and castle for the remainder of the year.[216]

Of the other Clifford clients, Dalston and Lowther were taken and sworn in October but then distanced themselves from the commons by taking refuge in Carlisle.[217] As for Thomas Curwen, client of Cumberland, ally of Wharton and opponent of John Leigh of Isel, he managed to remain unsworn and present in the region but "with no gentlemen about him to trust to", tucked away from the scenes of action in his manor of Workington.[218] Finally there was Edward Aglionby, a cousin of Sir William Musgrave, an opponent of Dacre, an ally of Wharton, who in 1537 was described as someone "whom the commons here dread most of all [in] this country".[219] Like Curwen, he remained unsworn and inactive. In late October he was lodged in Carlisle, incapable of organising any counteraction and reliant upon the capacity of the town to hold out. The passivity of these key figures affected the rest of the gentry, leaving them leaderless and therefore without much option but to submit to the commons. As John Leigh put it in his own defence, the king's officers – by whom he meant Wharton, Curwen, Lowther and the Cliffords – "had full policy to have commanded us in the king's name to have given attendance for the subduing of the king's enemies which commandment they gave none". Thus, he and his tenants, according to his account of what happened in October 1536, waited to be commanded by the warden or the justices of the peace or the sheriff, but they waited in vain.[220]

The Cumberland uprising, then, whilst similar to the other Cumbrian revolts, was characterised by certain distinctive features. In its four allegorical captains, its fondness for processions, its captain's mass, it possessed an organisation which was more religious in appearance than elsewhere. Moreover, as articulated, its grievances were

---

215 SP1/112, f. 133 (*L.P.* XI. 1242). The purpose was to report on the state of affairs in the West March, an aim in which he succeeded; and, as a result, through Musgrave's servant, the government learned of what had happened on the borders. See B.L. Harleian MSS, 6989, f. 60 (*L.P.* XI. 1228).

216 *L.P.* XI. 1228.

217 For Lowther, see above, p. 348. Dalston was sworn on 28th October (SP1/117, f. 57) and made a rebel delegate to Carlisle. But a day later he appeared to have made his escape and to have taken refuge in Carlisle (SP1/117, f. 48). For his connexion with the Cliffords, see Bindoff, I, pp. 7–8.

218 Curwen remained at Workington until January when he fled to Yorkshire. See SP1/114, f. 259b (*L.P.* XII{1}. 185). Also see Bindoff, I, p. 742.

219 Bindoff, I, pp. 296–7; *L.P.* XII{1}. 18.

220 SP1/118, fos. 129–129b (*L.P.* XII{1}. 904).

unusual in failing to specify the issue of government exploitation, objecting neither to the robbery of the church nor fiscal reform. Unusually, but not surprisingly, the threat to the commonwealth was conceived as a border problem, essentially created by the inability of the Crown's officers to prevent disorder and robbery and by the inadequacy of the system of tenant right to provide the lord warden with a proper force for defending the border against the Scots and for controlling the lawless society that inhabited the frontier uplands. Finally, the uprising was different from most of the October uprisings in being dissociated from the issue of Dissolution in spite of having a relatively large number of lesser monasteries dissolved or under the threat of Dissolution, two of the suppressions (of Calder and Armathwaite) passing unopposed and the two instances of monastic resistance (the one to restore Seton, the other to prevent the suppression of Lanercost) failing to implicate the uprising itself. Otherwise, it was a rising of the commons which raised a very large army. This force included an impressive display of gentlemen and clerics, the latter having a directing role but not at the expense of a lay leadership vested in the upper peasantry and embodied in the four captains of Penrith.

X

■■■►

THE CONVOCATION
OF THE HOSTS

The Doncaster confrontation

Having taken Pontefract Castle on 20th October, Aske proceeded to convoke the outlying hosts, alleging in his summons that a great force under the Earl of Shrewsbury was approaching fast and urging them to speed to the pilgrims' relief.[1] The response was swift. The Percy host, a force of 5,000 recruited from the Yorkshire wapentakes of Pickering Lythe, Dickering and Buckrose, joined him at Pontefract on 21st October; and the next morning two other armies arrived: the Stapulton host, its 2–3,000 troops recruited from the East Riding wapentakes of Holderness and Harthill, by nine o'clock; the Bowes host, variously reckoned at 4,000, 5,000 and 10,000 men, and recruited from the palatinate of Durham and the deanery of Cleveland, followed two hours later.[2] In addition, there was the host raised by Aske and his agents for the siege of Pontefract Castle, now enlarged by extensive recruitment in the southerly parts of the West Riding.[3]

The convened army was a massive gathering, variously estimated

---

1 E.g. for the Stapulton host, see Stapulton, p. 99. Aske's letters to the Bowes and Percy hosts were presumably similar.

2 For the arrival of the hosts, see Stapulton, pp. 99-100; Bateson, p. 336; P.R.O. SP1/115, fos. 259b-260 (L.P. XII{1}. 393 {2}). For the size of the Percy host, see Bateson, p. 336. The Stapulton host was put at 2–3,000 by Aske (Bateson, p. 336) and 3,000 by Thomas Percy [SP1/115, f. 260 (L.P. XII{1}. 393 {2})]. The Bowes host was reckoned at 10,000 by Aske (Bateson, p. 336), at 3–4,000 by Thomas Percy (SP1/115, f. 259b) and at 5,000 by Stapulton (Stapulton, p. 100).

3 See above, pp. 94ff.

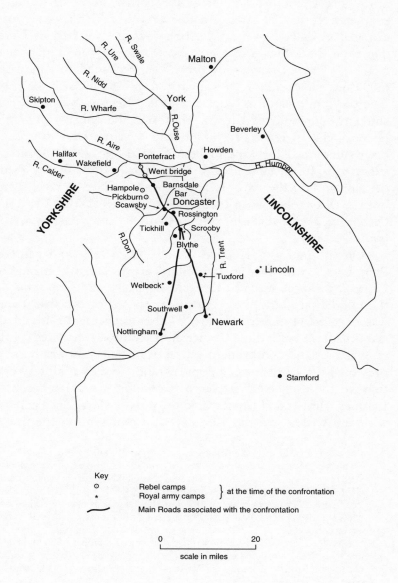

Map 11 The confrontation at Doncaster

at 28–35,000 men.[4] Yet it was not the full complement of rebels in arms. Elsewhere in the north were other hosts: the huge army, estimated at 15,000 strong, active in Cumberland; the two armies engaged in defending Sawley Abbey against the Earl of Derby, the one from the lordship of Dent and the barony of Kendal, the other from the Craven honour of Percy Fee, reckoned to comprise some 6,000 men; and the force, estimated at 12–20,000 men, besieging the Earl of Cumberland in Skipton Castle.[5] Recruited from Richmondshire, the lordship of Kirkby Malzeard, the Liberty of Ripon and possibly the baronies of Skipton and Westmorland, this force had been summoned by Aske to Pontefract. From 22nd October it was expected to form the rearward in the pilgrim host. But delayed by its decision to take the Earl of Cumberland, it failed to reach Pontefract until 27th October when it found, to its disgust, that the Truce had been agreed and that, in keeping with it, the pilgrims were going home.[6]

On the morning of 22nd October, the lords and gentlemen at Pontefract Castle met in council to create a battle formation, the Percy and Bowes hosts in the van, the Aske and Stapulton hosts in the middleward, and the rearward composed of the absent host that was engaged at Skipton Castle.[7] This arrangement allowed the pilgrims to form behind the banner of St. Cuthbert, donated by the Earl of Westmorland and brought to the front by the Bowes host.[8] It also presented the army not as a popular rabble but as a military organisation led by lords, since it placed to the fore the three barons, Lords Latimer, Neville and Lumley and the putative lord, Sir Thomas Percy, with the twelve-year-old Lord Neville representing the earldom of

---

4 Put at 34-35,000 by Aske [Bateson, p. 336]; at 30,000 by Norfolk [R. W. Hoyle, "Thomas Master's narrative of the pilgrimage of grace", *Northern History*, 21 (1985), pp. 70–71]; at 28,000 by Marmaduke Neville on one occasion [L.P. XII{1}. 29] and 30,000 on another [SP1/112, f. 244 (*L.P.* XI.1319)].

5 For Cumberland, see above, p. 352. For the defence of Sawley Abbey, see above, ch. VI(n. 26) and ch. VII(n. 3). For the siege of Skipton Castle Aske and Neville agreed on a force of 12,000, see Bateson, p. 337 and *L.P.* XII{1}. 29.

6 See M. L. Bush, "The Richmondshire uprising of October 1536 and the pilgrimage of grace", *Northern History*, 39 (1993), pp. 88–95. For the possibility of a contingent from the barony of Westmorland, see above, p. 302; and from the barony of Skipton, see above p.156.

7 Stapulton (see Stapulton, p. 100) gave a somewhat different account to that of Aske (see Bateson, pp. 336-7), placing the Beverley host in the van, whereas Aske placed it in the middleward; and placing the Bowes host in the rearward whereas Aske placed it in the van. The differences, however, can be reconciled because of changes temporarily made in response to practical difficulties in the period 22nd–27th October (see below).

8 *L.P.* XII{1}. 946 {118}; Bateson, p. 336; Hoyle, "Master's narrative", p. 71.

Westmorland, and Sir Thomas representing the earldom of North-umberland.[9] Moreover, in giving prominence to forces which were tried and tested from warring against the Scots and which were well horsed and harnessed, largely because they were recruited from regions of border service tenant right, the same arrangement gave the impression that the pilgrim host was capable of effective combat and a quick ride on London.[10]

Initially, however, the battle arrangement proved unworkable since the Bowes host refused to move from Pontefract on the day of its arrival, not because its leaders disagreed with the pilgrims' plans but because its men and horses were exhausted, having just come down from Spennymoor in the Durham palatinate. As part of the van it was required to defend, in conjunction with the Percy host, the crossing at Wentbridge on the night of 22nd October.[11] This precaution sprang from the fear that the Earl of Shrewsbury was planning a night march on Pontefract to take Lord Darcy, a fear generated by a sinister message delivered to the castle on 21st October which had read: "Son Thomas, this night the Earl of Shrewsbury intendeth to take you sleeper". That night Aske had manned the Wentbridge crossing but nothing had happened.[12] Now it was felt that Shrewsbury might attack on 22nd October; and so the crossing had to be defended again. Following the refusal of the Bowes host to leave Pontefract, it was replaced in the van by the Stapulton host.[13] Yet this was only a temporary rearrangement, for on 23rd October the rest of the pilgrim host came to Wentbridge and together the Bowes and Percy hosts, as the designated vanguard, proceeded southwards to Hampole Nunnery, about six miles north of Doncaster, whilst the Stapulton host remained behind with the middleward, that is, until the following day when it appeared to rejoin the van.[14] By the

9 Bateson, pp. 336–7.
10 For accounts that the army was well-horsed, see the charge brought against Lancaster Herald for spreading the news of 10,000 northmen, each with a horse worth twenty angels [St.P. I, pp. 487-8, n. 1 (L.P. XIII{1}. 1311)]; and Norfolk's remark on 29th October of his army "having no horsemen and they all the flower of the north"[Dodds, I, pp. 268-9 (L.P. XI. 909)]; and Neville's description of the pilgrim host as well-horsed [SP1/112, f. 244 (L.P. XI. 1319)]; and Aske's presentation of the army as "well-tried on horseback" (Bateson, p. 336). See also Appendix I.
11 Bush, "The Richmondshire uprising", p. 93. There were two Ferrybridges, one on the Aire and the other on the Went. The Ferrybridge referred to here is Wentbridge. See Map 11.
12 SP1/118, fos. 47-48b (L.P. XII{1}. 852/iv).
13 Stapulton, p. 100; SP1/115, f. 260 (L.P. XII{1}. 393 {2}).
14 P.R.O. E36/118, f. 115b (L.P. XII{1}. 29); SP1/115, f. 260 (L.P. XII{1}. 393{2}); Stapulton, p. 101.

night of 25th October the middleward had moved to Hampole and, to make room for it, the van, including the Stapulton host, moved to Pickburn which overlooked Doncaster.[15]

By this time Lancaster Herald, whom the rebels had last encountered at Pontefract on 21st October, had reappeared with a letter from the commanders of the royal army.[16] This he delivered, on 24th October, to the vanguard of the pilgrim host now assembled at Barnsdale, half way between Hampole and Wentbridge. It proposed that four of the rebels should meet the Duke of Norfolk in Doncaster to declare "the causes of their assembly" and that, to pledge their safety, four gentlemen would be placed as hostages in the rebels' custody.[17] At the time, Aske was with the van and conferred with its leaders on what to do. But he appeared to find their advice unsatisfactory, probably because it advocated battle, and therefore decided to consult Lord Darcy. In view of the hostility of the commons of the van towards Darcy for remaining, along with the Archbishop of York, in Pontefract Castle, Aske also needed to persuade him to come to the front. He therefore made a quick ride to Pontefract.[18] The outcome of his consultation with Darcy was to reject Norfolk's proposal but not to insist on battle. The message taken to Doncaster by the herald was that the rebels wanted a meeting, "betwixt the hosts", of delegates in equal number, to allow them to "declare their griefs and petition".[19] This was unacceptable to the king's commanders, especially because it would have revealed how unequal the two armies were. On 25th October, they returned the herald with a letter rejecting the pilgrims' terms and challenging them to battle, that is, unless "ye do, incontinent, draw home, every man to his house". Whilst the same letter also promised that "if ye go home, ye may be assured to have us most humble suitors to his highness for you", it threatened unequivocally: "And if ye do not, then do your worst to us for so we will do to you".[20] This challenge of battle was immediately acceptable to the rebel vanguard whose appetite for action had been further whetted that morning by a minor victory in the field. A scouting party of thirty horse had left Doncaster to view the pilgrim army and took captive two

15 L.P. XII{1}. 29; Stapulton, p. 101; SP1/120, f. 35b (L.P. XII{1}. 1175).
16 Stapulton, p. 101. Also see SP1/120, f. 35b (L.P. XII{1}. 1175).
17 Bateson, p. 337.
18 Stapulton, p. 101; SP1/118, f. 192b (L.P. XII{1}. 946).
19 Bateson, p. 337.
20 Ibid. For the letter, see St.P. I, pp. 495–6 (L.P. XI. 887).

rebels. It was then spotted by the van and chased back to Doncaster, leaving behind the two men.[21]

To consider the herald's challenge, the rebels convened a council that evening at Hampole Nunnery. It was attended by Lord Darcy and the Archbishop of York.[22] At the council Bowes reported upon the challenge, revealing that the lords of the vanguard wished to take it up and had already declared as much to the herald.[23] A debate on the wisdom of war followed in which Lord Darcy, the archbishop, Sir Robert Constable and Aske argued for negotiation, reasoning that, if a battle were fought, serious damage would necessarily ensue, no matter who was the victor; and that what the pilgrims essentially wanted was not loss of life but the opportunity to present their grievances to the king, so that they could expose the councillors of base blood who were "in error of the people" and who were endangering "the person of the prince". This, they proposed, was the best way to get the evil ministers punished and their policies undone. Another argument for avoiding a battle was provided by Darcy who said: "It were better [to] have garrison war than hosting war in time of winter".[24] For the second time in two days the policy of negotiation advocated by Darcy and Aske prevailed over the belligerence of the vanguard. As a result, the pilgrims accepted the original proposal that Norfolk and Shrewbury had put to them. Accordingly, the same night Sir Ralph Ellerker, Sir Thomas Hilton, Robert Bowes and Robert Chaloner were selected to act as the pilgrims' delegation and with this news, the herald was dispatched to Doncaster.[25] Indicating a willingness to avoid battle, the royal commanders immediately honoured their part of the agreement, sending, during the course of the night, four pledges to the rebel headquarters at Hampole.[26]

Having accepted a policy of negotiation on the terms proposed by the commanders of the army royal, the pilgrims, on the morning of 26th October, sought to bring pressure upon the negotiations by arraying their host at Scawsby Leys, in full view of Doncaster.[27] This was repeated on 27th October, when, according to Aske and upon his orders, "the whole host [was] standing in perfect array to

21 Bateson, p. 337; L.P. XII{1}. 946{118}.
22 SP1/112, f. 227 (L.P. XI. 1300);L.P. XII{1}. 946{2} and 1175.
23 L.P. XII{1}. 946{2} and 1175.
24 For the archbishop, see SP1/119, f. 7 (L.P. XII{1}. 1022). For Constable, see SP1/112, f. 227 (L.P. XI. 1300). For Aske, see Bateson, p. 337. For Darcy, see ibid., p. 554.
25 Bateson, p. 337; Stapulton, p. 101.
26 Bateson, p. 337.
27 Ibid., p. 336; Hoyle, "Master's narrative", p. 71; L.P. XII{1}. 1175.

within night" and only retired to their billets with the return of the rebel delegates. This behaviour, according to Darcy had a second purpose: to bring pressure upon the rebel negotiators whom the host felt might otherwise betray the cause.[28]

Given its size, a force of something like 30,000 men, and that it was well-horsed, led by lords and in possession of a miraculous banner – that of St. Cuthbert, which had conferred upon the English so many victories against the Scots – the pilgrim host must have offered a terrifying spectacle. However, on the night of 25th October, heavy rain had fallen, making the River Don too deep to ford and obliging the rebels, if they wished to occupy the town, to take Doncaster bridge which was now defended with artillery.[29] For the rebels, the state of the weather created two conflicting points of view. The one, dear to the warring party, was that a glorious opportunity to secure a decisive victory in the field had been missed, thanks to the pilgrims' willingness to negotiate and their failure to attack the town itself on the morning of 25th October following the skirmish and chase, when the ford across the Don had been only two feet deep and the town appeared to be theirs for the taking.[30] The point of view dear to the peace party was that the decision to negotiate rather than to fight had proved to be correct. For the army royal, the rain was a source of great relief, safeguarding its grossly inferior numbers against immediate attack and suggesting that saints were of no avail and that God was for the king.[31]

The Truce

The Truce resulted not simply from the might of the pilgrim host but also from the weakness of the army royal. Both Aske and Norfolk had good reason to exaggerate the disparity between the two forces, Aske in order to present the Truce as an act of magnanimous loyalty extended by the rebels to the king; Norfolk in order to present it as an act of wisdom on the part of him and his fellow commanders.[32] Between them they produced a corroborative picture, with the rebel army vastly superior to the king's in manpower, horses and provisions, so much so that, for the government's troops, the Truce seemed the only alter-

28 Bateson, p. 338. For Darcy's view, see Dodds, p. 303.
29 SP1/120, f. 35b (*L.P.* XII{1}. 1175) and Hoyle, "Master's narrative", pp. 70–71.
30 Hoyle, "Master's narrative", pp. 70–71.
31 Ibid. Also see *L.P.* XI. 936.
32 For Aske's account, see *L.P.* XII{1}. 1175. For Norfolk's account, see L.P. XI. 909 and Hoyle, "Master's narrative", pp. 70–71.

native to defeat in battle and, for the pilgrim host, it was taken as a gesture of respect extended, not under compulsion but willingly, towards Henry VIII. Exaggeration, however, did not mean total misrepresentation. In both accounts of the military situation there resided a good deal of truth.

For the government the problem was the manner in which its army was scattered across the midlands in the critical period from 24th to 27th October, with the troops led by Suffolk, Norfolk, Shrewsbury and Exeter all detached from each other and miles apart. The point was vividly made by Norfolk on 28th October when he reasoned that he had been forced to treat with the rebels "because our men were not yet joined but some eighteen, some nine, some thirty miles off".[33] When Norfolk finally joined Shrewsbury in Doncaster on 26th October, his army remained at Tuxford, some twenty-five miles away. Moreover, in the course of that vital day it got no further than Scrooby, which was still six miles off.[34] On the same day Exeter was at Nottingham while Suffolk was occupied at Lincoln.[35] Since these armies were relatively small – with Norfolk's company amounting to no more than 3,000 men, Shrewsbury's to about 6,000, Exeter's to 2,000 and Suffolk's to about 4,000–each was in danger of being routed in turn by the rebels.[36] The scattered nature of the army royal stemmed partly from the need to hold down Lincolnshire – the special task of the Duke of Suffolk – where the rebellion was over but fears persisted of further outbreaks. Commissioned to administer the handing in of arms, to identify ringleaders and to establish a garrison to hold the county down, Suffolk and the forces at his disposal could not be spared.[37] But the fragmentation of the army royal also resulted from the separation of the two lieutenants commissioned to deal with the pilgrimage. This came of Shrewsbury's decision, made at the time when Norfolk was as far south as Cambridge, to leave the sanctity of Newark, where he was protected by the width and depth of the Trent, and to push on towards Doncaster.[38]

Whilst at Newark on 17th October, Shrewsbury received, along with his commission of lieutenancy, instructions from the government

33 Ibid., p. 71.
34 Dodds, I, pp. 259–60; *L.P.* XII{1}. 1175.
35 *L.P.* XI. 864/ii; Dodds, I. p. 259.
36 For Norfolk, see SP1/108, f. 23b (*L.P.* XI. 803). For Shrewsbury, see *L.P.* XI. 758, 768; Hoyle, "Master's narrative", pp. 70–71. For Exeter, see *L.P.* XI. 803. For Suffolk, see *L.P.* XI. 768.
37 See *L.P.* XI. 765, 766, 817, 833 and 850. For fears of further revolts, see *L.P.* XI. 780. For the garrison plan, see Hoyle, "Master's narrative", p. 67.
38 *L.P.* XI. 864, 909, 1241.

to proceed against the Yorkshire rebels in order "to give them the stroke".[39] To consolidate his achievement in sorting out the Lincolnshire uprising, and knowing that Norfolk was now joined with him in the commission of lieutenancy and that he could call upon him and his troops, Shrewsbury responded promptly. He resolved to march to Doncaster the next day, believing that Norfolk would soon follow and that, although very much outnumbered, he could, in the meantime, hold the rebels back "by policy or otherwise".[40] But on 18th October letters from Lord Darcy and Brian Hastings imparted the horrifying news that the rebel army was 40,000 strong and, led by the lords and gentlemen of the north, had taken York and was about to take Pontefract Castle.[41] In addition, he learned that the citizenry of Doncaster had enthusiastically taken the rebel oath and that rebel musters were being held just north of the town, at Barnsdale, a recognised muster point for the wapentake of Osgoldcross.[42] This news stopped Shrewsbury in his tracks, persuading him to wait at Southwell unto Norfolk arrived.[43] However, after informing Norfolk of this, he changed his mind, presumably as a result of receiving, between 18th and 20th October, further instructions from the government. These instructions ordered him to advance "with all your possible diligence", reasoning that, although his force amounted to 6,000 men and seemed "too weak to encounter with the forces of the traitors now arisen in Yorkshire", he had the backing of Norfolk and Exeter whose 5,000 chosen men had been dispatched to join him "with all possible speed"; and, anyway, it was likely that the rebels would disperse upon sight of his army. Since Pontefract Castle still held out, this order made some sense.

Accompanying the instruction to act was an order to use against the Yorkshire rebels the device that Shrewsbury had so successfully used in Lincolnshire. This consisted of a proclamation, delivered by a royal herald, ordering the rebels to disperse or else.[44] In response,

---

39 See the undated instructions (*L.P.* XI. 716) which were received on 17th October (ibid. 758). Further instructions composed on 15th October (ibid. 715), which urged him to act once the Lincolnshire business was sorted, must also have reached him on 17th October (ibid. 757)
40 *L.P.* XI. 716; E36/121, f. 133 (*L.P.* XI. 758).
41 *L.P.* XI. 758 and 759.
42 *L.P.* XI. 759 and 774. That it was a recognised muster point, see *L.P.* XIV{1}, 652 (p.318).
43 *L.P.* XI. 773 and 774.
44 SP1/108, fos. 191–191b (*L.P.* XI. 771). Other instructions, composed on 17th October, must have reached him in this period but were out of date upon arrival since they took the form of a plan to rescue York from falling to the rebels, when it had already fallen (*L.P.* XI. 748).

Shrewsbury by 21st October had reached Scrooby only to learn that Pontefract Castle had yielded. From Scrooby he dispatched Lancaster Herald to the rebel headquarters in Pontefract with the proclamation. This has not survived; but Aske's description of it has. According to him, it contained "neither of pardon nor of no demand what was the causes of their assembly", which suggests that it was simply an order to disperse.[45] The rejection of this proclamation caused Shrewsbury, by 23rd October, to move close to Doncaster, even though he knew at the time that he was grossly outnumbered and that Norfolk and his army stood no chance of reaching him before 25th October.[46] Perhaps he was encouraged to do so by the comforting, if misleading, news that Sir Henry Savile, Sir Brian Hastings, Lord Dacre, Lord Scrope, the Earl of Cumberland and Sir Richard Tempest had remained "true subjects" and that he could expect support from them.[47] In the meantime, the order urging him to march upon the rebels had been countermanded: on 21st October the government had issued further instructions requiring him to guard the Trent by manning the bridges at Nottingham and Newark.[48]

Compounding the problems created by Shrewsbury's rapid advance to Doncaster was the painful slowness of Norfolk's progress north. By 23rd October, when Shrewsbury was camped close to Doncaster, Norfolk had only reached Newark, but ahead of his army and accompanied by no more than four servants.[49] By the night of 25th October he had only reached Welbeck, nearly twenty miles south of Doncaster, and still apart from his army which now lay at Tuxford, some twelve miles to the east.[50] Norfolk, in fact, reached Doncaster in the early hours of 26th October, in response to the news that Shrewsbury had agreed to negotiate with the rebels and goaded on by Shrewsbury's accusation that he was "a laggard"; but he was still

---

45 See G. W. Bernard, *The Power of the Early Tudor Nobility* (Brighton, 1985), p. 41. For Askes description, see Bateson, p. 336. This suggests that the proclamation used was not *L.P.* XI. 826{2} which offered a pardon. For the governments directions to Shrewsbury on the sort of proclamation he should issue and which he most likely followed, see SP1/108, f. 273 (*L.P.* XI. 826 {4}). If so, the proclamation used was very much like the Lincolnshire proclamation [see *St.P.*, I, pp. 462-3 (*L.P.* XI. 694 {2})],with the difference that it probably suggested that the rebels were moved by wild rumours [see SP1/108, f. 272 (*L.P.* XI. 826 {3})]. For the government's instructions to Shrewsbury on how to make a proclamation, see SP1/108, f. 191b (*L.P.* XI. 771), which refers to the minute *L.P.* XI. 826 {3 and 4}.

46 *L.P.* XI. 846 and 850.

47 *L.P.* XI. 846.

48 *L.P.* XI. 816.

49 SP1/109, f. 60 (*L.P.* XI. 845).

50 *L.P.* XI. 864.

separated from his army which, in the course of that day, made its way
not to Doncaster but to Scrooby.[51] As for the Marquis of Exeter, his
journey northwards was even slower than Norfolk's; and if he ever
reached Doncaster it was not before 27th October.[52] This meant that
on 26th October, the first day of the confrontation, when the rebel
army displayed itself in battle formation on the north bank of the Don,
it faced a force impressively captained by the three earls, Shrewsbury,
Rutland and Huntingdon, but one that amounted to no more than
one-fifth of the pilgrim host.[53]

Norfolk's slowness in moving northwards was due to not simply a
lack of appetite for battle but also certain plans he had concocted in the
light of information received from the north and of directions sent him
from the government. Thus, on 20th October, whilst still in Cambridge, Norfolk learned from Shrewsbury's letter of 18th October that
he would wait near Newark for Norfolk's arrival.[54] On the basis of this
information, Norfolk produced his "politic device", a plan centring
upon the belief that putting down the pilgrimage would be a much
tougher proposition than suppressing the Lincolnshire uprising; and
that it could be best achieved by guarding the line of the Trent, rather
than by advancing against the rebels. As part of the plan Norfolk
thought they should employ in the first instance a letter, composed
by the two lieutenants. This letter would seek either to persuade the
rebels to lay down their arms or to damage the rebels' cause by creating
divisions with their army. If this letter failed to terminate the revolt,
Norfolk felt that the onset of winter and a shortage of victuals would,
sooner or later, bring it to an end; that is, so long as the rebels were
prevented from using the bridges at Newark and Nottingham to cross
the Trent and press southwards.[55] By the 21st October the government

51 See Dodds, I, pp. 259-60 (*L.P.* XI. 864).
52 That he eventually arrived is made evident in a letter of 28th October signed by
    him and Norfolk and sent from Doncaster. See Hoyle, "Master's narrative", pp.
    70–71. He also received coat and conduct money from Gostwick at Tickhill on
    29th October (*L.P.* XI. 911).
53 Hoyle, "Master's narrative", pp. 70–71. Norfolk put the rebel army at 30,000 and
    the royal army in or around Doncaster at 5,000. The latter figure was an
    underestimation: by 27th October, with Norfolk and Exeter's 5,000 troops and
    Shrewbury's 6,000 the royal army amounted to 11,000 (*L.P.* XI. 750 and 771).
54 *L.P.* XI. 773 and 802.
55 The plan was set out in Norfolk's letter to Henry VIII of 20th October. Only a
    fragment of this letter has survived. See Hoyle, "Master's narrative", p. 68. Hoyle
    misdates it as 26th/27th October. For its correct dating, see *L.P.* XI. 816. The plan
    can be pieced together from the king's reply of 21st October (*L.P.* XI. 816). For the
    first page of this reply, see SP1/108, fos. 255–255b. For the rest of it, see E36/121,
    fos. 65–67b. Another aid in working out the nature of the plan is Norfolk's letter of
    25th October to Henry VIII. See Dodds, I, pp. 259–60 (*L.P.* XI. 864).

had warmly welcomed the plan; and by 22nd arrangements had been made to fortify the two bridges; and it seemed likely that the plan could be fully implemented by 23rd/24th October, with the armies of Norfolk and Shrewsbury joined together at the Trent and ready for defensive action.[56] But not so. Arriving in Newark in the early morning of 23rd, Norfolk received a brief letter, delivered at five a.m., indicating that Shrewsbury and his army were now at Scrooby.[57] His plan therefore collapsed. All it remained good for was a holding operation, in the event of Shrewsbury's defeat in the field.[58] However, in the course of the day, it seemed that Norfolk persisted with the idea of sending a letter to the rebels, not to persuade them to disperse but rather to stop Shrewsbury from chancing a battle and also to give the various scattered parts of the royal army time to come together. The letter proposed a procedure of negotiation which would permit the rebels to declare their grievances and allow the two lieutenants to intercede for them with the king.[59]

The effects of Shrewsbury's march to Doncaster were disastrous for the government: in splitting up the army royal commissioned to deal with the Yorkshire rebels: in galvanising the rebels to unite and advance south of Pontefract; in wrecking Norfolk's plan, which the government had backed, for holding a defence line at the Trent.[60] Moreover, the yielding of Pontefract Castle had rendered Shrewsbury's march pointless. A humiliating truce became inevitable. A further problem for the army royal was that, prior to its arrival, and a testimony to the proselytising dynamism of Sir Thomas Maunsell, vicar of Brayton, the rebels had already reached Doncaster and had sworn its inhabitants.[61] With the river fordable and the townsmen disloyal, and with news that in the town the pestilence was rife, the prospects of establishing a garrison there, which was capable of resisting the rebel army, were far from good.[62] For these reasons, Shrewsbury appeared to delay his entry to Doncaster, making his

56 For the government's enthusiastic support, see *L.P.* XI. 818. For fortifying the bridges, see *L.P.* XI. 834.
57 *L.P.* XI. 802 and 845.
58 Ibid.
59 Norfolk's letter is lost. It was sent on 23rd October, either first thing (*L.P.* XI. 845) or after his meeting with Lord Talbot (*L.P.* XI. 846). For its presentation as a ploy to gain time, see Hoyle, "Master's narrative", p. 76; *L.P.* XI. 864 and 884.
60 See above.
61 *L.P.* XI. 774; and see above, p. 94.
62 *L.P.* XI. 846 and 909; Hoyle, "Master's narrative", pp. 70–71. The problems facing the army are adumbrated by Bernard (see Bernard, op. cit., p. 42).

stand at Rossington bridge, three miles or so south of the town.[63] The pilgrim host was thus able to approach Doncaster without meeting any opposition, and to have the first pick of the provisions located in the region north of the Don. The army royal was consequently left so short of hay, oats, peas, beans and fuel that, if it had managed to unite its forces on the Don, it could not have fed them.[64] In addition, the royal forces at Doncaster were short of good horsemen.[65] This created two problems. It meant that they could not harry the pilgrim host; nor could they prevent the rebel horsemen from harrying the army royal.[66] As a result, it was impossible to make a stand at Doncaster without resorting to battle or to make an orderly retreat to the Trent for the purpose of reviving Norfolk's "politic device". A final problem for the commanders of the royal army was the poor motivation of their troops, with some thinking they were inadequately paid and others sympathising with the pilgrims' cause.[67] In the circumstances, the army royal had little choice but to make an appointment (i.e. treat) with the rebels. The threat of battle that it made on 25th October was mere bluff.[68]

Norfolk presented the decision to negotiate as a device for allowing the dispersed components of the army royal the opportunity to get together.[69] However, the negotiations, which started on 24th October and culminated in the truce of 27th October, formed part of a series of non-military measures employed by the government and its officers in the course of the month, either to persuade the rebels to go home or to limit the extent of the uprising. Thus, the government had already made concessions, both in stopping the collection of the subsidy and in suspending the new act for the regulation of the cloth industry.[70] Moreover, as well as planning military action, it had also sought to pacify the rebels by declaring that the news concerning new taxes and the demolition of parish churches amounted to no more than false rumours maliciously spread. To this effect, a royal proclamation was produced, a letter was sent to Darcy and the Archbishop of York on 18th October, and instructions were issued to Norfolk and Shrews-

63 *L.P.* XI. 850.
64 *L.P.* XI. 909 and 1241.
65 SP1/108 (*L.P.* XI. 774). What was lacking was not mounted troops (see *L.P.* XI. 930) but horses of sufficient quality to serve as scourers (*L.P.* XI. 846).
66 For the inability to retreat, see *L.P.* XI. 909. For the inability to harass the enemy, see SP1/120, f. 35b (*L.P.* XII{1}. 1175).
67 *L.P.* XI. 909.
68 See above, p. 378.
69 Dodds, I, p. 260 (*L.P.* XI. 864); *L.P.* XI. 884; Hoyle, "Master's narrative", p. 70.
70 For postponement of subsidy, see *L.P.* XII{1}. 152 and 594. For suspension of the act relating to cloth, see *L.P.* XI. 603.

bury, all asserting that such rumours were unjustified and should be denied. In the same cause, the government published a tract condemning rebellion and had copies distributed in the north.[71]

Undoubtedly, in dealing with the pilgrims, the government was influenced by its success in Lincolnshire. Following its termination of the Lincolnshire uprising, achieved peacefully by a proclamation composed and dispatched by Shrewsbury, the government about 18th October instructed the earl to try something similar with the Yorkshire rebels.[72] As a result, Shrewsbury composed a second proclamation which was taken by Lancaster Herald to Pontefract on 21st October.[73] The rebels, however, had likewise learned a lesson from the Lincolnshire episode. When the herald reached Pontefract and wished to make the proclamation public, Robert Aske refused him permission to do so.[74] The plan for pacifying the rebels without resort to battle, then, was not simply concocted on the eve of the Truce, in response to the disparity of resources clearly evident at that point in time between the two armies. Moreover it was a policy that stemmed not only from the government's success in ending the Lincolnshire uprising but also from the fact that, having recruited and organised a large army of over 19,000 men at Amptill, designed to be led by Henry VIII in person, it had dismissed this force on 19th October, after hearing of the final submission of the Lincolnshire rebels, only to realise, within a day or two, that it was needed after all to deal with the pilgrimage.[75] But by then the army had returned home, with the exception of certain troops reserved for the Duke of Suffolk in Lincolnshire and for the Duke of Norfolk and the Earl of Shrewsbury in Yorkshire.[76] Thereafter, the government dithered over whether to resummon it, in the meantime hoping for a non-military settlement.[77] Its preference for policy was first made evident in the instructions that the government issued to Shrewsbury on 18th October, ordering him to try something like the proclamation which had ended the Lincolnshire uprising; then it

---

71 For proclamation of 18th October, see Hughes and Larkin, I, pp. 244–5. For its use by Norfolk and Shrewsbury, see SP1/108, 191b (*L.P.* XI. 771), *L.P.* XI. 816 and SP1/108, f. 272 (*L.P.* XI. 826{3}). For letters to Darcy and Lee, see *L.P.* XI. 769 and 781. For the circulated tract, see *L.P.* XI. 816 and 822.

72 *L.P.* XI. 771.

73 For Shrewsbury's Lincolnshire proclamation, see *St.P.*, I, pp. 462–3 (*L.P.* XI. 694 {2}). For his Yorkshire proclamation, see E36/118, f. 92 (*L.P.* XI. 826{2}). In thinking that the same proclamation was used in both cases, the Dodds are wrong (Dodds, I, p. 228).

74 *St.P.*, I, p. 486 (*L.P.* XI. 826).

75 SP1/108, fosf. 23-23b (*L.P.* XI. 803).

76 *L.P.* XI. 799 and 825.

77 *L.P.* XI. 799, 821, 825, 884, 906 and 910.

resurfaced in the "politic device", proposed by Norfolk on 20th October and enthusiastically adopted by the government a day later when it told him, in compliance with his scheme, to use force only if other means failed.[78]

The plan which eventually pacified the pilgrims was, in all likelihood, set out in a letter from the Duke of Norfolk which Lord Talbot took to his father, the Earl of Shrewsbury, on the 23rd or the 24th October. Talbot had travelled to Newark on 23rd to assure Norfolk that his father would not engage in battle until Norfolk's force had joined him which, according to Norfolk's reckoning, could not be before 25th October.[79] In response to Norfolk's letter, Shrewsbury dispatched Lancaster Herald to the pilgrim host to propose to the rebel army, in Norfolk's name, an armistice.[80] When the rebels rejected the proposed terms and suggested others, a second letter was dispatched, in the name of Norfolk, Exeter, Shrewsbury, Rutland and Huntingdon, challenging the rebels to battle unless they dispersed.[81] Delivered by Lancaster Herald, this order closely resembled the proclamation which had terminated the Lincolnshire uprising, suggesting that, like the Lincolnshire proclamation, it was the work of Shrewsbury.[82] However, it was, in fact, a composition of Norfolk which was probably delivered to Shrewsbury along with the letter proposing negotiation so that it could be used (as it was) in the event of the rebels' rejection of the negotiating terms.[83] Although the outcome was quite different, its effect was as decisive as that of the Lincolnshire proclamation. In response, the pilgrims accepted the original terms, principally in order to avoid a battle and to escape

---

78 L.P. XI. 771; Hoyle, "Master's narrative", p. 68; L.P. XI. 816.
79 L.P. XI. 846. As early as 18th October, Norfolk had predicted that he would not get to Doncaster before 26th October (see L.P. XI. 776).
80 Bateson, p. 337.
81 St.P., I, pp. 495-6 (L.P. XI. 887).
82 The Lincolnshire proclamation differed simply in ordering the rebels to go home "or else we shall surely dispatch you" [St.P., I, pp. 462–3 (L.P. XI. 694 {2})], whereas the letter of challenge promised to make suit to the king if the rebels dispersed.
83 SP1/109, f. 221 (L.P. XI. 887, printed in full in St.P., I, pp. 495–6). Aske presented it as coming from Norfolk (see Bateson, p. 337). It is not written in Norfolk's own hand, as were many of his dispatches, but it is in the same hand as another letter he sent from Newark on 23rd October [SP1/109, f. 60 (L.P. XI. 845)]. His signature on the letter is genuine, although Exeter's is forged. The letter was undoubtedly brought from Newark to Doncaster on 23rd/24th October by Lord Talbot, along with the letter proposing negotiation. Shrewsbury, Huntingdon and Rutland then added their signatures.

the weaker option of dispersing without the chance to specify their grievances.[84]

The Truce came about, however, not just because of the army royal's inadequate resources but also because the rebels chose to accept it, in spite of enjoying the military advantage. The two camps resembled each other in having a war and a peace party. In the government camp the former was led by Shrewsbury, the latter by Norfolk; in the rebel camp the van was for military action whereas the middleward wanted a peaceful settlement. Since the absent rearward was also for war, the peace party represented the northern lowlands and the war party the northern uplands.[85] Essentially, the Truce was decided by the supremacy of the peace over the war party in the rebels' camp. Yet the compliancy of the rebels was not simply due to a preference for peace. After all, the rebels were not defenceless pilgrims reliant upon God's grace. Had they not raised and organised a massive, well-equipped army? Moreover, they had frequently declared their intention of marching upon London.[86] What is more, they had already begun the journey southwards. However, although far superior to the opposing army in manpower, cavalry, coordination and commitment, the pilgrim host had an obvious weakness. This lay in the absence of the rearward which was still at Skipton Castle. Aske had summoned it to join him, but without effect. Furthermore, the rearward was part of the same insurrectionary movement as the war party. Both were separate strands of the Richmondshire uprising.[87]

In the debate over peace or war, as it was conducted in Hampole Nunnery on the night of 25th October with the rain beating down, the case for peace could be the more effectively made (even though this entailed overcoming the humiliation of accepting previously rejected terms) simply because the rearward's absence deprived the war party of the weight of its support whilst giving the peace party the persuasive argument that battle should be avoided since a third of the army had yet to turn up. Also serving the cause of the peace party was the advocacy of Lancaster Herald and the assurances he gave the rebels that, if they submitted, the king would grant them "the lord privy seal and all other their demands", so much so that he was eventually

84 The letter proposed that "if ye go home ye may be assured to have us most humble suitors to his highness for you" [St.P., I, p. 496 (L.P. XI. 887)].

85 See above, pp. 378–9 and below.

86 As recently as 21st October when Aske put it to Lancaster Herald (L.P. XI. 826). Percy vouched for it as an expectation of the commons [SP1/115, f. 261 (L.P. XII{1}. 393{2})].

87 See above, pp. 161–2.

blamed for the Truce, convicted of treason and executed, his severed head set alongside the remains of Robert Aske in York.[88] According to Aske, the commons had told Lancaster Herald near Hampole, presumably on either 24th or 25th October, that "their griefs" all stemmed from Cromwell and the bad advice he had given the king. The herald's reply to their complaint might well have persuaded them to support a settlement.[89] Furthermore, whilst the council of pilgrims debated the issue into the night, the heavy rain doused the ardour of the rebel army as it sheltered in the nearby woods and prevented a rapid crossing of the Don by large numbers of troops.[90] Darcy, the archbishop, Constable and Aske could thus rest their case. Earlier the war party had been incensed to find the peace party dealing with Lancaster Herald without consulting it. Now, however, and winning it over to a policy of appeasement, was the peace party's willingness to allow the war party a foremost part in the negotiations of 27th October and its grievances a prominent place in the pilgrims' petition.[91]

Did the rebels accept the Truce because, in spite of differences of opinion between the orders, the gentlemen managed to take control of the commonalty? This was the scenario proposed by Darcy and Constable. According to Constable, battle was avoided because the gentlemen stayed "the fury of the commons".[92] According to Darcy, on 28th October, the day after the Truce was agreed, it was extremely difficult to hold back and disband the rearward. At that time, he alleged, the van and middleward were easier to control because in them "were great numbers of well-willed lords and knights of worship to help and, in the rearward, nothing like so many of worship and wild people evil to order". The rearward, he suggested, was brought to accept the Truce by the gentlemen who led it.[93] A similar point was made by William Stapulton who, after describing the skirmish on 25th October, in which the government's troops were chased back to Doncaster, declared that it was "with much pain" that "they stayed the people from setting upon Doncaster".[94] On the other hand, Aske denied that "there was any policy devised for the tarrying of the commons by the gentlemen".[95] Yet there was probably a strong,

88 St.P., I, pp. 487-8 (n.1) (L.P. XIII{1}. 1311); Dodds, II, p. 300.
89 Bateson, p. 340.
90 SP1/120, f. 35b (L.P. XII{1}. 1175); Hoyle, "Master's narrative", pp. 70–71.
91 For war party incensed, see E36/118, f. 118 (L.P. XII{1}. 29{2}). For war party won over, see above, p. 161.
92 SP1/120, f. 136 (L.P. XI{1}. 1225).
93 SP1/110 (L.P. XI. 928); SP1/111 (L.P. XI. 1045).
94 Stapulton, p. 101.
95 SP1/120, f. 36b (L.P. XII{1}. 1175).

upward pressure for war, created by the popular fear that, in the Lincolnshire manner, the gentlemen would abuse their position as negotiators of a settlement to betray the commons.[96]

What is clear is that the membership of the war and peace parties in the pilgrim host did not represent different orders. The war party, after all, included gentlemen, notably in the van. Furthermore, Constable's evidence is suspect simply because it was furnished in an attempt to save his own skin, principally by showing that his involvement in the uprising, rather than being an act of gross irresponsibility, "did the king good service" through dissuading the pilgrim host from exercising its military advantage. The same could be said of Stapulton's evidence, provided in the confession he made under examination in early 1537. Running through his account of the pilgrimage is the theme of a furious commons held in check by himself. Darcy's evidence, moreover, although provided at the time of the Truce rather than under examination, tendentiously presented a picture of genteel responsibility. Supplied in a letter to the king's lieutenants, Shrewsbury and Norfolk, it was designed to show that the gentlemen caught up in the uprising had, in effect, brought it to an end. What is more, his comments appertained to the problems he and Aske had encountered not with the pilgrimage as a whole but specifically with the rearward which, having been excluded from the making of the Truce, therefore, not surprisingly, found its terms difficult to accept. Nonetheless, what is also clear is that the Truce was made by the gentlemen. Even Aske was left out of the Doncaster deliberations of 27th October; and there is nothing to suggest that the commons were consulted at any stage of this settlement. Yet the radical change in rebel policy which the Truce brought about – one centring upon a supplication to the king through the medium of the king's lieutenants, rather than a march on London to confront the government – was not foisted upon the commons by the men of worship. Although the work of gentlemen, it did not appear to go against the commons' wishes. The rebels, it seems, accepted the Truce because of what it conceded. The generosity of its terms pacified the war party, as did the onset of winter and the obstacle of an unfordable Don and a bridge packed with artillery.[97]

The Truce was agreed on 27th October at two meetings, one held in Doncaster and the other, on Doncaster bridge. The first meeting complied with the terms initially proposed by Lancaster Herald on 24th October; the second, held in sight of the two armies, resembled

96 For Darcy, see Dodds, I, p. 303.
97 Hoyle, "Master's narrative", pp. 70–71.

the proposal initially put forward by the rebels.[98] Both meetings took place in the shadow of the pilgrim host which, as ordered by Aske, stood throughout the day "in perfect array".[99] At the first meeting, Sir Ralph Ellerker, Sir Thomas Hilton, Robert Bowes and Robert Chaloner, entered the town as the pilgrims' ambassadors.[100] There, in a meeting with the Duke of Norfolk and the earls of Shrewsbury, Rutland and Huntingdon, they put forward five points. Robert Bowes acted as spokesman.[101] Then, in response to a request from the lords to hear the rebels' grievances declared and detailed by, in Robert Aske's words, "the baronage and certain worshipful men of the north of their own mouth", a second meeting was held, this time on Doncaster bridge, with the four pilgrim ambassadors accompanied by the three rebel barons, Lords Latimer, Lumley and Darcy, and a number of rebel knights, including Sir Robert Constable and Sir John Bulmer.[102] Little is known of either meeting, apart from the outcome, the venue, the parties present and the fact that, at the first meeting, Norfolk ordered the rebels to put their points in writing and, at the second meeting, Lord Darcy declared to Shrewsbury: "Hold up thy long claw and promise me that I shall have the king's favour and shall be indifferently heard, and I will come to Doncaster to you", only to receive the uncompromising reply: "Then ye shall not come in".[103] Shrewsbury was simply making clear that the lords could not bind the king with promises to which he had not consented. This the rebels were prepared to accept.

It was agreed that Norfolk and Shrewsbury's son should present to the king the pilgrims' grievances, now set out in five articles, and plead for a pardon.[104] It was understood that the king would reply to the

98 Bateson, p. 337.
99 Ibid., p. 338.
100 *L.P.* XII{1}. 946 {118}.
101 SP1/119, f. 6b (*L.P.* XII{1}. 1022).
102 Bateson, p. 337.
103 Dodds, I, p. 302 (*L.P.* XI. 1086). For the writing down of the five articles, see below, pp. 394–5.
104 The government's understanding of the agreement was set out in the instructions issued to Norfolk in mid-November for the second appointment. See *St.P.*, I, pp. 498–9. The rebels' understanding was set out by Aske, see Bateson, p. 338 and *L.P.* XII{1}. 946 {118}, and by Darcy, see *L.P.* XI. 1045. In the matter of the pardon, Norfolk and the other commanders admitted to the king that adverse conditions "have made us condescend to a treaty with them, promising to be humble suitors to your majesty for their pardon" (Hoyle, "Master's narrative", pp. 70–71). But this was simply a plea for a pardon, not the granting of one. The letter that appears in the *L.P.* for 28th October and refers to "the declaration of your most gracious free pardon" is misdated (*L.P.* XI. 902). It belongs to December and the second appointment, not October and the first appointment.

rebels' complaint and that, until he did so, the rebels would hold their peace. For the "more sure declaration" of these grievances, Norfolk was to take with him Bowes and Ellerker, whose task was to elaborate upon the five articles. The procedure adopted, then, mirrored the manner in which the Lincolnshire letter of supplication of 3rd October and the petition of 9th October had been presented at Court, as well as implementing a proposal put twice to the rebels of the Beverley region by Sir Ralph Ellerker when he had offered to take their grievances to the king.[105] Also agreed was an immediate disbandment of the two armies. In addition, various solutions were tabled for consideration: notably the special summons of parliament to examine the rebel grievances; an invitation by royal proclamation for subjects to make complaints against harmful statutes and orders of council, with the promise that, if they could prove their complaints, the king should make reformation; and the grant of a pardon which, without exception, would apply to everyone involved in the uprising.[106]

Norfolk presented the agreement as merely a device for getting the government out of a tricky situation, in which it had been landed by the Earl of Shrewsbury's reckless march to Doncaster.[107] He also proposed, in an attempt to assure the king that he had not been committed to anything without his consent, that what had been offered to the rebels could easily be withdrawn.[108] But on this point Norfolk was wrong. The appointment of 27th October held, especially because, in compliance with its terms, the army royal had been disbanded. Realising as much, Norfolk divulged to the council on 29th October: "Now enforced to appoint with the rebels, my heart is broken".[109] The Truce was honoured until early December when it was terminated not by an act of repudiation but by a free and general

---

105 For presentation of Lincolnshire petitions, see Dodds, I, pp. 99, 114 and 123. For Ellerker's earlier proposals, see above, p. 67.

106 The demand for a parliament was made in the articles which proposed that the pardon might be authorised by enactment (see below, p. 396); was presented on 11th November by Darcy as "the thing they most desired" [SP1/111, f. 69 (L.P. XI. 1045)]; was proposed on 19th November by John Hallom, writing in the name of the commons, as the means by which the pardon was to be authorised (Hoyle, "Master's narrative", p. 73); appeared in the imperial ambassadors' accounts of what the rebels wanted (L.P. XI. 1143 and 1204); and featured among a list of devices for quietening the commons (L.P. XI. 1410 {4}). For the proposed complaints procedure, see ibid. The demand for a pardon which was general and admitted no exceptions was made in the five articles (see below, n. 116).

107 L.P. XI. 864, 909 and 1241.

108 Dodds, I, p. 260 (L.P. XI. 864).

109 Dodds, I, p. 268 (L.P. XI. 909).

pardon and the promise of a parliament at York to consider the detailed grievances of the rebels.[110] In a letter to his ambassadors Gardiner and Wallop, Henry VIII sought to sweep the October settlement into the same category as the one employed to terminate the Lincolnshire uprising, arguing that in both cases the rebels had dispersed neither with a pardon nor with "any certain promise of one", implying that the October rebels, in both Lincolnshire and Yorkshire, had withdrawn unconditionally and the king's honour was consequently unsmirched.[111] This was true of the Lincolnshire uprising, not of the pilgrimage of grace. Whereas the one ended with a submission, the other ended with a treaty. To the pilgrims the king's lieutenants, acting in the king's name, had, in effect, made binding concessions. A vital difference existed between the two uprisings and this determined the government's treatment of them: in Lincolnshire the rebels dispersed whilst a royal force under Suffolk remained in the vicinity and ready for action; whereas in Yorkshire the rebel and the royal armies disbanded simultaneously.

The five articles

Characterising the October activities of the pilgrimage of grace was not simply the mobilisation of the pilgrim host but also the eventual production of a petition. The latter was not a task easily accomplished. Whereas, within a day of its outbreak, the Lincolnshire rebels had dispatched to the king a supplicatory bill, with a set of articles composed the following day and dispatched to Court five days later, the rebels of the north had produced nothing equivalent, even after a fortnight of revolt, although their intention from the start had been, in the Lincolnshire manner, to petition the king.[112]

Delaying the production of a petition was first the northern rebels' reliance upon the Lincolnshire articles. When they were repudiated by the government and another declaration of grievance was therefore required, the pilgrims were, for some time, unable to formulate anything. This was not for want of trying. Following the embarrassment of the meeting with Lancaster Herald on 21st October, when the herald had asked for the rebels' articles in writing and Aske had to admit that they had none and could only offer a copy of the oath

110 See below, p. 401.
111 *L.P.* XI. 984.
112 See above, p. 91.

instead, attempts had been made to set something down.[113] About 22nd October the Archbishop of York was approached to help out, first by George Darcy and Ralph Ellerker and then by Aske, but refused to oblige.[114] When the pilgrim council accepted the offer of a treaty on 25th October, it still had no petition to present. One was created, in fact, only at the last minute: that is, in the morning of 27th October, prior to the meeting at noon in Doncaster. It was composed by a council meeting at Scawsby Leys where the pilgrim host was arrayed; but, perhaps because of a lack of time, it was not put into writing before the actual meeting with Norfolk. Declared by Robert Bowes who had committed it to memory, it was first penned on the Duke of Norfolk's command.[115]

The resulting document began with the oath, which Aske had composed on 17th/18th October and had presented to Lancaster Herald on 21st October as a true statement of the rebels' grievances. It ended with five articles. The oath, as it appeared in this petition, was slightly different from the one previously shown to the herald. Towards the end it contained the additional remark that those who had joined the rebellion should seek to suppress "the subverters of the just laws of God" and further added that no one should leave "our devout pilgrim-age" unless authorised to do so by the captains and council of each battle and that there should be no return "without the assent of the grand captain".[116] Why this oath was included in the petition is not clear. In all likelihood, its purpose was to declare to the government the rules by which the rebels abided, so as to give the impression that the uprising was efficiently and responsibly organised, as well as to make use of the oath's justification of the term "pilgrimage of grace for the commonwealth", with its emphasis on the need not only to maintain Christ's faith and his church against heresy but also to preserve the commonwealth against evil ministers from base backgrounds who, in contempt of the society of orders, were threatening its component parts, the royal family, the nobility, the church and the commons. That the document was meant to have this dual purpose is evident in Aske's reference to it as "our petition on faith and commonwealth".[117]

113 *L.P.* XI. 826.
114 SP1/119, f. 6 (*L.P.* XII{1}. 1022).
115 Ibid., f. 7.
116 The one surviving copy of this petition is badly mutilated. See SP1/109 (*L.P.* XI. 902{2}). The missing passages, however, can be mostly worked out from a summary of the petition provided in a letter from John Hallom to the pilgrims York council (see Hoyle, "Master's narrative", p. 73).
117 SP1/111 (*L.P.* XI. 1079).

The five appended articles sought to do two things: to put the rebels' concerns in a nutshell and to propose a remedy. Thus the essential grievances of the pilgrimage were presented as the Henrician government's abuse of the faith of Christ, of the church and its liberties, of the common laws and of the commonwealth. In the articles, as opposed to the oath, the term commonwealth appears to be used in the sense of the wealth of the commons rather than the wealth of all subjects of the realm. The last clause of the articles implies as much by referring to "the surety of the baronage and commonwealth" and in article three the requirement that "the commonwealth . . . may be used as it hath been" reflects Aske's remark to Lancaster Herald on 21st October that "the commonty to be used as they should be" and echoes a phrase from his first proclamation which obliged those supporting the uprising "to be true to the commons and their wealths".[118] The remedy the articles proposed was threefold: to restore matters to what they had been at the start of the reign "when his nobles did order under his highness"; to correct those who had subverted the laws of God and the laws of the realm – specified as Cromwell, Cranmer and Latimer – and to grant a general pardon, either by act of parliament or "otherwise" (i.e. by letters patent), excusing all offences of deed and word that the rebels had committed. The petition closed by affirming the need to preserve both the faith and the society of orders, presenting the articles as being "to the honour of God and his faith, reformation of the church militant, preservation of the king and his issue, for the honour and surety of the baronage and commonwealth of this realm".[119]

This petition appeared to bear little relationship either to the declarations of grievance produced by the Lincolnshire rebels or to the pilgrims' second petition, the twenty-four articles submitted to the government in December.[120] For example, it failed to mention either the Dissolution or the fiscal grievances, which had dominated the Lincolnshire complaint and which reappeared in the December statement. However, this was not because the pilgrims at this point in time were unmoved by such issues. The aim of the pilgrims' October

---

118 *St.P.*, I, p. 485 (*L.P.* XI. 826); SP1/107, f. 116 (*L.P.* XI. 622). Aske was also capable of using the term to mean "the wealth of all", as for example when he told the herald on 21st October that he should inform the lords in charge of the king's army "it were meet that they were with me, for it is for all of their wealth that I do" [*St.P.*, I, p. 487 (*L.P.* XI. 826)].
119 SP1/109 (*L.P.* XI. 902{2}).
120 For Lincolnshire grievance statements, see *L.P.* XI. 534 and 705. For the December articles, see *L.P.* XI. 1246.

petition was to produce broad categories of grievance which could be used in the first instance to highlight the rebels' basic complaint and remedy. The more detailed grievances were to be provided orally: first by the four pilgrim ambassadors who met Norfolk in Doncaster; then by the rebel barons and knights who met Norfolk on Doncaster bridge; and finally by Robert Bowes and Ralph Ellerker in their various meetings with members of the government during their trip to London to meet the king. What they were is made evident in two foreign ambassadorial reports, both composed in November to dispatch information to the Emperor on the dealings between the government and the pilgrims' representatives, Bowes and Ellerker. Included in fifteen to twenty proposed articles was the demand for the repeal of certain statutes, all enacted within the previous two years: i.e. the Act of Supremacy, in order to restore the pope's headship of the English church, the Act of Succession, in order to legitimise Princess Mary; the Act of Suppression in order to restore the religious houses so far dissolved, the Act of First fruits and Tenths; the Act of Uses; and the act making words a treasonable offence. Also contained in the articles was the demand that subsidies be granted only for the purposes of war; and that parliaments, in accordance with tradition, should be free of the control of pensioners and royal officers.[121]

The five articles, then, differed from the other submitted petitions in presentation rather than in content. A second difference lay in their formulation. The other petitions were put to the commons for their assent.[122] Although the five articles were seen as "coming from the commons" and "for the commons", the commons appeared to have no say in their production.[123] What is clear is that, in determining the presentation of the grievances, the vanguard of the pilgrim host had an important part to play. Of the four pilgrims who first went to meet Norfolk in Doncaster on 27th October, three (i.e. Ellerker, Bowes and Hilton) were from the van; and not only did two of its leaders, Ellerker and Bowes, receive the pre-eminent role of taking the articles to Court and of explaining them to the king and council, but it was the hosts that composed the van, moved as they were by constitutional irregula-

---

121 *L.P.* XI. 1143 and 1204. These accounts of grievance can be validated and their meaning further educed by comparing the grievances they identify with the lists of articles produced by the rebels in early December for the second appointment. See "the articles to the lords of the king's council at our coming to Pontefract" (*L.P.* XI. 1246) and a related list of articles put to the pilgrims Pontefract Council out of which the twenty-four articles emerged (*L.P.* XI.1182{2}).

122 For Lincolnshire articles, see *L.P.* XII{1}. 70/xi. For pilgrim articles of December, see Bateson, p. 340.

123 *L.P.* XI. 957 and 1117.

rities, which appeared to produce the complaint about the subversion of the law and to propose the remedy of restoring the constitution to what it had been on Henry VIII's accession.[124] In this way a trade-off occurred between the middleward and the van, with the latter won over from the cause of war, thanks to being granted a foremost role in the making of the peace.

The December agreement

The first appointment of late October led to the second appointment of early December; and the government's reception of the first five articles was followed by its reception of another twenty-four. For the rebels the second appointment represented a magnificent achievement. For the government it marked a humiliating climb-down. What was granted or allowed was: firstly, a free and general pardon absolving all participants in the pilgrimage of grace; secondly, the promise of a parliament, to be held by free election and in York, to consider the rebels' complaints; and thirdly, an understanding that, until this parliament had deliberated, nothing would be done to implement policies to which the rebels objected. Thus, until then, the collection of the taxes condemned in the twenty-four articles would be suspended, whilst the restored lesser monasteries would be allowed to stand.

None of this accorded with the government's intentions. Rather than a general pardon, the government wished to grant a pardon with exceptions. This was made clear during the Truce in a draft royal proclamation of 2nd November which offered to remit all offences committed by the pilgrims before 1st November, except for those of ten men, six of whom were named and one of whom was Aske.[125] As set out in the proclamation, the condition of the pardon was submission before the king's lieutenant, the Duke of Norfolk. The only alternative on offer was military action: the dispatch to the north of an army led by the king himself. The pardon with exceptions remained the central plank of the government's policy throughout November. As late as 4th December the privy council wrote to Norfolk, who was again in Doncaster, stating the king's keenness on preserving his honour "which will be much touched if no man be reserved to punishment".[126] Yet no pilgrim appeared to accept the limited par-

124 See above, pp. 166–8(Richmondshire uprising) and 50–3(Beverley uprising).
125 L.P. XI. 955.
126 B.L. Harleian MSS 6989, f. 62 (L.P. XI. 1237).

don; and, on 6th December, at the Whitefriars meeting between the rebels' representatives and Norfolk, the free and general pardon was allowed.[127]

The terms of the first appointment obliged the government to consider and answer the pilgrims' five articles. In fact, the purpose of the Truce was to allow it time to reply. The understanding was that the king's answer would be conveyed north by the pilgrims' emissaries, Robert Bowes and Ralph Ellerker. The king's inclination was to repudiate all five. In fact, within a day or two of meeting Bowes and Ellerker and after listening to their elaboration of the articles, he had composed, apparently without assistance, a lengthy and literate reply which dismissed the rebels' complaints as improper and misinformed and insisted that the pardon to be granted should not excuse all.[128] The initial aim was to dispatch the king's answer to the rebels; but this never happened. Deterring the government was news of further disturbances. Thus on 6th November Norfolk informed Darcy that, having composed the answer and having intended to send it north with Bowes and Ellerker, the king had decided to hold it back upon learning that Aske was stirring up the commons in the East and West Ridings.[129] Henry's refusal to send his answer was presented as a punishment for the pilgrims' breach of the peace; but, in all likelihood, its retention came of realising that the north was still, at a moment's notice, ready for militant action and that such an unconciliatory reply might trigger off the dreaded march on London. And so the king's answer was kept under wraps and for the time being Bowes and Ellerker were retained in London.[130]

Instead, the government attempted, deviously, to have certain ringleaders apprehended. For example, by 6th November it was seeking to persuade Lord Darcy to hand over Aske, in return for being acquitted of the charge of willingly yielding Pontefract Castle to the rebels in October. It was put to Darcy by Norfolk; but without effect. On 11th November Darcy replied, saying that it went totally against his honour to betray Aske and insisting that the terms of the first appointment should be respected, with the king's reply to the five articles delivered to the people of the north by Bowes and Ellerker. In addition, he recommended the summoning of parliament to deal with the issues raised by the articles since that was "the thing

---

127 Bateson, p. 341; *L.P.* XI. 1271.
128 *L.P.* XI. 995 and 1009; *St.P.*, I, pp. 506–10 (*L.P.* XI. 957).
129 *L.P.* XI. 995.
130 *L.P.* XI. 985, 986, 995 and 1064.

they most desire" and proposed, in the meantime, "an abstinence with assurance".[131]

The problem for the government was that, following the Truce, it felt it could only proceed by negotiation. This was because its four thousand troops based in Lincolnshire were required to hold that county down; and because the rest of the army royal had been dissolved on 27th October and nothing could be quickly put in its place.[132] Before hearing of the Truce, Henry VIII had issued plans to advance in person against the rebels. He had even summoned a fresh muster of troops. But upon hearing that the two armies had demobilised, in accordance with the first appointment, he acted on 30th October to discharge the troops who had been summoned only the previous day.[133] Thereafter, a major drawback for the government against raising more troops lay in the inflammatory effect the news of it would have upon the north. In addition, a fear was held in government circles that, if recruited, the commons of the south might share the pilgrims' cause and go over to the rebels. This fear was made explicit in the advice Norfolk pointedly offered to the king on 26th November when he remarked that, if the king persisted in rejecting the rebels' request for a general pardon and a free parliament, then he had no choice but to take military action against the rebels. However, this would have to be accomplished with an "army of gentlemen and household servants" since the commons could not be trusted.[134]

The idea of a second appointment came from the government, the result of the failure of its various policies to deal with the uprising. It was first proposed on 14th November, the date upon which a pardon was issued to the Lincolnshire rebels, except, that is, for the 140 in prison.[135] Presumably the king still hoped to secure a similiar settlement with the pilgrims: a submission followed by a partial pardon and the promise to consider, without obligation, the grievances so far formulated. The government's plan was set out in the instructions it issued to Bowes, Ellerker and Norfolk. Ellerker and Bowes were to announce that, as the king had found the five articles "general, dark and obscure", Norfolk would return to Doncaster to signify the king's response to them. This would take place at a colloquy in Doncaster

---

131 *L.P.* XI. 995; Hoyle, "Master's narrative", p. 73.
132 For the Lincolnshire problem, see *L.P.* XI. 909, 1103 and 1155(5/ii).
133 *L.P.* XI. 906 and 910.
134 Hoyle, "Master's narrative", p. 74.
135 *L.P.* XI. 1061 and 1065. By misdating *L.P.* XI. 1014 as 8th November, the editors of *L.P.* have given the impression that the plan had been formulated much earlier than it actually was.

consisting of three hundred delegates from each side.[136] Norfolk was instructed to adopt with the rebels a strong, censorious line.[137] If the rebels agreed to the colloquy, he was to declare, when it met, that the king took their proceedings "in very unkind part"; that they had compounded their offence by breaching the Truce with further assemblies and agitations; that their actions contradicted their claim to maintain the faith and commonwealth; and that they had offended against the body politic, by assuming that feet and hands could rule the head, and also against the society of orders, by disobeying the king and by obeying instead "a traitorous villein" (i.e. Robert Aske), "calling him captain". Norfolk was to require of them an acknowledgement of their crime and he was to tell them that, if they wished to see the king's answer to the articles, they must first "submit themselves to his mercy and laws", which in practice meant accepting the pardon with the ten exceptions. Only then "shall he deliver unto them copies of his grace's said answer". Yet, although firmly and precisely instructed, Norfolk was licensed "to use his discretion" and to proceed in whatever way was "most expedient for his Grace's honour".

The king thus remained insistent upon exceptions to the pardon and upon submission before allowing his answer to the five articles to reach the pilgrims. The pilgrims' reaction was to accept the proposal of a second appointment but to insist on a general pardon and a free parliament, and, as a rejoinder to Henry's perverse stand in finding the five articles too general and obscure whilst refusing to receive additional complaints, to propose further articles. All this was agreed at the pilgrims' York council, held on 21st–24th November to formulate a policy in the light of the information that Bowes and Ellerker had brought from the south. It was confirmed by the pilgrims' Pontefract council, held on 2nd–4th December, which produced a petition of twenty-four articles for presentation, through Norfolk, to the king.[138] At the December appointment the pilgrims had their way almost completely. Norfolk used his discretion to receive the twenty-four articles, to grant the general pardon, to promise a parliament at York and to withhold the king's rejection of the five articles. Norfolk also gave a broad hint, presumably with the king's approval, that some of the recent religious reforms were about to be undone. The only rebel demand he failed to comply with was a pardon enacted by parliament.

136 E36/121, fos. 1-5b (L.P. XI. 1064).
137 St.P., I, pp. 498–505 (L.P. XI. 1064).
138 For York council, see Dodds, I, pp. 311–18. For Pontefract council, see ibid., pp. 344–6 and 376–7. For decision to produce particular articles, see SP1/120, f. 36b (L.P. XII{1}. 1175).

In the five articles it was proposed that it should be authorised "by act of parliament or otherwise as surely as can be devised". In the course of November it seemed that the preference among the commons was for an enacted pardon. In December the pardon granted was simply under the great seal.[139] But this might have been regarded by the rebels not as a rejection of what they wanted but as a stop-gap until parliament next sat.

How did this submission to the rebels come about? By 26th November Norfolk was resigned to complying with the pilgrims' demand for a general pardon and for a free parliament to consider their complaint. Yet the king was strongly opposed to granting either. Norfolk by this time had reached Nottingham. The news he was receiving from the north made it clear to him that the rebels were determined "instantly to proceed in their pilgrimage" if the negotiations broke down. He was also aware of their commitment to die for the cause if the king failed to offer some redress.[140] The pilgrims, moreover, were gathering again in very large numbers. As he put it on 30th November, "the rebels are so strong and our forces so small that if this meeting take no effect and war follow, we are in an ill case". Therefore the grant of a pardon without exceptions and of a parliament to consider the rebels' grievance was "necessary for the present".[141]

Then the king made a number of concessions, in a series of fall-back policies concocted by his advisers to avoid the deadlock which might lead to war. Thus, on 2nd December a free and general pardon was drawn up and dispatched northwards with Sir John Russell, after the government had heard that the rebels had a host of 20,000.[142] Yet the accompanying order was that it should not be used: on 2nd December letters from both the king and the privy council emphasised that the free general pardon had to be withheld and that the rebels ought to receive instead the earlier pardon with its ten exceptions. Moreover, at this late stage the king remained adamant that the rebels should not present him with further articles, so much so that if the rebels insisted on it military action should be taken, deploying the

---

139 For pilgrim success, see Bateson, pp. 341–2; Hoyle, "Master's narrative", p. 75 (49); *L.P.* XI. 1319; *L.P.* XII{1}.137, 146 and 1175. For pardon, see SP1/109 (*L.P.* XI. 902{2}); Hoyle, "Masters narrative", p. 73; and *L.P.* XI. 1276. For the government's intimation of religious reaction, see below, p. 403.
140 Hoyle, "Master's narrative", p. 74.
141 Ibid., p. 75; ibid., p. 74.
142 *L.P.* XI. 1227.

forces of the Duke of Suffolk in Lincolnshire and the Earl of Derby in Lancashire.[143] Two days later he grudgingly accepted that the general pardon might have to be issued if "very extremity shall enforce the same" and it seems that he was now prepared "to condescend to a parliament"; but he remained opposed to the production of further articles "as our honour may in no wise grant".[144] The same day Norfolk reported that the rebels had produced further articles "which . . . be far from all reason", receiving them nonetheless for the king.[145]

Finally, some hope was raised that the traditional practices and beliefs of the church would be preserved. This came in the form of a letter from the king to Cranmer which was made available to the pilgrim leadership at Doncaster. In all likelihood, it was a version of a letter of 19th November in which the king ordered the bishops, on the one hand, to enforce the Ten Articles but, on the other, to proceed against radical preaching and married priests. The rebel leadership was deeply impressed by it, perceiving in it a turning of the tide, so much so that Darcy informed the Archbishop of York, to whom he sent a copy, that, because of it, "all true catholics may joy". Clearly signalled to the rebels, then, was the prospect of a religious reaction which soon materialised in the Bishops' Book of 1537 with its recognition of the lost sacraments, the four unmentioned in the Ten Articles.[146]

In determining the December agreement Norfolk had a vital part to play. It was he who managed to overrule the king. This was achieved when Suffolk and the other members of the privy council came to accept Norfolk's concessionary policy of pardon and parliament. As the king declared to Suffolk in a letter of 4th December, he had agreed to accept Norfolk's advice "seeing that you agree" and "yielding to the advice of our council".[147] In addition, there was the pressure apparently brought upon the proceedings by the commons of the north. Norfolk was aware not only that the commons were untrustworthy but also that they were deeply suspicious of the gentlemen pilgrims, believing that, in the Lincolnshire manner, they might betray the rebel cause by an act of unconditional submission. As Norfolk observed, the commons were bent on battle if their demands were

143 Ibid., and *L.P.* XI. 1228.
144 *St.P.*, I, p. 521 (*L.P.* XI. 1236).
145 Hoyle, "Master's narrative", p. 75.
146 *L.P.* XI. 1336. Also see M. Bowker, *The Henrician Reformation: the Diocese of Lincoln under John Longland, 1521–1547* (Cambridge, 1981), p. 161 and E. Duffy, *The Stripping of the Altars* (New Haven and London, 1992), pp. 398–401.
147 *L.P.* XI. 1236.

not met: "The commons are so many and so well provided and so stubborn-minded" that, without an agreement, he warned, "they will instantly proceed in the pilgrimage and they will all die in case their articles . . . be refused".[148] This was confirmed in a number of ways. Thus the yeoman John Hallom wrote to the pilgrims' York council "in the name of the commons" setting out the five articles, "requiring them to be granted by the king" and declaring in conclusion: "or else we are fully determined to spend our lives and goods in battle".[149] It was also underlined by the hostility of the commons shown towards the Archbishop of York on the 3rd December in Pontefract church for preaching the doctine that subjects were not entitled to take up the sword against their prince.[150] The same impression was conveyed by Sir Anthony Wingfield who, reporting on the York council, wrote: "the gentlemen be very weary of the matter but the commons cry still that if they have not a good end they will fight".[151]

Their basic demands were made clear at the York council: a general pardon and a parliament They were declared in Hallom's letter which required "a general pardon by act of parliament". In reporting upon the York council's proceedings to Lord Darcy, Aske revealed the importance attached by the commons to a general pardon; as did the report from Sir Anthony Wingfield who revealed how the demand was made for an enacted pardon. Apparently a petty captain named Walker warned all the gentlemen present "to look substantially in the matter so they might have a good end" and then told Aske: "Look ye well upon this matter for it is your charge, for if you do not ye shall repent it".[152]

As well as noting the determination of the commons not to submit, Norfolk also observed their unwillingness to be passive followers of the gentlemen. On 30th November he remarked that the "lords and gentlemen have no such power as they had among them" and that the commons were so suspicious of the gentlemen that they would not allow them to talk together in private.[153] On 3rd December he commented on the rebels assembled in Pontefract: "The people bear the rule and not the nobility but in manner have them so suspect that

---

148 SP1/112 (L.P XI. 1234); Hoyle, "Master's narrative", p. 75.
149 Ibid., p. 73.
150 Dodds, I, pp. 379–80.
151 L.P. XI. 1170.
152 Hoyle, "Masters narrative", p. 73; L.P. XI. 1170; L.P. XI. 1128. Aske's version differs in that he says the commons' priority was to have the pardon granted by Cromwell and that noblemen should rule again (ibid.).
153 Hoyle, "Master's narrative", p. 75.

they are in half-captivity".[154] That the commons were forcing the gentlemen to make a firm stand was evident in Robert Aske's narrative of the second appointment in which he showed how, fearful of the commons, the gentlemen left three peers at Pontefract on 5th December specifically to control them whilst the pilgrim representatives rode to Doncaster to treat with Norfolk; and how, in order to quell the suspicion of the commons, half the delegates chosen to treat with Norfolk at the Whitefriars on 6th December were of the commonalty.[155] With an agreement reached on a general pardon, a free parliament and the right of the restored religious houses to continue until parliament had deliberated in the matter, Aske personally reported back to the 3,000 commons at Pontefract who at first received the news joyfully but then, once Aske had returned to Doncaster, became suspicious, reasoning that, before the pilgrimage was called off, certain conditions had to be affirmed, notably that the pardon should be seen before it was accepted; that the restored monks should remain in possession of their houses; and that the promised parliament should be at York.[156] All this was reported to the delegates at Doncaster in a letter from Lord Lumley which closed with the threat that, if no assurance was given in these three matters, "they would burn beacons and raise the whole country". In response, Aske raced back to Pontefract to calm the commons. Agreement was finally reached between the delegates and the commons on 8th December when Lancaster Herald arrived in Pontefract, the pardon was read out and confirmation was given on the York parliament and the restored abbeys. Only then did the commons disperse.[157] With that accomplished, the gentlemen led by Aske humbly submitted, ritualistically tearing off their pilgrims' badges; and the king was left in a state of fury because none had been reserved for punishment and because, with the restored abbeys left standing, the way was now open for a permanent undoing of the Dissolution.[158]

The December appointment, with all that it entailed, was, then, specifically determined by the pressures the pilgrims brought upon the king's lieutenant, the duke of Norfolk, to comply with their wishes and by the singleminded resolution of the commons to go to war unless they received the pardon and the parliament. But directing it were also the promises made at the first appointment; and responsible for both

154 SP1/112 (*L.P.* XI. 1234).
155 Bateson, p. 341.
156 Ibid.
157 Ibid., pp. 341–2.
158 *L.P.* XI. 1271.

appointments were the October hosts, an overbearing fact in October and a potent, influential memory in December, coupled with the government's fear that, if negotiations failed, the rebels would, under compulsion from the commons, rehost, march on London and, in the manner of 1381 and 1450, achieve their purpose by force.

XI

━━━━━━━━━━━━━━━━━━━━━━━━━━━━━━━━━━

CONCLUSION

The pilgrimage of grace collapsed in March 1537. With its adherents divided between those keen to preserve the December agreement and those keen to stage further revolts and march on London, the government was able to secure a submission without needing to resort to either force or negotiation. Yet the situation had been totally different in late 1536. Then the government had been obliged to submit to the rebels. The secret of success for the pilgrims had lain in their mobilisation of a huge force, consisting of nine separate hosts, all recruited from the region north of the Don. Of these armies, some remained within the regions from which they were recruited. Their role was to resist loyalist elements, notably the Earl of Derby and his gentlemen supporters in Preston, the Earl of Cumberland and the gentlemen hiding in Skipton Castle, Lord Clifford and the gentlemen who had taken refuge in Carlisle, and the borderers of neighbouring Eskdale. But others converged at Pontefract to form the pilgrim host which so dwarfed the opposed army royal that the king's commanders readily agreed to a truce.

Each of the rebel armies began with a confederation summoned by bells, beacons and bills. Each of the confederations was bound by an oath to be true to God, the king, the faith and the commonwealth or commons. The confederations became hosts as a result of holding musters in which, following the procedure for raising the militia, all men between sixteen and sixty were called upon to assemble in arms. The best troops were then selected and each community was obliged to see that the troops it provided were properly equipped, waged and provisioned, raising money for the purpose by taxing the inhabitants who stayed behind. Formed in this way, the armies were not a rabble of peasants; nor were they the retinues of lords and gentlemen. Overall, they were impressively weaponed and well-horsed, with many of the troops experienced in war through service on the northern border. Many were equipped with horse and harness because they held their farms by tenant right and therefore were under permanent obligation to serve the lord warden of the marches in the defence of the frontier.

The armies presented themselves, and were perceived as acting, in the name and cause of the commonalty. Each was the military expression of a rising of the commons. Yet these movements were not simply popular revolts. They began, in every case, as a protest of the people, but developed into formidable movements – affecting regions rather than mere localities – because the county establishment of lords and substantial gentlemen made no serious effort to resist them. There is a marked contrast between the northern uprisings of 1535 and 1537, both of which the gentlemen put down, and those of 1536, to which the same gentlemen responded by either flight or submission.[1] In 1535 and 1537 the gentlemen had good cause to take counteraction, in 1535 because the rebel grievance was simply against harsh landlordship and in 1537 because they wished to preserve the December agreement. In contrast, moved by an antipathy to the government, many gentlemen in October 1536 had no incentive to suppress uprisings whose grievances they shared. Their attitude was best described by Robert Aske when he advised Stephen Hamerton in November 1536: "If they be rising of themselves, hinder them not of their good will".[2] The strategy of many gentlemen was to allow popular revolts to become so impressive that they might persuade the government to change its policies. In this manner, they hoped to effect something which they had failed to achieve through the normal channels of parliament and faction, without having to go to the lengths of mounting an aristocratic rebellion.

Although a series of risings of the commons, the pilgrimage of grace was imbued with a firm belief in the society of orders. The commons hoped to enlist the support of the other two orders, the gentlemen and the clergy, and to get them to perform the social

---

1 For the uprisings of 1535, contained by the actions of the earls of Westmorland and Northumberland, Lord Monteagle, Sir Marmaduke Tunstall and Sir Richard Tempest, see *L.P.* VII. 1314–15 (misdated); *L.P.* VIII, 863, 893, 946, 970, 984, 991–5, 1046, 1030{2} and 1133; *L.P.* X. 77; *L.P.* Add. 996; P.R.O. KB9/534/77; R. B. Manning, *Village Revolts, Social Protest and Popular Disturbances in England, 1509–1640* (Oxford, 1988), pp. 49–50. For the 1537 revolts, see D. Bownes, "The Post-pardon Revolts" (M. Phil., Manchester, 1995).
2 *L.P.* XI. 1115.

obligations of leadership and direction which the notion of orders expected. Their disobedience and initiative was not an abandonment of belief in the society of orders but rather a corrective mechanism used to compensate for the fact that the government could not be restrained by the normal means. With the clergy and gentlemen unable to curb the government's tyrannical and heretical ways, it was now up to the commons to rise to the occasion. All three orders shared the belief that the government was showing contempt for the society of orders: by exploiting rather than nurturing the commons; by allowing men of base blood to run the government and to secure noble status; by taking away the privileges of the clergy and the liberties of the church. Whatever gave meaning to society and its relationship with the body politic, it was felt, was being spurned. Moreover, the success of the uprisings was seen as depending upon the rebels' abilities to enact the society of orders in the defence of its very principles. Considerable efforts were made by the rebels to enlist the gentlemen and clerics. However, once recruited the higher orders were not placed in complete command. They were expected to serve the commons' cause and to remain answerable to the commonalty. For this reason they were in constant danger of being labelled "traitors to the commons". When they were compliant they were ecstatically appreciated; but the commons treated instances of independence and non-cooperation with deep suspicion and outbursts of rage.

Gentlemen and clerics could serve the commons by leading the hosts, by formulating petitions and by negotiating with the government. In parts, notably Cumberland and Westmorland, service to the commons meant respecting the system of tenant right. Here, with agrarian grievances dividing commons and gentlemen, the captaincy of the hosts was not conferred upon the latter. Yet they were still expected to participate, basically by submitting to what the commons decided. As for the clergy, contrary to the principles of the society of orders, pressures were occasionally brought upon them by the commons to serve at arms; and some (notably Thomas Maunsell, Thomas Johnson and William Tristram) were willing to comply. But normally it was accepted that their task should accord with the one allocated to them by the society of orders: that is, to minister to the hosts and to lead them, not as captains commanding an army but as crossbearers leading a pilgrimage.

The pilgrimage of grace became a great rebellion because all three orders were involved and because, either through fear of, or sympathy for, the commons' cause, the gentlemen failed to perform their expected task of keeping order in their localities. In most cases the gentlemen failed to organise resistance and fled. As a result, Carlisle, Scarborough, Preston, Skipton, Hull and Pontefract became nests of fled gentlefolk. In fact, the majority of gentle pilgrims were enlisted as the rebels brought pressure upon these refuges to give up their prestigious denizens. Vitally important for realising the society of orders in revolt was the taking of Hull and Pontefract, coupled with the siege of Skipton Castle by the 12,000 troops from Richmondshire and Ripon which, although failing to take it, succeeded in persuading some of the gentlemen within its walls, notably Lord Scrope, to join the pilgrimage. Other gentlemen yielded, following visits to their houses by bands of armed men.

The gentlemen pilgrims, like the clerical participants, claimed that they were enforced to join the uprising. This was largely true. But the contribution they made to the uprising also stemmed from their sympathy for the rebel cause. Their hope was that, unresisted, the commons would achieve their basic aim: to persuade the king to dispose of Thomas Cromwell and all that he stood for. But, forcibly drawn in by the commons, they became actively committed as organisers and captains of the host and as negotiators with the government because they subscribed to most of the rebels' grievances. These fell into two basic categories: those concerned with the defence of the faith and those concerned with the defence of the commonwealth. Linking the two was partly the belief that the "faith of the church" was maintained by "the profit of the church" and partly, and more importantly, by the belief that the government under Thomas Cromwell was damaging both the faith of Christ and the commonwealth of the realm.[3]

The faith issue centred upon a general objection to heresy. But it also complained specifically of the way heresy had already affected the church through a religious settlement that had condemned as superstition the power saints were assumed to possess in the remission of sin and in gaining God's grace; that had caused the replacement of the pope by the king as head of the English church; and that had cast doubt upon the existence of purgatory and, *ipso facto*, the whole system of intercession and its attendant beliefs in the efficacy of prayers for the dead, the taking of the sacraments and the veneration of relics and images. Yet, whilst the opposition to heresy itself was made repeatedly explicit, any opposition to its implications, as they were specified in the Ten Articles, in the royal injunctions enforcing these articles and abrogating holy days, in the new order of prayer and

3 For the connexion made between faith and profit, see below, n. 12.

in the Act of Supremacy, was very rarely stated. Presenting the rising as a pilgrimage was a religious protest in itself, for the royal injunctions of 1536 had disapproved of pilgrimages, largely because they raised false expectations of what the saints' could reasonably do.[4] Moreover, the abrogated saints days were clearly an issue in the Cumberland uprising, which specified them as a grievance in a proclamation that it produced; in the barony of Westmorland where the failure to announce the forthcoming St. Luke's Day during the Sunday service in the parish church of Kirkby Stephen marked the first sign of unrest; in the East Riding lordship of Watton whose inhabitants, prior to providing the company of troops which linked up with the Beverley and Holderness rebels, objected to the priest's failure to announce the forthcoming St. Wilfred's Day; and in Richmond where the abrogation of holy days was raised as a grievance at one of the assemblies held in the town.[5] But that is the tally: the grievance was not evidently associated with any of the other regional revolts comprising the pilgrimage of grace.

Similarly, complaint was made against the new order of prayer (which omitted prayers for the pope and his cardinals) in Cumberland, Kendal, the barony of Westmorland and in Percy Fee, but nowhere else; and only two of the references appertain to October 1536, the others belonging to January, 1537.[6] In the pilgrims' twenty-four articles papal overlordship in matters spiritual was specifically defended but the abrogation of holy days and the new order of prayer failed to figure as sources of objection.[7] True, the clerical representatives at the pilgrims' Pontefract convocation (held in the first week of December, at the same time as the Pontefract council, to deliberate on the articles to be presented to the king) opined: "We think that preaching against purgatory, worshipping of saints, pilgrimage, images" and "all books set forth against the same or sacraments" should be condemned; and went on to declare that the holy days should be observed "according to the laws and laudable customs"

---

4 For the attack on pilgrimages in the injunctions, see G. Burnet, *The History of the Reformation of the Church of England* (Oxford, 1829), I(ii), pp. 252–3.
5 For Cumberland, see P.R.O. SP1/117, f. 55b (*L.P.* XII{1}. 687 {2}). For the barony of Westorland, see ibid., f. 53. For Watton, see *L.P.* XII{1}. 201/iv. For Richmond, see *L.P.* XII{1}. 789; also see ibid. 163 (article 3).
6 For Percy Fee, see *L.P.* XII{1}. 792 and for the schedule mentioned in it, *L.P.* XI. 655(misdated). For Kendal, see *L.P.* XII{1}. 914. For Cumberland, see SP1/117, f. 55b (*L.P.* XII{1}. 687 {2}). For barony of Westmorland, see ibid., f. 59b–60 and also P.R.O. E36/119, f. 81 (*L.P.* XII{1}. 687{4}).
7 *L.P.* XI. 1246 (article 2).

and that "the bidding of beads" may be "as hath been used by old custom".[8] But this expliciteness was not typical of the pilgrims' religious complaint. There was little defence of the sacraments. True, the Archbishop of York had reported to the king on 10th December, that, when he had shown them the Ten Articles, the rebels had objected to them on the grounds that they mentioned only three sacraments; but the fact that the Ten Articles had reduced them from seven to three went largely unopposed. Apart from the objection declared by the clergy in the pilgrims' Pontefract convocation, their defence featured only in one early draft of the pilgrims' December petition where opposition was declared to "all who teach against Christ's faith and the sacraments of Christ's church". Yet in the same article a commendation was made of the articles recently issued by the king with the advice of "his catholic bishops", presumably the Ten Articles. Moreover, this complaint about the sacraments was edited out before the December petition was submitted.[9]

The Archbishop of York also informed the king in his letter of 10th December that the rebels had objected to the repudiation of purgatory. However, apart from the objection made by the Pontefract convocation, nowhere else in the surviving evidence of the pilgrimage is this key religious issue mentioned; and it is possible that, in the matter of both the sacraments and purgatory, the archbishop was putting grievances into the mouths of the rebels as a means of securing what he himself wanted. Furthermore, there is little defence of saints, apart from the concern for holy days. In the surviving evidence is very little reference to relics, shrines or images. Aske made the point, both in his address to the lords in Pontefract and again in his examination, that the Dissolution was found objectionable because it had involved the violation of relics and in a general muster proclamation used in the north-west in late October 1536, the recent religious reforms were accused of "blaspheming our lady and all other saints in heaven".[10] But that is about it. The first five articles that the pilgrims submitted to the king were perceived in parts of the north as calling for a restoration of the religious usages practised upon Henry VIII's accession; but the articles actually submitted made no such

---

8 L.P. XI. 1245, printed in D. Wilkins (ed.), Concilia Magnae Britanniae et Hiberniae (London, 1737), III, pp. 812–13.

9 For York's letter to the king, see R. W. Hoyle, "Thomas Master's narrative of the pilgrimage of grace", Northern History, 21 (1985), p. 76. For the draft articles, see SP1/112, p. III (L.P. XI. 1182{2}).

10 For Aske, see Bateson, pp. 335 and 561. For the muster proclamation, see Toller, p. 48.

point. They merely called for a restoration of "the commons laws and commonwealth" as was practised in 1509.[11]

Much more prominent in the pilgrims' complaint was concern over the spoiling of the church: in other words, the government's onslaught upon the wealth of the church through expropriation (the suppression of religious houses and churches and the confiscation of their treasures) and exaction (the levy of first fruits and tenths). At only one point was spoliation connected specifically with the faith: in the bill found circulating in the Richmond area in January 1537.[12] Otherwise, the spoiling of the church was presented as a common-wealth issue. It was objected to because, deprived of its wealth, the church would be less able to dispense charity and hospitality. In this respect, the complaint belonged to a broad category of grievance which charged the government with showing contempt for the wealth of the king's subjects, for the constitution and for the society of orders; and therefore accused it of bad governance.

On the issues of the faith and the commonwealth decayed, and because of the rebels' general willingness to lay the blame upon the government, the three orders of society found agreement and the nine hosts found a common cause. But also important as sources of motiva-tion were the complaints confined to particular localities. Most of the uprisings had their very own grievances which they might share with neighbouring revolts but which did not move the pilgrimage of grace as a whole. Thus, in the north-west, the hosts formed in Westmorland and Cumberland were especially moved by an agrarian grievance: i.e. the custom of tenant right and its ill-treatment by the landlords.[13] In Richmondshire the rebels were moved by the Wycliffe case and the government's high-handed treatment of the Yorkshire jury which, for refusing to find him guilty, was heavily fined in Star Chamber.[14] In Howdenshire and in the region about Malton, the imminent dispos-session of the Percy family was one cause of revolt.[15] In Percy Fee the granting of Sawley Abbey to a stranger, Sir Arthur Darcy, was a prominent grievance; and in Beverley the conflict between the town and its lord of the manor, the Archbishop of York, over respective rights and privileges was a source of complaint that worked its way

11 See E36/119, f. 81 (*L.P.* XII{1}. 687{4}) and SP1/111 (*L.P.* XI. 1059/ii).
12 *L.P.* XII{1}. 163.
13 See above, pp. 276–7(Kendal), pp. 309–10(barony of Westmorland) and pp. 336–8 (Cumberland).
14 See above, pp. 106–7.
15 See above, pp. 205–6.

into the revolts of October 1536.[16] None of these local grievances, however, stood alone; they were but part of a parcel of grievances which included complaints common to all the uprisings. Moreover, in many cases the local grievances were merely fuelling the general grievances to which they related. Thus the Wycliffe case, the town-versus-mitre struggle in Beverley, and the dispossession of the Percies simply sustained the belief that responsible for the ills of the realm was Thomas Cromwell; whilst the Arthur Darcy issue in Percy Fee simply provided another reason for subscribing to the generally-held grievance against the dissolution of religious houses. The strength of the pilgrimage of grace lay in the existence of grievances common to all the revolts and shared by all three orders. Essentially, they centred upon a complaint against bad governance. The point the rebels made and reiterated was that Cromwell had abused the king's trust to subvert the laws of God and of the realm. As a result, tyranny and heresy had been licensed to rule and, with the constitution impugned, the society of orders contemned and the realm plundered, the faith and the commonwealth were placed in dire peril.

Besides the socially unifying grievances, there were others which were socially divisive. Agrarian complaints were widely spread among the uprisings of October 1536, figuring not only in the uprisings in Westmorland and Cumberland but also in some of the Yorkshire revolts, notably in Richmondshire and Cleveland as well as around Dent, Beverley and Seamer.[17] The issue was tenant right and its infringement through the raising of gressums. Another factor was the decision of the Percy family to extend the tenant-right custom of the Honour of Cockermouth to its Yorkshire estates.[18] For various reasons the agrarian complaint failed to impair the pilgrimage. Agreements were reached between lord and tenant to respect the custom; concessions were promised by lords. In this manner the agrarian grievance was pushed into the background, in the interest of maintaining a common front against the government. In fact, only in the West March did it affect the nature of revolt, notably by preventing an enactment of the society of orders. In that region three hosts came into being which were not led by members of the county establishment. In this region the landlords were neutralised, not turned into captains.

Eventually the hosts appeared to fall under the control of lords and

16 For Percy Fee, see above, pp. 217ff. For Beverley, see above, pp. 50–3.
17 For the extent, see above, n. 13(Westmorland and Cumberland), pp. 54–5(Beverley), pp. 202–4(Seamer), pp. 170–3(Richmondshire), pp. 276–9(Dent).
18 See above, pp. 54–5.

knights, especially as they came together at Pontefract and were organised to form the pilgrim host, with the leadership of the van comprising of Sir Thomas Percy, Sir Thomas Hilton and Lords Lumley, Latimer and Neville; the middleward led by Lord Darcy, Sir Robert Constable and Sir Richard Tempest and the rearward led by Lord Scrope and Sir Christopher Danby. But this only resulted from dressing up a rising of the commons in the respectable cloak of the society of orders. Earlier the hosts had arisen from below led by captains who were not part of the county establishment. This was clearly evident in Cumberland where the four captains (all commoners apart from one who was soon replaced by a commoner) remained in charge. It was also evident in the barony of Westmorland where the captaincy lay with Nicholas Musgrave and Robert Pulleyn; in the barony of Kendal where William Collyns and John Atkinson provided the leadership; initially in Percy Fee where Jacks and Fawcett were the leaders; in the Beverley region where Stapulton and Hallom were prominent as captains and in Howdenshire where Aske soon came to the fore. This leadership was not drawn simply from the commonalty: among its members were minor gentlemen such as Atkinson and Pulleyn and younger sons of gentry families such as Stapulton and Aske. Moreover, the commoner leadership was drawn from well-off peasants, such as Jacks of Buckden, Hallom of Watton and Ombler of Holderness. What this group had in common was a greater freedom to vent their grievances than was possessed by the county establishment, lured as the latter was by the patronage the Dissolution had placed in the hands of the Crown. A remarkable feature of the pilgrimage of grace was that it should object to the Dissolution when it was perfectly clear that the laity would make enormous gains from it. This is to be explained by the fact that the uprising was intrinsically a popular movement which was first led by men who were beyond the scope of the Crown's patronage and therefore had no reason to believe that if they remained quiet they would be rewarded. Another remarkable feature of the uprising was the enlistment of the substantial gentlemen, many of whom had grievances against the government but were strongly inclined against direct implication. The fact that they were taken reflected the force and effectiveness of the commons licensed to act by a northern aristocracy which, disgruntled with the government, was not prepared to restore order and consequently found itself placed in charge of an insurrection which it had neither founded nor funded but rather had merely permitted.

Within the history of late medieval and early modern rebellions, the pilgrimage of grace occupies a special, if not a unique, place. The tendency to regard it as an aristocratic uprising has led to the assertion that, rather than a baronial revolt, it was the first of the country *versus* court uprisings and a forerunner of the English civil war.[19] This misses the point. Generically, it was a rising of the commons. As such, it belonged to a tradition of revolt established in the late middle ages as the society of orders came to fruition and "commons" came to mean commonalty rather than community. In organisation and idiom, it subscribed to a genre of revolt expressed first in 1381 and finally in 1549. Within this tradition were two strands of revolt, one driven by agrarian grievances, exclusively popular and mainly directed against landlords; and the other driven by political grievances, which permitted the positive involvement of gentlemen, and was mainly directed against the government. In the pilgrimage of grace, both strands were present, creating during the month of October 1536 revolts which differed in character but shared a conceit that they were by and for the commons.

Distinguishing the rebel armies which were mobilised in the north in October 1536 was firstly, their very size and efficiency; and secondly, an almost complete absence of fatalities, which rather suggests that they were firmly led and that their principal purpose was demonstration, not war. Whilst they clearly had a profound effect upon the government in late 1536 (and this was made evident in the October and December treaties agreed between the pilgrims and the king's lieutenants, and in the granting of a general pardon and the promise of a special parliament), the question remains: did the breaking of the December agreement render the northern uprisings ineffectual? The matter is debateable but good reasons exist against dismissing the pilgrimage of grace as a failure. After all, Cromwell had fallen by June 1540. Moreover, the protest against fiscal change was largely successful, arguably stopping a genuine Tudor revolution in government.[20] Furthermore, thanks to the pilgrimage of grace, the English Reformation became a complicated and drawn-out process. As things were developing in the early 1530s, it seemed that the break with Rome would be quickly followed by the establishment of a protestant regime. In practice, the pilgrimage of grace inspired a

19 See G. R. Elton, "Politics and the pilgrimage of grace" in B. Malament (ed.), *After the Reformation* (Manchester, 1980), pp. 47–52. The case for an aristocratic uprising was earlier made by R. B. Smith, *Land and Politics in the England of Henry VIII* (Oxford, 1970), ch. 5.
20 M. L. Bush, "Up for the commonweal: the significance of tax grievances in the English rebellions of 1536", *E.H.R.*, 106 (1991), pp. 314–15.

conservative reaction: within a few months the intimations made by the government at the start of December to undo the Ten Articles had materialised in the Bishops' Book.[21] And this reaction was so durable that the attempted revolution in religion was postponed until the following reign. Finally, a major agrarian development of the sixteenth century was the consolidation of customary rights of tenure, an achievement on the part of the peasantry that obliged the landlords to abandon, rather than operate through, the manorial system and to seek the replacement of the customary tenures by demesne leaseholds. Promoting the consolidation of custom and signalling its success were the privileges obtained by copyholds and by tenant-right tenures. At the time of the pilgrimage the tenant-right tenures tended to owe arbitrary gressums. However, by the late sixteenth century their gressums tended to be fixed. This is precisely what the pilgrims had wanted, both in the articles that they submitted to the government and in the custumals they forced lords to sign and seal. Moreover, the size of the gressum, set at twice the rent in the December petition, had become, by the late sixteenth century, the typical amount due.[22] In these respects, then, the formation of the pilgrim armies in October 1536 has to be appreciated not only as a spectacular achievement in itself but also as a major influence upon the religious, political, fiscal and agrarian changes of the time.

21 See above, pp. 401–3.
22 M. L. Bush, "Tenant right under the Tudors: a revision revised", *Bulletin of the John Rylands Library*, 77(1995), pp. 161–88.

Appendices

▪▪

I: The size and equipment of the rebel hosts

As one might expect, the estimates furnished by both sides on the size of the rebel armies were prone to exaggeration, because of the rebels' need to appear overwhelming and because of the loyalists' need to find excuses for their own ineffectiveness in resisting the uprising. But were these estimates far removed from reality; or can they be taken as plausible approximations? As the estimates suggest, the pilgrimage of grace was undoubtedly a massive uprising, securing support throughout much of the north and sweeping up the whole manred of each affected region rather than enlisting some individuals from the occasional community. But are they useful guides to the size of the rebel armies?

The surviving muster certificates of January 1535 and April 1539, commissioned by the government to assess the numbers of those over sixteen able to bear arms for the defence of the realm, are helpful for answering this question. Those for the north principally relate to Yorkshire. The broadest and most useful coverage was provided by the returns made in 1539, although, for the West and North Ridings, the returns for 1535 are also extensive. In addition, muster returns from 1535 have survived for Cumberland, but there is nothing from the 1530s for either Westmorland or the palatinate of Durham. For Durham there is the return of 1569, which is of some use. For Westmorland no returns have survived from the Tudor period.[1]

1 For Yorkshire musters of January 1535, see P.R.O. E36/32 (York and Ainsty); E36/37 (Claro); P.R.O. E101/549/5 (Barkston) and 6 (Skyrack); E101/62/8 and 9 (Agrigg and Morley); E36/44, f. 57 (Gilling East), f. 2 (Gilling West), f. 15 (Hang East), f. 26 (Hang West), f. 52 (Hallikeld) and f. 67 (Allertonshire); E101/58/59 (Birdforth); E101/549/7 (Langbaurgh); and E101/549/4 (Ryedale). For Yorkshire musters of April 1539, see E36/37, f.50 (Claro with Knaresborough Forest); E36/38, for the liberties of Claro: i.e. Kirkby Malzeard (f. 49), Ripon (f. 17) and Knaresborough Soke (f. 31)) and f. 1 (the liberty of Bradford) ; P.R.O. SP1/145, f. 170 (Skyrack); SP1/146, f. 1 (Osgoldcross), f. 82 (Ewcross) and f. 110 (Barkston); E36/30, f. 85 (Ouse and Derwent), f. 56 (Dickering), f. 84 (Holderness), f. 11 (Buckrose), f.1 (Howdenshire); E36/39 (Harthill); E36/23, f. 38 (Gilling West), f. 60 (Pickering), f. 13 (Hang East), f. 13 (Hallikeld), f. 1 (Birdforth); E36/41, f.1 (Hang West), f. 48 (Ryedale) and f. 27 (Langbaurgh); SP2/S p. 296 (Whitby and Whitby Strand); E101/549/22 (Allertonshire). For the Cumberland muster, see E101/549/13 and E30161/33. For the Durham muster, see P.R.O. SP12/51. The 1539 muster returns are summarised in *L.P.* XIV{1}. 652 (M26–9), apart from the one for Allertonshire (E101/549/22). The 1535 muster returns were overlooked by *L.P.*, apart from the one for Allertonshire (E36/44, p. 133) which the *L.P.* editors misdated as 1539.

The pilgrim host that Aske convoked to face the king's army at Doncaster – all of it drawn from Yorkshire and Durham – was reckoned to be at most 47,000 and at least 40,000.[2] Contemporary muster returns for Yorkshire indicate that the county could produce a force of something like 37,000 armed men.[3] However, since certain Yorkshire wapentakes, although up in revolt, did not supply troops for the pilgrim host (i.e. Staincliffe and Ewcross), this total has to be reduced accordingly to about 33,000. On the other hand, still to be taken into account is the muster return for the palatinate of Durham. Moreover, the returns for Yorkshire in the 1530s are incomplete: lacking are certificates for the North Riding wapentake of Bulmer as well as for the southerly West Riding wapentakes of Staincross, Upper Strafforth and Lower Strafforth. Could these regions have supplied the shortfall of 7-14,000 men? Without a doubt, the Durham militia was capable of providing at least 5,000 troops, and, if the Bowes host had consisted of 10,000, the Durham men must have contributed 7,500.[4] This latter figure was hardly possible: the nearest surviving muster return (for 1569), indicates a force of 6,500.[5] Furthermore, the return from the missing Yorkshire wapentakes, given their size and populousness, might easily have added 5,000, although this figure has to be reduced somewhat since it is normally understood that Upper Strafforth remained under loyalist control and did not participate much, if at all, in the pilgrimage.[6] A conservative estimate would reckon, then, that, if the military resources, as evident in contemporary muster returns, had been fully deployed, a pilgrim host of at least 40,000 armed men could have been raised. In this respect the contemporary estimates were exaggerations, but the lower estimate was well within range.

As for the size of the various regional hosts: the army recruited from Richmondshire and the West Riding that marched on Skipton Castle was drawn from an area with a muster return of 5,725 for the year 1535 and of 6,683 for 1539.[7] The estimate of 12,000 therefore must be a gross exaggeration. Yet this particular host was far from being a small force. After all, it alone was designated as the rearward in the pilgrim host. Moreover, there is

---

2 For the host assembled at Doncaster, see above p. 376. To these figures of 28,000 and 35,000 one needs to add the rearward which failed to arrive in time for the confrontation, a force estimated at 12,000 men.
3 See table below.
4 On the grounds that the militia capacity of Cleveland (i.e. Langbaurgh, Allertonshire and part of Birdforth) which also provided men for this host must have amounted to 2,500. See table below.
5 SP12/51. In 1569 4,000 were without horse, harness and even weapons, but this might have resulted from a decay of the border defences over the previous thirty years.
6 See R. B. Smith, *Land and Politics in the England of Henry VIII* (Oxford, 1970), pp. 175–6 and 197–8; G. W. Bernard, *The Power of the Early Tudor Nobility* (Sussex, 1985), ch.2; and above, p. 133.
7 See above, p. 153. It recruited from the Richmondshire wapentakes of Gilling East, Gilling West, Hang East, Hang West, Hallikeld and the West Riding wapentake of Claro. See table below for 1539 and E36/37 and 44 for 1535.

good reason to believe that, whilst at Skipton, it recruited from Craven (i.e. Staincliffe wapentake) and perhaps even from the barony of Westmorland. By the time it reached Pontefract it could not have equalled the 20,000 proposed by Darcy but it may well have approached the estimated 12,000.[8] Another likely exaggeration was the estimate of 17,000 for the force under Aske and Darcy's leadership, recruited as it was from an area with a known muster return of no more than 15,000.[9] The extent of this exaggeration, however, is concealed by the absence of muster returns for the wapentakes of Staincross, Lower Strafforth and Bulmer, all likely recruitment areas for Aske.

Moreover, whilst the estimate of 10,000 for the host from Cleveland and Durham was an overstatement, this could not be said of the alternative estimates provided for the same host, reckoned at 5,000 by Stapulton and 3–4,000 by Thomas Percy.[10] Between them, the Cleveland wapentakes of Langbaurgh and Allertonshire and the semi-Cleveland wapentake of Birdforth possessed just short of 3,000 able-bodied and armed men in 1539.[11] And the palatinate undoubtedly had the means to make up the difference of 3,000. As for the Percy host of 4–5,000, it was certainly within the military capacity of the wapentakes from which it was recruited: the total muster for Pickering Lythe, Whitby Strand, Ryedale, Dickering and Buckrose amounted to 5,000 in 1539.[12] The Stapulton host, calculated at 2–3,000 was well within the muster returns for the wapentakes of Harthill and Holderness which, including Hull and Hullshire, amounted to 6,000 for 1539.[13] The estimate for the Hamerton Tempest host from Percy Fee in Craven was probably exaggerated at 3,000, but the military resources of Staincliffe and Bowland were considerable, amounting in 1539 to just over 3,000 able and armed men, with at least 1,800 drawn from the region caught up in the revolt.[14] In addition, there was the contribution made to this host by the men from the Lancashire hundred of Blackburnshire, for which there is no contemporary muster return. The remaining muster figure of some use is that for the West Riding wapentake of Ewcross which, in conjunction with the barony of Kendal and the Lancashire hundred of Lonsdale, produced an estimated rebel force of about 3,000.[15] The military capacity of Ewcross alone was about 1,300 in 1539. Although Tunstall and Monteagle took with them 677 men to join the army raised by the Earl of Derby, it is

8 See above, p. 156.
9 This was an implied, not an explicit, estimate calculated by taking Aske's estimate of the force assembled (i.e. 35,000) and by deducting the estimates for the Percy host (5,000), the Bowes host (10,000) and the Stapulton host (3,000). The recruitment area was Howdenshire, Osgoldcross, Stainforth Lower, possibly Staincross, Agrigg and Morley, Barkston, Skyrack, Ouse and Derwent, Harthill, York and the Ainsty, possibly Bulmer. Also see table below.
10 See above, p. 160.
11 See table below.
12 See above, p. 195; and see table below.
13 See above, p. 58. For Hull and Hullshire, see E101/60/1.
14 See above, p. 223.
15 See above, p. 248.

conceivable that the combined effort of the barony of Kendal, of north Lancashire and of Ewcross could have raised the estimated host.[16]

Finally, the incomplete muster certificates for Cumberland, taken in 1535 and revealing a force of 7,500 men, would suggest that the rebel army of 15,000, reckoned to have arrayed outside Carlisle at the end of October, was very much an overestimation.[17] Unknown is the extent of the Westmorlanders' involvement in this venture; and, in the absence of muster returns, also unknown is the military capacity of the barony of Westmorland.[18] Yet making allowances for the Westmorlanders' possible contribution, and for the fact that certain parts of Cumberland, notably Eskdale ward, remained loyal to the Crown, the estimate for the rebel host remains well beyond belief.

The hosts were presented as well-horsed and harnessed,[19] yet another overstatement. But the muster returns suggest that the manred in parts of the north was very well-horsed indeed. This was certainly the case in the North Riding: for in Richmondshire, notably in the wapentakes of Hang West, Hang East and Gilling West, and in the wapentakes of Langbaurgh and Birdforth, half the troops certified as able were described as horsed. In the East and West Ridings, with the exception of Craven and Ewcross, the horsemen represented less than one-third of the troops returned. On the other hand, large numbers of horsed troops were available, the muster certificates of the 1530s revealing over 10,000 for Yorkshire alone, whilst Cumberland could provide another 2,300.[20]

According to the muster certificates, the horsed men were mostly fully harnessed: that is they were equipped with sallet (a leather or metal helmet reaching down to protect the back of the neck, jack (a leather or resined linen sleeveless jacket) and a pair of splints (i.e. plated armour for the arms). In sharp contrast, the foot men were mostly unharnessed. Very few were described as in "full harness for a man". Yet there were considerable numbers described as "parcel harnessed" in that, besides their weapons, they possessed some protective armour: just a sallet, or just a jack or just a pair of splints. Rarely mentioned in the muster certificates were steel bonnets, gorgets (throat-protectors), plate armour, mail or bucklers. Of the regions involved in the revolts of October 1536, the one with easily the most substantially harnessed militia was Cumberland, with 71 per cent of its able manhood in possession of some harness, followed by Richmondshire with 59 per cent having harness. Two of the latter's five wapentakes had a militia with over 70 per cent harnessed. In the East and West Ridings the percentage of able men with harness was only around 30 per cent, but in these Ridings were wapentakes with exceptionally high proportions of able men in

16 For troops taken by Tunstall and Monteagle, see above, p. 275. For Ewcross militia, see table below.
17 See above, p. 352; and see table below.
18 For Westmorlander involvement, see above, pp. 304–5.
19 See above, ch. IV(n. 222).
20 See table below.

harness, notably Harthill in the East Riding, with 47 per cent, and Staincliffe and Ewcross in the West Riding, with 48 and 47 per cent respectively.[21]

As recorded in the muster returns, the foot resembled the horse in being mainly armed with either bows or bills. In the possession of the gentry, all mounted, was the occasional spear, demi-lance and pole-axe, but most gentlemen carried bow or bill. As for the rank and file, only a very small minority at the musters was presented as equipped with staves, swords, daggers or lead malles; and the handguns recorded amounted to no more than six, four of them in the possession of the York militia. Again, the principal weapons were the bill and the bow; so much so that, in the muster certificates and books, the troops were designated either billmen or archers. Since the rebel troops were raised in the militia manner through formal musters, and since their numbers bore some resemblance to those found in the muster returns, it is reasonable to assume that the pilgrims were likewise armed; and given the military resources of the north, with large numbers of horse, considerable amounts of harness, and a huge amount of bills and bows, it would seem that the pilgrim hosts were genuine armies, not civilian rabbles.

Muster returns for Yorkshire:
numbers of able men and their equipment[22]

Wapentake	With horse	With harness[23]	With weapons
West Riding			
Skyrack(1539)	316 (all harnessed)	514 (198 foot)	986
Claro(1539)			
Claro with Knaresborough Forest	327 (ditto)	482 (190 foot)	1250
Kirkbyshire and Nidderdale	88 (ditto)	88 (no foot)	355
Liberty of Ripon	146 (ditto)	146 (ditto)	574
Liberty of Knaresborough	103 (ditto)	103 (ditto)	382

21 For York, see *L.P.* XIV {1}. 652, M26 (p. 307). Of the remainder, one handgun was possessed by a Cumberlander, see E101/549/13, f. 194; the other was possessed by someone living in the wapentake of Osgoldcross, see SP1/146 (*L.P.* XIV {1}. 652 {M29/7 Fockerby}).

22 For Yorkshire, the returns of 1539 have been used rather than those of 1535, although on occasion, notably with Gilling East and Agrigg and Morley, where

Wapentake	With horse	With harness[23]	With weapons
Barkston(1539)	316 (ditto)	316 (ditto)	2155
Staincliffe and Bowland(1539)	1247 (778 harnessed)	1463 (685 foot)	3141
Osgoldcross(1539)	456 (370 harnessed)	481 (111 foot)	1494
York and Ainsty(1539)	493 (477 harnessed)	568 (91 foot)	1931
Agrigg and Morley(1535)	284 (239 harnessed)	619 (287 foot)	1270
Ewcross(1539)	406 (322 harnessed)	619 (287 foot)	1270
Totals for the West Riding	4166	5468	18225
East Riding			
Howdenshire(1539)	82 (all harnessed)	82 (no foot)	605
Ouse and Derwent(1539)	137 (ditto)	137 (ditto)	928
Buckrose(1539)	148 (144 harnessed)	311 (167 foot)	727
Dickering(1539)	136 (129 harnessed)	430 (301 foot)	1112
Holderness(1539)	575 (all harnessed)	594 (19 foot)	2769
Harthill(1539)	733 (724 harnessed)	1312 (588 foot)	2859
Totals for the East Riding	1811	2866	9000

there are no surviving returns for 1539, the 1535 returns have been used instead. This preference is because the 1539 returns are more complete (i.e. for 1535 there are no surviving returns for the East Riding or for Osgoldcross, York and Ainsty, Ewcross, Craven, Pickering and Whitby). Moreover, the returns for 1539 tend to be more specific. For example the 1535 returns for Skyrack, Barkston and Claro fail to specify the horse. The returns for 1539 indicate greater numbers of armed men than those for 1535 and can therefore be regarded as more reliable on the grounds that there could have been good reasons for underestimating, but not for overestimating, the numbers available for militia service. Nonetheless, the 1539 returns are not without problems. The format into which "the view" was set tended to create two categories of troops only: horsed and harnessed horse and those without horse or harness, thus concealing sometimes the existence, sometimes the actual number, of horse without harness and footmen with harness. The references to the muster returns are given above, n.1.

23 Included in this category are not only the fully harnessed but also the partially harnessed.

Wapentake	With horse	With harness	With weapons
North Riding			
Richmondshire wapentakes			
Hang West(1539)	788 (all harnessed)	788 (no foot)	1451
Hang East(1539)	388 (ditto)	442 (54 foot)	603
Gilling West(1539)	660 (ditto)	660 (no foot)	1380
Gilling East(1535)	127 (ditto)	161 (34 foot)	366
Hallikeld(1539)	117 (ditto)	242 (125 foot)	322
Birdforth(1539)	388 (ditto)	388 (no foot)	800
Ryedale(1539)	267 (ditto)	267 (ditto)	1178
Langbaurgh(1539)	702 (ditto)	702 (ditto)	1455
Pickering Lythe (1539)	291 (ditto)	291 (ditto)	1017
Whitby(1539)	123 (ditto)	123 (ditto)	946
Allertonshire(1539)	245 (ditto)	245 (ditto)	636
Totals for the North Riding	4096	4309	10154
Totals for Yorkshire	10073	12643	37379

Muster returns for Cumberland(1535): numbers of able men and their equipment[24]

	With horse	With harness	With weapons
	2336 (all harnessed)	5272 (2936 foot)	7426

II. Chronology of events associated with the uprisings of October 1536

1534: Passing of a subsidy act, with a subsidy to be collected in 1535 and 1536 and a fifteenth and tenth in 1537; the Act for First Fruits and Tenths; the Act of Supremacy; a succession act; an act making words treason: all offensive to the pilgrims.

1535: Valor Ecclesiasticus compiled between January and July. The Leigh/ Layton visitation of religious houses between September and January.

February–April 1536: Passing of an act for the dissolution of the lesser monasteries; the Act of Uses, an act for ending the jurisdictional

24 See E101/61/33 and E101/549/13. Both relate to 1535. The surviving return is incomplete.

independence of Liberties and franchises, an act of succession allowing the king to will his successor: all offensive to the pilgrims.

May: Suppression of Sawley Abbey and Marton Priory.

20th May: Yorkshire jury summoned before Star Chamber and fined for acquitting William Wycliffe of murder.

June–July: In Convocation the clergy reject purgatory, accept the Ten Articles and enact the abrogation of holy days.

12th July: General order issued by the king to the bishops revising the order of prayer.

22nd July: Death of the Duke of Richmond.

August: Royal Injunctions issued instructing the clergy on the changes in religion and ordering a reduction in the number of holy days. Dissolution of the priories of Nunburnholme, Haltemprice, Holy Trinity and St Clement's in York, North Ferriby, Warter, Drax, Sinningthwaite, Healaugh, Armathwaite, Nun Monkton, Ellerton, Grosmont, Rosedale, Keldholme, Moxby, Arden and Baysdale and the abbeys of Easby and Coverham.

September: Dissolution of the priories of Conishead, Cartmel, Seton and the abbeys of Calder and Newminster.

25th September: Confederation through oath-taking in the West Riding lordship of Dent.

28th September: Commissioners resisted when attempting to dissolve Hexham Priory, inspiring the restoration of the recently dissolved Newminster Abbey and preparations for resistance at Lanercost, the next in line for suppression.

1st October: Treasures of Louth church locked up, their confiscation feared.

2nd October: Subsidy commissioners in Yorkshire and Lincolnshire set about collecting the second instalment of the subsidy granted in 1534.

————: Outbreak of the Lincolnshire rebellion, with bell-ringing and assemblies in Louth.

3rd October: Lincolnshire rebels capture subsidy commissioners and dispatch a letter of complaint to the government.

4th October: Aske leaves Yorkshire, crossing the Humber by the Hessle/ Barton Ferry, and is sworn by the Lincolnshire rebels.

5th October: Appointed captain of the West Ancholme strand of the Lincolnshire uprising, Aske meets the Louth host at Hambleton Hill, near Market Rasen.

5th/6th October: Archbishop of York writes to his Liberties of Beverley, York and Ripon. Telling them of the Lincolnshire uprising and Shrewbury's military preparations to deal with it, the letter orders the Liberty officials to look out for trouble.

6th October: Confederations are formed by oath-taking in Upper Wensleydale (North Riding); also in the Greta valley of South Ewcross (West Riding) and Lonsdale (Lancashire), under direction from the Dent men. Gentlemen are pressured to take an oath of allegiance to the commons.

———— Aske returns to Yorkshire, crossing the Trent at Burton-upon-Stather and the Ouse at Whitgift, and finds the commons of Howdenshire and Marshland ready to ring the bells to signal revolt. The same day the Louth and Horncastle hosts enter Lincoln, and Edward Dymmoke orders a rebel assembly at Ancaster Heath for 8th October, so that the Lindsey rebels can link up with those of south Lincolnshire.

7th October: Warned that the sheriff of Yorkshire is after him, Aske returns to Lincolnshire, probably by the Hessle/Barton Ferry. The same day two religious, Bowton and Mowde, cross by the same ferry into Yorkshire with a letter from the Lincolnshire rebels.

8th October: In the East Riding John Hallom and other parishioners force the priest of Watton church to acknowledge and announce the forthcoming St. Wilfred's Day, one of the abrogated holy days. The same day revolt breaks out in nearby Beverley, stirred by Woodmancy's arrival from Lincolnshire with the rebel articles and also by a letter from Aske to Raffles. The Beverley men send a letter to the Lincolnshire rebels and hold a muster on Westwood Green. The same day Aske returns to the East Riding, to dine with Babthorpe at Osgodby.

—— Sir Arthur Darcy allegedly confiscates the tithe corn and church ornaments belonging to Tadcaster parsonage, having been granted the possessions of Sawley Abbey, to which the parsonage had belonged.

By 8th October Lord Darcy and his son, Sir George, the outgoing sheriff of Yorkshire, have taken refuge in Pontefract Castle.

By 9th October letters of support have reached the Lincolnshire rebels in Lincoln from the townsmen of Beverley and Halifax; in response to which they send their latest articles not only to the king but into Yorkshire as well.

9th October: The Earl of Cumberland mentions "the misdemeanours of Gilsland", presumably a reference to preparations made to defend Lanercost against its prospective suppression. He is under instruction to go to the borders to deal with resistance there, notably at Hexham and probably at Newminster and Lanercost.

—— Beverley rebels hold a second assembly at Westwood Green and swear the Stapultons, making William Stapulton their captain. That night Hunsley beacon is fired, alerting the lowlands of the East Riding.

—— Aske passes into Lincolnshire again, returning to Yorkshire at midnight via the ferries at Burton-upon-Stather and Whitgift.

10th October: King's reply to the Lincolnshire rebels' letter of 3rd October reaches Lincoln.

—— The friar of Knaresborough seeks to raise Ryedale and Pickering Lythe in the North Riding, as well as parts of the East and West Ridings. This he does by spreading rumours of new taxes and plundered churches.

—— Commons rise in Malton region, taking captive the chancellor and registrar of the Archbishop of York who are then released through the intervention of Sir Ralph Eure.

——— Third assembly of Beverley rebels on Westwood Green. A second letter is sent to the Lincolnshire rebels.

——— Bell-ringing in Howdenshire (East Riding) and Marshland (West Riding), occasioned by a letter from Sir Brian Hastings, the incoming sheriff of Yorkshire, calling upon the gentry to organise themselves to prevent disorder.

——— Start of the four day minster horse fair at Ripon (West Riding) where the warning letter from the Archbishop of York (see 5/6th October) was read and the Richmondshire uprising probably has its beginning.

By 11th October there is friction in the barony of Kendal between the tenantry and its acting steward, Sir James Layburn, over the issue of tenant right and the exaction of gressums, causing the tenantry to present him with a petition.

11th October: Men from the lordships of Masham (North Riding), Kirkby Malzeard (West Riding) and Ripon (West Riding) occupy Jervaulx Abbey and restore Coverham Abbey, impose an oath to be true to the commons, burn beacons and recruit support from Nidderdale, Colsterdale, Coverdale, Wensleydale and the Vale of Mowbray.

——— Rebel musters are held on Hook Moor in Marshland and at Ringstone Hurst in Howdenshire. The Lincolnshire articles are read to the assembled. Aske issues his first proclamation ordering a muster at Skipwith Moor in the wapentake of Ouse and Derwent for the following day.

By 11th October the Archbishop of York, William Babthorpe and Robert Creke have left Cawood to take refuge in Pontefract Castle.

11th October: Fourth assembly of Beverley rebels on Westwood Green, attended by three delegates from Lincolnshire (Kyme, Curtis and Dunne), who deliver a letter from the Lincolnshire rebels with a copy of the articles that they had sent to Court. The same day Hunsley and Tranby beacons are fired. Summoned by bells, the Holderness men assemble at Nuthill to take the oath.

12th October: Restoration of Sawley Abbey.

——— Because of the unrest in Yorkshire, the Earl of Cumberland decides to disobey orders and to stay at Skipton Castle rather than, as instructed, to go to the borders to deal with the resistance at Hexham.

——— Lincolnshire uprising collapses, in response to a proclamation from the Earl of Shrewsbury.

——— St. Wilfred's Day. Muster at Skipwith Moor in wapentake of Ouse and Derwent. The Lincolnshire articles are read at the gathering. Afterwards, Acklam and Edwyn march up the Ouse into the Ainsty and Claro, mustering in the next three days at Acomb and Bilbrough; Maunsell proceeds to raise the wapentake of Barkston, mustering at Hillam, while Aske leads a march to Market Weighton in order to meet up with the Beverley rebels. The same day, the Beverley rebels muster at Hunsley

beacon. Hallom from the lordship of Watton with a company of woldsmen joins them; and then holds a second muster at Arram to link up with
men from Holderness. The same day the men of south Holderness hold a
muster at Sutton Ings, and the following day they march to Beverley.

By 12th October Gascoigne, Fairfax, Ryther and Ughtred have fled from
the region in and about the Ainsty.

12th/13th October: Lord Scrope flees from Castle Bolton in Wensleydale
(North Riding) to Helbeck in Westmorland and eventually to Skipton
Castle in the West Riding.

By 13th October Sir Ralph Eure has taken refuge in Scarborough Castle;
and so have George Conyers, Tristram Teshe and Edmund Copindale.

13th October: In the North Riding the first of the Richmond assemblies is
held and formulates a plan to recruit the local gentlemen by sending
parties to their houses. Easby Abbey is restored.

——— Conference between Aske and Stapulton on Weighton Hill. The
earliest use of the term "pilgrimage" is recorded, uttered by Aske to
describe the rebel purpose in conversation with Kyme and Dunne, the
delegates from Lincolnshire.

14th October: Travelling towards York, Aske's host spends the night of the
13th at Shiptonthorpe and all day of 14th October at Pocklington,
possibly becoming involved in the restoration of nearby Nunburnholme
and Warter Priories.

——— Second of the Richmond assemblies held, attended by recruited
gentlemen, notably Lord Latimer and Sir Christopher Danby. A letter
is composed condemning the dissolution of religious houses and calling
for the defence of the commonwealth. It is stuck to church doors in the
region.

15th October: Having joined up with the Holderness rebels, the Stapulton
host attends a meeting at Wyndeoak in the lordship of Cottingham. From
there it proceeds to besiege Hull.

——— Aske holds a muster at Kexby Moor (East Riding). He places a guard
on the bridges across the Derwent at Kexby and Sutton. At the muster
the Lincolnshire articles are read out.

——— Third of the Richmond assemblies is held. Robert Bowes arrives and
takes charge. Letters are composed: one for Cleveland ordering attendance at a muster on 16th to be held in the palatinate of Durham at
Oxen-le-Fields; others, written in the Captain Poverty idiom and
attached to a set of articles, are sent to Northumberland, Westmorland,
Cumberland and Pickering Lythe.

——— Curate of Kirkby Stephen church in Westmorland fails to announce
St. Luke's Day. The parishioners oblige him to do so.

16th October: Westmorland rebels hold their first muster at Sandford
Moor, in response to the Captain Poverty letter from Richmondshire.
Four captains are appointed: Pulleyn, Musgrave, Hilton and Blenkinsop.

——— Oath-taking assembly held at Malton (North Riding), incited by the friar of Knaresborough and the arrival of delegates from the Richmond-shire rebels. Deputed by this assembly, men, including the Richmond-shire delegates, visit the Percy house at Seamer (North Riding). They swear and enlist Sir Thomas Percy, brother of the sixth Earl of Northumberland.

——— Submission of York. Aske makes his triumphal entry at 5 p.m., after holding a muster outside the walls.

——— Richmondshire rebels hold their first muster in the palatinate at Oxen-le-Fields with the purpose of joining up with companies from Cleveland.

By 16th October: Conishead Priory has been restored.

——— Over fifty Yorkshire gentlemen (including one peer and nine knights) had taken refuge in Pontefract Castle: drawn from the West Riding Wapentakes of Barkston (e.g. the Darcies, Sir Henry Everingham, Henry Ryther); Skyrack (e.g. Sir William Gascoigne); Morley (e.g. Sir Robert Neville); Osgoldcross (e.g. Sir John Dawnye and Sir John Went-worth); the Ainsty (e.g. Sir Robert Ughtred); and from the East Riding wapentakes of Ouse and Derwent (e.g. William Babthorpe and John Acklam) and Harthill (e.g. Sir Robert Constable).

16th/17th October: Order for restoration of suppressed religious houses is nailed to the door of York minster. Holy Trinity and St. Clement's Priories, both in York itself, are restored; as is Healaugh Priory in the Ainsty.

17th October: Richmondshire rebels hold their second muster in the palatinate at Bishop Auckland. Finding that the Bishop of Durham has fled, they sack his palace. George Lumley is visited at Sedgefield, brought to Bishop Auckland and sworn.

——— Second meeting of the Westmorland rebels at Sandford Moor. They go to swear Sir Thomas Wharton. In his absence, they take his son and heir, removing him to Kirkby Stephen, and spend the night in Wharton Hall.

——— Muster of Malton rebels on the wold beyond Spital, attended by Thomas Percy. The rebels then plunder the property of the Cholmley family, close to Pickering.

——— Muster of Clevelanders at Carling Howe near Guisborough. They receive a message from the Richmondshire rebels not to march into the palatinate but to await further instructions.

——— Suffolk occupies Lincoln and supervises the submission of the Lincolnshire rebels; and the Earl of Shrewsbury is ordered to advance into Yorkshire "to give them the stroke".

17th/18th October: Aske composes the oath of the honourable men and issues his second proclamation, in the name of the baronage and com-monalty. He meets Thomas Strangways, steward to Lord Darcy, and presents him with the oath. Further musters are held on 18th October around York.

18th October: Musters in Barnsley and at Barnsdale, close to Doncaster.

―――― St. Luke's Day. The Westmorlanders assemble in Kirkby Stephen and visit Lammerside Hall to enlist the Warcops, who have fled.

―――― Following the arrival of Maunsell and his report on the support secured in the West Riding wapentakes of Barkston and Osgoldcross, Aske marches south to Pontefract, ordering the gentlemen and clerics in the castle to submit to the rebels and to take their oath.

―――― Government issues a proclamation, and sends letters to the same effect to Darcy and the Archbishop of York, asserting that the rumours of new taxes and demolished churches are totally false, maliciously spread and should be denied. It also urges Shrewsbury to advance against the rebels in Yorkshire and to use against them what had proved so successful in ending the Lincolnshire uprising: a proclamation composed by Shrewsbury and delivered by royal herald ordering the rebels to disperse or else.

―――― Two men from Dent(George Willan and William Garnet) enter the town of Kendal. In the course of the day they visit the understeward of the barony, Sir James Layburn, and William Collyns, bailiff of Kendal town. They also meet a number of the townsmen.

18th October/19th October: Richmondshire rebels hold a third muster in the palatinate at Spennymoor. The decision is made to divide the rebels into two hosts, the one composed of Durham men and Clevelanders, the other of troops from Richmondshire, Kirkby Malzeard and the Liberty of Ripon; the one to join Aske, the other to impress the Earl of Cumberland at Skipton Castle. To connect the two armies a secretariat is established at Jervaulx Abbey. On 19th October the Earl of Westmorland comes to the Spennymoor gathering, takes the oath and deputes his son, Lord Neville, to go in his stead on the march south.

―――― Thomas Percy is engaged in raising the East Riding wapentake of Dickering. George Lumley, having been sworn by the Richmondshire rebels in Durham, returns to his seat at Thwing on 18th October and joins this strand of revolt.

19th October: Townsmen of Kendal submit to the persuasion of the two men from Dent, taking an oath revised to replace "the commons" with "our ancient, laudable customs".

―――― Hull submits to the rebels.

―――― In barony of Kendal, the landlords Layburn and Strickland approve a declaration of custom drawn up by the tenantry, allowing their seals to be put to it.

―――― Westmorland host, led by Musgrave and Pulleyn, marches along the Eden to Penrith. On the way Musgrave visits Lowther Hall to recruit Sir John Lowther, but finds him out. Pulleyn finds Penrith already in revolt. Aroused earlier that day by the Captain Poverty letter from Richmondshire, it has appointed four captains (Beck, Burbeck, Hutton and Whelpdale) allegorically named Charity, Faith, Poverty and Pity and termed "the four captains of Penrith".

———— Aske enters Pontefract Castle, lambastes the lords within and sets out the terms for the yielding of the castle.

———— Bill on Giggleswick church door announcing a muster at Neals Ing in the northerly part of Percy Fee (West Riding).

———— Government dismisses its army of 19,000 troops stationed at Ampthill, which the king had intended to lead in person against the Lincolnshire rebels. It does so upon hearing of their final submission.

20th October: First muster in Percy Fee, at Neals Ing. The same day the rebels visit Sir Stephen Hamerton's house at Wigglesworth. He is steward of Percy Fee. He is enlisted and sworn.

———— Westmorland rebels hold an assembly at Eamont Bridge which some minor gentlemen attend, taking the oath. The same day the Cumberland rebels meet on Penrith Fell where they produce a proclamation which orders the restoration of the traditional practice of bidding holy days and beads and calls for a proper defence of "this country" against Scottish attacks and border reiving. At the same meeting the Captain Poverty letter is read and then sent to the communities which have failed to attend the meeting, notably Edenhall. There Sir Edward Musgrave takes the oath and the whole parish does likewise.

———— Letter from Aske reaches the Richmondshire rebels at Spennymoor, calling for assistance against Shrewsbury.

———— Muster at Northallerton where the Bowes host on its march to Pontefract is joined by the commons of Langbaurgh accompanied by Sir John Bulmer and the Rokebys.

———— Second assembly at Malton. Sir Nicholas Fairfax of Gilling Castle in Ryedale joins the Percy host.

———— Pontefract Castle is handed over to the rebels at 8 a.m., the inmates taking the rebel oath.

———— The Duke of Norfolk in Cambridge produces his "politic device". This advocates holding the line of the Trent rather than advancing into Yorkshire against the rebels; and of writing to the rebels to persuade them to disperse or, at least, to create division within the rebel ranks.

———— Beverley/Holderness rebels meet at Hunsley with the gentlemen taken from Hull. They appoint a council to formulate a petition. Before this can be composed a messenger arrives from Aske summoning assistance at Pontefract because of the approach of the Earl of Shrewsbury.

———— Percy host reaches York where it is joined by Sir Oswald Wilstrop of the Ainsty. Aske races back from Pontefract to greet Sir Thomas. Dining together, they rail against Cromwell; and then Aske returns to Pontefract.

21st October: Percy host parades through York and travels on to Pontefract.

———— Resident in Alnwick Castle, Ingram Percy, in response to the Captain Poverty letter, takes the oath and imposes it upon the gentlemen of Northumberland who at the time are in the castle.

———— Cumberland rebels hold a third muster, near Great Salkeld to draw in the townships east of the River Eden.

———— Percy Fee rebels enlist Nicholas Tempest, acting steward of Blackburnshire and acting forester of Bowland. The same day a deputation of nine men, including Hamerton, go to Skipton Castle to persuade the Earl of Cumberland to become a rebel. He refuses.

———— Shortly after the deputation from Percy Fee has departed, Skipton Castle is besieged by the Richmondshire rebels, leading to the surrender of Lord Scrope and the sacking of Cumberland's houses at Barden and Carleton, the robbing of his parks and the destruction of his estate records.

———— Muster is held in the West Riding lordship of Dent. A host is formed.

———— Shrewsbury with 6,000 troops has reached Scrooby and dispatches Lancaster herald to Pontefract with a proclamation stating that the Lincolnshire rebels have dispersed and the Yorkshire rebels must do likewise. Aske meets the herald in Pontefract Castle, refuses to allow him to make public the proclamation and employs his own oath to present to the herald the rebel grievances. That night Aske mans the crossing at Wentbridge, fearing that Shrewsbury might spring a surprise attack on the rebels in Pontefract.

———— Government has welcomed Norfolk's politic device and accordingly issues further instructions to Shrewsbury telling him not to enter Yorkshire but to guard the Trent at Nottingham and Newark.

22nd October: Bowes and Stapulton hosts arrive that morning in Pontefract. A council meets in a window of the castle to order the battle. The Percy and Stapulton hosts man Wentbridge as a further safeguard against Shrewsbury.

———— Second muster is held in Percy Fee, at Monubent in the southerly part of the honour.

23rd October: Percy Fee rebels march into Lancashire, imposing the oath and occupying Whalley Abbey. They use an oath which has been specially composed for them by Aske, in response to a supplication from the monks of Sawley Abbey.

———— The Earl of Derby receives the king's instructions, issued on 19th October, to levy Lancashire. Told to crush the revolt in Percy Fee and to execute the monks in Sawley Abbey, in the next four days he raises a force of 7,000 men and takes up a position at Preston.

———— Cumberland rebels hold a muster at Cartlogan Thorns, a meeting place for the inhabitants of Inglewood Forest. It draws support from the parish of Caldbeck, the lordships of Castle Sowerby, Hutton and Skelton and the barony of Greystoke. Barnard Townley and other gentlemen are allegedly brought in by the commons.

———— At Endmoor, the Kendal rebels meet the Dent host which notices that they have not yet been joined by the gentlemen of the barony.

―――― The Duke of Norfolk has just reached Newark, although ahead of his army. Learning that Shrewsbury has pushed on to Doncaster, he realises that his politic device is now inoperable. At Newark Norfolk meets Lord Talbot, Shrewsbury's son. Norfolk provides him with a letter proposing an armistice and also a back-up letter threatening battle if the armistice is rejected. Talbot takes the letters to Doncaster, giving them to his father.

―――― Middleward of the pilgrim host goes to Wentbridge; the vanguard moves to Hampole Nunnery.

24th October: Lancaster herald arrives with Norfolk's negotiating terms and hands them to the vanguard assembled at Barnsdale. Aske races back to Pontefract to consult Darcy. The rebels seek to revise Norfolk's plan, proposing a meeting of delegates between the hosts rather than in Doncaster.

―――― Assembly is held in Kendal town "to know the Lord Poverty's pleasure". For next three days the Dent host targets Sir James Layburn in order to persuade him to take the oath.

25th October: Cumberland rebels muster at Kylwatling How, a beacon and assembly point for the barony of Greystoke. Cuthbert Hutton, a recent sheriff of Cumberland, is recruited and four chaplains of poverty are appointed (Slee, Townley, Threlkeld and Blenkow).

―――― Middleward of the pilgrim host moves to Hampole; the van moves to Pickburn, overlooking Doncaster.

―――― Skirmish occurs that morning outside Doncaster, in which government troops are routed, inspiring the Bowes host to consider taking Doncaster immediately.The same day the herald returns with a letter rejecting the pilgrims' terms and challenging battle unless they disperse. The letter also proposes that, if they disperse, the commanders of the royal army will be suitors for them to the king.

―――― That evening the pilgrims convene a council at Hampole: the wisdom of war or peace is debated. A policy of negotiation prevails. The rebels accept Norfolk's original proposal for a meeting in Doncaster. That night heavy rain causes the Don to rise, making it unfordable.

25th/26th October: Cumberland rebels stage the captains' mass in Penrith church.

26th October: Norfolk reaches Doncaster in the early hours, without his army.

26th and 27th October: pilgrim host is arrayed before Doncaster at Scawsby Leys.

27th October: Siege of Skipton Castle is called off and the Richmondshire rebels march to Pontefract.

―――― First Appointment at Doncaster is made, A truce is agreed whilst the rebels' five articles are taken to the king by Norfolk accompanied by the pilgrim leaders, Bowes and Ellerker. It is also proposed that there should be a parliament to consider the pilgrims' grievances and that a general pardon should be granted.

By 27th October Cartmel Priory has been restored.

27th October: Layburn and other leading gentlemen of the barony of Kendal came to the town and take the rebel oath.

———— Cumberland rebels muster at Sandale Hill to recruit the Honour of Cockermouth.

27th/28th October: Second muster at Monubent in Percy Fee to plan resistance to approaching earl of Derby.

28th October: Cumberland rebels muster at Moota Hill. Attending are the gentlemen John Leigh of Isel, Sir John Lamplugh, John Skelton, Thomas Dalston and Richard Blenkow and also the Abbot of Holm Cultram. A council sits to work out what to do with Carlisle which remains unsworn.

———— Designated rearward of the pilgrim host (the rebels from Richmondshire, Kirkby Malzeard and Ripon who had gone to besiege Skipton Castle) reaches Pontefract.

———— Robert Pulleyn meets Aske in Pontefract, hands him the letter composed by the Westmorland commons, learns of the First Appointment, receives a copy of the articles and is warned by Aske not to mistreat the gentlemen of the barony, especially Sir Thomas Wharton.

———— Taking of Lancaster by the Dent and Kendal rebels.

———— Muster is held at Hawkshead to recruit the lordship of Furness Fells.

By 28th October the Earl of Derby has moved from Lathom to Preston. Among others, he is joined by Lord Monteagle and Marmaduke Tunstall, leaving a vacuum of authority in north Lancashire and in south Ewcross.

29th October: With Pulleyn declaring to it the five articles, the Appleby council decides to issue a proclamation ordering the clergy of Westmorland to bid the holy days and beads in the traditional manner.

30th October: Muster on Clitheroe Moor, arranged by the Percy Fee rebels who march down the Ribble into Lancashire. They occupy Whalley Abbey, following news that the Earl of Derby planned to stay there.

———— Massive muster of Cumbrians at Burford Oak in the Broadfield. The plan is to attack Carlisle if it refuses the oath. The same day Dacre and William Musgrave offer support to Lord Clifford in defending Carlisle against the rebels. News of the Truce, produced by the townsmen, causes the rebels to disband.

———— In spite of the Truce, Sir Marmaduke Constable of Everingham is driven out of the East Riding by a band of commons who seek to make him take the oath.

31st October: Sent by Atkinson, Captain Gilpin arrives in the Furness peninsula. He is greeted at Swartmoor by a deputation of monks from Furness Abbey. Hearing of his approach to swear the region, Roger Piles, the Abbot of Furness, and its steward William Fitton flee by boat to Derby's manor of Lathom, near Liverpool.

1st November: Muster is held at Furness Abbey of the tenantry who are instructed to attend with horse and harness.

2nd November: Government drafts a proclamation pardoning all the rebels, apart from ten men, six of them named, and requiring submission before Norfolk as a condition of its being granted.

3rd November: Believing the Truce to be an invention, the Cumbrians again muster on Broadfield to besiege Carlisle but are dissuaded by Sir Christopher Dacre.

By 6th November the king has composed his answer to the rebel articles. It dismisses them as misinformed and calls for exceptions to any pardon granted. But he has decided not to send it north with Bowes and Ellerker, as originally planned, because of news of further disturbances in Yorkshire. Bowes and Ellerker are to be kept for the time being in London.

6th November: Government seeks to persuade Darcy to hand over Aske. Darcy refuses insisting that the first appointment should be respected, with the king's reply to the articles delivered to the north by Bowes and Ellerker. He recommends a special parliament to deal with the rebels' grievances.

11th November: In spite of the Truce, 3–4,000 commons gather at Skipton to harass the Earl of Cumberland; and reprisals are taken at Hatfield against Sir Brian Hastings and in Wakefield against Sir Henry Savile, both of whom are thought to be planning a capture of the pilgrim high command.

14th November: Government proposes a second appointment, a colloquy of 300 delegates from each side, but insists on a pardon with exceptions and a submission of the pilgrims before the king's answer to their articles is made known. It also refuses to receive further articles.

15th November: The rebels capture a ship sailing from Grimsby to Scarborough. On board are provisions and money for the castle and a letter of instruction from Cromwell for Sir Ralph Eure suggesting government reprisals to be taken through garrisoning the north. As a result Scarborough Castle is besieged in spite of the Truce.

21st–24th November: Pilgrims convene their York council, with 800 delegates, to consider the information brought by Ellerker and Bowes. The council insists upon a general pardon, a free parliament and the right to propose further articles. It arranges for a pilgrim council and a pilgrim convocation to meet in Pontefract to draw up a full list of grievances.

26th November: From Nottingham Norfolk shows the king that, if he persists in rejecting the rebel request for a general pardon and a free pardon, he will have no choice but to resort to military action, for which he lacks the resources in view of the untrustworthiness of the commons.

2nd December: Government draws up a free and general pardon, dispatching it northwards but ordering Norfolk not to use it. Instead the earlier pardon with the ten exceptions is to be presented.

2nd–4th December: Pilgrims hold their Pontefract council, in the castle, to produce a set of articles which are to be presented, through Norfolk, to the king.

2nd–5th December: Pilgrims hold their Pontefract convocation, in Pontefract Priory.

3rd December: Archbishop is barracked in and chased out of Pontefract church when he preaches on the immorality of subjects taking up the sword against their prince.

4th December: Privy council writes to Norfolk stating the king's keenness to reserve some of the rebels for punishment rather than allowing all to escape with a general pardon. But on the same day the king concedes to Norfolk that, as a result of being overruled by the council, a general pardon might have to be issued and a parliament might have to be granted to consider the rebel grievances.

——— Pilgrims send their twenty-four articles to Norfolk in Doncaster.

5th December: Delegation of three hundred pilgrims rides to Doncaster.

6th December: In the Whitefriars forty pilgrim delegates meet Norfolk and his party. It is agreed that a general pardon be granted, the restored abbeys for the moment be allowed to stand and the articles be taken to the king.

7th December: In the early morning Aske reports to the commons at Pontefract and then returns to Doncaster. But a message is brought to Doncaster that they require certain conditions: the pardon to be seen, an assurance that the restored monks can remain in possession of their houses; the promise of a parliament at York. Aske returns to Pontefract.

8th December: Pilgrims assemble at Pontefract. Lancaster herald brings the general pardon and confirmation is given of a York parliament and that the restored abbeys should for the moment stand. The commons disperse. The gentlemen meet Norfolk in Doncaster and humbly submit themselves, tearing off their pilgrim badges.

Index

‹▰▰▰▰▰▰▰▰▰▰▰▰▰▰▰▰▰▰▰▰▰▰▰▰▰▰▰▰▰▰▰▰▰›

[E.R., N.R., W.R. – East, North and West Ridings of Yorkshire]